Flat-Tops and Fledglings

Flat-Tops and Fledglings

A History of American Aircraft Carriers

Gareth L. Pawlowski

South Brunswick and New York: A. S. Barnes and Company
London: Thomas Yoseloff Ltd

© 1971 by Gareth L. Pawlowski
Library of Congress Catalogue Card Number: 76-112765

A. S. Barnes and Co., Inc.
Cranbury, New Jersey 08512

Thomas Yoseloff Ltd
108 New Bond Street
London W1Y OQX, England

ISBN 0-498-07641-5
Printed in the United States of America

Dedication

A cool breeze flows across the white caps of the Pacific Ocean as the *Langley*, two hours out of North Island, lumbers in a wallowy motion in what appears to be a steady course. At first glance, you might think the old covered wagon was ready to roll over and meet Davy Jones. But to the crew, this wallow was normal as the ex-collier churned through the sea with a bone in her teeth. Inside the salt sprayed hull, the routine of at-sea life was taking shape. The deck force was securing all moveable objects and made the ship ready for rough weather. Down in the galley, the ship's cook was telling the mess cooks to square away and make ready for noon chow. You could bet your salt hook that "cold cuts" was on the menu for today!

So it went throughout each and every compartment as it had gone on for years and years in hundreds of other US Navy ships. But the *Langley* was no longer like any other ship. Her superstructure had been stripped and replaced with a wooden flat top. This flat top was soon to be dubbed "flight deck."

Up on the flight deck a new scene was taking place. A young pilot sat restlessly in the cockpit of a single-seated chasing plane, waiting for the signal to fly off. As the signal was given, the shaky biplane began to pick up speed as she rolled along the wooden planks that made up the 534 x 64 foot sea-going airfield. Suddenly, a gust of wind jerked the plane hard to port and the strong winds of the Pacific threw the plane into the choppy sea. There was no time for rescue as the twisted hulk that once was an airplane slipped beneath the waves.

The year was 1922, and this scene was to be repeated often as the struggle for Naval Air power continued. There was no glory, no medals, no fanfare. But the essence was there and this essence, which led to a new type of ship—the fleet aircraft carrier—was the will and determination of a handful of Navy men who had the foresight and the initiative to visualize sea-air power as a vital and powerful deterrent force second to none.

To those who gave their lives in a time when skeptics still joked about "the funny flying machine," their epitaph was to be written twenty years later in the skies of Coral Sea, Midway, Guadalcanal, the Philippine Sea, and many other famous battles now obscure in the pages of dusty history books.

It is with deepest respect that I dedicate this book to the pilots and men of the *Langley*, who during the period 1922–1927 were the only leg that sea-air power had to stand on, gave the supreme sacrifice, above and beyond the call of duty, while the Nation was on a "ten year toot."

Gareth L. Pawlowski
Burbank, California

Contents

Preface

Andrew J. Volstead pushed the Eighteenth Amendment through Congress and its enforcement became effective at 12:01 July 16, 1920. Four months later, radio station KDKA announced the election returns of the Warren G. Harding–James M. Cox Presidential campaign. A small and almost insignificant announcement by today's standards, but it marked the birth of the radio.

Thus the era of the lost generation and bathtub gin began—a decade that almost got out of hand, as flagpole sitting and goldfish swallowing became the main attraction. Eyes at breakfast tables were glued to the morning newspapers to read about the latest developments in the death of William Desmond Taylor and the trials of the silver screen comic Roscoe "Fatty" Arbuckle. Rudolph Valentino caused women to faint when he appeared as The Sheik and you couldn't get a ticket to see Frank Bacon in *Lightin'* on Broadway. Atlantic City held its first Miss America Bathing Beauty contest and bread was a nickle a loaf. *The Birth of a Nation* was banned in Boston and everyone was reading Sinclair Lewis's *Main Street* and F. Scott Fitzgerald's *This Side of Paradise*.

The war to end all wars was all but forgotten. The last great parade of the A.E.F. down Fifth Avenue in New York was staged 18 months after the war's end. Certain elements proposed almost total cutbacks in the Armed Forces. Funds allocated for experimentation and testing disappeared like John Barleycorn.

Yet, as in every generation when the majority seems to run afoul, there are those who put aside the contemporary strains of life and think above the turmoil. Those who have not forgotten the precious heritage of our Nation, utilizing to the fullest the freedom that history has shown is not a word to be taken for granted but a way of life founded on the battlefields of those striving for territorial gains and the lives of our Nation's young.

It was in those early days of the 1920s that a select group of Navy men realized that the aircraft carrier would play a prominent part in maintaining the freedom of the seas and the air above and to help insure world peace. On March 20, 1922, the experimental aircraft carrier *USS Langley CV-1* was commissioned. Despite the fact that the carrier had gotten off to a slow start, things were happening. By 1927, the *USS Lexington CV-2* and *USS Saratoga CV-3* were commissioned, and built from ex-battle cruiser hulls. These three carriers would pave the way for advancement of aviation on the seas throughout the late 1920s and early 1930s. Fledgling aircraft were designed for carrier suitability and task organizations were formed that evolved around the carrier. The familiar sight of the carrier trailing behind the battleship would soon fade away. Though the carrier proved promising in theory and training, the battleship had been combat-proven. It wasn't until the Second World War that the aircraft carrier had the chance to prove its worth. And it did so, far above original expectations. The fast carrier task forces swept across the Pacific Theatre of war, unleashing their deadly arsenal of aircraft swifter than any faraway land base could ever hope to.

A new chapter in the history of the aircraft carrier unfolded during the postwar period. On November 2, 1946, the *USS Franklin D. Roosevelt CVB-42* had the distinction of being the first US carrier to launch and land a jet. Thoughts of the carrier becoming obsolete vanished as the trend to modernize existing carriers to handle the new propless fledglings materialized. The *USS Valley Forge CV-45* was the first carrier to launch jet aircraft into actual combat, on July 3, 1950. It was up to the wartime-designed carriers to bring the Navy jets to the Korean scene of conflict, but a change was in the air.

In 1951, the Navy authorized the construction of the *USS Forrestal CV-59*. She became the first of the postwar carriers to be constructed and the first carrier designed to operate jet aircraft. The *Forrestal* class set a new precedent in carrier history but an even greater advancement came in 1958 when construction of the first nuclear aircraft carrier, the *USS Enterprise CVA(N)-65* began.

Today, some 47 years since that almost forgotten beginning in 1922, the carrier is our Navy's number-one line of defense. *Flat-Tops and Fledglings* is their story—the full story of each aircraft carrier and the distinguished role they have played to serve our country in peace and war.

Gareth L. Pawlowski
Burbank, California

Acknowledgments

A history book could not be compiled without the assistance of certain organizations. I wish to express gratitude and acknowledge the Naval History Division, Washington, D. C.; the Naval Air Systems Command; Public Affairs Office of ships that are in commission; the National Archives and the Naval Photographic Center, Washington, D. C. for supplying historical information and photographs. The National Archives is credited with all photographs taken prior to 1958 and the Navy Department for all official photographs taken from 1959 to the present.

Abbreviations and Terms

ASW	Anti-submarine Warfare	HMAS	Her Majesty's Australian Ship
BB	Battleship	HMCS	Her Majesty's Canadian Ship
CA	Heavy Cruiser	HQ	Headquarters
CAP	Combat Air Patrol	HUTRON	Helicopter Squadron
CarDiv	Carrier Division	IOIS	Integrated Operational Intelligence System
CASU	Carrier Aircraft Support Unit		
CAW	Carrier Air Wing	JCS	Joint Chiefs of Staff
CIC	Combat Information Center	NAS	Naval Air Station
CincPac	Commander in Chief, Pacific	NOB	Naval Operating Base
CL	Light Cruiser	NRA	National Recovery Act
CL(AA)	Light Cruiser, Anti-Aircraft	NTDS	Naval Tactical Data System
CNO	Chief of Naval Operations	ONI	Office of Naval Intelligence
CO	Commanding Officer	ORI	Operational Readiness Instruction
ComCarDiv	Commander Carrier Division	PriFli	Primary Flight Control
Cominch	Commander in Chief, United States Fleet	SAM	Surface to Air Missile
		SOPA	Senior Officer Present Afloat
CONUS	Continental United States	SS	Submarine
CTF	Commander Task Force	SS (N)	Submarine, Nuclear
CTG	Commander Task Group	TBS	Talk Between Ships
CV	Aircraft Carrier	TF	Task Force
CVA	Attack Aircraft Carrier	TG	Task Group
CVA (N)	Attack Aircraft Carrier, Nuclear	TU	Task Unit
CVB	Aircraft Carrier, Large	UDT	Underwater Demolition Team
CVE	Escort Aircraft Carrier	VA	Attack Squadron
CVL	Aircraft Carrier, Light	VAH	Heavy Attack Squadron
DCC	Damage Control Central	VAW	ASW Early Warning Squadron
DD	Destroyer	VCP	Composite Photographic Squadron
DE	Destroyer Escort	VF	Fighter Squadron
DLG (N)	Nuclear powered Guided Missile Destroyer	VMF	Marine Fighter Squadron

JAPANESE AIRCRAFT

Allied Code Name	Manufacturer	Type
Betty	Mitsubishi	Navy Zero-1 high level or torpedo-bomber
Fran	Nakajima	Navy, all purpose bomber

Allied Code Name	Manufacturer	Type
Frances	Nakajima	Navy, bomber
Frank	Nakajima	Army, fighter
Jake	Aichi or Watanabe	Navy, reconnaissance bomber
Jill	Nakajima	Navy, torpedo-bomber
Judy	Aichi	Navy, dive bomber
Kate	Nakajima	Navy, torpedo-bomber
Nate or Oscar	Nakajima	Army, fighter
Nick	Kawasaki or Nakajima	Zero-2, Army, fighter
Sally	Mitsubishi	Army, medium bomber
Tojo	Nakajima	Zero-2 Army, fighter
Tony	Mitsubishi	Zero-3 Army/Navy fighter
Val	Aichi	Navy dive-bomber
Zeke	Mitsubishi	Zero-3 Navy fighter

PART I

The Flat-Tops

USS Langley CV-1 Aerial oblique port broadside, 1922.

1

USS Langley AV-3

The Congress of the United States passed an act on May 13, 1908, which authorized the President to issue construction orders for two fleet colliers. The vessels were to maintain a trial speed of 14 knots and carry not less than 12,500 tons of cargo. The price tag was not to exceed $1.8 million each, and for the construction of both, $1.5 million was provided.

In May of 1919, Captain Thomas B. Craven became Director of Naval Aviation. He said: "One day when someone suggested that shoveling coal was becoming unpopular, we proceeded to angle for the colliers *Jupiter* and *Jason*. Although some conservative seniors frowned on the plan, in time and with the Secretary of the Navy's approval, we persuaded congressional committees of the wisdom of converting one ship, the *Jupiter*, into an aircraft carrier."

As a result, a Congressional Act dated July 11, 1919, included naval aviation and stipulated "$25,000,000 to be expended for the conversion of the United States steamship *Jupiter* into an aeroplane carrier."

On October 18, 1911, the keel of the *USS Jupiter*

AC-3 was laid down at Mare Island Naval Shipyard, Vallejo, California. She was launched on August 24, 1912, and commissioned on April 7, 1913. The Navy's first experimental aircraft carrier began her naval service as a fleet collier, assigned the task of supplying coal to the fighting ships of the fleet.

The *Jupiter* displaced 19,300 tons, had a mean draft of 27 feet 8 inches with an overall length of 542 feet, and carried a crew of 12 officers and 101 enlisted men. Her trial speed was 14 knots.

Following successful sea trials the *Jupiter* began the subservient duties for which she was built. The job was difficult and uneventful and it is unlikely that any sailor would find pleasure in relating his days aboard a collier. Transferring coal to the big battleships meant hours of strain for all concerned. Still, there was an element of pride in knowing that the job was essential. When the last load was aboard a fighting ship, the *Jupiter* would slowly edge away to assist other ships of the line.

In April of 1914, the *Jupiter* departed San Francisco

with a detachment of U. S. Marines and steamed to Mazatlan, Mexico. She arrived on April 27 to participate in the Vera Cruz operation and continued in this duty until May 25, for which she received the Mexican Service Medal. The collier then returned to San Francisco to resume hauling coal.

On October 10, 1914, the *Jupiter* became the first naval ship to pass through the then newly built Panama Canal. She was heading for Philadelphia and arrived on October 19.

The *Jupiter* was inactive at the New York Navy Yard from December 11, 1914, to May 4, 1915, while undergoing repairs. Afterwards, until the outbreak of World War I, she cruised the Atlantic and the Gulf from Portsmouth to Vera Cruz, Mexico.

On October 17, 1916, the *Jupiter* collided with the Italian bark *Doris* in Lynnhaven, Virginia. The collier was damaged above the water line, but was repaired during the following week.

Throughout 1917, the faithful *Jupiter* continued carrying coal to various ports, with the exception of one cruise in which she hauled a cargo of wheat and flour to France.

On June 5, 1917, the day before entering Gironde River, the *Jupiter* was surprised by an attacking German submarine. The sub sent a pair of torpedoes towards the collier, but they missed. Seven rounds of ammunition were fired at an object resembling a periscope. The object quickly submerged. However, some of the bullets exploded, which indicated they had found their target.

The *Jupiter* sailed into Pauillac, France, on June 5, 1917, carrying the first U. S. Military unit sent to Europe in World War I. This was the First Aeronautic Detachment, consisting of seven officers and 122 enlisted men, commanded by Lieutenant Kenneth Whiting.

On January 9, 1918, the *Jupiter* was assigned to the Naval Overseas Transportation Service (NOTS) at New York. After repairs to her main turbine bearings, she proceeded to Hampton Roads, Virginia, received cargo and returned to New York.

The *Jupiter* was released from the NOTS on August 17, and resumed duties with the Training Force.

On July 11, 1919, Congress authorized the conversion of a naval ship for the purpose of handling aircraft on the high seas. The navy pilots requested the *USS Jupiter AC-3* or *USS Jason*. The *Jupiter* won. Although the collier could not fulfill all the requirements, she could be used for experimental purposes

USS Jupiter AC-3 being moved by tugs, Mare Island, California, October 16, 1913.

The *Langley* conducting flight operations in 1922. Note second smoke duct added shortly after commissioning. July 31, 1925.

until larger ships could be converted into aircraft carriers. Hopefully, in the near future, ships would be designed and built from the keel up for the sole purpose of operating with aircraft.

The *Jupiter* entered the Norfolk Navy Yard in March 1920, to begin her metamorphosis. Her official designation was changed on the same day from AC-3 to CV-1.

There were numerous reasons for selection of the *Jupiter* as the ship to be converted into an aircraft carrier. She was the first naval vessel built with the Melville–McAlphine electric drive system, which proved so successful that the Navy adopted it for all capital ships. Her cargo spaces were large, which would permit the stowage of aircraft, and she was of sufficient length to accommodate a wooden deck capable of launching planes.

A significant portion of the *Jupiter's* superstructure and booms were removed. The remainder was assembled with a massive wooden flat-top placed across the full length of the ship. All equipment used for hauling coal was removed, for the ship would soon play a more important role for the Navy.

The ship had originally been commissioned with one smoke duct; a second was now added. Both were horizontal and interconnected, which enabled smoke to be discharged on the leeward side. One duct had a hinged extension and could be lowered close to the waterline; smoke from the other duct was discharged through waterspray.

During the conversion period on April 21, 1920, the ship was renamed *Langley*, in honor of Samuel Piermont Langley (1865–1906), known for his experiments on the problems surrounding mechanical flight.

An historic moment came on August 11, 1921, when practical development of carrier-arresting gear was initiated at Hampton Roads. Lieutenant A. M. Pride had taxied an Aeromarine onto a dummy deck and engaged the arresting wires. These tests resulted in the use of arresting gear for the *Langley*, consisting essentially of wires attached to weights plus additional wires positioned fore and aft.

On March 20, 1922, the unveiling came as the *USS Langley CV-1* was commissioned at the Norfolk Navy Yard. This was a momentous day for the Navy, for it ushered in the inauguration of carrier aviation.

During her first year of service the *Langley* was little more than a sea-going guinea pig. One of the special problems during the early days was to evaluate the characteristic requirements for operating aircraft aboard ship, and to discover or develop aircraft suitable for such operations.

All available aircraft that could be equipped with wheels were tested on the *Langley*'s flight deck. Lieutenant Virgil C. Griffin was at the controls of a VE-7-SF when he made the first takeoff from the *Langley* on October 17, 1922. Rear Admiral William A. Moffett, the first chief of the Bureau of Aeronautics, said of this memorable event: "The air fleet of an enemy will never get within striking distance of our coast as long as our aircraft carriers are able to carry the preponderance of our air power to sea."

Lieutenant Commander Godfrey de Chevalier accomplished the first landing on October 26, 1922.

The first catapult launch from the *Langley* came on November 18, 1922 when a PT piloted by Commander Kenneth Whiting was launched.

An order signed by the *Langley*'s executive officer, Kenneth Whiting, dated February 1, 1923, is an excellent illustration of the carrier's shipboard routine during those early days of naval aviation.

"The weather permitting, the ship will get underway at 9:00 A.M. tomorrow, February 2, 1923, and will proceed out of the harbor for the purpose of flying planes off and on the ship.

"The tug Alleghany will accompany the ship and take station one hundred yards out and two hundred yards astern of the starboard quarter, steaming at the same ratio of speed as the *Langley*—about six knots.

"When flying off and on, both life boats will be lowered to rail and manned; the first or second motor sailing launch, depending upon which stack is in use will be lowered to the level of the poop deck, manned and equipped with grapnels, crash kits and six men in addition to the crew. The Boatswain will be in charge of this boat and will go in the boat.

"The flight surgeon will fly over the ship in a flying boat piloted by O. M. Darling, ACR, USN. This plane will maintain station two hundred yards behind and two hundred feet above the plane which is flying on and off.

"This seaplane will start from the Naval Air Station upon a radio signal from the ship. Boatswain Fehrer will go into the tug accompanied by three men from the Fourth Division and a crash kit.

"In case of fog tomorrow, the ship will not get underway, but will stand by until noon; in the event that the fog is cleared up by that time, will proceed.

"Steam will be kept in three boilers and engines in maneuvering condition. In case the plane goes into the water, the first boat to get to it shall at once attempt to rescue the aviator, at the same time making a line fast to some strong part of the plane, in order to hold the cockpit above water. This line, if possible, should be passed around one of the 'A' frames or engine section, or later on in the vicinity of the cockpit."

Such a set of instructions seem crude by today's standards, yet in 1923 they evidently proved to be effective.

On February 21, 1923, tests of aircraft handling were conducted aboard the *Langley* with Aeromarines operating in groups of three. Results revealed that two minutes were required to prepare the deck following each landing. During the fastest time recorded for the day, three planes were landed in seven minutes.

In December 1924, the *Langley* joined the Aircraft Squadron Battle Fleet as a second-line combat ship. She could carry 12 single-seat chasing planes, 12 two-seater spotting planes, four torpedo planes, and six torpedo seaplanes.

The *Langley* had a unique method of handling aircraft. The original cargo spaces were altered to provide maximum space for housing the planes. Travelling cranes, located below the flight deck, hoisted the planes from the hold and moved them fore and aft, or simply lifted them to the flight deck.

An electric lift raised the planes topside. Her flight deck measured 534 by 64 feet and was 56 feet above the water line. The catapults could deliver torpedo planes into the air at 60 mph with only a 60-foot run.

Two cranes were located on each beam to pick up seaplanes from the water and place them on the flight deck.

The *Langley* could receive aircraft approaching at 60 mph and bring them to a safe stop within 40 feet.

On January 22, 1925, VF-2, the first squadron trained to operate from a carrier, began landing practice on the *Langley* positioned near San Diego. This was the finale of her role as an experimental carrier.

Fleet Problem V began in March, 1925, and the *Langley* entered the second phase off the coast of Southern California. The Problem was not unlike others practiced by the Navy. Relations between the Blue Force (U.S.) and the Black Force (an imaginary enemy) were split. The *Langley* was assigned to the Black Force along with the *USS Aroostoock CM-3* and the *USS Gannet AM-41*.

The force was supported by planes stationed aboard battleships. Blue Force was comprised of the *USS Wyoming BB-32* and cruisers. The action began with the Black Force declaring "war" on the Blue Force. The Black commander-in-chief was ordered to proceed from its imaginary country around the Hawaiian Islands to Guadalupe Island and establish a base of operations against the Blue Force. The *Langley* became the center of attraction for most of the air activity.

Aircraft were to be launched at 5:30 A.M. on March 11 to make an aerial reconnissance flight. This was one day prior to the Black Fleet's scheduled entrance into Guadalupe. However, the chief observer for the Fleet Problem cancelled the exercise at 5:08 A.M. thus precluding any activity by either Force.

On April 2, 1925, the feasibility of using flush-deck catapults to launch landplanes was aptly demonstrated from the *Langley* while moored at San Diego. Lieutenant-Commander C. P. Mason and a passenger, Lieutenant Braxton Rhodes, were successfully catapulted from the wooden deck in a DT-2 landplane.

Lieutenant John D. Price, flying a plane from VF-1, made a night landing on the *Langley* while the car-

rier was at sea off the San Diego coast; he was followed by Lieutenants D. L. Conley, A. W. Gorton, and R. D. Lyon that evening of April 8, 1925. With the exception of an unintentional landing on February 5, when Lieutenant H. J. Brow accidentally stalled while making night approaches, there were the first night landings aboard a U.S. carrier.

In February 1927, a joint Army-Navy problem was conducted in the Panama Canal area and the *Langley* was assigned to protect the fleet against land-based attacks. Although the exercise was not considered very effective, a distinctive feature was that an aircraft carrier for the first time had protected the battleships and concomitant fighting forces.

Fleet Battle Problem VII got underway during March 1927, as the Blue Force was escorting a con-

USS Langley CV-1 Elevator and (below) flight deck. Norfolk, Virginia, February 1922.

voy and set up a base under enemy opposition. Again the *Langley* was to protect the convoy and the Black Force was ordered to attack and destroy the Blue Force.

On the final day of the exercise, the Black Force launched a surprise attack of 25 land-based planes against the Blue convoy. The *Langley* previously had a protective air cover over the convoy, but discontinued it prior to the attack by the "enemy." Before the Black aircraft could reach their target the exercise was terminated. Observers stipulated that the attack was successful and from this exercise evolved an Act to allow the Commander, Air Squadrons more authority to use his planes in maintaining maximum efficiency during air operations.

For five years (1922–1927) the *Langley* held the distinction of being the Navy's only aircraft carrier. When the *USS Lexington CV-2* and *USS Saratoga CV-3* were commissioned in 1927, the *Langley* no longer commanded the limelight. Much had been learned from her decks, and the way was paved for newer and larger aircraft.

In September 1931, the XOP-1 Autogiro was purchased by the Navy for test purposes. The craft was a converted fixed-wing plane, but a free-spinning rotor was mounted atop the fuselage. The XOP-1 could not hover, but could take off and land on a short runway. Some of these tests were carried out aboard the *Langley*. Afterwards, the fixed wings were removed and the XOP-1 became the first naval aircraft to fly completely dependent upon a rotor for lift.

For ten days in December 1931, the *Langley* operated in the Cape Cod and Bar Harbor areas with temperatures below the freezing mark. Flight operations were conducted with O3Us and F3Bs. Additional tests included cold-weather experiments with engine starters and cold-weather clothing worn by pilots and flight deck crews.

On July 30, 1935, the first blind landing aboard a carrier was made by Lieutenant Frank Akers, who departed NAS San Diego in an OJ-2 with a hooded cockpit. He located the *Langley*, which was underway in an unknown position, and landed, catching the number four arresting wire. For this flight, Lieutenant Akers received the Distinguished Flying Cross.

When the year 1937 was ushered in, the usefulness of the *Langley* as an aircraft carrier was ushered out. Newer carriers like the *USS Ranger CV-4* and the *USS Yorktown CV-5* had joined the fleet. The *USS Enterprise CV-6*, *USS Hornet CV-7*, and *USS Wasp CV-8* were already on the buildingways or authorized for construction.

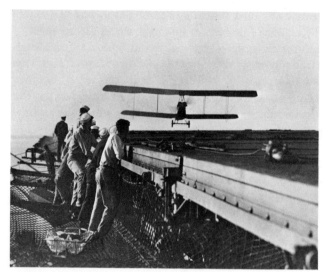

Aeromarine 39-B making a landing approach on the *Langley* during practice October 19, 1922.

The *Langley* was ready for conversion and the decision was that she became a seaplane tender. During her time in the yards, half of the famous wooden flat-top was removed. When the conversion was complete, she was reclassified AV-3 and served in the Pacific until the Japanese hit Pearl Harbor. At the time of the attack, the *Langley* was serving as a mobile base for two patrol bomber squadrons in the Philippines with Patrol Wing Two.

In February, 1942, the *Langley* sailed for Fremantle, Australia, to ferry Army P-40s to Java. The mission was extremely important, since many P-40s had been lost in bitter combat.

On February 22, 1942, the *Langley*, along with the British *Seawitch*, was ordered to detach from her present convoy after leaving Fremantle, and transport the fighter planes to Java at top speed. The *Langley* left the convoy before the *Seawitch*, but could not wait for the British ship to catch up; the delivery of the planes was paramount. The seaplane tender set course for Tjilatap, escorted by the *USS Whipple DD-217* and the *USS Edsall DD-129*. The *Edsall* would be lost in action only a few months later south of Java.

At 9:00 A.M. on February 27, 1942, the *Langley* requested air cover after spotting unidentified aircraft. Two hours later an answer came back in the form of nine twin-engine Japanese bombers. When the enemy planes reached their release point the *Langley* swung hard to starboard and the bombs exploded only 100 feet off her bow. On the second run, the bombers turned when the *Langley* did and resulted in five bombs smashing directly into the old seaplane tender.

Aircraft on the *Langley's* deck were now in flames and the ship was listing ten degrees with water rushing into her hull. After the fires were brought under control the planes were pushed over the side.

At 1:32 P.M. the order was given to abandon ship. All hands went over the side in typical "Blue Jacket Manual" fashion, which was a rare event aboard any sinking combat vessel.

The *Whipple* provided the final *coup de grace* by firing nine 4-inch shells into the smoking, twisted hull.

Thus, the career of the Navy's first aircraft carrier, a one-time collier and seaplane tender, slipped silently beneath the waves.

Many pilots who served as ensigns on her wooden decks would later become admirals and would always remember the ship that had contributed greatly to the progress of carrier aviation.

The *USS Langley AV-3* received the following awards during her 29 years of naval duty: Mexican Service Medal; World War One Victory Medal; American Defense Service Medal with one star; American Area Campaign Medal and the Asiatic-Pacific Area Campaign Medal.

LEXINGTON CLASS: EX-BATTLE CRUISERS OF 1916

Congress authorized the construction of six battle cruisers on August 29, 1916. They were to be the most powerful in size and armament to be built up to that time. Each ship was estimated to cost $16.5 million, exclusive of armament. No work was done on the ships until after the ending of the first World War.

The six battle cruisers were laid down as follows: USS *Lexington CC-2* on January 8, 1921, at Fore River, Mass.; USS *Constellation CC-2* on August 18, 1920, at Newport News, Virginia; USS *Saratoga CC-3* on September 25, 1920 at the New York Shipbuilding Company; USS *Ranger CC-4* at Newport News on July 23, 1921; USS *Constitution CC-5* at the Philadelphia Navy Yard on September 25, 1920; and the USS *United States CC-6* at Philadelphia on September 25, 1920.

The battle cruisers were originally designed to displace 35,000 tons and have a speed in excess of 25 knots. The main battery was to consist of ten 14-inch guns. The ships were to have seven funnels, the second, third, and fifth set abreast. The main armament was to be housed in twin tripple turrets while the secondary guns were to be placed in a double storied pod, two on each side of the bridge and three aside on the superstructure around the funnels and four placed aft at the upper deck level abreast of the "Y" turret.

Before the keels were laid down, the battle cruisers underwent a change. Their displacement was raised 8000 tons. The overall length was 874 feet; Beam, 90 feet. The main armament was altered to eight 16-inch 50-calibre mounts and a secondary battery of sixteen 6-inch 53-calibre guns; four 3-inch 50-calibre antiaircraft guns and eight 21-inch torpedo tubes, four above the waterline and four below the waterline. The ships were to have a triple bottom and antitorpedo protection.

The *Constellation* and *Lexington* were to be fitted out with flag quarters.

On February 6, 1922, the Washington Naval Treaty limiting naval armament was signed by representatives of the British Empire, France, Italy, Japan, and the United States. The treaty established a tonnage ratio of 5–5–3 for capital ships of Great Britain, The United States, and Japan respectively, and a lesser amount for France and Italy. The same ratio for aircraft carrier tonnage was set at 135,000 tons for Great Britain and the United States and 81,000 tons for Japan. The treaty also limited any new carrier to 27,000 tons, and if this amount were not exceeded by one carrier then two carriers could be built with a tonnage not over 33,000 tons, or obtain them by converting existing or partially constructed ships which would otherwise be scrapped by the treaty.

Rear Admiral William A. Moffet, who organized the Bureau of Aeronautics and became the first Chief of the Bureau of Aeronautics (Appointed September 1, 1927), realized the future importance of carrier warfare, and through his influence two of the battle cruisers under construction were saved from the scrap heap.

The *Lexington* and *Saratoga* were ordered to be completed as aircraft carriers on November 2, 1922, and October 30, 1922, respectively. The *Saratoga* was commissioned on November 16, 1927 and the *Lexington* on December 14, 1927.

As aircraft carriers, the vessels had an inclined deck armor belt 8½ feet, 7 inches thick at the top and four inches at the bottom. Standard Displacement, 33,000 tons; Full load displacement, 39,000 tons. Speed, 33 knots; Overall length, 888 feet; Beam, 105 feet 6 inches; Draft, 32 feet; Armament, eight 8-inch 55-calibre guns housed two each in four turrets, two forward and two aft of the island structure; Secondary battery, twelve 5-inch 25-calibre antiaircraft mounts. They could handle 90 aircraft and were equipped with one fly wheel type catapult. The complement was 195 officers and 1927 enlisted men, with a wartime complement of 3000 men. The *Lexington* and *Saratoga* had a unique hull structure: the hull plates extended up to the flight deck and the bridge and funnel were two separate structures. Each carrier had two centerline elevators.

Both ships retained their battle cruiser machinery. During the thirties, the *Saratoga* carried a two-plane flag unit and both carriers formed Carrier Division One.

In 1942, shortly after America's entry into the Second World War, the *Saratoga* had her 8-inch flight deck gun turrets removed and replaced with twin mount dual-purpose 5-inch 38-calibre mounts. Over one hundred 50-calibre 40mm mounts and thirty-two 20mm antiaircraft mounts were added. The tripod mast was replaced with a pole mast and the flight deck was enlarged. The *Lexington* had her 8-inch flight deck turrets removed and plans were formed to replace them with twin mount dual-purpose guns as the *Saratoga* but the carrier was lost following the Battle of Coral Sea on May 8, 1942, before this could be effective. The *Saratoga* survived the war and was used in the atomic bomb tests at Bikini, and was sunk on July 25, 1946 as a result of the underwater tests.

USS Lexington CV-2.

2

USS Lexington CV-2

The *USS Lexington CV-2* was the fourth naval vessel to bear the name honoring the famous Revolutionary War Battle. Originally designed as a battle cruiser, her keel was laid on January 8, 1921. Construction was suspended February 8, 1922, in accordance with the Washington Treaty regarding the limitation of naval armaments. Congress authorized conversion of the *Lexington* to an aircraft carrier on July 1, 1922, and work was resumed 11 days later.

Mrs. Theodore Douglas Robinson, wife of the Assistant Secretary of the Navy, christened the carrier on October 3, 1925, as it slid down the ways at Bethlehem Shipbuilding Corporation in Quincy, Massachusetts.

The *Lexington* had an overall length of 888 feet; extreme beam, 106 feet; mean draft, 24 feet 1½ inches. Her full load displacement was 41,000 tons. Trial speed was 34.24 knots and she could accommodate 195 officers and 1927 enlisted men. Armament consisted of eight 8-inch 55-caliber breech loading guns, twelve 5-inch 25-caliber antiaircraft guns plus four 6-pound saluting guns.

The *Lexington* was built at a cost of $45,952,644.83.

Under the command of Captain Albert W. Marshall, USN, the new carrier was commissioned on December 14, 1927. Following a normal shakedown cruise, the *Lexington* steamed for the Pacific to join the Battle Fleet at the San Pedro, California, naval base, arriving April 7, 1928. With San Pedro as her new home port, the *Lexington* became a floating laboratory for the Navy and from her flight deck numerous early aviation experiments and advancements were accomplished.

From June 9 to 12, 1928, the *Lexington* completed her first long voyage at sea, sailing from her home port to Honolulu. The 2229 nautical miles were covered in 74 hours at an average speed of 30.7 knots. During the 1928 Hawaiian cruise, the Navy developed

carrier tactics and trained the crew in tactical exercises with the fleet.

The 1929 fleet problem was a mock attack on the Panama Canal. The *Lexington*, along with the *USS Langley CV-1*, was assigned to the defending force while the *USS Saratoga CV-3* represented the attacking force, a Japanese fleet. Thus, the carrier striking force became a reality and the results of this hypothetical attack proved highly successful, resulting in several other fleet problems.

During the winter of 1929, freezing conditions suspended the entire electrical power supply of Tacoma, Washington. The *Lexington* rallied to the rescue, tied up alongside the Old Coleman pier, where for three months, the ship's dynamic power plants furnished all the electrical power required by the city.

The *Lexington* left Tacoma on January 16, 1930, and resumed operations off San Diego with the Battle Fleet. She was in port San Diego from February 9 to 14, then left the following day for Guantanamo Bay, Cuba. Maneuvers were conducted with the Battle Fleet and with the U.S. Army on February 27. Upon completion of these exercises, the *Lexington* arrived at the Norfolk Navy Yard on April 26 for military exhibition for Military and Public information. On May 21, the carrier proceeded to the West Coast to rejoin the Battle Fleet.

In April 1931, the *Lexington* withdrew from Guantanamo Bay, Cuba to assist the city of Managua, Nicaragua some 900 miles away, suffering from the aftermath of an earthquake.

Cruising at 30 knots, the *Lexington* dashed 700 miles across the Caribbean and arrived 150 miles off the coast of Nicaragua on April 1, 1931. Five aircraft were launched carrying indispensable medical supplies, four doctors, plus 1200 pounds of rice and beans. Another flight was sent the following day.

The *Lexington* was always considered a capable leader at sea and the crewmen labored endlessly to justify her great name. However, the men of *Lexington* were not content merely with taking bows for their ship's reputation on the high seas; they were also second to none at capturing awards for athletic competition.

The *Lexington* was first among all athletic events she entered, but the most important game to the crew had to be baseball. During the 1933–34 season, the *Lexington* had a very proud baseball team. Her team won every one of the 14 official games played. The "Minute Men" won their first game against the *USS West Virginia BB-48*, edging them 8–7. Coach "Pop" Fenton had a right to boast, for then the *Lexington* team fol-

The *Lexington* after being launched on October 3, 1925, at the Bethlehem Shipyard, Quincy, Massachusetts.

lowed through to garner the All-Navy Championship Baseball title from the USS *Wright AV-1*, which had tenaciously held the title for the seven previous years. The *Lexington* had shattered another long established fleet record.

Throughout the 1930s the *Lexington* remained an integral part of the Aircraft Battle Force, assigned to Carrier Division One. From San Pedro, she conducted fleet maneuvers in the Hawaiian area, in the Caribbean, off the Panama Canal Zone, and in the Pacific between the Aleutians and the West Coast.

In July 1937, the *Lexington* was anchored off the coast of Santa Barbara, California, when word came to begin a search for the famous aviatrix, Amelia Earhart. During a 27-day search, the *Lexington* covered 25,000 miles in the failing effort to locate Miss Earhart.

During their heyday, the *Lexington* and her sister ship the *Saratoga* majestically ruled the seas. Most of the early naval vessels, including the light cruisers, would completely exhaust their fuel supply trying to keep up with the big carriers. Each carrier displayed symbols for easy identification by other vessels. The *Lexington* prominently displayed the letters LEX on the after-end of the flight deck and all of her aircraft had their tails painted yellow.

On December 7, 1941, the *Lexington* was operating with Task Force Twelve, transporting Marine aircraft to the Island of Midway. At 7:58 on that fateful morning, the *Lexington*'s radio shack was humming with activity as the operators received the following message: "INTERCEPT AND DESTROY ENEMY BELIEVED RETREATING ON A COURSE BETWEEN PEARL HARBOR AND JALUIT. INTERCEPT AND DESTROY."

The sneak attack by the Japanese on Pearl Harbor was deeply felt in the hearts of all Navy men. Fourteen years of planning, training and hard work was justified as the United States entered the Second World War. The *Lexington* was fully prepared.

An immediate search began as the carrier rendezvoused with the *USS Indianapolis CA-35* and the *USS Enterprise CV-6* Task Force at mid-morning to seek out the Japanese Task Force, believed to be some 200 miles south of Pearl Harbor. The search continued until December 13, but no trace of the enemy could be found. The carrier returned to Pearl Harbor.

The *Lexington* steamed out of Pearl Harbor on December 14 with orders to raid the Japanese forces on Jaluit Island and relieve the pressure on Wake Island. The mission was cancelled due to heavy air reinforcements on the Marshall Islands.

Lexington then joined the *Saratoga*'s Task Force to help reinforce Wake Island, but when Wake fell to the Japanese on December 23, the two sea-going airfields were recalled and journeyed back to Pearl Harbor, arriving December 27, 1941.

The *Lexington* conducted offensive patrols in the Oahu-Johnston-Palmyra triangle to prevent possible enemy raids until January 31, 1942. She joined Task Force Eleven at that time as the flagship of Vice Admiral Wilson Brown, Commander, Task Force Eleven. After a conference between Rear Admiral J. G. Crace, RN, and Rear Admiral T. C. Kinkaid, USN, and Vice Admiral Brown aboard the *Lexington* on February 16, 1942, Task Force Eleven steamed in a north-northwesterly direction for an attack on the Japanese forces at Rabaul, New Britain.

On February 20, two enemy patrol planes were destroyed by the carrier's combat air patrol. Later that afternoon, a wave of nine Japanese bombers were intercepted and five were downed before reaching the task force. The four remaining aircraft made unsuccessful bomb runs on the *Lexington*. Three more enemy planes fell to the *Lexington* pilots and one from the carrier's gun crews.

A second wave of enemy planes approached from the east. All, except two fighters, were in pursuit of the first wave. One of the plane's guns jammed but the second fighter, piloted by Lt. Edward ("Butch") O'Hare shot down five Japanese twin-engine bombers, similar to the Army B-25s. For this action, Lieutenant O'Hare was awarded the Congressional Medal of Honor.

Four enemy planes eventually reached their dropping point as the *Lexington* radically maneuvered to avoid the bombs splashing miles astern. The *Lexington* suffered no casualties in this attack but the Japanese lost 17 of 18 aircraft.

The *Lexington* returned to the Coral Sea to conduct offensive patrols until March 6, when she teamed up with Task Force Seventeen headed for New Guinea. The carrier task force arrived in the Gulf of Papua on March 10 and the *Lexington* launched her aircraft against Japanese shipping and installations at Salamaua and Lae. The attack was a complete surprise to the enemy and after inflicting heavy damage, the planes returned to the task force without casualties. Following the Salamaua-Lae raid, the *Lexington* returned to Pearl Harbor, arriving March 26, 1942. Six days later, Rear Admiral Aubrey W. Fitch, USN, relieved Vice Admiral Brown as Commander, Task Force Eleven.

On April 15, the *Lexington* sailed from Pearl Harbor to join Task Force Seventeen, which included the USS

The Flight deck officer waves the go-ahead for a takeoff aboard the *Lexington*.

Yorktown CV-5. The ships rendezvoused May 1 southwest of the New Hebrides Islands. The two mighty forces refueled until the following afternoon, when the *Yorktown* departed for an attack on enemy landing forces at Tulagi, Solomon Islands. Heavy Japanese naval concentration in the Coral Sea made it obvious that the Japanese were planning amphibious operations, most likely against Port Moresby, New Guinea. Admiral Fletcher sent an attack group of cruisers and destroyers under the command of Rear Admiral Crace, RN, to the Louisiades to intercept the enemy should he attempt a move toward Port Moresby. The *Lexington* and *Yorktown* cruised northward into the Coral Sea in search of the enemy force.

The *Yorktown's* search planes reported contact with the enemy on the morning of May 7, 1942. Two carriers and four Japanese cruisers were sighted and strikes were immediately launched against the force.

Although the original reports were erroneous, the Japanese light carrier *Shoho* and her escorts were near the reported position given by the air groups. The enemy carrier was sent to the bottom with the loss of only three American planes. Unknown to the American task force, the unlocated Japanese carriers *Skokaku* and *Zuikaku* launched 12 bombers and 15 torpedo planes later that afternoon. These enemy aircraft made an unsuccessful search for the *Lexington* and *Yorktown*. However, while returning to their carriers, they were intercepted by American fighters. Nine enemy planes were destroyed in a wild dogfight. Three of the

Japanese planes mistook the *Yorktown* for their carrier but managed to escape her gunfire as they crossed her bow. Twenty minutes later, three other Japanese pilots joined the *Yorktown's* landing circle, making the same mistake; and one paid for the blunder with his life.

A *Lexington* search pilot spotted Admiral Takagi's carrier striking force on the morning of May 8, 1942, and an attack was launched. Severe damage was inflicted on the carrier *Shokaku*. The *Lexington* and *Yorktown* prepared for a return attack by the Japanese from an intercepted message that the enemy was aware of the location of the American carriers.

May 8, 1942, was to be a sad day for the men of the *Lexington,* for as the carrier added another achievement to her proud record, the Battle of Coral Sea was just about to begin.

This was the first naval engagement fought entirely by aircraft. Of all the ships in the combined fleets; not one single ship fired at another. One hour before noon, the expected attack came. One hundred Japanese aircraft were spotted coming towards the *Lexington* and *Yorktown*. The action that followed was one of the heaviest and most desperate ever to strike American carriers. Seventeen enemy aircraft were shot out of the sky by the carrier's combat air patrol while the *Lexington* zig-zagged to evade torpedo attacks. In a four-minute period, the *Lexington* was hit by five torpedoes—all on the port side! The first one struck the ship at 11:20 A.M., just foward of the port forward gun gallery. One minute later another tin fish smashed into the same side opposite the bridge. The torpedo attack was coordinated with a dive bomber attack which

The *Lexington's* Number Three 8" turret deck guns firing, January 27, 1928.

This rare photograph shows the port side, looking aft, near the forward boat pocket of a torpedo hit that the *Lexington* took on May 8, 1942, during the Battle of the Coral Sea.

scored three hits on the carrier. Following the air battle, the *Lexington* had a seven-degree list to port. Three engineering compartments were partially flooded, several fires raged furiously, and the ship's elevators were useless.

By 1:00 P.M., Damage Control Center reported the *Lexington* back on an even keel. Three fires had been extinguished and a fourth was under control. The steering gear was intact and the ship was cruising at 25 knots. At this time, her air group returned to the ship and landed.

Forty-seven minutes past one the *Lexington* was shaken by a heavy explosion as gasoline ignited below decks. A fire roared out from the ship's main deck and travelled down near the central station area. Every effort was made by the gallant firefighting teams to control the fire but it spread aft and communications were lost.

Captain Frederick C. Sherman ordered personnel who were below decks to move to the flight deck at 3:58 P.M. Internal explosions were bursting more fre-

quently and it was feared that the danger of torpedo heads and bomb detonating was imminent.

At 5:07 P.M., Captain Sherman gave the order to abandon ship and the crew started their descent down the ropes or jumped into the sea. The last three men to leave the *Lexington* were a Marine corporal, the Executive Officer, and Captain Sherman.

Soon afterwards, the mighty *Lexington* became a raging inferno as flames skyrocketed hundreds of feet into the air. The gallant ship, often called, "Lady Lex" by her crew, remained a lady to the end as she slipped beneath the broiling waters of the Coral Sea. At first, she settled slowly on an even keel, neither dipping in the stern or bow. Her glowing hull continued to blaze far into the darkness of night and as the sun brought the dawn of another day, the merciless fires still ravaged her twisted and shattered hull. Within the compartments and passageways, new explosions erupted, tearing at the very heart of the ship herself.

Just before the task group was ordered to reform due to an impending attack from Japanese submarines, the *USS Phelps DD-360* passed final judgment on the *Lexington* by firing four torpedoes into what remained of her hull. She settled more rapidly now as the waves swallowed the great ship.

As one old timer, tears glistening his eyes, put it: "She was a lady to the finish, never showing her skirts."

It was a painful sight for the *Lexington's* survivors to watch helplessly as their ship went under. Some of those watching had served on her since her commissioning back in 1927. In those days it was not unusual for a sailor to report aboard a ship as a Seaman Ap-

A destroyer picks up survivors from the *Lexington* as explosions continue to erupt from the ill-fated carrier.

Abandoned and afire, the *Lexington* burns from stem to
stern on May 8, 1942, following the Battle of Coral Sea.

prentice and retire a Chief Petty Officer, serving his
entire naval career on the same ship. A great ship like
the *Lexington* was a real home for the sailors in those
bygone days—not just another duty assignment to
gripe about.

The *Lexington* had accumulated 345,000 miles and
covered 43,311 miles from December 7, 1941, until her

death in the Coral Sea at Latitude 15°–20′ South, Longitude 155°–30′ East.

The *USS Lexington CV-2* was awarded the Ameri-
can Defense Service Medal with one bronze star, the
American Area Campaign Medal, and the Asiatic-
Pacific Area Campaign Medal with two battle stars.

USS Saratoga CV-3 oblique port bow. Planes spotted on the
flight deck, one landing. June 6, 1935.

3

USS Saratoga CV-3

The *USS Saratoga CV-3* was the fifth naval vessel to bear the name honoring the decisive victory of the Revolutionary War, after which General Burgoyne capitulated his army to the Continental forces commanded by General Gates, on October 17, 1777, at Saratoga, New York.

Originally designed as the battle cruiser *USS Saratoga CC-3*, one of six battle cruisers in the Lexington class of 1916, she and her sister, the *Lexington CC-1*, survived the torches of the scrap yard and were completed as aircraft carriers.

The *Saratoga's* keel was laid on September 28, 1920, at the New York Shipbuilding Company, Camden, New Jersey. Mrs. Curtis D. Wilbur, wife of the Secretary of the Navy, christened the new carrier with waters from Saratoga Springs, New York, on April 7, 1925.

The first officer to command the new *Saratoga* was Captain H. E. Yarnell, USN, when the new carrier was commissioned on November 16, 1927.

The *Saratoga's* air officer, Commander Marc A. Mitscher, USN, completed the first landing in January 11, 1928, flying a UO-1 assisted by a passenger named S. B. Spangler.

The new carrier had an overall length of 888 feet and was 130 feet across the flight deck. She held a complement of 195 officers and 1676 enlisted men. She displaced 33,000 tons with a draft of 24 feet, 2 inches. Trial speed was 33.4 knots.

USS Saratoga CV-3: General view September 30, 1922.

Armament from commissioning until 1941 consisted of eight 8-inch 55-calibre breech loading rifles in four twin mounts, located fore and aft of the island structure. Accompanying, were five 5-inch 25-calibre antiaircraft guns and four 21-inch single above-water torpedo tubes.

The price tag for the *Saratoga* was $43,856,492.59.

In 1942, her flight deck was enlarged to 901¼ x 103 feet. At this time the 8-inch flight deck gun turrets were removed and replaced by eight 5-inch 38-calibre dual-purpose guns, paired in four turrets and controlled by a pair of combined high angle/low angle direction control towers. The original 5-inch 25-calibre antiaircraft weapons were replaced by four 20mm AAs plus warning radar system and gunnery control. A pole mast replaced the tripod and a deep bulge protruded along the portside.

When the *Saratoga* joined the fleet, the transition period of converting existing aircraft and designing specific carrier planes was nearly completed. The massive pursuit of developing carrier aircraft was formidable. The limited distance for landing and launching, the area of elevator platforms, the square and cubic feet of usable space on the hanger deck, and other restrictions set by the size of an aircraft carrier presented intricate problems that had to be solved, and aircraft designers and engineers attacked the situation enthusiastically.

The arresting hook, catapult launching gear, aircraft wing folding mechanisms, and a specifically constructed frame to absorb the shock of landing at high speeds added weight to an airplane. This, naturally, increased the difficulty of designing planes with low stalling speeds plus adequate load carrying capability.

During the 1930s, the *Saratoga* served in two capacities: first, as a fleet combat vessel, then as an experimental seagoing laboratory, right up to the time when the United States entered World War II.

The *Saratoga* was a duplicate of her sister, the *Lexington CV-2*. A black stripe ran down the center of each side of her huge stack. Aircraft aboard her wore white tail colors. The letters SARA were displayed on the after section of the flight deck.

Both the *Saratoga* and *Lexington* contributed greatly to the development and progress of naval aviation. The multitude of tests conducted from their decks further demonstrated the practical value of aircraft carriers.

The *Saratoga* joined her sister ship for the 1929 Fleet Problem IX. This exercise was the most significant exercise until the United States entered the Second World War. As in previous fleet problems, the

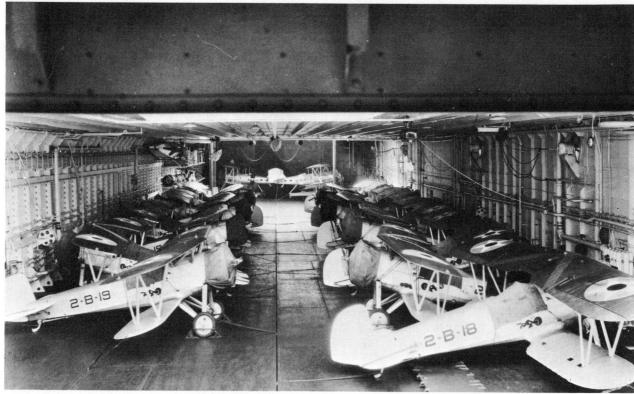

Hangar deck of the *USS Saratoga* March 9, 1929.

Panama Canal served as the "target" of enemy aggression. The force comprised a Blue Team (U.S.) and two "enemies"—Black in the Pacific and Brown in the Atlantic.

Blue Force had the *Lexington* while Black Force had the *Saratoga*. The *Langley CV-1* was in the yards for repairs so the *USS Aroostook CM-3* assumed the part of the *Langley,* as an RS-3 amphibious plane represented the *Langley's* airpower.

Actually, the Brown force was nonexistent, but comprised a "paper force." While the war game was in action, Brown Force ceased to pose a problem for the Blue force. The Black Force was determined to destroy the Panama Canal before the Blue Force could transit the Pacific and launch a surprise attack on the Black Force.

On January 25, 1929, the Black battleships spotted the *Lexington* and opened fire. Under actual battle conditions the mighty ship would have been sunk. However, since a sinking would end the carrier's participation, a restriction of 18 knots was imposed and the carrier was declared damaged.

During progression of the war game, the Blue Force had previously failed to advise the Army and Coco Solo of the *Aroostook's* substituting for the *Langley.*

The lone amphibious plane of the *Aroostook* began a bombing mission on the Atlantic side of the canal. The pilot had no opposition, and upon completion of his flight he landed and told the astonished "enemy" of their death.

The *Lexington* fell error to another action when her planes mistook her for the *Saratoga* and began a bombing attack. The error was understandable since both carriers were operating within a 12-mile radius. In later years the *Saratoga* would carry a black stripe along the sides of her stack and two white stripes parallel to the axis of the 8-inch gun turrets. This would be an identification symbol. Although confusion was prevalent in the exercise, it paved the trail for future developments in carrier aviation.

Fleet Problem IX marked the initial appearance of a large carrier striking force. Most significant was the utilization of an aircraft carrier as a single effective striking force.

From 1930 up to the early 1940s, the *Saratoga* would join with newer carriers to perfect this carrier striking force. When the *Ranger CV-4* and the *Yorktown CV-5* joined the fleet, the carriers had taken a more realistic role in war games.

U.S. Marine Scouting Squadrons VS-14M and

37

USS Saratoga CV-3: View of a part of the bridge structure and stack forward of the palisades January 28, 1933.

VS-15M reported aboard the *Lexington* and *Saratoga* respectively on November 2, 1931. They would function as an integral part of the Atlantic Battle Force. These squadrons remained aboard until late 1934. From that time until 1941, other Marine squadrons periodically operated from the two carriers.

On June 3, 1938, the *Saratoga* and the tanker *USS Kanawha AO-1* completed a two-day underway refueling test off the Southern California coast. Thus, the feasibility of refueling carriers at sea was successfully demonstrated.

On December 7, 1941, the *Saratoga* was undergoing a yard period at San Diego. The following day she steamed for the Hawaiian Islands, arriving on December 15. Two days later she was underway with Marine Fighter planes to assist the defenders of Wake Island. However, Wake fell to the Japanese on December 23, and the planes were delivered to Midway Island.

On January 11, 1942, the *Saratoga* was cruising some 500 miles southeast of Oahu when a Japanese submarine scored a successful torpedo hit. The steel fish struck the Flat-top's port quarter. Three firerooms were inundated but the engineering plant was not seriously damaged. She was able to proceed to Pearl Harbor under her own power. She was temporarily repaired at Pearl, then steamed to Puget Sound Naval Shipyard, Bremerton, Washington, for permanent repairs and modernization.

In view of the Pacific Fleet transmutation, coupled with the low morale of the American populace, the torpedoing of the *Saratoga* remained a well-guarded secret for a long time.

The *Saratoga* returned to the Pacific War Zone in late May 1942 and on June 8 delivered replacement aircraft to other carriers subsequent to the Battle of Midway. Following this operation, she became a member of Task Force 17, as the flagship of Vice Admiral J. F. Fletcher.

The *Saratoga's* air group supported the Marines on August 7, 1942, when they landed on Guadalcanal in the Solomon Islands. Her torpedo and dive bombers sank the Japanese carrier *Ryujo* and heavily damaged the seaplane carrier *Chitose* during the Battle of the Eastern Solomons on August 24.

She emerged from the attack unscratched, but on August 31, the powerful carrier became the victim of an enemy torpedo for the second time.

A Japanese submarine scored a direct hit on her starboard quarter inflicting irreparable damage to the engineering and electrical systems. The *Saratoga* sat dead in the water.

The heavy cruiser *USS Minneapolis CA-36* took the helpless *Saratoga* in tow until her power was restored. Temporary repairs were made at Tongatabu Harbor, then she returned to Pearl Harbor for completion of battle repairs.

Captain G. F. Bogan took command of the *Saratoga* on October 27, 1942. By December the ship was heading for Noumea, New Caledonia, to launch air attacks against Munda, Kolombongara, in the Solomons.

On April 7, 1943, Captain Bogan was relieved by Captain H. M. Mullinnix.

During May–August 1943, the *Saratoga* operated with the British carrier *Victorious*. The combined air groups of both ships struck enemy positions at Bougainville Islands, coordinating attacks with Marine landings at Empress Augusta Bay.

The *Saratoga's* efficient air group disabled eight enemy cruisers and a pair of destroyers on November 5, 1943. Upon conclusion of the action, Admiral Chester W. Nimitz said of the *Saratoga*: "You are the mainstay of the fleet."

The carrier returned to San Francisco on December 1, 1943, carrying survivors from the escort carrier *USS Liscombe Bay CVE-56*. After the happy survivors were put ashore, the *Saratoga* entered drydock for repairs. Afterwards she sailed to the Pacific War Zone for participation in the Marshall Islands operation.

For three days, beginning January 29, 1944, the *Saratoga's* air group sent continuous attacks against enemy installations on Wotje, Maloelap, and Taroa Islands.

In February, attacks were launched against Eniwetok. After covering the Eniwetok landings on Febru-

Saratoga in Tonga Tabu September 1942 after the torpedo hit. Listing 9½ degrees to Port.

Forward section of *Saratoga* showing extent of damage from February 21, 1945, attack, taken the following day.

ary 17, the carrier's air group supported the Marines who had landed ashore for the remainder of the month.

The *Saratoga* joined the Combined Eastern Fleet of allied vessels in March 1944, in Australia. While with this fleet she participated in strikes against enemy bases at Sabang, Sumatra and Surabaya, Java.

A lengthy cruise began for the *Saratoga* in May 1944, when she steamed from the Indian Ocean to Bremerton, Washington. Upon arrival she entered the Puget Sound Naval Shipyard for a complete overhaul.

The yard period was completed in September and the *Saratoga* sailed for Pearl Harbor to conduct training for air groups for both day and night carrier operations.

After joining Admiral Marc A. Mitscher's famed Task Force 58, she began the first carrier strikes on Tokyo, Japan, February 16–17, 1945.

Three years of service had resulted in only minor damage, except for the two torpedo hits. Then on February 21, 1945, the *Sarasota* became the victim of a Kamikaze attack.

Four suicide planes slammed into her and seven bombs found their mark, inflicting severe structural damage accompanied by savage, devastating flames. As a result 123 men were killed and 192 were wounded.

After many hours of heroic fire fighting, the *Sara-*

View from island of the *Saratoga* as firefighting is going on after the ship received seven direct hits off Iwo Jima on February 21, 1945.

toga was able to arrive at Eniwetok where she could be readied for a trip stateside.

The wounded carrier arrived at Puget Sound Naval Shipyard on March 16, 1945. She was not yet to be taken out of battle action. Following repairs she was

USS *Saratoga* CV-3 going down on July 25, 1946, in Bikini lagoon during operation "Crossroads." Forward Port side is showing.

once again sent to Pearl Harbor, where she completed her wartime duties as a training carrier.

From the date of commissioning in 1927 until August 15, 1945, the *Saratoga*'s flight deck received 89,195 plane landings. She joined the "Magic Carpet" fleet, bringing thousands of Pacific war veterans back home. During this time, her cruises brought back 29,204 personnel—more than any other single ship.

Nearly a year after World War II, the *Sara Maru*, as she was nicknamed by her crew, was designated to serve as a target vessel for the Bikini Atomic Bomb test. Many people were chagrined and complained against using the grand old carrier and wondering why she was even selected.

The reason was simple: The *Saratoga*'s huge island structure and stack limited her flight deck space more than any other carrier. Her deck was considerably more narrow, her elevators were smaller, and aircraft development had increased the size of newer planes. Her hangar deck contained less space than her contemporaries.

These, as well as other reasons, justified the sacrifice of the once gallant ship to the atomic test.

When the initial blast occurred the giant stack on the *Sara Maru* slowly tumbled into the sea and she quietly slipped beneath the boiling waves. Visible only for a brief glimpse was a figure 3 on the forward section of the flight deck.

And so it ended on July 25, 1946. The career of the Navy's third aircraft carrier became a myriad of memories sustained by the crew who served aboard her. No doubt, there were tears in the eyes of some veterans who cherished the memory of the *Sara Maru* during her reign in the 1930s when she had made naval aviation history.

The *USS Saratoga CV-3* received the following awards during her active service in the Navy: American Defense Service Medal with one star; American Area Campaign Service Medal; Asiatic-Pacific Campaign Service Medal with seven battle stars and the World War II Victory Medal.

USS Ranger CV-4, aerial oblique forward, port view, airplanes on flight deck. Cristobal, Canal Zone, April 6, 1935.

4

USS Ranger CV-4

On February 13, 1929, Congress authorized the construction of an aircraft carrier, the cost, including armor and armament, not to exceed $19 million. Experiments conducted aboard the first three probationary carriers, *Langley, Lexington* and *Saratoga,* became key factors while designing the *Ranger,* which was the first ship to be built as a carrier from the keel up.

Construction began on September 26, 1931, at the Newport News Shipbuilding Company. Original plans dictated a flush deck, but a small island structure had been included in the plans.

The *Ranger* was launched on February 25, 1933,

and commissioned on July 4, 1934. Captain A. L. Bristol became her first commanding officer.

The new carrier's overall length was 769 feet with a beam of 80 feet 1 inch. Mean draft was 19 feet 8 inches, and her full load displacement was 14,500 tons. She provided living and working spaces for 178 officers and 1610 enlisted men.

Lieutenant-Commander A. C. Davis made the first landing aboard the *Ranger* on June 21, 1934. He was flying a Vought O3U-3 with a passenger, H. E. Wallace, ACMM.

On August 17, the *Ranger* departed Norfolk for

shakedown operations that took her to Rio de Janeiro, Buenos Aires, and Montevideo. She returned to Norfolk on October 8, where she conducted air operations near the Virginia Capes until March 28, 1935.

Orders had been received transferring the carrier to the Pacific Fleet. After transiting the Panama Canal on April 7, she arrived at North Island Naval Air Station, San Diego, on April 15, 1935.

For the next four years the *Ranger* participated in Fleet problems reaching to Hawaii; western seaboard operations took her as far south as Callao, Peru, and northwards to Seattle.

On January 4, 1939, the *Ranger* steamed from San Diego for winter fleet operations in the Caribbean. She then headed for Norfolk, arriving on April 18, 1939.

In the autumn of 1939, the *Ranger* began service with the Neutrality Patrol. Based at Bermuda, she cruised the trade routes of the middle Atlantic and up the eastern seaboard to Argentina. While returning to Norfolk on December 7, 1941, her crew learned of the tragedy at Pearl Harbor.

On December 8, she docked at Norfolk. On the 21, she headed for the South Atlantic, where she operated until March 22, 1942. At that time she came back to Norfolk for overhaul and repairs.

Rear Admiral Ernest D. McWhorter and his staff came aboard on April 7, 1942. The carrier immediately set course for Quonset Point, Rhode Island, where 68

The *USS Ranger* sliding down the ways on February 25, 1933.

ABG-1 clears the *Ranger*, March 17, 1937.

Respotting aircraft aboard the *USS Ranger CV-4* (March 17, 1938).

Army P-40 Warhawks and men of the 33rd Army Pursuit Squadron were put on board.

On April 22, she sailed from Quonset Point and launched the Army aircraft on May 10; they would land at Accora, on the Gold Coast of Africa. The carrier returned to Rhode Island on May 28, made a short trip to Argentina, then returned.

On July 1, 1942, she was on the move again with 72 Army P-40s and participated in the same operations as before. The planes were launched on July 19 off the coast of Accora and the carrier returned to Norfolk, where she conducted air operations off the Atlantic seaboard until October 1, 1942.

At this time the *Ranger* was the only large carrier in the Atlantic Fleet. Her task force comprised four *Sangamon* class escort carriers and furnished the crushing air superiority that enabled the Atlantic Fleet Amphibious Force to place men in a position to seize the German dominated French Morocco. This capture came three days prior to the invasion which began on November 8, 1942.

The Task Force left Bermuda on October 25, and joined the invasion armada three days later for the approach to the Moroccan coast. The *Ranger* and her escort carriers had 28 TBF Grumman *Avengers;* 36 Douglas *Dauntless* dive bombers plus 108 F4F-4 *Wildcats.* In addition, 76 P-40s were being ferried to a base in Casablanca to be used subsequent to its capture. The *Ranger* also carried three Piper Cubs that were flown by Army Artillery officers to Fedela, where they searched for future artillery sights.

USS *Ranger* CV-4 F4F taking off in invasion of North Africa, November 1942.

On November 8, 1942, at 6:15 A.M., the *Ranger* launched her planes some 40 miles northwest of Casablanca. Nine *Wildcats* attacked the Rabat and Rabat-Sale airdromes, Headquarters of the Vichy French Air Force in Morocco. Without suffering any losses they demolished seven grounded planes on one field plus 14 bombers on another. Another flight destroyed seven planes at Port Lyauten and strafed four French destroyers in Casablanca.

During the three-day operation, the *Ranger* launched 496 combat sorties. Her SBDs scored two direct hits amidships on the Vichy French destroyer *Albatros.* A direct hit on the bridge killed the destroyer's commanding officer and his exec.

Aircraft from the *Ranger* also attacked the Vichy French cruiser *Primaugust* as she tried to escape from Casablanca Harbor. More than 70 enemy aircraft were destroyed on the ground and 15 were downed in aerial dogfights. Some 86 military vehicles were destroyed, most of which were troop carrying trucks.

Former *Ranger* crewmen still talk of the time when Lieutenant R. A. Embree and J. M. Eardley, his First Class Radioman, escaped death. While concentrating on a strafing run of an enemy truck, the aircraft failed to clear a roadside tree and the underside of the plane was badly damaged. Despite this, Lieutenant Embree safely brought his plane back to the *Ranger.* Adding to the danger was the fact that his plane was still loaded with one 500 pound bomb and two 100 pound bombs.

On the afternoon of November 10, 1942, the Vichy

View of the *Ranger's* island structure April 11, 1942, at the Portsmouth Naval Shipyard.

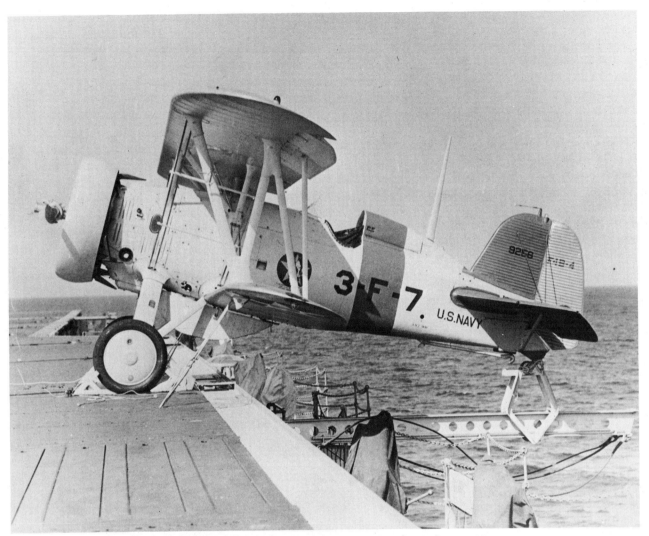

To save flight deck space, the *Ranger* used a unique outrigger system to park aircraft like this F4B-4.

French submarine *Tonnant* fired four torpedoes, which passed under the stern section of the *Ranger*.

Casablanca capitulated to American forces on November 11, 1942. The carrier departed Morocco the following day and arrived at Norfolk on November 23.

The Moroccan invasion might have been a lengthy and expensive struggle had it not been for the air support provided by the *Ranger* and her escorts. This support neutralized French Air Force cover of the landings and attacks on enemy shipping.

This engagement proved that carrier-based air power could play a formidable role during future amphibious landings, especially in the Pacific battles waged against Japan.

From December 16, 1942, to February 7, 1943, the *Ranger* received an overhaul at Norfolk. Afterwards,

she transported 75 P-40s to Casablanca and launched them on February 23.

After training pilots along the New England coast, north to Halifax, Nova Scotia, she left the latter port on August 11, 1943, and joined the British Home Fleet at Scapa Flow, Scotland, on August 19. She would be used to patrol the approaches to the British Isles.

The Home Fleet was commanded by Admiral Sir Bruce Fraser aboard the battleship HMS *Duke of York*. Under his command were HMS *Anson*, three cruisers, six destroyers, and Admiral Hustvedt's task force, comprised of the *Ranger*, the cruiser *Tuscaloosa* plus a destroyer division.

With the British Fleet the *Ranger* exited Scapa Flow on October 2, 1943, to attack German shipping in Norwegian waters. The Task Force's objective was the

Norwegian port of Bodo, south of the Lofoten Islands—a rendezvous for German and Quisling sea traffic.

The *Ranger* was at launch position off Vestfjord before dawn on October 4, 1943. At 6:18 A.M., the carrier launched 20 SBD *Dauntless* dive bombers and 8 *Wildcats* to protect them. The planes cruised low over the North Sea until they spotted the Myken Light, 18 miles south of the target.

Upon reaching the target, one division of SBDs attacked the 8000-ton freighter *La Plata*. Then they hit a small German convoy, severely damaging a 10,000 ton tanker and a 4300 ton troop-laden transport.

A second group of 10 *Avengers* along with six *Wildcats* destroyed the 5000-ton German freighter *Topeka*. Three *Ranger* aircraft were lost to antiaircraft fire during the battle.

By late afternoon on October 4, German planes finally located the *Ranger*, but the carrier's combat air patrol immediately shot down two of the attackers. The other lone raider turned 180 degrees and hastily retreated. The *Ranger* returned to Scapa Flow on October 6, 1943.

Along with the British Second Battle Squadron, the carrier patrolled the waters reaching to Iceland.

The *Ranger* departed Hvalfjord on November 26 and arrived at the Boston Navy Yard on December 4, 1943. The crew was able to enjoy Christmas and New Years at home, a rare occasion during wartime.

On January 3, 1944, the *Ranger* was designated a training carrier and would operate from Quonset Point. This duty was interrupted on April 20, when the carrier steamed to Staten Island, New York, to receive

An aerial oblique view of *USS Ranger CV-4*, at Guantanamo Bay, Cuba.

76 P-38 Lightning aircraft. Also quartered aboard were Army, Navy, and Free French sailors for transportation to Casablanca.

Staten Island slipped away on April 24 as the carrier sailed to Casablanca, arriving May 4, 1944. Damaged Army planes and military personnel were taken aboard and brought back to New York on May 16, 1944.

The *Ranger* entered Norfolk Navy Yard on May 19 to have her flight deck strengthened and a new type catapult system installed. Her Combat Information Center (CIC) received new radar and other equipment to provide sufficient night fighter interceptor training.

She departed the yard on July 11 and sailed through the Panama Canal on July 16. Several hundred Army passengers were embarked at Balboa, then the carrier proceeded to San Diego, arriving on July 25. Night Fighter Squadron 102 came aboard and the *Ranger* headed for Hawaii three days later.

Upon arrival at Pearl Harbor, some 1000 Marines were released from the ship. For three months to follow, intensive day and night air operations was conducted to train pilots and increase their proficiency.

The *Ranger* departed Pearl Harbor on October 13 and provided combat pilot training near San Diego until the end of World War II.

On September 30, 1945, the carrier sailed from San Diego to Balboa where she took on civilian and military passengers.

The *Ranger* participated in the Navy Day celebrations at New Orleans, then departed on October 30 for brief operations off Pensacola, Florida.

On November 18, she entered the Philadelphia Navy Yard for overhaul.

She remained in port on the eastern seaboard until October 18, 1946, at which time the Navy's first carrier built from keel up was decommissioned.

On January 28, 1947, the *Ranger* was sold to the Sun Shipbuilding and Drydock Company of Chester, Pennsylvania. She arrived at that shipyard on February 6, 1947; scrapping was completed in October. The builder's plate and ship's bell were presented to the Navy.

The *USS Ranger CV-4* received the following awards during her career. American Defense Service Medal with bronze "A"; American Area Campaign Medal; European–African–Middle Eastern Campaign Medal with two battle stars; and the World War II Victory Medal.

USS *Yorktown* CV-5 aerial oblique forward port view, at anchor, in the harbor of St. Thomas, Virgin Islands, January 17, 1938.

5

USS Yorktown CV-5

On April 22, 1930, a naval treaty was signed at London by the signatories of the Washington Naval Treaty, which carried forward the general limitations of that earlier agreement and provided for additional reductions of naval armament.

Under the terms applicable to naval aviation, the definitions of an aircraft carrier was expanded to include ships of any tonnage primarily designed for aircraft operations. It was further agreed that installation of a landing-on or flying-off platform on a warship that had been designed or used primarily for other purposes would not render that vessel an aircraft carrier, and also that no capital ship in existence as of

April 1, 1930, would be fitted with such a platform or deck.

The Senate ratified the treaty on July 21, 1930, and signed by the President on the following day.

During the early 1930s, President Franklin D. Roosevelt created the National Recovery Act (NRA) to revive American industry. Included in this program was the construction of two aircraft carriers.

Executive Order 6174 of June 16, 1933, stated: "During the thirty days the Federal Emergency Administrator of Public Works shall have the authority to allot the sum of, but not to exceed $238,000,000 to the Department of the Navy."

Following completion of the *Lexington* and *Saratoga* the Navy intended to build five carriers of the *Ranger* type from the remaining balance of tonnage provided for aircraft carrier construction by the Washington Treaty limiting naval armament.

Even before the *Ranger* was launched, the Navy recognized that the minimum effective size of a carrier was 20,000. Thus, the *Yorktown* and her sister the *Enterprise* were designed to be larger and generally more satisfactory in overall design than the *Ranger*.

The keel of the *USS Yorktown CV-5* was laid down on May 21, 1934, at the Newport News Shipbuilding Company. She was sponsored by Mrs. Franklin D. Roosevelt and launched on April 4, 1936.

Captain Ernest D. McWhorter assumed command on September 30, 1937, as the carrier was commissioned at the Naval Operating Base, Norfolk, Virginia.

The *Yorktown*'s overall length was 827 feet; extreme beam, 83 feet 1 inch; trial speed was 34 knots. She carried 207 officers and 2072 enlisted men. This included the ship's company, squadrons, Marines, and staff. She displaced 19,800 tons.

An improvement over the *Ranger* type was to be found in the *Yorktown*'s class. The machinery was more conventionally arranged, with boiler rooms forward of the engine rooms; the boiler intakes were led to a single large funnel on the island superstructure, and the flight deck overhung the stern.

Three elevators connected the hangars to the flight deck. Compartmentation was highly improved and there was a more durable patch of armor plating around the machinery spaces.

USS Yorktown CV-5. Hangar deck of the *Yorktown* looking aft, September 29, 1937.

A tripod foremost and polemost were fitted with two high-angle direction control towers on the island structure. The main battery comprised eight 5-inch 38 calibre guns while the secondary battery consisted of sixteen 1.1-inch AA machine guns.

Early in the war the boats and derrick outboard of the island were removed. The light AA batteries were reinforced with numerous 20mm AA guns.

A large "Y" was painted on each side of the *Yorktown*'s island. The letters YKTN were placed in white on the after section of the flight deck. All aircraft assigned to the ship had red tail colors.

Following an extensive shakedown cruise, the *Yorktown* remained at the Norfolk Navy Yard for further alterations until January 1939. She then became flagship of Carrier Division Two, Aircraft Battle Force, U.S. Fleet, and steamed the eastern seaboard south into the Caribbean Sea until April 1939. The carrier then headed for San Diego to serve in the Pacific as flagship of Aircraft Battle Force and Carrier Division Two.

Following maneuvers and tactics from along the west coast to Hawaii, *Yorktown* departed Pearl Harbor April 20, 1941, for neutrality patrol in the Atlantic and Caribbean as a member of Carrier Division Three, Aircraft Battle Force.

She arrived at Bermuda May 12, for patrols in the Caribbean Sea whereupon she moved northward and sailed off Newfoundland and the coast of New England.

The carrier was back at Norfolk December 2, 1941, and was in that port when the Japanese Navy accomplished its attack on Pearl Harbor five days later.

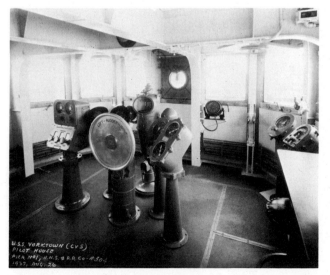

The pilot house of the *USS Yorktown CV-5*, August 26, 1937.

Less than nine days after the enemy attack on Hawaii, the *Yorktown* became battle ready and departed Norfolk December 16, 1941, arriving in San Diego on the 30th. She was the flagship of Rear Admiral Frank Jack Fletcher, commanding the newly organized Task Force 17. The carrier steamed from San Diego on January 6, 1942, to cover troop ships transporting Marine reinforcements to the Samoan Islands. The Leathernecks were put ashore at Samoa on January 23.

Two days later the *Yorktown* was underway along with the *Enterprise CV-6* Carrier Task Force. Near nightfall on January 31, the two carriers parted company. The *Yorktown* was ready for action and had her first taste of combat on February 1, when she sent

air strikes against Jaluit, Mili, and Makin. A lone four-engine Japanese bomber made an unsuccessful attempt at glory when it tried to attack the destroyer screen. When this proved futile, the enemy air crew headed for the *Yorktown*, and was shot down by pilots of the carrier's combat air patrol.

At Makin the *Yorktown*'s pilots left one auxiliary ship burning from two direct hits and they also destroyed additional enemy bombers. The results were costly for the *Yorktown*'s group, for seven planes and 16 men did not return.

After a short rest at Pearl Harbor the *Yorktown* returned to the war zone. On March 10, 1942, she participated in the Salamaua Lae raid. The strike target for the *Yorktown* was Lae. From a position in Huon

The *USS Yorktown* taking planes above on March 29, 1940.
Notice "Y" on island structure.

SBD's take off the *Yorktown* April 18, 1942.

Gulf the carrier sent her planes to attack the Japanese ships and installations situated in the eastern end of New Guinea. The only opposition during the Salamaua-Lae raid was a single seaplane fighter which went down very fast. Following the raid an accounting was made and it was learned that the enemy had lost two heavy cruisers, one light cruiser, one destroyer, and five transport ships. The *Yorktown's* pilots had sunk the cargo ship *Yokohama Maru*. One American plane was lost during this action.

The *Yorktown* departed Tongatabu Island April 27, 1942, and was southwest of the New Hebrides Islands May 1, when joined by the *Lexington*, which led Task Foorce 11 under Rear Admiral Aubrey W. Fitch.

At 3:45 P.M., May 2, the *Yorktown's* air scout sighted an enemy submarine on the surface. Bombers from the carrier began an attack, but unfortunately the sub escaped any serious damage from the aerial depth charges and was able to report the presence of the task force to her superiors.

At this time, a powerful Japanese task force had been organized in hopes of gaining control of the Coral Sea, and thus cut off Australia from the war. An amphibious task group of 11 troop-laden transports guarded by a Japanese destroyer force was to seize Port Moresby. A smaller amphibious group hoped to capture Tulagi Island in the Salomons and establish a seaplane base. A support group built around a seaplane carrier was to organize a seaplane base in the Louisiades. These Japanese invasion forces were covered by the light carrier *Shoho*, four heavy cruisers and a destroyer, plus an aircraft carrier task force com-

prising the carriers *Shokaku* and *Zuikaku,* screened by a pair of heavy cruisers and a half dozen destroyers.

On the morning of May 3, 1942, the *Yorktown* and *Lexington* task forces were 100 miles apart and engaged in refueling operations. A few hours before midnight, Rear Admiral Fletcher learned that Australia-based planes had spotted enemy transports debarking troops at Tulagi. He ordered a northerly course at 27 knots and by daybreak of May 4, was in striking distance of the island.

Three attack groups sped off the *Yorktown's* deck to hit the invasion force at Tulagi, and soon the harbors of Tulagi and Gavutu felt the sting of the American forces. Their bomb and torpedo hits sank the enemy destroyer *Kikusuki,* three minesweepers, and four landing barges. Five Japanese seaplanes were destroyed and numerous vessels including the destroyer *Yuzuki* were damaged. That same day a cruiser and destroyer force (Task Force 44), under Rear Admiral Crace's Royal Navy, joined the *Lexington* Task Force.

On May 6, all the forces were combined to form a single group known as Task Force 17 under tactical command of Rear Admiral Fletcher aboard the flagship *Yorktown*.

At daybreak on May 7, an attack was launched to the Louisiades to intercept any enemy attempts to move toward Port Moresby. This force was made up of cruisers and destroyers under the command of Rear Admiral Crace. His carriers headed north into the Coral Sea in search of enemy covering forces.

Three hours later, fleet oiler *USS Neosho AO-23,* which had fueled Admiral Fletcher's force, and her escort, destroyer *USS Sims DD-409* were located by planes of the Japanese Carrier Force. After dodging bombs from 25 enemy planes, they were attacked at noon by 36 Japanese dive bombers. The *Sims* took three direct bomb hits, two of which exploded in her engine room. She sank stern first with a large loss of life.

The *Neosho* received seven direct hits and became a lifeless hulk. She drifted until the afternoon of May 11, at which time her 123 survivors were taken off by the destroyer *USS Henley DD-391,* which then scuttled the *Neosho*.

While the *Neosho* and *Sims* drew off the attacking enemy planes, the pilots from the *Lexington* and *Yorktown* sank the Japanese light carrier *Shoho*.

On the afternoon of May 7, 27 enemy bombers and torpedo planes were launched from the still unlocated Japanese heavy carriers *Shokaku* and *Zuikaku*. They made an uneventful search for the American carriers and were on their way home when intercepted by fighters from the *Lexington* and *Yorktown*. Nine enemy pilots were shot out of the sky in the ensuing dogfights.

As night approached, a trio of enemy pilots mistook the *Yorktown* for their own carrier but were able to escape the barrage of gunfire aimed at them while crossing the carrier's bow. Three other enemy flyers made the same mistake 20 minutes later and one was shot down.

The great carrier air Battle of the Coral Sea was born on the morning of May 8, when a *Lexington* pilot sighted the enemy carriers, the striking force of Admiral Takagi. The *Yorktown* and *Lexington* immediately sent their planes at the heavy Japanese carriers *Zuikaku* and *Shokaku,* which were screened by a pair of heavy cruisers and several destroyers.

During this first American attack of the war on a large enemy carrier, the *Shokaku* took two bomb hits from the *Yorktown* pilots. This damaged her flight deck to such a degree that she was unable to launch any planes. Furious gasoline fires erupted, destroying her repair compartment containing aircraft engines.

The *Lexington* dive bombers added another hit, killing 108 enemy sailors and wounding 40 others.

While the American planes were attacking the Japanese carriers, the *Yorktown* and *Lexington* made ready for a second attack. An intercepted enemy message indicated that the Japanese knew of their location.

At 11:18 A.M. on May 8, the anticipated attack arrived as nearly 100 enemy planes began dives on the *Lexington* and *Yorktown*. Seventeen enemy planes were shot down, but others broke through and dropped torpedoes on both sides of the *Lexington*'s bow. Two of the steel fish smashed into her port side as a dive bombing attack scored three hits.

Meanwhile, the *Yorktown* maneuvered to dodge eight torpedoes and came under dive bomber attacks. The skillful hands of Captain Buckmaster steered the carrier clear of several near misses and evaded all but one 880-pound bomb, which slammed into the flight deck.

The hail of explosions were taking their toll on the *Yorktown*. Her stern was literally lifted so high that the ship's screws were visible. Forty-three men were dead, forty-three were seriously wounded and one was missing.

The fires were brought under control, and the *Yorktown* escaped any damage that would impair flight operations.

The *Lexington* was not so lucky. About an hour following the battle she was on an even keel. Three fires were out and a fourth under control. Her steering gear was intact and she was making 25 knots with

nearly normal flight operations. Her planes returned and landed. Then at 12:47 P.M., she was shaken by a large explosion caused by ignition of fuel vapor below her decks. Captain Frederick C. Sherman and his men now began a final fight of supreme courage to save their stricken home. The fire slowly spread aft and communications were lost as internal explosions became more rapid and the danger of torpedoes and bombs detonating was imminent. Only then, at 5:07 P.M., did Captain Sherman give the order to abandon ship. Captain Sherman was the last man to leave the raging inferno. The destroyer *USS Phelps DD-360* came within 1500 yards and fired a pair of torpedoes into the *Lexington*. With one last explosion the great carrier slipped beneath the waves at Latitude 15°-20′ South; Longitude 155°-30′ East.

The Coral Sea Battle was a tactical victory for the enemy in terms of losses inflicted, but a strategic victory for the United States. The Americans had stopped the Japanese thrust toward Australia. Not one of their ships would ever cross the barrier of the Louisiades safely. Tulagi, the sole objective attained by the enemy, was nullified by the arrival of American troops during August 7–8, 1942. Now the United States had the time to strengthen its forces in the Southwest Pacific.

The *Yorktown* returned to Hawaii for repairs. Battle damage had been inflicted to such an extent that in peacetime three months would have been required for repairs. Now, however, the work was completed in only two days. Afterwards her decks were still torn from bomb hits and some hull plates still leaked. However, no time was wasted in preparations to repel an expected full-scale attack by the enemy in their attempt to capture and occupy Midway Atoll.

The *Yorktown* sailed on May 30, and rendezvoused northeast of Midway on June 2, 1942, with the *Enterprise* Task Force 16, commanded by Rear Admiral Raymond A. Spruance. This task force held a position 10 miles to the south of *Yorktown*'s Task Force 17.

Two days later the Japanese armada was encountered and the Battle of Midway began. The carriers *Yorktown, Enterprise,* and *Hornet* launched their planes, which were soon involved in savage combat.

The first contact reports of enemy carriers and word that enemy planes were headed for Midway the morning of June 4 were intercepted by Rear Admiral Fletcher of the *Yorktown*. At 6:07, he directed Rear Admiral Spruance of the *Enterprise* to proceed southwesterly and attack the enemy carriers as soon as they were definitely located.

Forty-one torpedo planes from the three American carriers were overwhelmed by swarms of enemy planes.

The *Yorktown* burning after the first air attack. Personnel man the flight deck as smoke begins to issue from the island structure June 4, 1942.

Fires continue to rage as men survey damage from three direct bomb hits on the afternoon of June 4, 1942.

Crewmen bring up fresh planks to replace bombed out section of flight deck during the Battle of Midway.

Crewmen walk the slanted deck as the *Yorktown* takes a 20 degree list to port following the second air attack.

Yorktown and *Enterprise* attacked three Japanese aircraft carriers.

The attack group from the *Yorktown* had taken off little more than an hour after the launch of the *Enterprise*'s and *Hornet*'s planes. However, her Air Group leader had figured out the shortest route to the enemy carriers and then selected the enemy carrier *Soryu* for a victim. The *Soryu* had just armed and fueled an attack group for a second strike at Midway.

Planes were lined up on the *Soryu*'s deck and she had turned into the wind to launch when the *Yorktown* dive bombers roared in for three waves of diving attacks, which scored three fatal hits.

The *Soryu* became a blazing inferno from stem to stern and was abandoned. As her hull became lifeless, her sister carriers *Akagi* and *Kaga* received their death blows from the *Enterprise* pilots. *Soryu* joined her sister carriers at the bottom of the sea assisted by torpedoes unleashed by the fleet submarine *USS Nautilus SS-168*. The Japanese had lost three aircraft carriers, but a fourth, *Hiryu*, was still around.

The *Yorktown* launched scouting aircraft at noon on June 4. Three hours later one of them sighted the *Hiryu* under the escort of battleships, cruisers, and destroyers. At the same time, 18 enemy planes, previously launched from the *Hiryu*, attacked the *Yorktown*. Many of the enemy planes were shot down, but eight managed to evade the American pilots. Two of these

Only six of the total would survive to return to their carriers, but they were used as magnets for the enemy's combat air patrols. As they fought enemy fighters at near water level, the American torpedo plane pilots drew attention away from the high-altitude *Dauntless* dive bombers of the *Yorktown* and *Enterprise* that appeared a few minutes later. Then, virtually unopposed by enemy planes, the dive bombers from the

A destroyer stands by as the carrier continues to list portside.

were downed by cruisers and destroyers, but the remainder scored hits on the *Yorktown*. As one enemy plane was ripped apart by AA fire, a bomb fell on her flight deck, where its explosions inflicted many casualties and engendered three fires below decks which enveloped the carrier in smoke. The fires were quickly smothered, but a second bomb exploded in the smoke stack to disable five out of six boilers, decreasing her speed to a mere six knots. A third bomb smashed into her fourth deck triggering a fire adjacent to the forward fuel tank and ammo lockers. The magazines were instantly flooded and efforts made to prevent the gasoline stowage from exploding.

When fire had disabled communications on the *Yorktown*, Rear Admiral Fletcher shifted his flag to the cruiser *USS Astoria CA-34* and directed the cruiser *USS Portland CA-33* to take the *Yorktown* in tow. The lifesaving towline was never passed. The four boilers of the *Yorktown* were back on the line within minutes after Admiral Fletcher's departure, and she picked up to 20 knots.

At this time a cruiser made radar contact with a second wave of aircraft from the *Hiryu* from 40 miles away. The *Yorktown* barely had time to launch eight fighters which joined four other planes in the air in an effort to intercept ten fast enemy torpedo bombers escorted by six fighters.

The American flyers were unable to cope with the onward rushing enemy planes. The Japanese torpedo bombers divided to attack from four angles at masthead height. Four penetrated the concentrated AA fire and released their steel fish 500 yards from the *Yorktown*. The carrier dodged two torpedoes, but another pair slammed into the portside and exploded. The *Yorktown*'s rudder was now immobilized and all power connections were severed. It was 4:20 P.M. as the rudder jammed at 15 degrees to port and the carrier took a 26-degree list. It appeared that the ship might capsize at any moment so Captain Elliott Buckmaster ordered the *Yorktown* abandoned and four destroyers closed to take off her crew.

While the *Yorktown* was fighting for her life, 10 of her dive bombers took off from the deck of the *Enterprise* and joined 14 dive bombers from the latter carrier. Together, they attacked the *Hiryu* and concomitant cruisers.

The *Hiryu* received four direct bomb hits and was finally consumed by flames and had to be abandoned. Japanese destroyers were ordered to finish off her dead hulk with torpedoes, but she continued to float until after daybreak of June 5. When she plunged to the bottom, the Japanese Striking Force lost the last of its four fleet carriers.

One strange incident happened aboard the *Yorktown* on the night of June 4. Machine gun fire was heard coming from the dead carrier. Were this not a modern age, one might think it was the ghost of many a deceased shipmate taking revenge. Logic, however, triumphed so the destroyer *USS Hughes DD-410* sent out a boarding party and returned with two men who had been in sick bay and presumed dead. They had crawled topside and fired the machine gun in hopes that someone would hear and rescue them from the carrier. One of the men died shortly afterwards.

As the remnants of the Japanese Fleet fled the Battle of Midway, one more effort was made to save the *Yorktown* and take her to port. On the morning of June 6, 1942, the captain returned to his stricken carrier with 29 officers and 141 men. A group of five destroyers formed an antisubmarine screen around the *Yorktown* while a fleet tug, *USS Vireo AT-144*, very slowly towed the carrier. The *USS Hammann DD-412* came alongside to furnish pumps for counter flooding and provide electrical power to operate submersible pumps to clear out the carrier's enginerooms.

By mid-afternoon of June 6, considerable progress had been accomplished in the attempt to salvage the *Yorktown*. Had the enemy not been lurking in the area, the *Yorktown* might have been saved. However, a plane from a Japanese cruiser spotted the crippled carrier and reported her adrift in the water. An enemy submarine *I-168*, spotted the *Yorktown* on June 6 and released its torpedoes at 3:36 P.M. A spread of four torpedoes approached the *Yorktown*'s starboard beam from beyond the circling destroyer screen. This deadly salvo found their target with devastating explosion.

One torpedo missed the carrier and hit the destroyer *Hammann* amidships. She was torn in half and sank in four minutes with great loss of life.

Two other torpedoes passed under the *Hammann*'s keel and smashed into the *Yorktown*. Survivors were rescued from the sea while other's went down the lines to the deck of the Fleet Tug *Vireo*.

One minute after the *Hammann* sank, a violent explosion was felt, probably a depth charge from the stricken destroyer. The explosion killed several men and seriously injured personnel from both ships who were awaiting rescue from the sea.

Since all ships were employed in searching for the enemy submarine, all further salvage attempts were cancelled until the next morning. By this time the skeleton crew had departed the *Yorktown*.

At 5:20 A.M. on June 7, the *Yorktown*'s list was rapidly increasing and by 7:01 she turned over on her port side and sank in 300 fathoms of water. Her two battle flags were still flying as she slipped under, and her position was Latitude 30°-46′ North, Longitude 167°-24′ West.

The *USS Yorktown CV-5* received the following awards during her active naval service: The American Defense Service Medal with Bronze A; The American Area Campaign Service Medal, and the Asiatic-Pacific Area Service Medal with four battle stars.

USS Enterprise CV-6.

6

USS Enterprise CV-6

When the keel of the *USS Enterprise CV-6* was laid on July 16, 1934, it established a precedent by being the seventh U.S. fighting ship to bear the name of a perpetual symbol in the great struggle to retain American liberty, justice, and freedom since the initial days of the American Revolutionary War.

The *Enterprise* was built by the Newport News Shipbuilding and Drydock Company of Virginia and launched on October 3, 1936, under the sponsorship of Mrs. Claude A. Swanson, wife of the Secretary of the Navy. As the new carrier slid down the ways, Mrs. Swanson quoted a line from Shakespeare's *Othello* that was to gain increasing significance in the years to follow: "May she also say with just pride—I have done the state some service."

The *Enterprise*'s overall length was 827 feet 4 inches with a maximum breadth of 114 feet about her flight deck. She had a full load displacement of 32,000 tons with draft measuring 27 feet 7 inches. Trial speed was 33.6 knots. The original complement at commissioning was 82 officers and 1447 enlisted men, exclusive of the air group.

The letters EN were prominently displayed in white on her flight deck and all aircraft operating with the *Enterprise* air group wore blue tail colors for recognition.

On May 12, 1938, the *Enterprise* was commissioned at ceremonies conducted at the Naval Operating Base, Norfolk, Virginia. Her shakedown cruise took her to Rio de Janeiro. Upon returning to Norfolk, she held winter maneuvers with the fleet in the Caribbean Sea.

Capt. N. H. White, Jr., was relieved by Capt. C. A. Pownall on December 21, 1938.

The *Enterprise* joined the Pacific Fleet in April 1939,

becoming an integral part of Carrier Division Two of the Aircraft Battle Force. When President Roosevelt declared a state of national emergency on September 8, 1939, the *Enterprise* headed for Pearl Harbor.

On March 21, 1941, Captain Pownall was relieved by Capt. George D. Murray. During the latter months of 1941, the *Enterprise* trained for war operations as a contingent of the Hawaiian Fleet Detachment. One of her main duties was ferrying planes and air squadrons to various Pacific Island bases.

As flagship of Vice Admiral William F. Halsey, Commander Task Force Eight, the *Enterprise* cleared the Pearl Harbor channel on November 28, 1941, to deliver 12 Marine fighter planes to the newly constructed airfield on Wake Island.

Captain Murray issued Battle Order Number 1, which read: "The *Enterprise* is now operating under war conditions." On December 2, the Leatherneck fighters were launched about 75 miles north of Wake Island, then the task force returned to Pearl Harbor. Estimated arrival date was December 6. Due to a storm, Vice Admiral Halsey ordered reduced speed, thus delaying the carrier's arrival in the Hawaiian port to December 7. This delay proved to be an angel in disguise for the *Enterprise* escaped possible total destruction when the Japanese made their sneak attack.

At 6 A.M. on December 7, 1941, scout planes were sent aloft from the *Enterprise* to sector the area ahead, then proceed to Pearl Harbor. At 8:15 A.M. the men in the radio room of the big carrier received this shocking message: "Air raid on Pearl Harbor . . . This is no drill!" The crew hoisted the battle flags and launched the remaining aircraft in an unsuccessful attempt to locate the enemy aircraft carriers who were sending death and destruction over the serene blue skies of Hawaii on that black Sunday morning.

The wartime career of the *Enterprise* had begun. Her history is virtually a complete record of the Pacific Theater of the Second World War from Pearl Harbor to Okinawa. She would become the first carrier to be awarded the Presidential Unit Citation and later win the Navy Unit Commendation. No other aircraft carrier received both of these recognitions for service during World War II. The "Big E" also earned 20 battle stars.

When the *Enterprise* entered Pearl Harbor one day following the Japanese attack, the scene her sailors witnessed was heartbreaking. The once proud and mighty Pacific Fleet lay in near ruin. The *USS Nevada BB-36* was beached; *USS Oklahoma BB-37*, capsized and sunk; *USS Arizona BB-39*, sunk and split in two; *USS West Virginia BB-48*, sunk. These and many other ships suffered greatly from the bombs and torpedoes released by Japanese planes; however, some would return to see the victory that lay waiting.

The crew of the "Big E" could not waste valuable time in remorse of what happened at Pearl Harbor. After taking on fuel and supplies, she patrolled the Hawaiian area providing anti-submarine air coverage against a possible return of the enemy.

On December 10, north of Oahu, her pilots bombed and strafed two submarines. At 1:45 P.M., one of the pilots sunk the Japanese submarine *I-70*.

The *Enterprise* steamed to a position west of Johnston Island and south of Midway to assist the U. S. Marines on Wake Island, but on December 23, 1941, the island fell to the Japanese and the carrier returned to Pearl Harbor, arriving eight days later.

On February 1, 1942, the "Big E" launched air strikes against Kwajalein and Maloelap in the Marshall Islands. Air installations of the enemy on Taroa and Wotje were damaged.

While returning from this action, the *Enterprise* was attacked by five Japanese twin-engine bombers. The planes were repelled but not without incident. A near-miss caused a serious fire on the port quarter gun batteries. One of the enemy flyers attempted to crash the carrier's flight deck but fortunately missed.

On February 5, the *Enterprise* sailed back to Pearl Harbor. Task Force Eight was redesignated Task Force Sixteen on February 14, and that same day the *Enterprise* left her Hawaiian port on a mission to destroy enemy airfields, fuel storage, and ammo dumps on Wake Island. She accomplished this mission on February 24.

While returning to Pearl on March 4, the "Big E's" pilot bombed Marcus Island. Six days later she reached Pearl and underwent a short alteration period.

Most of her ancient .50-caliber machine guns were replaced with 20mm anti-aircraft mounts and 10 boats were removed. Additional radar equipment was installed to aid in finding the enemy at sea.

The *Enterprise* departed the Hawaiian port on April 8, 1942, and rendezvoused with the *USS Hornet CV-8* four days later off Midway Island. The two carriers steamed to a point only 500 miles from the coast of Japan and the *Hornet* launched 16 Army B-25s while the *Enterprise* provided air coverage. Following that now famous Halsey-Doolittle Raid, the "Big E" returned to Pearl Harbor on April 25.

Five days later, the *Enterprise* went to assist the *USS Yorktown CV-5* and *USS Lexington CV-2* in the Battle of the Coral Sea. The action was finished before the task force arrived, and on May 26 the *Enter-*

prise was at port in Pearl Harbor, for day and night preparations to engage the enemy at Midway.

The *Enterprise,* as flagship of Rear Admiral Raymond A. Spruance, Commander Task Force Sixteen, left Pearl on May 28, 1942. Rear Admiral Spruance informed his forces that the "expected enemy attack on Midway may be composed of all types of ships including four aircraft carriers." He further stated: "Great value to our country will come from the successful conclusion of the operations now commencing."

The *Enterprise* Task Force Sixteen rendezvoused with the *Yorktown* Task Force Seventeen on June 2, northeast of Midway; two days later, the Battle of Midway erupted.

A patrol plane from Midway spotted enemy aircraft heading for that island at 5:45 A.M. that morning. Another patrol pilot reported Japanese carriers 180 miles off Midway. All available planes on the island were sent into the air and the first contact reports were intercepted by the *Yorktown* at 6:07 A.M.

Rear Admiral Frank J. Fletcher directed Rear Admiral Spruance to "proceed southwesterly and attack enemy carriers as soon as definitely located. I will follow as soon as planes are recovered." Thus, Rear Admiral Spruance was placed in major tactical command of the crucial battle.

The *Enterprise* sent her aircraft into the skies at the time Rear Admiral Spruance calculated that the Japanese would be involved with reservicing their planes following the first strike against Midway.

The "Big E" and the *Hornet* dispatched 119 planes as the *Yorktown* launched 35 and held the remainder in reserve for attacks on enemy carriers still unlocated.

The torpedo squadrons became separated from their fighter escorts and suffered a severe beating. Ten of fourteen torpedo planes from the *Enterprise* were lost and from the total of 41 torpedo planes launched from all three carriers, only six returned. Their sacrifice drew enemy fighters away from the *Enterprise* and *Yorktown* dive bombers which were almost unopposed when they began their incursion on the trio of Japanese flat-tops.

The *Akagi,* Flagship of Admiral Nagumo, was set ablaze from stem to stern and damaged to such extent that a Japanese submarine finally sank her.

The *Enterprise* pilots scored four direct hits on the carrier *Kaga* and she sank the same evening after a terrific explosion. The carrier *Soryu* was under attack by 17 *Yorktown* dive bombers and three successful hits left her so severely damaged that the American submarine *Nautilus* sank her with torpedoes.

At 2:50 P.M. on June 4, a *Yorktown* scout pilot located the fourth enemy carrier *Hiryu,* escorted by battleships, cruisers, and destroyers. Eighteen dive bombers from the *Hiryu* attacked the *Yorktown* and all but five were shot down. However, before going into the sea, they managed to break through and score successful hits on the *Yorktown.* Rear Admiral Fletcher then transferred his flag to the heavy cruiser USS *Astoria CA-34.*

Aircraft assigned to the *Yorktown* were now operating off the *Enterprise* and *Hornet* and were launched upon knowledge of the location of the *Hiryu.* After a magnificent battle in the air, the *Hiryu* became a blanket of flame and soon found refuge on the ocean floor.

On June 6, 1942, the *Enterprise* air group devastated the cruiser *Mikuma* and another cruiser, the *Mogan,* suffered heavy damage. Additional enemy shipping felt the explosive bite of American bombs.

The Battle of Midway finally came to a dramatic close on June 6, 1942, with the American victory precluding any possibility of Japanese domination in the Pacific.

The gigantic armada of invading enemy troop transports and naval ships had been destroyed by the American air groups, but the greatest single factor was the destruction of the aircraft carriers, a crucial loss from which the Emperor's Navy never fully recovered.

In addition to the four large carriers which found berths on the coral reefs, the Japanese lost some 250 aircraft plus a large percentage of their highly trained and combat experienced carrier pilots.

Midway Island, measuring only 1¼ square miles in area, was secured and later served as an important submarine base for U. S. operations in the western Pacific.

The *Enterprise* returned to Pearl Harbor on June 13 to undergo a four-week period of battle repairs. She then cleared the harbor on July 15 as flagship of Rear Admiral T. C. Kinkaid, Commander Task Force Sixteen.

During August 7–9, her veteran air group supported the Guadalcanal-Tulagi Landing, including the first Savo. From August 10–25, she supported the capture and defense of Guadalcanal.

On August 24, during this operation, the "Big E" received three direct bomb hits and four near misses, resulting in the death of 74 men and the wounding of 89. Normal flight operations, however, resumed in one hour's time.

The exact number of enemy planes destroyed is difficult to ascertain, but 70 to 80 percent of the attacking planes were downed. The *Enterprise* air group was credited with splashing 29 planes while the ship's crews shot down 13.

The *Enterprise* went back to Pearl Harbor on September 10 for more repairs.

During the Santa Cruz battle on October 26, 1942, 24 enemy dive bombers made 23 bomb drops on the *Enterprise*. Two were direct hits; the first penetrated 50 feet through the forecastle deck and side before exploding. The second landed abaft of the forward elevator, breaking in two at the hangar deck where one-half exploded and the remainder pierced the third deck before erupting into a ball of flame.

As a result of the action, 44 men died and 74 suffered injuries.

On October 30, the carrier headed for Nouema for repairs, remaining there until November 11, at which time she returned to the Guadalcanal area when it became apparent the Japanese were prepared to strike the island again.

Torpedo pilots from the "Big E" found the Japanese battleship *Hiei* along with her escorts north of Savo Island. After several torpedo and bomb runs, the battleship sank amid fiery explosions.

By November 15, the *Enterprise's* air group had assisted in sinking the enemy cruiser *Kinugasa*, three destroyers and 11 auxiliary vessels. Four other cruisers were heavily damaged.

On November 16, the *Enterprise* went to Noumea for repairs. From January 12–15, 1943, the "Big E" launched her air group against Rennel Island.

On the 15th, Task Force Sixteen was redesignated Task Force Fifteen, but was short-lived. The task force was dissolved on April 30, and on May 1 the *Enterprise* returned to Pearl Harbor.

On May 27, while still at port in Hawaii, Admiral Chester W. Nimitz presented the *Enterprise* a Presidential Unit Citation, covering its activities from December 1941 to November 1942, when the carrier participated in nearly every major engagement, including the Gilbert and Marshall Islands raid; Wake Island raid; Battle of Midway; Occupation of Guadalcanal; Battle of Stewart Islands; Battle of Santa Cruz Islands and the Battle of the Solomon Islands.

The "Big E" then proceeded to Puget Sound Naval Shipyard, Bremerton, Washington, and upon arrival on July 20, 1943, she underwent a much needed overhaul period.

On November 6, she was back at Pearl Harbor, and three days later became the flagship of Rear Admiral A. W. Radford, USN, Commander Task Group 50.2.

The carrier departed Pearl the same day to participate in the Gilbert Islands operation. Direct air support was provided during the landings on Yellow Beach, Makin, from November 19–21.

A new page in naval history was written on the night of November 25 when one Avenger and two Hellcats were guided by ship's radar to within a few miles of the enemy. The Avenger then used its own radar to direct the Hellcats within visual range of the Japanese. The "Bat Team" came into existence and the *Enterprise* became a leading exponent of night fighting.

On December 9, 1943, the *Enterprise* was at Pearl for upkeep and preparation for the Marshall Islands operation. She slipped out of port on January 29, 1944, as the flagship of Rear Admiral J. W. Reeves, Commander Task Group 58.1.

Steaming in company with the new Essex class carrier, *USS Yorktown CV-10*, she accomplished bombing and strafing attacks over Taroa in the Maloelap Atoll and Wotje. These raids were in support of the occupation of Kwajalein and Majuro Atoll in the Marshall Islands.

As our troops landed on Behh, Nimmi, Ennylabegan, and Enubuj Islands, the "Big E" pilots strafed the beaches ahead and destroyed ammunition dumps.

The *Enterprise* proudly dropped her anchor into the azure waters of the newly won Majuro Lagoon on February 4, 1944.

Task Force Fifty-Eight, under the command of Vice Admiral Marc A. Mitscher, departed Majuro on February 12 and arrived off the island of Truk undetected four days later. A dozen torpedo planes were launched from the *Enterprise* before dawn on the 17th, marking the first night-radar bombing attacks involving U. S. carrier operations. The pilots scored 13 direct hits, sinking eight ships and inflicting damage to others. The group accounted for one-third of the total damage wrought by the entire Carrier Task Force. Of 55 enemy vessels at Truk, only 10 escaped damage. A pair of cruisers, four destroyers, and 24 auxiliary ships were completely destroyed(!); 211 enemy aircraft were destroyed, another 104 damaged.

Truk, the once powerful Japanese stronghold, received the first of many such attacks during the Asiatic-Pacific Raids of 1944.

From March 30 through April 1, 1944, the *Enterprise* struck Palau, Yap, Ulithi, and Woleai. Truk, Satawan, and Ponape were hit from April 21 to May 1. From April 21 to 24, the *Enterprise* provided air cover in support of the amphibious landing at Tanahmerah Bay. The "Big E" returned to Majuro Atoll on May 4, 1944, and two days later steamed towards the Marianas to support its capture and occupation.

The *Enterprise* launched attacks against Saipan from June 11 to 13, 1944. The following day, raids were directed against Saipan, Guam, and Rota. When the actual landings were made on June 15, the "Big E" provided air cover which persisted until June 17. Reports filtered through about the Japanese Mobile Fleet heading for the Marianas. The submarine, *USS Cavalla SS-244* reported that a major portion of the enemy was aiming for Saipan.

Two days later, the Battle of the Philippine Sea began. On the afternoon of June 20, 1944, search planes from the *Enterprise* located the enemy fleet steaming some 280 miles from our task force.

At 4:24 P.M., the "Big E" launched her air group and attacked the Japanese fleet. The U. S. pilots scored ten direct hits on two carriers and damaged a pair of tankers. By the time the pilots returned to the task force location, many planes were badly damaged or low on fuel. It was an evening of utter confusion and the pilots were ordered to land on the first carrier they approached.

Vice Admiral Mitscher gave the command to "light ships" to aid the exhausted fliers in finding the carriers. After the war, it was learned that Admiral Ozawa's air strength after the defeat was 35 operational aircraft of a total of 427 that he had sent out during the Battle of the Philippine Sea.

Raids against Volcano Bonin and Yap Islands were conducted from August 31 to September 8, 1944. Between October 6 and 24, the *Enterprise* supported the capture and occupation of the Southern Palau Islands.

While supporting the Leyte operation on October 30, 1944, the *Enterprise* had a close call when a Japanese suicide plane missed the ship and plunged into the sea just off the port quarter.

On October 23, 1944, the *Enterprise* proceeded to Ulithi but received orders to return to the area off Samar where Japanese Fleet units were reported closing in on Leyte in the Philippines. The enemy attack was three-pronged: one force came up from the south through Sulu Sea toward Surigao Strait, south of Leyte; a central force passed north of Palawan into the Sibuyan Sea, headed for San Bernardino Strait, north of Samar, while a northern force came in south from Japan directly towards Samar and Leyte.

The *Enterprise* saw action with all three Japanese forces. She launched aircraft on October 24 and the pilots helped cripple the battleships *Fuso* and *Musashi*.

The "Big E" then steamed westward about 120 miles from the San Bernardino Strait on October 25 and engaged with other American ships in the battle off Cape Engano. The enemy lost four carriers, a cruiser, and four destroyers during action.

On October 27, 1944, the *Enterprise* air group sank the enemy destroyers *Hayashimo* and *Shiranuhi* off Mindoro. This loss depleted the Japanese naval strength and precluded any hopes of their being able to hold the Philippine Islands or to maintain any effective strength for the defense of their homeland.

The *Enterprise* returned to Ulithi on October 30 for rest and replenishment, and sailed again on November 5 as flagship of Rear Admiral Ralph E. Davison, Commander Task Group 38.4.

Strikes were directed against Manila from November 10–11 and following a one-day attack on Yap, the carrier proceeded to Pearl Harbor, arriving on December 6, 1944.

Night Air Group 90 came aboard the *Enterprise* on December 24 and she departed the Hawaiian port for Luzon, where she arrived on January 5, 1945. Air strikes were directed against Luzon on the nights of January 6 and 7.

On January 12, the *Enterprise* air group attacked an enemy convoy near Cape Des Hirondelles, north Camranh Bay, Indo China.

During the period February 23 to March 2, the pilots of the *Enterprise* maintained 175 hours of air cover over Iwo Jima in the support of U. S. landings.

On March 2, zero weather conditions caused a delay of 24 hours and a total of 198 of 200 hours were chalked up.

The "Big E" sailed into Ulithi on March 12 and the crew rested while she underwent normal maintenance. Three days later she was on her way to strike Kyushu, southwestern Honshu, and shipping in the Inland Sea of Japan.

After effects of the direct bomb hit, temporary repairs were completed and the "Big E" was back in action.

While operating in the Kyushu area on March 18, a 250kg bomb hit the carrier flight deck, killing one man and injuring two others. Carl J. Smith AMM1/c described the incident: "I was standing on the flight deck enjoying the sunshine. All at once this Jap bomber came out of the clouds and made his run over the ship. He dropped the bomb and when I saw the bomb coming down, I took off down the flight deck, up over a catwalk, and down a ladder. That bomb hit about five feet from where I had been standing and rolled along the same path that I had taken along the flight deck. I couldn't have been more surprised or scared if it had followed me down the ladder too. The reason I'm able to tell the story is because that bomb was a dud. That Jap was so low over our deck that the bomb was still falling in a flat position when it hit. It

never did get the detonating head pointed down."

On March 24, the *Enterprise* returned to Ulithi for repairs sustained in battle. She left again on April 5 to support the assault and occupation of Okinawa.

During operations against Kikai, Tokuno, and Miyake Shima on April 11, the *Enterprise* was again under attack. A lone suicide plane plummeted over her flight deck and glanced over the side and its engine damaged the ship off the waterline. The bomb from the plane exploded beneath the carrier, lifting and whipping her violently, rupturing eight fuel tanks.

"The explosion was under the ship and it lifted us about three feet," stated Lieutenant-Commander C. H. Meiggs, the chief engineer.

"The noise and shock were terrific. We suffered major damage to the machinery, but our veteran 'black gang' regained full cruising speed within a few minutes."

Three additional enemy planes crashed close to the carrier. The *Enterprise* returned to Ulithi for repairs on April 19.

On May 6, the "Big E" headed for the Okinawa area to resume support operations.

When the *Bunker Hill* was severely damaged by suicide and bomb attacks on April 11, Vice Admiral Marc A. Mitscher transferred his flag to the *Enterprise*. Admiral Mitscher would soon be forced to move the flag again.

On May 14, a suicide plane dived at the *Enterprise* in what seemed certain to be an overshoot, however, the plane flipped over on its side and dived into the forward elevator, which was blown hundreds of feet into the air. Fourteen men were killed and 34 wounded. The admiral then transferred his flag to the *USS Randolph CV-15*.

It was obvious that the damage from the suicide plane could not be repaired in the forward area, so the "Big E" was ordered back to the United States.

Prior to returning stateside, the *Enterprise* made a short visit to Pearl Harbor. As she steamed through the channel, a flight of fighter-bombers flew over, forming the letter E. Then they descended and passed on the side of the ship and the sailors could read the words painted on the airplanes: For . . . Carrier . . . Champ . . . Take . . . *Enterprise*.

The planes were flown by pilots who had served on

The "Big E" takes a suicide hit on May 14, 1945 during the Okinawa Gunto operation. Note bits of the forward elevator flying into the air.

the "Big E" during the initial eight months of the war.

For the period November 19, 1943 to May 14, 1945, the *Enterprise* was awarded the Navy Unit Commendation. Previously awarded the Presidential Unit Citation, she was cited by the Navy for her gallant and heroic participation in nearly every major battle of the Pacific War Area. Her air groups had crushed many enemy aircraft and sent thousands of tonnage to the bottom. Her actions aided greatly in the ultimate defeat of the Japanese Empire.

The *Enterprise* was still in the Puget Sound Naval Shipyard undergoing repairs when the Second World War ended. After repairs were completed, she was fitted out for duty with the "Magic Carpet" fleet. On September 23, 1945, she headed for Pearl Harbor with 1141 "Magic Carpet" passengers. The carrier transited the Panama Canal on October 12 and arrived in New York City five days later.

She was out to sea and back in New York again on December 24 on the last of two "magic carpet" cruises that carried her to Southampton, England.

Shortly after the war ended, Secretary of the Navy James V. Forrestal proposed that the *Enterprise* be preserved as a naval relic to take her place with such other great naval ships as the *Constellation, Constitution, Hartford, Olympia,* and *Oregon.*

Ammunition was unloaded from the *Enterprise* at Gravesend Bay, after which she entered the Bayonne Annex of the New York Naval Shipyard on January 18, 1946, for deactivation process. She was officially decommissioned on February 17, 1947.

In July 1953, she was redesignated CVS-6: Antisubmarine Warfare support carrier.

The "Big E" remained in reserve, out of commission, from February 17, 1947 to October 20, 1956. On the latter date she was stricken from the lists of Navy ships to be sold for scrap.

Lipsett, Incorporated bought the *Enterprise* on July 1, 1958 for $1,561,333.00. When the cutting torches began taking the grand old carrier apart, they accomplished something the Japanese had never been able to do. Six times the "Big E" was reported sunk by the enemy, but she survived every battle. The scrapping process was completed in March 1960.

The "Big E's" war record will always remain unbreakable: 911 Japanese planes destroyed, 192 enemy planes damaged. During the war she sailed 275,000 miles.

The *Enterprise* was also the first American ship to sink a Japanese combat vessel. This occurred when the carrier sent the submarine *I-70* to a watery grave on December 10, 1941.

The *USS Enterprise CVS-6* received the following awards during her active duty: The Presidential Unit Citation; the Navy Unit Commendation; the American Defense Service Medal with one star; the American Area Campaign Service Medal; the Asiatic-Pacific Area Campaign Service with twenty battle stars; the World War II Victory Medal; Philippine Liberation Campaign Ribbon with one Bronze star; Republic of the Philippines Presidential Unit Citation Badge.

The *Enterprise* is gone, but her heroic exploits in the Pacific Theater of World War II will remain in the hearts and memories of many Americans forever. To some 10,000 men who served on her, they will always be *Enterprise* men.

A Seaman Second Class once expressed the true feelings of being an *Enterprise* man when he said: "I wouldn't take any other ship in the fleet. The *Enterprise* has a soul."

USS Wasp anchored in Guantanamo Bay, Cuba, Oct. 27, 1940.

7

USS Wasp CV-7

Within the realm of the Washington Naval Treaty of 1922, which limited the total tonnage for aircraft carriers to 135,000 tons, the Act of Congress dated March 27, 1934, authorized construction of one aircraft carrier of approximately 15,000 tons standard displacement to replace the experimental carrier *Langley.*

A total of 66,000 tons was used to build the *Lexington CV-2* and *Saratoga CV-3*. Another 14,500 tons

went for the *Ranger CV-4;* 39,000 tons for the *Yorktown CV-5, Enterprise CV-6,* and 19,000 tons had been reserved for the *USS Hornet CV-8.*

Thus, the size of the *Wasp* was arbitrarily restricted to the remaining balance. The *Wasp* could stow as many aircraft as the *Yorktown* types, but her speed was slower and she was not protected as well, owing to the principle of not sacrificing aircraft carrying to ship qualities.

Smallest of the prewar carriers, the *Wasp* had an overall length of 739 feet; she displaced 14,700 tons; Beam, 80 feet 9 inches; Draft, 20 feet, and her trial speed was 30 knots. She carried 1800 officers and men.

Armament consisted of eight 5-inch 38 caliber guns, sixteen 1.1-inch AA's, and twenty-four .5-inch AA guns.

Due to her short life, the *Wasp* received only a modicum of alterations consisting of the removal of fifteen .5-inch antiaircraft guns and the addition of thirty 20mm weapons and radar for gunnery control.

Her hull resembled that of the *Yorktown* class, but her smaller island structure and slimmer funnel were unique. Two High Angle Direction Control Towers were supported above the island by a tripod foremast and a pole mainmast.

Two elevators connected the open hangar with the flight deck. One elevator at the edge of the deck was a new innovation introduced by the *Wasp*. Four catapults were installed on the hangar and flight decks. Her boiler rooms were located between the forward and after engine rooms.

On April 1, 1936, the keel of the *Wasp* was laid down at the Bethlehem Shipbuilding Company at Quincy, Massachusetts. She was christened by Mrs. Charles Edison, wife of the Assistant Secretary of the Navy, and launched on April 4, 1939. Captain John W. Reeves, Jr., took command on April 25, 1940, as the *USS Wasp CV-7* was commissioned at the Boston Navy Yard.

The *Wasp* completed a shakedown cruise off the East Coast shortly after commissioning. During this time on March 7, 1941, she rescued crewmen of the schooner *George E. Klenck* of South Harbor, Maine.

The *USS Wasp CV-7* going down the ways, April 4, 1939.

The civilian ship had foundered in a heavy gale off Cape Hatteras.

The carrier joined the Atlantic Fleet as a unit of Carrier Division Three, Aircraft Battle Force. The planes assigned to her wore black tail colors for identification and the letters W-A-S-P were prominently displayed on each end of the flight deck.

The *Wasp* remained in the Atlantic Fleet conducting training exercises and routine patrols for 18 months of peacetime service. She would see only nine months of combat when the United States declared war on Japan, December 8, 1941, but during that time the carrier would play a vital role in the bitter conflict.

During an early convoy run, the destroyer *USS Stack DD-406* collided with the *Wasp* during a period of extremely low visibility on March 17, 1942. Fortunately there was no serious damage.

In the spring of 1942, the *Wasp* was engaged in her most famous mission. This was the relief of besieged Malta, a key allied island located about 60 miles south of Sicily in the Mediterranean. Nazi and Italian air raids were increasing, which resulted in the grave need for reinforcements. The nearest British airbases were beyond fighter range and German Field Marshal Rommel had pushed the British Eighth Army back to Cairo. The safest method of relieving Malta was to send in planes prepared to fight upon arrival.

On March 26, 1942, the *Wasp* joined Task Force 99, commanded by Rear Admiral Robert C. Griffin, Jr. The task force departed Casco Bay, Maine, for Scapa Flow the same day.

In company with the *Wasp* was the *USS Washington BB-56*, *USS Wichita CA-45*, *USS Tuscaloosa CA-37*, and Destroyer Squadron Eight. The *Wasp* was the first American aircraft carrier to enter the Mediterranean. On April 15, 40 *Spitfire* aircraft and pilots were embarked. During the night of April 20–21, the carrier slipped through the Strait of Gibraltar and passed Axis agents in Spain and Spanish Morocco, then into the Mediterranean.

On April 22, the *Spitfires* were launched as a Nazi radio broadcast stated that the *Wasp* was in the Mediterranean and German forces were on their way to sink her.

The operation was so successful that the *Wasp* returned to Scotland, loaded more aircraft and repeated the same maneuver on May 3, 1942. Sailors on the *Wasp* had a big laugh when they heard from a Nazi broadcast that the *Wasp* had been sunk.

On May 11, 1942, the carrier received the following message: "To the Captain and company of the *USS Wasp*. Many thanks to you all for the timely help.

USS Wasp CV-7: Spitfires, spotted in hangar deck, looking aft, April 1942.

F4F's ready for takeoff from *Wasp* Aug. 7, 1942, during the Guadalcanal-Tulagu Landings.

Who said a wasp couldn't sting twice?" The message was signed by Winston S. Churchill.

The *Wasp* departed Norfolk, Virginia, on June 6, 1942, in company with Task Force 37, to join the Pacific theater of battle. She transited the Panama Canal on June 19 and sailed into San Diego on July 1. During the next few weeks the *Wasp* prepared for her first Pacific war engagement—the Guadalcanal-Tulagi Landings.

On July 18, the carrier arrived at Nukualofa, Tonga-tabu, where a three-day engine repair took place.

The *Wasp* screened two cruisers and four destroyers as they steamed into position to launch their first strikes. At 6:31 A.M., on August 7, 1942, the *Wasp* air group arrived at Tulagi where her dive bombers attacked enemy seaplanes. The strike was successful and the planes returned to the carrier.

August 7, 1942, was D-Day for Tulagi. Torpedo bombers from the *Wasp* smashed enemy positions near Makambo and Saspi. An enemy attack on the task force was repelled before any damage was inflicted.

On September 15, 1942, the *Wasp* was operating off Espiutu Santo, New Hebrides, when a Japanese submarine scored three direct hits on the carrier. As her hull was ripped open by the tremendous blasts, many fires erupted throughout the ship. Courageous sailors fought the fires in a desperate attempt to save their stricken ship, but new explosions constantly added to the already serious condition. By nightfall, the situation appeared hopeless. The initial blast had left 26 officers and 167 enlisted men dead or missing.

Ruptured gasoline lines fed the vicious fires and

Sinking of the *Wasp* CV-7 September 7, 1942. The ship is listing, smoke pours from the deck and side.

The *Wasp* burns furiously on September 15, 1942.

spawned new ones with flames leaping 150 feet. Aircraft on the flight deck and inside the hangar deck were tossed into the air by explosions, then dropped onto the deck with such force that the landing gear was snapped off. Planes stored above the hangar deck tore loose and crashed onto the deck.

Ammunition exploded and water mains were ripped open under great pressure. Internal explosions increased, and about 3:05 P.M., a tremendous blast tore a gun mount loose, killing nearly everyone on the port wing of the bridge.

Fires were spreading throughout the hangar deck and explosions became more frequent. It was now necessary to abandon the dying carrier as soon as possible. When all of the crewmen had left the *Wasp*, her commanding officer departed at 4:00 P.M.

To prevent the *Wasp* from reaching enemy hands, the Task Force commander gave the order to sink the carrier.

The *USS Lansdowne DD-486* fired three successful torpedo hits into the burning hulk and the once proud veteran of two war theaters slowly plunged to the bottom. The hissing fires gave an eerie sound throughout the air off Guadalcanal, thus bringing to a close the career of America's seventh aircraft carrier.

The *Wasp's* crew had fought desperately to save the ship, but the damage was too great. Lieutenant-Commander John J. Shea of Arlington, Massachusetts, was one of the multitude of heroes who gave his life fighting the fires on the crippled carrier. He was fighting such a fire when a terrific explosion was heard, and he was never seen again. A letter he had written to his five year old son, explaining the ideals for which he was fighting, was widely published throughout the United States. It read:

Dear Jackie:

This is the first letter I have written directly to my little son. I am thrilled to know you can read it all by yourself. If you miss some of the words it will be because I do not write very plainly. Mother will help you in that case, I am sure.

I was certainly glad to hear your voice over the long distance telephone. It sounded as though I were right in the living room with you. You sounded as though you missed your daddy very much. I miss you, too, more than anyone will ever know. It is too bad this war could not have been delayed a few more years so that I could grow up again with you and do all the things I planned to do when you were old enough to go to school.

I thought how nice it would be to come home early in the afternoon and play ball with you and go mountain climbing and see the trees, brooks, and learn all about woodcraft, hunting, fishing, swimming and other things like that. I suppose we must be brave and put these things off now for a while.

When you are a little bigger you will know why your daddy is not home so much any more. You know we have a big country and we have ideals as to how people should live and enjoy the riches of it and how each is born with equal rights to life, freedom and the pursuit of happiness. Unfortunately there are some countries in the world where they do not have these ideals, where a boy cannot grow up to be what he wants to be with no limit on his opportunities to be a great man such as a great priest, statesman, doctor, soldier, business man etc.

Because there are people in countries who want to change our nation, its ideals, its form of government and way of life we must leave our homes and families to fight. Fighting for the defense of our country, ideals, homes and honor is an honor and a duty which your daddy has to do before he can come home and settle down with you and mother.

When it is done he is coming home to be with you always and forever. So wait just a little while longer. I am afraid it will be more than the two weeks you told me on the phone.

In the meantime take good care of mother, be a good boy and grow up to be a good young man. Study hard when you go to school. Be a leader in everything good in life. Be a good Catholic and you can't help being a good American. Play fair always. Strive to win but if you must lose, lose like a gentleman and a good sportsman.

Don't ever be a quitter, either in sports or in your business or profession when you grow up. Get all the education you can. Stay close to Mother and follow her advice. Obey her in everything, no matter how you may at times disagree. She knows what is best and will never let you down or lead you away from the right and honorable things of life.

If I don't get back you will have to be Mother's protector because you will be the only one she has. You must grow up to take my place as well as your own in her life and heart.

Love your grandmother and granddad as long as they live. They, too, will never let you down. Love your aunts and see them as often as you can. Last of all don't ever forget your daddy. Pray for him to come back and if it is God's will that he does not, be the kind of a boy and man your daddy wants you to be.

Kiss Mother for me every night. Goodby for now.

With all my love and devotion for Mother and you.

Your Daddy

The USS Wasp CV-7 received the following awards during her service: The American Defense Service Medal with Bronze "A"; The American Area Campaign Service Medal; the European-African-Middle Eastern Area Campaign Service Medal with one battle star, and the Asiatic-Pacific Area Campaign Service Medal with two battle stars.

USS Hornet CV-8.

8

USS Hornet CV-8

The hostilities waged by Japan in the Pacific and Germany during the early 1930s incited increased alarm for world tensions. War was inevitable—it was just a matter of time.

The 1922 Treaty of Limitations concerning war armament and the London Conference on April 22, 1930 terminated on December 21, 1936, when Japan abrogated. Thus, the Naval Expansion Act of May 17, 1938, provided 40,000 additional tons for aircraft carrier production.

The *USS Hornet CV-8* was authorized for construction before the ink was dry on the signatures of the Naval Expansion Act.

The *Hornet's* keel was laid on September 25, 1939

at the Newport News Shipbuilding and Drydock Co., Newport News, Virginia. The new addition to the fleet was christened by Mrs. Frank Knox, wife of the Secretary of the Navy, on December 14, 1940.

Capt. Marc A. Mitscher, USN, took command on October 20, 1941, and the *Hornet* was fully commissioned. She had a short-lived career, sinking only 371 days after Captain Mitscher accepted her. However, her gallant actions in the Pacific Theater of War will forever remain an enduring inspiration to all who sail the seas.

The *Hornet* was 809 feet long and had a beam of 83 feet 3 inches. Her mean draft was 21 feet 6 inches and she could travel at 34 knots. The *Hornet's* armament consisted of eight 5-inch 38-caliber mounts and a secondary battery with 40mm and 20mm antiaircraft guns; after World War II, 1.1-inch "Chicago Piano" Pom Poms were added.

The *Hornet* came into active service only six weeks before the Japanese attacked Pearl Harbor and the usual peacetime shakedown cruise was cancelled. The *Hornet* was deprived of sailing into a foreign port such as South America or the Caribbean to exhibit her proud lines, fresh grey paint, gleaming and untarnished from salt spray. A war was imminent so only small red battle lamps glowed inside her quiet hull. No bright lights were ever shown.

An accelerated but intensive shakedown cruise was completed on January 31, 1942, when the new carrier returned to the Norfolk Navy Yard for a final fitting-out period.

An Army B-25 clears the deck of the *Hornet* on April 18, 1942, in the daring Halsey-Doolittle Raid over Japan.

Strange events were happening aboard the *Hornet*. Scuttlebut of an important mission drifted like ominous air throughout the crew's lounge. No one could figure out why two B-25s were hoisted on deck.

On February 2, the *Hornet* steamed from Norfolk astern to conduct experimental flight operations off the Atlantic seaboard. The two Army bombers were successfully launched and the carrier reappeared at Norfolk.

On March 4, the *Hornet* set a course for the Pacific via the Panama Canal. Excitement surrounded the ship as the intended mission was still a mystery to the crew.

The *Hornet* arrived at the Naval Air Station, Alameda, California, on March 20, 1942. All of the carrier's normal aircraft was stowed below decks and 16 B-25 Mitchell bombers took their place on the flight deck. On April 2, the carrier silently slipped away from Alameda, nudged under the Golden Gate Bridge, and Captain Mitscher read the orders to the anxious crew that afternoon. The mission: A bombing raid on Japan. In less than four months after the U.S. had declared war on Japan, the enemy was to feel the sting of American air power.

Approximately 1000 miles east of Midway Island, the *Hornet* met with the *USS Enterprise CV-6* on April 13. As Task Force Sixteen, the two carriers and their escorts headed towards Japan. The "Big E" was engaged to provide combat air cover for the *Hornet* when the ships reached enemy waters.

On the morning of April 18, 1942, the *Nitto Naru*, a Japanese patrol craft spotted the task force. The enemy ship was sunk by the *USS Nashville CL-43*, but managed to send a message of the sighting before going under.

Admiral William F. Halsey, Commander of the Task Force, ordered the immediate launching of the Army bombers. At 8:00 A.M., the first B-25, piloted by Lt. Col. James H. Doolittle, USA, roared off the *Hornet's* flight deck at 35°-45′ North, 153°-40′ East or 620 miles east of Inuko Saki, Japan. The sixteenth plane was airborne at 9:20 A.M. All the bombers cleared the *Hornet's* deck despite a gale of more than 40 knots and 30-foot crests that violently pitched the ship.

The psychological strike against the Japanese homeland was to be the last until February 1944. With the mission accomplished, the task force began a rapid retirement from enemy waters. Six hours after the Army bombers had been sent aloft, a Japanese-English broadcast was intercepted confirming the success of the daring raid.

The *Hornet* returned to Pearl Harbor on April 25 for replenishment. The Halsey-Doolittle Raid remained a secret for one year and whenever President Roosevelt was questioned as to the destination of Doolittle's bombers, he would reply, "Shangri-la."

The *Hornet* departed Pearl Harbor on April 30, with orders to conduct offensive operations against the Japanese. She steamed rapidly toward the Coral Sea to aid the *USS Lexington CV-2* and the *USS Yorktown CV-5* in combat, but the battle had ended by the time she arrived, so she was ordered back to Hawaii and reached there on May 26, 1942.

Since the U.S. had broken the Japanese code, it was possible to determine that a huge enemy fleet movement was underway. The Japanese referred to a target area designated "AF." The Commander in Chief of the Pacific, Admiral Chester W. Nimitz, USN, stated that "AF" was Midway Island. However, Admiral Ernest J. King, USN, in Washington surmised that the designation was Pearl Harbor. The radio station on Midway transmitted a plain language message stating that the island's fresh water distillation plant was inoperable. Within three days, Japanese traffic was decoded and one message stated that "AF" was low on fresh water. Admiral Nimitz was correct and the Navy prepared for the expected Japanese attack on Midway!

On May 28, 1942, the *Hornet* sailed from Pearl Harbor. Her Task Force Sixteen rendezvoused with the *Yorktown*'s task force seventeen six days later, 325 miles northeast of Midway. The enemy fleet was located at 6:03 A.M., June 4, 1942.

The Battle of Midway got underway at 7:02 A.M., when the *Hornet* launched 35 dive bombers and 15 torpedo bombers with fighter escorts. The air group missed the enemy at the anticipated location and turned southeastward assuming the Japanese were still closing in on Midway. Actually, the enemy had steered north to converge on the American task force. The *Hornet*'s torpedo squadron became separated from its fighter escorts while en route to the strike point. The resolute actions of Torpedo Squadron Eight earned a Presidential Unit Citation and an eternal berth in the hearts of all Americans who knew of their heroic deed.

When the torpedo squadron finally located the enemy striking force, LCDR. John C. Waldron, Commander of *VT-8*, lead his unescorted air group to meet the enemy. The *Hornet*'s pilots sighted four carriers, the *Akagi*, *Kagi*, *Soryu* and *Hiryu* about eight miles away, and Japanese fighters commenced an attack on the torpedo bombers. Without the necessary escort, the American planes begin to fall one by one from the sky. However, *VT-8* pursued the enemy and before the enemy force had shot down the last plane, the remnants chopped their torpedoes at close range. The Japanese carriers had been protected by a screen of

cruisers and destroyers. However, the men of *VT-8* valiantly began their diving runs. All 15 torpedo planes fell to the enemy guns and only one pilot, Ensign George H. Gay, USNR, survived the battle. When his plane hit the water, Ensign Gay took refuge under a rubber seat cushion to avoid being hit by strafing runs. Actually, he had a reserved seat for the world's greatest naval battle, as history unfolded before his astonished eyes.

Captain Mitscher later said in tribute to *VT-8*: "They made certain for the Task Force and for the Navy, that Japanese air power was crippled at the start."

Ensign Gay later accepted for the squadron the Presidential Unit Citation and Navy Crosses "for extraordinary heroism and distinguished service beyond the call of duty."

The greatest importance of the Battle of Midway was the damage inflicted upon the Japanese carriers and their striking force. All four carriers and over 250 enemy planes were sent to the bottom of the ocean, along with a high percentage of highly trained and battle experienced pilots. This was a severe blow from which the Japanese never fully recovered. The result of this battle and other defeats such as the Marianas "Turkey Shoot" of June 19, 1944, in which 392 enemy planes were destroyed (360 in aerial combat) in a single day, lead the Japanese to use the "Divine Wind" Kamakaze Squadrons as the last resort in October 1944.

Before the *Hornet*'s aircraft took off for the Battle of Midway, the pilots sat in the ready rooms receiving last-minute briefings. As the men of Torpedo Squadron Eight studied their flight plans, they read this inspiring letter from their squadron leader, LCDR. John C. Waldron:

"Just a word to let you know that I feel we are ready. We have had a very short time to train and we have worked under the most severe difficulties. But we have truly done the best humanly possible. I actually believe that under these conditions we are the best in the world. My greatest hope is that we encounter a favorable tactical situation, but if we don't and the worst comes to the worst, I want each of us to do his utmost to destroy our enemies. If there is only one plane left to make a final run in, I want that man to go in and get a hit. May God be with all of us. Good luck, happy landings and give 'em hell."

Minutes later, Torpedo Squadron Eight was involved in their final battle of the war.

A U.S. submarine, the *USS Tambour (SS-198)* reported sighting an enemy force on the morning of June 5, 1942. The *Hornet* sent her pilots upstairs at 11:25 A.M., but a four-hour search failed to locate the

Japanese. On June 13, she returned to Hawaii for repairs and upkeep.

Training operations were conducted in the Hawaiian area until August 17. On that day, the *Hornet* went to join the *USS Saratoga CV-3* and arrived twelve days later. The *Saratoga* received a torpedo hit and was forced to retire for repairs. The *Hornet* conducted patrol duties with the *USS Wasp CV-7* off Guadalcanal. While engaged in these operations on September 15, the *Wasp* was severely damaged by enemy torpedoes and had to be sunk by U.S. destroyers.

The *Hornet* proceeded without escort to continue the patrols. On September 26, she arrived at New Caledonia to receive supplies. Shortly thereafter, she returned to the Solomons area and began air strikes against Japanese shipping along the Shortland Islands, south of Bougainville. Enemy air installations were bombed at Rekata Bay on October 16.

Eight days later, a four-carrier Japanese Combined Fleet was reported steaming southward to reinforce their land forces. The *Hornet* and *Enterprise* rushed between Guadalcanal and Santa Cruz Islands to intercept the fleet. At 7:30 A.M. on October 26, the *Hornet* launched her air group to fly an estimated 200 miles to the target. A large flight of enemy aircraft attacked the *Hornet's* task force shortly after ten o'clock. At 10:12 A.M., a Japanese bomber released two bombs on the starboard side of the *Hornet* which violently shook

The *Hornet* under enemy attack off Santa Cruz moments before a Japanese dive bomber plunges into the carrier's flight deck. Two enemy torpedo planes are seen attacking the ship.

The *Hornet* moments after the Japanese dive bomber crashes
into the flight deck. An explosion erupts from the flight deck
during the Battle of Santa Cruz on October 26, 1942.

the whole ship. One minute later, an enemy plane struck the tip of the stack and crashed into the flight deck. The plane's 100-pound bomb exploded into a large fireball causing considerable damage to the island superstructure. Before the stricken carrier had stopped trembling from the first bomb hits, two torpedoes rammed the starboard armor plating and exploded their fury in the engine room. At the same time, two more 500-pound bombs ripped up the carrier's flight deck! A severely damaged enemy torpedo plane plunged into the forward gun gallery! Its engine was driven into the junior officers' bunk room as bits of the plane and its pilot were thrown into the forward elevator shaft.

The burning *Hornet* had a 10-degree list but shortly corrected to seven degrees. Her engines were dead. Communications were dead. Fire mains were ruptured and power lines were sliced to ribbons. As the ship sat helpless in the water out of control, huge fires gutted her hull.

There was an order to abandon ship. However, the flames were soon brought under control and the order was belayed.

The cruiser *USS Northhampton CA-26* pulled up in an attempt to take the *Hornet* in tow. Japanese fighters then unleashed another attack and the tow lines were chopped for the safety of other ships; this tow line was to be drawn again and again.

As a third attack began, the *Northhampton* cast away the lines and her guns began firing. A torpedo from one of the planes slammed into the starboard side of the *Hornet* and the list doubled. At 3:40 P.M., when the ship's dangerous list had reached 18 degrees, the abandon ship order was given and the crewmen slid down ropes or jumped over the side and waited in life rafts until nearby destroyers picked them up.

While the abandon procedures were carried out, a Japanese pilot dropped his bomb on the starboard corner of the *Hornet's* flight deck. By now the fires began to envelop the entire ship, twisting the hulk like a giant pretzel. A radioman, preparing to leave the vessel, stopped to man a 30-caliber machine gun for one more shot at the enemy who had destroyed his ship.

Captain Mason was the last to leave the *Hornet*, at 5:27 P.M. To prevent the ship from falling into Japanese hands, the order was given to sink her. The *USS Dustin DD-413* and the *USS Anderson DD-411* fired

Hornet **damage of signal bridge as seen by destroyer on port side.**

over 500 rounds of 5-inch 38-caliber shells and twelve torpedoes into the burning hull, but the proud old carrier adamantly stayed afloat, burning from stem to stern.

The Japanese forces were closing in fast, so the task force was ordered to get underway. Upon arrival at the ghastly scene of the flaming carrier, the enemy destroyers *Akigumo* and *Makigumo* sent four torpedoes into the *Hornet,* and finally she slowly rolled over and slipped under the waves.

The Japanese were the last to see the *Hornet* go under, thus bringing a close to the career of the heroic carrier . . . the first Navy ship to accomplish the "impossible mission" of delivering bombs on the Japanese homeland.

The *USS Hornet CV-8* received the following awards during her naval career: The American Defense Service Medal with one star; The American Area Service Medal and the Asiatic-Pacific Area Campaign Service Medal with four battle stars.

View **of fire aboard the** *Hornet.*

ESSEX CLASS: (HULL NUMBERS 9-21)

The first eleven Essex class carriers were ordered in July of 1940. Average cost of each ship was estimated at $68,932,000. Later ships of the class were improved with stronger flight decks and were more thoroughly subdivided. With the commissioning of the *USS Valley Forge CV-45* on November 3, 1946, the Essex class was complete and contained 24 ships.

*CV-9 *Essex*	*CV-17 *Bunker Hill*
*CV-10 *Yorktown*	*CV-18 *Wasp*
*CV-11 *Intrepid*	CV-19 *Hancock*
*CV-12 *Hornet*	*CV-20 *Bennington*
*CV-13 *Franklin*	CV-21 *Boxer*
CV-14 *Ticonderoga*	*CV-31 *Bon Homme Richard*
CV-15 *Randolph*	CV-32 *Leyte*
*CV-16 *Lexington*	CV-33 *Kearsarge*

CV-34 *Oriskany*
CV-36 *Antietam*
CV-37 *Princeton*
CV-38 *Shangri La*
CV-39 *Lake Champlain*
CV-40 *Tarawa*
CV-45 *Valley Forge*
CV-47 *Philippine Sea*

---

* Short hull type

Original statistics of the Essex class carriers when built were: standard displacement, 27,100 tons; full load displacement, 33,000 tons; extreme beam, (at or about the flight deck) 147 feet 6 inches; speed, 33 knots; complement, 360 officers and 3088 enlisted men. Armament, twelve 5-inch 38-calibre guns plus many 40mm antiaircraft and 20mm antiaircraft quadruple gun mounts. Each carrier varied in length but the average overall length of each ship was 872 feet, and had the facilities to hold between 85 and 100 aircraft. Ten of the Essex class carriers were of short hull type. The only difference between the short hull and long hull ships was that the long hull type had a pointed bow extending beyond the flight deck.

One starboard bow and one hangar deck catapult were installed in six of the first Essex class carriers completed. The H-1VB (bow) catapult had a 96-foot power stroke and could launch an 18,000-lb. landplane at 90 mph while limited to 72.5 feet by the beam of the

ship, and it had a capacity to launch a 16,000 lb. airplane to 85 mph. Because of delays with catapult production, none were installed on the *USS Essex CV-9* when she was commissioned and only a starboard flight deck catapult on the *USS Lexington CV-16*. The next six ships commissioned had starboard bow and hangar deck catapults installed. They were *USS Yorktown CV-10*, commissioned April 15, 1943; *USS Bunker Hill CV-17*, commissioned May 25, 1943; *USS Intrepid CV-11*, commissioned August 16, 1943; *USS Wasp CV-18*, Commissioned November 24, 1943; *USS Hornet CV-12*, commissioned November 29, 1943; and the *USS Franklin CV-13*, commissioned on January 31, 1944.

Until mid-1943, the fast carriers made little use of their catapults, as is shown by the fact that in the spring of 1943 the Commanding Officer of the *USS Enterprise CV-6* recommended that all catapults be removed from that ship. In May 1943, a decision was made to install a second flight deck catapult (portside) in lieu of the hangar deck catapult in later ships of the Essex class. The proximity of these dates indicates that the decision to rely upon flight deck catapults and to abandon the hangar deck catapult was based primarily upon experiences with smaller CVL and CVE classes which had flight deck catapults only. The limited capability of the hangar deck catapult was a factor of some significance; eddy currents off the sides of an aircraft carrier were another.

The official order to install two flight deck catapults in lieu of a hangar deck catapult on all Essex class carriers after the *USS Franklin CV-13*—that is CV-14, 15, 19, 20, 21 and 31 through 40—came through on May 17, 1943, from the Bureau of Aeronautics. On December 23, 1943, the Chief of the Bureau of Ships authorized the installation of a second flight deck catapult on the *USS Lexington CV-16*. Completion of this alteration was reported by the Puget Sound Naval Shipyard on April 14, 1944.

The actual conversion from athwartships hangar deck to bow catapults would have depended upon the time that the carriers went into the Navy yard and upon the availability of the proper catapult equipment.

Unnamed carriers—designated CV-50 up to and including CV-55—were cancelled in March of 1945. Two carriers under construction, the *USS Reprisal CV-35* and *USS Iwo Jima CV-44* were cancelled in August 1945.

The supremacy of the carrier task force was proved beyond all doubt during the Second World War. In 1946, Navy planners were faced with the problem of designing a carrier that could handle the larger and heavier aircraft being produced. It was proposed to design and build a new carrier with an eye towards the future. It was to be a trial-and-error experiment. The Chief of Naval Operations stated in 1947, "In a war whose pace was at all times governed by what was logistically possible, the carrier task force was an economical weapon independent of the investments in time, personnel, and priceless shipping space required for construction of airfields and facilities soon to be left behind the advancing front. Its mobility gave to the attacker the advantage of continuous initiative and surprise."

A second thought was to cancel plans for a new, costly carrier and make the changes and improvements on existing Essex class carriers. Thus, Project 27A—Shipbuilding and Conversion Program, Essex Class Development—was instigated on June 4, 1947. Basically, Project 27A provided changes that would make the carriers capable of operating newer jet aircraft. A special weapons capability was included, plus increased aviation fuel capacity, jet blast deflectors, enlarged bomb elevators, and hangar deck subdivision fire doors. Three pilot ready rooms were relocated below the flight deck to provide better pilot protection. An escalator was installed abreast of the island structure, enabling pilots to get to their planes faster and allowing them to avoid running into the ship's crew as normal battle stations were being manned.

Construction of the *USS Oriskany CV-34* was held up in August 1946 due to a recasting of plans. When completed, the *Oriskany* looked slightly different from her other sister ships. The island structure was streamlined and the flight deck was much stronger. The *Oriskany* was the first carrier to be modernized under Project 27A. Between October 1947 and October 1953, eight more Essex class carriers were modernized under this program. They were the *Essex, Wasp, Kearsarge, Lake Champlain, Bennington, Yorktown, Randolph,* and *Hornet.*

When the steam catapult development was successful, Project 27C Axial Deck was begun. Changes in this program called for the installation of two C-11 steam catapults, double reeved arresting gears, an improved barrier system, plus features employed in the 27A program. The *USS Hancock CV-19* was the first carrier to be modernized under this program and was

followed by two more Essex class carriers, the *Intrepid* and *Ticonderoga.*

While the three mentioned ships were being converted, a new experimental angle (canted) deck was installed in the *USS Antietam CV-36.* Her flight deck was extended outboard on the port side from the normal flight deck, allowing aircraft to land at a 10-degree angle from the ship's centerline. The advantages of these experiments were soon recognized. Flight deck safety was greatly increased. The pilot no longer was in danger of crashing into the island structure or parked aircraft on the forward section of the flight deck. While one plane was landing, other aircraft could be taxied on the starboard side without halting air operations. Out of the experiments conducted on the *Antietam* came Project 27C Angle Deck. Also included in this new conversion program was the installation of an enclosed hurricane bow, an enlarged forward elevator, air conditioning, and sound proofing of the island structure. The *Lexington, Shangri La* and *Bon Homme Richard* were modernized and converted under this program.

Of the 15 Essex class carriers modernized all but one returned to the yards for the installation of an enclosed hurricane bow and angle flight deck. The *USS Lake Champlain CVS-39* still maintains an open bow and axial flight deck.

While the actual detailed considerations whereby some ships were selected for modernization were very complex, the selection process appears to have fallen into a pattern of operating those ships with the highest capability for handling modern aircraft while other ships of the class were being modernized. As a result, the last ships of the class to be commissioned (ie., *Boxer, Leyte, Valley Forge, Philippine Sea, Tarawa*) and one given a straight deck modernization (*Lake Champlain*) were in operational use when the angle deck modernization and hurricane bow modernizations were being made on older Essex class carriers.

On October 1, 1952, all 24 Essex class carriers, many now formed into the Oriskany-Hancock conversion class, were reclassified CVA—Attack Aircraft Carriers. In July of 1953, the *Franklin, Bunker Hill, Leyte,* and *Antietam* were again reclassified CVS—Antisubmarine Warfare Support Carriers. During the period January 1954 to October 1962, 15 other CVA's were reclassified CVS's.

The *Boxer CVS-21* was the first former Essex class carrier to undergo conversion to an LPH Amphibious Assault Ship in January of 1959. A new hull number, *LPH-4,* was assigned. Two more former Essex class carriers joined the ranks of Amphibious Assault Ships, the *Princeton CVS-37* to *LPH-5* in March 1959 and the *Valley Forge CVS-45* to *LPH-8* in June 1961. Now operating with amphibious assult task groups, they carry and operate between 30 to 40 RH2S helicopters.

On May 15, 1959, four former Essex class CVS's were again reclassified to AVT—Auxiliary Aircraft Support Transports; they were the *Franklin CV-13* to *AVT-8, Bunker Hill CVS-17* to *AVT-9, Leyte CVS-32* to *AVT-10* and the *Philippine Sea CVS-47* to *AVT-11*. The *Tarawa CVS-40* was reclassified *AVT-12* in May of 1961. All of the carriers were reclassified while decommissioned and none have actually served in the capacity of auxiliary aircraft support transports.

The *Antietam* (with the exception of the experimental flight deck), the *Franklin, Bunker Hill, Boxer, Leyte, Princeton, Valley Forge, Tarawa,* and the *Philippine Sea* have never undergone any major conversion. The *Philippine Sea* had a slight modification of her island structure which included a twin mast and clinker screen.

Only three of the original 24 Essex class carriers remain active as Attack Aircraft Carriers CVA. They are the *Hancock CVA-19, Bon Homme Richard CVA-31* and the *Oriskany CVA-34.*

USS Essex CVS-9.

9

USS Essex CVS-9

When authorization came through to build the *USS Essex CVS-9* on July 3, 1940, it was the beginning of an unprecedented era of aircraft carriers. The *Essex* along with her sister ships established the elite carrier task forces that charged defiantly across the Pacific during the Second World War, bolstered our depressed naval armada, and eventually brought down the curtain on a costly war.

Her keel was laid on April 28, 1941, at the Newport News Shipbuilding and Drydock Co., Newport News, Virginia. Mrs. Artemus L. Gates, wife of the Assistant Secretary of the Navy for Air, christened the *Essex* on July 31, 1942, and the first in a new class of carriers gracefully slipped down the building ways.

Capt. D. B. Duncan, USN, took command on December 31, 1942, during commissioning ceremonies at

The *Essex* on May 10, 1943, underway with planes spotted on flight deck.

the Norfolk Navy Yard. Later that day the captain addressed his crew prophesying: "It is my intention and expectation that between us, we shall make the name of *Essex* carry fear and destruction to our enemies, with praise to our friends and be an everlasting credit to our country and our flag."

No time was wasted in putting the new carrier through shakedown operations and qualifying Air Group Nine. The *Essex* departed Norfolk Navy Yard, eased through the Panama Canal, and on June 8 arrived at Pearl Harbor amidst the twisted wreckage of fire-gutted ships, still smoldering from that day of infamy.

Training operations took place in the Hawaiian area in preparation for the offensive actions which began August 31, 1943, when the *Essex* air group attacked Marcus Island. For ten hours, Marcus was embraced by dense smoke and fire from American bombs, which devastated enemy air facilities.

During October 5–6, 1943, Wake Island felt the agony wrought by the *Essex* and other carriers. American fighter pilots crisscrossed the island at dawn of the 5th, leaving buildings, ground installations, and underground stores in ruins. It was back in December of 1941 that an undermanned Marine garrison, weary from continuous battle, despondently surrendered Wake Island to the Japanese, so the U.S. pilots had a special determination in their hearts while flying over the target.

In November 1943, the Navy received information that a vast number of Japanese ships were positioned in the harbor of Rabaul. This was a potential threat to our newly established beachhead on Bougainville

and had to be eliminated. The carrier force arrived some 100 miles off the Rabaul coastline November 11. All available aircraft were sent against the enemy stronghold. The initial approach of attacking planes went undetected and Japanese warships attempting to get underway were hit and left blazing as they sank into watery graves. The air groups returned to their carriers ready to begin a second attack when a large group of enemy aircraft were reported en route towards the task force. More than 125 Japanese fighters and dive bombers were determined at sinking the carriers, but when the 40-minute battle was over the attacking force had been annihilated. The efficient pilots of Air Group Nine blasted 42 aircraft from the air. The ship's antiaircraft crews sent a half dozen of the Emperor's planes trailing fire into the sea or exploding into fireballs against the pale blue Pacific sky.

The *Essex* participated in the Gilbert Islands operation from November 13 through December 8, 1943. Air strikes were ordered on the morning of November 18 and the first engagement concentrated on Bititu Island. The task force was under constant attack by enemy planes and the *Essex* skillfully dodged several torpedo attacks.

The *Essex* tallied over 700 sorties and dropped more than 300,000 pounds of bombs and rockets, pulverizing ground installations. The battle for one tiny island in the Gilbert's chain, Tarawa, became the bloodiest in the history of any previous engagement by U.S. forces. The excellent training received by the task force in amphibious operations in the Gilberts proved a valuable asset in the occupation of Kwajalein during the next major operation—seizing the Marshall Islands.

A replenishment and well needed rest period was taken at Pearl Harbor before the assault of the Marshalls. Rearmed and battle-ready, the *Essex* sailed from Hawaii on January 16, 1944. The occupation of the Marshall Islands was the first time that land owned by the Japanese before the war had been taken from them. On January 29, Roi and Namur of the Kwajalein Atoll were hit in a pre-dawn attack. The encounter was so successful that by noon of the same day, every Japanese plane in the air or on the ground was just so much junk. Aerial attacks continued for two more days and on February 1, 1944, American troops swarmed ashore. By the eight day, the Marshalls were officially announced as captured.

Truk was a large Japanese fortification supplying their South Pacific forces with planes, ships, and men. This would soon cease! On February 16, 1944, more than 100 American planes were airborne and smashed the target area in a surprise attack. Strike after strike was launched against Truk Island. Aircraft returned to the carriers, refueled and rearmed, then began a second attack the following day. The *Essex* air group blasted 36 enemy planes in the air plus many on the ground. They sank four ships and severely crippled 24 others with repeated torpedo and bomb runs.

Truk was the first of two targets designated in the Asiatic-Pacific Raids of 1944. With that island devastated, the carrier's refueled and proceeded to their second target, the Marianas.

The *Essex* possessed the element of surprise in her first six battles. The Marianas attack was the first where the carrier had to fight her way to the target area. A Japanese search pilot sighted the task force and disappeared before he could be silenced. General Quarters was sounded shortly after sundown. Enemy

planes sent waves of attacks on the carrier throughout the night and when morning came, we launched our planes. When the bright orange sun rose over the horizon, most of the Japanese retreated and the *Essex* pilots concentrated on the airfield at Saipan. Tinian and Guam were hit by other carriers. The attacks were so successful that not one enemy plane was able to retaliate as the fighters withdrew from the area. The *Essex* returned to Majuro Atoll on February 23 for a 24-hour recuperation prior to sailing for the U.S.

On March 10, 1944, the *Essex* dropped anchor in San Francisco Bay. A few days later, she entered the Hunters Point Naval Shipyard. Repairs were completed on April 16 and the *Essex* journeyed to Pearl Harbor for several weeks of training exercises. By May 8, she had rejoined the task force at Majuro. The *Essex*,

An SB2C crashed into the barrier aboard the *Essex* in June 1944.

F6F "Hellcats" on the *Essex* are ready for takeoff to strike the coast of Tinian in June 1944.

in partnership with the *USS Wasp CV-18* and *USS San Jacinto CVL-30*, launched air strikes over Marcus during May 19–20 and battered Wake Island on the 23rd. Air Group Fifteen, who relieved Air Group Nine while the ship was in the yard, swallowed their first taste of combat while ravaging the enemy installations, aircraft, and ships in the area.

The carrier task force supported the Marianas operation from June 6 to August 13, 1944. Air Group Fifteen destroyed 104 enemy planes in the air and 136 on the ground. They sank 22 ships and demolished an additional 38. Following the action, the *Essex* returned to Eniwetok for a two-week rest prior to supporting the occupation of Palau.

The Palau air strikes came on August 29, 1944. A considerable amount of Japanese shipping was wiped out as far north as Manila Bay.

The *Essex* sent sweeping fighter patterns against Nansei Shoto, Formosa, and the Philippines from October 11–14, 1944. Ships remaining in Manila Bay were sunk. During the month, 138 enemy planes were shot out of the air, 117 never got off the ground, and five warships greeted the ocean floor.

On October 12, the *Essex's* supply officer was given the job as battle announcer and personnel below decks could visualize the action topside as the speaker voice described: "Four raids coming in . . . neared on port quarter . . . it's heavy! Oh, there is a Betty burning . . . tremendous fire. Raid over 38.2, port quarter. AA fire port quarter very heavy. Another Betty down . . . they burn beautifully, thirty seconds and then fade out . . . three of them . . . another raid on starboard bow 14 miles. AA astern of us straight up in the air. They're all over the place now . . . *Essex* is about to

open fire . . . it's getting darker by the minute now . . . Be very dark soon, we hope . . . It's very low. Babies closing in now. AA fire coming from all directions. Raid astern apparently opening now. Raid closing in on our port beam now. This is the sixth performance for the *Essex* on these night shows with these little monsters and it's the darkest night yet . . . and getting darker by the minute . . . so don't get excited about it. There are night fighters in the air . . . trying to break off this raid. So far, night fighters from the *Independence* have splashed five Bettys! This is Columbus Day and Task Force 58 is giving them a wonderful fireworks demonstration. This is also National Fire Prevention Week, so don't drop any matches in the dry grass. They're dropping flares now . . . just dropped two off the port quarter . . ."

That's the way it remained the rest of the night until all invading aircraft had been splashed or driven away.

On November 6, 1944, while the *Essex* was conducting raids against Manila, a torpedo bomber damaged by antiaircraft fire landed on the carrier. One antiaircraft shell had exploded in the plane's gun turret, killing the gunner instantly. The *Essex* Chaplain gave last rites to the brave airman, whose body remained at his post of duty. The plane was dropped over the aft end of the flight deck as crew members stood reverently at attention while the bugler sounded taps in solemn respect.

The task force sortied from Ulithi on November 22 to strike Luzon and destroy the last remnants of the weakened Japanese air force. Sorties were sent on the 25th and Air Group Four, newly arrived aboard the *Essex*, began their first combat mission. On November 25, the *Essex* received her first major battle damage when a lone Kamikaze charged through thick antiaircraft fire, skimmed along the flight deck, and crashed into the port side. A simultaneous explosion of the enemy plane and fully armed aircraft on the flight deck shook the *Essex* like an earthquake. Fifteen men were killed and 44 were wounded. In less than 30 minutes, the fires had been smothered and the flight deck was again operational.

On December 11, 1944, the Third Fleet left Ulithi for a three-day attack on Luzon in support of the occupation of Mindoro. A larger number of fighters were used to offset the kamikaze tactics. Fighters were directed over Formosa, Sakishima Gunto, and Okinawa Gunto in preparation for the landings at Lingayen Gulf. Flight operations were often restricted due to inclement weather but substantial damage was inflicted on airfields and installations.

**A closeup view showing damage to the *Essex* following a
Kamikaze hit, November 25, 1944.**

The *Essex* along with other carriers steamed to the South China Sea via Bashi Channel and began striking Japanese shipping in the Saigon-Camranh Bay area. Hainan and the China coast from Swatow to the Luichow Peninsula, including Hong Kong, were heavily hit by the carrier air groups on January 15–16, 1945.

February 10, 1945, was one of the most significant "firsts" for the famed Task Force 58, for on that day the giant carriers launched the initial air attacks against the Japanese homeland. Tokyo was blasted, neutralizing the enemy air strength in advance of the U. S. Marine landings on Iwo Jima. During the actual Iwo Jima landings, the *Essex* struck Chichi Jima and nearby islands. A one-day strike on March 3 over Okinawa Gunto ended the final phase of the Iwo

Jima operation. Extensive photographic reconnaissance flights were made for aerial mapping in preparation of the final engagement of World War II—the Okinawa Gunto operation.

After two weeks at Ulithi replenishing supplies, the speedy carrier task force, with *Essex,* departed the huge staging area on March 14, 1945. The *Essex* was at sea for 79 consecutive days. Air Group Eighty-Three flew 6460 missions, dropped 1041 tons of bombs and fired a million rounds of 50-caliber ammunition. Many enemy planes fell to the *Essex's* competent antiaircraft crews. On May 29, the carrier sailed for Leyte Gulf for a well-deserved rest.

Task Force 58 resumed strikes in massive strength against Tokyo on July 10, 1945. Hokkaido and Northern Honshu were bombed on July 14–15. Tokyo and the Kure Naval Base were hit on July 24–25 and 28 and Tokyo itself suffered relentless attacks up to July 30. Air strikes continued against the Japanese homeland right up to August 15, 1945, the day that fighting in the Second World War finally came to an end.

During the last engagement of the war, the Third Fleet actions against Japan found the *Essex* air group flying 2595 sorties, sinking 24,300 tons of enemy merchant shipping and damaging the battleship *Nagato*. The daring pilots also delivered successful attacks on a light cruiser of the *Kuma-Natori* class. They sank the light carrier *Kaiyo*, the minelayer *Tokima*, three destroyers, and five destroyer escorts.

Defensive air patrols were flown until December 13 when the *Essex* set course for Puget Sound Naval Shipyard, Bremerton, Washington. Upon embarking from Japan, the crewmen hoisted a homeward bound pennant 1538 feet in length. It was lost to the sea shortly after clearing the Japanese port but a duplicate was constructed and proudly flapped in the crisp wind as the *Essex* entered Bremerton.

For extraordinary heroism in combat action against enemy forces in the most forward areas of the Pacific, the *Essex* was awarded the Presidential Unit Citation for the period August 31, 1943, to August 15, 1945. The great ship completed 17 months of continuous operations and supported every major Pacific engagement from Tarawa to Tokyo Bay. Her valiant air groups inflicted insurmountable losses upon enemy

aircraft, fleet and merchant shipping, and rendered loyal service in achieving the ultimate defeat of the Japanese Empire. On January 9, 1947, the *Essex* was decommissioned with the Bremerton Reserve Group of the Pacific Reserve Fleet. It was short lived.

Less than 20 months after being mothballed, the *Essex* shed her cocoon, was removed from the reserve fleet and a 27A modification began September 1, 1948. The $40 million face lifting included a streamlined island structure, a stronger flight deck to handle jet aircraft, and the latest sophisticated electronic equipment.

Under the command of Capt. Austin W. Wheelock, USN, the *USS Essex CV-9* was recommissioned on September 15, 1951 at Puget Sound Naval Shipyard.

The *Essex* transited the Panama Canal and arrived in San Diego, California, June 26, 1951. Next, she went to Pearl Harbor where a brief training maneuver was conducted. On August 21, 1951, she joined Task Force 77 in Korean waters.

The *Essex* was designated the flagship of Rear Admiral John Perry, USN, Commander, Carrier Division One. Air Group Five (CAG 5) assigned to the ship flew 6600 combat missions, destroyed 640 sections of railroad tracks, snarled 80 highway bridges, 820 buildings and made kindling wood of 1218 railroad cars. During this time, the *Essex* became the first carrier to launch the F2H twin-jet fighter into combat.

The *Essex* returned to San Diego on March 22, 1952, from her first Korean war cruise. Only one serious accident occurred during the entire cruise. On the night of September 16, 1951, a Banshee jet smashed through the barriers crashing into numerous aircraft spotted on the forward end of the flight deck. Fire fighting teams quickly extinguished the blaze, but seven men had died in the mishap.

On June 16, 1952, the *Essex* left San Diego for her second Korean War cruise. This time the air group delivered 31,000 tons of explosives on enemy positions and flew more than 7000 sorties. The carrier took part in coordinated United Nations strikes all the way from the front lines to the Yalu River in North Korea. On October 1, 1952, the *Essex* was redesignated CVA-9— Attack Aircraft Carrier. After completing her fifth Korean engagement, she returned to the United States on February 6, 1953, arriving at the Puget Sound Shipyard. The haggard crew enjoyed a well-deserved rest while their ship underwent more alterations and repairs.

The *Essex* deployed from San Diego on December 1, 1953, for a third tour of duty in the Far East. There was no fighting this trip and the carrier began working

The Essex's chaplain delivers a brief funeral service to an airman whose body remains at his post of duty on January 5, 1945. Later the plane was pushed into the sea.

with the United Nations Peace Patrol.

Aboard the *Essex* was Rear Admiral Robert E. Blick, USN, Commander Carrier Division Three. After chalking up 57,000 miles, the ship headed for San Diego arriving on July 12, 1954.

For exceptional meritorious service during her operations against enemy forces in Korea from August 21, 1951 to March 5, 1952, the *Essex* was awarded the Navy Unit Commendation. Her air groups carried out highly successful defensive and offensive missions with distinction and contributed in large measure to the success of friendly forces against the enemy. Displaying the courage of her past actions during World War II, the *Essex* provided inspiring and unyielding devotion to the fulfillment of vital tasks in the Korean War Zone.

On November 3, 1954, the *Essex* left San Diego to begin her fourth Western Pacific cruise. With other units of Task Force 77, she took part in the Tachen Islands evacuation in Formosan waters. When the *Essex* anchored in the Menam Chao Phraya River in Bangkok, Thailand, in March 1955, she became the first carrier to visit that country since World War II.

Fleet maneuvers were held off Okinawa during April and May.

On June 21, 1955, the *Essex* stopped briefly in San Francisco Bay. Air Group Two was disembarked at Alameda Naval Air Station, then the carrier continued down the coast to her home port in San Diego on June 23.

The *Essex* entered Puget Sound Naval Shipyard on July 28, 1955 to undergo another major conversion, which took eight months to complete. Included in the modernization was a new angle flight deck and an enclosed hurricane bow. On March 2, 1956, the radically altered *Essex* left Bremerton Shipyard to rejoin the Pacific Fleet.

The *Essex* operated off the coast of Southern California throughout the first half of 1957. Orders were then received to join the Atlantic Fleet. The carrier rounded South America and arrived at her new home port of Mayport, Florida, in August, where she finished the year off conducting carrier air operations.

In February 1958, she departed for the Western Mediterranean, grouping forces with the Sixth Fleet. She participated in "Operation Green Cobra," a NATO exercise, until May and then shifted to the Eastern Mediterranean.

While in Athens, Greece, July 14, 1958, the *Essex* was alerted during the Middle East crisis and supported the U.S. Marine landings at Beirut, Lebanon on the following day. For six weeks, the *Essex* pilots flew

2780 reconnaissance and patrol missions over the troubled nation.

The *Essex* was once again pulled away from Naples, when she went through the Suez Canal on emergency orders to join the Seventh Fleet in Formosan waters, as another trouble spot erupted. The pilots flew 591 missions in this area.

In March 1959, the *Essex* received orders for recall to Mayport, Florida. During the tedious journey home, stops were made at Subic Bay, Philippines; Singapore; Malaya; Colombo, Ceylon; Capetown, South Africa; and Rio de Janeiro, Brazil. She had tallied 75,000 miles during the eight-month deployment. She joined other Sixth Fleet units to cover President Eisenhower's at-sea period of his 22,000 mile goodwill trip to the Middle East and Europe, then returned to Mayport in February 1960.

On March 8, 1960, the *Essex*, a long-time leader in her class, bowed out of the attack carrier classification and was redesignated CVS: Anti-Submarine warfare carrier. She now assumed a new role in keeping the sea lanes open and free.

Following six weeks of overhaul at the New York Naval Shipyard, she steamed for a new home port at Quonset Point, Rhode Island. Throughout the summer of 1960, she engaged in three anti-submarine warfare exercises. One of these, called "Operation Swordthrust," was with NATO forces in the Norwegian Sea and the Bay of Biscay.

The *Essex* operated continuously out of Quonset Point until October 1961. In the latter part of the month, she sailed to the Eastern Atlantic during the Berlin Crisis. At this time the large carrier visited Hamburg, where more than 70,000 civilians toured the vessel. The *Essex* also became the first U.S. carrier to successfully transit the Elbe River.

When the ship returned to the States, she entered the Brooklyn Navy Yard on March 25, 1962, to undergo a FRAM II conversion. The fleet Rehabilitation and Modernization program extended the carrier's service to about seven additional years. The latest electronic and sonar equipment, including a *Conorama* greatly increased her combat effectiveness.

On September 25, 1962, the *Essex* left the yards and a month later began a six-week training period off Guantanamo Bay, Cuba. While at sea on October 21, President Kennedy announced the naval quarantine of Cuba. For the next 26 days, the *Essex* conducted 624 consecutive hours of flight operations. When tension had settled around Cuba, the *Essex* resumed normal training exercises off Quonset Point.

The *Essex* left her home port on October 1, 1963,

for a three-month cruise to the Mediterranean and the Middle East. On October 29 she transited the Panama Canal for the fourth time. She then journeyed through the Red Sea and stopped at Jidda, Saudi Arabia, where a demonstration of ASW tactics was reviewed by prominent Arabians. The highlight of this cruise was "Operation MIDLINK VI," a Central Treaty Organization exercise involving Pakistan, Iran, Turkey, the United Kingdom, and the U.S. During the two week engagement, the *Essex* operated out of Karachi, Pakistan.

After transiting the Suez Canal for a fifth time, the *Essex* visited Naples, Italy. In December 1963, she returned to her home port of Quonset Point.

In June 1964, the *Essex* took 312 midshipmen for a seven-week training cruise to Northern Europe. The "middies" came from various colleges and the Naval Academy. Liberty calls were made at LeHavre, France, Copenhagen, and Portsmouth, England.

Following her return from this cruise the *Essex* resumed ASW operations off Quonset Point. When the Naval Training Carrier *USS Lexington CVS-16* entered the yards for overhaul, the *Essex* spent three weeks at Pensacola, Fla., performing carrier qualification for new pilots. While in this capacity, the *Essex* logged in her 120,000th arrested gear landing and launched her 32,000th aircraft from the starboard catapult.

A joint Canadian-American ASW operation began on July 20, 1964, off the Atlantic seaboard and was continued until December. Anti-Submarine Squadron VS-880 of the RCAF embarked on the *Essex* for the duration of the exercise.

In January 1965, the *Essex* resumed her ASW operations. She steamed to Mayport, Fla., in March 1965 to conduct carrier qualifications for pilots from the Naval Air Training Command. More than 700 "touch and go" landings were logged in, as well as 2143 arrested gear landings.

The *Essex* underwent an Operational Readiness Inspection (ORI) off Guantanamo Bay to examine her ability as a top combat unit of the fleet. The ORI is an annual affair for all naval ships. Included in the inspection party was the Commander, Hunter-Killer Force, Atlantic Fleet Training Group and the Commander of ASW Group Fifty from Key West, Florida. A short visit to Kingston, Jamaica, followed the ORI, then the *Essex* returned to Quonset Point in April 1965.

From June through September 1965, the *Essex* once again hosted the midshipmen on their annual training cruise. Two of these cruises were made in which the *Essex* participated with NATO forces in training operations. The *Essex*, along with four other ships, under-

went an exercise to test a multi-nation force operation over an extended period of time. On September 3, 1965, she returned to her home port and normal duties.

On January 7, 1966, the *Essex* entered the Boston Naval Yard for an extensive overhaul which cost $6.2 million. The necessary work was completed on June 10, 1966, and the *Essex* began a six-week refresher cruise off Cuba.

She was a few hundred miles off the North Carolina coast the morning of November 6, 1966, engaged in search and destroy tactics with fleet units, including the nuclear submarine *Nautilus (SS[N]-571)*. During an opposed refueling exercise, the submarine penetrated the destroyer screen and steamed in submerged toward the *Essex*. The carrier set course to take on fuel from the tanker *Salamonie AO-26*. A sudden severe shock reverberated throughout the *Essex* as the *Nautilus* collided with the carrier's hull and left an 8-foot gaping hole. The *Nautilus* immediately surfaced. One crewman from each warship suffered slight injury and the exercise was terminated with damage to each vessel. The *Essex* returned to Norfolk for repairs at the Boston Naval Shipyard, November 14–December 28, 1966.

When yardwork was completed the *Essex* sailed for Quonset Point on May 29, 1967, then on to Northern Europe for a four-month cruise. Various training exercises were held, as well as participation in combined operations with defense units of Norway, Denmark, the Netherlands, West Germany, and England. More than 10,000 flight hours were logged while the carrier steamed 26,000 nautical miles. Ports of call were Norway, the British Isles, Holland, and West Germany. Then she went to the Islands of Malta and Sicily in the Mediterranean.

On September 22, 1967, the *Essex* returned to Quonset Point from where she operated the remainder of the year.

Between February 15 and June 13, 1968, the carrier made another Mediterranean cruise and visited Naples, Italy; Golfe Juan, France; Valletta, Malta; Rotterdam, the Netherlands; Portsmouth, England; and Hamburg, Germany.

The *Essex* substituted for the training carrier *USS Lexington CVT-16* during July near Pensacola, Florida. She also participated in FIXWEX operations in August, then held practice maneuvers for the proposed recovery of Apollo 7.

On October 22, Astronauts Captain Walter Shirra USN, Air Major Donald Eisele USAF, and civilian Walter Cunningham splashed down in the Atlantic and were brought aboard the *Essex*.

The carrier departed Quonset Point on January 3, 1969, and headed once again to Pensacola to substitute for the training carrier *Lexington*. This was the final cruise for the *Essex*. On February 6, 1969, she was back at Quonset Point.

In March the *Essex* headed for Boston for a deactivation process and on July 30, 1969, the grand old lady of the fleet was decommissioned.

The *Essex* was the forerunner of the largest class of carriers ever built. However, by the time she was ready for the mothballs she herself had been reclassified. Of the 24 ships that had once belonged in the *Essex* class, today only five remain in the status of Attack Carrier CVA.

The men aboard the *Essex* called her the "Fightin'est Ship in the Fleet." This was more than just a nick-name. It was an honor that the carrier repeatedly earned during long and faithful service. On December 31, 1968, she had completed 26 years of naval service.

The *USS Essex CVS-9* received the following awards: The Presidential Unit Citation; Navy Unit Commendation; American Area Campaign Service Medal; Asiatic-Pacific Area Campaign Service Medal with 13 battle stars; World War II Victory Medal; Navy Occupation Service Medal; China Service (extended) Medal; Korean Service Medal with 4 battle stars; United Nations Service Medal; National Defense Service Medal; Armed Forces Expeditionary Medal; Navy Expeditionary Medal; Philippine Liberation Campaign Service Ribbon with 2 stars; Republic of the Philippines Presidential Unit Citation Badge; and the Republic of Korea Presidential Unit Citation Badge.

USS Yorktown CVS-10.

10

USS Yorktown CVS-10 (CV-10)

On December 1, 1941, the keel was laid down for the *USS Bon Homme Richard CV-10*, at the Newport News Shipbuilding Company in Virginia. On September 26, 1942, the name of the carrier was changed to *Yorktown*, in honor of the *USS Yorktown CV-5*, which was sunk after the Battle of Midway on June 7, 1942.

Mrs. Franklin D. Roosevelt was just about ready to christen the new ship on January 21, 1943, when to the surprise of everyone the carrier began to slide down the launching ways—seven minutes ahead of schedule.

Mrs. Roosevelt stepped forward and swung twice to break the champagne bottle on the ship's prow. From that moment, the *Yorktown* was known as an eager ship.

The *Yorktown* was commissioned on April 15, 1943 and Captain Joseph J. Clark became her first commander. In view of the urgent requirement for aircraft carriers in the Pacific forward area, no time was wasted in preparing the ship for her ultimate destination.

Original statistics of the *Yorktown* at the time of commissioning were: standard displacement, 27,000 tons; full load, 33,000 tons; extreme beam, at or about the flight deck 147 feet 6 inches; speed 33 knots; complement, 360 officers and 3088 enlisted men. Armament, twelve 5-inch 38-caliber gun mounts and many 40mm and 20mm antiaircraft gun mounts. The *Yorktown* could handle between 85 to 100 aircraft depending on the size.

Following a rapid but complete shakedown cruise, the *Yorktown* slipped through the Panama Canal and arrived at Pearl Harbor on July 11, 1943. Training exercises began with emphasis on flight operations and gunnery practice.

On August 31, the carrier departed Hawaii in company with the *USS Essex CV-9* and the *USS Independence CVL-22*. Assigned to Task Force 51, the *Yorktown* launched air strikes against Marcus Island on August 31 and left vital enemy installations in rubble.

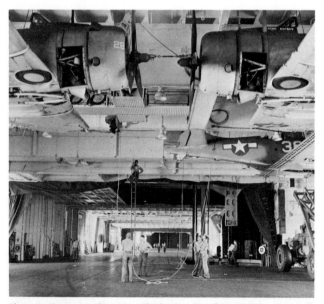

The *Yorktown's* hangar deck in October 1943. Aircraft overhead are SBD's.

From Marcus, the carrier proceeded to Wake Island where at 4:45 A.M. on October 5, 1943, air assaults were directed at the island; a second strike was made the next day.

Due to previous photographic coverage made by the Army, the pilots had memorized the general terrain and important installations which greatly contributed to the success of the mission. On October 23, the carrier returned to Hawaii for replenishment.

Assigned to Task Group 51.1, the *Yorktown* cleared Pearl Harbor on November 10, to strike Mille and Jalutt. The carrier arrived some 80 miles south of Mille and 150 miles east-southeast of Jalutt. The carrier launched her air group against Jalutt, concentrating on seaplanes and shipping in Jalutt Harbor and also hit enemy fortifications in the path of the strike route. Heavy damage was inflicted on airfields and the harbor area.

On December 4, 1943, the fast carrier force began air strikes against Kwajalein, where the primary targets were enemy shipping and aircraft installations. The *Yorktown's* earlier raids on Marcus and Wake had been pre-dawn strikes, but the Kwajalein assault was launched after dawn with excellent results due to catching the enemy by abject surprise. This particular raid was a stab against the heart of the Marshalls defense. Many ships in the northern and southern part of the lagoon were either sunk or severely damaged. With her air group safely on board, the *Yorktown* headed back to Hawaii where the crew enjoyed a Hawaiian Christmas.

On January 16, 1944, the *Yorktown* departed Pearl Harbor with Task Group 50.15. At 4:30 A.M., January 29, air strikes were launched against Taroa and Wotje; two combat air patrols were made against Taroa and three over Wotje. The next day strikes were made on Kwajalein and Ebeye Islands. The Marshall Islands operation was at full swing with many ground installations and airfields destroyed. Enubuj Island in the Kwajalein Atoll was smashed on January 31 and American troops rushed ashore.

By February 8 the Marshalls operation was concluded and the fast carrier force refueled and prepared for its first target of the Asiatic-Pacific Raids of 1944—Truk.

Admiral Marc Mitscher, Commander of Task Force 58 and his staff, boarded the *Yorktown* and the admiral's flag was hoisted to designate the carrier as the flagship of the mighty task force.

On February 16–17, Truk received a severe beating from the carrier's air groups. The giant Japanese staging area was hit for the first time and the enemy knew it wouldn't be the last.

A TBF being catapulted from the hangar deck of the *York-town* in May 1943.

Tinian and Saipan in the Marianas were hit on February 21–22. Japanese fighter and torpedo planes repeatedly struck our task force, but all attempts were in vain due to the accurate antiaircraft barrage from the gun batteries.

The *Yorktown* was in the Majuro Lagoon during March 1–8, but on the 8th she was underway for training operations and gunnery practice. A brief stop was made at Espiritu Santo, after which training resumed.

On March 23, the carrier rejoined the fast carrier force and struck the Palau Islands and Woleai Atoll from March 30 to April 1, 1944.

Airfields, shipping, hangars, and fuel dumps were nearly completely destroyed. The U.S. Army landed at Humboldt Bay and Tanahmerah Bay on the northern coast of New Guinea April 21–24.

The *Yorktown's* pilots flew support missions and 73 sorties were flown over the target areas with over 25 tons of bombs delivered on the enemy. The *Yorktown's* air group destroyed three enemy planes on the ground, sunk 12 barges and four landing craft, and left two fuel dumps aflame.

The first engagement of the Marianas operation began on June 11, 1944, with the fast carrier force supporting the capture and occupation of Saipan. Enemy ground positions took a heavy beating as fuel depots and warehouses were completely destroyed. Air strikes continued on Saipan until June 20 when reports were received that a massive enemy fleet had been sighted

A TBF is loaded for another combat mission on the *Yorktown* in October 1943.

approximately 300 miles from the task force.

The *Yorktown* and other carriers had their flight decks loaded with planes and in less than one hour the *Yorktown* launched her air group, which joined others and headed towards the enemy fleet.

Upon arrival at the target area the *Yorktown's* pilots concentrated on the enemy aircraft carriers. The largest was hit by three 1000-pound bombs and one 250 pounder. Two smaller carriers were hit with four 500-pound bombs and a light cruiser was severely damaged. This surprise attack was a complete success. Many of the returning fighters were low on fuel and badly damaged. Some landed on other carriers while some were ditched and the pilots picked from the sea by destroyers.

On June 24, the *Yorktown* participated in the Second Bonins Raid, which was followed by a third on July 3–4. The last two weeks of the month concluded the Marianas operation with air assaults over Palau, Yap, and Ulithi.

With five major campaigns behind her, the *Yorktown* began showing signs of wear and was ordered stateside. On August 18, 1944, she was in drydock at Puget Sound, Bremerton, Washington, where she received a complete overhaul. Fifty-one days later she was headed for Alameda Naval Air Station in California where Air Group 3 was embarked. The carrier was back with the task force at Ulithi on October 24.

Task Group 38.1 (*Yorktown* included) steamed from Ulithi Atoll for strikes on the Philippine Islands. Fighter sweeps were launched against enemy shipping in Manila Harbor from November 11–14. More than 38 enemy ships were sunk or severely damaged during these raids. Air strikes continued over southern Luzon and the Mindoro Strait, and airfields in the central Philippines were hit on November 19. The task force then retired to refuel, and returned to the Philippine area on December 14 for a three-day assault in support of the Mindoro landings. Airfields and storage houses were smashed and the war in the Pacific was a step closer to the end.

As the new year began, the *Yorktown* joined other carriers of the Third Fleet and supported the Luzon operation. The carrier sent air strikes against Luzon on January 6–7, 1945. Alternating periodically, the *Yorktown* sent strikes on Formosa on January 3, 4, 9, 15, and 21; the China coast on January 12–16, and the Nansei Shoto on the 22nd. The primary objective of these raids was to seek out and destroy the Japanese Second Diversionary Attack Force and eliminate enemy shipping in the South China Sea.

Prior to the U.S. Marine landings on Iwo Jima, the *Yorktown,* as a unit of Task Force 58, steamed from Ulithi on February 10 for air strikes against Japan and the Nansei Shoto. The main enemy air strength in Tokyo was hit to preclude any serious air attacks upon American forces at Iwo Jima.

On February 21, approximately 11 enemy planes approached the task force. As two planes came within firing range of the *Yorktown's* batteries, they were splashed without inflicting any damage. The *York-*

An F6F crashed on the *Yorktown* in May 1943.

town continued providing combat air patrols in support of the attack and occupation of Iwo Jima until March 1, 1945. A one-day air strike against Okinawa came on the last day of the Iwo Jima operation. The purpose was to obtain photographic coverage for an upcoming invasion of that island. The carrier force then went to Ulithi Atoll for rest and supplies.

The carrier force's final major assignment of World War II was the Third and Fifth Fleet raids in support of the Okinawa Gunto operation. The *Yorktown* sortied with the task force from Ulithi and launched air strikes against southern Kyush, Shikoku, western Honshu, and Nansei Shoto on March 18, 1945.

While en route to their objective on March 18, the task force was attacked by a large force of enemy planes. One fighter came in fast and scored a direct hit on the *Yorktown*. The bomb smashed into the starboard signal bridge, ripped through the deck and number two battery, and exploded near the second deck. A pair of gaping holes, 12 and 19 square feet, were gouged in the ship's side and three men died when the bomb exploded. However the *Yorktown* remained operational at all times despite the damage.

The *Yorktown* provided heavy air support to the American amphibious forces landing on Okinawa on April 1, 1945. A search plane from the *USS Essex CV-9* reported the presence of an enemy fleet southwest of Kyushu on April 7. The *Yorktown* immediately sent her air group to join other air groups and issued a devastating attack to the enemy fleet. The prize battleship *Yamato* came under direct attack of the *Yorktown*'s torpedo squadron and five direct hits between the bow and stern split the *Yamato* in half.

The carrier's air group also sank a light cruiser and seriously damaged two destroyers. The *Yorktown* then resumed support to the Okinawa assault until June 11, 1945, at which time the island was officially secured by the U.S. Marines.

On July 13, the *Yorktown* arrived at San Pedro Bay, Leyte Gulf, in the Philippines, where a two-week replenishment took place. The carrier was then underway to join the task force for the final assaults against the Japanese homeland. Air strikes continued until August 15 when the Japanese surrendered unconditionally. City after city came under attack from the carrier's air group during the last month of the war. Shipping, aircraft, and prime military installations were hit from northern Kyushu to southern Hokkaido. The strike groups flew back and forth destroying all sighted installations. As soon as one mission was ended, the planes were rearmed and refueled and headed for attacks on other coastline targets. Aircraft construction factories, warehouses, large staging areas, and ammo dumps became a shambles.

The *Yorktown*'s pilots were on their way for routine strikes on August 15, 1945, when CINCPACFLT ordered a cease to all offensive operations. The planes dropped their bombs and returned to the carrier.

The carrier proudly entered Tokyo Bay on September 16, 1945, and dropped anchor. Her air group switched from a "seek and destroy" unit to a more humanitarian task of transporting food, medical supplies, and clothing to all prisoner of war camps throughout the Japanese homeland.

On October 1, the *Yorktown* departed Tokyo Bay and proceeded to Okinawa. Only four months earlier the carrier had helped to free the island from Japanese domination. The carrier boarded 1600 veterans and steamed out of Buckner Bay on October 6. A thousand foot homeward-bound pennant was hoisted and held aloft by balloons donated by the ship's aerologist office. High winds demanded the pennant's recovery a short time later.

On October 20, 1945, the *Yorktown* pulled up alongside the pier at Alameda, California, Naval Air Station. Six days later, on Navy Day, 1800 civilians visited the carrier during open house. For many, this was the first time they had seen or boarded an aircraft carrier. Evident to all visitors was the ship's scoreboard which read: "118 enemy ships, including the battleship *Yamato*, destroyed or damaged along with 2358 aircraft and ground installations throughout the Pacific campaign."

The *Yorktown* arrived at Hunters Point Naval Shipyard, San Francisco, on October 29. Additional galley facilities and bunks were installed in the hangar deck, and on November 2 she began the first of two "Magic Carpet" cruises. The carrier arrived at Guam 16 days later, where 4312 veterans came aboard for return to the states, arriving at Alameda on November 29.

Upon completion of the final "Magic Carpet" cruise, the *Yorktown* had transported more than 10,000 servicemen back to the land they had fought for.

The carrier set course for the Puget Sound Naval Shipyard, arriving on February 1, 1946.

On January 9, 1947, she was decommissioned in the Bremerton Group of the Pacific Reserve Fleet.

In May of 1951, the *Yorktown* was moved from her berth in the reserve group into a Puget Sound Naval Shipyard drydock. The communist aggression in Korea was a decisive factor for recommissioning the carrier. First, the fighting lady of World War II fame had to be modernized to handle the latest jet aircraft. While the *Yorktown* was asleep in mothballs, naval aviation had progressed rapidly. Now the carrier had to be molded into a stronger fighting ship. During the face lifting, the *Yorktown* received a streamlined island structure and her flight deck gun mounts were removed. New electrically operating steel doors were installed to divide the hangar deck into three sections. She also became the first carrier to have a complete prosthetics laboratory for making dentures for crewmen who needed them while at sea.

On December 15, 1952, the *Yorktown* was recommissioned with Captain William M. Nation commanding. Two months before, the carrier had been redesignated Attack Aircraft Carrier—CVA.

During the first part of 1953, the *Yorktown* went through a complete shakedown cruise, followed by a post-shakedown yard period and operational training. On August 2, the "Fighting Lady" set course for Hawaii. Her bow sliced the warm waters of the South Pacific on August 31, where 10 years earlier she had launched strikes against the Marcus Islands.

The *Yorktown* became the flagship for Task Force 77 on September 15, 1953. Arriving too late to participate in the actual fight against communist aggression in Korea, she became a formidable barrier against the communists.

Her embarked Air Group Two conducted daily drills and numerous flight operations and practiced bomb runs and rocket firing at simulated targets. Their night flying exercises helped maintain a high state of operational readiness.

During her seven-month tour of duty in Korean waters, the *Yorktown* logged 5000 catapult launches.

On March 3, 1954, she arrived at Alameda, California. While at Alameda the *Yorktown* presented a $25,000 check to the Shrine Hospital for crippled children; this was the largest single donation ever collected aboard a Navy ship for charity. The carrier then moved across the Bay to Hunters Point for an overhaul.

On March 31, 1954, the *Yorktown* became the principal subject for a 20th Century-Fox motion picture, "Jet Carrier." The cinemascope film covered all phases of carrier operations.

The *Yorktown* deployed on her second Western Pacific cruise since recommissioning on July 1, 1954. With one brief stop at Hawaii, the carrier arrived at Manila Bay on August 2.

Throughout September, October and November, the *Yorktown* patrolled the South China Sea and spent Christmas at Yokosuka, Japan. Joint maneuvers were conducted with other Seventh Fleet units until January 23, 1955. On that day she steamed to the Tachen Islands near Nationalist China Formosa to evacuate

the troubled islands. In a twenty day period, the carrier's air group flew 1,355 sorties to provide protection to thousands of Chinese Nationalists who were withdrawn to Formosa.

Having logged 59,000 miles since the cruise began, the *Yorktown* returned to Alameda on February 28, 1955.

The mighty carrier set course for Puget Sound Shipyard, arriving on March 17, 1955 for a major conversion and overhaul. During this period the *Yorktown* received an enclosed hurricane bow, angle flight deck plus improved living quarters. The overhaul was complete by October 14 and the carrier resumed operational training along the California seaboard until March 19, 1956.

On that day she headed for the western Pacific and joined Task Force 77 for operations throughout the Far East. Highlighting this cruise was the *Yorktown's* participation in the American-Philippine Independence Day celebration at Manila on July 4, 1956.

On September 13, she returned to Alameda and spent a brief period at the San Francisco Naval Shipyard, where a mirror-light landing system was installed.

The *Yorktown* made another Western Pacific cruise from March 9 to August 25, 1957. Familiar ports in Japan and the Philippines were revisited and five months were spent operating with the Seventh Fleet.

On September 25, she entered the yards at Puget Sound for another conversion to enable her to take on a new role as an antisubmarine warfare carrier. The designation from CVA-10 to CVS-10 became effective September 1, 1957.

On February 7, 1958, the *Yorktown* steamed to her new homeport at Long Beach, California where she arrived on February 12. Intensive hunter-killer and other ASW operations took her from the California seaboard to Hawaii and the Canadian northwest. Her mission was to qualify the newly embarked air group in the skill required for searching and destroying hostile submarines in any weather day or night. In addition to her primary role as a CVS, the *Yorktown* also served as a mobile command communications center and logistics depot for task group formations. At times, this included not only a screen of destroyer type warships, but also killer submarines and other naval support units.

As an ASW support carrier she served as home base for fixed wing "Tracker" aircraft, a helicopter squadron and several airborne early warning radar-equipped planes. Her far-ranging airbase runways can be quickly aimed in any direction with devastating results to an enemy.

To complement her arsenal of weapons, the *York-*

town carried electronic rockets, homing torpedoes, depth charges, and atomic depth bombs.

On November 1, 1958, the *Yorktown* departed her home port for her first overseas cruise as an ASW carrier. Air Anti-Submarine Squadron 37, Helicopter ASW Squadron 2 and Detachment "A" of Fighter Squadron 92 were aboard for the trip. On May 13, 1959, she returned to San Diego, California.

The *Yorktown* departed California on January 5, 1960, as flagship for Commander Carrier Division 17 with Air Anti-Submarine Squadron 23, Helicopter ASW Squadron 4, and Carrier Airborne Early Warning Squadron 11.

With Destroyer Division 232 and embarked squadrons, the *Yorktown* deployed as the first permanent HUK Group in the Pacific area.

On March 3, 1960, the carrier arrived at Yokosuka, Japan, to relieve the *USS Kearsarge CVS-33*. During the deployment, routine ASW exercises were conducted with the *Yorktown* involved in three major operations. They consisted of "Operation Blue Star," an amphibious exercise conducted during March 1960 near Formosa; Seato Exercise "Sea Lion," an ASW convoy exercise held during May 1960 in the South China Sea; and "Operation Cosmos," which provided radio and communication support for the Presidential Press Party plus helicopter support for the entire Presidential Party during his state visit to the Far East.

On June 10, 1960, "The Fighting Lady"—a sobriquet for the *Yorktown*—played a major role in rescuing 53 merchant seamen from the ill-fated British freighter S.S. *Shun Lee*. The stricken vessel had run aground on Paratas Reef as a result of high winds and an angry sea spawned by Typhoon Mary in the China Sea.

On July 15, 1960, the carrier was relieved on station by the *USS Hornet CVS-12*, and arrived in Long Beach, California, on July 28. At this time the *Yorktown*'s communication department was awarded the Green "C" for excellence for the second consecutive year.

From September 20, 1960, to January 23, 1961, the *Yorktown* received an overhaul at Puget Sound Naval Shipyard. She sailed from the yard at Bremerton, Washington, on January 27 and reached Long Beach on the 29th for refresher training along the California coast.

"The Fighting Lady" was exposed to show business again on March 31, 1961, when the *Tennessee Ernie Ford* show was televised from her flight deck in a salute to the 50th Anniversary of Naval Aviation.

She cruised the Far East again from July 29, 1961, to March 2, 1962, followed by ASW training. On October 25, 1962, she steamed from Long Beach to cruise

with the Seventh Fleet in waters ranging from the shores of Japan to Okinawa, Taiwan, and the Philippines.

She got underway on June 5, 1963, and returned to Long Beach on June 18 for an overhaul that was not completed until March 30, 1964. She then put to sea from San Diego on October 23 for brief operations in Hawaiian waters. She joined the Seventh Fleet again at Yokosuka on December 3, 1964.

On January 26, 1965, the carrier departed Hong Kong to begin an at-sea period maintaining surveillance of the Soviet submarine tender *Bakmuht* and a trio of her submarines. During this time, on January 29 the *Yorktown* participated in combined exercises with the British attack carrier *HMS Victorious -R38*.

Early in February the *Yorktown* was sailing to the South China Sea for special operations in the area of South Vietnam. During this sojourn she took part in "Operation Candid Camera," with three other carriers and a variety of other surface vessels. She was part of the largest massed naval force since the Korean War.

After cruising for 37 consecutive days at sea, "The Fighting Lady" came into Sasebo, Japan, for several weeks of maintenance. Then it was back to the South China Sea where she remained from March 16 through May 3, 1965, when she arrived at Yokosuka, Japan.

After being relieved by the *USS Bennington*, the *Yorktown* exited Yokosuka on May 7 and arrived in Long Beach ten days later after a brief stopover in San Diego to release the air group.

From June 20–23 she supervised carrier qualifications. From July 7–12 the *Yorktown* hosted a group of Sea Cadets. "The Fighting Lady" was on her way again on July 14 with a cargo of vitally needed materials to the South China Sea. This was known by the crew as "Magic Carpet II," because it resembled in reverse the return of veterans from overseas at the end of the fighting in World War II. The carrier arrived at Pearl Harbor on July 20 with supplies picked up at San Diego five days before. The *Yorktown* departed Hawaii on July 22 with additional supplies and unloaded them at Subic Bay, the Philippines, on August 2.

The *Yorktown* was off again on August 3 and stopped August 7–11 at Yokosuka, then on to San Francisco where she arrived on the 20th. Three days later she headed for San Diego arriving on the 24th and proceeded directly to Long Beach.

A maintenance period was held until September 20, when she became involved with carrier qualifications.

October 23–30, 1965, was spent in training for an Operational Readiness Inspection (ORI) which was scheduled from November 29 to December 4.

When the Christmas leave period had ended, the

Yorktown sailed from her home port at Long Beach on January 5. She sailed to San Diego and picked up her air group plus 14 guests of the Secretary of the Navy. Six days later she arrived at Hawaii. Her guests went ashore and the carrier conducted operations near the Hawaiian Islands January 13–21. The hearty *Yorktown* crew enjoyed a visit to the islands of Hawaii from January 21 to February 9, at which time the carrier steamed for Japan and arrived at Yokosuka on the 17th. On February 21 she relieved the *USS Hornet CVS-12* and headed for the South China Sea where she cruised for 36 straight days before returning to Subic Bay for maintenance and four days relaxation.

During April the *Yorktown* was a Yankee Station for ASW and Search and Rescue operations with a brief two-day visit to Cebu City, Philippines.

On May 2 the carrier arrived at Sasebo, Japan, for two weeks of relaxation plus a change of command. A cruise to Manila on May 16 was a preparatory motion for an important SEATO exercise known as "SEA IMP." Its purpose was to practice assigned forces in their operational roles for safeguarding a convoy against surface, subsurface, and aerial attacks. "The Fighting Lady" entered Bangkok, Thailand, on June 5 and departed four days later with her escort, bound for Yokosuka and relief by the *USS Kearsarge CVS-33*.

On July 15, the "Lady" was headed for the states. Three days out of San Diego she was requested to aid in searching for General Stillwell, U.S. Army, and his crew aboard a downed DC-3.

The *Yorktown* arrived at her destination on July 27, released her air group, and continued to her home port at Long Beach.

The remainder of the year saw the *Yorktown* in six separate periods at sea for carrier qualifications and training. "Operation Baseline II" was held October 12–27. This was a major First Fleet exercise with an emphasis on antisubmarine warfare.

January 9–19, 1967, "The Fighting Lady" was again conducting carrier qualifications, but on the 26th she was host to 450 representatives of the American Ordnance Association. Carrier qualifications resumed from January 30 to February followed by a two-day period (February 6–7) at Seal Beach where ammunition was unloaded.

Her final carrier qualification session was carried out on February 13–15, after which she returned to home port for an open house in honor of the Beverly Hills Council of the Navy League. Eleven guests of the Secretary of the Navy were in attendance for this affair.

While preparing for a major overhaul at the Long Beach Navy Yard, the carrier made a high-speed run and unloaded oil on February 23–24. On April 7 she entered drydock, where on June 4 the mighty carrier celebrated the 25th Anniversary Memorial Service of CV-5. A change of command was effected on July 20 and her drydock period terminated on August 5 when she was moved to a yard pier.

October 10 marked the *Yorktown's* reentry into the First Fleet. She moved from Pier 2 at Long Beach to Pier E. The carrier began sea trials on the same day, which included tests in engineering, communications, radio, and radar.

The *Yorktown* received ammunition at Seal Beach on October 13 and from October 16 to November 10 she was busy with refresher training off San Diego. Just before Thanksgiving in port at Long Beach, she held additional training sessions near Seal Beach from November 13–17.

A Dependent's Cruise was held on November 25. With 4096 dependents and friends aboard the carrier sailed around Santa Catalina Island, then returned to home port.

From November 27 to December 8, she completed refresher training which included another ORI December 5–8. The carrier was in home port for Christmas leave from December 8 through 27, but on the 28th she headed for the western Pacific.

On the same day she embarked CVSG-55 in San Diego. After receiving planes from VS-23, VS-25, HS-4 and VAW-11, she headed for Hawaii.

The *Yorktown* took a diversion course into the Sea of Japan following the seizure of the *USS Pueblo AGER-2* off Wonsan, North Korea, on January 28, 1968. Here she continued a readiness patrol for 48 days before arriving at Subic Bay on March 12, 1968. She departed the Philippines immediately and arrived on Yankee Station March 16 for duty in the Gulf of Tonkin.

"The Fighting Lady" was in port at Yokosuka, Japan, April 12–22; in port at Hong Kong April 25–30; on station at the Tonkin Gulf May 10–25; and in port at Singapore May 29–June 3. June 7–15 the *Yorktown* was on station in the Gulf of Tonkin and spent June 18–21 in port at Sasebo, Japan. The *Yorktown* arrived stateside on July 5 where CVSG-5 was debarked in San Diego. Dependents came aboard for the final journey to Long Beach where the *Yorktown* arrived on September 15, 1968.

Since commissioning the *USS Yorktown CVS-10* has received the following awards: The Presidential Unit Citation; the American Area Service Medal; the Asiatic-Pacific Area Campaign Service Medal with eleven battle stars; the World War Two Victory Medal; the Navy Occupation Service Medal, with Asia clasp; the China Service (Extended) Service Medal; the Korean Service Medal; the United Nations Service Medal; the Armed Forces Expeditionary Medal; the Viet-Nam Service Medal with four stars; the Republic of the Philippines Presidential Unit Citation Badge; and the Viet-Nam Campaign Service Medal.

USS Intrepid CV-11. Broadside-port, underway, August 16, 1943.

11

USS Intrepid CVS-11 (CV-11)

On December 1, 1941—six days before the Japanese slipped through Kole Kole Pass and bombed Pearl Harbor—the keel of the *USS Intrepid CV-11* was laid down at the Newport News Shipbuilding Company in Virginia. Mrs. John H. Hoover, wife of Vice Admiral Hoover, sponsored the carrier during the christening ceremonies on April 26, 1943, and the new fighting ship was commissioned. (11/8)

The first plane to touch down on *Intrepid*'s deck was flown by Commander A. McB. Jackson, on September 16, 1943, and on October 7 he brought his pilots of Air Group 8 on board.

The *Intrepid* departed the Naval Operating Base at Norfolk for shakedown operations off Trinidad. During this period the pilots received extensive training in carrier takeoffs and landings. Shakedown procedures were completed on October 27 and the carrier returned to Norfolk for post-shakedown trials November 25–26 off Rockland, Maine. On November 30 she reembarked Air Group 8 at Norfolk, then sailed on

December 3 for her ultimate destination—the Pacific Forward Area.

While transiting the Panama Canal on December 9, the *Intrepid* ran aground, sustaining minor damage. A hole in her rudder was temporarily repaired while at anchor in the Balboa Canal Zone. She was underway on December 14 and edged into Alameda Naval Air Station eight days later where her air group departed. On the 23rd, the carrier was in drydock at Hunters Point in San Francisco where complete repairs were made to the damage resulting from the Panama Canal incident.

The air group came aboard on January 5, 1944, as the carrier was docked at Alameda. The next day, the navigator plotted a course for Hawaii where the ship arrived on the 10th. Air Group 6, led by Commander H. L. Miller, relieved Air Group 8, which had been reassigned to the naval air station at Maui, Hawaii.

On January 16, the *Intrepid* departed Pearl Harbor astern, in company with the *USS Essex CV-9* and *USS*

F4U's ready for takeoff from the *Intrepid* on a strike against Truk, February 1944.

Cabot CVL-28, to support the occupation of the Kwajalein and Majuro Atolls.

The *Intrepid* launched her first combat strikes against small islands of the Kwajalein chain on January 29. The primary mission was to conduct bombing and strafing attacks for the Marine landing forces. The carrier dropped anchor in the newly seized Majuro Lagoon on February 4.

Truk Island, in the Western Carolines, was the *Intrepid's* target on February 16. At this island the Japanese supplied their forces with ships, aircraft, and troops. Although the main elements of the enemy fleet had moved closer to their homeland, numerous ships and planes had been destroyed at Truk.

While a golden sun slipped below the horizon, the *Intrepid's* pilots flew back for a second strike. Later that night, Japanese torpedo planes advanced undetected upon the task force. A direct hit struck the *Intrepid's* starboard side, aft, approximately 15 feet below the waterline. Five men were killed when the "tin fish" ripped a large gash in the hull and exploded. The ship's rudder was jammed hard to port and Captain Sprague gave the order to steer the ship with her engines. This was done by revving the port engine while idling the starboard screws.

Captain Sprague said: "She was like a giant pendulum, swinging back and forth. She had a tendency to weathercock into the wind . . . turning her bow towards Tokyo, but right then I wasn't interested in going in that direction."

Commander Philip Reynolds and Frank Johnson, BMC, improvised a makeshift sail composed of hatchcovers and canvas and attached it to the forecastle at hangar deck level. The sail helped to reduce the strain on the screws and wind resistance was created by spotting all aircraft forward and all cargo aft. This put the ship's stern low in the water.

Eight days later, February 24, the *Intrepid* arrived at Pearl Harbor where Captain Sprague said: "No enemy could have ever figured out her zig-zag plan. As a matter of fact, there was no plan. The pattern was created as we went along and no one knew for sure how long she'd keep on anything like a straight course."

Temporary damage repairs were made until March 16, then the carrier set course for Hunters Point, arriving six days later. Air Group 6 disembarked, leaving a remarkable record of 55 enemy planes destroyed in the air and on the ground; five enemy ships sunk, five probably sunk and two heavily damaged.

On June 4, 1944, the *Intrepid* slipped away from Hunters Point and moored across the bay at Alameda where additional aircraft and equipment was put aboard.

Five days later she was at sea again and arrived at Pearl Harbor on June 14. A sojourn of rest was enjoyed until June 22 at which time Air Group 19 came aboard for transportation to Eniwetok in the Marshalls.

On June 23 the *Intrepid* headed towards that atoll and arrived on July 1. The air group was catapulted from her deck while at anchor. Hundreds of U.S. servicemen were taken aboard and three days later the big ship headed back to Hawaii, arriving on July 11.

When President Franklin D. Roosevelt visited the naval shipyard at Pearl Harbor on July 27, *Intrepid* sailors lined the railing to see their Commander-in-Chief.

On August 16, the *Intrepid* celebrated her first birthday and a 300-pound cake was enjoyed by her crew. That evening, with Air Group 18 aboard, she departed with the *USS Enterprise CV-6* and the *USS Independence CVL-22*, and arrived at Eniwetok eight days later.

The *Intrepid* was again facing combat on September 6, participating in the capture and occupation of the Southern Palau Islands; Peleliu was the main target, and every airfield was destroyed along with gun emplacements on the coast. September 9–10, the carrier, as a unit of Task Group 38.2, struck Mindanao's airfields, leaving them a pockmarked burning rubble. Japanese bases in the Visayan Sea were hit from September 12–14.

Word was received that a heavy concentration of enemy shipping was at Coron Island. The task force was 300 miles from Coron, but this did not prevent the fast carrier force from missing such an impressive target. Air strikes were launched on September 24, and, despite the extreme distance, none of the planes ran out of fuel. A quintet of enemy ships was sent to the bottom while three were burning on the water.

After a short replenishment at Saipan, the *Intrepid* arrived at Ulithi Atoll on October 1, 1944; she sailed again on the 6th, arriving at Okinawa four days later, where enemy airfields and shipping took a terrific pounding. October 12–14 a large seaplane base at Tansui on Formosa and the airfield at Shinchiku were targets for Air Group 18. The fast carrier force then shifted the attacks to northern Luzon.

Reports said that the Japanese Fleet was converging off Leyte Gulf. The intense battles that followed destroyed the remaining, and once mighty, Japanese naval armada.

The *Intrepid* refueled before joining other carriers in the Sibuyan Sea, where the central force of the enemy had been spotted. Aircraft were launched on October 24 resulting in a heavy beating from bomber and torpedo attacks. A battleship of the *Yamato* class was sunk. A few hours later, American search planes reported the location of the Japanese northern force. This comprised one large carrier, three light cruisers, two battleships, five cruisers, and six destroyers.

Mighty Task Force 38 shifted northward to intercept!

At dawn, October 25, the fast carrier force began attacking the enemy northern force off Cape Engano. Word was received that the central enemy force, hit by the *Intrepid* on the 24th, had passed the San Bernadino Strait and was steaming southwards, hitting our escort carriers near Samar.

Task Group 38.2 (including *Intrepid*) rushed at full speed to intercept the central force again, but upon arrival found no evidence of the enemy ships. The Japanese Fleet had backtracked through San Bernadino but had not escaped. On October 26, the central force was hit as it passed through the Subuyan Sea and Air Group 18 inflicted extensive damage to the fleeing enemy fleet.

On October 29, 1944, the *Intrepid* was sending air strikes against enemy shipping at Manila and Clark Field when she became the victim of a suicide hit. A Kamikaze, ablaze from antiaircraft hits, crashed into a portside 20mm gunmount. Ten men, including several stewards mates acting as volunteer gunners, died in this action. The crash area halted flight operations momentarily, but strikes were soon resumed on Manila Harbor and Clark Field.

November 19–25, the *Intrepid* continued air sorties over southern Luzon and the Visayans. Strike after strike was launched against the Philippine Islands right up to November 25, when once again the Kamikaze group attacked the task force.

At 12:18 P.M., two *Vals* (single engine dive bombers) made suicide dives on the USS *Hancock CV-19* and also the USS *Cabot CVL-28*. Both planes were splashed in a close call for the two ships. Twenty-four minutes later, the *Intrepid's* after-director spotted a pair of enemy planes approaching. Since many American planes were airborne, gunnery attempts were almost hopeless. Each plane had to be positively identified before AA batteries could open fire. At 12:53, the *Intrepid's* guns unleashed their ammo and disintegrated one of the enemy planes. The remaining intruder came in low from the stern. Starboard guns blazed away, but the pilot bored through the blanket of bullets. The plane went into a power-on stall 1000 yards astern, did a wingover at 500 feet, and smashed into the *Intrepid's* flight deck at 12:55 P.M. Its bomb penetrated the deck and exploded in a pilot readyroom. The room was vacant but an adjoining compartment was occupied and 32 men were killed.

The *Intrepid* maneuvered with starboard turns, spilling water and flaming gasoline over the side. Fire fighting parties continuously ducked exploding ammunition.

At 12:57 P.M., two more enemy planes were spotted and fired upon by the port AA batteries. One plane was splashed only 1500 yards away, but the other drove through the barrage of fire, power-stalled and crashed into the *Intrepid's* flight deck at 12:59 P.M. The bomb on the plane exploded in the hangar deck. For the next three hours, fire fighting teams battled the raging inferno.

Airborne pilots of Air Group 18 were forced to land on other carriers or airfields at Leyte. Sixty-five men died during this third suicide attack and the ship was dubbed with an unfortunate sobriquet: "Hardluck I."

Conditions were serious aboard the carrier's flight deck, which was now ripped apart. A mass of twisted hot steel now represented the hangar deck. The disfigured warship was forced to withdraw towards Ulithi on November 26.

Admiral "Bull" Halsey inspected the *Intrepid's* battle damage four days later. One glance told him the carrier had just won a free ticket stateside—the hard way.

Air Group 18 was released on November 31 and could pride themselves on a good combat record. Enemy planes destroyed in the air totaled 154 with 169 more demolished on the ground. They had also sunk

Following a Kamikaze attack in April 1945, Intrepid crewmen fight the fires after the initial crash and bomb explosions.

and assisted in sinking 53 enemy vessels.

On December 2, the *Intrepid* sailed away and stopped briefly at Pearl Harbor from the 11th to 16th. Then onward to California and Hunters Point Naval Shipyard where she arrived on December 20.

After post-repair trials off the California coast, she went to Alameda NAS on February 11, 1945. Air Group 10, lead by Commander John J. Hyland, came aboard five days later.

The *Intrepid* returned to Hawaii on March 2. Assigned to Task Group 12.2, the *Intrepid* joined the *USS Franklin CV-13* and *USS Bataan CVL-29* and departed on the 3rd for Ulithi Atoll where she arrived on March 13.

Task Group 12.2 was disbanded and the *Intrepid* joined Task Group 58.3. On March 14, the fast carrier force departed Ulithi and four days later arrived just east of Okinawa for air strikes against Kyushu.

A twin-engine Japanese bomber, identified as "Betty," broke through a flaming sheet of antiaircraft fire at 8:06 A.M., and began a suicide glide towards the *Intrepid*'s waterline. Starboard 5-inch guns and 40mm weapons began to speak. When the plane was about 1500 yards away the ship's 20mm's opened fire. It seemed frighteningly evident that the carrier was going to get hit again, but as the aircraft was 50 to 100 feet from the carrier's forward boat crane, it upended and splashed into the sea.

The *Intrepid* was not completely spared, however, for the explosion of the Kamikaze's bomb showered the carrier with fragments of the disintegrated plane.

Minor gasoline fires were born, but soon died at the hands of skilled firemen.

Okinawa was invaded by U.S. Marines on Easter Sunday, April 1, 1945. The *Intrepid* and other carriers flew support missions over the island and neutralized raids over Kyushu, Shikoku, and southern Honsho.

The Kamikaze force approached in full strength, hoping to penetrate the task force screen. About noon on April 16, one lucky suicide pilot managed to slip through the screen. As fate would have it, the determined flyer chose "Hardluck I" as the means to fulfill his "supreme sacrifice" to his Emperor. At 1:36 P.M., the plane smashed into the *Intrepid*'s flight deck at a vertical attitude and parts of its engine and fuselage penetrated the deck. In fact, the impact was so terrific that an exact imprint of the plane's wings was smashed into the deck. The plane's bomb exploded in the hangar deck, but by now the firefighters were accustomed to suicide hits and the fires were soon out.

This had been the fourth Kamikaze hit and resulted in the death of eight crewmen. On April 20, the injured carrier steamed to Ulithi for damage estimates. Previously unseen damage to her elevators was also discovered, which necessitated more than temporary repairs.

So, once again, the *Intrepid* cruised to Hunters Point, arriving on May 19 where a drydock awaited her. Shipyard workers began to talk of the ill-fated ship as their very own.

On June 29, the *Intrepid* received Air Group 10 again at Alameda and arrived at Pearl Harbor on July 5. Provisions were stored and training operations were held July 8–13. On July 30 she headed for Eniwetok and reached that island on August 7. The fleet was ordered to cease offensive operations eight days later. Task Unit 30.3.9 was formed on August 21. Along with the *Intrepid* was the *USS Antietam CV-36* and *USS Cabot CVL-28*. The Unit was sent to join the fleet now positioned east of Japan. They arrived, minus the *Antietam*, on August 26. The missing carrier was forced to stop at Guam due to structural damage. The *Intrepid* began duties correlated with the occupation of the defeated Japanese Empire, and remained in this duty until October 24 when she entered Yokosuka Naval Base. She stayed there until December 2.

The *Intrepid* sailed into San Pedro, California, on December 15 for an inactive period. On February 4, 1946, she went to San Francisco and was placed in reserve on August 15, 1946. The mothball process was completed on March 22, 1947 and the *Intrepid* was officially decommissioned and assigned to the San Francisco Group of the Pacific Reserve Fleet.

USS Intrepid, hole in flight deck. As seen from hangar deck,
April 16, 1945.

On February 9, 1952, the *Intrepid* was commissioned in reserve prior to her transfer to the East Coast. On hand was Vice Admiral Thomas L. Sprague, the ship's first commanding officer.

The carrier slipped through the Panama Canal on March 12 and arrived at Norfolk 17 days later. She was decommissioned once more on April 9 and a two-year modernization period began. While in the yards, the *Intrepid* was reclassified to CVA-11 on October 10, 1952.

She was placed in commission on June 18, 1954 but it was a reserve status while she awaited further orders at Portsmouth Naval Yard.

Captain W. T. Easton took command at the re-commissioning ceremonies and Mrs. John H. Hoover who had christened her in 1943 was present.

The long awaited day arrived on October 15 when the *Intrepid* relinquished her reserve status and became an active member of the Atlantic Fleet.

The *Intrepid* started shakedown operations near Guantanamo Bay, Cuba on January 9, 1955. During February, Air Group 4 reported aboard to begin extensive flight operations.

The carrier began her first Mediterranean cruise on May 28 and during the trip Sixth Fleet exercises were held. The carrier visited Naples, and Greece.

On November 24, she returned to the states and conducted a training period until December, at which time a holiday leave period began.

In January 1956, Air Group 8 relieved Air Group 4 and preparations were made for another Med cruise. Only 98 days after returning from her first trip, she was again steaming towards the Mediterranean area. The usual ports of call were made and the *Intrepid* participated in NATO and Sixth Fleet exercises.

On August 28, the "Big I" returned to Norfolk and 24 days later entered the Navy yard for a major conversion.

When she emerged in April 1957 she exhibited a new angle flight deck replete with a hurricane bow and a minor landing system. She remained at home port in Norfolk, where, during early May, she began refresher training cruises near Cuba.

Attack Squadrons 25 and 66 plus Heavy Attack Squadron 11 came on board for flight operations.

During an administrative inspection on August 8–9, the Commander of Carrier Division Six remarked that the ship's company was a "can do" outfit. The phrase has remained the ship's motto ever since.

The *Intrepid* departed Norfolk on September 7, 1957, for her first tour of duty in Northern Europe. She participated in "Operation Strikeback," a NATO exercise and the largest Naval exercise up to that time since World War II. Along with ships representing five other countries, the *Intrepid* tested the efficiency of a carrier strike force.

On September 20, she crossed the Arctic Circle and her crew became members of the "Royal Order of the Bluenose."

A4B streaming down the starboard catapult.

By late October the carrier returned to Norfolk and spent the remainder of the year operating off the Virginia Capes. In December the *Intrepid* was active in "Operation Crosswind," an experiment to determine wind effects on carrier launches. The results proved that, under any conditions, a carrier could safely launch aircraft without having to turn into the wind and could send her planes skyward while steaming downwind.

On January 22, 1958, she entered the Norfolk Navy Yard for an overhaul. The task was completed by June and she began a two-month European cruise.

The major exercise held during the time was called LANTFLEX 1–58, after which a visit was made to Lisbon, Oslo, and Rotterdam.

She returned to the Caribbean in November and joined units of the Second Fleet engaged in LANTFLEX 2–58. A four-day visit to Bridgetown, Barbados, British West Indies, relieved the strain of training. Late in November she was again at Norfolk for holiday leave.

During January and February 1959, the *Intrepid* continued normal training and air operations, then left Norfolk for another tour with the Sixth Fleet.

On March 1, she arrived at Gibraltar. Later, while in Naples, the carrier participated in the 10th Anniversary of the North Atlantic Treaty Organization.

The *USS Essex CVA-9* relieved the *Intrepid* at Mallorca's Pollensa Bay on August 19 and a course was charted for the states on August 30.

The *Intrepid* checked into the Yard at Norfolk on October 8 for a four-month overhaul. The engineering plant was renovated, including the screws and rudder. Her communications antenna system was modernized and the hull was strengthened.

In December, the "Big I" was ushered into a berth at Norfolk for the holiday season. A post-yard shakedown cruise was made in January 1960. Before returning to port a visit took her to what was then known as Ciudad Trujillo, capital of the Dominican Republic.

A fleet record was set in July when the *Intrepid* launched 11 jets in 8 minutes. Each aircraft remained on its catapult no longer than 32 seconds.

The carrier steamed towards the Mediterranean on August 4, 1960, where she soon visited Fiumicino and Genoa, Italy; Cannes, France; Gibraltar; and Roga, Spain. She was back at her Virginia port in January 1961 to begin another overhaul at Portsmouth.

On August 3, 1961, after three months of flight operations off the Atlantic seaboard, the *Intrepid* was scheduled for yet another Med cruise, where NATO and Sixth Fleet exercises became the daily routine. On February 17, 1962, the USS Shangrila CVA-38 took over and the Intrepid went home to Norfolk, arriving March 1.

The Intrepid relinquished her attack carrier status on March 31 when she was reclassified to CVS-11. She would undertake new duties as an anti-submarine warfare (ASW) support carrier and immediately slipped into the Navy yard at Norfolk to be fitted out for future missions.

Her jet planes were replaced with S2F Trackers, E1AE Skyraders and SH3A helicopters. These planes belonged to squadrons VS-24, VS-27, VAW-33, and HS-3. She departed the yard on April 2 and moored alongside her Norfolk pier. April 9–12 a carrier qualification period was taken to familiarize the new squadrons in carrier operations.

In May 1962, the Intrepid was the only carrier selected to participate in the recovery of Lieutenant-Commander Malcom Scott Carpenter and his Mercury space capsule, Aurora 7.

The carrier proceeded 200 miles east of Turks Island, Bahamas, to retrieve her space package. Besides this position, two additional impact areas were located 350 miles east and 325 miles south of Bermuda. The three positions varied, depending on the number of orbits the astronaut would complete prior to reentry.

Auroa 7 blasted off the launch pad at 8:45 A.M. (EDT) on May 24, 1962, and splashed down in the Caribbean at 1:41 P.M., after three orbits around the Earth. Astronaut Carpenter was the second American to experience an orbital flight in the space program. His capsule had landed several hundred miles away from the Intrepid, so two helicopters were immediately on their way. Upon their arrival, Carpenter was resting in a life raft which had been dropped by an Air Force Sea Rescue team. A helicopter from the Intrepid plucked the astronaut from the raft at 4:28 P.M. When he came aboard the carrier, Carpenter said he had been lacking in flight requirements for the past two months. After logging five hours in space, plus the hour helicopter ride, he was now in excess of requirements.

Following a cursory medical exam, he was flown to Grand Turk Island, Bahamas. With the historic space mission completed, the Intrepid sailed back to Norfolk on May 31.

On June 26, 209 midshipmen reported aboard for their two-month cruise. The carrier departed home port on July 6 and arrived at Quebec City, Canada, on the 20th. The midshipmen were drilled in carrier operations, then returned to Norfolk on August 5

where they said goodbye to the Intrepid.

On September 7, the carrier went to her second "home"—Norfolk Navy Yard. It was repair time once again. Work was completed on December 28, and the refreshed carrier docked at her old berth on January 4, 1963.

From January 23 to March 23 the Intrepid was engaged in antisubmarine warfare training off Guantanamo Bay. When Captain J. C. Lawrence assumed command of the ship on April 20 he felt almost at home. Many years had passed since he had served on the carrier as commander of Torpedo Squadron 10 during World War II.

During the summer of 1963 the carrier was host to the Annapolis midshipmen for their annual cruise. The carrier arrived at Halifax, Nova Scotia, on June 28. Unknown to the crew, a young Halifax girl stowed aboard the ship. Four days out of the city the girl was discovered in an electronic storage space. She expressed a desire to come to America, but fortune was against her. To her dismay, she was returned to Nova Scotia, thus closing a memorable episode aboard the Intrepid.

From July to November, the carrier completed a second midshipmen cruise (Aug. 3–Sept. 3) and conducted ASW operations off the Virginia Capes. She departed Norfolk on December 3 to participate in "Operation PHIBASWEX" off the Caribbean. After her biological-chemical competitive exercise, the "Big I" received a score of 95 of a possible 100. She was back in home port on December 17.

On January 13, 1964, the Intrepid slipped from her Norfolk berth and was active in "Operation Springboard" in the Caribbean. This exercise is held annually when weather is favorable and maximum training is assured. A brief visit was made to Puerto Rico and the Virgin Islands and British West Indies. While in Bridgetown, Barbados, on February 1–2, more than 1500 Barbadians were visitors to the ship during open house.

A NASA team came aboard on March 16 to evaluate recovery procedures for Gemini and Apollo spacecraft. Five practice recoveries were successfully completed.

Captain Joseph G. Smith, assumed command of the Intrepid on April 29. He had begun his military career in 1939 as an Army second lieutenant, then received his Navy commission as an ensign in October of that year and designated a naval aviator at Pensacola, Florida. During World War II, Captain Smith served aboard the USS Lexington CV-2 and is credited with sighting and reporting the position of the Japanese Fleet in the Battle of the Coral Sea. Another high-light during his career was assisting in sinking the first Japanese carrier. His plane was last in line to take off from the old *Lexington* before her fatal explosions below decks. He later landed on the *USS Yorktown CV-5*. Captain Smith holds the Navy Cross among his many awards.

The *Intrepid* departed Norfolk on June 11, 1964, for a two-month Mediterranean cruise with the Sixth Fleet. Rigid training programs were conducted using Hunter-Killer ASW procedures. During the cruise, the *Intrepid* and *Pawcatuk AO-108* broke a long standing approach and rigging record. This was accomplished on August 31 off the Straits of Gibraltar when the

tanker's rigging was completed in 3.24 minutes and the rigging to the oiler was managed in 6.39 minutes.

On September 15, the *Intrepid* sailed for home and on November 29 was designated the prime recovery ship for an unmanned Gemini launch into space. She arrived off station on December 4, but a missile launch failure postponed the shot. When it was known that the spaceshot was indefinitely scheduled, the carrier went back to Norfolk. She began a holiday leave on December 12. The *Intrepid* was the last carrier to be renovated at the Norfolk Navy Yard before it was closed.

As primary recovery ship for the first manned Gemini space flight, GY-3, the *Intrepid* arrived at the des-

Astronauts John Young and Virgil Grissom pose with the "Molly Brown" in the hangar deck of the *Intrepid* on March 23, 1965, following their recovery in the first manned Gemini space flight.

ignated position 800 miles downrange from Cape Kennedy on March 19, 1965.

The Gemini space capsule, nicknamed "Molly Brown," lifted off the launch pad at 9:24 A.M., on March 23 and was under the command of Major Virgil Ivan Grissom, USAF, and co-pilot Lieutenant Commander John Watts Young, USN. This epic event marked the first American two-man orbital flight.

After completing three orbits, the space craft splashed down in the Atlantic at 2:18 P.M., 50 miles short of the planned touchdown point. One hour later the two astronauts were picked up by a Navy helicopter and flown to the *Intrepid* for medical examinations.

On April 9 the carrier departed home port bound for the New York Navy Yard to receive a $10 million Fleet Rehabilitation and Modernization (FRAM) overhaul. Major work included flight deck planking, evaluation of the propulsion system, hull reinforcement, catapult and arresting gear improvements, and renovation of the ship's Combat Information Center (CIC). The carrier received a sonar system, a centerline anchor, data processing equipment plus new radar, radio, and electronic equipment and a new refueling rig. To improve flight operations the carrier received a Fresnel Lens Landing System known by its acronym PLAT (Pilot Landing Aid, Television).

The *Intrepid* moved for final touchups at Bayonne, New Jersey, on September 12 and was back at Norfolk on October 16 to begin a five-week training cruise off Guantanamo Bay. This cruise ended on December 20 when a holiday leave period began.

During January 1966 the *Intrepid* underwent a restrictive availability at Portsmouth. She departed the yard on February 1 for training operations preparatory to an unknown classified deployment. While refueling on February 22 the *Intrepid* was rammed on her starboard side by the oiler *USS Sabine AO-......*. The oiler's collision course was caused by a steering defect. Repairs were completed on March 18 and training resumed. While in the yard for repairs an announcement of the ship's secret deployment was made public by the Secretary of Defense, Robert S. McNamara, who said: "In order to maintain the attack carrier force off Vietnam, we are, as I noted, deploying one of the Atlantic based carriers, the *Intrepid* to Southeast Asia. Very minor modifications were required on this vessel to permit it to operate light attack aircraft and it can be quickly reassigned to its ASW role. What is involved is mainly a change in aircraft. The antisubmarine air group is being retained in the active fleet, thus giving us the capability to operate the carrier as CVS on short notice."

An F6F-3 is catapulted from the *Intrepid's* hangar deck February 24, 1944.

The *Intrepid* departed Norfolk on April 4, 1966 and on May 4 entered the South China Sea, where more than 20 years earlier she had earned her soubriquet, "The Fighting I." A short visit was made to Subic Bay, Philippines, for supplies, then she joined other Seventh Fleet ships on Dixie Station off South Vietnam.

The carrier launched her initial strikes against the Viet Cong on May 15. As a result of the 59-days of duties as an in-country support carrier she captured the personal praise of General Westmoreland, then Commander of all U.S. forces in Vietnam.

Air Wing 10 flew 5000 attack sorties, averaging 67 per pilot for a total of 12,540 combat hours flown over South Vietnam. More than 5500 tons of ordnance was dropped which destroyed 1400 structures, sunk 145 Junks, and eliminated numerous bunkers.

The pilots faced a more dangerous phase of operations while flying over North Vietnam. During 41 days on station, the air wing flew 2595 sorties, dropping 3704 tons of ordnance. Their bombs destroyed 141 railroad cars and 82 bridges. The petroleum oil lubricant centers at Vinh were also hit.

During September and October 1966, the *Intrepid's* air group joined other Yankee Team carriers to strike Ninh Binh, Thah Hoa, and Phy Ly.

Search and rescue operations became a continuous phase of combat. On one particular mission four of

Intrepid's propeller-driven A1 *Skyraiders* were attacked by North Vietnamese Russian-built MIG-21's. After an intense air battle one MIG was downed, one was severely damaged, and the remaining pair fled the area. The *Skyraiders* returned to the carrier unscratched.

Between combat operations, the *Intrepid* visited Subic Bay, Philippines; Sasebo, Japan; and Hong Kong, B.C.

On two separate occasions the carrier was paid a visit by Vice Admiral John J. Hyland, Commander of the Seventh Fleet. During World War II, Vice Admiral Hyland had commanded the current air wing on the *Intrepid*.

During the *Intrepid*'s 1966 Western Pacific cruise, a number of "firsts" were logged. On September 6, the 100,000th arrested landing was made. G Division, along with other ordnance divisions built and delivered a daily average of 125 tons, and during an underway ammo replenishment, the carrier received 400 tons of ordnance from the *USS Vesuvius AE-15*.

On October 25, the *Intrepid* cleared Subic Bay to begin her long journey home. She crossed the Equator on the 27th and 2800 "pollywogs" became "shellbacks." The alteration was received by sailors crossing the Equator for their first time and has long been a naval tradition.

When a Naval vessel crosses the Equator, all men that have never done so, become "Shellbacks." Those who have never crossed the Equator are called "pollywogs." The initiation is an experience never to be forgotten. The senior shellback is appointed the mythical Neptune Rex and presides over the affairs. All of the shellbacks get together and initiate the pollywogs as the ship crosses the Equator. Any man who comes through the ordeal with his hair intact on his head and not too red a bottom is a very lucky man. The proceeding is all in fun and after it is over, each man is given a card certifying him as a shellback. Because it is an unofficial tradition and not entered into a man's service record, the card is guarded carefully. When he leaves the ship for assignment to another ship that crosses the Equator, he shows the card and is then able to administer the ritual with other shellbacks to pollywogs crossing for the first time. Rank and rate are suspended during the time of the initiation and every pollywog from seaman to captain is treated the same way, and pity the shellback who does not have a card to prove he crossed the Equator!

The carrier arrived at Mayport, Florida, on November 21 to unload the air wing. Two days later she edged alongside Pier 12 at Norwolk to be greeted by a crowd of 2500. After engaging in combat for eight months, the carrier entered the Norfolk Navy Yard for a much needed overhaul.

By early March 1967, the "Big I" left the yards to resume training operations preparatory to her next overseas assignment. She celebrated her 24th birthday on April 26, 1967.

The *Intrepid* operated out of the Norfolk Naval Base from January to June 1968, in preparation for her third deployment to Vietnam. She left Norfolk on June 4 with Carrier Air Wing Ten embarked. After one week of Operational Readiness Inspection off the Virgin Islands, the *Intrepid* arrived at Rio de Janeiro on June 22.

On July 24, the "Fighting I" arrived on Yankee Station to commence a 106-day period of air strikes against enemy targets in which 12 million pounds of ordnance were dropped. Air Group Ten flew 5812 sorties. On September 8, 1968, strikes were successfully directed against the Vinh Son military complex 21 miles south of Vinh. Air Group Ten joined with air groups of other carriers in striking and destroying a SAM surface-to-air military site and a military headquarters. A second strike leveled a major North Vietnamese Headquarters.

Lieutenant Tony Nargi flying an F-8 Crusader was credited with downing two MIG-21 jets on September 19. Sparked by this victory, the air group turned their attention to petroleum pipelines outside of Vinh, leaving them a mass of rubble.

Between her lulls in combat operations on Yankee Station, the *Intrepid* made ports of call at Hong Kong, B.C.; Sasebo, Japan; the Philippines and Singapore. During this deployment, the *Intrepid* received word that she had been awarded her fourth consecutive Battle Efficiency "E" for combat excellence. After steaming some 90,000 miles, the *Intrepid* returned to Norfolk in February 1969. While en route she visited Australia, as well as Wellington, New Zealand, and Rio de Janeiro.

After two weeks in the Norfolk Navy Yard, the carrier entered the Philadelphia Naval Shipyard to undergo an extensive $15 million overhaul to convert the ship back to her former role as an antisubmarine warfare carrier. Although she retained her CVS designation, the *Intrepid* made three Vietnam cruises as a special attack carrier operating as a CVA. In August 1969, the "Fighting I" left the shipyard and steamed to her new home port of Quonset Point, Rhode Island, to resume training in ASW carrier warfare.

Since her commissioning, the *USS Intrepid CVS-11* has received the following awards: The Navy Unit Commendation; the Meritorious Unit Commendation; the American Area Campaign Service Medal; the

Asiatic-Pacific Area Campaign Service Medal with five battle stars; the World War Two Victory Medal; the China Service (extended) Medal; the National Defense Service Medal; the Vietnam Service Medal; the Philippine Liberation Campaign Ribbon; the Republic of the Philippines Presidential Unit Citation Badge and the Republic of Vietnam Campaign Medal.

USS Hornet CVA-12 May 10, 1955. Axial deck.

12

USS Hornet CVS-12 (CV-12)

The keel of the *USS Kearsarge CV-12* was laid on August 3, 1942, at the Newport News Shipbuilding and Drydock Co., Newport News, Virginia. A few months later the carrier-to-be was renamed *Hornet* in honor of the previous *USS Hornet CV-7*, which was sunk off Santa Cruz Island on October 27, 1942.

The new vessel slid down the launching ways on August 30, 1943, after being christened by Mrs. Frank Knox, wife of the Secretary of the Navy. Mrs. Knox also had the honor of sponsoring the previous *Hornet*.

On November 29, 1943, the *USS Hornet CV-12* was commissioned at the Norfolk Navy Yard, and

Capt. Miles R. Browning, USN, took command.

Due to the urgent need for aircraft carriers in the Pacific Theater, the *Hornet* was rushed through a two-week shakedown cruise between Norfolk and Bermuda. Tests were rigorously conducted in the engineering and communications departments as well as extensive flight operations.

The ship's new 5-inch 38-caliber 40mm and 20mm gun mount crews conducted calibration tests plus practice firing. The deck force was active with fueling procedures.

The new carrier then steered for the Pacific war zone to join the mighty Task Force 58 in the Marshalls.

On March 20, 1944, the *Hornet* anchored in the recently occupied Majuro Atoll, Marshall Islands. Less than five weeks earlier, the fast carrier force had completed the occupation of Kwajalein and Majuro Atolls during the Marshall Islands operation.

After two days, the *Hornet* departed Majuro for her first combat mission, which was the third phase of the Asiatic-Pacific Raids of 1944. Air strikes were launched against the Palau Islands on March 31. The carrier's air group participated in aerial mining operations to block the main harbor entrance on Palau. Strikes were sent against Woleai in the Western Carolines on the following day.

A brief replenishment period was taken at Majuro from April 8–13, then the fast carrier force sent its pilots to bomb enemy airfields and ground installations on Wadke-Sarmi and Sawar. The designated targets took a heavy plastering.

Truk Island, in the Western Carolines, was Japan's largest staging area and supplied ships, planes, fuel, and materials to various islands they were occupying.

The fast carrier force first hit Truk February 16–17. The *Hornet* missed out on that action but was there to launch a second strike on April 29–30. Once again, the Japanese on Truk felt the power of Task Force 58 as fuel depots, warehouses, and underground stores were reduced to smoking rubble.

The *Hornet* concluded the Asiatic-Pacific Raids with air assaults against Satawan, Ponape, Moen, Eaton, and Dublon Islands.

Throughout May 1944, the *Hornet* conducted training operations and took on supplies prior to the Marianas operation. On June 6, 1944, the task force sortied from Majuro. Word had been received that the Allied forces had landed on the Normandy beachhead in the European Theater, so spirits were high as the ships steamed toward the Marianas.

On June 11, the *Hornet* sent her air group to assist in the attack and occupation of Saipan. The next day

strikes were launched against Guam, Rota, Volcano, and Bonin Islands. The strategic value of these air strikes was to destroy enemy aircraft and landing fields, which were a threat to our northern invasion forces. On June 16, while striking Iwo Jima and Chichi Jima, the *Hornet's* pilots blasted 63 enemy aircraft from the sky.

At noon two days later, the *Hornet's* Task Group 58.1 met with other fast carriers 200 miles west of Saipan. The task force then steamed westward to provide air cover for U.S. invasion forces, which had landed on Saipan three days earlier.

Reports that the enemy fleet was steaming towards the Marianas were received, which could only mean that there was a possibility that the carriers would get a crack at the Japanese Fleet which had been in hiding for over a year and a half!

The enemy ships were not found by June 18, so the carriers were ordered to guard Saipan against a possible enemy flanking maneuver.

On June 19, the *Hornet's* air group began a two-day air battle over the Philippine Sea with a massive enemy force; the Japanese had orders to destroy the American task force and attacked the ships in four concentrated air strikes.

The *Hornet's* pilots were airborne at 7:20 A.M., to hit Crote Field on Guam. The first wave of enemy planes was sighted at 10:40 A.M., and the "Marianas Turkey Shoot" had begun. Fighters from the USS *Essex CV-9* teamed up with the *Hornet's* air group for the final battle, which ended about 6:45 P.M. The total Japanese aircraft destroyed numbered 392 with the U.S. losses at 29. This successful air battle broke the back of the Japanese air force, which had lost almost 400 combat trained and seasoned pilots; The battle was also a major reason why from that point on the Japanese turned to the Kamikaze tactics used so effectively during the last ten months of the Second World War.

The Japanese Fleet was sighted some 300 miles west of Rota on June 20, 1944. The *Hornet* launched her air group along with strike groups from other carriers and the long flight to smash the enemy ships was begun.

The *Hornet's* air group was given full credit for the single destruction of a large carrier of the *Shokaku* class. By the time the surviving aircraft had returned to the task force it was pitch dark and the exhausted pilots couldn't see their carriers cruising somewhere below. It was a touchy situation because many of the badly damaged planes were low on fuel and some were forced to ditch at sea. About that time, Vice Admiral

Marc A. Mitscher, Commander of the Task Force, gave the order to "light ships" so the planes could land. It mattered little to the battle-weary pilots what ship they landed on—they were just glad to be safely home.

On June 24, 1944, the *Hornet's* veteran air group struck Iwo Jima and Chichi Jima.

The month of July was spent conducting daily air strikes on Guam and the Bonins. Enemy airfields, shipping and ground fortifications were heavily damaged. Carrier strikes on the Bonins became so familiar that a "Toko Jima Development Corporation" was formed for the purpose of selling shares and developing real estate, advertised to be 500 miles from downtown Tokyo!

On August 26, Vice Admiral Mitscher came aboard the *Hornet* and personally presented more than 200 decorations to the carrier's air group.

The capture and occupation of southern Palau Islands, began on September 6, 1944. The *Hornet's* fliers struck Palau for the next two days then headed for the Philippine Islands to begin a five-day bombing of key airfields. Davao, Mindinao, Cebu, and the Negros Islands were hit in the southern and central parts of the Archipelago. On September 21, the fast carrier force arrived off the eastern coast of Luzon to destroy enemy shipping in Manila Harbor and airfields. Six days later, the *Hornet's* island scoreboard listed 27 ships sunk; 128 probably sunk and damaged. This scoreboard was later immortalized in the motion picture, "The Fighting Lady."

Sorties were sent against Okinawa, Formosa, and Northern Luzon from October 10 through 19.

The *Hornet* resumed attacks on the Philippine Islands on November 5. Clark Field, north of Manila, received a two-day pounding in which 29 enemy planes were downed in the air and another 133 destroyed on the ground.

The carrier air group struck Japanese shipping in Ormoc Bay, Leyte, on the 11th. One transport was sent to the bottom and three others were left burning.

The "Plan of the Day" for the *Hornet* on November 26, 1944, is now a treasured souvenir for former crewmen, who during the tiring battles of war still found time to lift morale in a moment of lull. It read in part: "Today will be Field Day. Air Department dust off all overheads, removing all snoopers which may be adrift and sweep all corners of the Philippines, sending to incinerator or throwing over the side (first punching hole in bottom) any Nip cans, AP's or AK's still on topside. Gunnery Department will assist as necessary. Engineering, Continue to pour on the coal.

Medics standby with heat rash lotion. Damage Control, observe holiday routine."

Strikes were directed at Manila Harbor on November 13–14, and on the 19, shipping in Subic Bay and Lingayan Gulf received heavy damage. One enemy freighter was sunk and 50 planes were destroyed at Clark Field.

On November 22, the *Hornet* retired at Ulithi for a short rest. Christmas Day was also observed at Ulithi Atoll, which was the springboard for the final U.S. assaults that forced the Japanese back to their homeland.

On December 30, the fast carrier task force began a three-week operation in the South China Sea where air strikes were launched against Formosa, Indo-China, and the Pescadores. An extensive photographic coverage of Okinawa was taken on January 22, 1945, for use in the future invasion of that tropic island.

Task Force 58 left Ulithi on February 10, 1945 and kept a date the old *Hornet* had made some 34 months earlier. Air strikes were sent against Tokyo in the first full-scale carrier attack on Japan! Operating 200 miles off Honshu, the *Hornet* was unchallenged as her pilots flew through bad weather to hit the Emperor's Domain. The *Hornet* took part in the Fifth Fleet Raids against Honshu and the Nansei Shoto on February 15, 16, and 25. Her air group supported the assault and occupation of Iwo Jima from February 15 to March 1, 1945.

At anchor in Ulithi Atoll March 4–14, the *Hornet* and other carriers prepared for the last major engagement of the war—the Okinawa Gunto Operation. All available aircraft were serviced and loaded with bombs and rockets. Leaving Ulithi astern on March 14, the fast carrier force arrived off the coast of Japan five days later.

The *Hornet* launched her air group against enemy shipping at anchor in Kure and Kobe naval bases. As the pilots made their daring bomb runs the *Hornet* was steaming only 40 miles off the Shikoku shoreline.

The U.S. Marines hit the beaches at Okinawa on Easter Sunday, April 1, 1945. The enemy had massed a large fleet, including the battleship *Yamato*, in a last-ditch effort to destroy the American task force. On April 7, the Japanese fleet was sighted entering the East China Sea and this is what Task Force 58 had so long waited for. The fast carrier force immediately shifted northward and by 11:00 A.M. the *Hornet* was sending her air group against the enemy fleet. The carriers launched a total of 280 planes and the battle began at 12:32.

The planes from the *Hornet* were first to arrive at

**F6F's returning from a strike on Formosa. One fighter on
flight deck, another taking a wave off, October 12, 1944.**

the target and scored four torpedo hits and three bomb hits on the *Yamato*. Two hours later, the once precious prize of the Japanese Navy went down with all but 269 of her 2767-man crew. The cruiser *Yahagi* and four destroyers met the same fate. None of the enemy ships were left unscathed.

The *Hornet* resumed air attacks on the Ryukyus and the Japanese home islands. The task force was now repelling desperate fighter and suicide attacks.

On April 16, the *Hornet*'s air group downed 54 planes. On April 30, the carrier returned to Ulithi, completing almost 40 days of continuous action. The *Hornet* had launched over 4000 combat sorties in 32 days and the ship was under attack more than 105 times!

Following a short two-week replenishment, the *Hornet* returned to the Ryukyus and her air group aided the destruction of a newly built enemy aircraft

plant at Kumamoto, Kyushu, on May 12. Not a single enemy plane would come from that factory, which was now a bomb shattered ruin.

Combat air patrols were continued over Okinawa throughout May. When Admiral Halsey relieved Admiral Spruance on May 27, the *Hornet* once more became part of Task Force 38.

On June 3, 1945, the *Hornet* retired east of Okinawa to begin at-sea refueling. Word was received that a typhoon was approaching and the refueling operations were postponed for the moment, and completed the next day.

There was nothing for the *Hornet*'s Task Group 38.1 to do now but face the oncoming fury of the typhoon, which tossed the sea with 60-foot waves while howling winds up to 100 miles an hour rolled and pitched the ships like rocking chairs. About 6:45 A.M. on June 5, a giant wave collapsed 25 feet of the *Hornet*'s forward flight deck; other relentless waves weakened an additional section of the deck.

The typhoon was over by late afternoon, leaving ships of the task force scattered about like toys; all the ships had suffered damage from the savage storm.

The *Hornet* launched search planes during the morning of June 6 to aid in rescue and recovery operations as the force began to reassemble. After she was unable to continue support operations, the carrier went to San Pedro Bay, Leyte.

The *Hornet* stayed at San Pedro Bay until June 19, then departed for Hunter's Point Naval Shipyard in San Francisco, where she arrived on July 7. Damage sustained in the June typhoon was repaired and the ship underwent an extensive overhaul. By the time yard work was completed, fighting in the Second World War had ended.

On September 13, 1945, the *Hornet* joined her sister ships in the "Magic Carpet Fleet" bringing home veterans from the Pacific Theater. The *Hornet* transported servicemen from Guam and Pearl Harbor, then returned to San Francisco on February 9, 1946. The carrier remained at Hunters Point Shipyard and on January 15, 1947, she was decommissioned in the Pacific Reserve Fleet.

The *Hornet*'s record of damage to the enemy during the war showed 688 planes destroyed in the air; 742 destroyed on the ground; 1 carrier sunk; 1 cruiser sunk; 10 destroyers sunk; 42 merchant ships sunk. She was also credited with an assist in the destruction of the battleship *Yamato*.

For this service, the *Hornet* and her proud air group was awarded the Presidential Unit Citation which read: "For extraordinary heroism in action against the

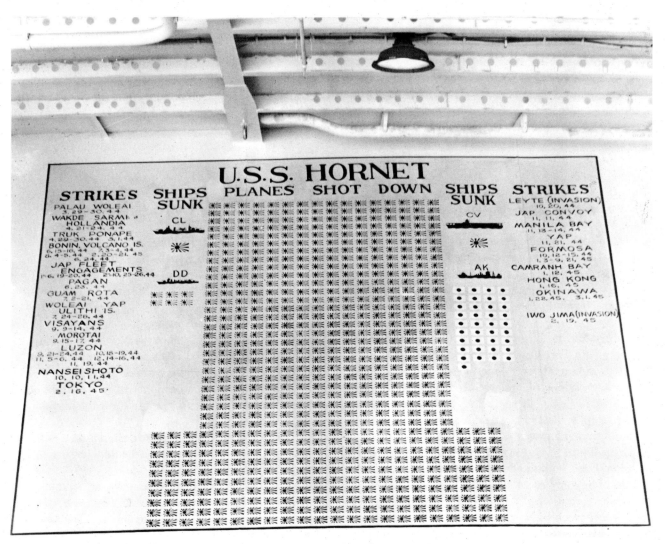

USS Hornet CV-12 scoreboard, May 1, 1945.

enemy Japanese forces in the air, ashore, and afloat in the Pacific War Area from March 29, 1944, to June 10, 1945. Operating continuously in the most forward areas, the USS Hornet and her air groups struck crushing blows toward annihilating Japanese fighting power; they provided air cover for our amphibious forces; they fiercely countered the enemy's aerial attacks and destroyed his planes; and they inflicted terrific losses on the Japanese in fleet and merchant marine units, sunk or damaged. Daring and dependable in combat, the Hornet with her wallant officers and men rendered loyal service in achieving the ultimate defeat of the Japanese Empire."

On March 20, 1951, the Hornet was moved to the Brooklyn Navy Yard, arriving May 12 to undergo conversion and modernization. Under the 27A modification program, the Hornet received a strengthened flight deck to handle jet aircraft. Her island structure was streamlined and the familiar flight deck 5-inch 38-caliber gun mounts fore and aft of the island structure were removed.

On September 11, 1953, the USS Hornet CVA-12 was commissioned and Capt. Milton A. Nation, USN, took command. Present at the ceremonies was Fleet Admiral William F. Halsey, USN, who had commanded the famed Task Force 38, in which the Hornet had been a vital element, during the war.

During January and February 1954, the Hornet conducted shakedown operations off Guantanamo Bay, Cuba. Following post-shakedown alterations, the carrier was assigned to the Atlantic Fleet.

On May 11, 1954, the Hornet departed Norfolk and began an eight-month global cruise. Her first port of call was Lisbon, Portugal, then Naples, Italy. The carrier crossed the Mediterranean Sea, through the Suez Canal and the Red Sea and the Indian Ocean and joined the Seventh Fleet, located in the South China Sea.

On June 24, the Hornet crossed the equator. While steaming with Task Group 70.2 on July 25, 1954, search planes from the carrier were attacked by two Chinese Communist fighter planes while conducting a search for a downed British airliner. Both Communist fighters were promptly blasted out of the sky, resulting in one of the hottest "cold war" incidents up to that time!

Rear Admiral S. C. Fing, USN, Commander Carrier Division One, embarked on the Hornet during the months of September and October. A four-day rest and relaxation period was taken at Hong Kong, B.C., during the first week in November. On November 29, the Hornet left Yokosuka, Japan, astern and returned to San Francisco Naval Shipyard arriving December 12, 1954.

The Hornet operated off the coast of Southern California until May 4, 1955, at which time she headed for another tour in the Western Pacific. She arrived at Yokosuka on June 13.

During this cruise, the Hornet visited Okinawa, Subic Bay, and Sasebo and Iwakuni, Japan. During "Operation Passage to Freedom" the Hornet assisted in the evacuation of citizens of North Viet Nam to the South, arriving at North Island, San Diego, on December 10, 1955.

In early January 1956, the Hornet entered the Puget Sound Naval Shipyard, Bremerton, Washington, to undergo a major conversion. Included in the face-lifting was the construction of an angle flight deck and an enclosed hurricane bow. The latest damage control and electronic equipment was installed. Following post-conversion trials, the Hornet returned to San Diego on August 15, 1956, and the remainder of the year was spent conducting flight operations in and around the San Diego area.

On January 21, 1957, the Hornet again deployed to the Far East for a seven-month tour with the Seventh Fleet. The usual visits to Yokosuka, Sasebo and Iwakuni, Japan; Manila and Subic Bay, Philippines; Buckner Bay, Okinawa and Hong Kong, B.C., were made between Seventh Fleet exercises in the South China Sea. On July 25, 1957, the Hornet returned to San Diego and conducted training exercises for the rest of the year.

On January 6, 1958, the Hornet once more deployed to the Western Pacific. During this cruise the carrier represented the United States in the annual Black Ship Festival in Shimoda, Japan. The festival celebrated the landing of Commodore Perry, some 104 years earlier.

The Hornet remained alert where trouble brewed—in Indonesia and Quemoy and Matsu, the Nationalist Chinese offshore islands.

On July 2, the Hornet completed the cruise when she tied up at the Quay Wall of the North Island Naval Air Station in San Diego. A little more than a month after returning to the States, orders came to proceed to the Puget Sound Naval Shipyard for a four-month overhaul and conversion to a CVS (Anti-submarine Warfare Carrier).

The Hornet received her new designation on July 27, 1958, and left the shipyard steaming for her new home port at Long Beach, California.

January and February 1959 were spent conducting ASW training as an efficient base for aircraft whose purpose is to detect and destroy enemy submarines.

On April 3, the Hornet deployed on her fifth Western Pacific cruise, her first as an anti-submarine warfare carrier.

The *Hornet* returned to Long Beach on October 9, 1959, where the usual training exercises resumed until March 17, 1960. She then sailed again for the Western Pacific. Joining the Seventh Fleet support operations, the ASW carrier conducted peace-keeping missions in Southeast Asia against potential Communist insurgency threatening that part of the free world. On November 29, the *Hornet* left Subic Bay astern and arrived at her home port on December 18, 1960.

The *Hornet* once more became involved in a major overhaul at the Puget Sound Naval Shipyard on February 17, 1961. Afterwards, she went to Tacoma on June 16, where Open House was held aboard ship. An estimated 25,000 people visited the carrier for the next three days. The hangar deck was jammed with curious sightseers viewing the aviation displays and exploring the flight deck. Over one million people in the Seattle-Tacoma area watched a 12-hour telecast from the *Hornet*, which presented a show in honor of the 50th Anniversary of Naval Aviation. Interviews with flight deck personnel, air operations, and an anti-submarine warfare demonstration were conducted to explain the mission of the *Hornet*. The carrier then set a course for her home port in Long Beach.

Fifty-four men from the *Hornet*'s deck and damage control divisions rendered aid in the devastating fires that scorched the Hollywood Hills in California on November 7, 1961. The men helped nuns and girls of St. Mary's College in Bel Air to clear away wreckage and restore damaged facilities.

In June 1962, the *Hornet* departed Long Beach for another Far East cruise. The Communist menace in Southeast Asia was still a threat, and the carrier remained on constant alert with the Seventh Fleet. On December 21, 1962, she returned to Long Beach and from January 4 to February 18, 1963, the *Hornet* underwent overhaul at the shipyard in Long Beach. Three of her 5-inch 38-caliber gun mounts were removed and yard work was completed on February 18.

On June 6, the *Hornet* was a unit of Task Force 10, demonstrating fleet weapons for President John F. Kennedy. The ASW carrier joined 18 other fighting ships in fleet maneuvers which were viewed by the President, who was aboard the *USS Kitty Hawk CVA-63*.

The *Hornet* deployed for the Western Pacific on October 9 during which cruise she participated in "Operation Backpack," a coordinated U.S. and Nationalist Chinese amphibious exercise off the coast of Taiwan. On April 15, 1964, the *Hornet* returned to Long Beach, California.

The *Hornet* departed her home port on June 29 to undergo a seven-month FRAM II conversion (Fleet Rehabilitation and Modernization). This was the carrier's second major conversion and it is estimated that her usefulness to the fleet has been extended to another ten years.

The FRAM II overhaul cost $10 million. Included in the work was an aluminum-covered landing area on the flight deck to increase landing efficiency and safety; a closed-circuit TV; complete modification of the ship's sonar equipment. In addition, the Communications Department was equipped with Gemini Space Recovery communications facilities. Boiler systems and the main propulsion gear were completely overhauled and air conditioning was added to the electronic spaces. The *Hornet*'s crew was elated to learn that new dining tables with individual chairs were to replace the traditional long tables and benches in the crew's mess decks. The FRAM II program was completed on February 19, 1965, and a 30-day refresher training period began off San Diego. On March 26, the *Hornet* returned to her home port.

The newly fitted *Hornet* deployed for her ninth Western Pacific cruise on August 12. The situation in the Far East had altered since her 1964 cruise; trouble erupted in the Gulf of Tonkin four months after the ship had returned to the States. As a CVS, the *Hornet*'s role in Vietnam now was to provide antisubmarine warfare, surface surveillance, and war zone search and rescue. She did not launch air strikes against the enemy. On August 19, the *Hornet* sailed into Pearl Harbor to begin an Operational Readiness Evaluation (ORE) test. It was to be the final phase of training prior to joining the Seventh Fleet.

A simulated enemy force of submarines was sent out to detect and destroy the *Hornet* as part of the ORE. The *Hornet*, with a team of destroyers, sought to eliminate the aggressive force. The ORE was completed with total success for the *Hornet*'s ASW team on August 28, 1965.

Following a two-week rest and replenishment at Hawaii, the *Hornet* with Antisubmarine Warfare Group One aboard, left the Pacific naval shipyard astern on September 13 and arrived in Yokosuka, Japan, 11 days later. Fighting in Vietnam had escalated, and on October 4, the *Hornet* left Yokosuka to join the Seventh Fleet in the South China Sea. The attack carriers of Task Force 77 were conducting air strikes over designated enemy targets and the *Hornet* began a 21-day round-the-clock search and rescue mission, which included deep inland flights in support of the strike aircraft flying from the attack carriers. The *Hornet*'s SH-3A helicopters provided this service. The helicopters' white markings were painted to reduce the possibility of visual detection. The SH-3As were armed with two M60 machine guns. On October 20, one of the *Hornet*'s choppers had to make a forced landing in the water due to mechanical problems. Later, the disabled chopper was picked up by the *Hornet*.

From October 19 to November 3, 1965, the *Hornet* operated with the *USS Midway CVA-41*. The *Hornet*'s detachment of four Marine jets flew 109 combat sorties against the Viet Cong forces in South Viet Nam. The Marine A-4 "Skyhawks" strafed designated targets with 20mm cannon fire and released napalm bombs over enemy targets.

The *Hornet* arrived in Subic Bay on November 4 for a ten-day rest that was followed up on November 17 by a resumption of operations in the South China Sea for nine days.

On November 26, the *Hornet* began a seven-day visit to Hong Kong; during this period, on November 29, she celebrated her 22nd birthday. The modern carrier had come a long way since her 1943 commissioning and the crew enjoyed a giant cake baked by the ship's bakers to celebrate.

On December 3, the *Hornet* steamed northward through the Taiwan Straits and began a refresher ASW drill, then joined ten units of the Republic of Korea Navy in a joint four-day exercise. Tactical maneuvering and coordinated ASW exercises were included.

The *Hornet* returned to Subic Bay on December 20 for the Christmas holidays.

Early in January 1966, the *Hornet* took a few days off from "Yankee Station," the term given to the American Seventh Fleet, to monitor the movements of a group of Soviet ships conducting operations in the Pacific between Taiwan and Luzon in the Philippines. The Soviet Fleet and the *Hornet*'s ASW group witnessed a fly-over and bombing practice runs from the *USS Kitty Hawk CVA-63*. The Soviet fleet was notified that the planes were only practicing before the actual practice drills began.

On February 8, 1966, the *Hornet* returned to Yokosuka, Japan, for upkeep and supplies. She left Yokosuka on February 17 headed for Sydney, Australia; en route the *Hornet* steamed on an 11-day journey through the famed battlefields of WW II. Now-familiar names like Iwo Jima, Guadalcanal, the Coral Sea, Truk, Lae, New Guinea, Rabaul, New Britain wrote a blazing chapter to American history as the advance of Japanese aggression came to a halt in August 1945. Men of the *Hornet* paid tribute to those who fought and died there.

On March 1, the *Hornet* arrived in Sydney, Australia, and following a six-day rest she departed, en route to her home port in Long Beach.

Four units of the Royal Australian Navy and the *Hornet* conducted a 36-hour antisubmarine warfare exercise off Sydney before the carrier started home.

The *Hornet* steamed into San Diego harbor on March 23, 1966, to unload her air group; she then moored at her home port the next day.

The *Hornet* departed long Beach on June 10 to begin a five-week Midshipman Cruise. "Middies" from various colleges and universities underwent a training period to learn about shipboard life and the art of seamanship.

The carrier returned to Long Beach on July 16 for maintenance, then on the 25th, a quick departure to search for a missing aircraft carrying General Joseph Stillwell, Jr.

Throughout the summer, the *Hornet* conducted simulated recovery practice of an Apollo space capsule, and on August 29, she returned to her home port for a repair period prior to another Western Pacific tour.

As flagship of anti-submarine Group Three, the *Hornet*, with CVSG-57 embarked, left Long Beach early in 1967 to support the combat operations of the Seventh Fleet off the coast of Vietnam. She returned to Long Beach in October 1967 and entered the Shipyard for an extensive overhaul. She emerged from the yard in 1968 and commenced training up to September, then deployed once again to the Western Pacific to support units of the Seventh Fleet. During this cruise, in April 1969, the *Hornet* was sent to the Sea of Japan where a US Navy reconnaissance plane was shot down by North Korea. The *Hornet* remained in the troubled area for two weeks, then returned to Long Beach on May 12, 1969.

A six-week period of maintenance and repairs was required, after which the *Hornet* left the Long Beach Navy Shipyard in June to prepare for her assignment as primary recovery ship for Apollo Eleven.

With a Saturn 5 booster rocket under them, Lt. Colonel Michael Collins, Neil Armstrong, and Colonel Edwin E. ("Buzz") Aldrin, were lifted off launch pad 39A at 9:32 A.M. EDT July 16, 1969, at Cape Kennedy to begin their historic flight to the moon. On July 20, 1969, Buzz Aldrin remained in the command ship *Columbia* while Armstrong and Aldrin inside the Lunar Module landed on the moon at 4:17:40 P.M. as most of the civilized world watched the live television show from 241,500 miles away. At the exact moment the LM touched down on the moon, Neil Armstrong remarked, "Houston, Tranquility Base here. The Eagle has Landed." At 10:56:20 P.M., Neil Armstrong became the first man to place his foot prints on the moon. As he planted his left foot in the soft surface

Armstrong uttered those now-historic words, "That's one small step for a man, one giant leap for mankind." For two and one-half hours, Armstrong and Aldrin walked, worked, performed experiments, collected samples of the lunar rocks, and took photographs before climbing back inside the Lunar Module. The total time on the moon was 21 hours 36¼ minutes before blasting off at 1:54 P.M. EDT July 21, 1969. The command ship *Columbia* and the *Eagle* module connected together on the dark side of the moon at 5:35 P.M. EDT and the three astronauts prepared for the long journey home.

The *Columbia* splashed down in the Pacific at 12:50 P.M. EDT on July 24, 1969, 11 miles from the *Hornet* and only 1¾ miles from the aiming point and 950 miles Southeast of Hawaii.

Two of the *Hornet*'s recovery helicopters took off and proceeded towards the capsule, which was wallowing calmly in the water. Seaman John M. Wolfram was the first of the recovery crew to dive into the water from one of the helicopters; he attached a sea anchor to the command module. He was joined seconds later by Lt (jg) Wesley T. Chesser and Michael G. Mallory, Quartermaster Third Class. A flotation collar was placed around the capsule. Lieutenant Clancey Hatleeberg was dropped from one of the helicopters and he donned the special garments to protect the men from possible contamination. After spraying the spacecraft, the astronauts, and a scrubdown, the three astronauts were hauled aboard the helicopter. Armstrong was the first to board, followed by Collins and Aldrin. As the *Hornet*'s band played "Columbia, the Gem of the Ocean," the helicopter with the astronauts landed on the carrier's flight deck. The astronauts quickly walked into a specially built trailer. The *Hornet* then proceeded to Pearl Harbor, where the trailer was placed aboard an Air Force C-141 cargo plane and flown to Ellington Air Force Base.

Following the historic recovery of Apollo Eleven, the *Hornet* returned to her duties in ASW.

On October 27, these duties were again interrupted when the *Hornet* was designated primary recovery ship for the Apollo 12 mission and steamed for Hawaii and the recovery area. At 11:22 A.M. EST November 14, 1969, Apollo 12 lifted off launchpad 39A at Cape Kennedy. President and Mrs. Richard M. Nixon and their daughter Tricia watched as a Saturn-5 booster rocket carried the spacecraft into the clouds. Apollo 12 went into lunar orbit at 10:32 P.M. EST on November 17. After circling the moon ten times, Charles ("Pete") Conrad, 39, Commander of the Apollo 12 crew, and Alan L. Bean, 37, pilot of the lunar module, climbed

into the LM, nicknamed Intrepid, while Richard F. Gordon, Jr., 40, remained inside the command module nicknamed Yankee Clipper. At 11:16 P.M. the lunar module separated from the command module and began its journey to the moon.

Intrepid landed on the moon at 1:54 A.M. EST November 19 exactly on target in the dry Ocean of Storms. The site was 954 miles west of the spot in which Apollo 11 had landed in the Sea of Tranquility. The distance from the earth was 233,450 miles. Surveyor 3, an unmanned US space probe that had landed in a lunar crater in April 1967, lay some 600 feet from the Intrepid. On November 19, Gordon in the CM Yankee Clipper said he could see both Intrepid and Surveyor 3 through a sextant as he passed in orbit above the landing site.

At 6:45 A.M. Conrad placed his foot in the moon's dusty surface and said "Whoopie! Man, that may have been a small one for Neil, but that's a long one for me!" Bean followed Conrad down, setting foot on the moon at 7:14 A.M. The two astronauts collected rock samples and conducted several experiments during a four-hour walk. They walked some 1300 feet from their LM, five times more than the Apollo 11 crew members had gone. During the second moon walk, Conrad and Bean climbed 155 feet into the crater in which Surveyor 3 had landed and removed the TV camera and other items for study back on earth.

After 31 hours and 31 minutes on the moon, Conrad and Bean fired the ascent engine of the LM at 9:25 A.M. on November 20 and rose from the moon's surface to lunar orbit. Intrepid and Yankee Clipper mated together at 12:58 P.M. while the CM was making its 31st orbit around the moon. After Conrad and Bean rejoined Gordon in the command module, the Manned Spacecraft Center in Houston transmitted a radio command that sent Intrepid back down towards the moon, where it crashed into the Ocean of Storms at 5:17 P.M. about 80 miles south of its initial landing site.

Yankee Clipper splashed down in the South Pacific at 3:58 P.M. EST on November 24 some 404 miles southeast of Pago pago and 2651 miles south-southwest of Honolulu, Hawaii, and only three miles from the *Hornet*. The three astronauts were hoisted aboard a waiting helicopter and flown to the carrier. The command module was brought aboard later.

The *Hornet* participated in various ASW exrecises and carrier qualifications for new pilots out of Long Beach up to March 30, 1970, then on that day left Long Beach for the last time and set course for the Puget Sound Naval Shipyard, Bremerton, Washington, arriving the first week in April to undergo the process of deactivation. Finally in June of 1970, the *USS Hornet CVS-12* was decommissioned and placed in the Bremerton Group of the Pacific Reserve Fleet at the Puget Sound Naval Shipyard, after almost 27 years of service to her country.

The *USS Hornet CVS-12* has received the following awards: The Presidential Unit Citation; the Meritorious Unit Commendation; the American Area Campaign Service Medal; the Asiatic-Pacific Area Campaign Service Medal with seven battle stars; the World War Two Victory Medal; the Navy Occupation Service Medal; the China Service (extended) Medal; the National Defense Service Medal; the Vietnam Service Medal; the Philippine Liberation Campaign Service Ribbon with one bronze star; and the Republic of the Philippines Presidential Unit Citation Badge.

With a fresh coat of camouflage, the *Franklin* leaves Norfolk, Virginia, on February 21, 1944.

13

USS Franklin AVT-8 (CV-13)

The keel was laid for the *USS Franklin CV-13* at Newport News Shipbuilding and Drydock Co., Newport News, Virginia, on the first anniversary of the sneak attack on Pearl Harbor.

Lt. Comm. Mildred A. McAfee, USNR, Director of the WAVES,[1] christened the *Franklin* and the carrier was launched on October 14, 1943.

1. Women's Auxiliary Volunteer Expeditionary Service

This massive vessel was one of the original ten *Essex* class carriers built. The *Franklin* displaced 27,000 tons. Her overall length was 872 feet with a beam measuring 93 feet. The extreme width of her flight deck was 147 feet 6 inches. She could travel at 33 knots carrying 3448 men. Armament consisted of twelve 5-inch 38-caliber guns, twelve quadruple 40 millimeter and fifty-seven 20 millimeter antiaircraft guns.

Capt. James M. Shoemaker, USN, accepted command of the *Franklin* as she was commissioned on January 31, 1944. Shakedown operations were held near Trinidad from March 20 to May 4. The carrier was assigned to Task Group 27.7 on May 5 and headed for San Diego to undergo intensive training prior to combat duty in the forward areas of the Pacific.

On June 1, the *Franklin* departed San Diego, passed through Pearl Harbor to Eniwetok, joining Carrier Task Group 58.2 on June 22, 1944. Eight days later, she exited Eniwetok to begin carrier air strikes on the Bonin Islands in support of the Marianas operations and the planned assault on Tinian. *Franklin's* air group participated in the third Bonin raid of July 3–4, inflicting heavy damage to Japanese installations. The pilots flew 190 air strikes against Iwo Jima, Chichi Jima, and HaHa Jima on July 4. As they headed back to their carrier, they left their calling card in the form of burned-out buildings, a sinking cargo ship, and three smaller ships burning in the water.

On July 5, the mighty *Franklin* steamed southward launching air strikes against Guam and Rota to soften up the islands for invasion forces. The sorties were flown on July 6.

The missions continued until July 21 with the daring pilots providing direct support to the troops landing in the first assault waves.

Following a two-day replenishment at Saipan, the *Franklin* arrived off the Palau Islands on July 25 to conduct air sorties plus photographic reconnaissance. The flights continued until July 27 and the carrier completed more than 350 Combat missions which provided valuable photographic information. When the *Franklin* departed the Palaus on July 28, she left a monument the Japanese could not erase from their memories—the destruction of military installations and shipping.

While en route to Saipan, the *Franklin* joined Task Group 58.1 under the command of Rear Admiral J. J. Clark. On August 4, the big ship sent her pilots against Chichi Jima and Ototo Jima. The latter target became a wasteland upon the destruction of the radio station, seaplane base, airstrip, and ships.

On August 9, 1944, the *Franklin* returned to Eniwetok for maintenance and supplies.

The *Franklin* left Eniwetok astern on August 28 in company with the *USS Enterprise CV-6, USS Belleau Wood CVL-24* and the *USS San Jacinto CVL-30.* As flagship for Rear Admiral R. E. Davison's Task Group 38.4, the *Franklin* prepared to launch neutralization and diversionary attacks against the Bonin Islands. The raids continued from August 31 to September 2,

1944. The Big Ben's air group peppered ground fortifications with their bombs, sank two cargo ships, and obtained good photographic coverage of Iwo Jima.

Following a short replenishment at Saipan, the *Franklin* conducted air strikes against Yap and supported the Peleiu landings on September 15 by providing direct air assistance for the ground troops.

During September 21–25, the *Franklin* took a brief recess from combat at Manus Island, Admiralties.

The powerful carrier returned to the Palaus on September 27 and began daily patrol and night fighter strikes. Later, she rendezvoused with other carriers of the Third Fleet to conduct air strikes against the Philippines, Formosa, and the Ryukus in support of the impending invasion of Leyte. Southwest of Formosa on October 13, the task group was attacked by four Japanese aircraft. Four torpedoes were aimed at the *Franklin,* but fortunately all missed.

While Lt. (jg) Albert J. Pope, USNR, was on final approach for a landing, he noticed a Japanese plane screaming at the carrier to deliver another death blow. Lieutenant Pope jammed the throttle to full power, took a wave-off, and blasted the enemy plane into flaming fragments.

"Big Ben's" antiaircraft crews sent all they could at the advancing enemy planes. This aerial show looked like some distorted kaleidoscope as AA shells intermittently exploded into black clouds against the blue sky, while enemy planes maneuvered to evade their destructive havoc.

A Japanese plane diving at the ship took a direct hit from the port battery, skidded out of control across the flight deck, and fell into the sea off the starboard side, causing little damage.

"Too close for comfort," was the description later given by Lt. Daniel M. Winters, who leaped for the deck when he saw the enemy plane zooming at him. As the burning craft passed over him, a wing ripped the seat of his trousers!

Following a fighter sweep against Aparri, Luzon, the *Franklin* steamed eastward to neutralize enemy installations prior to the Leyte landing invasion.

On October 15, three enemy planes attacked the *Franklin.* One managed to slip through "Big Ben's" firepower and scored a hit on the after outboard corner of the deck edge elevator, killing three men and wounding 22.

On October 24, 1944, the *Franklin* participated in the Battle of Sibuyan Sea. The carrier's active pilots sank the Japanese destroyer *Wakaba,* west of Panay, and aided the destruction of the battleship *Musashi* off Sibuyan. Later in the afternoon, the *Franklin* steamed northward with Task Force 38 to intercept Japanese Vice Admiral Ozawa's advancing forces.

The first combat air strikes were scheduled for October 25 and the Battle of Cape Engano began. Negligible air opposition was encountered by the American air crews and when the battle had ended, four enemy aircraft carriers plus a destroyer became additional inventory for Davy Jones's Locker.

The *Franklin* retired with her task group to refuel, then returned to combat off Leyte on October 27. When the Battle of Leyte got underway, the carrier's fliers provided support for ground forces, launched fighters against enemy shipping, and conducted search and rescue patrols for survivors.

The *Franklin* was steaming some 100 miles from Samar on October 30 when five enemy dive bombers approached. Two planes were quickly eliminated, while the remaining three continued their charge through thick antiaircraft fire. One plane missed the ship and splashed near the starboard side. Another plane crashed into the *Franklin's* flight deck and its aerial bomb set the deck ablaze. A flighter plane close by penetrated the flight deck, continued through to the hangar deck, and set off many additional fires. A third aircraft slipped within 30 feet of the *Franklin* and splattered into the after-end of the *Belleau Wood's* flight deck.

All fires were under control in less than two hours, thanks to the fire fighting crews, who were not going to let their ship down in a crisis. It was discovered that the damage was too severe for repairs in the forward area of battle, so the *Franklin* was ordered back to the United States. The price of this particular battle cost 56 men their lives and 60 were wounded.

The *Franklin* retired to Ulithi, Western Carolines on October 31 for temporary repairs and on November 11 she sailed for the States, arriving at Puget Sound Naval Shipyard on November 28, 1944.

Repair work was conducted day and night to make the *Franklin* ready for action quickly. "Big Ben" left the yard on February 2, 1945, and arrived near Ulithi on March 13 to join Task Group 58.2 for strikes against the Japanese homeland.

While searching for the remains of the Japanese fleet and flying successful air sorties, terror struck the *Franklin* again. The day was March 19, 1945. On the flight deck, planes were fueled, loaded with bombs and rockets, and waiting for the order to get airborne for action against Honshu and shipping in Kobe Harbor. Without warning, an enemy dive bomber sped in fast and low. Despite heavy fire from "Big Ben's" forward 5 inch and 40 millimeter mounts, the plane

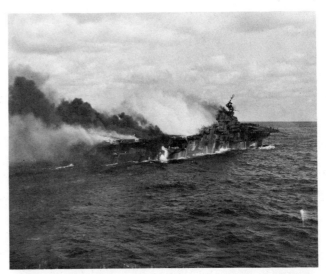

The near fatal bomb hit of March 19, 1945 left the *Franklin* helpless in the water and burning from the island structure to stern.

broke through and released two 500-pound bombs. One of the bombs exploded below the flight deck where armed planes were resting, and the second bomb went off on the hangar deck where additional planes were awaiting launch.

The one enemy plane was destroyed within 60 seconds. However, the damage had been done. Bombs were exploding everywhere, each explosion bigger than the one before. When the 5-inch service magazines blew up, it was a living nightmare; airplane engines with the propellers still attached, jagged pieces of steel, and anything not tied down, including human beings, were hurled the length of the ship, tossed hundreds of feet into the air to rain down like a hailstorm.

The entire after-end of Big Ben was a sheet of flame! Aircraft, pilots, and crewmen became human torches as aviation fuel poured over the side of the burning vessel. Survivors could do nothing more than seek cover where they stood while rockets, bombs, and ammo mixed with twisted steel and deck splinters saturated the air around them.

The Damage Control Manual has everything systematically listed on what to do in case of an emergency, but one vital section is deleted. Most of the men in the damage control parties are already dead or wounded when the emergency arrives!

On the *Franklin*, as well as on other ships in distress, the so-called privileges of rank surrender to the task of staying alive; a pilot, a mess cook, line officers, and stewards can all be found holding the same firehose, trying to control an angry blaze.

Crewmembers of the *Franklin* are seen fighting the raging
fires as the carrier burns from gasoline and bomb explosions.

Lt. Comm. Joseph O'Callahan, USNR, was one of the real heroes on the *Franklin,* and the only Chaplain to be awarded the Congressional Medal of Honor. He rushed over the tilted decks of the injured carrier, administering last rites to his dying shipmates. He was seen carrying hot bombs and shells to the side of the ship for jettisoning. Crewmen who witnessed this were deeply inspired by his bravery. Chaplain O'Callahan personally lead a damage control party into the main ammunition magazines to wet them down. He was seen to risk his life on ten different occasions; no one can tally up the brave acts which went unseen by this noble man.

A 19-year-old Marine corporal, Wallace L. Kimkieweiz, requested and received permission to man a 40mm antiaircraft gun, when ordered to abandon the ship. He and others stayed at their battle stations to strike back at the enemy who were still attacking the crippled, burning carrier.

James P. Odem MM1c, USNR, was in the fireroom when the first explosion occurred. Disregarding his own life, he found a gasmask and remained at his post, keeping up steam in one of the ship's boilers for three hours. When overcome by smoke, he finally had to leave for some air. Upon reaching the flight deck, he helped man a hose spraying a fire. Next, Odem volunteered for rescue party duty and worked hours freeing trapped shipmates. Throughout the five-day ordeal of saving the *Franklin,* he managed to sleep six hours. For his devotion and heroism, James Odem was promoted to the rate of Chief Machinist Mate on the spot.

Gerald Smith F1c, USNR, risked his life to keep a firehose in service during the desperate hours when "Big Ben" was dangerously spreading flames. As the USS *Santa Fe CL-60* came alongside the reeking *Franklin* to receive wounded, one of the firehoses which had been pumping water on the flight deck was slashed into. This didn't hinder Smith, who removed the fouled hose and brought a new one into action. While two men held his ankles, Smith dangled head down over the deck edge to unfasten the damaged hose. All the time, the *Santa Fe* was violently bumping against the gun sponsons of "Big Ben."

The *Santa Fe* crew showed remarkable courage as rescue operations continued. Once, the light cruiser came in moving at 22 knots and ripped off the radio mast, gun emplacements, and catwalks on her starboard side! The *Franklin* was nothing more than a sitting duck only 50 miles off the Japanese coastline. In less than 30 minutes, a squadron of enemy planes *could* have attacked!

Meanwhile, the crews fought the topside fires as death quickly took the lives of men far below the scorching hull.

A warrant officer, walking along a passageway, was thrown 40 feet against a steel bulkhead by an explosion. Other men were blown clear of the vessel to drown or die from the initial blast and concussion.

The *USS Hunt DD-674* and *USS Marshall DD-676* picked up 600 men from "Big Ben"; the *USS Hickox DD-673* and *USS Miller DD-535* took on several more.

Franklin as the *Santa Fe* stands by, March 19, 1945.

Damage to the *Franklin* is seen from the air on April 22, 1945. Internal hangar deck explosions left the flight deck completely destroyed.

The first few hours of a disaster are the worst and the *Franklin's* plight was no exception. Men were trapped in the stern; others jumped over the side when it became imminent that delay would mean death. Damage control parties below decks succeeded in flooding some of the volatile magazines.

Men were transferred from the smoldering *Franklin* to the *Santa Fe* by various ways: makeshift mailbags and breeches buoys were used, while some wounded were hoisted out on the horizontal radio mast and lowered into waiting arms on the cruiser.

Rescue operations were suddenly halted as one of the *Franklin's* 5-inch gun mounts caught fire. The cruiser drew away until the threat of explosion had passed, then edged back alongside and took the remaining wounded men. One hour later, the *Santa Fe* moved slowly away from the stricken carrier.

Captain Gehres of the *Franklin* sent a message to all nearby ships, vowing, "If you can save us from the Japanese, we will save the ship."

The *USS Pittsburg CA-72*, with all guns blazing, closed in on "Big Ben's" port bow and took her in tow. Fighter aircraft flew continuous combat air patrol for the two ships, trudging along at six knots. While crewmen still fought to control the fires, the gallant *Franklin* headed for Ulithi. While en route, Admiral Davison, whose flag had flown from the carrier's mast during the attack, sent the following message: "I am on a stranger's doorstep, but I claim you again with pride. Battered though you may be, you are still my child. Great Work!"

By the morning of March 28, the "Big Ben's" crew had one of the carrier's boilers and a fireroom operational. Other boilers were put into shape during the day, but the ship was still in trouble. The electric power was useless and food shortage was a problem. The steering gear was completely destroyed. The only way to control the ship's heading was by varying the speed of the main engines!

The skeleton crew of the *Franklin* toiled day and night to ensure that the ship would stay above water. She was finally able to increase her speed to 23 knots.

On March 21, 300 of the *Franklin's* sailors came aboard. Additional crewmen, food, and supplies were offered, but the brave men who had saved their ship replied: "We have plenty of men and food. All we want to do is get the hell out of here!"

When a count had been completed, it was established that 724 men had been killed and 265 were wounded.

On April 3, 1945, the *Franklin* steamed proudly into Pearl Harbor, where 706 crewmen mustered on the ship's forward section, which had been scorched from the actions of battle. A solemn expression on the faces of dockside personnel knew there was immeasurable pride in the crew of a ship that refused to die.

Ashore, some of the men described unusual events that had occurred on that fateful day of March 19, 1945.

Louis Vallina MM1c, USNR, was on the fantail when the first explosion went off. Twice he started to jump, but feared he would be sucked under the ship's giant screws to drown. So he waited. Suddenly a second jolt erupted and rocked the carrier so badly that he had no chance for any further decision. The force of the blast threw him so far out from the ship that he didn't have to worry about being pulled into the screws.

Edward D. Mesial SK2c said, "I managed to crawl on my stomach to our carrier's catwalk after being trapped below. I could hear people yelling for me to crawl over the side onto a cruiser that was picking up wounded personnel, but my legs would not respond anymore. So, I just lay there on the catwalk, hoping my strength would return when the ship listed heavily to starboard and I tumbled right onto the cruiser's deck!"

Julius F. Payak, USMC, retold what it was like aboard the *Franklin* during the disaster. At the time of the violent explosion he was brushing his teeth. "I looked up; the mirror in front of me was gone and I decided it was time for me to go too. I ran into a compartment, just about 75 feet from where the bomb had hit. The smoke was starting to get me. My mattress was nearby and it occurred to me that there should be some air in it. I tore off the cover and buried my nose in the mattress. After a while, I tried to get out, crawling along the deck and finally made it to the ammunition transfer room where it was possible to get some fresh air because the intakes were open. When I regained some strength, I found a hose and helped fight fires."

On April 28, 1945, with a cruiser escort, the *Franklin* steamed on her own power and arrived in New York Harbor. The big carrier's main mast leaned at a sharp angle, her foremast was a jagged stump, and gnarled

A proud and brave group of officers and men of the *Franklin* stand at attention as the carrier enters New York Navy Yard on April 28, 1945.

steel plates, buckled and torn, could not be hidden. The flight deck was completely unrecognizable as a result of battle damage.

The crew assembled on the flight deck's remains for awards and the largest number of decorations ever presented upon a single ship in the history of the Navy began.

There were 393 medals bestowed that day. Nineteen Navy Crosses, 22 Silver Stars, 5 Gold Stars in lieu of second Bronze Star awards and 235 Commendation Ribbons were awarded.

Wreckage on *Franklin's* flight deck May 28, 1945, as ship passes through the Panama Canal.

On January 23, 1946 President Harry S. Truman presented the Medal of Honor to Chaplain O'Callahan, the first time in the history of the Armed Forces that a military chaplain received the nation's highest decoration. (Lieutenant Vincent R. Capodanno, USNR was awarded, posthumously, the Medal of Honor, January 7, 1969, becoming the third chaplain to receive the Medal of Honor and the second Navy chaplain to be so honored. Lieutenant Capodanno was in direct line of enemy fire when he ministered a dying corpsman in Vietnam. He dashed to the wounded sailor's side and in doing so made the ultimate sacrifice. Chaplain Capodanno's actions were an inspiration to the Marines who saw him and his words of faith strengthened morale and provided encouragement to those who heard him.)

Chaplain O'Callahan retired from the Naval Reserve a Captain and passed away a few years ago. On February 14, 1964, the keel of destroyer escort DE-1051 was laid. She was launched on October 20, 1965, and in the summer of 1968, commissioned the USS *Joseph T. O'Callahan DE-1051* in honor of the late Navy chaplain. The O'Callahan was built by the Defore Shipbuilding Company at Boston and is now stationed at San Diego.

The damage suffered by the *Franklin* was too great for the carrier to return to the war. Savage fires had taken the life of the once majestic carrier and all that remained was mangled, jagged steel, scorched from the blaze and blackened from the smoke of battle.

On February 17, 1947, the *Franklin* was decommissioned at Bayonne, New Jersey, in the Atlantic Reserve group. "Big Ben" was reclassified three different times while in mothballs. First to Attack Aircraft Carrier CVA-13 on October 1, 1952, then to Anti-Submarine Warfare Carrier CVS-13 on August 8, 1953 and finally to Auxiliary Aircraft Transport AVT-8 on May 15, 1959.

The *Franklin* was removed from the manifest of Naval vessels on October 1, 1964, becoming the first of the *Essex* class carriers to be labelled unfit for further service.

During her three short years of active service, the *Franklin* received The American Area Campaign Medal; the Asiatic-Pacific Area Campaign Medal with four battle stars; the World War II Victory Medal; the Philippine Liberation Campaign Ribbon and the Republic of the Philippines Presidential Unit Citation Badge.

USS Ticonderoga CVS-14 at present.

14

USS Ticonderoga CVS-14 (CV-14)

The present *USS Ticonderoga CVS-14* is the fourth naval vessel to be named after the historic fort on Lake Champlain captured on May 10, 1775. Ethan Allen and his Green Mountain Boys seized this strategic British post, which was a plethora of artillery and military supplies.

Ticonderoga, meaning "between two waters," was the name given by the Iroquois Indians to the land separating Lake George from Lake Champlain. Ethan Allen, acting on his own initiative, gathered his troops and attacked the British-held fortress. In 1755, when the fort was built, its name was Fort Carillon. It had been constructed by the French, but the English renamed it Ticonderoga when they captured it in 1759.

The keel of the *USS Ticonderoga CV-14* was laid down on February 1, 1943 at the Newport News Ship Yard in Virginia. Mrs. Roger de Chame, the former Miss Stephanie Sarah Pell, christened the carrier on February 7, 1944. Mrs. de Chame is the daughter of Robert T. Pell and the granddaughter of Stephen H. Pell, through whose valiant efforts Fort Ticonderoga was restored to its original condition.

Captain Dixie Kiefer assumed command and the *Ticonderoga* was commissioned on May 8 at Norfolk. To start at the bottom and progress up the long ladder of rank to command an aircraft carrier is the ultimate goal and dream of all carrier pilots. It is even more rewarding if the person is commanding his ship during wartime when his many years of training are put to the ultimate test.

Captain Kiefer was no stranger to the advancements made in aviation. On November 11, 1924, Lieutenant Kiefer had flown a plane in a successful night catapult launch from the battleship *USS California BB-44*. The ship was at anchor in the harbor at San Diego and the 9:46 P.M. launch was aided only by searchlights aimed about 1000 yards ahead. As aviation advancements continued, newer and bigger aircraft came on the scene. At last, Captain Kiefer was prepared to take his ship to war.

On June 19 the carrier received her fighter and torpedo squadrons of Air Group 80. A bomber squadron came aboard two days later and carrier qualifications began for the pilots in the Chesapeake Bay. The air group simulated attacks against their ship and newly assigned watch officers logged over 100 hours of tactical training time.

Shakedown operations began on June 26 in the

Ticonderoga firing number 1 and 2 flight deck gun turrets, July 7, 1944.

Gulf of Paria, and the air group underwent a rigorous training session preparatory to action in the Pacific. On July 16 the *Ticonderoga* departed Trinidad and returned to the Norfolk Navy Yard for post-shakedown alterations.

On August 30 the big carrier headed for her ultimate destination in the Pacific to team up with the fast carrier task force. While en route to the Panama Canal, her air group went through strafing and bombing practice in addition to photographic reconnaissance maneuvers on Great Exhuma Island.

A joint exercise with the U.S. Army began on September 3. The carrier launched simulated air assaults on the Panama Canal, approximately 150 miles off shore. The confused defending Army forces were overtaken by the air group.

The *Ticonderoga* transited the Panama Canal on September 4 and arrived at North Island Naval Air Station, San Diego, the following day. She took on supplies plus 77 aircraft and personnel who would later be assigned to a light carrier. She departed again on September 19 and steamed into Pearl Harbor on September 24.

While in Hawaii the carrier conducted experimental tests, transferring bombs from a cargo ship (*USS Carina AK-74*) to an aircraft carrier. The next day both vessels went to sea for another test under normal operating conditions. The overall results were favorable, so the carrier went back to day and night air operations.

On October 18, the *Ticonderoga* sailed from Hawaii and arrived at the Advanced Fleet Base, Ulithi Atoll on October 29. Four days later she was off again to rendezvous with Task Force 38. The "Big T" launched her first combat strikes during a two-day air attack on Luzon in the Philippines on November 5–6. Air Group 80 flew 127 sorties and 50 combat air patrol sorties the first day, striking Zablan, Mandaluyong, and Pasig airfields plus enemy shipping near Manila. The air group assisted in sinking the heavy cruiser *Nachi* and damaged over 50 other ships.

Around 4:00 P.M. the dreaded Kamikaze force began an attack on the task force. One crashed into the signal bridge of the *USS Lexington CV-16*; another made a dive at the *Ticonderoga's* port quarter, but was shot down by *Lexington* gunners. The "Big T's" combat air patrol also downed a suicide plane cruising six miles from the action.

On November 6 the air group concentrated their fighter sweeps on airfields and smashed the ships in Manila Bay again. The next day the carrier rendezvoused with a fleet tanker for refueling and also ac-

cepted replacement aircraft from the baby carrier *USS Cape Esperance CVE-88*. By November 11 the "Big T" was some 80 miles off Samar where her air group went after Japanese shipping in Ormoc Bay, Leyte. Three destroyers and two cargo ships were eliminated from the Japanese inventory.

Manila Bay shipping once again became targets for the "Big T's" pilots on the 12th. The light cruiser *Kiso*, four destroyers, and a submarine chaser were all sunk. On November 14 the Ti had launched 643 combat strikes in support of the Leyte operation. Vital enemy airfields were ravaged; ground installations became infernos—including antiaircraft batteries, oil tanks, warehouses, and supply depots. The carrier returned to Ulithi on the 17th.

Three days later the Ti took on supplies, aviation gasoline, ammunition, and fuel oil. Anchored 600 yards away was the fleet oiler *USS Mississinewa AO-59*. The serenity was broken as a Japanese submarine scored a direct torpedo hit on the oiler, which sank with a devastating explosion.

The Ti went to sea two days later; then on November 23 she logged the 4000th landing made on her flight deck. Air strikes resumed on Luzon and shipping off Santa Cruz and Lingayen Gulf. During these attacks on November 25, the air groups sank two Japanese heavy cruisers, the *Kumano* and *Yashojima*. The suicide planes were ubiquitous, but the carriers' AA batteries were successful in repelling many attacks. One carrier was not so fortunate. A Kamikaze plane crashed into the *Essex* despite the blanket of antiaircraft fire. Many of her aircraft were forced to land on the *Ticonderoga*.

On December 2, 1944, the task force returned to Ulithi for provisions, then departed eight days later to send a final air strike at Luzon from December 14–16. Airfields, installations, and shipping northwest of Luzon came under heavy attack and helped support the U.S. Army landings on Mindoro on the 15th.

The Ti managed to escape the wrath of a typhoon that hit the Third Fleet east of the Philippines. On December 24 she anchored at Ulithi for the Christmas holidays.

Five days later the fast carrier force sailed from Ulithi and began a two-day attack against Formosa on January 3–4, 1945. The U.S. Army rushed ashore at Lingayen Gulf on the 9th while the carriers provided air cover.

The task force entered the South China Sea on January 11 to destroy shipping which traveled from Saigon to Hong Kong and Formosa.

On January 15 the Ti's air group returned to the

Carrier under attack by Kamikaze planes as seen from a distance by *USS San Jacinto*, January 21, 1945.

Formosa area and resumed strikes on airfields and shipping, plus attacks on the Ryukyus and Pescadores Islands.

While conducting air strikes over Formosa on January 21 the *Ticonderoga* fell victim to the dreaded Kamikazes. At 12:01 P.M., a single-engine Japanese fighter plane came out of the sun and crashed into the Ti's flight deck, abreast of the Number Two 5-inch gun mount. More than 100 men were killed or wounded when the plane's bomb exploded just above the hangar deck and started many fires. Many of the men were trapped in the deck spaces.

On the bridge, Captain Kiefer ordered an immediate change in course to prevent the wind from spreading the fires. This maneuver also kept the acrid smoke from entering the ventilation intakes. The course change was maintained until the conflagration was extinguished, except for one short moment to permit the rescue of men trapped in the deck ready rooms.

Meanwhile, the Ti's executive officer, Commander William O. Burch, went below decks to supervise compartment flooding to overcome the ship's starboard list, and give her a ten-degree portside list. Such an angle would increase the possibility that the fire would carry itself overboard. The gasoline floated on the water—the very water being used to fight the fire.

Badly burned aircraft were pushed overboard as firefighters struggled with the blaze. Smoke curled

upwards hundreds of feet, making an easy target of the carrier; and the Ti was still in the thick of battle. Three more suicide planes were splashed by skillful gun crews. Then, at 1:00 P.M., a Kamikaze roared through the gunfire and crashed into the Ti's superstructure. Captain Dixie Kiefer, severely wounded, remained on the bridge for 12 hours after the attack until assured that all injured crewmen had been cared for. The executive officer was also suffering from serious wounds and it became necessary for the engineering officer, Commander Harmon V. Briner, to take command of the stricken ship. All fires were under control and extinguished in less than two hours after the first suicide crash.

On January 24 the *Ticonderoga* limped into Ulithi, at which time it was learned that 143 men were dead and 202 were wounded from the two Kamikaze hits. The carrier required stateside facilities to repair the massive damage, so Air Group 80 was transferred to the *USS Hancock CV-19* and the Ti proceeded to Washington's Puget Sound Shipyard, arriving February 15.

In addition to battle damage repairs the carrier received a much needed overhaul and work was completed on April 20, 1945. The next day the Ti departed the yard and sailed to the Naval Air Station, Alameda, California, arriving May 1. Air Group 87 came aboard, and the carrier headed for Hawaii the next day. Two weeks of training awaited the crew

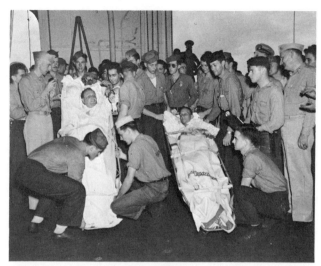

USS Ticonderoga CV-14. Captain Dixie Kiefer and Commander W. A. Burch, Jr. on stretchers awaiting transfer to hospital ship (January 25, 1945).

upon arrival at Pearl Harbor and the new air group underwent rigorous tactical problems in aerial and torpedo bombing.

The *Ticonderoga* departed on May 11 and joined Carrier Task Group 38.4 eleven days later at Ulithi Atoll. On May 24 the fast carrier force was steaming away and sent air strikes during the Okinawa Gunto operation. Installations at Minami Daito Shima and Kita Daito Shima received heavy bomb hits. On June 6 the air group downed enemy fighters heading towards the task force.

The Third Fleet operations against Japan from July 21 to August 15, 1945, completed the finishing

touches on a war that had begun for the United States three years and eight months earlier. Daily bombardment of the Japanese homeland had completely devastated the once-powerful enemy fighting machine.

The *Ticonderoga* joined other fast carriers for daily assaults on shipping and camouflaged airfields. A two-day strike on the Inland Sea area began July 24 in which the giant naval base at Kure was all but obliterated. Japanese warships like the battleships *Hyuga, Ise,* and *Haruna,* the escort carrier *Kaiyo* and two heavy cruisers were all sunk. Mammoth bomb craters gutted the airfields at Nagoya, Osaka, and Miho. Kure Naval Base was hit again on July 28, leaving a carrier, three cruisers and a destroyer sinking in flames. Industrial factories in central Honshu were leveled on July 30.

Air Group 87 of the Ti had just completed a bombing mission over Tokyo on August 15 when word was received to cease all offensive operations. At last, fighting in the Second World War had come to an end. Another wave of fighters jettisoned their bombs and returned to the carrier.

As defensive maneuvers the fast carrier force launched patrol sweeps over Japanese airfields and military installations until September 2, at which time the official signing of the peace treaty took place on board the *USS Missouri BB-63* at Tokyo Bay.

Medical supplies, food, and clothing were dropped on allied prisoner of war camps during the next three days. On September 6 *Ticonderoga* entered Tokyo Bay and remained for 19 days. She headed for Hawaii on September 20 where 1916 veterans came aboard for transportation to the states.

The Ti arrived at Alameda, California, on October 5. Four days later she returned to Hawaii and brought a thousand military men back over to Tacoma, Washington.

On October 27–28, open house was held aboard the Ti during Navy Day celebrations, and more than 60,000 Tacoma citizens toured the big carrier. One of the most outstanding sights noticed by the visitors was the carrier's wartime scoreboard. It revealed that 358 enemy aircraft were destroyed; 11 enemy warships were sunk; 30 merchant vessels were sunk; and damage was rendered to 12 enemy warships and 87 ships.

On October 29 the *Ticonderoga* headed for Pearl Harbor and Air Group 87 was launched to mark the official detachment of the victorious fighter squadron.

At Pearl Harbor the Ti received alterations for service with the "Magic Carpet" fleet. Additional berths were set up in the hangar deck and the mess deck was extended to serve a maximum number of

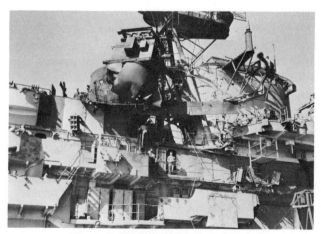

View of damaged *USS Ticonderoga.*

personnel. Then the carrier steamed to Guiuan Roadstead, Samar, Philippines, arriving November 20 where 3746 troops were embarked. She returned to Alameda on December 6 and the passengers went ashore, happy to be on American soil again.

Another Magic Carpet cruise was conducted by the Ti from December 13, 1945, to January 21, 1946. On this cruise 1759 passengers were transported from Buckner Bay, Okinawa, to Seattle, Washington. Then the Ti entered Puget Sound Naval Shipyard for a deactivation process and on January 9, 1947, she was decommissioned with the Bremerton Group, Pacific Reserve Fleet.

There was an unusual sight at the Bremerton Group of the Pacific Reserve Fleet. Seven of the aircraft carriers, the backbone of Famed Task Force 58, were juxtaposed in serene idleness: *Essex CV-9, Yorktown CV-10, Lexington CV-16, Bunker Hill CV-17*—all of which had received the Presidential Unit Citation—and the *Ticonderoga* and *Hancock CV-19*. These once active carriers remained in their comatose state throughout the late 1940s while their future usefulness was being decided by the Navy Department.

In the years to come, all but one (*Bunker Hill*) of these seven carriers would rejoin the active fleet. On January 31, 1952, after five years in mothballs, the *Ticonderoga* was moved from the Reserve Fleet and placed on a reduced commission. She departed Puget Sound Shipyard on February 27 and sailed to the Navy yard at New York, arriving April 1. This was her first visit to Atlantic waters since commissioning in 1944. She was decommissioned three days later to undergo a modernization.

Basically, the alterations included new steam catapults, a new deck-edge elevator, nylon barricade, streamlined island structure and the latest communications, electronic, and fire control equipment. While undergoing this face-lifting, a planning stage was established under which she would return to the yards in 1956 for an angle deck conversion and the Ti was redesignated CVA-14—Attack Aircraft Carrier.

On September 11, 1954, the *Ticonderoga* was recommissioned with Captain William A. Schoech in command. She proceeded to Norfolk and embarked Air Group 6. Lieutenant Joseph N. Malnerich made the first arrested landing on January 20, 1955. Commander John E. Lacoutre accomplished the first takeoff using a steam catapult flying an F9F-8 *Cougar* jet.

Shakedown operations began off Cuba on February 3, and afterwards the carrier received repairs at Norfolk. Routine flight operations were held during the next five months.

On September 1, 1955 the *Ticonderoga* arrived at the Philadelphia Navy Yard to participate in the National Air Show. The Chief of Naval Operations, Admiral Arleigh A. Burke, boarded the carrier on September 4 to observe air operations. Carrier aviation history was made on the *Ticonderoga* September 12–16 when experimental jet evaluations were conducted. Military and civilian aeronautical experts watched the first take offs and landings of the new A4D-1 *Skyhawk* and F4E-1 *Skyray* from a carrier.

The Ti departed Mayport, Florida on November 4 to join the Sixth Fleet. This would be her only cruise to the Mediterranean. Upon arriving at Gibraltar, the Ti relieved the *USS Intrepid CVA-11* and visited such romantic ports as Nice, Naples, and San Remo, and also Rhodes, Beirut, Istanbul, and Valencia.

On August 2, 1956, the *Ticonderoga* returned to the Norfolk Navy Yard for an angle deck conversion including an enclosed hurricane bow. Work was completed seven months later and trials were conducted off the Virginia Capes.

On April 15, 1957, she steamed for a new home port at Alameda to join the Pacific Fleet. On May 30 she arrived there and conducted air operations until September 16 when she then headed for her first Western Pacific cruise.

The Ti joined the Seventh Fleet at Yokosuka Navy Yard on October 15. Battle problems and Seventh Fleet exercises became her daily routine while operating from the east coast of Honshu to the Philippines. She returned to home port on April 25.

Three cruises were made in the troubled waters of the Far East from October 4, 1958, to February 16, 1959; March 5, 1960, to October 11, 1960, and May 10, 1961, to January 15, 1962. During the latter cruise the Ti received the Armed Forces Expeditionary Medal for support given to military operations at Laos, Quemoy, Matsu, and Vietnam.

From 1960 to 1962 the Ti was the outstanding carrier of the Pacific Fleet, having garnered the coveted Battle Efficiency "E" for three consecutive years. This award is the highest peacetime recognition bestowed on a ship and all attack carriers of the Pacific Fleet competed for it. The Ti also captured the Departmental "E" for excellence in Engineering, Weapons, Air Operations, and the Green Communications "C" for the fleet's top radio personnel.

On January 19, 1962, the *Ticonderoga* departed North Island and went to Puget Sound Shipyard, Bremerton, Washington, for a much needed overhaul. Major improvements included aluminum decking, renovation of the steam catapults, and the new Van

Zelm bridle arrestors for catapult launches. All work was completed on July 23. Following a brief participation at the annual Sea Fair celebration at Seattle, the Ti sailed for home port at San Diego on July 30, 1962.

She was sailing again on January 3, 1963, for her fifth Western Pacific cruise and for the next six months operated with the Seventh Fleet. The Ti came back to San Diego on July 15 and operated off the California coast the rest of the year and early 1964.

In April 1964, the Ti was off for sixth visit to the Far East. A routine stop was made at Pearl Harbor for readiness exercises, then she proceeded to Japan, arriving at Sasebo May 16. Some 8000 Japanese guests toured the carrier during open house on Armed Forces Day. Rear Admiral R. B. Moore, Commander, Carrier Division Five and also Commander of the Carrier Striking Forces of the Seventh Fleet, shifted his flag to the *Ticonderoga* in June.

On July 5 the "Big T" went to sea for two months to meet the requirements of an increased tempo of operations. On Sunday, August 2, she came to the assistance of the destroyer *USS Maddox DD-731*. The destroyer was on special assignment some distance from the task force and had flashed a message that while in international waters about 30 miles off the North Vietnam coast, in the Gulf of Tonkin, she was attacked by three high speed PT-type boats. They had fired torpedoes at the *Maddox* and raked the destroyer with machine gun fire.

The *Maddox* answered the attack with gunfire from her 5-inch 38-caliber and 3-inch gun mounts. Within minutes after the attack the *Ticonderoga* advised that she was sending four F8E *Crusaders* to assist in repelling the PT boats.

When the jets arrived they unleashed Zuni rockets and strafed the PT boats with machine gun fire. Two of the boats were damaged and a third was dead in the water. The latter boat had received a direct hit from the 5-inch guns on the *Maddox*.

Afterwards, the destroyer *USS C. Turner Joy DD-951* joined the *Maddox* in the Tonkin Gulf Patrol. At 9:30 on August 4 a second deliberate PT boat attack was directed against these two ships. The destroyers were then 60 miles off the North Vietnam coast. Aircraft from the *Ticonderoga* were again launched and immediately arrived on the scene to join in repelling the enemy torpedo boats. Two were sunk and two were damaged.

In retaliation for the unprovoked aggression against American ships on the high seas, President Johnson—backed by a Congressional Resolution—on August 5, 1964, directed the Navy to conduct strikes against bases used by North Vietnamese naval craft.

During the day some 60 attack sorties were launched from the *Ticonderoga* and the *USS Constellation CVA-64* against four Vietnamese patrol boat bases plus an oil storage depot that supported them. The oil depot was 90 percent damaged and about 25 PT boats were destroyed or damaged. The objective of these air strikes was to unequivocally show the intentions of the United States to maintain its right of freedom of operation on the high seas.

Carrier Air Wing Five's squadrons flew 130 sorties August 2–6. In September the carrier visited Yokosuka and Beppu, Japan, then returned to the southern waters for further operations.

While on station in the South China Sea in October, the Ti received notification that she, and other units, had been awarded the Navy Unit Commendation by Secretary of the Navy Paul H. Nitze. The award was for "Exceptionally meritorious service in support of operations in the Gulf of Tonkin during the period August 2–5, 1964."

The "Big T" completed the month of October and part of November in the South China Sea, conducting operations and maintaining a ready alert in case of any additional trouble. Then a long awaited visit was made to Hong Kong followed by one more short cruise in the South China Sea. The *Ticonderoga* returned to North Island, San Diego on December 15, 1964.

She entered the San Francisco Navy Yard on January 27, 1965, for five months of overhaul and repairs. After a refresher training cruise, the Ti departed San Diego on September 28. She was soon operating in the South China Sea between Yankee and Dixie stations, and launched combat tours off North and South Vietnam from November 5 to December 1; December 22 to January 13, 1966; January 24 to February 17; March 5 to April 1; and April 10 to 21.

Between these periods the Ti made ports of call at Subic Bay, Sasebo, and Hong Kong. She had launched 10,118 sorties during her combat tours. The Ti returned to San Diego May 13, 1966.

On July 9 the Ti participated in training exercises near Southern California and continued in this program until October when, once again, she set course for the Western Pacific. After a brief stopover at Hawaii on October 20–22, she steamed to Japan, arriving at Yokosuka on October 30. She departed on November 5 and made a two-day stop at Subic Bay on November 10–11, and finally arrived in the Gulf of Tonkin on the 13th.

Air strikes were launched from January 4 to February 4, 1967, February 15 to March 15, and March 29 to April 27. Familiar ports were visited between combat periods and on May 29 the *Ticonderoga* returned to San Diego.

In June she steamed for Puget Sound Naval Shipyard for overhaul which was completed on September 8, and she resumed training operations near Southern California.

The *Ticonderoga* departed home port December 28 and went to Pearl Harbor for operational readiness instructions. She departed Hawaii on January 9, 1968, and returned to the South China Sea for air operations against North Vietnam.

During this deployment, the Big "T" launched more than 16,500 sorties in 120 days of action. At one time, she launched 20 A4 "Skyhawks" in eight minutes. Commander Samuel Chessman became the holder of the record for the most sorties over North Vietnam when he returned from his 306th mission. Lieutenant Commander John Nichols became the *Ticonderoga's* first pilot to shoot down an enemy Mig jet fighter.

Pilots of the carrier's Air Wing dropped 9500 tons of ordnance, destroying or damaging 119 bridges, 118 truck parks, 424 barges, and 28 radar sites. For her fourth combat cruise to Vietnam, the *Ticonderoga* was awarded her third Navy Unit Citation. She returned to San Diego on August 17, 1968.

On February 1, 1969, the *Ticonderoga* left San Diego for her tenth deployment to the Western Pacific. Her Air Wing continued to support the Republic of Vietnam by striking the enemy. While in Subic Bay, Philippines, the Ti celebrated her 25th birthday. She returned to San Diego on September 18, 1969, the first ship of her class to complete five Vietnam combat cruises.

In mid-October, the Ti shifted her home port from San Diego to Long Beach and entered the Naval Shipyard for overhaul and reconfiguration to an ASW antisubmarine warfare support carrier. Her classification was changed to that of a CVS, effective October 1, 1969. She left the yard in mid-1970 to join the antisubmarine task force of the Pacific Fleet.

The *USS Ticonderoga CVS-14* has received the Navy Unit Commendation (two times); American Area Campaign Medal; Asiatic-Pacific Area Campaign Medal with five battle stars; World War II Victory Medal; Navy Occupation Medal; National Defense Service Medal; Armed Forces Expeditionary Medal with four stars; Vietnam Service Medal with three stars; Republic of the Philippines Presidential Unit Citation Badge; Philippine Liberation Ribbon; and the Vietnam Campaign Medal.

USS Randolph CVS-15.

15

USS Randolph CVS-15 (CV-15)

When the original order for the proposed *Essex* Class carriers was authorized, President Franklin D. Roosevelt issued a memo to the Secretary of the Navy requesting that the anticipated CV-15 be christened *Randolph*.

On May 10, 1943, the keel of the carrier was laid at Newport News, Virginia. The new flat-top was named in honor of the Continental Navy's Yankee frigate. The frigate had received its name from PAYTON RANDOLPH (1721–1775)—statesman, soldier and President of the First Continental Congress from September 5 to October 20, 1774.

The *USS Randolph CV-15* was launched on June 28, 1944, sponsored by Mrs. Guy M. Gillette, wife of the Senator from Iowa.

On October 9, 1944, the *Randolph* was fully commissioned in ceremonies conducted at Norfolk Navy Yard, Portsmouth, Virginia. Captain Felix Baker assumed command of the eleventh *Essex* Class carrier to gain membership in the Fleet.

Two days later the *Randolph*'s crew took on stores and ammunition preparatory to shakedown operations. Test runs plus drills began November 6, 1944, off Chesapeake Bay.

Commander L. C. Simpler, USN, accomplished the first landing on November 12.

The *Randolph* returned to the yards where Air Group 87 came aboard for duty. The ship anchored in the Gulf of Pania, Trinidad, West Indies on November 27. While in that area, she underwent a rigorous period of combat training, flight operations, gunnery practice, damage control, and engineering tests until December 16, when she prepared for return to the yards for a post-shakedown availability.

However, on December 17, as sealed orders were opened, the carrier found orders to proceed to San Francisco via the Panama Canal. Thus, the *Randolph* became the first carrier to enter combat without benefit of a final inspection by her builders, subsequent to the shakedown cruise.

On December 20, 1944, the *Randolph* arrived at Cristobal, C.Z., transited the Panama Canal the following day, and dropped anchor in San Francisco Bay on December 31.

Air Group 87 was relieved by Air Group 12 and training began near the San Francisco coast with primary attention on damage control, fire fighting and gunnery practice.

The *Randolph* sailed from the Bay Area on January 20, 1945. Seventeen days later she joined the famed Task Force 58 at Ulithi Atoll in the Western Carolines.

The Task Force sorties on February 10 from Ulithi commenced the initial aircraft carrier attacks on Japan proper. The *Randolph* launched her unprecedented combat strikes five days later against an air installation in Tokyo plus a Tachikawa engine plant.

Chichi Jima was blasted on February 18. The *Randolph*'s air group provided combat fighter sweeps for the ground forces landing on Iwo Jima on February 20. Twin aerial sweeps were launched against HaHa Jima and combat air patrols were continuously flown over Iwo Jima until the island was secured.

On February 25, another strike was directed against Tokyo and Nansei Shoto. The task force returned on March 1 at Ulithi for replenishment. The *Randolph* had ended her baptismal combat assignment in the Iwo Jima operation, which included the first and second carrier strikes on the face of Japan.

Kamikaze—a word capable of reducing the saltiest sailor's composure to spasms—was born during the Battle of Leyte Gulf. The Japanese suicide planes were the most harrowing and hazardous weapon conceived by the Nippons. Prior to their existence, 80 to 90 percent destruction by our fighters during aerial battles was considered a successful feat; this truism was now nullified, for that 10 to 20 percent could become a human death-bomb capable of rendering serious damage or total destruction to allied shipping.

Scattered incidents of Japanese aircraft crashing into our ships occurred prior to the Leyte invasion. However, these were in no way related to the Kamikaze units.

As a result of the new brutal tactic the Japanese lost 1500 highly trained and seasoned pilots during the Battle of the Philippine Sea (June 10–20, 1944); a disaster from which they never fully recovered.

Several high-ranking Japanese Naval officers felt that the American carriers were a serious threat to the ultimate victory plans of the Imperial Navy. One man in particular was Admiral Takijiro Onishi, Commander of the First Air Fleet. He often thought of how to deal with the problem of immobilizing the carriers so that the Japanese battleships could deal with the enemy more effectively.

On the evening of October 19, 1944, Admiral Onishi told his executive officer of the Mabalacat Airfield on Luzon, Asaichi Tamai and Commander Rikihei Inoguchi, senior staff officer of the First Air Fleet, his plan.

To organize the *Tokubetsu Kogeki Tai* (Special Attack Force), a special suicide force comprised of Zero fighter aircraft, each carrying a 250 kilogram bomb that would crash dive into the American carriers, was organized.

It took only six days for the plan to become effective. On October 25, 1944, the first Kamikaze attack force took off from the Mabalacat Airfield after a reported sighting of an American carrier task force. A group of escort carriers was sighted and the attack commenced. A single suicide plane crashed into the *USS St Lo CVE-63* immediately igniting gas below decks. In two minutes the light baby flat-top was rocked by a violent explosion and sank 21 minutes later. From then on, the omnipresent Kamikaze death-blow was felt everywhere in the Pacific Forward Area, including the Ulithi Staging area. So successful were the new suicide squadrons that the strikes were no longer limited to the carriers but to any enemy ships hindering the Imperial advancement.

The evening of March 11, 1945, was placid in the

USS Randolph, looking down flight deck at point of impact (March 11, 1945).

Ulithi Atoll as ships of the Fifth Fleet relaxed. The *Randolph's* crew began a normal routine, enjoying what comfort could be found.

Like other ships anchored in Ulithi, the *Randolph* was showing movies in the hangar deck. The projectionist was busying himself in preparation for a second showing of the film.

Weary sailors shuffled onto the hangar deck searching for good seats. For a brief period of time they would be able to forget the horrors of war and watch Cornel Wilde, Paul Muni, and Merle Oberon in *A Song to Remember*.

Suddenly, at 8:07, a Kamikaze took precedence over

Damage to overhead hangar and flight deck of carrier after a Kamikaze hit, March 1945.

the entertainment by crashing into the starboard side of the ship, below the flight deck. The twin-engined Japanese bomber exploded, instantly erupting fires everywhere.

Fire fighters leaped into action impulsively while damage control parties applied their valuable training. The flames were under control at midnight and completely extinguished by 6:00 A.M.

Twenty-five men had been killed and 106 wounded from the Kamikaze visit. The sultry yet annoying voice of Tokyo Rose poured out loud and clear over the ship's radio. Japan's lady broadcaster announced that the prearranged attack had been planned for the *USS Yorktown CV-10* and added: "Think you're nice and safe at Ulithi don't you? Well, we're fixing a little surprise for *Yorktown*."

Even though the *Randolph* had received the "surprise," she returned to action in less than three weeks.

On April 5, 1945 the *Randolph* departed Ulithi and joined the *USS Enterprise CV-6* and *USS Franklin CV-13* of Task Group 58.2 to support the Okinawa Gunto operation. She rendezvoused on April 7, one week after operations began, due to the suicide attack of March 11. Various islands in the Okinawa group were hit by combat air patrols until April 14 at which time the air groups shifted to Okinawa, IeShima, and Kakeroma Islands. Bomber and torpedo squadrons combined with fighter sweeps left all targets destroyed or heavily damaged. Airfields in southern Kyushu on the Japanese mainland were smashed on April 15.

Just before dawn on April 17, a low flying enemy plane positioned for an attack on the *Randolph*. The pilot never made his glorious mark due to accurate gunfire from the ship. Four additional attacks were attempted during the day on the task group. One enemy plane was seen to explode in the air before inflicting any damage.

The *Randolph* continued support operations against Okinawa for the remainder of April. On April 20 a total of 14 different types of combat air patrols were flown, which included patrols over the task group in support missions for combat over Okinawa. Early in May the fast carrier force returned to Ulithi.

On May 15 the *Randolph* became flagship for Task Force 58 as Vice Admiral Marc A. Mitscher and his staff came aboard. On May 29 the carrier was off again for support operations in the Okinawa campaign, then proceeded to Guam where Admiral Mitscher and staff debarked.

Air Group 16 relieved Air Group 12 and the *Randolph* joined Admiral William Halsey's Third Fleet operations against the Japanese homeland. On July 10, 213 flights were launched at Tokyo. Bad weather detained operations on the 13th, but next day weather conditions were favorable. Strikes were sent against an area of Honshu never hit before.

Two prominent Honshu-Hokkaido train ferries were sunk and three damaged. On July 18 the *Randolph* launched three strikes: two against airfields in the Tokyo area and one against the battleship *Nagato*, which was camouflaged alongside a pier at Yokosuka Naval Base. Inland sea shipping became primary targets on July 24. Air Group 12 assisted in heavily damaging the carrier-battleship *Hyuga* and other ships were sunk. Enemy airbases on Kyushu, Honshu, and Shikoku were also hit: Since the initial attack July 10 right up to July 25, the *Randolph's* air group established an impressive record. Despite adverse weather the *Randolph's* pilots destroyed 34 planes on the ground, damaged 27 more, sank between 25 to 30 ships and damaged 40, destroyed 5 locomotives and rendered considerable damage to shore installation, bridges, and a railroad yard.

On August 14 the carrier's air group was blasting Kisarazu airfield when ships of the Third and Fifth fleets received the word—Japanese forces had surrendered unconditionally to the allied powers. The pilots safely discarded their remaining ordnance and headed for the carrier. Fighting in the war was over and the *Randolph* was only ten months old, but her battle scoreboard listed 143 enemy planes destroyed in the air, 160 on the ground, and 87,000 tons of shipping sunk.

The *Randolph* teamed with other carriers in the

An F6F is launched on an air strike over Japan from the Randolph in July 1945.

immediate occupation of Japan and dropped food and medical supplies to prisoner of war camps. In September 1945 the *Randolph* departed Tokyo Bay and steamed to Pearl Harbor where over 1000 veterans came aboard for transportation home.

On October 1 the carrier sailed for Hawaii, transited the Panama Canal on the 16th, and arrived at Norfolk where she celebrated Navy Day on October 21 at Baltimore. She was the largest vessel to dock there.

The *Randolph* returned to Norfolk Navy Yard for alterations preparatory to duty with the "Magic Carpet" fleet. She completed two cruises to the Mediterranean bringing home thousands of war veterans. She subsequently became part of the Atlantic Fleet as a training carrier operating along the eastern seaboard and Caribbean until the summer of 1946.

The carrier took a short cruise to the Mediterranean and visited Italy, Turkey, Lebanon and Greece, then returned to the states in December. Peacetime training duties resumed off the Atlantic seaboard the first few months of 1947. One more cruise was made to northern Europe with Annapolis midshipmen aboard.

In company with the carrier during this trip was the *USS New Jersey BB-62* and *USS Wisconsin BB-64*. The task group visited England, Scotland, Norway, Sweden, and Denmark. When she returned from this training cruise the *Randolph* was decommissioned in the Atlantic Reserve Fleet in June 1947.

The *Randolph* was moved to the Newport News Shipbuilding Company in January 1952 for modernization under Project 27A. This was required due to the many advancements made in carrier aviation while the *Randolph* had been resting in mothballs. Her island structure was streamlined: flight deck strengthening to handle heavier and faster planes, installation of the latest electronic equipment, and special weapons systems were all included.

During the yard period the *Randolph* was reclassified CVA-15—Attack Aircraft Carrier. On July 1, 1953 she was recommissioned at Newport News and Captain Robert S. Quackenbush took command.

Shakedown operations were held off Guantanamo Bay, Cuba, until February 3, 1954, when the carrier joined the Sixth Fleet in the Mediterranean. During this cruise she visited Spain, Italy, Greece, France, and Algeria. Subsequent to the cruise she conducted flight operations off the Atlantic coast.

On August 1, 1955, she entered Norfolk Navy Yard for a major conversion. She departed in January 1956 wearing a new look. Included in the conversion program was an enclosed hurricane boy and angle flight deck.

For the next six months the *Randolph* conducted flight operations between Virginia and Florida. A "first" was accomplished when she became the first Atlantic Fleet carrier to launch a Regulus Guided Missile from her flight deck.

On July 14, 1956, the *Randolph* deployed on another Mediterranean cruise where NATO and Sixth Fleet exercises were conducted until October.

When Israel invaded Egypt the carrier was ordered to stand ready. Her aircraft provided cover during the evacuation of U.S. nationalists from Alexandria. On February 19, 1957, she returned to home port at Norfolk, Virginia.

The *Randolph* remained at Norfolk until July 1, when she returned to the Mediterranean for another tour of duty with the Sixth Fleet. Christmas holidays were celebrated in European ports and from August through December the carrier was mainly in the Mediterranean area during the Syrian uprisings.

On February 24, 1958, the *Randolph* came home and entered the naval yard at Portsmouth for a routine overhaul that took four months.

In June she began shakedown training near Guantanamo Bay, Cuba, then resumed air operations from Norfolk. On September 2, she started on her fifth Mediterranean cruise; this would be her final European deployment as a CVA. Her efficiency as an attack carrier was unmatched—she had received the cherished Battle Efficiency "E" for the years 1955–57. In 1958 she made a clean sweep and garnered all excellency awards for air operations, gunnery, and engineering. The majority of this cruise was spent in the Western Mediterranean with brief stops at Malta and Rhodes. NATO and Sixth Fleet maneuvers were conducted with great success and on March 12, 1959 she came home.

She entered the yards on April 1 for installation of antisubmarine warfare equipment and was then reclassified CVS-15. A six week refresher training cruise began on June 1. On August 2 she returned to Norfolk and was once again the winner of the Battle Efficiency "E"—this time as the top rated CVS in the Atlantic Fleet.

In September she became the flagship of Task Group Alpha and began training as a special ASW Hunter-Killer force, a training which continued throughout November.

The carrier celebrated Christmas at Norfolk—her first Christmas in the states in more than four years.

During the first two months of 1960 the *Randolph* conducted training as flagship of the Atlantic ASW task group. A short visit to New York highlighted the month of March when 15,000 residents visited the ship on St. Patrick's Day.

In September she again won the Battle Efficiency "E" for the fourth year. This was a feat never previously accomplished by a carrier.

The *Randolph* entered Norfolk Navy Yard in October for installation of additional equipment and became the first carrier to have sonar installed. Also received was new electronics for her Combat Information Center. She emerged to resume training off the Virginia coast during early 1961.

A sojourn in Kingston, Jamaica, gave the weary crew a chance to relax from the tedious drills. The month of July will be remembered by all who served on the *Randolph*. It was the carrier's first participation in the NASA space program in recovering an astronaut. Virgil Ivan (Gus) Grissom, 35, USAF, blasted off the pad in the Mercury space capsule *Liberty Bell* 7 at 8:20 A.M. EDT, July 21. During his 16-minute flight the *Liberty Bell* 7 soared 118 miles up and touched down in the Atlantic at 8:36. When the capsule hit the water the explosive cord blew off the hatch prematurely. Grissom leaped out and started swimming. A Marine helicopter picked him up, but the space capsule sank. Grissom was flown to the *Randolph* where he talked with President Kennedy via ship-to-shore telephone. The astronaut remained aboard overnight and was transferred to Grand Bahama Island.

After the space recovery the *Randolph* stopped briefly at New York before returning to home port. The remainder of the year was spent in ASW duties along the Atlantic coast.

On February 20, 1962, the carrier stood ready as primary recovery ship for John Glenn's historic space flight. Lieutenant Colonel Glenn, a 40-year-old Marine, became the first American to orbit the earth. His craft, a Mercury capsule named *Friendship* 7, lifted off at 9:47 A.M. EDT on February 20 and Glenn made three orbits before splashdown in the Atlantic off the Bahamas at 2:43 P.M. The destroyer USS *Noa DD-841* retrieved the capsule and placed it on deck. Glenn stepped out and said, "It was hot in there." Later, the astronaut was flown to the *Randolph* by helicopter.

After receiving medical exams, Glenn was flown to Grand Turk Island. Once again the carrier resumed her ASW duties until May, when she took on supplies preparatory to a Mediterranean cruise.

The *Randolph* was again teamed with units of the Sixth Fleet and active in NATO exercises as the flagship of the ASW force in the Atlantic. By the time she returned home in October, a crisis had erupted in Cuba. President Kennedy ordered a naval blockade on

Cape Canaveral, Florida. Astronaut John Glenn transferred from the destroyer *Noa* to the carrier *Randolph*. Glenn receives the plaque of task force Alpha by its commander, Radm. E. R. Eastwold, USN, aboard the *Randolph* (February 20, 1962).

and plunged into the sea. Five sailors, one C2D *Tracker* aircraft, and a tractor were on the elevator. The *USS Holder DD-819* rushed to the scene and promptly rescued three of the men. After a long and extensive search all hope was lost for the other two crewmen.

On August 27 the *Randolph* entered the yard at Norfolk for a major overhaul and all departments received extensive renovating. The carrier also got a fresh coat of paint. Work was completed on January 29, 1965, and the carrier conducted refresher training near Cuba.

On April 12 she resumed her duties as flagship of Task Group Alpha and so continued until October 12, 1966, when she celebrated her 22nd birthday. The various conversion and modernizations to the *Randolph* gave her a longer lifespan than originally predicted. She continues to live up to her "can do" spirit as the top rated antisubmarine warfare support carrier of the Atlantic Fleet.

On June 11, 1965, the *Randolph* left Norfolk for three months of duty with the Sixth Fleet in the Mediterranean. She returned to Norfolk on September 2, 1965, and resumed operations in the waters stretching north to Canada and south along the eastern seaboard into the Caribbean. The *Randolph* continued these operations up to May 16, 1966, then she began a Northern European training cruise which took her to Bergen, Norway; Rotterdam, Holland; Hamburg, Germany; Copenhagen, Denmark; Portsmouth, England; Edinburgh, Scotland; and Belfast, Northern Ireland. On September 2, 1966, the *Randolph* returned to Norfolk.

From October 7 to November 14, she remained in the Boston Naval Shipyard for repairs and upkeep. She returned to Norfolk on November 20, 1966, and took over the duties of the *USS Essex CVS-9* that had been damaged in a collision with the submarine *Nautilus*. With antisubmarine Air Group 54 embarked, the *Randolph* left Norfolk on the 29th and commenced operations off the eastern seaboard. She joined with units of the Second Fleet south of Puerto Rico in a simulated attack that resulted in the ship "sinking" 20 submarines. On her return to Norfolk on December 16, 1966, the *Randolph* took part in an experiment to test the feasibility of landing nonoperational aircraft on carriers at sea. A CH-53A helicopter took off from the Naval Test Center, Patuxent River, Maryland, towing an A4B jet aircraft which landed on the *Randolph's* flight deck at 9:20 A.M. by the towing helicopter. The nonoperational jet was relaunched by helicopter at 9:47 A.M. for towing back for a landing at Naval Air Station Norfolk on the same day.

Upon arrival at Norfolk, the *Randolph* resumed her

Cuba and the *Randolph* operated in Cuban waters until the situation had calmed and all known Soviet weapons removed from the island.

In January 1963 the carrier entered Norfolk Navy Yard for a routine overhaul. In March she conducted refresher training and provided carrier qualifications to new pilots. She also won the coveted Battle Efficiency "E" for the year; engineering also captured their "E" for the sixth consecutive year.

A six-week midshipman cruise began in July during which time the carrier visited St. Thomas, Virgin Isles; Port of Spain, Trinidad; Colon, Panama; and Guantanamo Bay, Cuba.

In September the *Randolph* returned to the Naval Operating Base at Norfolk and operated near the southwest Atlantic course the remainder of the year.

The carrier was back in action during February 1964, assigned to Task Group Alpha for ASW operations. Tragedy struck the *Randolph* on April 1 when her Number Three elevator tore loose from the ship duties as flagship of Task Group Alpha, under the command of Rear Admiral Edward C. Outlaw, Commander Hunter-Killer-Forces, U.S. Atlantic Fleet. The *Randolph* left Norfolk on January 16, 1967, to conduct tests with new detection systems for ASW ships and also on Operational Readiness Instruction (ORI). She returned to Norfolk on January 27. Similar operations were conducted off the Virginia Capes up to September 27th, then the *Randolph* left Norfolk for a three-month cruise to the Mediterranean, returning to Norfolk on December 17, 1967. She immediately entered the Norfolk Naval Shipyard for restricted availability up to the 29th, then resumed operations off the eastern seaboard.

On February 13, 1969, the *Randolph* was decommissioned at the Boston Navy Yard and placed in the New York Annex of the Philadelphia Reserve Fleet.

The *USS Randolph CVS-15* has received the following awards: American Area Campaign Service Medal, the Asiatic-Pacific Area Campaign Service Medal with Three battle stars; the World War Two Victory Medal; the Navy Occupation Service Medal; the National Defense Service Medal; and the Armed Forces Expeditionary Medal.

USS Lexington CVT-16.

16

USS Lexington CVT-16 (CV-16)

On July 15, 1941, the keel of the *USS Cabot CV-16* was laid at the Bethlehem Steel Co., of Quincy, Massachusetts. A month before the ship was to be launched, the *USS Lexington CV-2* was lost following the Battle of the Coral Sea. CV-16 was renamed *Lexington* in honor of her famous predecessor.

Mrs. Theodore D. Robinson, who sponsored the first carrier so named, also christened the new *Lexington* during launching on June 16, 1942.

Capt. Felix B. Stump, USN, assumed command on February 17, 1943, and the new carrier was commissioned.

The *Lexington* departed the Boston Navy Yard on April 14 for shakedown operations off Trinidad, British West Indies, then returned to the Navy Yard on June 8 for post-shakedown alterations and repairs.

On August 9, 1943, she arrived at Pearl Harbor for final preparations before joining the Fast Carrier Force in the Pacific Theater. The *Lexington* presented a unique appearance in as much as she was the only carrier in the Pacific not wearing a camouflage at the time. She was thus nicknamed "The Blue Ghost."

On September 18, 1943, the "Lady Lex" launched her first combat strike during a one-day raid of Tarawa Atoll, then returned to Hawaii for two weeks of training. She resumed action in the Pacific Raids by

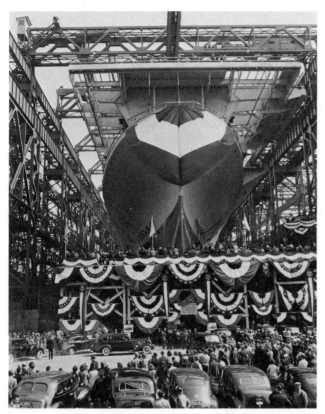

Originally named *USS Cabot*, CV-16 was renamed *Lexington* and launched on June 16, 1942, at the Bethlehem Steel Co of Quincy, Massachusetts five weeks after her predecessor went down after the Battle of the Coral Sea.

The *Lexington*'s air group destroyed 23 enemy aircraft in aerial combat plus three on the ground and damaged two heavy cruisers plus a cargo vessel.

About noon, Japanese torpedo planes attacked the task group. Three were splashed by the *Lexington*'s skillful antiaircraft batteries and the remaining planes were driven away. Just before midnight a second wave of enemy planes began a concentrated run on both sides of the *Lexington*'s bow. A continuous stream of AA fire drove away many of the attackers; however, one "Betty" came in fast off the carrier's starboard side and released its deadly torpedo, which slammed into the *Lexington*. The torpedo hit succeeded in disabling the steering gear and the ship settled five feet by the stern and began to circle to port while dense clouds of smoke erupted from ruptured smoke tanks aft. Two men were killed, seven were missing, and 34 were wounded. The *Lexington* was brought under control by an emergency hand-operated steering unit designed by one of the ship's ingenious officers. The carrier then set a course for Pearl Harbor and arrived December 9, 1943.

Emergency repairs were completed and the *Lexington* returned to the United States for more extensive repairs, arriving at the Puget Sound Naval Shipyard, Bremerton, Wash., on December 22, 1943. The battle-weary crew offered no complaints as shore leave began for the Christmas holidays.

Upon completion of repairs the "Lady Lex" left Puget Sound on February 10, 1944, and arrived at Majuro Atoll on March 8. One month before she returned to the Pacific forward area, the Marshall Islands operation had begun. On March 18, the *Lexington*'s air group hit Mille Atoll, destroying air installations and storage depots in support of this operation. In conjunction with the Asiatic-Pacific Raids of 1944, the *Lex* departed Majuro on March 22 and launched air assaults against enemy shipping in Palau Island on March 30–31. Woleai was hit on April 1, then the carrier returned to Majuro five days later for replenishment. One week later, the task force steamed off Hollandia, Dutch New Guinea, to support the Army landings.

The *Lex* launched her aircraft on April 22 to cover the landing forces and also provide support for the ground forces. The Carrier Task Force operated in the Hollandia area until April 27, then returned to Majuro Atoll on May 6.

The *Lexington*, in company with the *USS Enterprise CV-6* and the *USS San Jacinto CVL-30*, as Task Group 58.3, deployed from Majuro Atoll on June 6, 1944, to commence the Marianas Operation. Air strikes were

striking Wake Island on October 5–6, 1943. Continued emphasis on combat training continued in the Hawaiian area after these raids.

The *Lexington* sailed from Pearl Harbor on November 10, 1943, to begin her first major engagement of the Second World War—The Gilbert Islands operation. The Gilberts were known to be strongly fortified and the primary mission of the Fast Carrier Force was to gain control of the air, thus clearing the way for U.S. Marine landings by destroying military installations and gun emplacements on Mille Atoll in the Marshalls.

A series of destructive strikes against Mille Atoll were made from November 19–24, destroying 17 of 20 enemy fighters. The pilots of Air Group Sixteen flew combat air patrols between the Marshall and Gilbert Islands and intercepted Japanese aircraft cruising to attack our landing forces on Tarawa and Makin.

Air strikes were launched against Kwajalein and Roi on December 4, 1943. These raids insured further protection to the Gilberts and also provided a damaging stab at the Marshalls defense setup.

launched on June 11 against airfields and shipping at Saipan. The Allied Forces landed on June 15 and the carrier's air group supported the amphibious landings and destroyed shore defenses and gun emplacements. The Task Group was under heavy attack by late afternoon.

Ten multi-engine Japanese aircraft approached the *Lexington* dead ahead on the port bow. Half of the enemy planes were downed and the remainder scattered to safety. Torpedo wakes were seen—two within ten yards of the carrier—but fortunately no contact was made.

The *Lex* joined other Fast Carriers to locate a reported enemy fleet on June 18; however, the fleet was not found until the following morning. The air groups engaged in combat with enemy planes over the Phillipine Sea. Many old-timers refer to the first-day Battle of the Phillipine Sea (June 19–20, 1944) as the "Marianas Turkey Shoot."

Air Group 16 of the *Lex* destroyed 45 planes from a total of 392. CDR. Paul D. Buie of the *Lex*'s VF-16 was credited by RADM Samuel Eliot Morison in his "History of United States Naval Operations in WW II," as the originator of the battle's famous nickname.

The enemy fleet was located on June 20 and air strikes were launched immediately. The Japanese warships were 300 miles from our carriers, however, this extreme range did not prevent them from assaulting the enemy task force which reportedly contained aircraft carriers.

Air Group 16 scored direct hits on two carriers and several escort destroyers. By the time the carrier air groups had returned to the vicinity of their ships, many were heavily damaged or extremely low on fuel. The exhausted pilots decided to set down on the first carrier they spotted. Several damaged planes splashed into the sea and the pilots were picked up by nearby destroyers.

The Task Force steamed toward the enemy fleet on June 21 but was unable to make contact by that evening and reversed course to resume air attacks against the Marianas.

Aerial sorties against Guam began on July 17 in support of the capture and occupation of that island. Primary targets were gun emplacements along the island's southern landing beaches. During the period July 25–27, the Fast Carrier Force hit Palau, Yap, and Ulithi in the Western Carolines chain. A two-day strike in the Bonin's on August 4–5, 1944, ended the *Lexington*'s Marianas campaign and the carrier retired at Eniwetok for rest and replenishment on August 9, 1944.

On September 6, the Fast Carriers of Task Force 58 began a three-day strike against Yap and Ulithi in another support of the Western Caroline Islands operation. Daily combat sorties continued until October 14 when the Carolines were captured.

The *Lexington*'s air group participated in air assaults against Mindanao and the Visayans on September 21 to soften up the Philippines for future landings on Leyte. Shipping in Manila harbor and along the west coast of Luzon was heavily damaged. On September 27, the *Lex* steamed into the recently captured Ulithi Atoll in the Western Carolines for rest and replenishment.

The task force put to sea on October 6, 1944, to resume air attacks against the Philippines and Okinawa. Four days after leaving Ulithi Atoll, the Fast Carrier Force launched air strikes on Okinawa where tremendous damage was inflicted. Formosa was hit on October 12 and enemy shipping and shore facilities suffered a three-day period of destruction. The Japanese launched concentrated air opposition against the task group but the mighty *Lexington* came through without even a scratch on her paint. Her antiaircraft crews destroyed three enemy aircraft and assisted in downing two others on October 14, 1944.

The *Lexington* joined other carriers in air strikes on the Philippines on October 21. Enemy airfields on Luzon were hit hard. A massive wave of Japanese planes attacked the task force on October 24. Many of the offenders were repelled or downed without serious damage to our vessels. One determined enemy pilot made it through the thick AA fire to score a direct hit

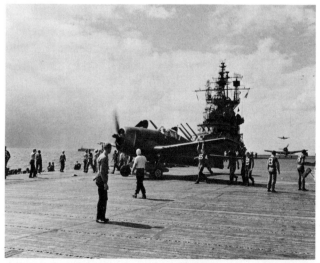

Fighter aircraft are launched on October 12, 1944, during the Northern Luzon and Formosa attacks.

on the *USS Princeton CVL-23*. Another enemy force had been sighted in the Sibuyan Sea and the carriers launched all available planes to converge on the Japanese fleet.

Air Group 16 assisted in sinking the battleship *Musashi* and scored hits on three enemy cruisers. The Japanese began a three-pronged attack as a last chance to destroy the U.S. Fleet off Leyte Gulf.

A scout plane from the *USS Essex CV-9* sighted the enemy carriers on October 25 and the *Lex* joined the *Essex* in strikes against the carriers *Chitose, Zuikako,* and *Zuiho.* One hour after launching, the carrier air groups threw all they could in a furious battle. The *Chitose* exploded and sank from direct bomb and torpedo hits. A second strike group began attacks on escort ships. The *Lexington's* air group concentrated on the *Zuikako,* and following a series of bomb and torpedo attacks the enemy carrier went on its final cruise—to the bottom of the ocean. With fighter aircraft assistance from the *Essex,* the *Zuiho* met the same fate.

A two-day strike against the Visayans was conducted on October 26–27, after which the Task Force sailed for Ulithi Atoll.

Mog Mog, a now-obscure name as are thousands of other small islands in the Pacific, was a haven for fighting sailors of the Task Force. It is the largest island in the Ulithi Atoll and became a scene of bustling activity during the war years. Many a baseball game was played under the simmering sun and "old salts" of the Third and Fifth Fleets still argue who were the *real* baseball kings. Beer flowed like water down the partched throats of weary sailors and partially removed the thoughts of what lay ahead and the memory of shipmates no longer with them.

Ulithi was the spring board for the Navy during the final campaigns of the war. It was here that battle-damaged ships received vital repairs following combat action.

On November 5, 1944, the *Lexington* was in the Philippines bombing Luzon airfields and shipping in Manila harbor.

The heavy Japanese cruiser *Nachi* received four torpedo hits, which disintegrated the stern and bow. A group of enemy planes evaded the combat air patrols by hiding in heavy clouds to strike the Task Force. At 1:38 P.M. a lone enemy pilot was splashed a thousand yards off the *Lexington's* starboard beam. Another determined Japanese flyer began a suicide dive for the carrier, and despite being hit several times was able to drop his bomb before crashing into the ship's island structure. The signal bridge received serious damage and several gun emplacements became nullified.

Forty-seven men were killed and 127 wounded. Within twenty minutes, all fires were under control and flight operations resumed. Air Group 16 hit Luzon on November 6, then the *Lex* returned to Ulithi three days later for repairs.

The *Lexington* sailed from Ulithi on December 11 to continue air strikes in the Philippine area. Luzon was hit December 14–16, resulting in considerable damage to ground installations. Additional sorties were cancelled when Nature attacked the Task Force in the form of a typhoon. The *Lex* received minor damage from dangerous seas and returned to Ulithi on Christmas Eve for the holidays.

The carrier began the New Year by sailing on January 3, 1945 from Ulithi for the Philippines to lend support to the Luzon operation. Formosa and Luzon were under attack January 3–8. On the 9th, the Task Force shifted into the South China Sea and began a series of strikes in Cam Ranh Bay, Saigon; Hong Kong, and the Pescadores. Fifteen enemy ships were hit at Cam Ranh Bay on January 12 and Air Group 16 assisted in sinking two of them. Only three enemy vessels escaped damage.

A one-day assault on Formosa and Okinawa was accomplished on January 20, after which the Fast Carrier Force retired to Ulithi seven days later.

As the flagship of Task Group 58.2 (Rear Admiral R. E. Davison commanding) the *Lexington* left Ulithi on February 10, 1945, to support the capture and occupation of Iwo Jima. Air strikes were directed against enemy aircraft defense plants in Tokyo February 16–17 and close ground support was provided during the actual landings on Iwo Jima two days later. These missions continued until February 22 when the Fast Carrier Force resumed sorties against the Japanese homeland. The Task Force then reappeared at Ulithi for repairs.

On March 7, the *Lexington* departed with orders to proceed to the Puget Sound Naval Shipyard, Bremerton, Washington, for an essential overhaul.

The yard period began on March 27 and on May 22, 1945, the *Lex* sailed away to receive her air group, then headed for Pearl Harbor for additional supplies.

On June 13, the *Lexington,* along with the *USS Hancock CV-19* and the *USS Cowpens CVL-24,* departed Pearl, bound for the Philippines.

Thirteen days later the trio arrived in San Pedro Bay, Leyte, where training operations began. The *Lex* joined other flat-tops of the Third Fleet for air assaults against Japan from July 10 to August 15, 1945. Her

Landing Signal Officer Lt (jg) J. W. Shuff waves an F6F "Hellcat" in on the *Lexington* following an air strike on the Philippines in December 1944.

air group was in the process of striking the Honshu area on August 15 when word was received to cease offensive operations.

The pilots jettisoned their bombs and returned to the ships. The last targets hit by the *Lex*'s air group were Honshu, Hokkaido, the Yokosuka and Kure Naval Bases, and industrial sites in the Tokyo area.

Air Group 16 flew combat patrols over Hokkaido, Northern and Central Honshu, and Tokyo immediately following the Japanese surrender in the event some units would not comply with the surrender terms.

Medical supplies, food, and clothing were parachuted over allied prisoner of war camps, and on August 29 patrols were airborne to protect the entrance of the U.S. Fleet into Sagami Wan and Tokyo

Bays. With only one brief replenishment period at Eniwetok from September 27 to October 7, the *Lexington* continued support operations in the Occupation of Japan until December 3, 1945. On that day, veteran troops were embarked and the *Lex* departed Tokyo Bay and arrived at the San Francisco Naval Shipyard on December 15, 1945.

The USS *Lexington CV-16* and her Air Group were awarded the Presidential Unit Citation which read: "For outstanding heroism in action against the enemy Japanese forces in the air, ashore, and afloat in the Pacific War Area from September 18, 1943, to January 22, 1945. Operating in the most forward areas, the USS *Lexington* and her air group struck crushing blows toward annihilating Japanese fighting power;

An SB2C "Helldiver" is catapulted from the *Lexington* while
other aircraft are being readied to go into action over
Formosa on January 25, 1945.

they provided air cover for our amphibious forces;
they fiercely countered the enemy's aerial attacks and
destroyed his planes; and they inflicted terrific losses
on the Japanese in Fleet and Merchant Marine units
sunk or damaged. Daring and dependable in combat,
the *Lexington* with her gallant officers and enlisted
men rendered loyal service in achieving the ultimate
defeat of the Japanese Empire."

The *Lexington* arrived at Seattle on May 23, 1946,
to await deactivation.

On April 23, 1947, she was decommissioned and
joined the Bremerton Group of the Pacific Reserve
Fleet at Puget Sound Naval Shipyard. While in mothballs, the *Lexington* was redesignated CVA effective
October 1, 1952. On September 1, 1953, she was in

drydock for a major conversion. An angle deck and enclosed hurricane bow were installed; her island structure was streamlined and the flight deck was strengthened. The massive job took one month short of two
years to complete and on August 15, 1955, the USS
Lexington CVA-16 was recommissioned.

Capt. A. S. Heyward, Jr., USN, assumed command
and a shakedown operation began off the coast of
Southern California. On January 29, 1956, the *Lex*
returned to the yards for post-shakedown alterations
and overhaul. She was now prepared to take her part
as an attack carrier of the Pacific Fleet.

In early March, the *Lexington* arrived at her new
home port of North Island Naval Air Station, San
Diego, California.

The "Blue Ghosts" Battle Scoreboard updated to March 18, 1945.

Training operations were conducted near the San Diego coast until May 28, 1956, after which the *Lexington* deployed on a tour of duty with the Seventh Fleet in the Far East. Her overseas homeport was Yokosuka, Japan. Ports of call were Buckner Bay, Okinawa; Subic Bay, Philippines; Hong Kong, B.C.; and Kobe, Japan.

On December 6, 1956, the *Lex* departed Yokosuka and sailed into San Diego two weeks later.

The first three months of 1957 found the *Lexington* on training exercises and battle drills off the San Diego coast. Simulated attacks were staged as part of the program to maintain the carrier's attack readiness.

On April 19, the *Lex* sailed from San Diego for her second Western Pacific cruise since recommissioning.

A three-week Operational Readiness Instruction (ORI) was held in the ship for duty with the Seventh Fleet. On June 1, the *Lexington* arrived at the Naval Shipyard, Yokosuka, Japan and tied up alongside Piedmont Pier. Rear Admiral H. D. Riley, USN, Commander, Carrier Division One, came aboard for the duration of the cruise. Training and evaluation programs were conducted near Japan, Guam, and the China coast with other crack units of the Seventh Fleet. A rest and relaxation call was taken at Hong Kong, after which the carrier returned to Yokosuka for supplies before sailing for the U.S.

The *Lex* departed Yokosuka on October 8, 1957, and pulled up aside Quay Wall, North Island Naval Air Station in San Diego nine days later. She was moved to Puget Sound Naval Shipyard in November to undergo a routine overhaul. Work was completed on March 26, 1958; then she returned to San Diego for additional training and carrier qualifications for various air groups. The training schedule was shortened due to the Lebanon crisis. Hence, on July 14 the carrier arrived at Alameda Naval Air Station to embark Air Group 21 and also received orders to join the Seventh Fleet off Taiwan.

Taiwan was the principal location of the *Lexington* during this Far East deployment. The carrier made short visits to Yokosuka, Japan; Subic Bay, Philippines; Okinawa and Guam. On December 3, 1958, she left Subic Bay and returned to her home port in San Diego, arriving 16 days later.

The *Lex* operated periodically with the First Fleet off California and the Seventh Fleet in the Western Pacific throughout 1959 and 1960.

While working with the Seventh Fleet, the carrier visited Yokosuka, Iwakuni, and Sasebo, Japan; Hong Kong, B.C.; Manila and Subic Bay, Philippines; and Buckner Bay, Okinawa.

As several hostile outbreaks erupted on Formosa when the Chinese Communists threatened the offshore islands and in the Laos crisis of 1960–61, the *Lexington* stood poised and ready in case world peace was threatened.

While in the United States, the *Lex* conducted training and carrier qualifications off the Southern California coastline.

On July 23, 1962, the *Lexington* received orders to report to the Atlantic Fleet to relieve the *USS Antietam CVS-36* as the Navy training carrier. En route, she conducted flight operations while rounding Cape Horn. It is believed that this was the first time a carrier performed flight ops in this area.

Upon arrival at the New York Naval Shipyard, the *Lexington* underwent a brief repair period. She was redesignated CVS-16 (anti-submarine support carrier) on October 1. The *Lex* was scheduled to arrive at Pensacola, Florida, by late November, but an unexpected outburst in Cuba changed her schedule. President Kennedy announced a blockade of Cuba and the *Lexington* left the yards despite two weeks of unfinished work.

With ammunition loaded at Norfolk and an air group on board, she operated in the Jacksonville area awaiting any sudden orders. After tension had diminished, the *Lex* sailed into Pensacola in December.

With the exception of a six-month overhaul at the New York Naval Shipyard (October 1964–March 1965) the *Lexington* operated exclusively off the Florida coast in the capacity of Naval training carrier. Her primary mission was to qualify Navy and Marine Corps pilots in carrier air operations. Pilots from Pensacola and Corpus Christi reported to the ship for extensive training. During these operations, as many as 500 carrier landings and takeoffs were recorded in a single day.

One week of each month the *Lexington* conducted refresher training for fleet squadrons. This program is called "Fleet Week" and breaks the monotony of daily routine as various fleet type aircraft are used rather than the normal student trainers.

The high priority of the *Lexington's* mission is understood as world problems have increased. More than 2000 pilots per year are qualified and since her December 1962 appearance in Pensacola, over 45,000 arrested gear landings have been logged, bringing the carrier's total landings closer to 150,000.

The daily training of student pilots is thorough. While at Pensacola, the student fliers learn to operate strikes from a floating mobile force (the carrier) and then return according to a prearranged location. The arrested landings conducted aboard the *Lexington* are the final examinations of the course.

The *Lexington* also provides relief duty during Florida hurricanes. In this role, food and medical supplies are delivered to disaster areas.

The "*Lady Lex*" fought for peace during the Second World War, and in recent years has stood by off Formosa, Laos, and Cuba. Though the *Lexington* is now a training carrier, she remains in a high state of combat readiness, able to move into a trouble spot should the occasion present itself.

On July 1, 1969, the *Lexington* was officially designated CVT-16, Navy Training Carrier.

The *Lexington CVT-16* has received the following awards during her naval service: The Presidential Unit Citation; The American Area Service Medal; The Asiatic-Pacific Area Campaign Service Medal with eleven battle stars; The World War II Victory Medal; Navy Occupation Service Medal; National Defense Service Medal; The Armed Forces Expeditionary Service Medal; Philippine Liberation Campaign Ribbon with two stars; The Republic of the Philippines Presidential Unit Citation Badge.

The *Bunker Hill* underway July 5, 1943.

17

USS Bunker Hill AVT-9 (CV-17)

Less than three months before the Japanese devastated Pearl Harbor, on September 15, 1941, the keel was laid for the construction of the *USS Bunker Hill CV-17*. Secretary of the Navy Frank Knox appointed Mrs. Donald Boynton of Highland Park, Illinois, to sponsor the ship. She christened the new carrier on December 7, 1942 at the Bethlehem Steel Company of Quincy, Massachusetts. On May 24, 1943, the *Bunker Hill* was placed in commission with Captain John J. Ballentine in command.

The war was two years old, and the *Bunker Hill* was ready to play her role in the tragic drama taking place in the Pacific area. She would leave an impressive record before the final curtain came down.

In August 1943 the *Bunker Hill* arrived in the Pacific Forward Area and joined Task Group 50.3; her

air group was launched on November 1, 1943, for their first combat strikes. The target was Rabaul. These strikes aided immensely in decreasing surface resistance to the U.S. assault forces in the Northern Solomons, New Guinea, and the Gilbert Islands. Heavy damage was inflicted and the pilots were credited with downing 50 enemy planes.

The capture of Tarawa was necessary, as the U.S. needed the island as a stepping stone for the forthcoming assaults on the Japanese homelands. The *Bunker Hill*'s air group participated in air strikes over this tiny isle in an attempt to lure the Japanese fleet from their stronghold—Truk, in the Carolines—in addition to preinvasion strafing.

Attacking at dawn on November 19, 1943, the island's gun emplacements, dugouts, and shore installations took a heavy pounding. Airfields were completely destroyed along with all aircraft. The U.S. Marines landed the following day and encountered a vicious enemy, for the Japanese were determined to keep the island under their control. The *Bunker Hill* remained in the Tarawa area until December, when the island was converted into an American base.

On Christmas Day 1943, the *Bunker Hill* conducted air strikes against Kavieng on the northern tip of New Ireland with the prime targets being harbor shipping. Enemy aircraft attacked the task force, but failed to do any damage. The task force was halfway back to base when word was received that a new enemy shipping had arrived at Kavieng Harbor. A second strike was launched on January 1, 1944. Although enemy air opposition was strong, it was not effective. Two cruisers and one destroyer were about to enter the harbor when the American planes began the attack. Both cruisers were abandoned and burning, while the destroyer was severely damaged from bomb and torpedo attacks.

The next target for the *Bunker Hill* was the Marshall Islands. The U.S. needed bases on the Marshalls to prepare for the forthcoming assaults on the Marianas. On January 29, the strikes began with the *Bunker Hill* pilots bombing Kwajalein and Ebeye Islands of the Kwajalein Atoll. Enemy bombers on the runways were obliterated.

Captain Thomas J. Jeter, USN, relieved Captain Ballentine as commanding officer in February, 1944.

On February 17, the *Bunker Hill* launched air attacks that smashed shore installations and sunk ships that crowded the lagoon of Truk in the Carolines. The surprise attack was so efficient that many enemy ships, like the cruiser *Naka,* were sent to the bottom by the *Bunker Hill's* Torpedo Squadron 17. Surface resistance from Truk was thus eliminated but raids on the Island continued until the following day. By this time, all targets had been reduced to rubble.

After a short stay at the Marshalls, the carrier proceeded to Pearl Harbor where she remained until late March. During the Hawaiian stay, the ship's Air Group 17 was relieved by Air Group 8.

Back in action again, the *Bunker Hill* penetrated deeper into Japanese-held waters than ever before. The targets were enemy installations on Palau, the westernmost island of the Carolines, east of Mindanao. The attack lasted two days and six cargo ships were sunk along with a list of many more probable sinkings, plus severe damage to the remaining vessels. During the fast carrier strikes on Palau, Hollandia, and Truk, from March 22 to April 30, Air Group 8

was given an unusual operation. The pilots were ordered to mine the two passageways in the main harbor of Palau. Those who flew this mission called themselves the "Flying Miners," and their emblem was a crossed shovel and pickaxe.

Admiral Frederick C. Sherman and his Flag came aboard and the ship prepared for the upcoming Marianas invasion. This island would provide an easy strike range at the Japanese homeland. Prior to the landing on June 15, 1944, the carrier conducted highly successful attacks leaving 200 enemy planes destroyed or down, and all island runways useless.

When the landing operations were in full swing, a Japanese fleet was located 750 miles from the task force. General Quarters was sounded and the carriers tensely waited for an enemy air attack. Two Japanese bombers attacked the *Bunker Hill,* but fell to this ship's AA fire. The planes had time to drop their bombs but they missed the ship. Explosions nearby in the water caused slight damage and shrapnel flew everywhere, killing two men and wounding 80.

Following the climax of the Battle of the Philippine Sea, a night recovery had to be made. With the night pitch black, Admiral Marc Mitscher made his famous decision to "light ships," so that the returning aircraft could spot the carriers. Many were badly damaged and all were low on gas. The pilots landed on the first available carrier spotted.

A Helldiver from the *USS Hornet CV-12* landed on the *Bunker Hill* despite a waveoff from the landing signal officer, who had indicated the deck was foul. The plane smashed into the deck and lodged its propeller. Moments later an Avenger pilot from the *USS Cabot CVL-28,* tried to land. He was also waved off. The plane careened into the deck and sheared off a wing on one of the gunmounts, then smashed into the stricken Helldiver. The *Bunker Hill's* air officer and four other men were killed while attempting to clear wreckage from the flight deck.

There was much confusion, and many of the planes ran out of fuel and ditched before they were ready to land. Destroyers picked up the men from the cold waters.

Steaming with other carriers of the mighty Third Fleet, the *Bunker Hill* returned to Palau to soften up the islands prior to an invasion. On September 9, assaults on the Philippines resumed when the air groups hit Mindanao. Three days later, shipping off Samar was hit. Two large cargo ships were hit and sunk. In addition, five were heavily damaged. Legaspi, Cebu, Alicante, and Fabric were hit the next day and ground installations took a terrific beating. Primary targets were ammunition and fuel dumps, hangars and barracks. Manila came under attack on September 21 and the enemy was caught completely surprised. Two cargo ships were sunk and assaults against the Philippines were concluded on September 24, 1944.

The task force anchored at Ulithi on November 6 but the *Bunker Hill* headed for the states to undergo a yard overhaul at the Puget Sound Navy Shipyard, Bremerton, Washington. Two months later, the *Bunker Hill* arrived at the Alameda Naval Air Station, took on aircraft, and then rejoined the fleet at Ulithi.

On February 10, 1945, the *Bunker Hill* joined with other carriers to begin the first air attacks on Japan proper. Tokyo was hit. Air action began for the *Bunker Hill* on the 16th, with four fighter sweeps that left hangars and installations ravished, including the Ota aircraft factory. Bad weather cancelled air missions for the 17th, but the next day, the pilots were again airborne and pounded Iwo Jima in support of the pre-invasion action.

The *Bunker Hill* refueled on February 20, then steamed to the Tokyo area for further attacks on Japan. Another bad day of weather hampered the air operations so the ships headed for Okinawa to fly photo reconnaissance missions.

April Fools Day 1945, was the day that the Marines landed on Okinawa. An enemy task force was dispatched to intercept and hit American shipping off Okinawa and on April 17, the Japanese received one of the most devastating blows. Fighters and torpedo

The *Bunker Hill* just after being hit by two Kamikaze planes only 30 seconds apart. The deck begins to smoke and flames billow up behind the island structure on May 11, 1945.

Bomb damage sustained on the flight deck as viewed
from the signal bridge on May 11, 1945.

bombers from the U.S. carriers located the enemy fleet and began to bomb the force. The battleship *Yamato*, the cruiser *Yahagi*, and nine destroyers were sunk. Air Group fighters from the *Bunker Hill* scored six direct hits with bombs and torpedoes on the *Yamato* and then sank a destroyer.

On May 11, 1945, the *Bunker Hill* met with a fate similar to that of the *USS Franklin CV-13*. A Japanese aircraft swooped in and released a 500-pound bomb on the *Bunker Hill*'s flight deck, aft of the number three elevator. Fires instantly erupted as the enemy plane crashed into parked aircraft. The bomb went through the flight deck into the topside gallery deck and exploded. About this same time, a second enemy plane smashed into the flight deck and spread fires throughout access passages and ladders of the ship's island structure. Three officers and eleven men of the Admiral's staff were killed. The Admiral's staff was trans-

ferred to the *USS Enterprise CV-6* and the *USS English DD-696*.

Smoke and fire curled from stem to stern and the dense smoke and flames leaped downward into three decks of the smoldering ship. In a situation such as this, the fire fighting training that every sailor had taken for granted was valuable knowledge which helped the men same their stricken ship . . . and their lives.

When the fires were finally extinguished and normal ship routine resumed, the disaster tally read 346 men killed, 43 missing, and 246 wounded. The *USS Wilkes Barre CL-103* came alongside the carrier to remove the wounded men. Although the *Bunker Hill* was severely damaged, she was able to steam for Pearl Harbor and then on to Puget Sound Naval Shipyard.

During June and July 1945, the *Bunker Hill* underwent extensive repairs. Upon leaving the yards, the carrier steamed to Alameda where aircraft were re-loaded. Then she departed for the Pacific war zone. But Japan surrendered before the carrier had arrived in the forward area.

As men reflected back to the combat days, they recalled that all of the carrier's major strikes had been conducted on a holiday, so the *Bunker Hill* was nick-named "Holiday Express." She raided New Britain on Armistice Day 1943; attacked Tarawa and nearby islands on Thanksgiving Day 1943; attacked Kavieng, New Ireland, on Christmas Day 1943; attacked the Marshalls on President Roosevelt's birthday—January 30, 1944; hit the Marianas on George Washington's birthday, 1944; conducted air strikes against Woleai in the Carolines on April Fools Day, 1944; struck Formosa on Columbus Day 1944; made assaults on Leyte on Armistice Day 1944; and participated in raids on Okinawa on April Fools Day and Easter Sunday 1945!

A proud day for the *Bunker Hill* was June 30, 1946, when she was awarded the Presidential Unit Citation for "Extraordinary heroism in action against enemy Japanese forces in the air, shore, and afloat in South-central, Southwest, and Western Pacific from November 11, 1943 to May 11, 1945. Spearheading our concentrated carrier warfare in the most forward areas, the *Bunker Hill* and her air groups struck crushing blows towards annihilating Japanese fighting power; they provided air cover for our amphibious forces; they fiercely countered the enemy aerial attacks and destroyed his planes; and inflicted terrific losses on the Japanese fleet, and merchant marine units. Daring and dependable in combat, the *Bunker Hill* with her gal-

Destroyed aircraft in the *Bunker Hill's* hangar deck.

lant officers and men rendered loyal service in achieving the ultimate defeat of the Japanese Empire."

The *Bunker Hill* established a combat record that still remains one of the top carrier scores with 430 enemy planes destroyed in the air; 230 enemy planes destroyed on the ground; 146,803 tons of enemy shipping sent to the bottom; and 20 enemy planes shot down by the carrier's antiaircraft batteries.

In January 1947, the *Bunker Hill* was decommissioned in the Bremerton Group of the Pacific Reserve Fleet at the Puget Sound Naval Shipyard. On May 15, 1952, the carrier received a new classification—Auxiliary Aircraft Transport AVT-9. She has never seen service in this capacity and remained in the mothball fleet for 18 years.

The *Bunker Hill* was detached from the Bremerton Reserve Group and arrived at the San Francisco Naval Shipyard on May 15, 1965. Here the old warrior was fitted out for her future assignment as a test ship for the Naval Electronics Laboratory in San Diego. The *Bunker Hill* left San Francisco on December 2, 1965.

On November 1, 1966, 23 years to the day that she launched her first combat strikes, the *Bunker Hill* was stricken from the list of Naval vessels and declared unfit for further service. Now referred to as the *ex-USS Bunker Hill*, she acts as a test ship for research, development, and engineering programs. Certain spaces and machinery have been activated to accommodate these programs but the ship is unable to get underway.

The nation has all but forgotten the *Bunker Hill*, but every year former crew members hold a reunion and discuss the ship's great moments in the Second World War.

A closer look at the *Bunker Hill's* flight deck following the bomb and Kamikaze hit of May 11, 1945.

Destroyed aircraft in the *Bunker Hill*'s hangar deck, May 11, 1945.

The *USS Bunker Hill AVT-9* received the following awards during her three years and seven months of active service: The Presidential Unit Citation; the American Area Campaign Service Medal; the Asiatic-Pacific Area Campaign Service Medal with eleven battle stars; the World War Two Victory Medal; the Philippine Liberation Campaign Ribbon; and the Republic of the Philippines Presidential Unit Citation Badge.

Aerial oblique stern view of the *USS Wasp CV-18* in April 1944.

18

USS Wasp CVS-18 (CV-18)

On March 18, 1942 the keel of the *USS Oriskany CV-18* was laid at the Bethlehem Shipbuilding Company at Quincy, Massachusetts. On November 13 the name was changed to *Wasp,* to honor the previous ship of that name, which was lost south of the Solo-mons on September 15, 1942. That gallant vessel had been torpedoed by the enemy submarine *IJN-I-19* and so severely damaged that is was finally sunk by the American destroyer *USS Lansdowne DD-486.*

Miss Julia M. Walsh, sister of Senator Davis I.

Walsh of Massachusetts, christened the new carrier on August 17, 1943. Captain Clifton A. F. Sprague took command on November 23 and the *USS Wasp CV-18* was placed in commission.

At that time the *Wasp* had an overall length of 872 feet, an extreme beam of 147 feet 6 inches, a full load displacement of 36,380 tons, and a maximum draft of 27 feet 7 inches. She could accommodate 360 officers and 3088 enlisted men. Her armament consisted of a dozen 5-inch 38-caliber guns and seventeen 40mm quadruple antiaircraft mounts. She was built at a cost of $40,009,400.

The *Wasp* wasted no time in preparing for her future task in the Pacific War Zone. A shakedown cruise was conducted between Norfolk and the British West Indies.

On February 27, 1944, she was ready to participate in the war in the Pacific. After transiting the Panama Canal she arrived at Pearl Harbor for a brief training period, then proceeded to the forward area.

Her first strikes were launched on May 19–20 with a raid on the Marcus Islands, followed by an attack on Wake Island.

Air Group 14 of the *Wasp* was active during the capture, occupation, and defense of Saipan, Tinian, and Guam June 7–24. The air group flew 220 miles to attack a Japanese force consisting of three aircraft carriers, two battleships, two escort carriers, and two light cruisers. After the attack many of the planes were low on fuel and some were damaged. Due to a miscalculation in navigation the distance back to the carrier was greater than the pilots thought. They were forced to land in the water or on the decks of other carriers. As it turned out, fifteen of the *Wasp's* planes landed on other carriers and nine planes from other carriers landed on the *Wasp.*

Throughout September the *Wasp* participated in action against the Philippines. Her air group struck Mindanao, Viscoyas, Luzon, Manila, Gebu, Negros, Panay, Morotai, and the Celebes. Many times the *Wasp* planes were attacked by enemy aircraft.

The carrier's mission was explicit: "assist in gaining control of the air and maintain it; destroy enemy aircraft in the areas of Palau, Mindanao, Palmas, Talaud, and Morotai; destroy enemy surface vessels, air facilities, coastal defense guns, antiaircraft batteries; provide tactical air support of amphibious forces and furnish protection for U.S. surface forces."

In October the action shifted to Luzon, Formosa, and Okinawa. To illuminate their targets the enemy dropped flares around ships of the task force. On one such occasion the *Wasp* gunners downed several en-

emy planes. After a raid on the Naha, Okinawa, airfield on October 10, the *Wasp's* air group returned, leaving the target a shambles with curling black smoke ascending.

Air Group 81 relieved Air Group 14 in November and their first strikes were concentrated in the Luzon area and Lingayen Gulf. Action continued to December in this region, then the carrier returned to Ulithi.

On January 3, 1945, she sailed again, this time with Task Group 38.1 to raid Formosa. Two days later the *Wasp* was off the Philippines once more striking Luzon. A short layover was made at Hong Kong when a violent typhoon lashed the fleet.

In February, the *Wasp's* sting was felt by the enemy when carrier based raids were launched at the Tokyo area with attacks on Honshu and Nansei Shoto on the 15th, 16th, and 25th. The air group next attacked Hachijo Jima, Chi Chi Jima, Iwo Jima, Ha Ha Jima, Okinawa, and Miyako Jima. During one of the Yokohama strikes the pilots encountered a medium-sized Japanese aircraft carrier. When the attack was over, the flat-top was seen to roll slowly over and slide under the water.

Bad weather hindered the task group and many scheduled strikes were aborted for a while.

As the curtains of war were slowly coming down, the *Wasp* was prepared to ram her fist into the enemy's face. Strikes would smash her homeland, destroy her airplanes and facilities. When General Quarters was sounded at 8:00 A.M., of the initial strike day, the *Wasp* was less than 100 miles from Honshu. On February 22 the air group supported ground troops at Iwo Jima and Air Group 86 reported aboard to assist in this final effort.

The *Wasp* received her first battle damage on March 19 when a bomb was released from a Japanese plane. It penetrated the flight deck and exploded in the hangar deck. The blast killed 102 sailors and caused considerable damage, but the carrier was launching aircraft in less than 60 minutes.

The weeks that followed proved to be the most active for the ship. In seven days she had destroyed 14 aircraft in the air plus six on the ground; scored two hits with 500-pound bombs on two enemy carriers; dropped two 1000-pound bombs on a battleship while under constant enemy attack. In addition to the combat sorties, the *Wasp* sent out combat air patrols, antisubmarine patrols, and recon patrols.

In April the *Wasp* returned to Puget Sound for extensive repairs. Afterwards, a new crew reported aboard and she returned to the Pacific fighting area via Hawaii, arriving on July 12. Six days later a strike

Aerial view of the *USS Wasp* underway, August 6, 1945.

was launched against Wake Island.

From July 26 to August 15 the *Wasp* was engaged in Third Fleet operations against Japan proper. Nearly all the strikes were accomplished with the absence of enemy air power. On August 9 a Kamikaze dived towards the *Wasp*, but an alert pilot from the carrier spotted the intruder and poured a stream of lead into its starboard wing. The enemy plane exploded and plunged into the sea near the carrier.

After the fighting was over, on August 15 two Japanese began a run at the *Wasp*. The carrier's planes were still maintaining combat air patrols and shot the would-be attackers.

The *Wasp* was caught in a typhoon shortly afterwards and 30 feet of her bow was pushed in by the storm's violence. Despite this severe damage, pilots flew off the shortened deck to conduct mercy patrols to American prisoners of war at Narumi, near Nagoya. The prisoners knew and appreciated the effort put forth by the *Wasp* in delivering food, clothing, and medicine, and on the roof of one of the tiny huts they had written: "Men of Bataan and Corregidor—thank *Wasp*."

The *Wasp* sailed into Boston Navy Yard on October 27 where open house was held on Navy Day.

By November 15, the *Wasp* had been fitted out for "Magic Carpet" duty. Her officer complement was reduced from 162 to 92 and the number of enlisted men dropped from 2469 to 1532. Much of the ship's fighting equipment was removed to facilitate her new transport duties. After helping to return American soldiers to the States, the *Wasp* was deactivated and placed out of commission in the U.S. Atlantic Reserve Fleet on February 17, 1947.

In the summer of 1948 the *Wasp* was moved to the New York Naval Shipyard for a three-year major conversion. Her flight deck was strengthened to handle jets. Her 5-inch, 38-caliber gun turrets were removed and her island structure was streamlined. New arresting gear equipment and catapults were installed and on September 10, 1951 the carrier was recommissioned with Captain Burnham C. MaCaffree in command.

Following a shakedown cruise to evaluate her new equipment, the *Wasp* returned to the yards for alterations.

While en route to Gibraltar on April 26, 1952, she collided with the destroyer-minesweeper *USS Hobson DMS-26*. This happened during night flying operations and 52 of the *Hobson's* men were picked up by the carrier. The *Hobson* had been split in two by the carrier's bow and sank rapidly. The *Wasp* returned to New York, then entered drydock at Bayonne, New Jersey, and the bow section of the decommissioned *USS Hornet CV-12* was grafted onto the *Wasp*.

On June 2, the *Wasp* relieved the *USS Tarawa CV-40* at Gibraltar and began duties as a member of Carrier Division Six. Various fleet training exercises were held and many ports were visited.

The *Wasp* was relieved by the *USS Leyte CV-32* on September 2 and departed the next day for Greenock, Scotland. Throughout the month the *Wasp* participated in the NATO "Operation Mainbrace" along with Task Force 175. After a visit to Portsmouth, England she sailed to Norfolk on October 13.

A seven-month overhaul began on November 7 and upon its completion in June 1953 she conducted a refresher training cruise to Guantanamo Bay, Cuba and Port-au-Prince, Haiti.

The *Wasp* departed Norfolk on September 16 for an around-the-world cruise that would take seven and one-half months. On the first leg she participated in NATO "Operation Mariner" in the North Atlantic, then steamed to the Mediterranean. She passed through the Suez Canal and joined Task Force 77 for training exercises in the South China Sea. On January 10, 1954, Generalissimo Chiang Kai-Shek spent four hours aboard the ship while it was in Formosan waters.

In March the *Wasp* was visited by President Ramon Magsaysay of the Philippines, as a guest of American Ambassador Raymond A. Spruance.

The carrier operated from Subic Bay, then steamed to Japan where she was relieved by the *USS Boxer CVS-21*. In April she arrived at her new home port, NAS North Island, San Diego, California.

In September 1954 the *Wasp* departed home port and one month later relieved the *USS Boxer* in the South China Sea. As a unit of Task Group 70.2 she conducted air operations and training exercises in the South China Seas, off the Philippines and Japan.

She provided air cover for the evacuation of the Tachen Islands by Chinese Nationalists and then returned to San Diego in April 1955 where she later entered the San Francisco Naval Yard for a major conversion. The most apparent changes were the addition of an enclosed hurricane bow and an angle flight deck. She departed the yards on December 7, 1955, to resume flight training off the California coast.

On April 23, 1956, the *Wasp* departed home port for another tour of duty with the Seventh Fleet. A visit was made to Guam on May 14 where her embarked Carrier Air Group 15 made a fly-over for Armed Forces Day ceremonies. While en route to Japan she joined Task Force 77 for "Operation Sea Horse," a five-day exercise involving day and night training maneuvers. The *Wasp* arrived at Yokosuka, Japan, on June 4. The carrier paid a visit to the Philippines, then participated in search for a Navy patrol plane that had been shot down on August 23 off the coast of Communist China. The *Wasp* returned to San Diego on October 15, 1956.

On November 1, 1956, she was reclassified as an antisumbarine warfare carrier, CVS-18. On January 31, 1957, she departed home port, and rounded Cape Horn for operations in the South Atlantic and Caribbean Sea. She then went to Boston, arriving March 21; and on April 6 she arrived at Norfolk to receive members of her crew from the Anti-Submarine Warfare School. During the next month the *Wasp* was busy with ASW tactics along the eastern seaboard down to Bermuda, which included a joint convoy escort exercise with American and Canadian units.

On September 3, the *Wasp* departed Boston for an extended cruise to the Mediterranean. Her first exercise with NATO forces was "Operation Seaspray" followed by "Operation Strikeback." During these operations the *Wasp* teamed with six attack submarines, land-based patrol planes, and two other hunter-killer groups to form a barrier patrol in the natural bottleneck area between the Faeroes Islands and Iceland. This maneuver was to keep "hostile" submarines of the North from penetrating within striking distance of the Underway Replenishment Group protected by the fleet. The *Wasp* returned to Boston on October 23 and took a yard period until March 10, 1958. Then came ASW training off Guantanamo Bay.

On April 29 she became the flagship of Task Force 66 and steamed for duty with the Sixth Fleet on May 12. She participated in a joint Italian-American ASW exercise off Sardinia and visited Naples on July 3. The *Wasp* departed that port on the 15th and patrolled the waters off Lebanon. As the crisis there increased, her helicopters set up camp at Beirut International Airport and flew reconnaissance missions interspersed with transporting injured Marine battalions to the evacuation hospital at the airport. The carrier remained in the Lebanon area until September 17, then returned to Norfolk on October 7. She unloaded supplies, then made a brief call to Quonset Point before returning to Boston four days later.

On November 26 the *Wasp* departed Rhode Island for a 17-day cruise in the North Atlantic. She was flagship of Task Group Bravo, one of two newly formed ASW defense groups to concentrate on specific ASW problems for the improvement of ASW readiness in the Atlantic Fleet. Day and night operations were conducted before she returned to Boston on December 13.

The *Wasp* continued operations with the experimental Task Group Bravo throughout the year of 1969 and most of the training took place out of Boston along the Atlantic seaboard.

On February 27, 1960, she was in the Boston Navy Yard for a four and one-half month overhaul. In mid-July she went to the South Atlantic area and stood ready when civil strife erupted in the newly independent Congo. The *Wasp* returned to Boston late in August and operated off the Atlantic coast until August 1961.

A three-month cruise to the Mediterranean was made and then she came home on September 1 and entered the yards for an overhaul. She then rejoined the fleet on November 6.

January 11–18, 1962, the *Wasp* was active in training exercises and submarine tactics off the east coast. After a two-day stop at Norfolk she continued training until February, then stopped briefly at Bermuda.

On February 17 she set course for another European cruise and made an eight-day visit to Portsmouth, England, before steaming to the Bay of Biscay for ASW operations. March 15–22 she was at Rotterdam, then steamed to Scotland for a five-day stopover. The carrier arrived at Keil, Germany, on May 3 and afterwards went to Norway and Iceland. Her final port of call was Argentina, Newfoundland, after which she headed for the States, arriving at Boston on June 16.

In response to a call from President Kennedy, the *Wasp* participated in the Cuban quarantine from November 1–22. December 21–29 she made a Midshipmen cruise to Bermuda.

On January 21, 1963, the *Wasp* departed Boston for ASW operations off the Virginia Capes. March 9–23 she conducted surveillance operations along the Caribbean coast off Costa Rica. A visit was made to St. Thomas, Virgin Islands, March 23–26, and she returned to Boston on April 4.

The next eight months were used for operations off the Atlantic seaboard and the Caribbean. After an extended overhaul the *Wasp* spent 1964 conducting ASW operations in the Norwegian Sea and the Bay of Biscay and was flagship of the Hunter-Killer group. She returned to Boston on December 18, 1964, and remained in port until February 8, 1965.

During the summer she conducted search and rescue operations for an Air Force C-121 that had gone down off Nantucket. On August 20 she began a two-day joint training exercise with German and French forces.

Major James A. McDivitt and Major Edward H. White orbited the Earth in *Gemini IV* June 3–7. The capsule was launched at 11:15 A.M. EDT on June 3 from Launch Pad 19 at Cape Kennedy.

McDivitt left the capsule on the end of a 25-foot lifeline and maneuvered in space with a small oxygen-jet propulsion gun for 21 minutes. McDivitt brought the craft out of orbit and splashed down in the Atlantic at 1:13 P.M. EDT on June 7 only 56 miles from the *Wasp* and 390 miles east of Cape Kennedy. The flight involved 62 orbits and covered 1,906,684 miles in 97 hours, 48 minutes.

Gemini VII was launched at Cape Kennedy at 2:30 P.M. EST December 4, with Lieutenant Colonel Frank Borman and Lieutenant Commander James A. Lovell. On December 15, *Gemini VI-A* was launched at 8:37 A.M. EST, ten days after *Gemini VII* was safely in orbit. The crew commanding *Gemini VI-A* was Captain Walter M. Schirra, USN, and Major Thomas P. Stafford, USAF. *Gemini VI-A* rendezvoused within one foot of *Gemini VII* and made 16 orbits before splashdown in the Atlantic 13 miles from the *Wasp* at 10:29 A.M. EST on December 16 after 25 hours, 52 minutes in space. The capsule, with the astronauts inside, was hoisted aboard the *Wasp* by helicopter. *Gemini VII* made the longest space flight at that time with 350 hours, 35 minutes logged before an Atlantic splashdown at 9:06 A.M. EST December 18, 17 miles from the *Wasp*. Borman and Lovell were flown by helicopter to the carrier having made 206 orbits around the Earth.

On January 24, 1966, the *Wasp* departed Boston for fleet exercises at Puerto Rico. En route heavy seas and high winds caused structural damage and she entered Roosevelt Roads on February 1 for a damage survey. Limited ASW operations were held February 5–8. After a brief stop at Quonset Point and the Navy Ammunition Dump at Earle, New Jersey, she went into the yards at Boston for repairs on the 18th.

Work was completed March 7, and operations were

Commander Donald R. Schaffer bids astronauts Thomas P.
Stafford and Eugene A. Cernan farewell as they depart for
Cape Kennedy, Florida.

conducted off Narragansett Bay until the 24th, at which time the *Wasp* underwent an ORI off Guantanamo Bay from April 18 to May 13.

From May 13 to June 8 the *Wasp* was the primary recovery ship for *Gemini IX*. Lieutenant Colonel Thomas P. Stafford and Lieutenant Commander Eugene A. Cernan blasted from the pad at 9:39 A.M. EDT on June 3. Cernan made an epochal 2 hour 9 minute walk in space and the capsule completed 44 orbits before splashing down in the Atlantic at 10:00 A.M. EDT June 6—345 miles from Cape Kennedy. The capsule was only three miles from the *Wasp* and was recovered with the astronauts inside by a helicopter, which placed the capsule on the *Wasp*.

The *Wasp* returned the space capsule to Boston on June 8 and remained there for 12 days before rejoining the fleet for ASW exercises from July 25 to August 5. Hunter-Killer operations were conducted with the Royal Canadian Navy from September 19 to October 4. After stopping at Halifax, Nova Scotia, the *Wasp* returned to Boston. On November 18 she unloaded her special Gemini support equipment and prepared for fleet exercises, which were conducted off Viegues from November 28 to December 16.

From January 24 to February 26, 1967, the *Wasp* served as a Carrier Qualification vessel for pilots at the Naval Air Training Command. While taking on fuel from the *USS Salamonie AO-26*, the oiler lost rudder control and slammed into the *Wasp*, damaging her Number Three elevator and refueling stations.

After repairs the carrier resumed operations on March 29 and returned to Boston on April 7. Four days later she unloaded ammunition at Earle, New Jersey then went to New York April 15–19 before returning to Boston for an overhaul. The work was completed early in 1968 and ASW operations resumed off the Atlantic coast until June 15. At that time she reported to her new home port at Quonset Point, Rhode Island.

The *USS Wasp CVS-18* has received the Navy Unit Commendation; American Area Campaign Medal; Asiatic-Pacific Area Campaign Medal with eight battle stars; World War II Victory Medal; Navy Occupation Service Medal; China Service (extended) Service Medal; National Defense Service Medal; Korean Service Medal; Armed Forces Expeditionary Medal; United Nations Service Medal; Philippine Liberation Campaign Ribbon; and Republic of the Philippines Presidential Unit Citation Badge.

The *Hancock* shows off her new coat of camouflage paint on May 19, 1944, 34 days after commissioning.

19

USS Hancock CVA-19 (CV-19)

The present *USS Hancock CVA-19* is the third vessel of the U.S. Navy to be so named in honor of John Hancock (1737–1793) the famous statesman and delegate to the first and second Continental Congresses. He later became President of the Continental Congress and the first to sign the Declaration of Independence.

On January 26, 1943, the keel of the *Hancock* was laid at the Bethlehem Steel Co., Quincy, Massachusetts. Mrs. DeWitt C. Ramsey, wife of Rear Admiral Ramsey, Chief of the Bureau of Aeronautics, christened the *Hancock* on January 24, 1944. Less than 15 months after her keel was laid, the *USS Hancock CV-*

19 was commissioned on April 15, 1944. Her first commanding officer was Capt. Fred C. Dickey, USN. The *Hancock* was then taken to the Boston Navy Yard where final fitting out was completed.

On May 22, 1944, the *Hancock* set course for the Norfolk Navy Yard and remained there until June 12, when she departed to begin shakedown operations off Trinidad and Venezuela. During this time, the *Hancock's* crew became familiar with night firing, anti-aircraft practice, short range battle tactics, and air operations.

On May 27, 1944, Commander W. S. Butts, USN, flying a TBF, completed the first takeoff and landing on the new carrier.

The *Hancock* returned to the Boston Navy Yard for final alterations on July 9, and 22 days later was bound for combat duty in the Pacific forward area. She arrived at Cristobal on August 8 and transited the Panama Canal. The *Hancock* made a short visit to San Diego, then steamed to Pearl Harbor for final instructions before joining the famed Fifth Fleet, commanded by Admiral William F. Halsey.

On September 14, 1944, the *Hancock* received Admiral of the Fleet Chester W. Nimitz; Lord Keyes of the Royal Navy, and Rear Admiral Forrest D. Sherman, USN, to observe air operations and examine the carrier's combat capabilities. Three weeks of training began near the Hawaiian Islands, and on September 24, the *Hancock* departed Pearl Harbor, ready to join the fighting. She arrived at Ulithi Atoll on October 5, 1944.

Upon entering the Ulithi staging area, the *Hancock* joined Task Group 38.2.1 of Carrier Task Force 38. On October 6, she left Ulithi to join other task units of the fleet located west of the Marianas then steamed for Okinawa to strike enemy installations.

The *Hancock* launched her first combat air strikes on October 10, 1944, and Japanese ground fortifications and shipping suffered heavy damage. The *Hancock's* Air Group 7 was credited with the destruction of seven enemy planes on the ground and assisted in the destruction of a sub tender, twelve torpedo boats, a medium freighter, and one small oiler. The powerful carrier then steamed north and east throughout the night to strike Formosa on Columbus Day. That evening, a large group of Japanese aircraft attacked the task force. During the seven-hour battle, the *Hancock's* antiaircraft crews got their first two confirmed kills.

On October 14, the *Hancock* sent fighter squadrons against Taien airfield on Formosa. An enemy dive bomber dropped a 500-pound bomb that penetrated a

The ordnance team is quick to land aircraft in October 1944 as the *Hancock* prepares to strike Okinawa on her first combat operation.

steel 20mm gun platform, but exploded harmlessly in the water. The carrier then steamed on to support amphibious landings in the Philippines.

On October 17, 1944, the *Hancock* aircraft began a series of combat strikes that continued until the 21st. Cebu, Panay, Negros, and Mastbate in Northern Luzon tremored from relentless air sorties delivered by the fast carrier force.

Rear Admiral T. L. Sprague's escort carrier took over on October 21 to provide close-in ground support and strategic bombing. The *Hancock* headed for Ulithi, but while en route word was received that an enemy fleet had been seen off Samar. The *Hancock* dispatched her planes in search of the enemy fleet. The Japanese task force advanced in a three-pronged deployment, resulting in the Battle of Surigao Strait, the Battle of Samar and the Battle of Cape Engano. The *Hancock's* pilots did not reach Samar in time to assist in the actual battle, but found enemy ships from the center force on October 25, cruising northeast of Samar. Air Group 7 scored direct hits on a *Nachi* class cruiser, a *Yamato* class battleship, an *Agano* class cruiser and a *Kongo* class battleship.

Other enemy ships were seen retreating through the San Bernardino Straits and the swift air group commenced a bombing run on the ships as they fled through Jintola Channel. The battleship *Musashi* was hit with a 1000-pound bomb and a *Mogami* class cruiser received heavy damage.

The *Hancock* rendezvoused with a fleet tanker to

refuel at sea before returning on October 29 to bomb Clark, Nichols, and Angeles airfields and Manila Harbor in the Philippines.

Air strikes were conducted from Manila Harbor to Mastbate Island, then the carrier force retired to Ulithi for rest and maintenance.

Hot dogs, beer, and baseball was the "Plan of the Day" on Mog Mog, a small island in the Ulithi Atoll.

On November 14, 1944, the *Hancock,* as a unit of Task Group 38.2, left Ulithi to resume air strikes on the Philippines. A surprise attack on Ryukyus and Formosa destroyed several enemy aircraft and supplies that would have been used to reinforce the Philippines. On the morning of November 17, the *Hancock* became the flagship of Vice Admiral John S. McCain, Commander, Second Carrier Task Force, Task Force 30. The following day, a fighter sweep was again launched against enemy shipping in Manila Harbor and Nichols airfield. While recovering aircraft from this operation, an F6F circled the *Hancock* and landed normally, then the plane's belly tank fell to the deck and exploded. A fire-fighting team quickly drenched the flaming Hellcat with fog foam; however it was too late to save the pilot. He was buried at sea on November 20.

Inclement weather hampered the carrier force until November 25, at which time the *Hancock* resumed air attacks against shipping in Manila Harbor. At noon, a large number of enemy aircraft attacked the task force. One Japanese plane came out of the sun towards the *Hancock.* The carrier's AA batteries opened

fire and disintegrated the plane only 300 feet from the ship. A section of the plane's fuselage careened into the flight deck and burst into flames. The fires were extinguished quickly with only minor damage.

Kamakaze tactics were in full force that day and scored hits on the *USS Intrepid CV-11, USS Independence CVL-22* and the *USS Cabot CVL-28.* Many of the *Intrepid's* aircraft safely landed on the *Hancock* upon returning from air strikes.

The fast carrier force returned to Ulithi for upkeep and replenishment. Admiral William F. Halsey came aboard and presented medals to many of the *Hancock's* pilots. On December 10, 1944, the *Hancock* sortied from Ulithi to strike airfields in the Philippines in support of the landings on Mindoro. The first wave of fighters cleared the deck on December 14 and Clark and Angeles airfields came under heavy attack.

The enemy airstrips could only be reinforced from China and nearby Japanese-held islands, so a continuous combat air patrol over the air fields prevented the enemy from bringing in reinforcements. The *Hancock's* air group supported our ground forces landing on Luzon and continued air assaults on Masinloc, San Fernando, and Cabanatuan on December 15, 1944.

The *Hancock* terminated her fourth combat operation the next day by destroying enemy shipping in Manila Bay and other nearby harbors. Air strikes scheduled for December 19–20 were cancelled due to a vicious typhoon. The Navy was cognizant of the storm, but because of the importance of the mission, operations continued until it became impossible to launch aircraft. At times, waves broke over the *Hancock's* flight deck 55 feet above the waterline. On December 24, 1944, the *Hancock* returned to Ulithi for a six-day rest.

On December 30, the Third Fleet's Task Group 38.2 sortied from Ulithi to help end the Japanese occupation of the Philippines. Along with the *Hancock* was the *USS Ticonderoga CV-14, USS Lexington CV-16,* and the *USS Independence CVL-22.* On January 3, 1945, the *Hancock* sent air strikes against airfields at Koshun and Heito on Formosa. A new carrier tactic was introduced during these raids in the form of night combat air patrols. The *Independence* launched nightly patrols to defend the task group against enemy attacks. January 6–7 the air groups hit Cabanatuan, Mabalacat, and Banban airfields on Luzon. As the sun slipped below the horizon, the *Enterprise* and *Independence* launched night strikes and round-the-clock bombing became routine. On January 9, the fast carrier force travelled north to hit airfields on Formosa. Heito, Kato, Koshun, and Giran were once again under at-

Hole in the *Hancock's* flight deck after a Japanese suicide crash. Shipfitter starts to cut away jagged edges of twisted steel.

tack. The *Hancock's* pilots attacked an enemy convoy north of Camranh Bay on January 12. Two auxiliary ships were sunk and only three of the 15-vessel convoy escaped damage. Later in the afternoon, strikes were directed over French Indo-China. Air sorties continued through January 16 against Hainan Island in the Gulf of Tonkin, the Pescadores Islands, and enemy shipping in Hong Kong Harbor. Assualts on Formosa resumed on January 20.

At 1:28 P.M. January 21, 1945, a *Hancock* torpedo bomber was returning from an air strike off Formosa. The plane made a normal landing and taxied to a point abreast of the island structure. Suddenly there was a deafening explosion and the ship trembled from keel to masthead. Seconds later the flight deck was a mass of flame and puddles of burning gasoline simmered around the wreckage. The galley deck, many officers' staterooms, and the flight deck received the full force of the mysterious explosion. The *Hancock* made a wide turn and moved away from other ships in the task force in the event that she might blow up and damage other ships. Fire-fighting parties had the fires under control by 3:10 P.M. and the *Hancock's* flight deck was repaired. Fifty men were killed and 75 wounded in the unfortunate mishap. On January 23, burial services were held for the dead crewmen.

On the same day as the tragic accident, while conducting air strikes off Formosa, the USS *Ticonderoga* CV-14 was hit by two Kamakaze planes.

Twenty-four hours after the explosion, the battle-weary *Hancock* steamed for Ulithi. The war operations just completed had been the carrier's most successful to date, but the loss of so many shipmates tempered the spirits of the men. The ship had sunk 7 enemy ships, four Japanese merchant ships, and 36 aircraft in ten strikes deep in Japanese-held territory.

On January 25, 1945, the *Hancock* became a member of the Fifth Fleet, concurrent with the reassignment of Vice Admiral Marc A. Mitscher from the Third to the Fifth Fleet. Vice Admiral McCain left the *Hancock* after giving kudos to all hands aboard. Rear Admiral Thomas L. Sprague, Commander Carrier Division Three, boarded the *Hancock* and the ship became part of Task Group 58.2. Three days later, Air Group Eighty relieved Air Group Seven.

Task Force 58 sortied from Ulithi on February 10, 1945, to begin the first of many fast carrier raids on the Japanese mainland. The famed task force was commanded by Vice Admiral Raymond A. Spruance, USN, Commander of the Fifth Fleet. The heaviest fighting occured over Chiba Peninsula. During the Battle of the Philippine Sea, the *Hancock's* "Fighting Eighty"

shot down 71 enemy planes, breaking the record set by the *Lexington* on June 19, 1944, while fighting the Mariannas Turkey Shoot.

Leaving the airfields on Luzon a maze of destruction. the *Hancock* sent her air group against Iwo Jima. Newly constructed airfields became primary targets and soon became newly destroyed airfields. Chichi Jima and Haha Jima were hits while 30,000 U.S. marines stormed the beaches north and east of Mount Suribachi. Air strikes continued on February 21–22.

Iwo Jima is a small island only five miles long and two and one-half miles across at its widest point, but the ground fighting was so thick that more than 60,000 American troops were engaged in the action to secure the island. On March 1, 1945, air strikes resumed on the Nansei Shoto Islands. Heavy destruction was inflicted on the Koniya Seaplane Base, Amai-o-Shima, Okinoyerabu, Tokuna and Takara Shima. The *Hancock* returned to Ulithi for a brief rest on March 4.

Air Group Eighty was transferred to the USS *Wasp* CV-18 on March 9 as Air Group Six reported aboard the *Hancock*. This veteran group had served on the *Enterprise* and was the first to see action in the Pacific when the war started. On March 14, 1945, the *Hancock* sortied from Ulithi on her seventh combat tour in support of U.S. landings on Okinawa.

While refueling the destroyer USS *Halsey Powell* DD-686, a nerve-wracking series of events were set in motion by a lone Kamikaze pilot as he began his death dive at the two ships. AA fire destroyed the intruder, but blazing fragments of the disentegrated plane fell like hot rain. The engine and bomb from the suicide plane tumbled over the starboard side of the *Hancock's* flight deck and fell onto the *Halsey Powell*, penetrating her deck and making it impossible to steer. As the destroyer started a turn to port, she was lost from sight as she swung across the carrier's huge bow, under the flight deck hangar. The startled sailors braced for the impact of grinding steel as the 33,000-ton carrier bore down on the helpless destroyer. Then the hand of fate took over, for the *Halsey Powell* cleared the *Hancock*, avoiding a collision only by inches.

On April Fools Day 1945, the U.S. Tenth Army landed on the western coast of Okinawa as the fast carrier force flew support missions over the island. Six days later, a suicide plane cartwheeled across the *Hancock's* flight deck and crashed into a cluster of spotted planes. The enemy fighter's bomb exploded on the port catapult, killing 62 men and wounding 71. Once again, the *Hancock* left formation to fight the fires covering her. In less than 50 minutes, the damage control parties had the fires under control and returning aircraft were able to land four hours later.

The *Hancock* returned to Pearl Harbor for a brief yard period and departed on June 13 to launch air strikes over Wake Island. During these attacks, the air group tested a new phosphorous, which suppressed the vision of enemy gunners and made things easier for succeeding waves of fighters and bombers.

The *Hancock* began her tenth combat operation on July 10, 1945, by striking airfields in the Tokyo area of Japan. The big naval base in Yokosuka was hit on July 18 and the battleship *Nagato* was left a burning hulk. Northern Honshu airfields were hit on August 10, 1945. About midnight, the first news that Japan had accepted the terms of the Potsdam Conference came in. Many shipmates were awakened to hear the welcome news. The fast carrier task force continued air strikes pending official recognition of the Japanese surrender.

On August 15, the Japanese capitulated. At 4:33 P.M., the *Hancock*'s planes were recalled before they had reached their assigned targets.

The *Hancock*'s photo squadron was attacked by seven aircraft over Sagami Wan. Three enemy planes were shot down during the incident. The carrier's air group parachuted medical supplies and provisions over prisoner of war camps, then sailed into Tokyo Bay on September 10, 1945.

Twenty days later, she departed and arrived in San Pedro, California, October 21, 1945.

The *Hancock*'s air and gunnery departments were relieved of all personnel and some 40mm mounts were removed to build temporary washrooms as the carrier was fitted out for "Magic Carpet" duty. On November 2, she left for Seeadler Harbor, Admiralty Islands then returned to San Pedro on December 4 with 3999 passengers. The *Hancock* set out on her second Magic Carpet cruise seven days later, arriving in Manila on December 30, where 3755 passengers were taken aboard. On January 3, 1946, the *Hancock* arrived at the naval air station, Alameda, California. After disembarking her passengers, she returned to San Pedro.

The *Hancock* sailed from San Diego on March 11 and took aboard Air Groups Eighty and Nineteen for transportation to Saipan. The planes were flown off on April 1 and the *Hancock* then anchored off Saipan. On April 29, 1946, the *Hancock* arrived at Seattle, to await deactivation. The final deactivation process was conducted at Everett, Washington, on September 24, 1946, after which the carrier entered Puget Sound Naval Yard on February 15, 1947. She was decom-

missioned on May 9, 1947 to the Bremerton Reserve Group of the Pacific Fleet.

As a result of her outstanding service during combat from October 10, 1944, to August 15, 1945, the *Hancock* was awarded the Navy Unit Commendation. Her scoreboard showed 723 enemy planes destroyed, 17 warships sunk, 31 merchant ships sunk, and 10 planes fell to the ship's gun crews. The *Hancock* lost 221 shipmates who were either killed or missing in action.

After four years in mothballs, the *Hancock* was moved to her berth in the reserve group and entered drydock for a complete modernization prior to recommissioning. Her island structure was streamlined, a new Mark VII arresting gear apparatus was installed, and the first steam catapult system to be put on an American aircraft carrier was established.

On February 15, 1954, the *USS Hancock CVA-19* was recommissioned at Bremerton, Washington, under the command of Capt. Whitmore S. Butts, USN. Throughout the early months of 1954, she was moored at North Island in San Diego, Calif., testing her new steam catapults. On June 1, an S2F-1 Sentinel became the first aircraft launched from a U.S. Navy ship utilizing a steam catapult. "Project Steam" came to an official close on February 18, 1955, with great success.

Air Operations and training continued off the Southern California coast until August 10, 1955, when the *Hancock* began an eight-month cruise in the Far East. As a unit of the Seventh Fleet, she patrolled the China coast and visited Yokosuka, Iwakuni, Japan; Buckner Bay, Okinawa; Subic Bay and Manila in the Philippines, and Hong Kong. On March 16, 1956, the *Hancock* returned to San Diego.

The *Hancock* entered the San Francisco Naval Shipyard on April 13, 1956, to undergo an $8 million conversion. Again, she was placed in reserve commission on April 16 as the face-lifting work began. On November 15, 1956, the *Hancock* was placed in full commission status and assigned to Carrier Division One, U.S. Pacific Fleet.

Old shipmates from World War II days could hardly recognize the *Hancock* as she steamed out of the yard. Included in the current conversion was the installation of an enclosed hurricane bow, a new angle flight deck, a mirror landing system, an enlarged forward elevator, and special weapons capabilities.

Following sea trails off the coast of San Diego, the *Hancock*'s home port was changed to Alameda, California. On April 6, 1957, the *Hancock* deployed for another tour of duty with the Seventh Fleet in the western Pacific. She arrived at Yokosuka on May 9 and operated out of that port to Okinawa, Formosa, and Hong Kong. The carrier conducted routine training exercises in the South China Sea and departed Yokosuka on September 6 arriving in Alameda on September 18, 1957.

The *Hancock* again entered the San Francisco Naval Shipyard for maintenance, then resumed normal flight operations along the California coast until February 15, 1958. At this time, she set a return course for the Far East. Continuous flight operations and exercises were conducted in the South China Sea and off the coast of Japan.

Quemoy had become a hot spot as the Communists were ready to pose a threat to the free world. The *Hancock* stood by during the tense months until the situation had eased down. On October 3, 1958, she edged under the Golden Gate Bridge while members of the crew spelled out "Our Town" on the flight deck. On November 14, the *Hancock* entered the San Francisco Shipyard for a third visit to undergo a four month overhaul, which included installation of new radar equipment.

The mighty ship was discharged from the yard to resume operations with the Pacific Fleet on March 18, 1959. In July she participated in the First Fleet Review in San Francisco. More than 146,124 persons toured the carrier and other ships. On the first day of Open House, the *Hancock* was host to 20,396 visitors.

The *Hancock* left Alameda on August 1 for a four-month duty tour with the Seventh Fleet operating in the western Pacific. After a two-week layover at Pearl Harbor for the annual Operational Readiness Inspection exercise, she proceeded to Subic Bay, Philippines. Due to unrest in the Laotian area, the carrier spent much of the cruise operating from the Philippines. On January 18, 1960, she returned home and entered the Hunters Point Shipyard for repairs.

In February 1960, the *Hancock* participated in the Moon Relay communications test. Ultra-high frequency waves were reflected off the moon, and with the use of teletype and photo facsimile transmission, a photograph of the *Hancock* with members of her crew spelling out "Moon Relay" on the flight deck became the first official photograph to be transmitted via the new moon relay system.

In August, the *Hancock* left on her fifth engagement of the Far East since recommissioning. Manila, Subic Bay, Okinawa, Hong Kong, Guam, Yokosuka, and Iwakuni were ports of call and the carrier took part in "Operation Handclasp," a people-to-people program. While in the Philippines, an Open House during Aviation Week celebrations led visitors to various displays of aircraft firepower and capabilities. Highlighting the celebration was the catapulting of two aircraft while at anchor in Manila Bay. One of the planes launched was a large A3D Skywarrior.

On March 19, 1961, the *Hancock* returned to Alameda, California. After the carrier air group was released, the ship steamed for the Puget Sound Shipyard in Bremerton, Washington. A $4 million overhaul included new steam accumulators for the catapults, reweaving of the arresting gear cables, rebricking the boilers, and new electronic equipment.

In September 1961, the *Hancock* left the yards in preparation for another Far East tour. Air operations were conducted off the California coast until February 2, 1962, when the carrier sailed to the western Pacific via Pearl Harbor. Violence had erupted in Laos and Vietnam so the *Hancock* remained in the South China Sea, conducting exercises or standing ready in case she was needed. While in port at Yokosuka on June 7, 1962, the *Hancock* made a hurried departure to stand by Quemoy and Matsu as tension mounted there. After the tension had dwindled, the *Hancock* resumed training out of Yokosuka, Japan. On August 14, the carrier left for home, arriving one week later at Alameda, California.

Following a brief six weeks in repair at the San Francisco ship yard, the *Hancock* began carrier qualification of new pilots. Operating between Alameda and Hawaii, she logged 1500 day and night landings. On December 21 she arrived at Alameda for the annual holiday period.

In March 1963, a new Pilot's Landing Aid Television (PLAT) system was installed. From June through December of 1963, the *Hancock* served as a unit of the Seventh Fleet. Upon returning to the Far East, she served again in standby duty or training exercises, then sailed back to the San Francisco Naval Yard for a four-month overhaul.

In May 1964, she resumed normal training operation near California.

The *Hancock* left Alameda on October 21, 1964, to join Task Force 77 of the Seventh Fleet working in the Far East. For three months, she enjoyed a normal cruise and took part in the annual people-to-people program, "Operation Handclasp."

In February 1965, the increased North Vietnamese involvement culminated in attacks upon U.S. personnel and the *Hancock* was called to action. On Sunday, February 7, 1965, she launched her first combat air strikes since World War II. The sorties were against Viet Cong barracks near the 17th Parallel, in direct reprisal for guerrilla attacks on U.S. installations at

Pleiku. The Carrier Air Wing CVW-21 struck deep into the heart of Communist Vietnam. Four days later, the *Hancock*'s pilots joined in a 150-plane raid against supply depots in North Vietnam.

The *Hancock* resumed strikes on March 15, 19, 26, and 31. A strategic bridge was destroyed by the *Hancock*'s air wing on April 3 south of Hanoi. With her mission accomplished, she left the area in early May and returned to Alameda on May 29, 1965.

A three-month yard period was taken for overhaul at the Hunters Point Shipyard in San Francisco the *Hancock* was ready for a second Vietnam war cruise.

Family and friends bid farewell, and on November 10, 1965, the *Hancock* departed for an extended tour of duty in the Far East. Carrier Air Wing 21 was also beginning its second tour with the *Hancock*.

On December 16, she teamed with other carriers of Task Force 77 off Yankee Station to strike enemy supply routes and troop concentrations throughout Central South Vietnam in support of American and South Vietnamese ground troops. On March 7, 1966, a Navy reconnaissance pilot met with two Russian-built anti-aircraft missiles over North Viet Nam. The RF8 Crusader from Photo Reconnaissance Squadron 63 (VFP-63) set out to photograph a stretch of road often used as a supply route to the south. The word "missiles away" (a term used by pilots to warn each other of approaching missiles) squawked over the radio. The Crusader pilot quickly made a 180-degree roll-out just as the missile burst above his plane. When he landed on the *Hancock*, the film was developed and the Navy had its first photo of in-flight enemy missiles used against our aircraft.

On June 12, 1966, Commander Harold L. Marr,

USS Hancock CVA-19.

USN, lead four Crusader jets on a combat patrol in support of ground attacks being delivered by CVW-21s 4A Skyhawks. Lt. (jg) Phil Vampatella of Islip Terrace, New York, who was Commander Marr's wingman, spotted a group of MIGS coming in for an attack. Commander Marr launched a Sidewinder Missile to blast the 13th MIG of the Vietnam war out of action!

The *Hancock*'s fighter Squadron 211, scored their second aerial victory on June 22, 1966, when Lt. (jg) Vampatella made a direct hit on a MIG with a Sidewinder Missile. The F8E Crusaders were so low on fuel that they were forced to break the engagement and return to the carrier. While returning, they were met by an airborne tanker and refueled prior to setting down on the *Hancock*'s deck.

On July 7, 1966, the *Hancock*'s air wing struck the Haiphong oil supply area. The target, located just over two miles northwest of Haiphong, was left a mass of fireballs and explosions. Geysers of flame shot hundreds of feet into the smoking air, and were visible to U.S. Navy destroyer men in the Gulf of Tonkin. The *Hancock* returned to the states shortly thereafter.

The *Hancock* operated off the coast of Southern California until January 5, 1967, on which date she left Alameda to begin her third Vietnam cruise. She arrived in the Gulf of Tonkin during the first week in February and commenced to launch her air wing against designated targets. During the six-month deployment, the carrier launched 8950 combat and combat support sorties of 102 days on the line on Yankee Station. Her air group totally destroyed the Nam Dinh thermal power plant and heavily damaged Kep Airfield. Other targets that received a heavy pounding included the Vin Loc highway bridge, the Chu Ne army barracks, Hai Dong rail bridge complex, Kien An Airfield near Haiphong, the Chu Son military storage area, the Cong My and Loi Dong petroleum trans-shipment points near Haiphong and the Doan Vi trans-shipment point. On July 22, 1967, the "Fighting Hannah" returned to Alameda, California.

She immediately entered the Naval Shipyard for a four-month yard overhaul. Her hull was completely renovated and a modified central air conditioning system was installed.

After a short post overhaul and training period, the *Hancock* left Alameda on July 18, 1968, for her fourth tour of duty in the Western Pacific and duty with the Seventh Fleet in the Gulf of Tonkin. After a brief visit to Japan and the Philippines, the carrier arrived in the Gulf of Tonkin on August 22. Her embarked Air Wing twenty-one destroyed a SAM (Surface-to-Air) site 25 miles northwest of the panhandle city of Vinh. After the November 1 bombing halt, the *Hancock* took part in an interdiction campaign against Communist supply lines in South Vietnam, providing close support to US troops. During this cruise the *Hancock* launched over 9000 combat support sorties and the air wing dropped 9000 tons of ordnance. The *Hancock* returned to her homeport of Alameda on March 3, 1969.

On April 15, 1969, the *Hancock* celebrated her 26th birthday. Through several modernization and conversion programs, the carrier's life expectancy with the fleet has been extended for several years.

The *Hancock* is one of the three original 24 *Essex* class carriers to still hold the designation of Attack Aircraft Carrier and has the distinction of being the oldest CVA in the Fleet.

For services performed in active duty status, the proud *Hancock* has received the following awards: The Navy Unit Commendation; the Meritorious Unit Commendation; The American Area Campaign Medal; The Asiatic-Pacific Area Campaign Service Medal with four battle stars; The World War II Victory Medal; The Navy Occupation Service Medal; The China Service Medal; The National Defense Service Medal; The Armed Forces Expeditionary Service Medal; The Vietnam Service Medal; The Philippine Liberation Campaign Ribbon; and the Republic of the Philippines Presidential Unit Citation Badge.

USS Bennington CV-20. Aerial oblique, forward starboard view, camouflage, Sept. 25, 1944.

20

USS Bennington CVS-20 (CV-20)

The current *USS Bennington CVS-20* is the second U.S. Naval vessel to bear the name commemorating the Battle of Bennington, Vermont, on August 16, 1777. Her keel was laid on December 15, 1942, at the New York Navy Yard. The *Bennington* was launched on February 26, 1944, and commissioned on August 6 of the same year. Captain J. B. Sykes assumed command at that time.

With Air Group 82 embarked, the *Bennington* departed New York Navy Yard on October 16 for shakedown operations in the Gulf of Paris. Emphasis was keyed to gunnery practice and flight operations in preparation for duty in the Pacific theater of war. A complete shakedown cruise was taken, and on November 17 the big warship returned to the navy yard in New York for a final post-shakedown inspection and alteration. The crew was divided into port and starboard liberty—i.e., half the sailors went ashore and the remainder left upon return of the first half. Ammunition was loaded at Gravesend Bay December 13 and two days later the carrier began her long journey to the Pacific.

The *Bennington* transited the Panama Canal on December 22. During this period simulated attacks were conducted in conjunction with the U.S. Army. Rough seas in the Gulf of Tehantepec postponed

The *USS Bennington* underway, flight deck loaded with aircraft, January 1 ,1945.

Christmas dinner. The *Bennington* arrived in San Diego for a brief sojourn, then departed for Pearl Harbor on January 1, 1945, arriving seven days later. While there the big ship was loaded with supplies and all available space was filled with extra aircraft on the hangar deck and flight deck. Three weeks later, she departed Pearl to join Task Force 58 at Ulithi Atoll in the Western Carolines. General Quarters was sounded for the first time as the carrier passed Truk Island under Japanese occupation. The expected attack failed to materialize and the *Bennington* steamed into Ulithi shortly afterwards.

On February 10, the *Bennington* sailed from Ulithi as part of the famed Task Force 58 to participate in her first combat strikes consisting of offensive raids over the Japanese homeland.

The *Bennington*'s air group flew continuous strikes over Iwo Jima beachheads on February 19 in support of the troop landings. Selected enemy positions were bombed including caves and blockhouses. The *Bennington* Task Group 58.1 was unmolested by suicide aircraft on February 22, but other task groups were not so lucky and suffered heavy damage.

On March 1, shipping in the vicinity of Naha, Okinawa, was destroyed and photo squadrons flew over the Kerama Phetto Islands. March 4–14 the *Bennington* was anchored in Ulithi Atoll, and during replenishment and maintenance the sailors managed to play a few baseball games on Mog Mog Island.

On March 18, the *Bennington* was only 80 miles off Kyushu (on Honshu, the Japanese "mainland"). An enemy plane made a vain attempt to crash the car-

Aircraft being serviced on the *Bennington*, February 1945.

rier. All starboard antiaircraft batteries opened fire and the craft splashed into the sea only 200 yards from the ship. The next two days were spent north of Kure Naval Base. The primary objective was to destroy as much of the Japanese Air Force as possible. A total of 57 confirmed enemy planes were shot down on March 18–19. The *Bennington*'s pilots damaged a Yamato class battleship off Kure, and the task force was under heavy kamikaze attack during this time.

A week of intensive fighter sweeps over Okinawa began on March 23 in preparation for the Easter Sunday landings by the U.S. Marines. An enemy convoy was spotted in the East China Sea heading toward Okinawa, and planes from Task Group 58.1 destroyed the entire convoy. One cargo ship—apparently burdened with ammunition—erupted in flame, sending debris 3000 feet skyward.

The bright early morning sun of the following day provided considerable daylight for a lone Japanese pilot wishing to establish his worth for the Emperor. The pilot began a shallow dive out of the clouds, aiming for the carrier, but the alert crew on the ship spotted the intruder.

Antiaircraft batteries immediately opened fire. The pilot must have thought the Emperor was personally protecting his frail craft, since he was not hit by the flaming incendiaries traversing all sides merely inches away.

The enemy pilot turned and completed a perfect pass across the *Bennington*'s flight deck, but to the surprise of everyone—including the invading flyer—no bomb ripped up the deck nor was there any explosion!

The relieved crewmen on the carrier surmised that the plane's bomb release system had malfunctioned and further believed that the enemy pilot, having lived through one deadly pass on the carrier as well as the antiaircraft fire, did not wish to tempt fate any further. The Emperor would have to wait for a next time as far as this particular pilot was concerned. He rapidly retreated, abandoning any desire to crash his plane into the ship.

When the Marines began to land on Okinawa April 1, 1945, the carriers had already destroyed many installations and machine gun emplacements. During the landings, the air groups flew in advance of the Marines, strafing forward positions and forcing the Nips to keep their heads buried.

On April 6, the *Bennington*'s air group destroyed 31 enemy planes with no U.S. losses. One week later, 34 Jap planes were downed to our one, and a rescue ship later picked up the *Bennington* flyer. On April 7, more than 300 planes from the fast carrier force began an attack on the final Japanese Capital ship in commission—the battleship *Yamato*. Many strikes were launched against this prize target and the *Bennington* air group assisted in the sinking. Later, the carrier's pilots sank a destroyer and made two torpedo hits on the cruiser Agano.

The *Bennington* participated in only one antiaircraft action from April 16 to June 8. This incident occurred early on the morning of May 14 when a single-engine unidentified "bogie" was seen behind a trio of Navy fighters eight miles away. The fighters turned and began runs on the enemy plane, but it managed to break through and dive on the *Bennington*. One of the carrier's 5-inch mounts scored a direct hit and the craft exploded instantly.

The mighty carrier steamed for 24 hours to avoid a typhoon, but the storm overtook the ship on June 5. Winds of at least 90 knots—the limiting mark on the instruments—were registered. The screaming winds whipped waves 40 to 50 feet from trough to crest, flooding the *Bennington*'s forward passageway, berthing spaces, and forecastle deck. The heavy seas buckled a 35-foot section of the big flight deck and both catapults were out of action. Despite the damage, the *Bennington* was able to launch fighter surveys against Kyushu airfield on June 8. The carrier dropped anchor in San Pedro Bay in Leyte Gulf three days later for repairs.

Work on the damaged flight deck began immediately. Air Group 82 was detached and returned to the states. Air Group 1 came aboard, and on July 1 the *Bennington* rendezvoused with other task groups. Nine days later, air strikes began 120 miles southeast of southern Honshu and fighter sweeps were directed over the Tokyo plains—Tsukuba, Hyakurigahara, and Ishioka. Air Group 1 destroyed over 85 enemy planes at their airfields and on July 28 the flyers struck Mitsuko Jima, where they damaged an Ise class battleship and an Amagi class cruiser. The Kobe-Nagoaya area was hit on July 30, August 9–10. On August 15, a second strike force was preparing to hit the Hyakuriga-hara airfield. However, word was received that the Japanese had surrendered. The news did not seem real until Admiral Halsey announced the surrender of all Japanese forces to the entire Fleet.

The *Bennington's* air group obtained good photographic coverage of the historical surrender signed aboard the battleship USS *Missouri BB-63.* On October 29, the carrier returned to Pearl Harbor and took passengers aboard. The mighty ship steamed for the United States and arrived in San Francisco November 7, 1945.

The *Bennington* completed one more voyage to Pearl Harbor to return aircraft and personnel stateside and returned from this mission March 30, 1946. April 13–17 she again passed through the Panama Canal, and arrived five days later at the Norfolk Navy Yard, where she was decommissioned with the Atlantic Reserve Fleet on November 8, 1946. She was shifted from Norfolk to the navy yard in New York on October 30, 1950, for modernization. Her flight deck was strengthened, her island structure was streamlined, and various gun mounts were removed. The mighty *Bennington,* with a new face, was recommissioned CVS-20 on November 13, 1952.

While conducting shakedown operations on April 27, 1953, a downcomer tube in the number one boiler room slipped loose with a deafening explosion that rocked the ship's lower decks. Eleven men died and four were seriously wounded. Following repairs, the *Bennington* resumed operations off the East coast. During the summer a midshipman cruise was held, with a visit to Halifax. In September she deployed on her first Mediterranean cruise where she participated in Exercise Mariner with NATO forces in the North Atlantic. In February 1954, the carrier returned to home port at Quonset Point, Rhode Island.

Disaster struck for a second time at 6:11 A.M., May 26, 1954, when the port catapult accumulator burst, releasing hydraulic fluid under tremendous pressure throughout the adjacent spaces. As a result of the accident 103 officers and men were killed and 201 of the ship's personnel were injured. However, the *Bennington* was able to return to Quonset Point under her own power.

The carrier entered the naval shipyard in New York on June 12 to begin a major conversion. Included was an angle-deck, an enclosed bow, and the latest electronic equipment. A third elevator was installed on the starboard after-section and the primary flight control, fire control, and ready rooms were refitted. The entire conversion was completed by March 19, 1955, and the carrier rejoined the Atlantic fleet.

On August 22, 1955, Commander R. G. Dose, commanding officer of VS-3, made the first carrier landing in an FJ3 *Fury,* using the Mirror Landing System. The first night landing followed on the 24th, by Lieutenant Commander H. C. MacKnight in an F9F *Cougar.*

The Secretary of the Navy boarded the *Bennington* on April 22, and presented medals and letters of commendation to 178 men, who were cited for heroic action during the disaster on May 26.

The carrier departed Mayport, Florida, September 8, 1955, to join the Pacific Fleet. She rounded Cape Horn and arrived in San Diego, California, on October 20. Eleven days later she headed for her first cruise to the Far East since World War II. The ship visited Yokosuka, Iwankuni and Sasebo, Japan; Buckner Bay, Okinawa; Manila and Subic Bay, Philippine Islands; and Hong Kong. Numerous Seventh Fleet exercises were conducted during this cruise, after which the *Bennington* returned to San Diego on April 16, 1956. There she entered Hunters Point Shipyard for overhaul. Routine flight operations were conducted from San Diego until October 12, when the *Bennington* left for a second tour in the Western Pacific. This cruise was highlighted by a visit to Sydney, Australia, and on May 2, 1957, she took part in the 15th Anniversary of the Battle of the Coral Sea.

Upon returning from this cruise on May 22, the carrier began a three-month overhaul at Hunters Point. For nine months the *Bennington* enjoyed stateside duty while conducting routine operations off the coast of Southern California. In May 1958, she steamed to Hawaii and underwent the annual Operational Readiness Inspection. She then proceeded to Vancouver, British Columbia, to attend British Columbia's Centennial and joined other U.S. and Canadian vessels, which were reviewed by Princess Margaret.

On August 21, the *Bennington* made another cruise to the Far East. This was done with less than a week's notice, and she joined a unit of the Seventh Fleet participating in the Quemoy crisis. During this time the carrier steamed for 43 days, launching aircraft continuously. She took time to visit the usual ports of call in Japan, the Philippines, and Hong Kong before her return home on January 13, 1959.

The *Bennington* entered Hunters Point for a five-month yard period and conversion to an antisubmarine warfare support carrier. She left the yards on June 30 and was redesignated CVS-20. A month later she began carrier qualifications and suitability tests of the Grumman WF-2 *"Tracker."* The carrier embarked Carrier Division 15 and conducted antisubmarine warfare exercises off the southern California coast until October 1, 1960, then got underway to join the Seventh Fleet in the Far East. Most of this cruise was in the South China Sea during the tense Laotian crisis. Visits were made to Yokosuka, Iwankuni and Sasebo, Japan; Buckner Bay, Okinawa; Manila and Subic Bay, Philippines plus Hong Kong. She sailed into port at San Diego on May 22, 1961. She remained on the west coast for eight months, conducting simulated ASW

operations. On January 2, 1962, she once again sailed to the Western Pacific. Operations in the South China Sea became routine.

The *Bennington* returned to San Diego in August, where her Air Group disembarked. On September 14 she entered Puget Sound Naval Shipyard in Bremerton, Washington, for a FRAM II conversion. Her ASW capabilities were increased with the addition of sonar equipment. After a refresher training period off San Diego, she rejoined the fleet on May 1, 1963, and tied up at her new home port of Long Beach, California.

A five-month Pacific cruise began on August 5 and from August 9 to 11 the carrier participated in Seattle's annual Sea Fair celebration. She then headed north to Alaska and stopped at Juneau and Kodiak. She was the first aircraft carrier to visit these ports. On August 30, she returned to Long Beach for ASW operations,

Aerial view of the *USS Bennington* taking on fuel from the
USS Chemung AO-30 (January 23, 1964).

USS Bennington entering Long Beach Harbor after ORI in San Diego, California, January 1965.

training, and carrier qualifications prior to her next overseas assignment.

On February 19, 1964, the *Bennington* went to the Western Pacific for six months of duty with the Seventh Fleet, and returned to home port on August 11 to resume training. On Christmas Eve of 1964 she made a hurried dash up the coastline to Eureka, California, to assist victims of a flood. December 25–28 her helicopters flew 102 mercy missions in which 161,000 tons of supplies were delivered and 167 persons evacuated.

Three months of training began near Long Beach on March 22, 1965, then the carrier set course for Vietnam. During this seven-month tour, the *Bennington* performed ASW operations and patrolled off South Vietnam. On October 7 she returned to Long Beach

for a six-month extended yard period, which included installation of advanced electronic and engineering equipment. In April 1966 the *Bennington* left the yards and continued normal training out of Long Beach in preparation for another overseas assignment.

The *Bennington* played host to the 1966 National Red Cross Board of Governor's reception and Open House in San Diego on May 8, 1966. This was followed by two weeks of continuous flight operations during which time the *Bennington* made naval history on May 18 when the revolutionary new vertical and short takeoff and landing (V-STOL) transport plane conducted first preliminary carrier trials on her flight deck.

On November 4, 1966, the *Bennington* left Long Beach for her tenth Western Pacific cruise. She conducted ASW operations in the Tonkin Gulf with Task

Force 77 and visited Sydney, Australia, for the 25th Commemoration of the Battle of the Coral Sea, then returned home to Long Beach on May 23, 1967.

The carrier went into the Long Beach Naval Shipyard for a short upkeep and repair period. She then made a (mid-pac) mid Pacific cruise to pick up the first Apollo capsule near Midway Island.

The *Bennington* operated off the California coast up to April 30, 1968, then deployed on her eleventh cruise to the Far East. On this her third Vietnam war cruise, the *Bennington* made the Sea of Japan Transit, in joint operations with the Japanese Maritime Defense Force. During the transit, several overflights by Soviet planes were observed and Soviet ships were in constant observation by the task force. The *Bennington* returned to Long Beach on November 9, and went into the shipyard for an extended overhaul, which lasted up to May 1969; then the carrier rejoined the First Fleet.

The *Bennington* continued to operate out of Long Beach until October 10, 1969; on that date she left Long Beach for the last time, steaming for the Puget Sound Naval Shipyard, Bremerton, Washington, where she arrived on October 13. On January 15, 1970, the *USS Bennington CVS-20* was decommissioned and placed in the Bremerton Group of the Pacific Reserve Fleet.

The *USS Bennington CVS-20* has received the following awards: The American Area Campaign Service Medal; the Asiatic-Pacific Area Campaign Service Medal with three battle stars; the World War Two Victory Medal; the Navy Occupation Service Medal; the China Service Medal (extended); the National Defense Service Medal; and the Armed Forces Expeditionary Medal.

USS Boxer LPH-4 (ex CV-21).

21

USS Boxer LPH-4 (CV-21)

The fifth naval ship to bear the name *Boxer* was ordered November 15, 1941. Her keel was laid down at the Newport News Shipbuilding Yard September 13, 1943.

Miss Ruth D. Overton, daughter of Senator John H. Overton, caressed the carrier's bow with the traditional magnum of champagne on December 14, 1944, and Captain Donald F. Smith took command when the ship was commissioned on April 16, 1945.

The *Boxer* commemorates the capture of the British Brig *HMS Boxer* by the *USS Enterprise* off Portland, Maine, on September 15, 1813. This particular seizure was the most gallant exhibition of action during the War of 1812.

USS Boxer CV-21. Aerial oblique, broadside, in harbor, May 24, 1945.

The *Boxer* is one of several *Essex* Class carriers to remain on active duty since 1945. Although she was completed too late for action in World War II, the "Busy Bee" gained fame as a top fighting unit during the Korean conflict and earned eight battle stars.

Following shakedown operations off the Caribbean, the *Boxer* slipped through the Panama Canal July 23, 1945, arriving at San Diego six days later.

On September 1, the day before the historical Japanese capitulation ceremonies aboard the *USS Missouri BB-63* in Tokyo Bay, the *Boxer* departed San Diego for her initial Far East cruise. She operated off the Yellow Sea and during the tenure, visited Hong Kong, Guam, Saipan, Okinawa, and Manila. On September 9, 1946, she returned to San Diego.

On March 10, 1948, the *Boxer* became the first *Essex* class carrier to launch jet aircraft. Two pilots from Fighter Squadron 5-A flew off the *Boxer's* deck and were closely followed by their leader, Commander Evan Aurand, who accomplished the first jet-operational takeoff and landing. These tests were conducted off the coast of Southern California.

The *Boxer* was off for another Far East cruise on January 11, 1950. During this period, South Korean President Syngman Rhee came aboard on April 8 while the ship was anchored at Inchon, Korea. On June 13, the carrier returned to Alameda, California.

On June 25, 1950, the Communist armies of North Korea decided to cross the 38th parallel and were soon faced by the United States which joined forces with the United Nations to aid the nearly defenseless South Koreans. On August 24 the *Boxer* steamed from Alameda to Japan after a brief stop at Pearl Harbor. She arrived at Sasebo on September 14 and the next day rendezvoused with Task Force 77. Air strikes were immediately launched against shore installations of the Inchon area. The *Boxer* supported U.N. forces in the liberation of Seoul and struck the North Korean capital, Pyongyang.

The fighter group tactics used in World War II were now being used by the *Boxer's* air group, which strafed the area forward of United Nations troops; the Commies were prudent in keeping their heads down. Photographic flights were made over large sections of combat zones.

On October 1 the air group destroyed an electric power plant. This particular target received the destructive effect of 36,900 pounds of bombs and 120 skyrockets. Ensign Claude Dorris of VF-23 was the only casualty; he was rescued when his plane crashed into the sea.

The *Boxer* teamed with the *USS Leyte CV-32*, *USS Valley Forge CV-45* and *USS Bon Homme Richard CVA-31*. This became the first occasion since World

HUS of Marine Squadron HMR-L-262, being landed by the LSE aboard the *USS Boxer LPH-4* while underway to Vieques island.

F4U's (Corsairs) from a combat mission over North Korea circle the *USS Boxer CV-21* as they wait for planes in the next strike to be launched from her flight deck. Helicopter hovers above the ship.

War II in which four *Essex* class carriers sailed side by side.

The *Boxer* participated in the Inchon invasion, known to the principals as "Operation Chronite." This decisive operation was conceived entirely by General of the Army Douglas MacArthur.

On October 14 the carrier shifted to the eastern coast of Korea to support the advancing United Nations forces near Wonsan. Her air group provided air cover between Wonsan and Hungnam. The carrier returned to Yokosuka on October 25 and departed five days later for San Francisco and a session in drydock.

With Commander Carrier Division One and Air Group 101 embarked, the *Boxer* departed San Diego on March 2, 1951 for a second Korean War cruise. On March 25, she rendezvoused with the *USS Rush DD-714* and *USS Thomason DD-760* off the Van Dieman strait, then joined Task Force 77 the following day.

From March 27 to April 8 she launched daily air strikes against cities and other designated targets in the Wonsan-Songjin areas. On April 7 close air support was provided to an amphibious landing of *HMS Royal Commands* south of Songjin. The carrier returned to the east coast of Korea on April 16 where her pilots concentrated on Hamhung, an important communications center.

Night harassment missions were conducted against the enemy transportation system after the New Communist Chinese offensive had been rendered impotent. On July 17 the targets were railroads, highways, and key supply routes.

The *Boxer's* pilots teamed with air groups from the *Bon Homme Richard* on July 6, and their collective efficiency inflicted severe damage on the North Korean port of Wonsan. Strikes were sustained over Korea until October 5, when the *Boxer* returned stateside.

Air Group 2 came aboard and the big carrier steamed again to Korean waters on March 10, 1952. The "Busy Bee" joined her sister ships *Bon Homme Richard CV-31* and *Princeton CV-47* June 23–24 to launch air strikes against one of the most prominent power plants in the world—the Suiho Dam. This large installation had provided North Korea and Manchuria with all of their power requirements—until the air group inflicted heavy damage.

While off the east coast of Korea on August 6 a gasoline tank in a parked plane exploded, causing fires to spread throughout the *Boxer's* hangar deck. Up on the flight deck were 58 planes loaded with rockets and bombs. Cruising speed was immediately reduced as the planes were rolled to the forward deck area. Ammunition was exploding everywhere in the

Bow view of *USS Boxer CV-21.*

hangar deck, but the courageous fire fighting teams were determined to save the ship. Then a 500-pound bomb exploded, enveloping the entire ship in a black shroud of smoke. Eight men were killed and two severely burned, but the mighty carrier managed to escape death.

She returned to Yokosuka on August 11 for temporary battle repairs, then sailed into combat again on the 28th, attacking storage areas near Wonsan and Songjin-Kilchu.

On September 25 the *Boxer* arrived at San Francisco for repairs and alterations. During the yard period she was reclassified CVA—Attack Aircraft Carrier. Repairs were completed in March 1953 and the renovated ship headed for San Diego preparatory to another Korean tour of duty. She departed March 30, engaged in a brief operational readiness inspection at Hawaii, then arrived at Yokosuka, Japan, on April 30.

From May 10 to June 21 the *Boxer* sent air strikes against enemy troop movement and supply areas resulting in heavy beatings to railroads, highways, and storage facilities.

Two months before the Korean truce the *Boxer*

established three records for the number of sorties flown; 592 the first day, 600 the next, and 635 on the third. Most of these fighter sweeps were in directed support of the weary ground troops resisting repeated Communist attacks.

The Military Armistice Agreement was signed in Korea July 27, 1953. The *Boxer* conducted training operations in the Sea of Japan until November 11, then returned to California, arriving at Alameda on the 28th.

On March 3, 1954, the "Busy Bee" began her first peacetime cruise to the Far East. Afterwards she returned stateside, arriving at San Francisco on October 11 for a routine overhaul. Work was completed in February 1955 and she began training operations off the coast of Southern California.

Another Far East cruise was taken from June 3, 1955, to February 3, 1956 and during the trip she was again reclassified, this time to CVS-Anti-Submarine Warfare support carrier. This designation became effective November 15, 1955.

The *Boxer*'s tenth Western Pacific deployment began June 9, 1956. It was during this cruise that she logged the 79,000th arrested gear landing, which at the time was a record for all active Pacific Fleet carriers. She also traveled 666,666 nautical miles and made 500 carrier control approach landings.

In October 1958 the *Boxer* was equipped as an Amphibious Assault Carrier and became the flagship for Amphibron 10. Her first ship-to-shore movements by helicopter began off the North Carolina coast.

The "Busy Bee" received another reclassification in January 1959 to LPH-4—Amphibious Assault ship—and her crew began immediate training for this new phase of ASW tactics. She became a part of the "Gator" Navy, and vertical envelopment problems were developed as tactics were improved. Such amphibious maneuvers proved more effective than the frontal beach landing assaults of World War II.

Throughout 1960 the *Boxer* engaged in various amphibious exercises with other Atlantic Fleet units. A new record for debarkation and embarkation of troops was set during each operation. She logged her 25,000th helicopter landing during early 1961 while returning from a three-month Caribbean cruise. In May another cruise was made to the same area with 50 midshipmen aboard for at-sea training.

From August 1961 to February 1962 the *Boxer* received an elaborate overhaul at the New York Navy Yard. Many changes were made to her engineering sections, mess decks, and ship's library.

On March 8 the carrier departed the yard and was assigned to Amphibious Squadron 10. She loaded supplies at Norfolk, then steamed on March 20 to Guantanamo Bay, Cuba, for refresher training. She returned to Norfolk on May 10.

During the first weeks of April she participated in a fleet review for President John F. Kennedy. On the *Boxer* was performed a demonstration of vertical envelopment amphibious assault operations.

"Quickkick," a joint military operation, gave the *Boxer* a chance to demonstrate her efficiency, as Marine troops were transported from Vieques, Puerto Rico, to Onslow Beach, N.H. Twenty-eight helicopters from Marine Squadron HMM-264 flew the troops ashore.

A goodwill cruise began in June. Ports of call included St. Thomas, Virgin Islands; Santo Domingo, Dominican Republic; St. Johns, Antigua; Bridgeton, Barbados; Fort de France, Martinique. The cruise ended with a celebration at Trinidad and Tobago.

When tension mounted over Cuba in October 1962, the *Boxer* joined two other LPH's, *Thetis Bay* and *Okinawa*, and stood ready as President Kennedy ordered a blockade around the Communist-controlled island. She came back to Norfolk in December for Christmas leave.

On January 7, 1963, she participated in PHIBULEX 1-63, an amphibious emergency test.

On February 21, units of Amphibious Squadron Ten completed the tests of the squadron's efficiency to re-embark marine units of the 30th Marine Expeditionary Unit, including Marine Air Group 26 of the *Boxer*.

The *Boxer* rested at Norfolk until April when she participated in PHIBULEX 2-63. This operation was terminated ahead of schedule due to hostilities between the Dominican Republic and the Republic of Haiti. For 30 days the *Boxer* steamed off the Gulf of Gonave with Marines of the Sixth Marine Expeditionary Unit.

From August to October the "Busy Bee" operated off the North Carolina coast. On December 20 she entered Portsmouth Naval Yard for a four-month overhaul.

In January 1964 the 300 members of her Marine detachment were sent ashore and on January 16 the *Boxer* went into drydock at Norfolk, where old machinery was replaced with modern equipment.

She left the yards on April 28 for 30 days of operational readiness and amphibious training near Guantanamo Bay, Cuba. During May, dependents of the crew were treated to a surprise cruise, which included a visit to Kingston, Jamaica.

As the anniversary of the Cuban Revolution was

being celebrated, the *Boxer* steamed south of that island July 24–29 to land Marines and evacuate civilians. Tension diminished and the carrier resumed training operations off Gitmo Bay.

The "Busy Bee" sailed from Norfolk on October 3, 1964, to participate in Operation Steel Pike I. There were 1800 combat-ready Marines aboard to carry out a full-scale amphibious "assault" on the beaches of southern Spain. This was the largest peacetime amphibious operation in history, involving 80 ships and 60,000 men in a demonstration of Navy-Marine Corps striking power. The exercise was completed in early November and the *Boxer* steamed to Plymouth, England. She crossed the English Channel to Le Havre where the crew enjoyed four days of liberty. The carrier returned to Norfolk November 28 where she remained the rest of the year.

On April 1, 1965 she resumed training exercises in the Caribbean. While refueling on April 25 she was alerted to proceed immediately to Santo Domingo, Dominican Republic, for possible evacuation of American civilians. The Dominican crisis was again raging. A decision was made two days later and U.S. Marines were landed to protect American lives. They became the first U.S. troops to go ashore and during the week 1000 American women and children were safely removed from danger areas. After 47 days of continuous operations the *Boxer* returned to Norfolk June 29.

The carrier went to Mayport, Florida, August 10 and received units of the U.S. Army's First Cavalry Division (Air Mobile) plus 200 helicopters. The *Boxer* next arrived at Cam Rahn Bay, South Vietnam, on September 9 and unloaded the Army. On the 15th the carrier departed for Subic Bay, Philippines, where the crew enjoyed liberty. While en route to Norfolk she made four-day stops at Hong Kong, Naples, and Barcelona. On October 28 the *Boxer* arrived at Norfolk after steaming some 26,000 miles.

During January 1966 the "Busy Bee" underwent normal maintenance at Norfolk and departed February 8 to serve as primary recovery ship for the first Apollo spacecraft test shot. The capsule was picked up on February 20 about 200 miles east of Ascension Island and the carrier headed back to shore, arriving at Norfolk April 6. She was on station to recover the Gemini 8 manned space capsule five days later, but the craft splashed down in the Pacific, depriving the *Boxer* of a recovery. She went back to home port March 19.

April 16 was a proud day for the "Busy Bee," for she celebrated her 21st birthday. A huge cake was enjoyed by her elated crewmembers. During the next

ten days provisions were stored as the ship made ready for another cruise.

She departed April 26 for the 27,000-mile journey to Vietnam via the Mediterranean Sea, Suez Canal, Indian Ocean, and the Straits of Malacca. This second Western Pacific cruise, coming only six months after her return from transporting the Army's First Cavalry (Air Mobile) Division to Vietnam, carried on the pace-setting tradition established by the *Boxer* at Korea.

Aboard for this cruise was Marine Medium Helicopter Squadron 265 from New River, North Carolina, commanded by Lieutenant Colonel H. E. Medenhaull, and destined for duty with the First Marine Air Wing in Vietnam. Also on board were units of the Marine 3rd Force Reconnaissance Company headed for Okinawa, and a pair of Navy Mobile Inshore Undersea Warfare units for Vietnam.

The "Busy Bee" arrived off Vietnam late on the afternoon of May 20. The next day was Armed Forces Day and the carrier anchored at Nha Trang. That same afternoon she went northwards to Qui Nohn.

At dawn May 22 the *Boxer* arrived off Danang and delivered Squadron 265. Fighting in the city of Danang at that time resulted in a last-minute change in plans and it was decided to fly off all possible equipment rather than barging it ashore for transportation through the city.

The CV-46A *Sea Knight* helicopters of Squadron 265 maintained a continuous series of flights to shore for more than five hours. Only a few pieces of gear were too bulky or heavy to be airlifted, and they were put on barges later that afternoon.

Departing Danang, the carrier rendezvoused with the Seventh Fleet oiler USS *Cacapon AO-52* for night refueling. On May 25 she arrived at Buckner Bay, Okinawa, and took an overnight break for the first time in a month. All hands were granted liberty.

Port visits to Yokosuka, Japan, and Hong Kong rounded out the Western Pacific tour.

The *Boxer*'s medical department was summoned to provide treatment to a sailor from the oiler USS *Chemung AO-30*, who suffered serious injuries while refueling the *Boxer* prior to her departure from the South China Sea. Because the treatment required surgery, an expeditious transfer by highline was made from the oiler.

The "Busy Bee" returned to Norfolk on July 13, 1966. She had steamed more than 67,000 nautical miles in the past 11 months.

The *Boxer* and other units of Amphibious Squadron Ten left Norfolk on September 12 for three months of operations in the Caribbean. Before her return to Norfolk, the "Busy Bee" aided hurricane-stricken communities in the countries of Haiti and the Dominican Republic after Hurricane Inez unleashed her fury.

After six weeks in her home port, the *Boxer* steamed for the Boston Naval Yard for an extended overhaul, which lasted until July 1967. In August the assault ship commenced a five-week training cruise off Guantanamo Bay. She returned home in September.

The *Boxer* operated out of Norfolk up to March 11, 1968, then returned to the familiar Caribbean area for a 3½-month training cruise, returning to Norfolk on June 29. On August 5, 1968, the *Boxer*, in company with seven other ships and with Marine Battalion Landing Team 2/6 and Marine Helicopter Squadron HMM-162 embarked, participated in Exercise Escort Lion, a riverine exercise conducted in South Carolina, and the first of its type to be conducted on the east coast.

In October 1968, the *Boxer* left Norfolk and began a four-month cruise which took her to Caracas, Venezuela, and Cartagena, Colombia. She returned to her home port of Norfolk in February 1969. The next three months were spent in Newport News, Virginia, then the *Boxer* commenced six weeks of refresher training out of Guantanamo Bay. She returned to Norfolk on August 15, 1969.

As newer amphibious assault ships were commissioned, it became apparent that the *Boxer* would soon outlive her usefulness to the fleet. She continued to operate out of Norfolk, conducting antisubmarine warfare experiments and exercises up to December 1, 1969. On that day she was decommissioned and stricken from the list of Navy ships and disposed of for scrap.

The *Boxer* is gone but her memory remains in those who served in her in time of war and peace. In statistics, the *Boxer* held records which are still unbroken to this day, and held many firsts in her years of active service. She was the first Essex class carrier to operate jet aircraft; the first ship to launch guided missiles in combat (Korea 1952); the first amphibious assault ship to conduct, control and support and recover a nighttime helicopter assault under combat conditions (Dominican Republic, 1965); the first amphibious assault ship involved in space recovery operations.

Among the unbroken records still held by the *Boxer* are: most number of missions during the Korean Conflict; the all-Navy record for transferring ammunition at sea (225.2 short tons transferred in one hour); most number of helicopter landings (over 86,000 since 1959); most number of helicopter landings in one day (946); she passed one million miles steamed in 1967.

The *USS Boxer LPH-4* received the following awards during her 24 years of continuous active service: The Korean Service Medal with eight battle stars; the United Nations Service Medal; the National Defense Service Medal; the Armed Forces Expeditionary Medal; the Vietnam Service Medal and the Republic of Korea Presidential Unit Citation Badge.

INDEPENDENCE CLASS OF 1940-1943

Due to the critical need for aircraft carriers in the Pacific Forward Area during the early part of the Second World War, nine ships originally laid down for construction as light cruisers (CL) were reordered to be completed as aircraft carriers (CV) on March 18, 1942. The actual dates on which each ship was reclassified CV varies. The first five carriers of the class were commissioned as CVs. To distinguish them from the larger carriers of the fleet, they were again reclassified, as CVL, on July 15, 1943. The remaining four light carriers were commissioned as CVLs.

As light cruisers, the first six ships were ordered on September 9, 1940. They were the *USS Amsterdam CL-59*, *USS Tallahassee CL-61*, *USS New Haven CL-76*, *USS Huntington CL-77*, *USS Dayton CL-78*, and the *USS Wilmington CL-79*. The *USS Buffalo CL-99* and *USS Newark CL-100* were ordered on December 16, 1940, and the *USS Fargo CL-85* was ordered on February 5, 1942.

During construction, there were two name changes. The *USS Crown Point CVL-27* was renamed *Langley* and the *USS Reprisal CVL-30* was renamed *San Jacinto*. With completion of the *San Jacinto* on December 15, 1943, the *Independence* Class was complete as follows:

> *USS Independence CVL-22*
> *USS Princeton CVL-23*
> *USS Belleau Wood CVL-24*
> *USS Cowpens CVL-25*
> *USS Monterey CVL-26*
> *USS Langley CVL-27*
> *USS Cabot CVL-28*
> *USS Bataan CVL-29*
> *USS San Jacinto CVL-30*

The Independence class carriers displaced 11,000 tons; 15,800 tons full load. Overall length, 623 feet; Beam, 71½ feet; Width, 109 feet; Draft, 26 feet. Speed, 32 knots; Armament, four 5-inch 38-caliber gun mounts, twenty-six 40mm and forty 20mm antiaircraft mounts. Aircraft, in excess of 45. Complement, 1569 men.

All nine of the light carriers saw extensive action in the Pacific. The *USS Princeton CVL-23* was lost in action on October 24, 1944, during the Battle of Leyte Gulf.

The *Independence* was designated a target ship for the atom bomb test "Operation Crossroads" in July 1945. She survived the test and was used in radiological experiments up to January 29, 1951, when on that day she was sunk off the coast of Southern California. The *Langley* was transferred to Great Britain under the Mutual Defense Assistance Program in January 1951 and renamed *LaFayette*. She was returned to the United States in March of 1963, stricken from the list of Navy ships, and scrapped.

When the *Independence* was stricken in 1951, the class was redesignated *Belleau Wood* class and so remained until September 1953; then the *Belleau Wood* was loaned to France and renamed *Bois de Belleau*. The loan was for five years but was extended to 1960. She was returned to the United States in September 1960 and stricken from the list of ships that same month and sold for scrap. The five remaining light carriers were then designated the *Cowpens* class.

On May 15, 1959, they were redesignated Auxiliary Aircraft Carriers (AVT) and received new hull numbers.

> *USS Cowpens AVT-1*
> *USS Monterey AVT-2*
> *USS Cabot AVT-3*
> *USS Bataan AVT-4*
> *USS San Jacinto AVT-5*

The *Bataan* was stricken from the Navy list of ships and scrapped in September 1959. The *Cowpens* was stricken on November 1, 1959, and sold for scrap. The *Cabot* underwent antisubmarine warfare conversion in the mid 1950s. Her flight deck and hangar deck were strengthened. She received a large port catapult and much of the latest electronic devices. She was transferred to the Spanish Navy on August 30, 1967 and renamed *SNS DeDalo PH-01*.

At present two of the original nine light carriers remain on the list of Navy ships. The *Monterey* and the *San Jacinto*. The *San Jacinto* has been in mothballs since decommissioning in 1946. The *Monterey* was decommissioned on January 15, 1965.

The *Independence*, six months old, underway in the San Francisco Bay on July 15, 1943.

22

USS Independence CVL-22

Construction on the *USS Independence CVL-22* began in Camden on May 1, 1941. She was the fourth naval vessel to carry the name. She was originally named *USS Amsterdam CL-59*, but due to the urgent need for aircraft carriers in the Pacific she was reclassified on January 10, 1942.

Mrs. Rawleigh Warner, wife of the president of the Pure Oil Company, christened the ship on August 22, 1942. The *Independence* was commissioned on January 14, 1943, and Captain George R. Fairlamb, Jr., took command.

The new carrier was 622 feet 6 inches long and displaced 11,000 tons. She had a beam of 71 feet 6 inches

and her draft was 26 feet. Trial speed was logged at 31.6 knots. Her crew comprised 159 officers and 1410 enlisted men.

Shakedown operations were conducted off Trinidad, then she sailed towards California, arriving at San Francisco on July 3, 1943. Eleven days later she departed for Hawaii where she underwent weeks of training exercises prior to combat duty.

On August 22, 1943, on the first anniversary of her christening, the carrier was sailing for the action areas of the Pacific. Teamed with her were the *USS Essex CV-9* and *USS Yorktown CV-10*. The naval trio struck Marcus Island September 1, destroying 70 percent of

**A TBF taxis to take off; other TBF's in background
(April 1943).**

its shore installations, then returned to Pearl Harbor six days later. During this brief rest period, the executive officer, Commander Rudolph L. Johnson, assumed command of the carrier from Captain Fairlamb on September 27.

Assigned to Task Force 44 the *Independence* sailed on September 29 and participated in the Wake Island strike October 5–6, returning to Pearl on the 11th.

On November 5 the carrier was anchored at Pallikule Bay, Espiritu Santo, New Hebrides. Her air group attacked Rabaul six days later along with air groups from the *USS Essex* and *USS Bunker Hill CV-17*. While the planes were away, approximately 120 Japanese aircraft attacked in three waves, and the *Independence* scored her first six kills with antiaircraft fire.

The carrier suffered her first taste of battle damage while operating as the covering force for amphibious troops at Tarawa November 18–20. A large group of Japanese "Bettys" came in low over the water for an attack. Six of the enemy planes were repelled, however some managed to release three torpedoes, which scored direct hits on the starboard quarter. Only one of the deadly torpedoes exploded and superb damage control actions made it possible for the carrier to withdraw under her own power. Fourteen men were recommended for the Distinguished Service Medal and Captain Johnson received the Silver Star.

The *Independence* departed Funafuti Ellice Island December 7, 1943, and sailed into San Francisco Bay January 2, 1944. During the next few months the crew received shore leave.

The _Independence_ at Pearl Harbor in December 1943.

When repairs were completed the big carrier sailed under the Golden Gate Bridge while the San Francisco skyline slowly disappeared. Many sailors on deck were contemplating the time they would return.

At Pearl Harbor the ship began operational training. On July 26, 1944, Captain Johnson was relieved by Captain Edward C. Ewen.

On August 17 the _Independence_ departed Hawaii for Eniwetok. September 6–22 she participated in the capture and occupation of Southern Palau and sent air strikes against the Philippines.

A two-day strike beginning September 9 was directed at the Visayans. This was the first time the carrier's night air group saw action. Raids were conducted at the Visayans October 12–14 and Clark Field was bombed on the 22nd.

The _Independence_ was active in the support of the Leyte operation and her pilots directed attacks on Nansei Shoto on October 10, Formosa on October 12–14, the Visayans on October 20–22, and Luzon on the 24th.

The enemy hurriedly utilized the remainder of their once-proud fleet in an attempt to destroy American supremacy at Leyte Gulf. U.S. submarines sank two heavy cruisers on October 23. Admiral Halsey believed the enemy battle force to be too damaged to continue the attack, and ordered the withdrawal of his Fast Carrier Force to meet the threat of Japanese carriers in the northeast.

In the Surigae Strait American forces destroyed the Southern Japanese force commanded by Admirals Nishimura and Shima.

At San Bernadino Strait the Japanese battle group reversed course and attacked 16 escort carriers. The enemy feared a trap was enshrouding them and retreated, but we had lost two baby flat-tops.

Thus, the Japanese fleet slowly approached its inevitable end; they had lost four carriers, three battleships, ten cruisers, nine destroyers, three submarines, and 35 aircraft. It was obvious that the Rising Sun was falling.

The _Independence_ remained in the thick of action and continued strikes on the Philippines November 14–16. She was lucky to enjoy short rest periods from combat at Ulithi Atoll.

Steaming from the atoll on January 30, 1945, she aimed for Pearl Harbor for minor repairs and an overhaul. Upon arrival on February 11, Captain Nolan M. Kindell took command.

The carrier departed Hawaii March 14 for a 62-day operation in support of the Okinawa invasion. This was followed by a ten-day relaxation period at Ulithi, after which her air group was active in 35 night attacks, patrols, and support missions over Kyushu and Nansei Shoto.

From July 9 to September 2, Air Group 27 took part in Third Fleet operations against the Japanese homeland. They were credited with sinking the enemy cruiser _Oydo_.

For outstanding service during October, November, and December 1944, the _Independence_ was awarded the Philippine Republic Presidential Unit Citation Badge.

With final victory over Japan firmly established, the carrier departed Tokyo on September 22 and arrived at San Francisco October 31.

On November 15 she began the first of several "Magic Carpet" cruises bringing war-weary G.I.s back home. Her final cruise of this campaign was completed at San Francisco January 28, 1946.

The _Independence_ was positioned at Bikini Atoll for the atomic bomb test on May 29. She had been selected as a target ship to determine the endurance of a carrier under such an explosion. The atomic blast on July 1 sank five ships. The _Independence_ was still afloat but gutted by fires and rocking from internal explosions. A sub surface blast on July 25 sank nine more vessels but the _Independence_ stubbornly remained afloat, although she was now highly radioactive. She was towed to Kwajalein and decommissioned on August 28, 1946. In March 1947 she was brought home, where, for the next four years, many radiological tests and experiments were conducted.

On January 29, 1951 she met a highly unromantic demise. In a special test of new aerial and undersea

Damage to the *Independence* after the A-Bomb tests at Bikini during Operation Crossroads.

weapons, she was sunk off the California coast. America's first light carrier was forever stricken from the naval inventory on February 27, 1951.

During her short 3½ years of active Naval service, the *Independence* received the following awards: American Area Campaign Service Medal, Asiatic-Pacific Campaign Area Service Medal with eight battle stars, World War II Victory Medal, Navy Occupation Medal, and the Philippine Republic Presidential Unit Citation Badge.

USS Princeton CVL-23.

23

USS Princeton CVL-23

On the evening of October 24, 1944, the *USS Princeton CVL-23*, emitted a final agonizing eruption, then violently plunged to the ocean's sandy foundations some 150 miles off the coast of the Philippine Islands. Thus ended the all-too-brief career of a worthy ship.

During her short-lived 622 days in commission, she participated in every major pacific engagement, earning nine battle stars as her air group "Fighting 23" wrote history across the blue Pacific skies.

Her keel was laid on July 2, 1941, at the New York Shipbuilding Corporation, Camden, New Jersey.

She was originally designed as a light cruiser, the *USS Tallahassee CL-61*. However, early in 1942, she was converted due to the necessity for carriers in the Pacific.

On October 8, 1942, the *Princeton* was launched under the sanction of Mrs. Harold Dodds, wife of the president of Princeton University. The name of the new carrier honored the Revolutionary War Battle of Princeton of 1777.

The new carrier displaced 11,000 tons, stretched out 610 feet, and had a 71-foot beam. She carried a complement of 159 officers and 1410 enlisted men. Her armament consisted of various 20mm and 40mm quadruple gun mounts. The *Princeton* operated with a single aircraft squadron of 45 planes, composed of fighter and torpedo bombers.

Captain George R. Henderson, USN, assumed command on February 25, 1943, and the *USS Princeton CV-23* was officially placed in full commission. A rigorous shakedown cruise was conducted off Trinidad to test all shipboard equipment and prepare the crew for battle. After a brief post shakedown period in the yards, the *Princeton* was rushed to the Pacific war zone via Pearl Harbor. She was reclassified CVL-23 on July 15, 1943. On September 1, 1943, the light carrier participated in her first combat mission when her air group provided air cover for U.S. troops landing on Baker Island. It was in this action that the new F6F "Hellcat" was used in combat for the first time in the Pacific area. The landing forces were unopposed but the fighters engaged in a skirmish with an "Emily" reconnaissance plane. The *Princeton's* air group provided air cover for the next twelve days and also supplied the fleet with its first photographs of the four engine Japanese bomber, the "Emily."

While the larger carriers conducted air strikes against Makin and Tarawa on September 18, 1943, the *Princeton* launched her air group to provide protection within the task force. The primary strikes helped also to relieve the pressure on our troops landing at Bougainville. Air Group 23, commanded by Lieutenant-Commander Henry L. Miller, USN, was the carrier's Sunday punch. Four strikes were flown over airfields at Buka and the Bonins in the northern Solomons. So effective were the bombardments that not one single enemy aircraft was able to take off from the airfields. These strikes contributed to the neutralization of those airfields at the time that U.S. forces were landing in Empress Augusta Bay.

To prevent the establishment of air power over Bougainville by the Americans, the Japanese had assembled a powerful concentration of cruisers and destroyers at Rabaul. The *Princeton* arrived at a point about 220 miles south-southeast of Rabaul on the morning of November 5, 1943. With other carriers of the task force, she launched her fighter and torpedo aircraft and scored two direct hits on the enemy cruisers and one destroyer. The carrier's fighters downed ten enemy planes, thus eliminating the Japanese threat to consolidate their positions on Empress Augusta Bay. Another strike was launched on Rabaul November 11th.

From Rabaul, the *Princeton* steamed north to help neutralize Nauru while other forces supported the

landings on Tarawa. Airfields were left useless and cratered after a strike November 19.

After a short rest from combat the *Princeton* resumed the offensive in the attack against the Marshall Islands. On January 29, 1944, a three-day strafing attack was launched against Wotje and Taroa. Another lull in combat was observed at Roi Island following this action, and during the rest Captain William H. Buracker, USN, relieved Captain Henderson as Commanding Officer of the *Princeton.*

The carrier was back in combat on March 9, when she launched strikes on Engebi Island, leaving airfields completely unusable. Support sorties were carried out until the atoll was in Allied hands. It was a little over a year since the "Peerless P" had been commissioned and she had steamed 70,701 nautical miles, made 44 air strikes, and dropped 444,000 tons of ordnance on enemy targets.

On March 1, 1944, the *Princeton* anchored at Majuro Atoll for maintenance and loading of supplies. Carrier qualifications for new pilots were conducted off Espiritu Santo before sailing for another combat mission on March 23.

The performance of Air Group 23 during the strikes against Palau and Woleai were something the *Princeton* could be proud of. Seventeen enemy planes were downed in aerial combat and six were destroyed on the ground. One of the most experienced air groups in the Pacific at that time, the air group earned the nickname "Fighting 23" by living up to the highest standards expected of them.

As part of Task Group 38.3, the *Princeton* anchored in Majuro Atoll in the Marshalls on April 6, where supplies were taken on and the ship refueled. On April 13, the carrier sortied with the task force and commenced strikes on Hollandia. During the period April 14th to May 3rd, her air group flew a total of 548 combat missions. Returning to Majuro Atoll on May 4th, only long enough to conduct minor repairs and receive supplies, she resumed operations in the Hollandia operation until April 24, 1944.

On May 11, the *Princeton* returned to Pearl Harbor for a much-needed overhaul. Air Group 23 was relieved by Air Group 27, commanded by Commander E. W. Wood, Jr., USN. The light carrier rejoined the task force off Majuro Atoll on June 4. A fighter sweep was launched against Saipan to support the landings on that island on June 6. Additional strikes were launched from the 12th to the 18th against Guam, Tinian, and Rota. The enemy made air strikes against US Forces during this period, including a dusk attack on Task Group 58.3 on the evening of June 15th. During the air battle of June 19, the *Princeton*'s air group alone accounted for 30 confirmed aerial planes shot down, including many probables and assists. A hunt for the crippled enemy fleet followed the battle, after which the *Princeton* returned to the Marianas to resume strikes against airfields and installations on Pagan, Rota, and Guam.

On June 19 one Judy was shot down from guns of the *Princeton* and the *USS Enterprise CV-6*. Immediately thereafter, two Jills making a torpedo run on the *Princeton*'s starboard beam were shot down by the ship's gunners. A third Jill torpedo bomber attacked from the starboard side. The *Princeton* began a hard turn to right in order to offer a smaller target, and one of the carrier's gunners shot a wing off the enemy

plane and it crashed into the waters dead ahead. A torpedo was seen to fall from the plane but no contact was made.

The *Princeton*, and other carriers and units of the fast carrier task force, anchored at Eniwetok for replenishment on July 9. The ships got underway on July 14 and proceeded to the vicinity of the Marianas Islands to furnish air support for the amphibious operations in the capture and occupation of Guam and Tinian Islands. During the four-day strikes on Guam, the primary objective was to prevent the Japanese from using their airfields on Guam and Rota by cratering the runways on each field daily. Enemy antiaircraft fire was accurate on Guam and the *Princeton* lost one of her pilots from a direct hit over the target area.

TBM "Avengers" are positioned for takeoff from the "Peerless P" for strikes against the Ryukus on October 10, 1944.

The *Princeton* returned to Eniwetok Atoll on August 2 for upkeep and replenishment and repair work on her boilers. Upon completion of the repairs the carrier conducted a short training period before rejoining the task force.

When the fast carrier strikes were launched during a raid on Mindanao in the Southern Philippines on September 9 and 10, the "Peerless P" was there as a unit of Task Group 38.3. While strikes were being conducted against Del Monte airfields in Northern Mindanao by carriers of other task groups, the *Princeton* maintained antisubmarine and combat air patrols over the task group.

Beginning September 11, 1944, the *Princeton's* air group shifted her targets to the Visayas, Central Philippine Islands. The air group struck targets as far west as Iloilo, on Panay Island, as well as airfields and miscellaneous targets on Negros, Cebu, and Mactan Islands. At Mastbate, shipping was again attacked. A large cargo ship was left dead in the water while three smaller vessels were damaged. One of the carrier's pilots had to make a forced water landing five miles west of Milagros and was later rescued by a Kingfisher from the battleship *USS Massachusetts BB-59*. Before returning the pilot to the *Princeton*, the plane made a one-aircraft raid over damaged ships and a pier.

The *Princeton* took part in the first strikes of the war against Japanese-held Manila on September 21–22. In a series of engagements on the morning of the 21st, the *Princeton's* air group shot down 38 enemy aircraft without a single loss. By the morning of the 22nd, enemy air opposition had virtually disappeared. The afternoon airstrikes were cancelled due to an approaching typhoon.

Air strikes against the Philippines were resumed on September 24. Air Group 27 struck Coron, Mastbate, and made fighter sweeps over Panay and Negros Islands. The Coron strikes was over 700 miles round trip and the longest strike launched by the carrier at that time. Three enemy ships were sighted, and when the smoke had cleared one oiler was sinking and the two other ships were afire and seriously damaged. An air battle was staged over Nichols field and extended over Manila harbor and Cavite, and finally ended over Laguna de Bay, southeast of Manila.

The task group retired to Kossol Roads, Palau Islands, on September 27 and remained there until October 10, then got underway for the first carrier strikes against Nansei Shoto. Her targets were aircraft, airfields, and military installations on Okinawa Jima as well as shipping in the area.

On the morning of October 24, 1944, the great Battle of Leyte Gulf began. All carrier task groups were alerted that the remaining units of the crippled Japanese fleet were approaching. The *Princeton's* job was to send a fighter sweep over Manila and to stand by to hit important enemy naval units and shipping at anchor in Manila Bay. The "Peerless P" prepared for action. As in the case of each battle, the carrier's crew made ready for the upcoming attack. Firehoses were stretched along the deck edge and the hangar deck. Gun crews looked sharp-eyed into the skies and all men knew that the enemy opposition was going to be formidable. They ate breakfast at their battle stations and the flight deck crews gassed up and crammed the planes with bombs and torpedoes.

The fighter aircraft were launched at 6:00 A.M. some 150 miles from Manila. Enemy aircraft were reported heading towards Manila, west of the task force, in a force of 75 to 100. The remaining group of Hellcats were launched from the *Princeton* and they grouped about 50 miles away from the general formation. At the same time, a large group of enemy aircraft was discovered some 15 miles beyond the first group that was sighted.

The *Princeton's* air group joined fighters from the *USS Lexington CV-16* and intercepted the second enemy air group and completely disorganized them. Fighter Squadron 27 of the "Peerless P" alone accounted for 34 enemy aircraft downed with only one loss in the battle.

While the *Princeton* was recovering her aircraft on the morning of October 24, 1944, a lone enemy aircraft

The first major explosions occurred at 10:02 a.m. when the torpedo planes in the hangar bay exploded, blowing out the Number Two elevator and buckling the flight deck.

The *Birmingham* maneuvers in to resume fire fighting on
the burning *Princeton* during the Battle for Leyte Gulf.

was spotted at 9:38 A.M. The plane was coming in on
the port bow and made a shallow dive as the antiaircraft batteries opened fire. But the attack was too
late and the enemy plane slipped through and released its deadly 500-pound bomb. The ominous object slipped through the air and exploded just forward
of the number two elevator. Meanwhile, the ship's
AA batteries downed the Japanese plane as it passed
over the ship, but the damage had been done.

The hole in the flight deck appeared so small that
it hardly seemed possible any major damage could
have been sustained. Unfortunately, the bomb knocked
out the after fire fighting system while passing through
the flight deck and exploded the gas tanks of a torpedo
plane. The after engineering spaces became a raging

inferno with smoke so thick that it completely blacked
out the after section of the sip. Intense heat and suffo-
cating smoke forced personnel on the fantail to jump
overboard. They were picked up by nearby destroyers.

When the bomb struck the *Princeton,* the ship was
making 24 knots. In view of the developing conditions,
Captain Buracker reduced the ship's speed to 14 knots.
The light cruiser *USS Reno CL-96* and the destroyers
USS Cassin Young DD-793, USS Gatling DD-671 and
the *USS Irwin DD-794* were ordered to stand by and
assist. The task force, meanwhile, steamed onward to
conduct air strikes.

At 10:02 A.M., the first major explosion occurred
when the torpedoes in aircraft in the hangar deck
exploded. Shortly thereafter the *Princeton* was jarred

by a second explosion, which destroyed the forward elevator and buckled the flight deck. Flying debris from the explosions rendered many casualties and the fires extended to the island structure and bridge.

As the light carrier lost all weight, she assumed a crosswind position and drifted leeward. Smoke was so thick the ship was completely obscured from the view of other ships. The *Reno* was relieved by the *USS Birmingham CL-61* and the *USS Morrison DD-560*, came alongside to assist in fire fighting. The *Morrison* did far more in her efforts to save the *Princeton* than could be expected under the circumstances. She was one of the fighting "tin cans" that was lost as a result of Kamikaze attacks off Okinawa later in the war.

Before the destroyer *Irwin* departed, she had picked up 600 to 700 of the *Princeton*'s survivors and aided in firefighting along the forward section and hangar deck of the stricken carrier.

At 10:19 A.M., a group of enemy planes approached the *Princeton* at low altitude. Two of the planes were downed by the *Reno* and the remainder scattered.

Soon, the *Princeton* lost pressure in the forward fire fighting system, leaving only the emergency equipment in use.

Due to the wind velocity and denseness of smoke, fire fighting could only be maintained on the windward side of the burning carrier. By 11:56 A.M., the situation seemed to be improving, but when the

When it seemed that fires were being contained, the *Birmingham* and destroyers fighting fires had to pull away when enemy aircraft were reported approaching.

Morrison came alongside she lost her forward mast when it wedged between the carrier's stacks.

Any time enemy aircraft were reported approaching, the cruiser and destroyer had to pull away from the *Princeton* to fight off the enemy planes. When the *Morrison* was alongside the carrier, debris was constantly dropping onto her. At one point, a jeep and a torpedo tumbled from the carrier onto the destroyer's deck.

By 1:00 P.M. it looked as if the carrier might be saved, as fires in the extreme after section had been contained. All fires were reported extinguished when a group of enemy aircraft was reported approaching. Once again the *Birmingham* and *Morrison* pulled away. Only one plane was actually sighted and the attack never materialized. It is believed that this one incident alone caused the loss of the *Princeton*. Every time the cruiser and destroyer had to pull away, flames leaped to new heights. The *Birmingham* pulled along side again and resumed fire fighting and tried to take the carrier in tow.

As the cruiser was approaching the port side of the *Princeton*, the carrier's reserve torpedo and bomb storage exploded. The carrier's crew had been unable to jettison the ammunition earlier, for the heat and smoke made it impossible for anyone to approach those areas. The entire after section of the *Princeton* was blown sky high and debris in massive chunks covered the *Birmingham*. At this same time, the *Princeton*'s stern was blown away and the carrier's prospective commanding officer (who had refused to leave the ship) Captain John M. Hoskins, USN, lost the lower part of his leg while fighting fires in the hangar deck.

The *Birmingham* suffered 220 dead and 420 wounded—far in excess of the total *Princeton* casualties, when the carrier's stern had blown free. As the crippled cruiser moved away, all hope of saving the carrier had dissolved. At 3:38 P.M., Captain Buracker sadly left his ship—the last man to leave. The *Reno* received a message to destroy the *Princeton* and the other ships to rejoin the task group.

One final search of the waters surrounding the burning carrier was made to make sure no stragglers were

At 5:46 p.m., the *USS Reno CL-96* fired the first of two torpedoes at the *Princeton*. Moments later, a geyser of smoke and flame was all that was visible as the *Princeton* went down.

left in the water. Night was approaching and the ships would soon be sitting targets for enemy submarines and aircraft.

The *Reno* fired the first two torpedoes at the ill-fated *Princeton* at 5:45 P.M. Flames and debris rose 2000 feet into the air. Survivors of the *Princeton* gathered at the railings of the various ships that picked them up to take one last glimpse of the smoke-filled area.

The after section of the carrier appeared momentarily, with the screws protruding, then sank deep into the waters of the Philippine Sea.

During her brief life span of one year, seven months and 23 days, the *USS Princeton CVL-23* earned the following awards: The American Area Campaign Service Medal; the Asiatic-Pacific Area Campaign Service Medal with Nine battle stars; the Philippine Liberation Campaign Ribbon; and the Republic of the Philippines Presidential Unit Citation Badge.

USS Belleau Wood CVL-24, aerial view, May 22, 1943.

24

USS Belleau Wood CVL-24

Although the *USS Belleau Wood CVL-24* was a light carrier of the *Independence* class and ranked second to the larger *Essex* class ships, she sailed home with a record hardly equalled by any of her counterparts when the Second World War came to an end.

Rear Admiral Sprague sent a message to the crew stating: "Your performance of duty has been outstanding on all occasions and you leave behind a distinguished chapter in war history. You have contributed more than your share in the final victory."

True credit was given when the *Belleau Wood* was awarded the Presidential Unit Citation for action in the Pacific.

Her keel was laid down as the *USS New Haven CL-76* on August 11, 1941, at the New York Shipbuilding Company, Camden, New Jersey. On February 16, 1942, her name was changed to *Belleau Wood* and construction was authorized for completion as a carrier.

The *Belleau Wood* was named for the World War I Battle of Bois de Belleau, fought near Soissons, France, in June 1918. The Fourth U.S. Marine Brigade had bravely fought through many bitter encounters during the struggle, and the new carrier would live up to this high standard during the months that followed her introduction to active naval service.

Mrs. Thomas Holcomb, wife of the Commandant of

the Marine Corps, christened the carrier December 6, 1942.

The *Belleau Wood* was 622 feet 6 inches of fighting potential and displaced 11,000 tons. Extreme beam was 71 feet 6 inches; armament consisted of numerous 20mm and 40mm quadruple gun mounts. She carried a crew of 159 officers and 1410 enlisted men with complement of 45 aircraft.

Captain A. M. Pride assumed command on March 31, 1943, and the carrier was placed in active commission. Captain Pride was a "mustang," having worked his way up through the ranks from Machinist Mate Third Class to Captain, and had earned his aviator's wings during World War I.

The *Belleau Wood* went through a shakedown cruise in Chesapeake Bay and post-shakedown alterations followed at the Norfolk Navy Yard.

On July 26, she passed through the Panama Canal and arrived at Pearl Harbor August 9 ready to join other fast carriers in the Pacific war zone. Her first combat assignment was Baker Island situated near the equator. The island was needed as a fighter base to disrupt Japanese raids out of Tarawa and Makin Islands. The attack came as a total surprise to the enemy and no effectual action was observed while the Army P-40s were landing. The *Belleau Wood* crossed the equator 32 times while providing the island with protective cover.

Tarawa marked the deepest advance of the Japanese and it was here that Air Group 24 received its baptism of fire by striking enemy bases.

The *USS Lexington CV-16* and *USS Princeton CVL-23* accompanied the *Belleau Wood* on this mission and the light carrier crossed the International Date line for the first time. The *Belleau Wood* then returned to Pearl Harbor for minor repairs.

On October 1, 1943, the *Belleau Wood*, along with the *USS Essex CV-9, USS Yorktown CV-10, USS Lexington CV-16*, and *USS Independence CVL-22*, departed Hawaii to strike Wake Island. Emotions were tense during the battle, since Americans were attacking soil that the Marines had valiantly fought for.

On October 5–6 Wake Island took a severe beating—twice as powerful as the one inflicted on Tarawa.

Afterwards, Admiral of the Fleet Chester W. Nimitz sent this message to the task force: "The thorough job well done on Wake Island by planes and ships of your task force will have results reaching far beyond the heavy damage inflicted."

As the task force prepared to destroy Japanese-held land defenses on Makin and Kwajalein, it was obvious the enemy was there to stay. The *Belleau Wood*, as part of Task Group 50.2, steamed through the waters of the Gilberts and raided Makin and Tarawa on November 23. The final organized resistance on Tarawa disappeared. The enemy was now removed in the Gilberts and the task force prepared for an attack against the Marshalls.

The *Belleau Wood* returned to Hawaii for a brief yard period, then sailed to battle off Kwajalein on January 29, 1944. She was teaming with Task Group 58.1 with Rear Admiral Marc A. Mitscher commanding.

Her planes were assigned to Taroa (Maloelap) on the opening day of fighting, then were moved to Kwajalein for air strikes from January 30 through February 3. By February 4, 1944, American control of Kwajalein was secured, and the task group anchored at Majuro Atoll for some rest.

Working with Task Force 58 the *Belleau Wood* participated in the attacks on Truk, Saipan, and Tinian during February 1944. Air battles began on the 16th and by the afternoon 204 enemy planes had been destroyed. This terminated Japanese supremacy over Truk. Even though the island was finally bypassed, her airpower had to be nullified prior to American assaults against Eniwetok on February 17. Maximum damage was inflicted on Tinian, Rota, and Guam in the Marshall chain. Enemy strength on Saipan had to be tested prior to final landings scheduled for June. The air group took off and flew towards the island, encountering heavy air action on February 22. As a result 200 enemy planes were destroyed with a loss of 45 to the task force.

Before the scheduled operations against the Western Carolines began, the *Belleau Wood* moved south to Espiritu Santo where the task force assembled for the strike. For the first time task groups were composed of four aircraft carriers in each group.

On March 15 the fast carrier force steamed from Palau, where they unleashed a tremendous assault, resulting in the sinking of 31 enemy ships and the damaging of 18 more. *Belleau Wood* pilots downed three enemy fighters, damaged a freighter and a minelayer, and destroyed an aircraft hangar. On March 31 the carrier celebrated her first birthday by destroying an enemy weather station at Ngulu Island and followed this up by sinking a cargo ship at Ulithi and downing two enemy planes cruising 22 miles from the ship.

Concluding these attacks in the Western Carolines her air group became the first American fighters over Woleai and where heavy damage was inflicted on ground installations.

USS Belleau Wood as seen from the USS Essex CV-9, bringing down attacking Japanese torpedo plane, February 22, 1944.

The Marianas Islands were the guarding sentinels of the Philippines as well as the Ryukyus and Japan itself. On June 11, 1944, the *Belleau Wood* launched her planes in an attempt to destroy Japanese air power over the Marianas. During the assault the task force repulsed a major enemy carrier force and destroyed 360 planes. Her pilots sank a carrier of the *Hiyo* class—a ship three times the size of the *Belleau Wood*. Few carriers, even the larger ones, could boast or receive full credit for sinking a major enemy warship.

Most of June was spent providing air cover during the occupation of Saipan and Tinian. Strikes were flown over Iwo Jima, HaHa Jima, and Chi Chi Jima. During the last week of June the *Belleau Wood* returned to Pearl Harbor for her first overhaul since beginning active service. Afterwards, she resumed her duties in the Marianas operation, assisting in the capture and occupation of Saipan up to August. While engaged in raids against Iwo Jima and the Nansei Shoto on October 12–13, the *Belleau Wood* was victim to 47 separate Japanese bombing, strafing, and torpedo attacks. Then she headed southward for strikes at Aparri, Laoag, and the Luzon Islands in the Philippines.

When the Leyte operation began October 20 a large Japanese task force of four carriers, two battleships, five cruisers, and numerous escorts was detected some 200 miles north of Luzon. The American task force immediately swung northwards where early the next morning the enemy force was caught unprepared.

The *Belleau Wood* and other carriers launched their planes and delivered everything they had to the enemy, encountering a minimum of resistance. The bombings, strafing, and torpedo attacks by American pilots were highly successful and the enemy could only get 15 planes airborne. After the battle all four enemy carriers were resting on the sea bottom while the two burning battleships and escorts headed north in full retreat.

The *Belleau Wood* was operating with Task Group 38.4 some 90 miles off the Leyte coast on October 30 when, shortly before noon, enemy aircraft were spotted. As the carrier sent her planes to attack, a kamikaze pilot crashed into the *USS Franklin CV-13* nearby. Another began an apparent suicide approach, but suddenly banked towards the *Belleau Wood.* The determined pilot rushed through heavy antiaircraft fire and it seemed success was his. "This is it," raced through the minds of *Belleau Wood* crewmen as the suicide plane smashed into the after-portion of the ship's flight deck. Ammunition and depth charges exploded and fires raged for hours, fed by burning gasoline. Finally, the fire fighting teams had control of the inferno and the carrier had survived her first major battle damage. Ninety-two men were dead or missing.

On October 31 the carrier limped back to Ulithi and results showed that damage was two severe for repairs in the forward area; she was ordered to Hunters Point Naval Shipyard in San Francisco. Upon her arrival at California she had sailed 141,178 miles since commissioning.

Repairs were completed by January 20, 1945, and

USS Belleau Wood CVL-24. View of flight deck and fires after a Kamikaze attack, October 30, 1944.

on that day she sailed for Hawaii in company with the newly commissioned *USS Randolph CV-15.* They arrived six days later and joined the fleet at Ulithi on January 29.

Assigned to Task Group 58.1 the *Belleau Wood* departed Ulithi on February 10 to begin the first strikes on the Japanese homeland. A series of strikes were also launched against the Bonins, Chi Chi Jima, and Iwo Jima; additional sorties were made on Tokyo and Nansei Shoto on March 1.

March 18–21, the *Belleau Wood* struck Kyushu where an enemy attacking force was annihilated. Two enemy destroyers, three cargo ships, and a submarine chaser were sunk on March 24.

On April 6, 1945, following a successful combat air patrol over the amphibious ships off Okinawa, Air Group 30 was landing aboard their carrier. Upon arrival they noticed an unusual "weather report" issued by the ship's aerological office. It read: "Weak Japanese front approaching Okinawa this afternoon was broken up by converging F6Fs. Scattered to broken Japanese planes at 2000 feet lowering to sea level. Large reduction in visibility was due to rising suns falling into Japanese current."

From July to August 15, 1945, the *Belleau Wood* bombed and strafed the Japanese homeland islands of Honshu and Hokkaido. These strikes continued through the invasion of Okinawa, Kyushu, and the *Belleau Wood* flyers were also dealt the task of intercepting and eliminating enemy planes and defense facilities in the Japanese Empire and Nansei Shoto.

The formal Japanese surrender ceremonies were held on September 2, 1945. The *Belleau Wood* was present as a visitor after two years of combat duty which took her 216,682 miles across the seas, accounted for the destruction of 502 enemy aircraft, sunk 12 heavy and 36 light Japanese vessels, and rendered damage to 83 others.

The *Belleau Wood* was assigned to duty with the "Magic Carpet" fleet returning thousands of G.I.'s from the war zones of the Pacific. She completed three such cruises, returning from the last voyage January 31, 1946.

When the *Belleau Wood* was awarded the Presidential Unit Citation, the article read: "For extraordinary heroism in action against the enemy Japanese forces in the air, ashore and afloat in the Pacific War Area from September 18, 1943, to August 15, 1945. Spearheading the concentrated carrier-warfare in the forward areas, the *Belleau Wood* and her air groups (24, 21, 30, and 31) struck crushing blows toward annihilating Japanese fighting forces; they provided air

Port bow view of *USS Belleau Wood CVL-24*, Jan. 19, 1945.

cover for our amphibious forces; they fiercely countered the enemy's aerial attacks and destroyed his planes; and then inflicted terrific losses on the Japanese Fleet and merchant marine units sunk or damaged. Daring and dependable in combat, the *Belleau Wood* with her gallant officers and men rendered loyal service in achieving the ultimate defeat of the Japanese Empire."

After a short period of active peacetime duty on the West coast, the carrier was decommissioned and placed in the Alameda Pacific Reserve Fleet on January 23, 1947.

She was removed from mothballs on September 5, 1953, and transferred to France under the Mutual Defense Assistance program. Her name was changed to *Bois De Belleau* while serving with the French Navy.

When she returned stateside in September 1960 she was stricken from the lists of Navy ships and sold for scrap. Thus ended the career of one of the fightingest ships of the Second World War.

The *Belleau Wood* received the following awards during her three years and nine months of active commission in the US Navy: The Presidential Unit Citation; the American Area Campaign Medal; the Asiatic-Pacific Area Campaign Medal with eleven battle stars; the World War Two Victory Medal; the Navy Occupation Medal; the Philippine Liberation Campaign Service Ribbon with two bronze stars; and the Republic of the Philippines Presidential Unit Citation Badge.

USS Cowpens CVL-25, aerial oblique view, July 17, 1943.

25

USS Cowpens AVT-1 (CVL-25)

On November 17, 1941, the keel of the *USS Huntington CL-77* was laid at the New York Shipbuilding Corporation at Camden, New Jersey. Events that occurred during the next 14 months altered the construction and the light cruiser was completed as an aircraft carrier.

Mrs. Margaret Halsey, daughter of Admiral of the Fleet William F. Halsey, christened the ship on January 17, 1943, as the *USS Cowpens CV-25*. The *Cow-*pens was named in honor of the famous battle fought during the Revolutionary War, when America defeated the British in the town of Cowpens, near Spartanburg, South Carolina. The light carrier's launching came exactly 162 years after the Battle of Cowpens.

The *Cowpens* displaced 11,000 tons, was 610 feet 6 inches long, had a beam of 71 feet 6 inches, and a speed, 33 knots. Her armament consisted of many

40mm and 20 mm quadruple gun mounts. The carrier operated with 45 aircraft and was home to 159 officers and 1410 enlisted men.

Captain Robert P. McConnell assumed command of the *Cowpens* on May 26, 1943, and the ship was commissioned at the Philadelphia Naval Shipyard. Captain McConnell had been the skipper of the ill-fated *USS Langley AV-3* when she went down on February 27, 1942, south of Java.

On June 20, the *Cowpens* conducted trial runs on Delaware Bay, returning to port five days later. Air Group 25 reported on board July 3, and the *Cowpens* began to shape up like a combat ship. She got off to a bad start and was burdened with being called a jinx ship for a while. On July 14, 1943, while returning to Norfolk, she ran afoul of an antisubmarine net near the Navy Yard, a day in drydock was needed to repair the damage.

July 21–August 8 the small carrier made a training run to the Port of Spain, Trinidad, and then back to Philadelphia; on August 26, the *Cowpens* departed for San Diego. She was still in training upon arrival on September 12, but due to the desperate need for carriers in the Pacific Theater, she only remained in San Diego overnight, then departed for Pearl Harbor the next morning.

On September 19, 1943, the *Cowpens* arrived at Pearl Harbor. Supplies were loaded, and on the 29th the carrier left Pearl as a unit of Task Group 59.18 to participate in her first combat action, striking Wake Island. The carrier's air group began air attacks on October 5, and for two days relentlessly smashed the island's defenses. There was no opposing air opposition, but antiaircraft batteries on the island gave U.S. forces a strong fight. Following the Wake Island raid, the *Cowpens* returned to Pearl Harbor, where bad luck again befell the ship.

On October 17, a destroyer rammed her starboard side, calling for another session in drydock. As if this were not enough, a gasoline fire broke out during the repair period. The cool efficiency of the crew soon had the fire under control and serious damage was prevented.

Next mission for the *Cowpens* was to join other fast carriers to soften Japanese defenses on Tarawa and prevent any enemy interference with the U.S. landings on the island. Most of the islands within range of Tarawa suffered heavy bombardment on November 20

USS Cowpens CVL-25, starboard broadside view, at sea, planes on deck; *USS North Carolina* in background, November 1943.

and 24, 1943. The *Cowpens*'s air group concentrated strikes on Makin and Mille.

The *Cowpens*'s pilots flew against Kwajalein and Eniwetok on December 4 and 5, where 11 enemy torpedo planes were destroyed on the island's airfields. On the 4th, the Japanese tried twice to penetrate the attack and destroy the carriers. All enemy aircraft attempting daylight attacks were shot down, but during the night many slipped through and caused considerable damage to ships in the task force.

Prior to the Marshall Islands campaign, the carriers demonstrated what they could do to help the amphibious operations.

On airfields in the Marshalls, 150 Japanese aircraft were poised in battle readiness. When the U.S. troops went ashore on January 31, 1944, not one single enemy plane was able to get off the ground.

As the carriers continued to play havoc with the enemy, each attack carried the offensive deeper into Japanese-held territory. Truk was an important Japanese strong point in the Western Carolines, and when word came that the island was soon to be designated a target, apprehension grew among the men in the fleet.

On February 16 and 17, 1944, the *Cowpens* and other carriers smashed two airfields, shipping, and other defenses on Truk. Air Group 25 from the *Cowpens* assisted in sinking one cruiser and downing three aircraft. From Truk, the task force headed for the Marianas and important photographic coverage of the island was accomplished as well as heavy damage to shore installations.

The "Mighty Moo," as her crew called her, had the element of surprise on her side in all combat operations up to the Asiatic-Pacific raids of 1944 on the Marianas. An enemy aircraft spotted the U.S. task force 420 miles away from their objective. The antagonists threw all they could at the advancing carriers, sending in waves of torpedo attacks. The *Cowpens* launched her air group under attack for the first time. Guam, Rota, and Saipan were hit until February 23, resulting in 168 aircraft shot down or destroyed on the ground.

The U.S. Army was preparing for a new invasion of New Guinea. Besides keeping the Japanese fleet away, the fast carriers were assigned to support the U.S. ground forces. The Japanese moved their larger ships back to Palau and Yap after the first Truk attack. The *Cowpens*, along with other carriers, had the task of preventing the enemy fleet from attacking the army in New Guinea. Assigned to Task Group 58.1, the *Cowpens* launched her aircraft against Palau and Yap.

The Japanese sighted our task force once again and night and day air battles were fought before our air groups could get within striking range of their targets. Palau was hit on March 30, and Yap on April 1, at which time Woleai also received heavy damage. The Japanese moved much of their larger ships again, this time farther back, but many of the smaller ships were destroyed. Heavy damage was also done to shore installations and aircraft.

On April 21 and 22, the carriers hit enemy airfields on Sarmi, Wake, Sarvar, and Humboldt Bay while the U.S. Army was landing on New Guinea. With New Guinea finally secured by the army, the *Cowpens* conducted more air strikes on Truk before returning to Majuro Atoll for replenishment.

On May 18, Captain Hubert W. Taylor relieved Captain McConnell as commanding officer.

On June 12, 1944, while the *Cowpens* was sending air strikes over the Marianas, Lieutenant Commander Robert Price, the ship's air group commander, was shot down. He was located in the water and a life raft was thrown to him, but night came before he could be rescued. Various searches the next day failed to locate him. Eleven days later, another task group spotted him and he was picked up feeling fine, but hungry.

As the tide of battle on Guam and Saipan shifted in favor of the U.S., the Japanese were making a final effort to save their possessions. On June 19, 1944, a large concentration of enemy aircraft were launched in a wave-after-wave move to destroy the U.S. fleet. Brilliant air-to-air combat by our pilots was shown in a one-day action later called "The Marianas Turkey Shoot" in which the Japanese lost 360 aircraft to our 20.

The *Cowpens* missed out on action that occurred the following day due to refueling operations away from the battle area. The carrier returned to combat and supported the invasion until July 6, then returned to Pearl Harbor for normal upkeep and repairs.

Air Group 25 had 950 combat sorties chalked up after the Marianas operation. The *Cowpens* left Hawaii in August 1944, with Air Group 22 on board under the command of Commander T. H. Jenkins, USN. The ship was also painted in zigzag camouflage.

As part of Task Group 38.1, the *Cowpens* hit Palau and struck Angaur, Ngesebus, and Malakai September 6–8, 1944. There was no enemy air opposition.

On September 24, the *Cowpens* participated in the opening phases of the Philippine Campaign, and during the whole period Air Group 22 shot down 41 enemy aircraft.

The carrier had steamed over 100,000 miles since

commissioning, and was beginning to show signs of wear from combat duty, but there was no time for an overhaul.

From October 12 to 14, the *Cowpens* conducted air assaults on Formosa. During action on the 13th, two U.S. cruisers, the *USS Canberra CL-81* and *USS Houston CA-30* were torpedoed, but every ship in the task group made it back to Ulithi. After taking on stores and prepared to strike again, the *Cowpens* received word that the Japanese fleet was heading back toward the Philippines. Three of our task groups destroyed the Japanese carrier force to the north and the *Cowpens*'s air group flew combat patrol and fighter sweeps over airfields in the Visayans. The *Cowpens*'s torpedo squadron scored three direct hits on a cruiser, which sent her to the bottom. The threat to our landings was now removed and the fast carrier force steamed to Ulithi for a well-deserved rest.

A typhoon smashed the task force off the Philippines on December 18 and 19, 1944, and carried more enmity than the Japanese had ever attempted. Wind speeds of 100 miles per hour struck and the *Cowpens* took her toll of damage and sustained rolls of as much as 45 degrees. Bombs in the forward magazine broke loose, and as men tried to secure them they had to hang from the overhead to avoid being crushed to death. A fighter plane's belly tank caught fire and the firemen had to lash themselves to the flight deck so they would not blow over the side.

Lieutenant Commander Price, who had escaped death six months earlier, was killed by tractors and planes moving wildly about the flight deck.

At the height of the typhoon, the *Cowpens* lost radar contact and was guided by the destroyer *USS Halsey Powell DD-686*. The only rewarding result of the typhoon was that the *Cowpens* remained in Ulithi for repairs on Christmas Day.

Air Group 46, led by Commander C. W. Rooney, USN, flew aboard on February 6, 1945, and relieved Air Group 22, which had left behind a proud record.

The *Cowpens* sortied from Ulithi on February 10, 1945, for air strikes about 125 miles from Yokohama. Little air opposition was encountered and strikes were conducted on the Ryukyus before the task force retired to Ulithi.

The *Cowpens* departed on March 7, 1945, and arrived in San Francisco on the 24th. A yard overhaul began at Mare Island.

While in the yards, the *Cowpens*'s executive officer, and all department heads except the first lieutenant and supply officer, were relieved.

On May 21, with Air Group 50 aboard, the *Cow-*

An F6F starts to crash into aircraft spotted at the forward end of the *Cowpens CVL-25* in March 1945. Two men jumped overboard and were lost. Five aircraft were smashed.

pens returned to the Pacific combat area. On July 10, 1945, she commenced air strikes on Japanese shipping and aircraft from Hokkaido to the Inland Sea.

The Second World War was slowly coming to an end and Air Group 50 did its share in helping sink the battleships *Nagato* and *Huruna*, the carrier-battleships *Ise* and *Hyuga*, and the cruiser *Oyodo*. Hostilities ceased on August 15, 1945, and *Cowpens* pilots, out to make more strikes on the Japanese homeland, jettisoned their bombs and returned to the ship.

On August 27, the *Cowpens* was assigned to the "Show of Force" group sent into the Sagami Bay. Her aircraft flew passengers ashore on the 28th and these were believed to be the first planes to land on Japanese soil subsequent to the war. The *Cowpens* fought gloriously for 22½ months in the Pacific Theater. Her scoreboard revealed 2452 combat sorties flown, 108 enemy aircraft destroyed in air combat, 198 enemy aircraft destroyed on the ground, 657 tons of bombs, and 3063 rockets dropped on enemy installations, and 39 merchant ships sent to the bottom.

The USS *Cowpens CVL-25* was awarded the Navy Unit Commendation which read: "For outstanding heroism in action against the enemy Japanese forces in the air, ashore, and afloat in the Pacific War Area from October 5, 1943, to August 15, 1945. Operating continuously in the most forward areas, the USS *Cowpens* and her air groups struck crushing blows toward annihilating Japanese fighting power; they provided air cover for our amphibious forces; they fiercely countered the enemy's aerial attacks and destroyed his planes; and they inflicted terrific losses on the

Japanese in fleet and merchant marine units sunk or damaged. Daring and dependable in combat the *Cowpens* with her gallant officers and men rendered loyal service in achieving the ultimate defeat of the Japanese Empire."

The *Cowpens* spent two years of peacetime duty with the fleet, and in January 1947, she was placed in the Pacific Reserve Fleet. On May 16, 1959, the *Cowpens* was reclassified AVT-1 (Auxiliary Aircraft Transport). The carrier was never to see active duty in this capacity, for on November 1, 1959, she was stricken from the list of Navy ships and sold for scrap.

The once great carrier was bought by Zidell Exploration Inc., on May 5, 1960, for $273,389.98. Scrapping began two weeks after purchase and was complete by October 19, 1961.

During her active service the *USS Cowpens AVT-1* received the following awards: The Navy Unit Commendation; the American Area Campaign Medal; the Asiatic-Pacific Area Campaign Medal with eleven battle stars; the World War II Victory Medal; the Navy Occupation Medal; the Philippine Liberation Campaign Ribbon with two bronze stars and the Republic of the Philippines Presidential Unit Citation Badge. Also received was the "Anti-Submarine Net Medal" for successfully snagging a net single handedly in 1943.

USS Monterey CVL-26, aerial oblique view, 1943.

26

USS Monterey AVT-2

On September 9, 1940, construction of the light cruiser *USS Dayton CL-78* was authorized. Her keel was laid at the New York Shipbuilding Corporation of Camden, New Jersey, on December 29, 1941. Due to the extreme shortage of aircraft carriers in the Pacific Theater, the *Dayton* was one of nine light cruisers under construction destined to become aircraft carriers. In *March* of 1942, the future carrier was renamed *Monterey CV-26*, in honor of one of the hardest battles fought during the war between the United States and Mexico, September 19–24, 1846.

Mrs. P. L. N. Bellinger, wife of Rear Admiral Bellinger, Deputy Chief of Staff to the Commander-in-Chief, Pacific Fleet, christened the ship on February 21, 1943, and the new carrier slid down the ways.

The *Monterey* was 622 feet 6 inches long; extreme beam, 26 feet. Armament consisted of two 40mm quadruple and nine twin 40mm antiaircraft gun mounts; she accommodated 159 officers and 1410 enlisted men, and operated with 45 aircraft.

Captain Lester T. Hundt, USN, assumed command of the *Monterey* at commissioning ceremonies conducted at the Philadelphia Navy Yard on June 17, 1943. A war-hurried shakedown cruise was carried out so that the ship could join forces with the fast carrier force in the Pacific forward area. In less than three months after her commissioning, the *Monterey* was in combat as she took part in the Makin and Marshall Islands attacks on November 19, 1943.

On December 25, 1943, and January 1, 1944, her air group struck the combined air and naval strength of Japan; these assaults continued up to January 4, resulting in the sinking of a cruiser and a destroyer.

The 1944 Asiatic-Pacific raids began on February 16. The *Monterey*, steaming in company with other carriers, launched a devastating attack on Truk for two days; the next target for the *Monterey* was the Marianas during February 21–22.

From March 30 to April 1, air strikes were flown over Palau, Yap Ulithi, and Woleai. The Asiatic-Pacific raids were completed on May 1, with hard hitting fighter sweeps over Satawan and Ponape. During these raids the *Monterey* was subjected to stiff air opposition, but no damage was sustained.

The *Monterey's* air group was sent against the Japanese carrier force when the enemy made an ill-fated show of strength on June 19–20, 1944. This event, called the Battle of the Philippine Sea, was a disastrous blow to the enemy. The veteran air group from the *Monterey* participated in the "Marianas Turkey Shoot," where 392 Japanese planes were downed on the first day of the battle. The carrier then sent air assaults against the Bonins, Wake, Yap, Luzon, Formosa, and the Ryukyus.

On December 18, 1944, the task force encountered a typhoon. The men knew the storm was coming, so everything was lashed down. The storm continued for

Gun crews of the *USS Monterey CVL-26* firing at an attacking Japanese airplane. The *USS Wasp CV-18* is seen in the background. June 26, 1944.

two days and the *Monterey* received heavy damage; several planes secured to the hangar deck were torn loose from their ¾-inch cables. Planes bounced around the deck, showers of sparks flew from the planes when they crashed into each other and the side of the ship. Fires broke out and immediately began spreading fore and aft of the ship. Captain S. H. Ingersoll ordered the *Monterey* steered to a position where the wind and seas would reduce the ship's motion so that the fire fighting teams could extinguish the fires. All fires were completely dead in 40 minutes from the time they began.

However, it wasn't an easy task for the men manning the hoses. They had to dodge burning aircraft that slid back and forth. Many sailors were overcome by the blinding smoke, but as one sailor fell, another picked up the hose to continue the fight.

A 100-knot gale lifted one sailor overboard into the raging sea. An officer who saw the man go over threw out a hose and the sailor grabbed it and clambered back on deck. The salt-soaked sailor candidly said it was "just enough to cool me off after the heat of the damned fire!"

The *Monterey* was ordered to Bremerton, Washington, and entered the Puget Sound Naval Shipyard in January 1945. For two months she underwent a complete overhaul and battle damage repairs.

By May 1945, the *Monterey* was back in combat, this time launching strikes against Japan proper. As part of the famed Task Force 58, commanded by Admiral Marc A. Mitscher, the fast carrier force launched air assaults over Kyushu and then supported the Okinawa offensive forces.

Strikes began for the carrier's air group over Tokyo in June of 1945. Hokkaido and northern Honshu were hit hard, then an attack was made on the Kure Naval Base. Many industrial facilities and ships under construction were under constant bomb and rocket attacks right up to August 15, 1945, when the Japanese surrendered. On that day, the *Monterey* had all of her available aircraft in the air ready for another strike on Tokyo. The Third Fleet received word to "recall all air strikes." The Second World War had finally come to an end.

The *Monterey* and the *USS Bataan CVL-29*, patrolled the Kyushu area up to September 4, in the event that diehard enemy troops would fail to abide by the surrender announcement. On the 6th, the *Monterey* steamed proudly behind the *USS Ticonderoga CV-14* into Tokyo Bay. When the light carrier dropped anchor, a total of 68 consecutive days of sea duty had been logged.

Aerial, broad on starboard stern, at anchor in Ulithi harbor, planes on deck, November 24, 1944.

Marines and naval personnel who had participated in the initial occupation of Japan were loaded onto the *Monterey* and that same evening, the carrier steamed out of the Tokyo Harbor.

After a short period at anchor in Buckner Bay, Okinawa, the *Monterey* went to Pearl Harbor, where the crew received the good news that liberty was granted. This is routine procedure, but for the *Monterey's* crew, this was their first liberty in 82 days. Passing through the Panama Canal on October 8, the *Monterey* then steamed into the New York Navy Yard on October 17, 1945.

The *Monterey* had an impressive war record to show to the people who came aboard during the Navy Day celebration. The carrier's scoreboard read: Five enemy warships sunk; 500 enemy aircraft destroyed in the air and on the ground; over 300 shore base targets destroyed; and thousands of Japanese shipping sent to the bottom.

With the war over, the problem of transporting the thousands of soldiers back from the fighting areas was solved by using aircraft carriers as transport ships. Additional berthing space was made by removing much of the combat equipment and hundreds of men could be accommodated in the hangar decks. This operation was called the "Magic Carpet Fleet" and the *Monterey* made several trips between Naples and Norfolk, Virginia, in this capacity.

Following her last "Magic Carpet" cruise, the *Monterey* proceeded to the Philadelphia Navy Yard for deactivation. On February 11, 1947, the light carrier was decommissioned in the Atlantic Reserve Fleet.

Damaged planes on hanger deck, which resulted from a storm and fire, December 19, 1944.

On September 15, 1950, a little over three years after being zipped up, the *Monterey* was recommissioned. Captain D. L. Mills, USN, assumed command and shakedown operations began off Norfolk, Virginia, until January 3, 1951.

On a later date, the carrier reported to Pensacola, Florida, and was assigned to the Naval Air Training Command Center. Her new task was to qualify new pilots for carrier operations.

During the period February 12–18, 1953, the *Monterey* participated in the traditional New Orleans Mardi Gras Festival. She became a familiar sight to the port cities of Florida and Louisiana and hundreds of local citizens visited her often.

Igor Sikorsky, in his own invention—a Navy helicopter—landed on the *Monterey's* flight deck on April 3, 1952. Helicopters were fast becoming important in the phase of air-sea rescue.

A brief overhaul was taken in January 1954 when she entered drydock for minor repairs at the Mobile, Alabama, Drydock and Shipbuilding Corporation.

A few naval aviation records were set by the *Monterey* while operating as a training carrier. During the week of April 12, 1954, 1632 arrested landings were made. On May 25, 799 arrested landings were logged and for the month of August, the *Monterey* had a total of 3062 arrested landings.

On Octover 1, 1954, the *Monterey* received an urgent message to assist in a rescue mission of flood-stricken Honduras. The carrier steamed to Puerto Cortez on the northern coast of Honduras. Rear Admiral M. E. Miles, Commander Panama Sector, Carib-

bean Sea Frontier and his staff were embarked and the *Monterey* became a flagship from which rescue teams had disembarked and supervision of the overall operation took place. When the final rescue teams finished, the President of the Republic of Honduras came on board the *Monterey* to inspect the crew and thank them personally for their fine and outstanding work.

On October 11, the *Monterey* proudly steamed back to Pensacola Bay with a stalk of green bananas dangling from her aviation crane. She moored alongside Allegheny Wharf while the air station band welcomed the crew back with music amid the greetings from their families on dock.

The *Monterey's* last visit to New Orleans was on December 31, 1954, but this time she was not a mere spectator. The purpose of this trip was to attend the annual Sugar Bowl classic and cheer the "Middies" from Annapolis to victory over the colorful University of Mississippi.

Upon completion of this hard-fought football game, won by Navy 21–0, the *Monterey* sailed from her berth at Esplanade Avenue and docked at 11:10 A.M., January 2, 1955. She later returned to the Alabama Drydock at Mobile for a short rest period.

This rest period was short lived when a British freighter, the *M.V. Hartismere*, suddenly loomed out of the treacherous fog laden Mississippi.

Despite desperate attempts, the two vessels collided bow-to-bow at 1:54 P.M. They were mid-stream north of Wilder Flats and careened port to port, scraping past each other.

Both ships dropped anchors immediately to determine the results. Damage to both ships was comparatively light and on January 3 the *Monterey* was underway to resume her call at the Mobile Alabama Drydocks.

When repairs were completed, she resumed her duties as the Navy's training carrier and continued qualifying pilots of the Naval Air Training Command for the next six months.

A much sought naval aviation "first" was made on the *Monterey's* flight deck when Captain Don W. Dickenson, USN, landed on February 2, 1955, thus marking the first 100,000th arrested landing on an aircraft carrier.

On May 15, 1955, the *Monterey* received orders to report to the Philadelphia Naval Shipyard for an overhaul and then proceed to the Philadelphia Group, Atlantic Rescue Fleet for inactivation processing and decommissioning.

All hands manned the rails on June 9, 1955, as the

light carrier eased off her moorings at Allegheny Wharf at the Pensacola Naval Air Station and slipped out of Pensacola Bay for the last time.

The occasion did not go unnoticed, for Vice Admiral Austin K. Doyle, Chief of Naval Air Training, and Rear Admiral Dale M. Harris, Chief of Naval Air Basic Training, were on hand with members of the Naval Air Training Command staff. They congratulated the officers and men of the *Monterey* for a job well done and wished the proud ship a bon voyage.

The *Monterey* joined the Philadelphia Group of the Atlantic Reserve Fleet on September 15, 1955 With deactivation completed, she was decommissioned on January 5, 1956.

The *Monterey* received a change of classification on May 15, 1959, to AVT-2, auxiliary aircraft transport.

During her active duty, the *USS Monterey AVT-2* received the following awards: The Asiatic-Pacific Area Campaign Medal with eleven battle stars; the American Area Campaign Medal; the World War II Victory Medal; the Navy Occupation Service Medal; the National Defense Service Medal; the Philippine Liberation Campaign Service Ribbon; and the Republic of the Philippines Presidential Unit Citation Badge.

Aerial oblique view of the *Langley* CVL-27 on October 12, 1945.

27

USS Langley CVL-27

On April 11, 1942, the keel of the light cruiser *USS Fargo CL-85* was laid at the New York Shipbuilding Corporation at Camden, New Jersey. The Navy Department then authorized the *Fargo* and eight other light cruisers then under construction to be completed as aircraft carriers. The *Fargo* was at first renamed *Crown Point,* but adhering to the policy of naming new carriers after other famous ships, her name was changed to *Langley* to honor the first *USS Langley CV-1,* which was lost south of Java on February 27, 1942.

Mrs. Harry L. Hopkins, wife of the special assistant to President Franklin D. Roosevelt, christened the new ship on May 22, 1943. On July 15 the nine light carriers were redesignated from CV to CVL, thus distinguishing them from the larger carriers of the fleet.

USS Langley CVL-27 being launched on May 22, 1943.

On August 31 the *USS Langley CVL-27* was commissioned with Captain W. M. Dillon in command. The new carrier displaced 11,000 tons standard and 15,800 tons full load. She had an overall length of 623 feet, width of 109 feet, and a beam of 7?½ feet. Her speed was 32 knots and her draft was 26 feet. She carried 159 officers and 1410 enlisted men, plus 45 aircraft. The main armament consisted of four 5-inch 38 caliber mounts and her secondary armament was made up of twenty-six 40mm and forty 20mm antiaircraft mounts.

A shakedown cruise was hurriedly completed off Trinidad, followed by post-shakedown alterations at the Philadelphia Navy Yard. The *Langley* then sailed for the Pacific via the Panama Canal and Pearl Harbor, stopping briefly at San Diego, California.

The *Langley* launched her first combat strikes on January 29, 1944, as Air Group 32 struck Wotje and Taroa. The next month the *Langley* supported the landings at Eniwetok and Kwajalein. She was a member of Task Group 58.2, under the command of Rear Admiral A. E. Montgomery at this time. The overall commander of Task Force 58 was Rear Admiral Marc A. Mitscher.

Steaming with the *USS Essex CV-9, USS Intrepid CV-11*, and *USS Princeton CVL-23*, the *Langley* participated in the raids against Palau, Yap, Ulithi, and Woleai from March 30 to April 1, 1944. Truk Island was barraged by the fast carrier force on April 29 and more than 2200 sorties dropped 740 tons of explosives during the attack.

While on patrol one morning, eight pilots from the *Langley* sighted about 30 enemy planes only a few hundred feet below them. The battle began immediately and during the ensuing dog fight 21 enemy planes were shot down without one single loss to the *Langley's* planes.

From June 11–24 the carrier was active in the capture and occupation of Saipan; and also attacked Tinian, Pagan, Guam, and Roga. Pre-assault operations against Saipan began June 3, as bombing strikes were directed at Palau and Truk, and the islands of Pulowat and Satawan were hit by land-based Army Air Force bombers.

At 1:00 P.M. June 11, the *Langley* launched 208 fighters and eight torpedo planes 200 miles east of Guam. The targets were enemy bases and airfields at Saipan and Tinian. Repeated attacks continued for the next few days, reducing enemy airpower to zero. One raid annihilated a sampan flotilla near Pagan.

Saipan was the key fortress to the inner defenses of Japan. Our assaults there on June 15 forced the enemy to expose his fleet, which had been hidden since the Battle of Midway. Admiral Raymond A. Spruance, Commander of the Fifth Fleet, embarked on the *USS Indianapolis CA-35*, made a wise decision in electing to cover the Saipan landings instead of to search for the Japanese fleet. He ordered the fast carrier force to the west. Battleships, cruisers, and destroyers were deployed 15 miles ahead of the carriers to meet the expected enemy fleet. On June 19 the two-day Battle of the Philippine Sea began. At the end of the first day, 366 enemy planes had been destroyed in aerial combat and 17 others on the ground.

On the afternoon of the 20th the enemy fleet was spotted so far westward that strikes were sent to an extreme range. The carrier launched the air group, which sank two enemy carriers, two destroyers, and one tanker. The backbone of the Japanese fleet was now suffering from severe injuries and would not again be capable of challenging the U.S. forces until the Battle of Leyte Gulf.

By June 21 the enemy fleet was so distant that the chase had to be abandoned. The Battle of the Philippine Sea had nullified the enemy's effort to reinforce the Marianas and the capture and occupation by allied forces proceeded without any serious threat of interference.

During the first weeks of July the *Langley* sent her air group against Guam preparatory to an invasion scheduled for the latter part of the month. Her pilots also engaged in preliminary strikes over various airfields in the Philippines prior to the Palau invasion on September 15–20.

Air Group 32 was relieved by Air Group 44 in October and the carrier was stationed off Formosa and the Pescadores. On October 25–26 they struck the crippled Japanese fleet as it retreated from the disastrous battles of the Surigao Strait and Southern Samar. From October 1944 to January 9, 1945, the *Langley* conducted raids on the Philippines and Formosa.

The fighting carrier became a unit of the Third Fleet, commanded by Admiral William F. Halsey, in December 1944. (Admiral Halsey's flag waved from the masts of the *USS New Jersey BB-62* at that time. The *Langley* was assigned to Task Group 38.3, which included the *USS Essex CV-9*, *USS Ticonderoga CV-14*, and *USS San Jacinto CVL-30*.

On January 3, 1945, the *Langley* participated in the Luzon operations, which included strikes against Formosa on January 3, 4, 9, 15, and 21. During this period the fast carrier force attacked Luzon and the China coast and charged into waters that the enemy had heretofore considered as their own private lake. Strikes were then conducted along the coast between Saigon and Camranh Bay, resulting in the massive destruction of enemy ships. The total score was 41 ships sunk and 31 damaged, 112 enemy planes de-

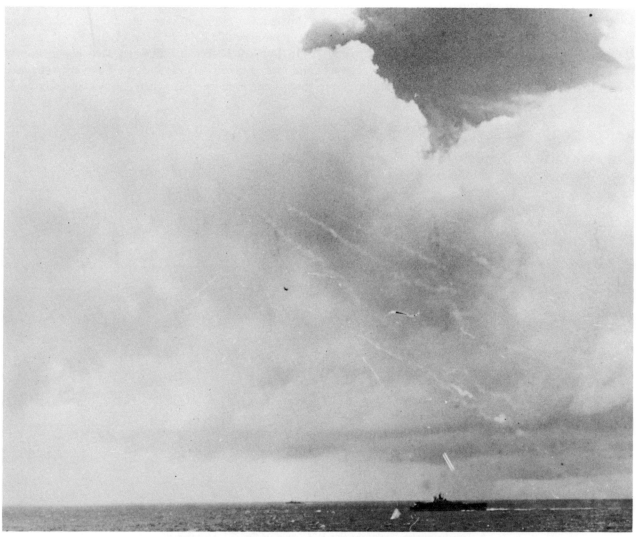

Japanese aerial attack on October 24, 1945. A dive bomber starts a run on the ship.

stroyed, and heavy damage inflicted to airfields, oil depots, and installations.

In February, Air Group 44 was relieved by Air Group 23 and the Formosa raids resumed with fighter sweeps directed against Amoy, Swatow, Hong Kong, and Hainan. During this action the fleet steamed unopposed through enemy waters and the *Langley* had penetrated 3800 miles into no man's land. At no time did enemy aircraft come closer to the fleet than a safe 20 miles.

The *Langley* was actively engaged in the Iwo Jima operation February 20–23, and on March 23 her air group attacked Okinawa. After that day the *Langley* divided her strikes between the Okinawa invasion and Kyushu in an effort to repel the desperate Kamikaze attacks being sent from that southern island under enemy control.

In May the *Langley* returned to San Francisco for a long-delayed overhaul. She was not destined to see further action in World War II. She was en route to Hawaii, cruising to the Pacific forward area, when word was received on August 15 that the war was finally over. The carrier operated as a training ship

out of Pearl Harbor and completed two cruises to San Francisco, transporting veterans to the U.S. for discharge.

On October 1, 1945, the *Langley* sailed from San Francisco to Philadelphia where 25,000 persons visited her during Navy Day celebrations. On November 15 she got underway for the first of several "Magic Carpet" cruises to Europe and brought thousands of weary, but happy, G.I.'s home.

The *Langley* had operated with three top Air Groups during her combat career—Air Groups 32, 44, and 23. She had sustained one bomb hit, which penetrated the forward end of the flight deck killing three crewmen. The pilots had downed 119 enemy planes in the air and destroyed over 100 on the ground, and had sunk 7 warships plus 31 enemy merchant vessels. For their gallant fighting the *Langley* and her air groups received the Navy Unit Commendation for "Outstanding Heroism," for action against the enemy from January 29, 1944, to May 11, 1945.

In January 1947 the *Langley* was decommissioned and placed in the Atlantic Reserve Fleet and remained there until January 1951 when she was transferred to

The *Lafayette*, formerly the *USS Langley CVL-27* arriving at the Philadelphia Navy Yard on March 6, 1963 after completing twelve years with the French Navy.

France under the Mutual Defense Assistance Program. During her duty with the French she was named *LaFayette*. The carrier was returned to the U.S. in March 1963, stricken from the list of Naval ships, and sold for scrapping.

During her brief but historic career, the *USS Langley CVL-27* received the following awards: The Navy Unit Commendation; American Area Campaign Medal; Asiatic-Pacific Area Campaign Medal with nine battle stars; the World War II Victory Medal; Philippine Liberation Campaign Ribbon; and the Republic of the Philippines Presidential Unit Citation Badge.

The *USS Cabot CVL-28* at the Philadelphia Navy Yard on October 29, 1943.

28

USS Cabot AVT-3

On August 16, 1942, the keel of the *USS Wilmington CL-79* was set down at the New York Shipbuilding and Drydock Co., of Camden, New Jersey. Due to the critical shortage of aircraft carriers in the Pacific Theater, the light cruiser *Wilmington* was renamed *USS Cabot CVL-28* in June 1942 and was converted to use as an aircraft carrier.

Mrs. Bess Berdine Read, wife of Rear Admiral Albert C. Read, christened the light carrier and she slid down the ways on April 4, 1943.

The *Cabot* was named in honor of the 10-gun brig of the Continental Navy. The original *Cabot* was one of the first ships assigned to the Continental Navy in October 1775. She was named after John Cabot (1450–1548), the Venetian navigator. Capt. M. W. Schoeffel, USN, assumed command of the Navy's second *Cabot* as she was commissioned at the Philadelphia Navy Yard on July 24, 1943.

Air Group 31 reported aboard in August and shakedown operations began in the Chesapeake Bay. Throughout September and October, the air group practiced flight operations and the ship's crew underwent intensive training in preparation for combat in the Pacific Theater of war. After a brief visit to the British West Indies, the carrier returned to the Philadelphia Navy Yard about mid-October for final fitting out.

On November 8, the *Cabot* loaded aircraft at Quonset Point, Rhode Island, and departed for San Diego. Upon arrival, passengers and additional aircraft were taken aboard for delivery to Pearl Harbor.

The *Cabot* sailed on November 24 and arrived in the Hawaiian port on December 2. A five-week training period took place near the Hawaiian Islands, with emphasis on Air operations, gunnery practice, and damage control procedures.

On January 16, 1944, the *Cabot,* as part of Task Group 58.2, left Pearl Harbor and steamed for the Marshall Islands for a series of attacks to neutralize the enemy air power concentrated in that area. On January 31, she suffered her first casualty when a torpedo plane crashed in the water astern. One of the plane's crewmen (T. J. Wolfe AMM2/c) who died after rescue was buried at sea the following morning.

The *Cabot's* air group raided Truk on February 16, hitting hard the mighty Japanese fortress in the Western Caroline Islands.

The task group was attacked by retaliating enemy planes later that evening. A torpedo struck the *USS Intrepid CV-11* on her starboard quarter and the *Cabot* was transferred to Task Unit 58.2.4 to escort the crippled carrier from the danger zone.

The *Cabot* returned to Pearl Harbor on March 4 for boiler repairs and overhaul. Provisions were stored and she sailed on March 15, anchoring five days later at the Majuro Atolls.

Enemy shipping, aircraft, and ground installations on Palau were prime targets for the Fast Carrier Force on March 22. The *Cabot's* air group provided antisubmarine and combat air patrols over the task force. On March 30, her combat air patrol shot down seven Japanese dive bombers, then gave chase to two others and downed them.

Task Force 58 proceeded to Truk on April 29 and began air strikes there as well as the adjacent islands.

Lt. (jg) A. R. Hawkins had just catapulted off the *Cabot* when a Japanese torpedo plane suddenly appeared in his gun sights. Hawkins—airborne only 15 seconds—nevertheless shot down the invader!

Training operations were conducted off Majuro Atoll during May and early June 1944. On June 11, the *Cabot* was south of Saipan and launched her aircraft against Saipan and Tinian prior to the amphibious landings. The next day, a torpedo wake approached the port bow of the carrier. An emergency turn was executed while tense crewmen watched from the flight deck as the torpedo passed harmlessly.

On June 15, the *Cabot* provided support for amphibious landings on Saipan. The task group was harassed by contacts with numerous enemy submarines, but the only ominous incident was a periscope sighting during the morning. Aircraft flying antisubmarine patrol bombed the periscope but no visible results were obtained from the attack.

Task Force 58 charged westward on June 17 to intercept a Japanese fleet reported heading towards Guam. Two days later, pilots returning from their first combat patrol of the day reported downing six enemy aircraft. Thus began the famous Battle of the Philippine Sea.

When the battle smoke disappeared and fighting had ended that first day, 392 enemy planes had been destroyed with a U.S. loss of 29 planes.

The task group commander sent the following message to the *Cabot*, following the action: "You are tops in the league today."

The next day, U.S. planes returning from a search for the Japanese fleet were low on fuel because the original reported distance of the enemy force had been underestimated. Several planes ditched in the water and the exhausted pilots were rescued by escort vessels. Planes from other carriers landed on the *Cabot* in addition to fighters from her own group.

The *Cabot* launched air strikes against Iwo Jima on July 4; 13 enemy fighter planes were intercepted and eliminated.

Three days later, strikes were conducted over Guam in preparation for the landing of American troops. During the actual landings, on July 21, the *Cabot's* air group provided air support and destroyed enemy land targets.

Ulithi and Yap were under attack four days later. Air strikes were launched against Chi Chi Jima and the Bonins on August 4. The *Cabot's* air group sank a destroyer, a supply ship, bombed two heavy ammunition barges, and damaged another destroyer.

The task group retired Eniwetok on August 5, 1944. On August 29, the *Cabot* was assigned to Task Group 38.2, which was part of Task Force 38, commanded by Vice Admiral Marc A. Mitscher.

On September 13, the *Cabot*'s air group shot 25 enemy aircraft out of the sky while conducting strikes over Luzon, Philippines. Several buildings and supply areas were completely ravaged.

Air support was provided for ground troops September 17–20 amidst the landings on Palau. Manila was under attack on the 21st and the *Cabot*'s pilots repeated their first victory by destroying 25 additional planes during an aerial battle over Clark Field, Luzon.

Rear Admiral G. F. Bogan, Commander, Task Group 28.2, sent a message to the *Cabot* saying: "Well done. Your back must be badly bent carrying the load for this group."

On September 29, the task group steamed for the Western Caroline Islands and dropped anchor at Ulithi Atoll on October 1, 1944.

The task group was underway two days later, moving south to avoid a typhoon reported approaching their position. The *Cabot* maneuvered through a series of violent rolls during the storm. Six fighters and a torpedo plane broke free and were lost over the side.

The *USS Barnes* supplied replacement aircraft on October 6, and also on that day Air Group 31 was relieved by Air Group 29. The task force then sailed to strike Okinawa and Formosa.

At 7:14 P.M., on October 12, while operating near Formosa, a Japanese "Betty" came in off the *Cabot*'s starboard beam. As the plane began attacking, the antiaircraft batteries opened fire and hit the enemy. As the harmless burning craft passed over the ship, it cast strange shadows on the flight deck. The plane went into the water some 300 yards off the starboard beam. The task group was harassed by enemy planes late into the night and they were finally driven away; however, some vessels received damage.

The *USS Canberra CL-81* was hit by a torpedo at 7:57 P.M., on October 13, and the *Cabot* joined the newly formed Task Group 30.3 to escort the damaged ship away from the danger area. The *USS Houston CA-30* also joined the ranks of the dispositioned ships when she took a torpedo the next day.

Waddling along at four knots, the sitting-duck towing group was about 75 miles east of Formosa by October 16. The Third Fleet commander hoped to lure the Japanese out of hiding and destroy them, using the stricken vessels as decoys.

At 1:25 P.M., a large group of enemy aircraft were reported 70 miles distant and closing. Two divisions of fighters from the *Cabot* were flying combat air patrol. All available aircraft were launched at once.

The enemy planes were coming from both north and south. It was estimated that each enemy group consisted of 60 planes.

The flight director informed the pilots at 1:35 P.M., "Your target is at 12 o'clock, 5 miles, look up."

Twenty-six minutes later, the pilots acknowledged, "Tallyho, many many bogies!"

The striking enemy force was now estimated between 60 to 75 aircraft of every type available. There were twin-engine bombers and torpedo planes in formation with fighter planes above them.

Against overwhelming odds, the *Cabot*'s eight fighters began an aerial battle. The majority of enemy planes destroyed during the ensuing dog-fight were downed by the original two divisions. The *Cabot*'s planes shot down 31 planes. A dozen enemy torpedo planes started attacking the helpless towing group. Nine were shot down before they could get close. The remaining three, more determined, managed to get closer before they too were downed. Unfortunately, one of the planes was able to release a torpedo at the *Houston*. All remaining enemy planes turned tail and retreated towards Formosa.

On October 16, a torpedo plane piloted by Ensign R. J. Maghan was flying a tedious antisubmarine patrol when a Japanese "Zeke," chased by two fighters, crossed in front of him. Ensign Maghan lined up the target quickly and said, "Splash one Zeke." Upon landing aboard the *Cabot*, the young officer shrugged off the kill, saying, "He got in my way."

The *Cabot* received several messages following the action, including kudos from Admirals Nimitz and Halsey. On October 30, the carrier was reassigned to Task Group 38.2.

Following air assaults on Luzon on October 29, a fighter made a horizontal landing approach but crashed into the catapult on the starboard side of the *Cabot* and burst into a ball of flame. Damage control parties were summoned and quickly extinguished the fires. In view of the flight deck damage, the remaining *Cabot* aircraft landed on the *USS Intrepid CV-11* nearby.

On November 25, the Fast Carrier Force launched other air strikes against Luzon. Japanese aircraft were pinpointed by radar and the force waited intensely for the on-coming attack. It erupted at 12:35 P.M., when the *Cabot*'s guns opened fire on a "Judy." The Japanese fighter plane approached the *Cabot*'s stern, aiming for the island structure as the 20mm and 40mm guns blazed away as rapidly as possible. As antiaircraft shells chewed into the plane, pieces started streaking in all directions. The plane came within six feet of the island structure, then slipped to the left and downward, dropping a wing as it crashed into the flight deck near a 20mm gun mount. The bomb on the plane exploded moments after the suicide crash, tearing the gun mount away while its crew disintegrated in the scorching fire. The blast tossed nine men overboard from the 40mm starboard mounts.

In less than one minute following the suicide crash, a second Kamikaze approached the starboard quarter. Every available gun opened fire, and the plane, stricken, began spinning radically out of control and finally crashed into the sea in a blazing spectacle.

It seemed to the crewmen that the entire Kamikaze force of the Japanese Empire was out to "get" the *Cabot* that day, for a third "Zeke" began a death dive towards the carrier. The pilot lost control, and it appeared the plane was going to plunge into the sea. But at the last moment, he swung back and smashed into the *Cabot*'s port blister near the water line. Violent explosions resulted from the plane's bomb and the port side was blanketed with sharpnel and debris from amidships to stern.

The attack was over at 12:56 P.M., and by 1:13 P.M., the damage control parties had extinguished all fires. As a result of the explosions, however, 62 men had been killed or seriously wounded, while another 49 were treated in sick bay.

As the men surveyed their ship to estimate damage, it was obvious the *Cabot* was in critical shape. Her catapult was useless, the main electrical control system was damaged, and there was a pair of six-foot holes in the flight deck. The gun sponson and adjoining catwalk forward of number two director had been blasted away and the radio antennae were destroyed. Another six-foot hole was located in the hull at the 03 level and the port side amidships, above the hangar deck level, was peppered with shrapnel.

A high-speed retreat from Luzon was underway the

An F6F crashed the barrier on the *Cabot* CVL-28 in December 1944.

morning of October 26. At 10:15 A.M., all ships slowed down and the *Cabot* held funeral services for the dead shipmates as they were committed to the deep.

The *Cabot* slipped alongside the repair ship *USS Jason ARH-1* on November 30 at Ulithi for repairs. Within ten days she rejoined the task force and was again in the combat area.

The carriers returned to resume strikes against the Philippines. Fighter sweeps were sent against Luzon in the Manila and Subic Bay areas until December 17, at which time air operations were cancelled due to a typhoon. The next day, several vessels suffered casualties from the storm and men were washed overboard.

The *Cabot* pitched and rolled violently in the roaring sea and some crewmen feared she would capsize— as had three destroyers!

Eventually, however, the storm diminished and the sea calmed. The *Cabot* came through with only minor damage. Recurrence of foul weather resulted in cancelling flight operations on December 19, and the task group sailed for Ulithi.

On January 3, 1945, the *Cabot*, in company with Task Group 38.1, resumed air strikes against Formosa. Unfavorable weather again cancelled flight operations. The task group cruised south overnight, then returned to Formosa the next day to hit the same targets.

The *Cabot*'s air group reached Pork and Neilson airfields on Luzon January 6-7. On the 9th, Task Force 38 struck Formosa. The *Cabot* was assigned the Karenko area and encountered little opposition during the attacks.

Enemy aircraft attacked the task force about noon on January 21 near Formosa. The *USS Ticonderoga CV-14* received two suicide attacks causing serious damage.

Shortly after sundown, a twin-engine Japanese bomber passed directly over the *Cabot*, port to starboard. Just as the plane cleared the ship, the *USS Boston CL-69* opened fire. The *Cabot*'s gunners were unable to pick up the target. As the plane reached the *Cabot*'s port quarter, it burst into flames. Thanks to the *Boston*, the light carrier had survived a suicide crash.

The task force was at Ulithi on January 26, and six days later the *Cabot* was assigned to Task Group 58.4.

On February 9, 1945, the famous war correspondent Ernie Pyle came aboard the *Cabot* to write about the Fast Carrier Force. Mr. Pyle remained until February 23, then transferred to the *USS Moale DD-693* leaving many new friends behind.

The *Cabot* was anchored at Ulithi Atoll the evening of March 11, 1945. A movie being shown on the hangar deck was suddenly interrupted by a terrific explosion. The executive officer jumped to his feet yelling, "Silence" and the crew quickly responded as any battle-experienced men would. Everyone was ordered to "stand fast" and give the gun crews the right of way. General Quarters was sounded 60 seconds later. Soon it was learned that a Japanese suicide plane had crashed into the *USS Randolph CV-15* some 2000 yards eastward. Ten minutes later the carrier secured from G.Q.

The task force sortied from Ulithi on March 14 to conduct operations against Kyushu and support the Okinawa troop landings. While receiving returning aircraft east of Okinawa on March 22, the *Cabot* experienced an unfortunate accident. One plane had landed and was being moved forward to make room for further recoveries. The pilot was still in the plane when

another fighter came in low, hit the deck, sheared off the arresting gear hook, bounced over the barriers, and crashed into the parked aircraft, whose pilot died in the plane. Six other planes were so badly damaged they were pushed overboard.

All of the carriers launched air strikes in support of the landings at Okinawa on April 1. As the U.S. Army and Marines surged forward in bitter ground fighting, aircraft overhead softened up the enemy positions. While a torpedo plane was being launched from the *Cabot*, the ship took a heavy roll to port. The plane went off the deck 50 feet short of the normal run. The pilot fought desperately at the controls as the right wing rubbed against the deck and the left wing and wheels were in the air. Crewmen on deck waited for a crash, but the skilled pilot fooled everyone as he demonstrated a top-notch job of flying the plane into

USS Cabot CVL-28 scoreboard April 17, 1945.

Fire breaks out aboard the *Cabot* as a result of bomb damage.

the air safely. He was later forced to land on the USS *Essex CV-9* because of damage during the wild takeoff. He returned to the *Cabot* the next day.

A Japanese plane began a run on the *Cabot* at noon on April 6. The carrier's AA's opened fire and a split-second after the pilot dropped his bomb burst into a flaming torch. It seemed as if the burning plane would crash into the carrier, so the AA batteries kept firing in an attempt to blow the plane to pieces. The enemy stayed airborne and passed over the starboard side, crashing into the sea off the bow.

Another Kamikaze began his attack one hour later and again the AA's fired continuously. The wing of the invader clipped the radar antennae before plunging into the water, showering the flight deck with shrapnel. It was a hectic day, and by evening the task force had accounted for the destruction of more than 85 enemy death-planes.

On April 7, search planes located Japanese fleet units steaming southeast to Kyushu and all available torpedo planes were sent after the enemy ships. Meanwhile, the *Cabot's* AA crews opened fire on an enemy fighter zooming towards the USS *Hancock CV-19*. The plane came in from the *Hancock's* starboard bow, but the *Cabot* was also positioned the same and had to cease firing to prevent hitting the *Hancock*. The suicide plane crashed into the *Hancock*, causing a large fire. Aircraft returning from combat strikes on the enemy fleet reported scoring three torpedo hits on the prize Japanese battleship *Yamato*. There were so many American planes, they had to attack the enemy in shifts; first the torpedo planes would come in low,

drop their tin fish and pull up and away. They would be followed in turn by the dive bombers and the fighters.

Lt. (jg) J. P. Speidel, USNR, was among the pilots directed to destroy the *Yamato*. He was worried about the mission because he was awaiting word from home on the birth of his first child. The fighter-torpedo group reached its target and Lieutenant Speidel was soon enveloped in pyrotechnics and missile fire. Luckily he wasn't hit. He dropped his torpedo, scoring a direct hit on the battleship's hull under the bridge structure. The remaining pilots unloaded their explosives on the *Yamato* and left it a burning mass sinking slowly beneath the waves. When Lieutenant Speidel landed on the *Cabot*, a message was awaiting with the news he wanted to hear: His wife had borne him a boy!

When the task group returned to Ulithi on April 11, it was dissolved and the *Cabot* was ordered home. The crew let out a wild cheer, as the carrier had not been stateside since November 1943 and had seen no civilization since leaving Pearl Harbor in March 1944.

On April 13, the *Cabot* bid farewell to the Fast Carrier Force and arrived at Pearl Harbor eight days later, where she stayed 48 hours. The navigator then set course for Alameda, California.

Upon arrival at the Alameda Naval Air Station, the first half of the ship's crew began a 20-day leave period. The *Cabot* entered Hunter's Point Shipyard on April 30 for overhaul and while the yard period was in session the remaining crewmen took their 20-day leave.

On June 20, 1945, the *Cabot* returned to Alameda to take on supplies and aircraft. She sailed seven days later and arrived at Pearl Harbor on July 4. Training periods were conducted until the 18th and five days later, the carrier went to rejoin the Fast Carrier Force at Eniwetok.

The *Cabot* launched air strikes against Wake Island on August 1, then returned to Eniwetok where a four-day training cruise began.

On August 15, word was received to cease all offensive operations, for fighting in the Second World War had finally ended.

The *Cabot* entered Buckner Bay, Okinawa, on August 30 and was assigned to Task Force 72. On September 1, 1945, the task force left Okinawa to display a show of strength and support amphibious landings in connection with the occupation of the Yellow Sea and Korean area.

The *Cabot's* aircraft flew over Shanghai, Tsingtau, Chefoo, Taku, Tientsin, Peiping, Dariren, and southeast Korea until September 13. On that day the task group returned to Okinawa.

The carrier continued operations in the Yellow Sea area until October 15, then was ordered to Guam to load passengers for transport to the states. On October 21, the *Cabot* arrived in Guam and all travelers were embarked; three days later she headed for home via Pearl Harbor, arriving at Alameda on November 9, 1945.

The *Cabot* accomplished an impressive war record, for which her crew was justly proud. Her scoreboard read 133,880 nautical miles of combat sailing, 4933 combat sorties flown, 252 enemy aircraft shot down by the air group, and 8 enemy planes destroyed by the ship's antiaircraft batteries. She had left 96 enemy planes destroyed on the ground, and 265 vessels were hit by torpedoes and bombs by the air group.

The *Cabot* did not go unrewarded for her combat exploits. She was awarded the Presidential Unit Citation which read in part for "extraordinary heroism in action against enemy Japanese forces in the air, ashore, and afloat from January 29, 1944 to April 8, 1945.

"The carrier and her air groups inflicted crushing blows toward annihilating Japanese fighting power; they provided air cover for our amphibious forces; they fiercely countered the enemy's aerial attacks and destroyed his planes and dealt out terrific losses to the Japanese fleet and merchant marine units. Daring and dependable in combat, the *Cabot* with her brave officers and enlisted men rendered loyal service in achieving the ultimate defeat of the Japanese Empire."

On February 11, 1947, the *Cabot* was decommissioned at the Philadelphia Navy Yard. However, she remained inactive only 19 months. She was the first carrier to be mothballed at the war's end and the first to be unzipped. Her state of preservation was highly successful and greater than anticipated. It was evident that the other reserve carriers could also be recalled to active duty whenever necessary.

On October 27, 1948, the *Cabot* was recommissioned. Three months later she was assigned to the Naval Air Training Command at Pensacola, Florida, where she took on the task of qualifying pilots in all phases of carrier air operations.

The *Cabot* led a rather quiet and uneventful life during her final years on active duty, but it was a well-deserved peaceful mission she performed. She remained at Pensacola and operated out of Quonset Point, R. I., from her recommissioning until late 1954. From January 9 to March 26, 1952, she completed a tour of duty to European waters.

The *Cabot* was decommissioned on January 21, 1955 in the Atlantic Reserve Fleet. On May 15, 1959, she was reclassified AVT-3—Auxiliary Aircraft Transport.

The *USS Cabot AVT-3* received the following awards during her active tour of duty with the Navy. The Presidential Unit Citation; The American Area

SNS *DeDalo PH-01*, ex- *USS Cabot AVT-3*. Aerial-astern view, August 1967.

The *USS Cabot CVL-28* on August 23, 1951 underway.

Campaign Service Medal; The Asiatic-Pacific Area Campaign Service Medal with nine battle stars; The World War Two Victory Medal; The Navy Occupation Service Medal; The National Defense Service Medal; The Philippine Liberation Campaign Ribbon; and The Republic of the Philippines Presidential Unit Citation Badge.

USS Bataan CVL-29. Port broadside view, underway, planes on deck, April 1943. TBF taxis to takeoff spot on flight deck, other TBF's in background.

29

USS Bataan AVT-4 (CVL-29)

The *USS Bataan AVT-4* was originally intended as the *USS Buffalo CL-99*. Work began on August 31, 1942, at the New York Ship Building Corporation at Camden, New Jersey.

The late Secretary of the Navy, Frank Knox said: "The *Bataan* has a rendezvous with destiny that shall not be denied."

On August 1, 1943, Mrs. George D. Murray, wife of

Admiral Murray, christened the light carrier and she slid down the ways, becoming the first ship to be named in honor of a World War II battle.

Manuel Quezon, President of the Philippine Commonwealth, said: "The valor of the American and Filipino fighting men who battled through the long months on Bataan will serve as an inspiration to the people of the Philippines, who live only for the day of victory and liberation. The *Bataan* will be a symbol of the inevitable defeat of Japan. Our fighting comradeship was sealed in the foxholes of Bataan and hallowed forever in the shallow graves of that bloodstained bit of land."

The *Bataan* was moved to the Philadelphia Navy Yard where fitting out was completed. She was commissioned on November 17, 1943, and Captain V. H. Schaeffer became her first commanding officer.

Between December 28 and February 14, 1944, the *Bataan* conducted a war-hurried shakedown cruise in the Chesapeake Bay and Caribbean Sea area. Following post-shakedown overhaul she sailed from Philadelphia to San Diego. Then she proceeded to Pearl Harbor, arriving on March 22 for a training period before deployment to the Pacific Theater.

The *Bataan* sailed from Hawaii on April 4, 1944 and arrived at Majure Atoll and anchored five days later with Task Force 58. She departed the same day with the Task Force and steamed across the equator on the 17th. She participated in air strikes on Sawar, Sarmi, Wake and New Guinea in support of the landings at Hollandia April 21–23.

The Task Force made a devastating attack on the

F6F Hellcat aboard the *USS Bataan CVL-29* removing chocks for takeoff.

Caroline Islands, hitting Truk and Ponape, then returned to Kwajalein on May 14. Due to a damaged forward elevator that could not be repaired in the Forward Area, the *Bataan* returned to Hawaii.

She rejoined the Task Group at Majure Atoll on June 2, and three days later set course for the Marianas. Guam and Rota were hit on June 11 and 13, and Chi Chi Jima on June 15–16.

While supporting the Marianas operation, Task Force 58 intercepted a large Japanese fleet cruising towards Saipan and Guam, intent on reinforcing their island garrisons. The enemy force was almost completely destroyed during the action which followed, primarily fought in the air. After the two-day Battle of the Philippine Sea on June 19 and 20, 1944, the Task Force found a Japanese surface force and sent three enemy aircraft carriers to the bottom.

Pagan, Marianas Islands, was the carrier's target for June 23, after which she steamed northward where her air group inflicted heavy damage to shore installations on Iwo Jima. After a five-day rest at Eniwetok, the fast carrier force attacked the Bonins on July 3–4, and heavy raids were launched against Guam and Rota.

The *Bataan* departed Eniwetok on July 16 and made a brief stop at Pearl Harbor before arriving in San Francisco on July 30, 1944. The carrier underwent a long awaited overhaul at Hunters Point.

On August 26, 1944, Captain J. P. Heath relieved Captain Schaeffer as commander.

The *Bataan* sailed from San Francisco on October 7 and reached Hawaii on the 13th. The air division began qualifying pilots for combat duty with the fleet.

On March 3, 1945, the *Bataan* joined the *USS Franklin CV-13, USS Intrepid CV-11* and the *USS Independence CVL-22* and set course for rendezvous with other ships of the fighting fleet.

The *Bataan* rejoined Task Force 58 on March 13 and the following day the air groups began strikes on the Japanese homelands. Kyushu was the victim on March 18, but there was a reversal on March 19 when disaster struck the Task Force.

The *USS Franklin CV-13* was wrecked by two bomb explosions, released from a lone enemy plane. The big *Essex*-class carrier burst into flames and sent a frantic radio message to the *Bataan* that she was coming in hard to starboard. The two ships executed sharp turns simultaneously to avoid a collision. Through great sacrifice and courageous efforts, the *Franklin* was saved after many hours of relentless fires and explosions.

On March 20, a Kamikaze began a dive on the *USS*

228

A Japanese plane makes a run on the *Bataan* off Okinawa as seen from the *USS Hancock CV-19* on March 20, 1945.

Hancock CV-19, but was splashed by the *Bataan's* antiaircraft fire. The intruder crashed into the fantail of the *USS Halsey Powell DD-*, causing minor damage. Two more suicide pilots made an effort to smash the *Bataan*, but were downed by pinpoint gunfire. The *Bataan* was earning a reputation as an antiaircraft carrier.

Okinawa was invaded on Easter Sunday, April 1, 1945. The *Bataan* began relentless attack against the enemy force on the island in support of ground troops in their struggle to take Okinawa. Wave after wave of aircraft were sent against enemy installations, planes, and shore defenses. On April 7, 1945, the American fleet began an encounter with the Japanese Navy's final attempt to stop the U.S. advance. The *Bataan* air group scored four torpedo hits on the *Yamato*, and the one-time prize of the Japanese Navy slipped to a watery grave.

During this operation the Kamikazes were in full force, striking any opposition they met. The *Hancock CV-19* was hit by a suicide plane that had slipped through heavy antiaircraft fire. On April 11, unsuccessful suicide dives were aimed at the *USS Enterprise CV-6*, *USS Bunker Hill CV-17* and the *USS Essex CV-9*, but the *Bataan* shot down two enemy planes and helped destroy many others.

A close call occurred when a Kamikaze approached the starboard beam of the *Bataan*, just missing the island structure and stack as it crashed into the sea off the port side.

On April 18, the *Bataan* air group sank a Japanese submarine while conducting antisubmarine patrols.

The Japanese struck the Task Force again on May 11, but the 20mm and 40mm guns of *Bataan* shot down 14 planes attempting to close in on the ship. This action did not pass without incident. Two suicide pilots scored bomb hits on the *Bunker Hill CV-17* before crashing into the carrier. The *Bunker Hill* started for the *Bataan's* beam, but a speedy emergency turn was successful, thus avoiding a collision.

The famed Task Force 58 received its share of major death blows from Kamikaze planes. While the Task Force was attacking Kikuchi and Waifu airfields on Kyushu on May 13, a suicide plane crashed into the *USS Enterprise CV-6*. Men on the "Big E" expertly handled the situation and the veteran of nearly 18 major battles continued operating without any interruption.

The *Bataan* steamed southward on June 1, 1945 and anchored in Leyte Gulf for replenishment and rest. On June 5, Captain Heath was relieved by Captain W. G. Gilbert.

The *USS Randolph CV-15* and the *Bataan's* air groups struck the airfields on Mobara, Miyakawa, Naruto, Yachimata and Yokosuka on July 10. Forty-one sorties were flown over Japan, but not one single enemy airborne plane was sighted.

On August 15, 1945, the *Bataan* launched a strike towards Tokyo. At 6:35 A.M., word was announced that hostilities had ceased and that the Japanese had accepted unconditional surrender. The *Bataan's* Air Group 7 broke radio silence for the first time as pilots sang "Oh What A Beautiful Morning" into their microphones.

When the hostilities ceased, the *Bataan* continued to fly patrols off the Japanese coast to keep the skies clear of do-or-die enemy flyers.

On September 6 the *Bataan* pulled into Tokyo Bay and anchored midway between the *Yokohama* and *Yokosaka*. Later that evening the light carrier set course for Okinawa, arriving September 8, 1945; 529 passengers came aboard; on the 10th the ship proceeded to Pearl Harbor, arriving ten days later.

On September 25 she was underway for the naval ship yard in New York. The *Bataan* was among the first carriers to transit the Panama Canal after the war and was featured in *Life* magazine as the "Picture of the Week" as she passed through Mira Flores Locks.

Following a sojourn at Cristobal, Canal Zone, the *Bataan* steamed northward, arriving in New York on October 17, 1945. Then she headed for Providence, Rhode Island, for an Open House ceremony honoring Navy Day.

Next she entered Boston Navy Yard for alterations for duty with the "Magic Carpet" fleet. She completed

Aerial view of the *Bataan* September 11, 1950.

two cruises to Italy, transporting Italian prisoners of war back to their homeland, and returning American army troops to the United States.

The first cruise was made November 21–December 8, 1945; the last one December 14, 1945–January 2, 1946.

The *Bataan* now underwent a deactivation period prior to decommissioning. Captain Gilbert turned over his command to Commander W. B. Short, who in turn was succeeded by Commander W. H. Davison in November 1946.

On May 11, 1947 the *Bataan* was decommissioned and placed in the Atlantic Reserve Fleet. She did not remain in this status too long, for on May 13, 1950, she was recommissioned at the Philadelphia Navy Yard. Captain Edgar T. Nesle took command and the light carrier was once again a member of the active Navy. She departed for San Diego on July 5 and arrived at North Island two weeks later.

After a brief training session near the Southern California coast, she headed for Japan, arriving in Tokyo Bay on November 16, 1950.

On December 15 the *Bataan* began her first combat air strikes of the Korean Conflict as a unit of the United Nations Task Force. She remained in the Korean area until June 2, 1951, then returned to San Diego. A course was set on July 9 for Puget Sound Naval Ship Yard, Bremerton, Washington, where she would be overhauled.

Upon completion the *Bataan* sailed to San Diego on November 20. Christmas and New Year's holidays were enjoyed by men of the carrier as a rare leave period began.

After taking on supplies and aircraft the *Bataan* headed again to the Korean War zone. A short training period was conducted off Buckner Bay, Okinawa, before actual combat strikes were launched.

The *Bataan*'s pilots were constantly engaged in attacks with the enemy. Many bridges, railroads, and combat installations fell to this seasoned group of aviators.

On May 10, 1953, the *Bataan* sailed for the United States. She moored alongside the Quay Wall at North Island Naval Air Station while a crowd of anxious families and friends of the crew members cheered from the dock.

The carrier remained in the San Diego area until July 31, after which she headed for Hawaii, Japan, and then back to Pearl Harbor. This cruise was used to complete various training exercises. Upon arrival in Hawaii, she underwent a deactivation process; early in 1954 she was placed in the Pacific Reserve Fleet.

On May 15, 1959, the *Bataan* was reclassified AVT-4 —Auxiliary Aircraft Transport. She was never to see duty in this capacity, for on September 1, 1959, she was stricken from the list of Navy ships and sold to Nicola Joffe Corporation of Beverly Hills, California and scrapped.

During her active career the *Bataan* received the following awards: The American Area Campaign Service Medal; the Asiatic-Pacific Area Campaign Service Medal with five battle stars; the World War Two Victory Medal; the Navy Occupation Service Medal; the Korean Service Medal with seven battle stars; the United Nations Service Medal; the National Defense Service Medal; and the Republic of Korea Presidential Unit Citation Badge.

USS San Jacinto CVL-30. Starboard broadside view, camouflage paint, anchored, January 1944.

30

USS San Jacinto AVT-5 (CVL-30)

On October 26, 1942, the keel for the *USS Newark CL-100* was laid at the New York Shipbuilding Corporation of Camden, New Jersey. At the time, only two carriers were active in the Pacific Theater—the *USS Saratoga CV-3* and the *USS Enterprise CV-6*. The need for additional carriers was obvious, so the *Newark* was completed as an aircraft carrier. Her name was changed to *USS Reprisal CVL-30,* but when the *USS Houston CA-30* was lost in the Sunda Strait of the Java Sea, the light carrier was renamed *USS San Jacinto CVL-30.*

The *San Jacinto* was launched on September 26, 1943, under the sponsorship of Mrs. Jesse H. Jones, wife of the Secretary of Commerce. The carrier was constructed from money collected during a warbond

drive from the people of Texas, who wanted another ship to replace the *Houston.* The light carrier became the third U.S. vessel to bear the name, which commemorates the Battle of San Jacinto on April 21, 1836. During this historic battle General Sam Houston's brave army, outnumbered two to one, defeated Santa Anna's forces and secured the Liberty of the Texas Republic from Mexico. On December 15, 1943, the *San Jacinto* was placed in commission under the command of Captain Harold M. Martin, USN.

Four months later the *San Jacinto* was at Pearl Harbor taking on supplies in preparation for assignment in the Pacific. She sailed from Pearl Harbor on May 3, 1944, for her first combat operation. On May 19, her air group struck the enemy-held islands of

Marcus and Wake. This was the deepest penetration of U.S. forces into Japanese-dominated waters at that time. The air strikes continued to May 23, when the carrier began a period of training and replenishment for her first major operation of World War II.

On June 6, 1944, the *San Jacinto* was steaming as a unit of Task Force 58 to support the Marianas Operation. From June 11 to 17, Air Group 51 participated in the capture of Saipan. A report of the Japanese fleet steaming eastward into the Philippine Sea was received and the *San Jacinto* headed westward with other carriers in hopes of engaging the enemy fleet. The task force came under constant attack, but the carriers launched a long-range offensive, which inflicted severe damage to enemy ships. VT-S1 from the *San Jacinto* sank a destroyer and damaged a *Hiyataka* class cruiser. By the time the aircraft returned to the task force, many were badly damaged or low on fuel and ditched into the sea. The fast carrier force returned to the Marianas and resumed support of that operation. On July 6, the *San Jacinto* resisted enemy air raids off Eniwetok; Guam and Rota came under attack July 14–22. The light carrier steamed southward for air strikes against Palau, Yap, and Ulithi. While conducting an anti-shipping patrol in this area, the *San Jacinto*'s air group sank a destroyer and was successful in obtaining reconnaissance photos.

The *San Jacinto* replenished ammunition and stores on July 28 at Saipan, then participated in the Fourth Bonin Raid August 4–5, 1944. On August 9, the carrier anchored in Eniwetok for rest.

The *San Jacinto* was next assigned to the Second Carrier Task Force of the Third Fleet. Her mission was to assist in the capture and occupation of the Southern Palau Islands. Before the actual assault of Palau, the carriers struck the Bonin and Yap Islands in a diversionary action. Shore installations on Ulithi and Yap were completely destroyed. From September 6 to October 14, 1944, enemy ground positions on Peleliu and Anguar were under constant attack. Runways became bomb craters and shipping in the harbors was sunk. The *San Jacinto* provided direct support to the Saipan occupation up to September 18, then returned to Seeadler Harbor, Manus, for repairs.

By October 11, 1944, the Leyte Operation was in full swing. We were back to regain the Philippines. When the *San Jacinto* arrived, Leyte was in the process of being captured by determined U.S. ground forces. The air group bombed northern Luzon and Formosa from October 11 to 14, 1944. This action was imperative if the Japanese were to be prevented from reinforcing their strongholds on Leyte. The *San*

Jacinto came under heavy aerial attack on October 15, and blazing antiaircraft batteries knocked down nine enemy aircraft. Operations continued to October 21, then the carrier proceeded to Ulithi for replenishment. On the night of October 24, 1944, the *San Jacinto* joined other carriers and hastened northward to intercept the Japanese Fleet's Northern Force. Again, long-range air strikes were launched. This historic event occurred the morning of October 25, 1944. The battle off Cape Engano at the northeastern tip of Luzon was a memorable event for the *San Jacinto*. Air Group 51 sank the Japanese carrier *Zuiho* and scored direct torpedo hits on another carrier and a cruiser.

Elements of the Japanese Central Force were reported breaking through the San Bernadino Straits and attacking our escort carriers off Leyte. The *San Jacinto*'s air group pursued the enemy fleet but results proved negative, although one crippled enemy cruiser was sighted and sunk. While steaming for the refueling area on October 29, word was received that the Japanese were ferrying planes into Los Negros

USS San Jacinto CVL-30. Texas flag flying from the mainmast. On flight deck TBM's and F6F's are being warmed up to strike at Palau Island, July 1944.

USS San Jacinto CVL-30.

and Cebru off Samar. The next day the *San Jacinto* returned to that area. While screening our destroyers, she endured her first Kamikaze attacks. The *USS Franklin CV-13* and *USS Belleau Wood CVL-24* were hit and only accurate AA fire saved the *San Jacinto* from being hit twice.

On November 2, 1944, the *San Jacinto* anchored in Ulithi for repairs and supplies, then returned to the San Bernadino Straits to fly defensive combat patrols. The *San Jacinto*'s air group hit Manila Bay on November 13–14, 1944. A floating drydock sank and damage was inflicted at the Cavite Japanese Naval Base. Returning to Ulithi on November 19, the carrier's air group scored a hit with a 500-pound bomb on an enemy destroyer. On November 20, the *San Jacinto* dropped anchor at Ulithi for rest.

The *San Jacinto* departed Ulithi and proceeded to Guam, where Air Group 45 relieved Air Group 51. The fresh air group underwent a week's training off Ulithi; then, on December 11, 1944, the carrier sailed to take part in the Luzon Operation. Her new air group helped neutralize enemy air facilities on Mindoro and destroyed a considerable amount of shipping. Daily air assaults were launched up to December 17, when the ship stopped for refueling.

On December 18, 1944, the *San Jacinto* rode out a terrific typhoon, believed to be the most severe ever

encountered by the fleet. Aircraft tore loose from mooring cables and were tossed around like toys. On December 22, the *San Jacinto* tied up alongside the repair ship *USS Hector AR-7* for repairs. Foul weather continued to be a stumbling block for the fleet, but despite the rough weather air attacks were successfully launched over northern Luzon to isolate the invasion force.

On January 3, 1945, the *San Jacinto* returned to Formosa and resumed strikes against enemy airfields; she launched attacks against Indo China on January 12, during which various ground positions were completely destroyed and shipping nearby was sunk. From January 12 to 16, enemy emplacements along the China coast were under attack. The Kamikaze force had returned to harass the task force, and on January 21, 1945, two suicide planes crashed into the *USS Ticonderoga CV-14* off Formosa. As damaged ships began retirement to Ulithi the *San Jacinto*'s air group obtained valuable photographs of the Okinawa area to be used in the up-and-coming assault of that island. With this mission accomplished the light carrier returned to Ulithi for maintenance and supplies.

The *San Jacinto* was active in a diversionary thrust off southern Honshu on February 16, in support of the Iwo Jima Operations. Industrial sites near Tokyo were hit twice, then the carriers steamed southward for

Iwo Jima. Air Group 45 commenced bombing and strafing runs over Iwo Jima and joined in more attacks against Honshu and Nansei Shoto. These attacks continued until March 16, 1945, when the task force returned to Ulithi in preparation for the last major operation of World War II—The Okinawa Gunto Operation.

While riding anchor in Ulithi on March 11, a suicide plane penetrated the staging area and crashed into the USS *Randolph CV-15*, anchored next to the *San Jacinto*. One week later mighty Task Force 58 steamed from Ulithi and attacked the Ryukyus. The *San Jacinto* was a part of Task Group 58.2 but was assigned to Task Group 58.1 after the *Wasp* was damaged. Ground installations and shipping were hit on March 23, 1945, against Okinawa and nearby islands. An enemy convoy in the East China Sea was completely smashed on the following day. While searching for a reported enemy fleet on the 25th, the *San Jacinto*'s air group sank six coastal cargo ships.

On April 1, 1945—Easter Sunday—U.S. Marines rushed ashore on Okinawa and the *San Jacinto* supplied direct support, destroying ground installations. The Kamikaze force returned on April 6, and launched an estimated 500 planes. None of the aircraft succeeded in hitting the *San Jacinto*, although the USS *Hancock CV-19* was hit the following day. The Japanese made one of their greatest mistakes on May 7, 1945, when they sent the battleship *Yamato* and her escorts to sea without air cover. The *San Jacinto*'s air group joined other fighters and quickly sank the once-proud ship and her escorts. The carrier's air group was occupied with downing enemy aircraft and offensive sweeps off the Ryukyus up to April 27; then the task force returned to Ulithi for rest.

Air Group 49 relieved Air Group 45, and shortly afterwards the *San Jacinto* returned to begin raids over the Japanese mainland. Kyushu was hit on May 13–14, Tokuno on the 19th, and Kikai on May 22, 1945. Air strikes over Okinawa resumed on the 23rd, but were cancelled on June 5, when another severe typhoon struck the fleet. On June 8, 1945, strikes against Japan proper were resumed.

Tokyo was bombed on July 10, Hokkaido-North Honshu on the 14th and 15th, and after a one-day pause due to bad weather, Yokosuka was hit on July 18. The battleship *Nagato* was heavily damaged at the latter port. Widespread attacks from Kure to Nagoya were carried out on July 24, 1945. Four days later, a survey saw the battleships *Ise* and *Hyuga* sunk, the *Karuna* beached; the cruiser *Oyoda* capsized; the carriers *Amagi* and *Katsuragi* burning out of control;

and a *Kobe* class escort carrier sunk. By July 30, the task force struck Tokyo again, leaving many military installations in flames.

On August 8, 1945, the *San Jacinto*'s air group spotted a camouflaged enemy airfield. The air group was officially credited with destroying more than 78 aircraft and possibly 71 others. These planes it was believed, were being held in reserve for use against our forces when we invaded the homeland. More air facilities were destroyed on the 13th and 69 enemy aircraft were added to Air Group 49's victories. The *San Jacinto* launched her air group against Tokyo on August 14, 1945. Seven enemy aircraft were shot down before the order to cease fire was released. Japan had surrendered unconditionally.

Shortly after the cease fire, the *San Jacinto*'s air group began to fly patrols over occupied Japan. From August 23 to 30, prisoner-of-war camps near western Honshu received medical supplies and food from the air group. On September 14, 1945, the *San Jacinto* sailed out of Tokyo Bay and returned to San Francisco. The light carrier was fitted out with additional berthing spaces for duty with the "Magic Carpet" fleet. On November 25, 1945, the *San Jacinto* embarked on the first of two such cruises, bringing back war veterans. The first cruise was to Guam and the second to Manila and Subic Bay. The *San Jacinto* brought back over 2500 passengers on her last "Magic Carpet" cruise.

The *San Jacinto* had a proud record of World War II service. Her scoreboard showed 712 Japanese aircraft destroyed, 17 ships sunk including the carrier *Zuiho*, an assist in destroying the battleships *Nagato* and *Ise*, plus many shore installations destroyed. Her most proud moment came when awarded the Presidential Unit Citation, which read as follows:

"The President of the United States takes pleasure in presenting the Presidential Unit Citation to the USS *San Jacinto* and her attached air groups for extraordinary heroism in action against enemy Japanese forces in the air, ashore, and afloat in the Pacific War Area from May 19, 1944, to August 15, 1945. Operating continuously in the most forward areas, the USS *San Jacinto* and her air groups struck crushing blows toward annihilating Japanese fighting power; they provided air cover for our amphibious forces; there they fiercely countered the enemy's aerial attacks; and they inflicted terrific losses on the damaged. Daring and dependable in combat, the *San Jacinto* with her gallant officers and men rendered loyal service in achieving the ultimate defeat of the Japanese Empire."

In January 1947, the *San Jacinto* was decommissioned and assigned to the Pacific Reserve Fleet. On May 15, 1959, she was reclassified AVT-5—Auxiliary Aircraft Transport.

During her three years and one month of active naval service, the *USS San Jacinto AVT-5* accumulated the following awards: The Presidential Unit Citation; American Area Campaign Service Medal; Asiatic-Pacific Area Campaign Service Medal, with seven battle stars; The Navy Occupation Service Medal; World War II Victory Medal; Philippine Liberation Campaign ribbon with two stars; and the Republic of the Philippines Presidential Unit Citation Badge.

ESSEX CLASS: HULL NUMBERS 31-40

USS Bon Homme Richard CVA-31.

31

USS Bon Homme Richard CVA-31 (CV-31)

The present *Bon Homme Richard CVA-31* is the second naval vessel to be so named. *Bon Homme Richard* is the French equivalent of "Poor Richard." The carrier was given the name to honor the Continental Frigate *Bon Homme Richard.*

No history of the current *Bon Homme Richard* is complete without mentioning the first vessel of the same name and sacrifices made by her crew. The original name of the frigate was *Duc de Duras,* but when Captain John Paul Jones took command he altered the name to *Bon Homme Richard* in honor of Benjamin Franklin. As a full moon illuminated the sea on September 23, 1779, the vessel engaged in combat with the *HMS Serapis*. This proved to be a tragic event for the frigate. The *Serapis* carried 50 guns comprised of twenty 18-pounders on her lower deck, twenty-two 9-pounders topside and eight 9-pounders on the quarterdeck. The *Bon Homme Richard* faced her adversary with 42 guns; twenty-eight 12-pounders, six 18-pounders, and eight 9-pounders.

Nine of the *Bon Homme Richard*'s weapons were rendered useless by the *Serapis* as well as the total number of her 18-pounders. Of the 144 men who manned the gun deck, only 64 were able to continue fighting. The stiuation appeared hopeless; then another British warship, the *Alliance*, arrived to add to the frigate's troubles.

Captain John Paul Jones thought the battle would surely end, but the *Alliance* fired only one shot, then sailed out of range. (Years later, the captain of the *Alliance* was court-martialed for his action and pleaded as his defense that extreme darkness had caused him to leave the area. He thought the *Bon Homme Richard* was an English warship.) Captain Pearson of the *Serapis* called, "Quarter, Captain, are you asking for Quarter?" It was then that Captain John Paul Jones replied, "I have not yet begun to fight." He then ordered several men aloft to the mainmast with grenades. They edged along the foot ropes on a spar until directly over the *Serapis*, where they dropped the grenades. One hit a powder keg and the *Serapis* literally came apart at the seams. From then on all combat was hand to hand.

Finally, Captain Pearson struck his colors and the battle ceased around midnight. The ropes holding the two ships together were severed and the *Bon Homme Richard* slowly started sinking. The American flag was the last of the gallant frigate to be seen as the ship slipped beneath the waves.

The aircraft carrier *Bon Homme Richard* thus carries a proud name in the fighting fleet. Her keel was laid down February 1, 1943, at the New York Naval Shipyard.

Mrs. John S. McCain, wife of Vice Admiral McCain, Deputy Chief of Naval Operations for Air, christened the ship on April 29, 1944. Captain A. O. Rule, Jr., took command and the carrier was commissioned on November 26, 1944.

Following shakedown operations in the Chesapeake Bay, she transited the Panama Canal and arrived in San Diego preparatory to departure for Hawaii.

Night Air Group 19 reported aboard while at Pearl

F6F turning over on back after crashing barrier on the *Bon Homme Richard* in January 1945.

Harbor and on May 21, 1945 the carrier went to join Task Force 38 at Ulithi.

On June 4 the "Bonnie Dick's" air group began a three-day bombardment of Okinawa, after which the carrier went to Subic Bay. She departed July 1 and sent her pilots against Hokkaido, Honshu, and Kyushu. The carrier was active in the final operation of World War II, participating in Third Fleet maneuvers against Japan right up to August 15 when hostilities ended.

The *Bon Homme Richard* sailed into Tokyo Bay September 16 after 78 continuous days at sea. Her air group dropped food and medicine on located P.O.W. camps throughout Japan. She made a brief stopover at Guam, then headed for home, arriving at San Francisco on October 20, 1945.

After another trip to the Pacific as part of the "Magic Carpet" fleet, the carrier returned to Alameda, California, December 2 with 3562 veterans. Her final trip came on January 16, 1946, when she sailed into Alameda with 4255 troops.

The *Bon Homme Richard* proceeded to the naval shipyard at Bremerton, Washington, for deactivation and was decommissioned January 9, 1947, with the Bremerton Pacific Reserve Group.

When trouble erupted in Korea she was recommissioned on January 15, 1951, and underwent a hurried shakedown cruise. On February 27 she arrived at Alameda for a short training period, then back to Puget Sound for alterations.

On March 6 the carrier pulled up alongside Quay Wall at North Island, San Diego, and embarked aircraft of VF-781, VF-784, VA-923, VC-3, VC-11 and VC-35. Unlike other *Essex*-class carriers, the *Bon Homme Richard* had not received any immediate modernization when recommissioned, and thus remained as she had been since 1944.

She departed on May 10 and crossed the International Dateline May 23. Her first combat strikes began at 3:01 P.M. May 31 when four F9F's were sent against Wonsan. Also hit were railroads at Changhungi and supply areas at Manchon.

For 17 consecutive days the air group hit rail bridges, highway bridges, truck convoys, warehouses, and troop barracks in North Korea. By June, over 149 offensive and 11 defensive sorties had been launched since the carrier's arrival in the Far East.

On June 18 she entered Sasebo, Japan, for a short rest that ended on the 30th when she departed and resumed air operations off Korea. Despite foggy weather, the air group managed to strike railroad cars, supply depots, factories, and highways at the Wonsan-Songjin area.

The *Bon Homme Richard* returned to Yokosuka on July 30 for minor repairs. In only two months she had launched 1433 offensive and 1306 defensive sorties. She resumed her position in Korean waters on August 10 and sent daily combat strikes against the usual targets.

The carrier operated with Task Force 77 until September 5 when she headed north to the Yalu River to assist U.S. Air Force bombers in destroying targets at Rashin and Najin. Two days later she went back to Yokosuka, Japan, where she rested ten days.

Her air power was needed to strike targets in the areas of Hungman, Paegam-Dong, Wonsan, Onyand-Ni, Kowon, Yangdok, and Tangchong. A vital enemy mining region was struck on October 9 about 35 miles from Songjin.

Two reconnaissance planes sighted a supply train near Songjin on October 10 and the air group's planes went in and demolished the train and its cargo. The "Bonnie Dick's" pilots made 4660 runs during a 29-day period; then the carrier returned to Yokosuka on October 20.

From October 31 to November 30 the air group came in contact with several MIG-15 jets. *Corsairs* and *Skyraiders* were flying protective cover on November 27 over a wounded pilot of another carrier who had crashed. Aircraft from both nations exchanged a short volley of fire but no kills were recorded by either side.

On November 20 the *Bon Homme Richard* was preparing for return to the states when the following message was received:

"Commander Seventh Fleet extends to officers, men and embarked air group of *Bon Homme Richard*, a hearty well done for the outstanding accomplishments in all types of weather and under difficult conditions. Happy voyage home."

During mid December the carrier returned to San Diego just in time for the crew to enjoy a well-deserved Christmas leave.

In January 1952 the *Bon Homme Richard* entered Puget Sound Naval Shipyard for an overhaul, then returned to San Diego for training preparatory to a second Korean war cruise.

The "Bonnie Dick" sailed again May 20 and joined Task Force 77 on June 23. Preparations began for a major strike on the North Korean hydroelectric power plants. Later that evening nine ADs, eight F4Us, and eleven F9F-2s were launched and headed for the Kyosen #2 Hydroelectric Plant 30 miles north of Hamhung. Another group comprised of six ADs, six F4Us, and seven F9F-2s went to strike the Fusen #2 plant west of Kyosen. The transformer yard and adjacent building were leveled and Fusen #2 was bombed out of commission.

The next day the complex was hit again, with attacks over Kyosen plant #4. This was followed by attacks on the railroad yard near Tanchon. Then bad weather hampered flight operations, and on June 26 the carrier headed for Sasebo, Japan.

By July 3, 1952, the "Bonnie Dick" was back in action striking the North Korean hydroelectric plants again. Kyosen #1 and #2 were the victims followed by

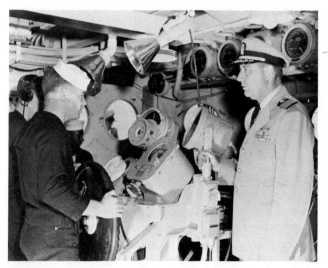

Captain P. W. Watson talks to the helmsman on board the "Bonnie Dick" May 22, 1952.

An F4U (Corsair) moves down flight deck of *USS Bon Homme Richard CVA-31* as another F4U moves into position for takeoff. The planes will make another Thanksgiving Day strike against the communists in Korea (November 1952).

a four-day strike at transportation supply warehouses and troop barracks in Wonsan Valley. On July 8 the powerhouse at Kyosen #2 received two 500-pound bombs.

A combined armed forces bombing effort was scheduled for the North Korean capital of Pyongyong. Aircraft from land-based U.S. Marines, the Australian Air Force, and the Royal Navy would participate. The *Bon Homme Richard* and *USS Princeton CV-47* were ordered to suppress flak units for aircraft. While the strikes were in progress a dense blanket of fog settled in at sea and the jets were diverted to fields in South Korea. The propeller aircraft made it safely back to the carrier. Bad weather continued until

July 19, resulting in little action except for a single strike against the Chosen #3 power plant.

For a three-day period, Wonson and the surrounding region took a beating and close air support was provided for the U.N. front-line troops, opposed by the 68th Chinese Communist Field Army.

On August 4 the hydroelectric complex was hit again as the "Bonnie Dick's" air group attacked Kojo #3, Chosen #1 and Kyosen. Severe damage was inflicted on transformer stations, switch houses and supply houses. Soon the carrier was en route to Yokosuka, but a message was received ordering her back to relieve the *USS Boxer CV-21*, which was suffering from damage caused by an internal hangar deck fire. Later, the

Bon Homme Richard pulled into Yokosuka when the Commander, Carrier Division One transferred to the *Princeton*. It was a short stay, for she was immediately sent back to Korea waters.

On August 9 her planes struck Hamhung, Pukchong, plus the Sindok Lead and Zinc Mines. Attacks were directed on troops and supply regions near Wonsan two days later, followed by strikes against Hodo Pando Peninsula where five coastal defense batteries were destroyed.

Inclement weather again hampered flight operations so the carrier headed for Yokosuka, arriving August 20. On September 4 she rejoined Task Force 77 at Korea and launched close support air strikes to assist the U.S. First Corps and the Second ROK. On September 9, the F4Us and ADs teamed with jet fighters in a strike against industrial areas. The next day the air group hit Kyosen #1 plant again and nullified all the repair work that had laboriously been accomplished.

The Sindok Lead and Zinc Mine was hit again September 12. Rail lines and boxcars in the area were destroyed and a strike was made against Hoeryong

near the Manchurian border. Two days later, the Sungjibaegam electro-metallurgical plant was leveled. A jet recon flight discovered a 130-foot communist naval vessel near Wonson and sank her, then Kojo #3 was hit again to disrupt repairmen.

On October 10 the "Bonnie Dick's" air group initiated a new phase of air strikes with emphasis against enemy front line positions. Particular attention was given to supply areas and retarding the enemy's capability to launch a major offensive while the truce talks were in progress.

For four days beginning October 12 the carrier participated in "Kojo Amphibious Feint," blasting targets of military significance in the Wonson-Kojo areas. One of the largest naval forces since WW II engaged in this operation, which caused considerable damage to enemy installations. The enemy leaders were forced to divert massive numbers of troops and equipment to the Kojo region in the belief that a major invasion was imminent.

Continuous strikes disrupted the Red railroad network and repairs were even more difficult because of

Aircraft spotted on forward section of "Bonnie Dick's" flight deck in the Gulf of Tonkin.

A4 Skyhawk being launched for a strike over North Vietnam.

the freezing weather and snow.

Once again the hydroelectric plants were bombed, and this time the damage inflicted was severe enough to preclude any repairs. Flights were then directed at railroads, highways and factories at Rashin and Taeyu-dong.

At Yokosuka on December 18, 1952, the "Bonnie Dick" was visited by Vice Admiral J. J. Clark, Commander of the Seventh Fleet. The same day the carrier got underway for the states and arrived at Alameda Naval Air Station January 8, 1953. After unloading her ammo and air group, she went to San Francisco on March 3. She was decommissioned May 15 and sent to the shipyard for a major conversion that would require two years to complete.

Captain Lamar P. Carver took command on September 6, 1955 and the "Bonnie Dick" was recommissioned at San Francisco. Noticeable improvements included an angle deck, enclosed hurricane bow, and a streamlined island structure. A pair of steam catapults replaced the former hydraulic types and a revamped operational control deck increased visibility

and decreased noise. Her total displacement was increased 5000 tons.

In August 1956 the *Bon Homme Richard* headed for the Western Pacific, during which time the Commander of Carrier Division Seven and Air Group 21 were embarked. For seven months the carrier operated in the South China Sea, then returned to Alameda in February 1957. Once again she was a guest at the San Francisco Naval Shipyard where she ran up a $450,000 bill for repairs and alterations.

On June 7 at 9:00 A.M., two A3Ds and two F8Us took off the "Bonnie Dick's" deck and landed three hours and 28 minutes later on the *USS Saratoga CVA-60* off the Florida coast.

President Dwight D. Eisenhower was among the guests who watched the arrival of the four jets marking the first time carrier-launched planes had flown cross-country from one carrier to another.

The carrier headed for the Western Pacific again on July 10. Her air group was now equipped with the new A3D *Skywarrior* and F4D *Skyray* aircraft. A highlight of the cruise came in the Formosa Straits when Generalissimo Chaing Kai Shek and Madam Chaing visited the ship.

After five months of duty with the Seventh Fleet, the "Bonnie Dick" returned to Alameda December 11, 1957. Seven days later she set course for Bremerton, Washington, where upon arrival she entered the Puget Sound Naval Shipyard for a four-month overhaul.

On May 21 she returned to Alameda. Then, on July 2, she was sailing toward San Diego from where she operated during August and September. Another Western Pacific cruise was taken from November 1, 1958 to June 18, 1959.

From July to November 21, 1959, the carrier operated along the western seaboard, then departed Alameda for one of the most extensive cruises ever conducted by a Pacific fleet carrier. First stop was at Pearl Harbor, then on to Guam, Okinawa, and Japan. In mid-March she participated in "Operation Bluestar"—the largest amphibious exercise in the Pacific since World War II. Hong Kong was visited on March 26, then she traveled south around the tip of Malaya, through the Malacca Strait, under the tip of Ceylon. At the latter port she accepted an invitation from the Indian Navy to remain in Bombay for five days. She departed Bombay April 16, 1960, for a two-day jaunt to Singapore, then on to Okinawa where the Commander Carrier Division Three, Rear Admiral Andrew McB. Jackson, and his staff transferred to the USS Ticonderoga CVA-14. The "Bonnie Dick" then went to Yokosuka for one day and on May 4 departed for a non-stop return to the states, arriving at Alameda May 14, 1960.

She traveled to Puget Sound for a four-month overhaul, which was completed on October 6, 1960. The carrier then returned to her new home port of San Diego.

After six months of intensive training she departed on April 26, 1961, for duty with the Seventh Fleet in the Far East. Upon reaching Hawaii a scheduled Operational Readiness Inspection was cancelled so she sailed for Subic Bay and took part in the "Fil-Am" fiesta on July 2–3. Among the celebrities from Hollywood that visited the ship were Shirley MacLaine and Paul Newman. During World War II Newman had served as a Radioman Third Class in the Navy and the surroundings were familiar to him. On December 2, the "Bonnie Dick" began a long voyage home and arrived at San Diego on the 13th, where she docked at North Island.

On July 17, 1962, the carrier departed home port for the Western Pacific and arrived at Subic Bay via Pearl Harbor, where she joined the Seventh Fleet.

During this cruise the carrier was mostly assigned to duty in the Philippine area. A visit was made to Sasebo and Beppu Japan, followed by a trip to Hong Kong before returning to the Philippine Sea.

Typhoon Diana cut short the Hong Kong visit. On December 25 the "Bonnie Dick" anchored at Buckner Bay, Okinawa. More than 200 underprivileged children were entertained by volunteer "Big Brothers" and a 30-foot Christmas tree was mounted on the flight deck. A roaring cheer came from the children when Santa Claus arrived by helicopter.

On February 11, 1963, the carrier returned to San Diego. A month later found her at Puget Sound for another long overhaul with a $7 million price tag.

She returned to San Diego July 25 and began training pilots of Air Wing 19. From July to January 1964 the carrier's crew underwent training for an overseas cruise. Following an Operational Readiness Inspection at Pearl Harbor the "Bonnie Dick" arrived at Subic Bay on February 23 and on March 30 she departed for a goodwill cruise to the Strait of Malacca and Indian Ocean.

Her first port of call was the French-speaking port of Diego Suarez on the northern tip of Malagasy. A week later she was at Mombasa, Kenya, in East Africa. After a brief stopover at Aden, on the tip of the Arabian Peninsula the carrier returned to Subic Bay.

The Bon Homme Richard arrived at Yokosuka, Japan, May 25 and remained until August 28, at which time she was sent to the South China Sea. Because of the Tonkin Gulf crisis she patrolled the waters off Vietnam for 45 days before returning to Subic Bay on October 12.

On November 21 families and friends of the crew came aboard as the carrier tied up alongside Quay Wall at North Island, San Diego, after ten months of overseas duty.

Carrier Air Wing 19 was embarked on April 21, 1965, and the carrier departed home port for her first complete tour of duty in Vietnam. Training operations were conducted from April 30 to May 5 in the Hawaiian area, then the carrier steamed away and arrived at Subic Bay on May 18.

Assigned to Task Force 72 she operated off Yankee Station in the Tonkin Gulf from May 26 to July 2. She then went to Subic Bay for maintenance until July 17, at which time she took position on Dixie Station off South Vietnam on July 19, remaining there through August 11. September 25–26 the carrier was active in Operation Dagger, then cruised to and from Subic Bay periodically. She came to rest at the latter port on October 30 after 53 days at sea.

View of A1H, piloted by Ltjg. S. E. Frederick, being launched off the *USS Bon Homme Richard* CVA-31, on a mission over North Vietnam.

On November 26 the *Bon Homme Richard* celebrated her 21st birthday with a special U.S.O. stage show. The crew then enjoyed a five-day visit to Hong Kong before sailing on to Yokosuka. On December 30 the "Bonnie Dick" departed Japan and sailed stateside, arriving at San Diego January 13, 1966. She had just completed 267 days of deployment in the Western Pacific and her crew were elated to be home again.

Three days later the "Bonnie Dick's" home port was changed to Long Beach, California, and entered the naval shipyard there on January 26 for a $22 million renovation. She was equipped with ship-wide air conditioning and a new flightdeck.

On October 4 she sailed to San Diego, but a mechanical failure en route forced a return to Long Beach six days later. On November 2 the carrier arrived at San Diego and learned this was again to be her home port. Training took place off the California coast until January 25, 1967, then on the 26th she headed for operations in the Western Pacific.

Among her feats during this cruise was the successful action of her air wing. The "Bonnie Dick" and Carrier Air Wing 21 became the first ship/air wing to shoot down nine North Vietnamese MIG-17 jet fighters. The first pair were blasted from the air over North Vietnam on May 1 during a strike on Kep Airfield, 35 miles north of Hanoi. While flying cover for the strike force, Lieutenant Commander M. O. Wright, in an F8 *Crusader* from Fighter Squadron 211, shot down one MIG with an air to air missile. An instant later, Lieutenant Commander Wright and his wingman, Air Force Major Ron Loro, spotted another enemy plane going after one of the strike force bombers. Major Lord, an exchange pilot, slipped down behind the MIG simultaneously warning the A4 *Skyhawk* to break away. When it did, Major Lord pressed his trigger and ripped the MIG's wing with 20mm gunfire. The enemy pilot could take a hint and immediately dived for the ground for the protection of North Vietnamese antiaircraft gunners.

During this same strike Commander T. R. Swartz, flying an A4 *Skyhawk* of Attack Squadron 76, was concentrating on his rocket run on Kep Airfield when he was jumped by two MIGs. He managed to down one of them and earned the honor of being the first Navy pilot in the Vietnamese conflict to down a MIG with an A4 light attack plane.

The main strike force of A4s, led by Lieutenant Commander Paul Hollandsworth, dropped their bombs and rockets with pinpoint accuracy, destroying five MIGs parked at Kep and seriously damaging several others. Excellent aerial photo coverage was obtained by Light Photographic Squadron 63, Detachment Lima.

During a strike on the thermal power plant at Hanoi on May 19, the "Bonnie Dick's" pilots shot down four MIGs in aerial combat. The F8 fighters met their quarry in the midst of heavy AA fire while escorting the bombers to target, only one mile from Hanoi.

On July 21 Carrier Air Wing 21 pilots scored their final kills of the cruise when they blasted three more MIGs over the Ta Xa oil depot 25 miles from Hanoi.

The *Bon Homme Richard's* numerous displays of aerial superiority over North Vietnam made her the Navy's first "ace" carrier and Fighter Squadron 211 became the first "ace" squadron of the Vietnamese conflict. The repeated raids on Hanoi's power plants, along with multiple strikes on the power plants at Haiphong, Than Hoa and Bac Giang, severely crippled North Vietnam's ability to produce electric power for her war effort. At one point the production capability was diminished 50 percent.

During the total Seventh Fleet cruise, the personal flags of two Rear Admirals waved from the "Bonnie Dick's" yardarm on separate occasions. On February 25 Rear Admiral Thomas J. Walker, Commander Carrier Division Three, broke his flag which was replaced on April 13 by the flag of Rear Admiral Vincent P. de Poix, Commander Carrier Division Seven.

Upon completion of her last line period, the *Bon Homme Richard* stopped at Yokosuka where on August 10 a change of command was conducted on her flight deck. Rear Admiral Frederick A. Bardshar relieved Rear Admiral de Poix.

Air Wing 21, led by Commander Albert J. Monger, dropped a total of 5506 tons of ordnance on military targets in North Vietnam with precision accuracy, as was proved by excellent aerial photography.

Under the command of Captain Charles K. Ruiz, the carrier returned to San Diego on August 25, 1967, then sailed to Long Beach Naval Shipyard on September 5. On November 3 she was back at San Diego where the rest of the year was spent operating off the coast.

During her 22 years of naval service, the *USS Bon Homme Richard CVA-31* has received the following awards: The Navy Unit Commendation, first in Korea, then in Vietnam; the American Area Campaign Medal; the Asiatic-Pacific Area Campaign Medal with one battle star; the WW II Victory Medal (Asia); the National Defense Service Medal with five battle stars; the Armed Forces Expeditionary Medal; the Vietnam Service Medal with three stars; the United Nations Service Medal; the Republic of Korea Presidential Unit Citation Badge; and the Republic of Vietnam Campaign Medal.

USS Leyte CVS-32 at anchor off Malta.

32

USS Leyte AVT-10 (CV-32)

Construction on the *USS Crown Point CV-32* was authorized on March 23, 1943 and her keel was laid on February 21, 1944 at the Newport News Shipbuilding Company.

On May 8, 1945 her name was changed to commemorate the Battle of Leyte Gulf. Mrs. James M. Mead, wife of the New York Senator, christened the ship as it was launched on August 23, 1945. Captain Henry F. Maccomsey took the helm and the *USS Leyte CV-32* was commissioned on April 11, 1946.

Original statistics of the new carrier at the time of commissioning revealed that she was 888 feet long with a standard displacement of 27,100 tons. Extreme beam at the flight deck was 147 feet 6 inches with a draft of 28 feet 7 inches. Her trial speed was 32.7 knots and she carried 360 officers and 3088 enlisted men. Her armament consisted of twelve 5-inch 38-caliber guns plus eighteen quadruple 40mm mounts.

On August 30 the *Leyte* departed Hampton Roads, Virginia, and arrived at Quonset Point, Rhode Island, where she welcomed aboard Air Group 18 and began carrier qualifications. Shakedown operations were held off Guantanamo Bay, Cuba, beginning September 16, after which she returned to the yards for post-shake-down alterations.

On October 20 she transited the Panama Canal and joined the battleship *USS Wisconsin BB-64* for a good-will cruise along the western seaboard to South America. The surgeon-general of the Chilean Army came aboard and the carrier steamed to Valpariaso where her crew attended the inauguration of President Gabriel Gonzales in Santiago. Afterwards the ship went to Callae, Peru.

The *Leyte* resumed shakedown operations off Cuba on November 18 and visited the Virgin Islands before returning to Yorktown, Virginia, on December 12.

During the next three years the *Leyte* participated in numerous exercises with the fleet and hosted Naval reservists. Three cruises were made to the Mediterranean, during which time she was the flagship of Carrier Division Four.

She arrived in the Mediterranean for a fourth time in May 1950. While in Beirut, Lebanon, in August she received word to join the United Nations Carrier Task Force 77 in the western Pacific. After a 15-day preparation period in Norfolk, she sped to the Pacific.

On October 3, the *Leyte* arrived in Korean waters and immediately got into action. For 52 consecutive days her air group struck against the Communist aggressors. Of 108 days in the area she spent 92 at sea and launched 3933 sorties. The air group logged 11,000 hours of combat flying while inflicting serious damage to the enemy.

Keeping ready to meet enemy planes should they appear, the USS Leyte "cuts loose" with her 5" guns during gunnery exercises en route to the combat area off Korea.

Lieutenant (jg) Thomas J. Hunder of the *Leyte's* air group was awarded the Congressional Medal of Honor for heroism during an attempt to rescue one of his fellow pilots down behind enemy lines.

On January 19, 1951 the *Leyte* was detached from Task Force 77 and sailed to Norfolk for an overhaul. The *Leyte* was affectionately nicknamed "Leading Leyte" by her crew, who were certainly proud of her when she received the Navy Unit Commendation. This was awarded for her meritorious service in Korea from October 9, 1950 to January 19, 1951.

The overhaul was completed and the next six weeks were spent in fleet training in the Caribbean. She then returned to Norfolk on August 21, 1951.

On September 3, she began another tour of duty with the Mediterranean's Sixth Fleet, after which she returned to the United States and operated with the Second Fleet along the Atlantic coast.

Another Mediterranean cruise was conducted from August 1952 to February 1953, during which time the *Leyte* was redesignated CVA—Attack Aircraft Carrier. Upon return from her sixth Mediterranean cruise in February 1953 she was scheduled for decommissioning. Her deactivation process was nearly complete when the Navy Department announced that she would be redesignated CVS—Antisubmarine Warfare Carrier and would serve the fleet in this capacity.

The CVS tag became effective in August 1953 and the *Leyte* was among the first five carriers to serve in Antisubmarine Warfare (ASW) duty.

The ASW Support Aircraft Carrier evolved from the lessons learned during World War II. Today submarines are a constant threat in both conventional and nuclear war. They are capable of launching nuclear missiles against our cities and industrial regions. With this in mind, there is an ever-increasing emphasis to use new tactics, new advancements, and specialized personnel training.

A major step took place in August 1953 when five attack aircraft carriers (CVA) were designated CVS. They were the *Enterprise CVS-6, Franklin CVS-13, Bunker Hill CVS-17, Leyte CVS-32* and *Antietam CVS-36* Eventually, 15 other carriers were so designated and 10 still remain in this classification.

The U.S. Navy views the submarine as a great threat to our use and control of the high seas as well as our national security. The aircraft carrier plays a prominent role in the ASW program, for it is capable of moving from one sea lane to another as required and there serving as a logistics center for ASW units and as a command post for "Hunter-Killer" teams.

ASW carriers use a variety of surface and air search

A Navy ad "sky raider" takes off from *USS Leyte* for strike on Korean targets.

radars plus the latest electronic equipment coupled with modern navigational plotters and high-speed communications.

The "Hunter-Killer" groups compose a highly technical complex of machinery and aircraft. As an offensive team, where an enemy submarine may be lurking, basic teamwork combining search and tracking enable the ASW sub surface units to destroy any threat with their attack capabilities.

At this writing, the ASW team includes the aircraft carrier, with a flag rank officer aboard as the Task Group commander; five to eight destroyers with a senior officer aboard one to serve as a Screen commander; and a carrier-based ASW Air Group flying Gruman S2F *Tracker*; Douglas EA-1E *Guppy*; Sikorsky SH-3A *Sea King*; a helicopter squadron; and a

detachment of early warning radar planes. The primary mission of an ASW Air Group is to conduct all-weather antisubmarine warfare operations. This is done by detection, tracking, and destruction of the enemy submarine. Continuous training in instrument flying, tactics and weapons, and delivery are vital for an effective ASW team.

The S2F *Tracker* is capable of delivering rockets, depth bombs, torpedoes, and aerial mines. The helicopters are primarily used for closer localization of an enemy submarine detected by the *Tracker* planes.

Backed up with our own submarines and land-based planes, the ASW team stands ready to meet any aggression which presents itself.

While the *Leyte* was undergoing her CVS conversion on October 15, 1953, an explosion in the port catapult machinery room killed 32 men and injured several more.

In January 1954 the conversion was completed and the *Leyte* began refresher training off Guantanamo Bay, Cuba. In February 1955 she began "Hunter-Killer" operations in the Caribbean. In May she participated in "Operation New Broom III," a combined NATO exercise.

During the major portion of her ASW career the *Leyte* was the flagship of Carrier Division 18 and operated from Quonset Point, Rhode Island. Her duty took her to the North Atlantic, down the eastern seaboard, and into the Caribbean Sea while cruising with submarines based at New London, Connecticut.

In January 1959 the *Leyte* sailed into the New York Naval Shipyard and was decommissioned on May 15, 1959. On the same day she was stricken from the list of naval ships and was destined to become scrap.

During her active career she was awarded the Navy Unit Commendation Ribbon; Navy Occupation Service Medal; Korean Service Meral with two battle stars; United Nations Service Medal; National Defense Service Medal; and the Republic of Korea Presidential Unit Citation Badge.

USS Kearsarge CVA-33.

33

USS Kearsarge CVS-33 (CV-33)

The *USS Kearsarge CVS-33* honors two famous predecessors of the same name, which have become an honorable attribute to our Navy's heritage. The name *Kearsarge* comes from an obscure mountain peak in the Southeastern ranges of New Hampshire's White Mountains.

The first ship to bear the name was commissioned on February 5, 1862, and saw action in the Civil War. One of her most memorable moments came on June 19, 1864, during a 65-minute skirmish with the Confederate blockade runner *CSS Alabama*. More than 370 rounds of ammunition were hurled at the *Kearsarge*, which had only 173 rounds to answer with. However this proved to be sufficient, because the *Alabama* was sunk.

Because of the record of the Civil War sloop-of-war, the Congress authorized construction of a battleship that would bear the name *Kearsarge. Designated BB-5*, the vessel served until May 1920 when she was decommissioned.

Three months later the *Kearsarge* was redesignated AB-1, a craneship. In this unglorious capacity she assisted in work on the *USS Saratoga CV-3, USS Essex CV-9,* and *USS Hornet CV-12*. She was deleted from the list of Navy vessels on June 22, 1955, and sold for scrapping on August 9.

The current *Kearsarge* is the only U.S. carrier to bear the name of a former battleship. Her keel was laid down on March 1, 1944, at the New York Naval Shipyard.

Mrs. Aubrey W. Fitch, wife of Vice Admiral Fitch, sponsored the new carrier during a gala launching ceremony on May 5, 1945. She was commissioned on March 2, 1946 with Captain Francis J. McKenna in command.

During her first year the *Kearsarge* underwent an elaborate shakedonw cruise and then operated along the eastern seaboard and the Caribbean Sea. She departed Norfolk on June 7, 1947, for her first European cruise, where she visited Rosyth, Scotland; Goteborg, Sweden; and Weymouth, England. On July 18 she departed England and sailed to the states. At Annapolis, midshipmen who had been on this cruise departed the ship and trudged to the Naval Academy on August 16.

The *Kearsarge* went to sea again on August 30 from Quonset Point, Rhode Island. She launched two of the Navy's latest FD-1 *Phantom* jets to participate in the National Air Races at Cleveland. This marked the first time a jet plane had taken off a carrier and landed at an inland base.

Training maneuvers continued until June 1, when 400 Marines came aboard at Hampton Roads, bound for the Mediterranean. During the next four months the carrier was assigned to the Sixth Fleet. On October 2, 1948, the "Mighty K" returned to Quonset Point.

Throughout November she participated in a special cold-weather exercise. This duty took her as far north as the Davis Straits, after which she made a return trip to Newport, where she arrived November 30.

An overhaul was taken from August 22, 1949, to January 27, 1950, at the Boston Navy Yard. Then she transited the Panama Canal, stopped briefly at San Diego, then proceeded to Bremerton, Washington, arriving February 23.

On June 16 the *Kearsarge* was decommissioned for another overhaul period.

Captain Louis B. French took command during re-

Aircraft operation aboard *USS Kearsarge* during carrier qualifications off San Diego, California. F9F-2 Panther being shot off port catapult halfway through run.

commissioning ceremonies on February 15, 1952, then sailed his ship to San Diego in early April for a shakedown cruise.

While the *Kearsarge* was being modernized, the war erupted in Korea, and now the carrier was ready to do her duty. On July 5, 1952, she departed San Diego, and following a cursory training period at Hawaii she reached Yokosuka, Japan, on September 8. She was assigned as flagship of Carrier Division Five, working with the United Nations forces in fighting Communist aggression in Korea.

During the Korean Summer-Fall defense and the Third Korean Winter of 1952 the *Kearsarge* launched more than 6000 sorties over North Korea. She returned from her first Korean war cruise on March 17, 1953.

The *Kearsarge* conducted training operations off the coast of Southern California until July 1, then deployed for her second tour to the Far East. On October 1, she was reclassified from a heavy carrier to attack carrier.

An uneasy truce had been signed but the carrier was still busy. In addition to her usual patrols with other carriers, she maintained a careful watch on the waters separating the Nationalist Chinese at Taiwan from the mainland of Communist China. On January 18, 1954, she came home to San Diego.

She entered the San Francisco Naval Shipyard on January 30, 1954, for a five-month overhaul, which was completed July 6. She immediately took a short refresher cruise near San Diego.

Her third Western Pacific cruise also proved to be memorable as trouble flared again in the Far East. On October 7 she joined a carrier task force, which included the *USS Wasp CVA-18*, in the South China Sea. The Chinese Communist forces had begun concentrated attacks on the Chinese-Nationalist-held Tachen Islands, located 120 miles northeast of Taiwan.

Based at Subic Bay in the Philippines, the *Kearsarge* stood ready to assist the Nationalists in evacuating the Tachen Islands. Orders came from President Eisenhower on February 6, 1955, to proceed with the operation. The *Kearsarge* supported Seventh Fleet units and the Chinese Nationalist Navy in a successful evacuation of more than 18,000 civilians and 20,000 military personnel from the islands.

After the evacuation the carrier visited Hong Kong before resuming her patrols from Subic Bay. On May 12 she sailed back to San Diego, California.

Five months of operational training was conducted from the California port, then on October 23 the carrier once again set course for the Western Pacific. Ports of call were made at Okinawa, the Philippines, Hong Kong, and Japan.

Kearsarge anchored in Subic Bay.

She returned to San Diego on May 17, 1956, and entered Puget Sound Naval Shipyard on July 5 to begin a series of Modernizations. During this seven-month yard period the *Kearsarge* received a new angle deck, hurricane bow, and a deck edge elevator.

Work was completed February 7, 1957, and she operated along the west coast until August 9 when she aimed for Hawaii, thence to the Marianas and Japan, arriving at Yokosuka on September 22. During this cruise the *Kearsarge* steamed 43,000 miles, launched 2531 sorties, and participated in the cold weather readiness exercise "Castle Rock," plus a massive amphibious warfare landing operation called "Strongback."

Her air group endured two weeks of intensive flying from the naval air station at Cubi Point in the Philippines. Twice the carrier hosted groups of Japanese government, military, and press representatives as they watched air operations during a day-long cruise.

The *Kearsarge* was always on the alert to aid in the defense of Taiwan as the Communist Chinese shelled the Kinmen group of islands near the Chinese mainland. On April 2, 1958, the *Kearsarge* returned to San Diego, then entered the shipyard at Long Beach where she received antisubmarine warfare equipment. In her new role she was reclassified from attack (CVA) to antisubmarine warfare (CVS) on October 1, 1958.

On September 26 Typhoon Vera passed over the central Honshu mainland. Nagoya and adjacent areas absorbed the brunt of Vera's furious wrath which injured 18,000 persons, killed 3000, and left over a million in dire distress.

The *Kearsarge* was 300 miles away from the disaster scene on September 29 and went to render assistance. Her planes were sent to the area with advance parties of medical and supply personnel who established a liaison and made ready to provide relief to the City of Nagoya. Relief efforts continued up to October 5, resulting in the evacuation of 4610 persons, an airlift of 148,000 pounds of supplies, and the inoculation of thousands of Japanese. The *Kearsarge's* ship's company and air group personally donated $3020 and 3000 pounds of clothing to the disaster victims.

Admiral Arleigh A. Burke, Chief of Naval Operations, sent a message to the carrier stating: "Your prompt and spirited action in providing humanitarian relief to the unfortunate typhoon victims in the Nagoya area was an impressive demonstration of the Navy's willingness and capability to relieve suffering . . . the aid you rendered in Nagoya will be long remembered. Well done."

Throughout November, a weapons demonstration for Asian leaders was held with the assistance of two attack carriers. The display covered the full range of offensive capabilities of the ships and aircraft of the Seventh Fleet. Representatives were present from Australia, Cambodia, Nationalist China, France, Indonesia, Japan, South Korea, Laos, Malaya, New Zealand, Pakistan, Republic of the Philippines, Thailand, South Vietnam, and the United Kingdom.

After a training schedule with other Seventh Fleet units of the SEATO nations, the *Kearsarge* visited Nagoya, Japan, on February 18, 1960. During a three-day period the crew had a chance to meet friends they had made five months before due to the typhoon. Governor Mikine Kuwahara of the Aichi Prefecture was the first to thank the Navy, adding that a large portion of the relief came from Los Angeles, California, which had declared itself Nagoya's sister city in March 1959. Mayor Kissen Kobayashi related how work restoring the Nagoya Castle, built in 1612, had been interrupted by the typhoon.

The *Kearsarge* held open house during the visit and hundreds of Japanese got a first-hand view of the ship via television after a tour had been scheduled.

After a short stop at Yokosuka the carrier went to sea on March 3, 1960. Three days later a storm forced her to head 1200 miles off Wake Island where a 50-foot Russian landing craft had drifted for 49 days in choppy waters. The four crewmen had survived the ordeal with three cans of beef, one loaf of bread, and whatever water could be saved from rainfalls. The Russians gave their names as Master Sergeant Victor Aygonschi, Private Anthony Kruchowske, Private Philip Poplavski, and Private Fredor Ivan. They were given food and medical attention until the carrier arrived at Alameda, California, March 15. They were then flown to Moscow via New York. Later a radio message was received from Odessa, Russia, which said: "Let us greet you for saving our compatriots who returned to their country and would like to shake hands with you. . . . Oldunov."

For almost a year the *Kearsarge* sailed the area of Southern California, operating mostly from San Diego while training with other units of the First Fleet. On March 3, 1961, she went to the Gulf of Siam near Bangkok when the Seventh Fleet prepared to deal with the Communist threat to Thailand in conjunction with the crisis at Laos. When tension ceased the *Kearsarge* resumed operations with the Seventh Fleet.

On September 19 the carrier arrived at the Long Beach Naval Shipyard, then transferred to the yard at Bremerton, Washington for modernization, which required seven months. The facelifting was completed

June 19, 1962, and the refreshed carrier went to San Diego for training maneuvers.

The *Kearsarge* sailed for Hawaii on August 2 to participate in her first Project Mercury operation.

Commander Walter M. Schirra, Jr., 39, orbited the earth nearly six times in his space capsule, *Sigma 7*. Commander Schirra had lifted off the pad on the morning of October 3 and splashed down in the Pacific 8¾ hours later at 5:29 P.M., EDT. *Sigma 7*, with Astronaut Schirra still inside, was placed upon the *Kearsarge's* flight deck at 6:15 P.M. Schirra later talked with President Kennedy and Vice President Johnson via ship-to-shore radio-telephone.

When the *Kearsarge* arrived at Honolulu on Oc-tober 6, Astronaut Wally Schirra departed and was flown to Houston, Texas. The carrier then proceeded to San Diego and resumed ASW training for the next six months.

On May 15–16, 1963, 36-year-old Air Force Major Leroy Gordon Cooper, Jr., made 22 orbits around the earth. His Mercury space capsule, *Faith 7*, had roared off the launch pad at 9:04 A.M., EDT, May 15 and touched down in the Pacific Ocean at 7:42 P.M., only 7000 yards from the *Kearsarge*. *Faith 7* was flown to the carrier and placed on the deck at 8:11 A.M. on May 16. Astronaut Cooper stepped on deck, sur-rounded by the exuberant cheers of the crewmen. He later talked with President Kennedy via telephone.

U. S. Air Force Major Leroy Gordon Cooper being helped from the space capsule that touched down in the Pacific four miles in front of the USS Kearsarge. This was the final and longest flight of the Project Mercury.

Saluting the 1964 Olympics in Tokyo upon its return to Japan is the crew of Seventh Fleet's antisubmarine aircraft carrier, *USS Kearsarge CVS-33*.

From June 1963 to December 1964, the *Kearsarge* made her eighth and ninth deployments to the Western Pacific. Highlighting the latter cruise on August 5, the "Mighty K" was ordered to proceed from Yokosuka, Japan, to provide antisubmarine warfare support to the Seventh Fleet ships involved in the Gulf of Tonkin crisis. She returned to Long Beach on December 16, 1964, to undergo a six-month yard overhaul. During the yard period, the *Kearsarge* received a new aluminum flight deck and the latest radar equipment.

The *Kearsarge* operated off the coast of Southern California until early 1966, then once again set course to the Far East to support units of the Seventh Fleet off Vietnam. During the 1966 cruise, the carrier steamed over 35,000 miles on Yankee Station, maintaining an around the clock surface and sub-surface vigil on the waters of the Gulf of Tonkin. The carrier's helicopters rescued 16 downed American fliers, many of whom had been heavily hit by enemy ground positions. In October, the *Kearsarge* transported President Johnson's helicopter through the Strait of Malacca while the President visited Malaysia. During her trip to Malaysia, the *Kearsarge* crossed the Equator and some 2000 men went through the transition from Pollywog to Shellbacks. The *Kearsarge* returned to Yankee Station on the 23rd, then after a short visit to Hong Kong and Japan returned to San Diego on December 26, 1966.

She operated off San Diego up to August 1967, then took part in training exercises off the Hawaiian Islands. Following the operations, the *Kearsarge* left Pearl Harbor to join with the Seventh Fleet in the Western

Pacific, arriving at Sasebo, Japan, on December 23, 1967. On her arrival, the carrier suffered a severe fire that broke out in an aviation store room. Three men were killed due to the intense heat and the fire was brought under control without affecting the operational ability of the carrier. The *Kearsarge* completed her eleventh WestPac cruise on April 6, 1968, arriving at Long Beach Naval Shipyard to undergo extensive repairs and overhaul. While in the yard, the ship received notification that she had been awarded the Meritorious Unit Commendation and the Battle Efficiency "E" Pennant for the highest degree of combat efficiency. This was the first time that an ASW carrier had received both awards simultaneously.

The *Kearsarge* conducted one final Western Pacific deployment in 1969. Upon her return to Long Beach, the carrier entered the shipyard for the process of deactivation. All usable equipment was removed and she began her final voyage to San Diego, where on February 13, 1970, the 24-year-old carrier was decommissioned and placed in the San Diego Group of the Pacific Reserve Fleet. Today, the *Kearsarge* slowly sways against her moorings in her berth near the 32nd Street Pier at the Naval Ship's Maintenance Facility, her fate in the hands of Navy officials who will deem the proper time when she will be considered useless to her country and disposed of for scrap.

The *USS Kearsarge CVS-33* has received the following awards: the Meritorious Unit Commendation, Navy Occupation Service Medal (Europe); Korean Service Medal with two battle stars; National Defense Service Medal (twice); Armed Forces Expeditionary Medal; the Vietnam Service Medal; the United Nations Service Medal; and the Republic of Korea Presidential Unit Citation Badge.

The *Oriskany* on her shakedown cruise in December 1950 off the Atlantic Seaboard. At that time, the "Big O" was the Navy's newest carrier and many former Essex Class carriers conformed to her style through modernization and conversion.

34

USS Oriskany CVA-34 (CV-34)

Congress authorized construction of the *USS Oriskany CVA-34* on August 7, 1943. Her keel was laid on May 1, 1944, at the New York Naval Shipyard.

The *Oriskany* was launched on October 13, 1945, under the sponsorship of Mrs. Clarence Cannon, wife of the Honorable Clarence Cannon, Member of Congress from Missouri.

The carrier's name commemorated the Battle of Oriskany on August 6, 1777, in which a British invasion was repulsed after attempting to divide the colonies. The battle, fought in the Mohawk Valley, derives its identification from an Indian village, "Oriska," which means "a place of nettles." "Any" indicates "the presence of water."

The *Oriskany* was decommissioned shortly after launching due to a recasting of plans. However, on September 25, 1950, Captain Perry H. Lyons assumed command and the carrier was again commissioned.

The *Oriskany*'s appearance differed from her sister *Essex*-class carriers. She had a smaller, more streamlined island structure and the thirty-eight 5-inch twin gun mounts were absent on the flight deck. Eventually, other *Essex*-class carriers were extensively modernized to conform to the *Oriskany*'s standards. Subsequent to the alteration, they were called "Improved *Essex*-class" or "*Oriskany-Hancock* conversion class."

Lieutenant Commander J. P. McGovern made the first landing on the *Oriskany*, flying an AD Skydiver.

During a two-week operation, Carrier Air Group One was qualified without a single accident.

The *Oriskany* then commenced a shakedown cruise near Guantanamo Bay, Cuba, and successfully passed all phases of gunnery, damage control, and other important drills.

On May 15, 1951, the *Oriskany* departed Quonset Point, R. I., for her first Mediterranean cruise. She joined the Sixth Fleet at Augusta, Sicily, on May 7 and relieved the *USS Saipan CVL-48*

During the cruise, stops were made at Athens, Greece; Irklion and Suda Bay, Crete; Tripoli, Libya; Ismit, Turkey; Naples, Genoa, and La Spezia, Italy.

The *Oriskany* returned to Quonset Point on October 4, 1951. On November 6, she steamed to New York and 1400 men stood at attention on her flight deck and spelled "Hi New York— *Oriskany* Can Do 100%— Can You?"

This was a response to a vital campaign for blood donations in which 2000 pints of blood were donated by the *Oriskany*'s crewmen and the nickname "Blood Vessel" is still remembered by former shipmates.

On November 16, the carrier was decommissioned at the Brooklyn Navy Yard. During this inactive period her flight deck was completely renovated. She was again placed in service on May 25, 1952. The *Oriskany* arrived at Norfolk Navy Yard to store supplies for a ten-day training voyage near Guantanamo Bay, Cuba.

On June 19, 1952, she steamed into Quanabara Harbor, Rio de Janeiro, Brazil. The following day President Vargas came aboard to watch flight operations.

On June 29, the *Oriskany* made history by becoming the first aircraft carrier to navigate around Cape Horn. She was prepared for rough weather as she reached the Falkland Islands, but the sea was unusually calm; the crew was able to observe a beautiful winter sunrise.

After 15,000 miles of travel the *Oriskany* docked at Quay Wall, North Island, San Diego, on July 21.

On August 28, the 17-year old King of Iraq, Faisal II, came aboard for a one-day cruise. The King was assassinated in a bloody coup d'état seven years later.

The *Oriskany* departed San Diego on September 15 and arrived in Korean waters to join Task Force 77; this followed two weeks of combat readiness drills near Hawaii.

She was redesignated CVA—Attack Aircraft Carrier —on October 1, 1952.

An F9F Panther jet was launched on November 2, marking the first sortie from the carrier. The *Oriskany*'s air group blasted the North Korean coast and

Lieutenant Edwin Kummer returning from a bombing mission over North Korea. One bomb which failed to come lose over target dangles from the wing.

enemy supply lines, destroying storage and manufacturing.

A quartet of planes from Fighter Squadron 121 assigned to the carrier encountered air-to-air combat with four MIG-15 jets. This is believed to be the first aerial dogfight in naval history involving jet aircraft.

Lt. Royce William and Lt. (jg) David Middleton downed a pair of the MIGs and Lt. (jg) David Rowlands damaged a third.

An F4U Corsair returning from a strike mission approached for a landing on March 6, 1953. When the plane touched the flight deck, a bomb that had failed to release during the mission was jarred loose and bounced twice across the deck and exploded. Two men were killed and 15 were injured. A photographer was one of the two men killed. He had been standing on the starboard catwalk taking photos of the landing plane and his film revealed the complete incident, including the flaming explosion which took his own life.

Airman Richard Donovan plunged into the flames with complete disregard for his own safety; he succeeded in rescuing the unconscious pilot, who had been trapped inside the burning wreckage.

An amusing incident that occurred during the Korean War, when the expression "give 'em everything but the kitchen sink" gnawed at the pilots' nerves. One morning a Douglas bomber took off from the *Oriskany* with a zinc bathtub strapped to her belly. The sink was dropped into an enemy position and the *Oriskany* was assured she had given them everything.

The *Oriskany* returned to San Diego on May 18, 1953 for a normal yard overhaul. On September 14, the carrier departed the yards and arrived in Korean waters on October 15. Although the truce had been signed, the *Oriskany* maintained a state of semi-alert-

This dramatic photo was taken by photographers mate Thomas Leo McGraw, 22, at his station when the bomb fell to the deck. He was killed instantly but his camera kept running.

Lt. Kummer was rescued from his Corsair by Airman Richard D. Donovan, who plunged through the explosions, cut him loose from the parachute harness. The pilot suffered burns and leg injuries.

Firefighters fought the huge flames and fires all night and by daylight the Oriskany had resumed air strikes over North Korea.

ness, launching 4422 sorties in the Sea of Japan, the East China Sea, and the Philippine Sea during the uneasy truce.

Yokosuka, Asaebo, and Kobe, Japan were some of the places visited, and the crew had more time to relax while visiting Kamakura and the ancient capital of Kyoto.

Throughout November and December 1954, the *Oriskany* went "Hollywood," playing the role of the fictitious carrier *Savo* for the motion picture of James Michener's *The Bridges at Toko Ri*.

Many of the ship's crew had bit parts and Air Group 19 supported the movie with authentic flight deck operations.

Paramount Studios rented the "Showboat" night club in Tokyo and invited 200 men from the ship's crew for the shooting of a nightclub scene.

On March 2, 1954, an F2H-3 Banshee was in the landing pattern, with Lt. F. J. Repp at the controls. The plane suffered a partial loss of power and the pilot had difficulty controlling the plane's altitude; the craft continued to drift downward until it was below the glide path. There was not sufficient power to raise the plane and it struck the after end of the flight deck, its fuselage breaking in half. Fuel tanks exploded into giant orange balls of flame. The nose and cockpit section of the plane had been thrown forward down the deck as the tail section tumbled into the sea. Lt. Repp climbed unhurt from the cockpit, with disbelief that he had survived.

During the summer of 1954, the *Oriskany* took part in another motion picture, titled *Men of the Fighting Lady*.

Upon completion, MGM premiered the film on the carrier's flight deck with the stars of the film, Van Johnson and Keenan Wynn, present.

The *Oriskany* entered the San Francisco Navy Yard in September 1954 for a six-month modernization. She received a new fuel system, improved arresting and barricade gear, plus the latest electronic equipment.

In the fall of 1954 the *Oriskany* said goodbye to a faithful shipmate. As is the custom with many ships, the *Oriskany* had a mascot—a dachshund named Tripoli Schatzie, USN K-911c. She finally took her leave after having served three years on the ship, one year of which was in combat.

Tripoli had sailed the waters of Formosa to Korea and rounded the Horn and crossed the Equator.

As a member of the crew, she was awarded the Korean Service Medal with two battle stars; the United Nations Service Medal; National Defense Service Medal; China Service Medal with European Clasp; and the Purple Heart.

The latter was awarded after the dog had sustained injuries from a gasoline burn during the Korean conflict, which left a scar on her shoulder.

Her retirement was depicted in a *Saturday Evening Post* feature article. While serving on the *Oriskany*, Tripoli produced three litters; the pups were raffled off to the crewmen and $22,000 was raised for charity.

In February 1955, the *Oriskany* resumed operations. In March she departed Alameda, California, for a third tour of duty in the Western Pacific.

Ports of call were Yokosuka, Japan; Subic Bay and Manila, P.I.; Buclney Bay, Okinawa; Hong Kong; and Pearl Harbor.

As a member of the Seventh Fleet, the carrier was active in numerous drills and exercises in preparation for any trouble that might flare up in the South China Sea.

On September 7, 1955, the *Oriskany* sailed from Yokosuka, Japan, and arrived in Alameda, California, 19 days later.

The *Oriskany* spent the remainder of 1955 operating near the California coast, qualifying pilots of Air Group Nine. On February 11, 1956, the carrier sailed to join the Seventh Fleet. During the four-month cruise she participated in various exercises in the South China Sea. On June 13 the carrier arrived at the Navy Yard in San Francisco, where on October 1 she was commissioned into the reserves and then decommissioned on January 2, 1957, to receive another major face lifting.

During the two-year period she was equipped with new steam catapults, an enclosed hurricane bow, and an angle flight deck; and the Combat Information Center (CIC) was relocated to a safer area of the ship.

The *Oriskany* was recommissioned on March 7, 1959, the last of the original 24 *Essex*-class carriers to be modernized.

Captain James M. Wright, who had served as her executive officer during 1951–1952, now took full command. The carrier returned to her home port at San Diego on June 11 and began refresher training and shakedown operations.

Throughout the summer the *Oriskany* passed a series of post-conversion tests, then, in December 1959, she returned to the San Francisco yards for a final touchup.

In January 1960, the *Oriskany* was again in San Diego, conducting carrier qualifications for various squadrons.

On April 30, 1960, Vice Admiral U.S. Grant Sharp relieved Vice Admiral R. E. Libby as Commander of the First Fleet. Admiral Libby was retiring after 42 years of active naval service. The ceremonies were held aboard the *Oriskany.*

The *Oriskany* departed her home port on May 14, 1960, for a seven-months tour of duty with the Seventh Fleet in the Far East. She donated 7500 tons of meat and clothing to flood victims in Luzon, Philippines.

On December 15, she returned to home port and operated off the San Diego coast until March 1961, then was again placed in the San Francisco yards for a five-month overhaul. She received a Fresnal Landing System, the Van Zelm Bridle electronic computer system, and a Naval Tactical Data (NTDS) System.

In September, the *Oriskany* returned to San Diego to resume training operations.

On June 7, 1962, the mighty carrier was again deployed to the Far East. On this cruise (August 12) she set another record during her annual Western Pacific movements when she refueled the *USS King DLG-10* and the *USS Mahan DLG-11,* simultaneously.

Excitement was high when the world-famous Bayanihan Dance group performed traditional dances of the Philippines aboard the *Oriskany* on November 24. At the time, the "Big O" was anchored in Manila Bay.

This was the dancers' first show aboard a U.S. Navy ship. The *Oriskany* returned to San Diego on December 17, 1962, for maintenance, and the crew was released for Christmas leave.

From January through April 1963, the *Oriskany* continued normal training schedules out of San Diego. She received a Pilot/Landing Aid Television System on May 7. This closed-circuit system (PLAT) is a tremendous aid to pilots. Dual cameras recessed in the flight deck and a third camera on a platform two decks above are fed into the closed-circuit television system.

President John F. Kennedy was on board in June 1963 to review the Pacific Fleet. He witnessed "Operation Gold Ball," a fleet exercise that involved 15 ships, including the *Oriskany.*

The Chief Executive saw most of the action from the carrier's flight deck. Also, during the exercise, the *Oriskany* recorded her 12,481st arrested landing and logged 65,439 miles of travel since her commissioning.

On August 1, 1963, the "Big O" set out for her sixth Far East cruise. While in Iwakuni, Japan, in October, she received orders to proceed, "as fast as possible" to the Vietnam area and patrol the coast during the days that followed the *coup d' état* that had caused the downfall and execution of President Diem.

The carrier operated from Yokosuka, where the *Oriskany*'s baseball team became the Seventh Fleet Champs on December 30.

After three months of duty with the Seventh Fleet in the South China Sea, the "Big O" returned to San Diego in March 1964.

Shortly thereafter, she entered Puget Sound Naval Shipyard for an extended overhaul.

In February and March 1965, the *Oriskany* was active in "Operation Silver Lance"—a massive amphibious landing exercise.

The carrier provided air cover for the Marines, fighting a mock battle.

On April 5, 1965, the *Oriskany* was sent on her seventh Western Pacific cruise. Two weeks of ORI were observed in Hawaii and then she headed to the Far East.

In May, the "Big O" arrived in the South China Sea, where on the 8th she launched her first combat sorties since the Korean conflict. This was her first combat air strike in support of the U.S. Marine landings at Chu Lai.

Four "Big O" aircraft teamed with planes from the *USS Coral Sea CVA-43* on May 9 to fly daily recon missions over North Vietnam, inflicting heavy damage to highways and bridges. More than 100 combat sorties were flown in which more than 100 tons of ordnance were dropped each day.

The *Oriskany*'s crew labored 15 to 24 hours daily to maintain the pace of the Vietnam air war.

In July, she arrived in Yokosuka, Japan, for an 11-day rest, which was the longest period in port during the cruise. At this time, the orphans from the *Oriskany Home* were invited aboard. Each child received a gift and the Mother Superior was presented a $1200 check from the crew.

The "Big O" won the Pacific Fleet "underway ordnance replenishment" record during the cruise. The ammunition ship *USS Pyro AE-24* came alongside and ammo was brought aboard at a rate of 196 tons per hour.

Throughout the winter months, the *Oriskany* continued to launch combat sorties over North Vietnam. On November 25, 1965, she completed her 12,000th combat flight launch. This was a record that no other carrier received in a single cruise, including World War II and Korea.

On December 16, 1965, the *Oriskany* returned to her home port. As she pulled up alongside the Quay Wall Pier, a thousand persons viewed the proud ship.

During her nine-month cruise in the Western Pacific, the "Big O" played an active role in the Vietnam conflict for 6½ of these months.

More than 100,000 miles were traveled and nearly 10,000 tons of bombs had been released over enemy targets.

The *Oriskany* was awarded the Navy Unit Commendation for outstanding duty and Captain B. J.

An F8E "Crusader" from Carrier Air Wing 16 is readied for a strike over Vietnam.

Connolly, III, the commanding officer, was presented the Legion of Merit.

As 1966 began, the *Oriskany* conducted training operations off Southern California in preparation for her next Western Pacific cruise.

With Carrier Air Wing 16 aboard, she sailed from San Diego on May 26. She passed the annual ORI inspection at Pearl Harbor, then departed on June 6 bound for Japan, arriving at Yokosuka eight days later.

On June 21, she tied up at the Fleet support base in Subic Bay, Philippines, for a two-day stay.

From June 30 to July 7, the *Oriskany* operated on Dixie Station, then went into action in Yankee Station from July 8 through the 28th.

A brief rest was taken in Subic Bay, then on August 7 she was in the Gulf of Tonkin supporting U.S. efforts in Vietnam. The sailors worked under adverse weather conditions and extreme tropical heat; however, a 15-hour day became normal routine and not one day of combat operations was lost.

The "Big O" established a new record for underway replenishment, transferring 437.5 short tons of ammunition per hour. The transfer was made from the *USS Mount Katmi AE-16*.

After 30 days on the line, the *Oriskany* returned to Subic Bay for a brief stay, then steamed to Hong Kong. While en route to the "Pearl of the Orient," she and *HMS Victorious* had an exchange where planes from each carrier landed on the opposite of their own.

On September 16, a merchant ship of British registry ran aground on the Pratas Reef, 175 miles southeast of Hong Kong.

Helicopters from the *Oriskany* lifted the stricken vessel's 44-man crew from the wreckage. One helicopter was engulfed in a giant wave and crashed into the sea, but all crewmen were picked up safely.

After a brief rest in Hong Kong, the "Big O" arrived on Yankee Station on September 24 to resume combat operations.

Commander Richard M. Bellinger, C.O. of VF-162, downed a MIG jet on October 9, thus evening up a score; only three months earlier, he had been shot down.

While engaged in combat operations in the Gulf of Tonkin on the morning of October 26, 1966, the morning launch was halted by the sudden sounding of the fire alarm at 7:28.

A fire was roaring near the flare locker of Hangar Bay One, and quickly spread—extending over the flight deck and trapping many officers who had returned from combat missions only shortly before.

The flight deck crews were rushing about, hastily moving aircraft aft away from the forward catapult area in an effort to save them.

Searching parties were formed to go through the various compartments and living quarters in attempts to save their trapped shipmates from the raging inferno now roaring out of control.

Aircraft that were in the *Oriskany's* hangar bay during the fire of October 26, 1966, and later evacuated to the flight deck, are surveyed for damage by crewmen.

An A4E "Skyhawk" from Attack Squadron 163 begins her launch from the *Oriskany* during the carrier's second Vietnam War Cruise.

Brave deeds became commonplace as crewmen fought to save others. Earl Houston, Engineman 2d Class, checked the starboard staterooms until driven away by the intense heat. He went through compartments on the port side until stopped by bulkheads warping into the passageways. Late into the night he worked, setting up emergency night lighting and running numerous equipment. Houston was a fine example of a crewman who knows his job. He had attended firefighting schools ashore, but, as he later stated, "I never thought I'd have to use what I learned."

Marine Pfc Peter Mora is credited with saving many lives during the tragedy, including an attempt to revive one fire victim with mouth-to-mouth resuscitation. He also directed hoses, checked hot spots, and noxious gases. Mora said: "I can't remember any specific actions I might have taken. I just kept moving, that's all."

When the terrible fires were finally extinguished, damage to the ship became visible. Two helicopters were lost; four Skyhawks damaged; minor damage to Hangar Bay Two and extensive damage to Hangar Bay One; forward officers quarters damaged as well as the forward elevator, catapults and aircraft.

The damage could have been worse, had it not been for the swift actions of the crew and their accurate knowledge of what to do.

Many sailors scoff at the weeks spent at school, with its daily dousing of water from various types of fires and the odor of sweat and black soot. However, when the time comes for the use of this knowledge to be applied, he's thankful for the weeks or drill.

The *Oriskany* steamed into Subic Bay, on October 28 with her colors at half-mast, she unloaded the flag and dropped the bodies of 44 departed shipmates. She departed on November 4 for the return home and repairs from the fire.

Steaming some 125 miles southeast of Iwo Jima on November 6, memorial services were held for the 44 fire victims and the body of LCDR Omar R. Ford was committed to the deep.

The *Oriskany* arrived at NAS North Island, San Diego, on November 16, 1966, to unload her aircraft prior to entering the yards at San Francisco.

Her cruise had been shortened by six months. She had logged 8535 total combat sorties, dropped 6727 tons of ordnance and spent 142 days on the line, covering 75,000 miles.

Brave shipmates were recognized for their actions. The awards included 3 Silver Stars, 35 DFC's, 666 Air Medals, and 15 Purple Hearts.

The *USS Oriskany CVA-34* has received the following awards since her commissioning in September 1950: The Navy Unit Commendation; the Navy Occupation Service Medal; the China Service (extended) Medal; the Korean Service Medal with two battle stars; the United Nations Service Medal; the National Defense Service Medal; the Armed Forces Expeditionary Medal; Korean Presidential Unit Citation Badge; Viet-Nam Service Medal and the Republic of Viet-Nam Campaign Medal.

USS Antietam. Port side, aft view of carrier at anchor, Norfolk, Va., May 23, 1945.

35

USS Antietam CVS-36 (CV-36)

The *USS Antietam* received her name from the Battle of Antietam Creek, which was waged between the U.S. Army and the Confederate Army near Sharpsburg, Maryland, on September 17, 1862.

On March 15, 1943, 80 years later, the keel of the *USS Antietam* was laid down at the Philadelphia Naval Shipyard.

Mrs. Millard E. Tydings, wife of the Maryland Senator, christened the new carrier August 20, 1944. Then on January 10, 1945, the first carrier to be built at the Philadelphia Navy Yard was commissioned. Captain James R. Tague became her first commanding officer. He also held another unique distinction—he was the only officer born in Japan to command a U.S. Navy

vessel. Captain Tague was born in Kobe, a region of Honshu Island in the Japanese Inland Sea. His parents were Methodist missionaries and returned to America when their son was five years old.

The *Antietam* was rushed to completion using various prefabrication techniques. Even so, she was completed too late for action in World War II. She did participate in the Occupation of Japan following the surrender.

Assigned to Task Force 72 of the Third Fleet, the carrier patrolled the Yellow Seas during September and October 1945. The *USS Intrepid CV-11* and *USS Cabot CVL-28* joined in this operation to protect our amphibious occupation landings in China and Korea.

First firing of 5" 38-cal. guns structural tests aboard Antietam March 5, 1945.

It was also meant as a show of strength to any inhabitants of occupied territories still reluctant to accept the end of the war.

Task Group 72.1 was organized October 15 and the *Antietam* deployed for Guam, arriving six days later. She was sailing again on October 31 and arrived at Tsingtao, China, in four days, where she conducted training maneuvers off the Shantung Peninsula and Gulf of Pohai. In late December the carrier returned to the naval yard at San Francisco.

From January 1946 to February 1949 the *Antietam* conducted training operations off the coast of Southern California in addition to patrols off Japan.

A directive dated February 1949 ordered the carrier to San Francisco. Upon arrival she entered the yards for deactivation and on June 21, 1949, she was decommissioned in the Alameda Reserve Group of the Pacific Fleet.

The Korean conflict erupted in June 1950 and the *Antietam* was among those sleeping carriers recalled to active duty. She was recommissioned January 17, 1951, under the command of Captain G. J. Dufek who

took her to San Diego on May 14. This would be her home port.

Before departing for overseas action she went "Hollywood" for one month while a large part of the movie *Task Force* was filmed aboard her. Actor Wayne Morris, a fighter pilot stationed on the *USS Bon Homme Richard CV-31* during World War II, co-starred with Gary Cooper in this thrilling, authentic movie depicting life aboard a wartime carrier.

On September 8 the *Antietam* departed home port and joined United Nations Task Force 77 in Korean waters. From October 15 to November 14, 1951 she participated in the United Nations Summer-Fall offensive.

She earned her second battle star during the period from November 21, 1951 to March 1, 1952.

More than 5000 tons of ordnance were dropped on designated enemy targets by the carrier's air group. She returned to the states in April 1952 and enjoyed semi-retirement with the Pacific Fleet.

In August the *Antietam* transited the Panama Canal and sailed to Bayonne, New Jersey, for an unusual "first." The *USS Shangri-La CV-38* had received orders to report to the Pacific Fleet, while the *Antietam* arrived for duty in the Atlantic area. To avoid moving hundreds of families at a cost of thousands of dollars, the Navy Department completely exchanged the crews.

The *Antietam* entered the New York Naval Shipyard in September 1952 to undergo an experimental conversion, which consisted of an angle deck. The official report from the Bureau of Ships announced during the same month that "the canted deck on the *Antietam* was finally installed at an angle of 10.5° to the centerline of the axial flight deck. The landing area is 525 feet long with a width at the landing ramp of 70 feet and narrowing to 32 feet 8 inches at the extreme forward end of the takeoff area."

This novel deck paved the way for later conversions of numerous other *Essex*-class carriers. The advantages of an angle deck were immediately recognized, for when a plane landed it could taxi to the starboard deck edge elevator without interrupting flight operations. Aircraft could be launched and recovered simultaneously with complete safety. The new deck also precluded the danger of landing planes crashing into the ship's island structure, or into planes loaded with ammunition and fuel parked on the forward end of the flight deck.

The *Antietam* greeted her new home port at Quonset Point, Rhode Island, in April 1953 after the conversion. For the next eight months she was busy with

Arrival of the *USS Antietam* from Korean Theatre, with reserve squadron aboard, oblique; taken during crew formation under the Golden Gate Bridge, San Francisco.

evaluation exercises, which proved the efficiency of her new angle deck.

On April 11, she was presented the colors of the 165th Infantry Regiment of the New York National Guard. The colors had been valiantly carried during the Battle of Antietam Creek while the Confederate flag waved over the statehouse at Montgomery, Alabama.

The carrier received a routine overhaul from June 1953 to January 1954. As the flagship for Commander Carrier Division Four, she participated in various fleet exercises throughout the year.

In January 1955 the *Antietam* steamed to the Mediterranean for duty with the Sixth Fleet. Upon her return to home port in March 1955 she was the site of the Atlantic Fleet Type Commander Conference.

Television personality Ed Sullivan filmed his popular show aboard the carrier on July 3.

In September 1955 the *Antietam* checked into Boston Naval Yard for maintenance, where she remained until January 1956. This was followed by a six-week training cruise off Guantanamo Bay, Cuba.

A one-day cruise was held June 16 for the benefit of 400 members of the Armed Forces Chemical Association, who watched the carrier's efficiency in hunter-killer tactics.

In July a midshipman cruise was taken to provide at-sea training for future naval officers.

The *Antietam* departed Norfolk October 1, 1956 to begin a goodwill and training cruise in the Eastern

F4U's on flight deck of *USS Antietam CV-36* in Korean waters.

Atlantic. Her first port of call was Brest, France, where French naval officers came aboard for a 24-hour cruise. Then the carrier steamed through the English Channel to Rotterdam, the Netherlands. The goodwill cruise was cancelled due to hostilities in the Middle East and the ship sailed to the Mediterranean for duty with the Sixth Fleet. A brief rest period was taken at Athens, followed by a demonstration of ASW operations for Italian military officers stationed at Taranto.

On December 13, 1956, the *Antietam* was released from the Sixth Fleet and returned to Quonset Point nine days later.

The *Antietam* was assigned to the Chief of Naval Air Training at Pensacola, Florida, on April 21, 1957

and relieved the *USS Saipan CVL-49* as the Navy's training carrier. Mayport, Florida, became the ship's temporary home port until dredging of the Pensacola Channel could be completed.

The carrier became the largest vessel to visit New Orleans when she participated in the May 1957 Armed Forces Day activities. More than 16,000 visitors toured the carrier.

From August 12 through 20 experimental tests were conducted on the carrier, using the new Bell Automatic Landing System. Commander D. Walker accomplished the first landing utilizing the system, then continued by making nine arrested landings and 45 touch-and-go landings in an F3D.

The *Antietam* returned to Boston for a six-month

overhaul in February 1958. Afterwards she made a stop at Norfolk on July 15, where 100 helicopters and 1400 U.S. Marines were embarked because of the crisis at Lebanon. The *Antietam* anchored off Vieques, Puerto Rico, until Arab tensions were alleviated, then she went to Norfolk to release the Marines.

In August the carrier was back at Pensacola for training operations. The dredging of the Channel was completed in January 1959 and the carrier bid hello to her new home port at Pensacola at that time. During the summer of 1959 the *Antietam* hosted Naval Academy midshipmen on their annual Aviation Training cruise. While returning from this mission the carrier recovered an air open-powered boat 60 miles southeast of St. Augustine, Florida. Its only occupant was a Cuban national who had fled Castro's Cuba in an effort to locate her brother in New York. The small craft had drifted 450 miles up the Gulf Stream from Havana.

The *Antietam* entered the Norfolk Navy Yard on February 26, 1960, for minor repairs, then continued training operations out of Pensacola.

On April 28 the carrier received the first manned balloon landing. A week earlier, Commander Malcom Ross and Lieutenant Commander Victor A. Prather set the world's balloon altitude record by ascending 68,000 feet. One month later the two pilots were launched from the *Antietam* in the Gulf of Mexico, and they broke their former record and established a new one by rising to 113,733 feet. Telemetering equipment aboard the carrier and at shore recorded scientific data of the upper atmosphere during this flight. The project was called "Operation Strato Lab High No. 5" and came under the direction of the Office of Naval Research. Tragedy came during recovery operations when Commander Prather fell from the helicopter's rescue hook and drowned.

On July 8, 1961 the *Antietam* sailed from Pensacola to the navy yard at Norfolk for routine maintenance. While en route on the evening of July 9, the carrier recovered a disabled 14-foot motorboat carrying eight Cubans. Three men and five women were fleeing Cuba in search of freedom in the United States.

The carrier entered the yards on July 12. During her overhaul she received the Chief of Naval Operations Safety Award for 1961.

Work was completed on September 10 and the *Antietam* prepared for carrier qualification training. While en route to Pensacola she received orders to proceed at full speed and embark Marine Helicopters plus medical supplies at the Florida port and transport them immediately to stricken areas of southeastern

Bow view of the USS Antietam, underway.

Texas—a scene of violence inflicted by Hurricane Carla. She arrived off Matagorda Island near the Texas coast and delivered the supplies, returning to Pensacola September 17. Among the personnel delivered to the disaster region were four Navy nurses; it is believed to be the first occasion that women sortied aboard a U.S. Navy man of war.

The *Antietam* logged her 100,000th arrested gear landing October 24.

A goodwill visit to New Orleans was made three days later, and over 10,000 persons toured the ship. During her return from New Orleans on October 31 the communications room received an ominous message relating another hurricane disaster, this time off British Honduras. The *Antietam* rushed to Pensacola, arriving November 1, and loaded 300 tons of emergency supplies, 23 helicopters, 50 doctors, 4 Navy nurses, and 73 hospital corpsmen. That evening she sped across the water and arrived at Belize, British Honduras, on November 3. The supplies were rapidly distributed and the medical team inoculated 25,954 persons in the Belize and Stann Creek areas. The carrier departed on November 6 and returned to Pensacola.

From January 1962 to April 1963 the *Antietam* operated from her Florida home port training pilots for the Naval Air Training Command.

In May 1963 the carrier was decommissioned and placed into the Philadelphia Group of the Atlantic Reserve Fleet.

The *USS Antietam CVS-36* received the following awards during her career: The Navy Occupation Service Medal; the China Service (extended) Medal; the Korean Service Medal with two battle stars; the United Nations Service Medal; and the Republic of Korea Presidential Unit Citation Badge.

USS Princeton LPH-5.

36

USS Princeton LPH-5 (CV-37)

On September 14, 1943, the keel was laid down at the Philadelphia Navy Yard of the *USS Valley Forge CV-37*. During the ensuing construction period the name was changed to *Princeton*. The purpose was to honor the previous *USS Princeton CVL-23,* which was lost subsequent to the Battle of Leyte Gulf on October 23, 1944.

Mrs. Harold Dobbs, wife of Princeton University's president christened the new *Princeton* on July 8, 1945, remembering that it was only two years and nine months earlier when she had christened the previous *USS Princeton CVL-23*. Captain James M. Hoskins took the helm on November 18, 1945, and the new carrier was commissioned into the Navy. Captain Hoskins had been aboard the old *Princeton* at the time of her sinking. He was the ship's prospective commanding officer and would have taken command the day after she went down. He became the first C.O. of a U.S. Navy vessel to wear an artificial foot.

The *Princeton* departed on December 13, 1945, and embarked Air Group 81 after a one-day cruise. On January 8, 1946, she began shakedown maneuvers off Guantanamo Bay, Cuba. Afterwards she was assigned to the short-lived Eighth Fleet and participated in Atlantic fleet maneuvers from April 18 to May 31, 1946.

Upon the Eighth Fleet's demise, the *Princeton* transited the Panama Canal and went to San Diego, where the body of the late President Manuel L. Quezon, wartime leader of the Philippines, was placed aboard for return to his homeland.

On September 28 the carrier arrived at Yokosuka, Japan, and became Task Force 77's flagship. Intensive training programs were conducted during this cruise, and on April 15, 1947, the *Princeton* returned to North Island at San Diego.

From July to October 1947 the *Princeton* underwent general maintenance at Puget Sound Naval Shipyard, Bremerton, Washington.

Another trip was made to the Western Pacific before the carrier returned to Bremerton preparatory to deactivation. On June 21, 1949, she was decommissioned with the Bremerton Pacific Fleet Reserve Group, where she remained for just over one year.

On August 28, 1950, the sleeping giant was recommissioned at Puget Sound and became the first capital vessel from the Pacific Reserve Fleet to be so honored. The purpose for her resurrection was the outbreak of hostilities in Korea, and following three arduous months of preparation, she was rushed into combat readiness with naval reservists comprising 75 percent of her crew. She was soon in the battle, along with her sister ships, launching maximum close-support air strikes day after day against the Communist aggressors.

On December 25, 1950, the *Princeton* became the flagship of Rear Admiral Ralph A. Ofstie, Commander, Carrier Division Five. Rear Admiral Ofstie had served as C.O. of the *USS Essex CV-9* during World War II, and under his direction the *Princeton* would soon send daily strikes to support United Nations ground forces in Korea. These aerial bombardments resulted in severe damage to railroads, bridges, and supply areas.

The *Princeton* launched her initial actual combat strikes April 2, 1951, and from that day jet planes became full fledged offensive and defensive weapons.

Lieutenant Commander George B. Riley led his *Panther* jets over numerous bridges, which supplied the enemy aggressors. Another "first" was garnered on May 1 when an AD *Skyraider* was launched against Hwachon Dam in central Korea. The propeller-driven plane scored five hits on the target. Commander Richard C. Merrick, who led the raid, was killed a month later when his plane was shot down on a close support mission.

On May 6, 1951 Rear Admiral George H. Henderson relieved Rear Admiral Ofstie as Commander, Carrier Division Five and Task Force 77. From July 14 to August 10 the *Princeton* was active in operations against the Communist Chinese Spring Offensive. On August 27 she returned to San Diego with an impressive scoreboard. During her first Korean war cruise Carrier Air Group 19 had destroyed 200 rail and highway bridges; and damaged or destroyed over 35 locomotives and 510 railcars, 1180 trucks, 70 airplanes, and 75 fuel and ammo depots.

The proud carrier disembarked her air group at San Diego, then proceeded to Puget Sound Naval Shipyard in Washington for repairs.

On April 30, 1952, the refreshed carrier rejoined Task Force 77. During her second encounter against the enemy, Air Group 19 was active in the Second Summer-Fall campaign and the Korean Defense Summer-Fall 1952 campaign during the periods April 30; May 1–13; June 4–6; July 6–August 3; August 18–September 20; and October 4–16. Vital ground installations, bridges, and storage depots were destroyed, including the Suiho Dam.

The *Princeton* returned to San Diego in November after 138 days in Korean waters. One month earlier she had been redesignated CVA-37—Attack Aircraft Carrier.

A third Korean cruise was taken in 1953 from March 13–31; April 17–30; May 1–15; and June 18–July 27. Air Group 15 flew 3468 sorties and delivered 2700 tons of ordnance on enemy troops and installations.

During flight operations on July 27 the truce was signed and the *Princeton* headed for home. On November 12 she received another reclassification, to CVS-37. Early in 1954 she entered the naval yard at Puget Sound for conversion to an antisubmarine warfare support carrier.

In May she began refresher training near Southern California where intensive operations with other Hunter-Killer groups continued until November 2,

USS Princeton CVA-37 alongside a tanker for refueling in Korean waters.

1954. The carrier then sailed to the Western Pacific and helped evacuate Chinese Nationalists from the Tachen Islands in February 1955. While assigned to the Seventh Fleet she was involved in various exercises until May 15 when she departed Yokosuka, Japan, and arrived in San Diego May 31, 1955.

The *Princeton* operated from this California port, conducting ASW drills until January 1956, then departed for another tour with the Seventh Fleet. She served as flagship of the ASW team that participated in the SEATO exercise *Firmlink* near Thailand.

A mock invasion of Thailand comprised the forces of the United States, Australia, Great Britain, and New Zealand.

The *Princeton* returned to San Diego on August 17 and headed for Puget Sound for an overhaul on September 13, 1956.

On January 20, 1957, the *Princeton* emerged from the yard and resumed ASW operations until July 12, when she joined the Seventh Fleet for six months of duty in the South China Sea.

Upon her return to San Diego on February 12, 1958,

she began a maintenance period followed by routine duties. Another Western Pacific cruise was conducted from June 20 to December 2, 1958.

Early in 1959 the *Princeton* was marked for decommissioning, but the U.S. Marine Corps requested conversion of the carrier to an amphibious assault ship—LPH. On March 2 the *Princeton* was redesignated LPH-5 and went to the Long Beach Naval Shipyard on March 16 for conversion, which was completed May 10.

Immediately upon leaving the yard she participated in an amphibious exercise, *Twin Peaks*, which landed Marines on the beach at Camp Pendleton, California. Over 1000 men of the First and Third Marine Air Wings departed the *Princeton* via helicopters and were flown behind "enemy" lines during the attack. This exercise demonstrated the important coordinated role of the Navy and Marines in vertical envelopment operations.

In February 1960 the *Princeton* made her first cruise to the Western Pacific as an LPH. She resumed amphibious operations upon her return to Long Beach.

LSO signals helos for landing on flight deck of *USS Princeton LPH-5* during first operations of *Princeton* as an LPH carrier.

USS Princeton CV-37.

These maneuvers continued until September 9, 1960, at which time the carrier rejoined the Seventh Fleet in the Far East.

The *Princeton* returned to the shipyard in Long Beach in December for a Fleet Rehabilitation and Modernization (FRAM) conversion. This massive job was completed June 1, 1961, and the carrier returned to normal operations.

In 1962 the carrier was involved in constant amphibious assault operations. Her last exercise, designated "Operation Dominic," was completed in November and the *Princeton* prepared for a nine-month tour in the Western Pacific.

She departed the California coast in February 1963. During operations off the Philippines on April 24, Major Ray Lemmons and First Lieutenant Phillip Goddard of Marine Helicopter Squadron HMM-163, made the 100,000th touchdown aboard the *Princeton*. The carrier became a member of Task Force 76.5 throughout this cruise and returned to Long Beach in October 1965, for routine operations.

On February 15, 1964, a national television audience saw the *Princeton* in a dramatic episode of *The Lieutenant*, which was filmed aboard the veteran carrier. Gary Lockwood starred in the show, with a large supporting cast of the *Princeton*'s sailors and Marines. The ship was docked at Long Beach for an overhaul during the filming.

In June 1964 the *Princeton* arrived at San Diego following a five-month yard period. She was the first ship to be fueled by the newly commissioned supply ship USS *Sacramento AOE-1* on June 30. A month later the carrier returned to Long Beach, where she remained for two months.

On September 16, she departed for the coastal waters of South Vietnam and joined Amphibious Ready Group 76.5. In November the *Princeton* anchored in Hong Kong harbor as her crew enjoyed a rest and relaxation period. While riding at anchor she was ordered to the flood-stricken areas off South Vietnam. For one week helicopters from the *Princeton*'s deck provided relief and also hosted many distinguished guests, including Dr. Oanh, Deputy Prime Minister of South Vietnam, who personally expressed his appreciation of "the kindness and courage" provided by embarked Marine Helicopter Squadron 162. Afterwards, the carrier went to Subic Bay.

The *Princeton* was scheduled to host Bob Hope's annual Christmas show in December 1964, but the carrier had to decline and rush to Yankee Station off South Vietnam.

On January 25, 1965, the *Princeton* was awarded the Armed Forces Expeditionary Medal for her participation in the Vietnam battles.

From May 7 to 14 the *Princeton* returned to Long Beach. During July she hosted midshipmen from various colleges for a summer training cruise, which took the future officers over 5500 miles of water. The "middies" departed on July 31 and went back to the scattered campuses.

A new assignment was given to the *Princeton* on August 11, 1965. It directed that she land Marine Air Group 36 and its equipment at Chu Lai. The force consisted of 1075 men, 320 tons of combat cargo, and 105 helicopters. Additional helicopters were picked up at Subic Bay to be delivered to the Army in Saigon. The Marine units were unloaded on September 1–2, which was the carrier's second major amphibious operation of the year. After the landings the *Princeton* participated in a five-day exercise, "Operation Piranha" near Cape Batangan.

She arrived in Hong Kong September 11 for a three-day rest and returned to Long Beach via Japan on October 3. An extensive yard period was then scheduled, which took three months.

The *Princeton* departed home port February 16, 1966, and sailed to the Western Pacific. She became the flagship of Captain J. D. Weslevelt, Commodore of the Seventh Fleet's Amphibious Ready Group. After a training exercise dubbed "HILLTOP IV," near Mindoro, Philippines, the carrier steamed toward the river approaches of Saigon.

On March 26, 1966, the *Princeton* participated in her first amphibious exercise of the cruise. Officially named "Operation Jackstay," General W. C. Westmoreland requested the Amphibious Assault Group's assistance in eliminating Viet Cong mortar fire aimed at shipping along the rivers. This operation was highly successful, and was completed April 6, at which time the *Princeton* went to Subic Bay.

During late April the carrier cruised the troubled waters between Hue and Danang. Viet Cong terrorists were continuously harassing friendly Vietnamese farmers. On April 27 "Operation Osage" began in an attempt to seek out and destroy these V.C. forces.

On May 4 the *Princeton* unloaded BLTs at Chu Lai, then steamed for Buckner Bay, Okinawa. On June 18 she began her third amphibious operation, called "Deck House." This took place in the Son Cau region, 25 miles south of Qui Nhon. During a search and destroy mission, many prisoners were taken.

Operation Hastings ended in July and the *Princeton* off loaded her Marine Battalion Landing Team in Chu Lai. After a brief stop in Hong Kong, Subic Bay, and Yokosuka, the ship returned to Long Beach on September 2, 1966.

On January 30, 1967, the Sweet "P" began a four and one half month deployment off the Coast of Vietnam. After a four-day stop in Chin Wan, the ship steamed to the Philippines where she relieved the USS Okinawa as flagship of the Seventh Fleet Amphibious Ready Group. During this cruise, the landing ship was the home of two battalion landing teams; First and Third Battalions, Fifth Marines. Marine helicopter squadrons HMM-362, HMM-363 and HMM-364 were also aboard.

From March 16 to April 1, the Princeton engaged in Operation Beacon Hill One. By the end of May, she had participated in Operations Beacon Star, Belt Tight, and Hickory. She left Yokosuka on June 5 and returned to her home port of Long Beach on the 19th, completing her 16th Western Pacific cruise. Sweet "P" entered the Long Beach Naval Shipyard for a major overhaul. She was in drydock from August 9 to November 16.

The Princeton left the shipyard in January 1968 and commenced training operations out of Long Beach up to March 17, then began her 17th and final cruise to the Far East. She set a new record on July 10, while off the coast of Vietnam. Pilots of Helicopter Squadron HMM-362 logged the 70,000th helo landing. During this deployment the Princeton conducted Operation Fortress Attacks III, and IV, Proud Hunter, Swift Pursuit II, Eagle Hunter and Liberty Canyon. During Operation Liberty Canyon, the landing ship moved elements of the Army First Cavalry Division from Da Nang to Vung Tau. On December 16, 1968, she returned to Long Beach.

During the month of April 1969, the Princeton served as host ship to the French Helicopter carrier Jeanne d'Arc and her crew when the ship visited Long Beach.

In May, the Princeton was designated primary recovery ship for the Apollo Ten mission. Apollo Ten lifted off launch pad 39B atop a 363-foot, 6,493,800 pound Saturn-5 rocket at Cape Kennedy on May 18, 1969, at 12:49 P.M. EDT. Inside the capsule, Colonel Thomas P. Stafford, 38, USAF; Commander Eugene A. Cernan, 35, USN, and Commander John W. Watts, 38, USN checked out equipment as the eight day "dress rehearsal," the final mission before the actual first manned landing on the moon, began.

Apollo Ten, with an apogee of 118 miles and perigee of 115 miles, circled the earth 1½ times, then with a speed of 24,200 mph left the earth's orbit and went into a transluner trajectory. The space capsule, nick-

named "Charlie Brown," went into lunar orbit around the moon at 4:45 P.M. EDT May 21. At 3:36 P.M. the following day, the lunar module, "Snoopy," separated from the command module and was brought within nine miles of the surface of the moon by Colonel Stafford and Commander Cernan. After 7½ hours, the LM linked back to the command module at 11:11 P.M.

Apollo Ten splashed down in the Pacific on May 26, 1969, at 12:52 P.M. EDT about 440 miles east of Pago Pago, American Samoa, only 7000 yards from the Princeton. The three astronauts were quickly flown aboard the landing ship via helicopter and the space capsule was hauled aboard shortly thereafter. Following the recovery of Apollo Ten, the Princeton returned to Long Beach to prepare for her final mission, which took her to an island few people have ever heard of, located near the extreme end of Alaska's Aleutian chain, roughly 3000 air miles from Long Beach. Amchitka Island, site of the Atomic Energy Commission's underground nuclear test, which the Princeton would support, is one of 70 named islands in the Aleutian chain, which reach out for a thousand miles from the Alaska Peninsula toward the Soviet Union's Kamchatka Peninsula in the Northern Pacific.

The Princeton left Long Beach on September 12, 1969, and ten days later, her crew got their first look at the Aleutian chain, as the ship joined Command Joint Task Group 8.3, along with the USS Small and USS Strauss, and other Amchitka military units. On September 24, helicopters from Marine Squadron HMM-163 began evacuating newsmen, civilian workers, and military personnel from the island, and operation MILROW, was underway.

The Princeton became the home to some 200 civilians including Commodore G. A. Gowen, Commander Joint Task Group 8.3, Major General de Saussure, Commander Joint Task Force 8, and Alaska's Secretary of State Robert Ward.

The Marine helicopters assisted the Atomic Energy Commission personnel in rescuing a "snow cat" from Semisopochnoi Island, northeast of Amchitka. Helo crews lifted the 2300 pound vehicle and returned it to the ship, where it remained only a day before it was flown off at Kiska Island to do work on a weather station.

The Princeton headed northwest on September 29 to outrun a storm moving into the area from the southeast at a fast pace. The ship raced almost 200 miles into the Bering Sea before the storm was left behind and the coast was clear to return.

By the first of October, the entire population of Amchitka was settled aboard the Princeton awaiting "zero hour" when the nuclear test device would be detonated far below the island's frozen surface.

On October 2, the *Princeton* assumed her position on station, seven miles off the northwestern coast of Amchitka, some 25 miles from the site of the blast. Personnel aboard the ship waited patiently up to 12:06 P.M. when the device was detonated. Seconds later, the *Princeton* felt the slight ripple of shock waves as they passed through the water. Shortly after the blast, officials were flown to the test site for observation and to collect necessary data.

The *Princeton* left Amchitka Island on October 3, 1969, and began her final cruise home, docking alongside Pier "E" Berth 24, at the Long Beach Naval Station Saturday morning October 11, 1969. Thus the *Princeton* completed 24 years of honorable service to her country. On January 30, 1970, the *Princeton* was officially decommissioned but fate would not allow her to join some of her sisters in the Reserve Fleet. She was stricken from the list of Navy ships and sold for scrap.

The *USS Princeton LPH5* received the Navy Unit Commendation; the Meritorious Unit Commendation; the Navy Occupation Service Medal; the China Service (extended) Medal; the Korean Service Medal with eight battle stars; the United Nations Service Medal; the National Defense Service Medal; the Armed Forces Expeditionary Service Medal; the Vietnam Service Medal; and the Republic of Korea Presidential Unit Citation Badge.

USS Shangri-La CVS-38.

37

USS Shangri-La CVS-38 (CV-38)

After the historic Tokyo Raid of April 18, 1942, the American Press asked President Roosevelt for the name of the base from which Lieutenant Colonel James H. Doolittle launched his B-25s that penetrated the very heart of Japan less than four months after Pearl Harbor. President Roosevelt replied with but a single word—"Shangri-la."

At that time the mission remained in the Top Secret category. Shangri-la stems from the mythical utopian retreat in James Hilton's novel *Lost Horizons*.

Actually, the Halsey-Doolittle Raid was launched from the *USS Hornet CV-8*, which was later lost at the Battle of Santa Cruz. In response to a nationwide war-bond drive, the American public wanted to make that mythical base a reality. During the month of the "Shangri-la" bond drive, over $900 million worth of bonds and stamps were purchased. A special fund drive organized by the U.S. Treasury Department was highly successful and $131 million was collected for construction of an aircraft carrier.

An *Essex*-class carrier bearing hull number 38 was laid down on January 15, 1943 at the Norfolk Navy Yard. On August 16, CV-38 was assigned the name *Shangri-la*. A crowd of 100,000 persons was on hand to witness the launching on February 24, 1944.

Upon being christened by Mrs. James H. Doolittle, the big carrier slid down the ways while Secretary of the Navy Frank Knox predicted that her mission would be to "strike the enemy fast, with surprising and devastating results."

On September 15, 1944, the *USS Shangri-la CV-38* was commissioned with Captain James D. Bainer in command. A preliminary trial run was conducted in Chesapeake Bay on October 15. That same day, Commander Wallace A. Sherrill of Carrier Air Group 85 made the first landing aboard her, flying a TBM *Avenger*.

By november 4 all shakedown maneuvers were completed and the carrier reported for duty with the Air Force's Atlantic Fleet operating out of Norfolk. Air Group 85 reported aboard.

A series of experimental flights was conducted on November 15, using an Army P-51 twin-engine *Tiger* plus an FBJ bomber. These airplanes had never before operated from an aircraft carrier. Upon conclusion of the tests the carrier returned to home port and stored provisions for a trip to Trinidad. While en route on November 21, Air Group 85's total complement *Corsairs, Helldivers,* and *Avengers* was flown aboard.

Six days later the *Shangri-La* arrived in the Gulf of Paria where a rigorous schedule of day and night flight exercises were conducted until December 16. In addition to this, evaluation tests were held in gunnery drills and damage control procedures. She returned to Norfolk just in time for the crew to take Christmas leave and the air group was shorebased until January 14, 1945, when they again came aboard. The carrier sailed for the Panama Canal the same day. Assigned to Task Group 21.12, she came under the tactical command of Rear Admiral Francis S. Low, the commander of Carrier Division Sixteen aboard the *USS Guam CB-2*.

The next day the carrier slipped through the Canal and tied up at Balboa. Orders came from the Commander, Panama Sea Frontier and directed the *Shangri-La* to proceed to the naval air station at North Island, San Diego. She arrived February 2 and Rear Admiral Ralph Jennings, Commander, Carrier Division Twelve, embarked for a two-day inspection at sea. This observation was meant to evaluate the carrier's readiness for combat.

The examination must have been favorably passed, for immediately thereafter 71 planes were placed aboard for transport to Hawaii, as well as 148 officers and 565 enlisted men, who were slated for duty in the forward area.

The *Shangri-La* departed San Diego February 7 and arrived at Pearl Harbor, where Air Group 85 was temporarily shorebased nearby at Barbers Point.

The carrier began two months of training various air groups which would serve in the Hawaiian Sea Frontier. Her combat career was postponed and she operated northeast of Oahu training new air groups and evaluating their strike effectiveness. These operations proved to be more important than placing the carrier in combat in view of the valuable training provided to the various air groups. On April 1, a total of 6315 landings had been logged without any major personnel casualties.

Air Group 85 came aboard once more on April 7 and three days later the *Shangri-La* was underway towards Ulithi to join Task Force 58 of the Fifth Fleet.

She dropped anchor at Ulithi on April 20. As a member of Task Unit 50.9.10, under the command of Commander, Battleship Division Seven aboard the *USS Iowa BB-61*, the carrier departed the Atoll and rendezvoused near Okinawa where she was reassigned to Task Group 58.4 commanded by Rear Admiral Arthur W. Radford aboard the *USS Yorktown CV-10*.

The third phase of the Okinawa Gunto operation was in progress as the *Shangri-La* prepared for her first combat strikes. The northern portion of the island had been secured and landings were being accomplished by American forces in the south against stubborn Japanese resistance. What remained of the once-powerful Japanese Fleet was now virtually immobilized and enemy suicide attacks became a definite menace to logistics personnel supporting the Tenth Army.

Okino Daito Jima was Air Group 85's first target, and on April 25 the carrier launched combat strikes against that island. Strikes were repeated until May 12 and the pilots concentrated on enemy air and ground forces, which were prolonging the American Tenth Army's advance.

On April 29 the carrier launched a night combat air patrol to splash a "Betty" that radar had detected. The Task Group returned to Ulithi May 12 and the crew took a brief rest while the ship received battle repairs.

Vice Admiral John S. McCain embarked as commander, Second Carrier Task Force, and from that day forward the *Shangri-La* was the flagship of Task Force 38.

When the armada returned to Okinawa, Vice Ad-

USS Shangri-La CVS-38.

miral McCain relieved Vice Admiral Marc A. Mitscher and the Fifth Fleet under Admiral Spruance became the Third Fleet under Admiral William F. Halsey.

On the first day of combat the *Shangri-La's* pilots shot down ten enemy planes over Okinawa.

While operating near Kyushu, Japan, on June 20, Air Group 85 met their most prominent resistance to date.

After returning to Okinawa to resume support for the Tenth Army a typhoon hampered flight operations and the group was forced to clear the area to avoid the violent storm.

The end of the Battle of Okinawa approached on June 8 and the carrier launched a strike against Kyushu. *Shangri-La's* pilots encountered only five enemy planes and the bombers were able to attack

southeast to southwest in a quick series of devastating blows, which completely saturated the enemy defenses.

Two weeks of rest began June 11, while the carrier was at Leyte Gulf. At this time preparations were made for the final major operation of the war and involved extensive action against the main islands of the Japanese homeland.

Task Force 38 departed Leyte on July 1 and steamed northward for attacks on Tokyo and adjacent targets. A unique ceremony occurred the second day at sea when John L. Sullivan took the oath of office as Secretary of the Navy—the first ever performed in a war zone.

During the final raids against Japan the *Shangri-La* carried the proud soubriquet "Tokyo Express." Her pilots made their first aerial attacks at the capital on

July 10, where they inflicted damage to airfields, railroads, and shipping.

On July 16 Captain Richard F. Whitehead relieved Captain Bainer.

The dreaded Kamikazes continued to hamper the task force while American pilots unerringly dealt out severe damage to airfields and shipping at Honshu and Hokkaido. Air group 85 flew over the naval base at Yokosuka and helped cripple the battleship *Nagato*, a prized remnant of the now-impotent Japanese Navy. At Kure Naval Base, the light cruiser *Oyodo* was capsized and the battleship *Karuna* was beached.

A short reprieve from daily bombing was observed as the U.S. Army Air Force dropped the powerful atomic bombs. Attacks were resumed immediately afterward and continued until official word told of Japan's unconditional surrender.

Air Group 85 then teamed with other groups and flew daily patrols over prisoner of war camps paradropping food and medical supplies.

While the air group flew over the USS *Missouri BB-63* in Tokyo Bay on September 2, 1945, the official surrender document was signed. Three air group officers and one enlisted man, who had been listed as missing in action, were returned to the carrier.

On September 16, 1945, the first anniversary of her commissioning, the *Shangri-La* dropped anchor in Tokyo Bay. Although she had operated in the Pacific forward area during the constant Kamikaze attacks, she suffered no damage to herself or her crew.

The *Shangri-La* participated in the "Magic Carpet" operations and brought thousands of American troops home.

The first atomic bomb tests at Bikini took place early in 1946 and were dubbed "Operation Crossroads." The *Shangri-La* launched and controlled the drones that flew through the blast area and were later recovered. The information from the drones provided vital data involving the military aspects of atomic power.

The carrier transited the Panama Canal twice during January, February, and March 1946. Following the atomic bomb tests she made a short cruise to Pearl Harbor, then proceeded to Puget Sound Naval Shipyard for the Christmas holidays.

After a cruise in the Pacific, which included a visit to Sydney, Australia, the carrier entered the navy yard at San Francisco and was decommissioned November 7, 1947.

She remained inactive from that date until her recommissioning on May 10, 1951. The *Shangri-La* spent spring and summer at the Boston Navy Yard Annex and exchanged complete crews with the USS *Antietam CV-36* at Bayonne.

In September 1952 she transited the Panama Canal and returned to Bremerton, Washington, to undergo a three-year conversion at Puget Sound.

The massive facelifting was completed on January 10, 1955, and the carrier was recommissioned with Captain Roscoe Newman at the helm. The *Shangri-La* now presented an appearance completely different

Note "Z" on flight deck of USS Shangri-La. Aerial-port bow view underway.

from the one known to her previous crew. She now sported twin steam catapults and her elevators and arresting gear had been improved. The major distinction was apparent on the flight deck, which had not only been lengthened and strengthened, but now revealed a new style—an angle deck.

The *Shangri-La* sailed from Puget Sound March 24 and proceeded, via Alameda Naval Air Station, to San Diego. During the spring she was engaged in training maneuvers at sea, then returned to Puget Sound for six weeks before arriving again at San Diego in August. The remainder of the year involved additional training off the California coast. In December a new commanding officer, Captain C. W. Lord, took the helm.

On January 5, 1956, the *Shangri-La* steamed with Task Force 16 to the Far East. Brief stopovers were taken at Pearl Harbor, Midway, Yokosuka, and Iwakuni, Japan, before she teamed with other ships for operations near Okinawa and Iwo Jima.

The big carrier arrived at Cubi Point, Subic Bay, February 25, where Rear Admiral Stoors, Commander of Carrier Division 5, hoisted his flag.

During the next seven weeks the carrier participated with Task Force 77 in various operations, with rest periods at Manila and Hong Kong. April 16 was a V.I.P. day. As the carrier approached the Okinawa operations area she was visited by Under Secretary of the Navy Thomas S. Gates and Vice Admiral Ingersoll, the Seventh Fleet commander.

The *Shangri-La* was at Yokosuka on May 7, then headed for more duty in the Pacific prior to returning home. The summer was used for normal operations off the coast of California.

In November the *Shangri-La* teamed with Task Force 11 at San Francisco and steamed westward, arriving November 20 at Pearl Harbor, where Captain Lord was relieved by Captain F. D. Foley.

After an Operational Readiness Inspection, the *Shangri-La* departed for Japan, arriving at Yokosuka December 14. Christmas was celebrated at sea, but a gala New Year's Eve celebration was enjoyed at Kobe, Japan.

Most of January 1957 was spent at sea operating with Task Forces 76 and 77 near Okinawa. Air Group 2 was able to log a lot of flying time, but the usual visits to familiar ports were taken in between.

On May 20 the crew were happy to see San Francisco come into view and on the next day the carrier docked at home port in San Diego. During June the *Shangri-La* steamed northwards for overhaul.

Captain W. C. Short assumed command in October, and upon completion of the overhaul took the ship back to home port where she remained for the rest of the year except for short-term exercises at sea.

The year 1958 became one of the most cherished peacetime periods for the carrier. On March 8, with the commander of Carrier Division 7 aboard, she steamed to the Far East.

In September, Captain K. E. Taylor took over as commanding officer and two months later the carrier returned to the states, where she remained until March 9, 1959. At that time she went to Hawaii, where she was active for a month, then began a trip to the Far East, assigned to Task Group 77.4.

At the end of April she was cruising the seas south of Korea, sojourning briefly in May at Yokosuka before sailing to Okinawa for exercises with two Japanese maritime destroyers.

The next stop was at Manila, then in early June the schedule called for operations off the coast of North Borneo.

During September the carrier along with Task Group 77.4 was maneuvering to avoid Typhoon Sarah off the coast of Okinawa. Afterwards, she sailed from Japan September 22 and steamed for home. Shortly after arrival at San Diego she went to Puget Sound for an overhaul requiring six weeks.

The well-known pattern of Far East cruises was altered in 1960 when the carrier departed for Callao, Peru, on March 16. There was a change of command ceremony, "shellback" initiations, and visits to Valparaiso, Chile; Rio de Janeiro, Brazil; Port of Spain, Trinidad; and stops at Bayonne and Norfolk before a return to Mayport, Florida.

Six weeks of rugged underway training at Guantanamo Bay preceded her first Atlantic deployment. This cruise began March 16 and closed November 25 when the carrier sailed back to Mayport. The ship's crew enjoyed a well-deserved rest period during December and early January 1961.

On February 2 the *Shangri-La* sailed eastward and relieved the *USS Intrepid* at Rota, Spain, eight days later. Then she slipped through the Gibraltar Straits into water under the responsibility of the Sixth Fleet.

After a week of operations near Golfo di Palmas, Sardinia, the *Shangri-La* sailed to Naples where she engaged in exercises at sea interspersed with liberty for the crew at select ports.

After farewell stops at Gibraltar and Rota, Spain, she crossed the Atlantic and arrived at home port May 15.

On June 2 she sailed once more for two weeks of normal operations near Galebra and the region south of Puerto Rico. When she came back to Mayport, however, her crew enjoyed three months leave while she underwent general maintenance.

The *Shangri-La* was hastily called to duty on September 11 as flagship of a task force that raced to Galveston, Texas, and assisted victims of Hurricane Carla. She dropped anchor seven miles off-shore and launched her helicopters on mercy missions to the stricken citizens.

She arrived back at Mayport September 20. With the exception of a six-week maintenance period at the Brooklyn Navy Yard, she continued normal operations near home port for the rest of the year.

On January 8, 1962, the carrier went to sea with Carrier Air Group 10 to participate in a ten-day At-

lantic Fleet exercise. On February 7 the carrier headed for Europe and passed through the Pillars of Hercules on the 17th. During March, the carrier was responsible to Rear Admiral F. T. Williamson, commander of Carrier Division 4.

While at Palermo, Italy, on March 14, Captain R. W. Rynd relieved Captain H. N. Houck in a colorful ceremony attended by numerous Italian military personnel.

The *Shangri-La* went to sea and teamed with the *USS Saratoga CVA-60* in a NATO exercise. At the end of March the carrier visited Rhodes, Greece.

She remained in the Aegean Sea during early April and visited Athens on the 7th. This Eastern cruise

Flight deck operations aboard the *USS Shangri-La CVA-38.* One of fighter squadron VF-62's aircraft F8U is shown being catapulted from the port cat, while one of VA-106's aircraft, A4D, is turned up on the starboard cat.

continued with a voyage through the Dardanelles and the Sea of Marmara with a brief rest at Istanbul. On April 25 Vice Admiral David M. McDonald came aboard. In late April the "Shang," as the crew called their ship, and Air Group 10 steamed westward, pausing for a visit to Valetta, Malta, on the 28th.

Following a six-day layover at Genoa, Italy, the carrier began its most formidable operation period of the entire cruise. On May 16 the "Shang" participated in "Power Drive," which was followed by "Quick Train" five days later. These exercises covered all phases of combat conditions and proved to be an excellent test of the carrier's ability to launch planes and fight in the same class as the newer and more massive carriers.

A welcome diversion came in May with a trip to Livorno, Italy, and the crew enjoyed the beaches and other facilities of the nearby Army base at Camp Darby.

The "Shang" cruised the Tyrrhenian Sea in early June and headed back to Cannes, where on the 18th a large mass of U.S. press correspondents came aboard for a two-day tour. After returning the press writers to Cannes, the carrier received a group of Midshipmen who were quickly integrated into the world of junior officers. On June 19 a reception was held for the "Middies" in Hangar Bay 1.

Attending the reception were a number of lovely young ladies, to the delight of all the crew.

Next came a visit to Naples on July 12, where the ship was visited by Admiral James L. Russell, Commander in Chief, Southern Forces Europe.

Three days later the carrier began a week of operations under the watchful eyes of Rear Admiral John R. Miner, commander of Cruiser Destroyer Flotilla 8.

During July 21–27 the "Shang" visited Livorno and then sailed to participate in her final major exercise with the Sixth Fleet—"Full Swing."

On Rugust 3 she was at Rapallo, Italy, where its citizens were impressed by the arrival of a U.S. aircraft carrier.

Being one of the oldest and smallest CVAs in the fleet, the "Shang" was honored when she was relieved by the newest and largest carrier, the USS Enterprise CVAN-65. The nuclear carrier took over for the Shangri-La in Golfo de Palmas on August 19 and two days later the "Shang" was heading for home, arriving at Mayport on the 28th.

After a month at home port the carrier went to New York for a major overhaul and arrived at Brooklyn on October 14. During this renovation she received a new air search and height finding radars, the Van Zelm Bridle Arrester system, plus improvements to her

Routine flight operations aboard the USS Shangri-La, as A4-C aircraft jockey into place for a cat shot.

electrical and engineering departments.

The Shangri-La was selected to be the host for the visit to New York of the Italian cruiser Garibaldi. The occasion was highlighted by an unending round of receptions during which the American officers got to know their counterparts very well.

The year came to a close with the carrier perched at the New York Shipyard suffering the effects of a violent winter. The crew didn't seem to care about the weather as they thoroughly enjoyed the entertainment spots offered by New York City.

On January 1, 1963 the "Shang" was still in the New York drydock.

On February 14, Captain Edward L. Dashiell, Jr., took command. Three weeks later, after completing sea trials, the carrier arrived at Bayonne, New Jersey, for final adjustments. A month later she sailed into Norfolk, where on March 17 she loaded ordnance; 900 tons were brought aboard in a three-day period.

The "Shang" then went to Mayport for a week, thence to Guantanamo Bay, Cuba. Rear Admiral Robert J. Stroh, commander of Carrier Division Six, was aboard along with Air Group 10. During the next ten days the carrier was active with day-and-night air operations.

The second week of April brought a liberty period for the crew at Guantanamo Bay. However, all liberty was restricted to the base in view of the political situation between America and Cuba. After the rest period the "Shang" resumed fleet training.

A three-day visit to Kingston, Jamaica, May 3–6

delivered the third act of terminal exercises in the Caribbean. Two more weeks were put to good use because the "Shang" successfully passed her Operational Readiness Inspection. She then sailed back to Mayport on May 25, and remained in port for maintenance while the crew took liberty.

On June 17 the "Shang" departed home port and arrived two days later at Norfolk, where she joined Task Force 23, a Midshipmen Training Squadron under the command of Vice Admiral A. G. Ward. On June 20, 512 Midshipmen from the U.S. Naval Academy reported aboard for 4½ weeks of at-sea training. On July 25 the future naval officers departed the ship and returned to Annapolis and the carrier went to home port, arriving three days later.

She remained in Mayport during August and conducted training exercises off the coast during August 26–31.

On September 3–4 the Shangri-La took its Operational Readiness Inspection for the year. A one-day guest cruise followed with 120 members of the National Security Council of the American Legion. On September 20, it was time for Air Group 10's ORI, but this was cancelled because of hurricane weather. The ship returned to Mayport on the 24th.

One week later the carrier departed for a seven-month Mediterranean cruise. She teamed with destroyers from Newport and Charleston and the USS Essex CVS-9 to form Task Force 25.

On October 13 she relieved the USS Saratoga CVA-60 as a component of the Sixth Fleet on Golfo di Palmas, Sardinia. The Shangri-La then went to Palermo, Italy and the crew went on liberty.

She departed on October 16 and conducted normal operations until malfunctions in the arresting gears forced the carrier into a five-day stop at Naples.

She weighed anchor on the 25th and began day and night operations during which time she logged her 54,000th arrested gear landing. On October 31 the carrier anchored in a wintery Cannes, France. High winds, coupled with rain and heavy seas, caused liberty to be cancelled.

On November 4 the carrier headed for Taranto, Italy, where she stayed nine days, while 700 persons toured the ship and a reception was held for officers of the Italian Armed Forces and their wives.

On November 15 the carrier embarked the staff and Class 24 of the NATO Defense College for a one-day cruise to demonstrate air power.

Upon leaving Taranto two days later the Shangri-La took part in a major fleet and NATO exercise involving close air support of a Marine division on the east coast of Spain. During these exercises the carrier recorded its 55,000th arrested landing.

Thanksgiving Day was celebrated at Cannes under an overcast sky.

At sea once more on December 7 the ship called flight quarters early the next morning and the air group engaged in two days of extensive task unit operations.

December 11–14 the carrier was in Marseilles prior to a major fleet and NATO exercise. Pilots of the "Shang" carried out high-altitude penetration techniques and simulated bomb runs. A vigilant and tenacious French Air Force opposed the "Shang" pilots during two days of maneuvers that strengthened the Allied defenses.

Afterwards the carrier transited the Straits of Bonifacio and directed simulated attacks against a French Naval Task Force. It was during these exercises that the Shangri-La recorded its 56,000th arrested gear landing.

On December 21 she was at Naples and provided the crew with an opportunity to visit Rome. On December 29 the carrier hosted the Bob Hope Christmas Show.

A two-day training period followed on December 30–31, after which the "Shang" returned to Naples.

Upon her return to the United States, the Shangri-La conducted flight operations off the Atlantic coast area. Throughout 1964 and into mid-1965, she operated as a unit of the Second Fleet in the Atlantic and with the Sixth Fleet in the Mediterranean. She visited the following ports while with the Sixth Fleet: Istanbul, Turkey; Athens and Rhodes, Greece; Naples, Genoa, Leghorn, Taranto and Rapallo, Italy; Marseilles, Toulon, and Cannes, France; St. Thomas, Virgin Islands; Rota, Palma de Mallorca, and Barcelona, Spain; and Quebec City, Canada. On November 16, 1965, the Shangri-La entered the Philadelphia Naval Shipyard to under go a $13 million overhaul. New equipment and the incorporation of technological advancements have renewed the carrier's capabilities to perform to the highest degree of efficiency.

In May of 1966, the Shangri-La left the shipyard and returned to Mayport, Florida. She left Mayport in June for six weeks of refresher training in the Guantanamo Bay area. She then returned to Mayport and loaded provisions, and on September 29, 1966, left Mayport for six months of duty in the Mediterranean. She returned home on May 20, 1967, and entered the Jacksonville Shipyard for two months of yard work.

The Shangri-La left Mayport for the Norfolk Naval Shipyard on July 10th for a ten-day stay where a routine inspection of the ship's screws and hull was performed. While at sea on September 3, 1967, the Shangri-La celebrated her 23rd birthday. She operated out of Mayport until November 13, training and conducting flight operations. On November 14 she set course for the Mediteranean. Familiar ports were revisited and training exercises were performed with NATO forces before the carrier returned to her home port on August 4, 1968.

From September 24 to 30, the *Shangri-La* was in drydock at the New York Shipyard. Upon completion of the yard period, she spent the remainder of the year training off the Caribbean. On January 7, 1969, the *Shangri-La* left Mayport for another tour of duty with the Sixth Fleet in the Mediterranean. The *Shangri-La's* designation was changed from that of an Attack Carrier (CVA) to an Antisubmarine Support carrier (CVS) on July 1, 1969.

The *USS Shangri-La CVS-38* has received the following awards: American Area Campaign Service Medal; World War Two Victory Medal; Navy Occupation Service Medal; China Service Medal (Extended); National Defense Service Medal; Armed Forces Expeditionary Medal; and the Navy Expeditionary Medal (Cuba).

USS Lake Champlain CVS-39.

38

USS Lake Champlain CVS-39 (CV-39)

On August 7, 1942, construction was authorized for the *USS Lake Champlain.* The carrier received its name from the victory of Commodore Thomas McDonough, who on September 11, 1812, with a squadron of 14 ships defeated a British squadron of 16 larger vessels on the New York State lake during the War of 1812.

She is the second ship to bear the honor; the first was a minelayer of World War I. On March 15, 1944, the carrier's keel was laid at the Norfolk Navy Yard, built by funds contributed by the citizens of New York State.

The *Lake Champlain* was wholly constructed in a drydock and her launching and commissioning were held simultaneously on June 3, 1945. Mrs. Warren Austin, wife of the Senator from Vermont sponsored the new carrier, whose first commanding officer was Captain Logan C. Ramsey.

Shakedown operations began July 1, 1945, off Guantanamo Bay, Cuba, where, with Air Group 150 aboard, she underwent intensive training and simulated attacks against Culebra Island. She returned to Norfolk for post-shakedown alterations and while there the Second World War came to an end.

The *Lake Champlain* joined the Atlantic Fleet about the same time the Japanese surrender ceremonies were being held onboard the *USS Missouri BB-63* in Tokyo Bay. September 1–8 the new carrier held an open house in New York. Another open house was conducted from September 27 to October 3.

On October 6, 1945 the *Lake Champlain* entered the Norfolk Navy Yard for alterations preparatory to serving with the "Magic Carpet" fleet, and her first cruise as a transport was made October 14–19 from Norfolk to Southhampton. On October 20, 296 Army and 32 naval officers plus 3367 enlisted Army troops and 19 sailors were embarked and returned to New York, arriving October 27. From that date to November 8 the carrier remained at the U.S. Port of Embarkation, Staten Island, where modifications were made to the passenger accommodations. She steamed for Naples on the 8th, arriving eight days later. The carrier truly earned her soubriquet "Champ," while serving as a troop transport. Returning from Europe with 5000 troops, she averaged 32 knots while sailing 3960 nauti-

cal miles with an en route time of 4 days, 8 hours, and 51 minutes. The area travelled was from Cape Spartel near Gibraltar to Chesapeake Bay off Hampton Roads, Virginia—the longest speed run on record. Since the carrier was a naval vessel she was ineligible for the "Blue Ribbon" award granted to commercial ships for the fastest Atlantic crossing. However, this unofficial record was unbroken until the summer of 1952, when it was bettered by the SS *United States*.

Upon completion of the "Magic Carpet" cruises, the *Lake Champlain* was decommissioned in March 1946.

When hostilities increased in Korea she was removed from mothballs and prepared for modernization at the Newport News Shipyard. She received a conversion that conformed to the standards of the *USS Oriskany*, which included a streamlined island structure and a strengthened flight deck to handle the big jets. On September 19, 1952, the *Lake Champlain* was recommissioned with Captain G. T. Mundroff in command.

From November 25 to December 25 the carrier conducted shakedown operations near Cuba. On April 26, 1953, she departed Mayport, Florida and sailed 20,000 miles—through the Red Sea, Indian Ocean and the China Sea, became the largest ship to transit the Suez Canal, and finally arrived at Yokosuka, Japan, on June 9.

F2H's (Banshees) flying over the *USS Lake Champlain* operating in Korean waters.

Lake Champlain crew members spell out greeting to midshipmen of Annapolis.

Two days later she departed as the flagship of Task Force 77 and arrived off Western Korea on June 14, where she immediately launched her air group at North Korean installations. *Lake Champlain* pilots flew escort for Air Force B-50 bombers while striking enemy positions. The air group also dropped a few bombs themselves during 2244 combat sorties. Enemy targets continued receiving ordnance until the truce was inked on July 27, 1953. On October 11 the *USS Kearsarge CVS-33* relieved the *Lake Champlain,* which headed for the South China Seas, arriving at Singapore 13 days later. She remained in port for 48 hours, then returned to the U.S. with brief stopovers at Columbo, Port Said, Cannes, and Lisbon. She arrived in Florida December 4.

For the next three years the *Lake Champlain* completed several cruises to the Mediterranean, where she participated in NATO exercises. On April 25, 1957, she joined other ships of the fleet in a high-speed trip to the tension-filled Middle East. She cruised the areas of Lebanon and reinforced Jordan's stand against the Communist threat. When tension had alleviated the carrier sailed back to Florida on July 27.

The *Lake Champlain* was redesignated ASW on August 1, and began training off the eastern seaboard to sharpen her skills as an antisubmarine warfare vessel.

She departed Bayonne, New Jersey, on February 8, 1958, for another Mediterranean jaunt and visited the usual ports of call between training maneuvers before coming home to Florida on August 9. She operated off the Florida coast and the Caribbean until June 15, 1959, at which time the Mediterranean beckoned once more. She returned to her new home port at Quonset Point, Rhode Island, on September 4.

Normal operations were conducted from home port until June 29, 1960, when she hosted a Midshipmen cruise to Halifax before returning on August 12. The carrier then resumed routine operations. In December she hosted members of the Armed Forces Staff College who observed a first-hand view of ASW techniques.

In February 1961, the *Lake Champlain* went to the Caribbean for a week of intensive training at Guantanamo Bay, Cuba, with calls at Kingston, Jamaica, and the Virgin Islands. During this cruise some 46 senior military officials of Latin American republics witnessed a demonstration of modern weapons systems during a ten-day Joint Chiefs of Staff program.

On May 1 the "Champ" departed homeport, after being selected the prime recovery vessel for *Freedom 7*. Four days later, Commander Alan B. Shepard, Jr., 37, became America's first astronaut when his spacecraft was launched at Cape Canaveral at 9:34 A.M. EDT. The *Freedom 7* soared upwards 115 miles during this initial suborbital effort by the United States.

Commander Shepard reentered the earth's atmosphere at 9:43 A.M., and decreased speed from 4227 mph to 341 mph in one minute's time, then plopped into the Atlantic at 9:49. Four minutes later Shepard climbed into the recovery helicopter, which flew back to the *Lake Champlain.*

The carrier began recovery tests many weeks prior to the space flight and conducted training exercises with a mock capsule.

Late in August the "Champ" visited Kingston, Jamaica, then conducted normal operations from home port the remainder of the year.

In November she was on-station to recover the first attempt by NASA to orbit a chimp, but technical difficulties aborted the operation. The next month found the carrier at the Boston Navy Yard for an overhaul.

In January 1962 she resumed normal ASW duties off the Atlantic coast. In May she participated in the New York Armed Forces Day celebrations during which 30,000 visitors came aboard. Another cruise to the Mediterranean came in June with Midshipmen aboard from the Naval Academy.

On October 24 the *Lake Champlain* was active during the Cuban Missile Crisis. To nullify this threat President Kennedy ordered a naval blockade, halting all ships carrying Soviet missiles and military supplies to the island and enforced American demands for the withdrawal of the missiles. On November 28 most of the demands were complied with and the quarantine was lifted. The "Champ" headed for home via St. Thomas, Virgin Islands, and returned to Quonset Point on December 4.

During February and March 1963 the *Lake Champlain* spent 18 days launching surveillance flights over all shipping arriving and departing Cuban ports. She then entered the Boston Navy Yard in April for a five-month overhaul. After the yard work a brief visit was made to Quonset Point, then she proceeded to Guantanamo Bay on September 10 for refresher training. The drill schedule was interrupted for ten days, when the carrier was to assist the government of Haiti in evaluating damage engendered by Hurricane Flora. The "Champ's" helicopters flew medical supplies and food to the storm victims in an operation called "Hand Clasp." She returned to home port on November 2.

The *Lake Champlain* hosted 250 members of the American Helicopter Society on a one-day cruise November 14, then spent the next two weeks in ASW training in the North Atlantic. The big carrier returned to Quonset Point on Thanksgiving Day.

NASA astronaut Alan B. Shepard, Jr. inspected his spacecraft after being returned to the U.S. Navy carrier *Lake Champlain*. Astronaut Shepard had just completed the first Project Mercury suborbital space flight.

From February 3 to March 8, 1964 the *Lake Champlain* joined other Atlantic fleet units for "Operation Springboard" in the Caribbean.

During the next two years she continued to operate from Quonset Point in various ASW training exercises with occasional Midshipmen training cruises during the summer. A special project interrupted this training schedule when the "Champ" was called to assist in the recovery of *Gemini 5* in August 1965. This was her second recovery of a space capsule. Airforce Lieutenant Colonel Leroy Gordon Cooper, Jr., 38, and Lieutenant Commander Charles "Pete" Conrad, Jr., 35, completed eight days in orbit before they splashed down in the Atlantic at 8:56 A.M. EDT, on August 29, 1965. The two astronauts were picked up by a Navy helicopter and taken to the *Lake Champlain* for debriefing.

The *Lake Champlain's* last major operation was the recovery of an unmanned Gemini-Titan spacecraft on January 19, 1966. On May 2 she was decommissioned and stored in the Atlantic Reserve Fleet.

Lieutenant Commander Charles J. Conrad, Jr., and Lieutenant Colonel L. Gordon Cooper, Jr., walking along *USS Lake Champlain* flight deck after helicopter recovery.

Prior to her deactivation she held the singular distinction of being the only *Essex*-class carrier whose axial (straight) flight deck had not been modernized to conform to the *Oriskany-Hancock* conversion class.

On December 1, 1969, the *Lake Champlain* was stricken from the list of Navy ships and disposed of for scrap.

The *USS Lake Champlain CVS-39* holds the following awards: The Navy Occupation Medal; Korean Service Medal with one battle star; United Nations Service Medal; National Defense Service Medal; Armed Forces Expeditionary Medal; and the Republic of Korea Presidential Unit Citation Badge.

USS Tarawa CV-40.

39

USS Tarawa AVT-12 (CV-40)

For a long time Tarawa was merely an insignificant barren lump of rock protruding the waters of the Pacific Ocean. When World War II came along the Japanese soldiers entrenched themselves upon this speck and it suddenly became a vital piece of real estate. The deed was very expensive—the price would be paid in blood, not money.

On November 20, 1943, the U.S. Marines charged ashore with one single purpose in mind—secure the island. During the next 76 hours, Tarawa was the stage for some of the bloodiest combat of the war, before the Marines finally secured it.

To honor the historic struggle during the Battle of Tarawa, Congress authorized the construction of an aircraft carrier bearing the name. The keel was laid down March 1, 1944 at the Norfolk Navy Yard.

Mrs. Julian C. Smith, wife of the general who had commanded the Marines at Tarawa, christened the new carrier on May 12, 1945.

On December 8, 1945, the fourth anniversary of our entry into World War II, the *USS Tarawa CV-40* was commissioned. General Julian C. Smith said: "It is eminently fitting that this great ship should be named for an operation that marked the turning point of the war in the Pacific and began a new era of amphibious warfare."

The same battle flag that had gone ashore with the Marines was presented to the new carrier. Under these colors 786 Marines and Navy medical personnel had given their lives in capturing the island. The flag was hauled down from a river coconut palm on February 13, 1944, by a color guard of men who had participated in the actual assault.

The *Tarawa* operated as a training center in the Atlantic and Pacific until October 1, 1948, at which time she began an around-the-world cruise. The voyage took five months, during which the carrier visited San Francisco, New York, Hawaii, Tsingtao, Hong Kong, Singapore, Ceylon, Bahrein, Suez, Greece, Istanbul, and Gilbraltar.

Upon conclusion of the trip a decision previously made to reduce the number of commissioned ships in the Navy was implemented. On March 3, 1949 the

Tarawa entered New York Shipyard from which she emerged decommissioned on June 30 to join the Atlantic Reserve Fleet.

The inactivity was very brief due to the outbreak of hostilities caused by the aggressive acts of North Korea. The *Tarawa* went to the navy yard in New York and was recommissioned February 3, 1951. On March 17 the State of Connecticut officially adopted the carrier as its own ship and the state flag was presented to the *Tarawa*'s commanding officer by the Governor. The ceremony was impressive for the two million citizens of the Nutmeg State, who had not been represented by any ship since the battleship *USS Connecticut* was scrapped in 1923.

The carrier then began shakedown maneuvers and

Marines prepare to board HRS helicopter on deck of *USS Tarawa CVS-40* during amphibious exercises.

training near Guantanamo Bay, Cuba.

In December she was sent to join the Sixth Fleet in the Mediterranean during which time she became the symbol of freedom and international goodwill to the citizens of France, Spain, Italy, Greece, and Turkey. The carrier returned to Boston in June 1952 and received her first overhaul.

On January 7, 1953, the *Tarawa* began another Mediterranean cruise and returned to the states in July. During the next three months she was actively engaged in qualifying pilots for carrier operations at sea.

The *Tarawa* started her second world cruise on November 12. It is normal for a major ship to conduct only one cruise around the world during its entire naval career, but the *Tarawa* exceeded this usual schedule, and enjoyed eight weeks visiting the Mediterranean ports and spent Christmas on the French Riviera.

On February 15, 1953, she arrived at Yokosuka, Japan, for five months of duty with the Seventh Fleet. First she went to Iwo Jima and Sasebo, Japan, thence to Australia where she represented the U.S. Navy at ceremonies commemorating the Tenth Anniversary of the Battle of the Coral Sea.

Throughout the summer she cruised the South China Sea. On August 19 the carrier slipped under the Golden Gate Bridge in San Francisco. Four days later she departed for the Panama Canal, which she transited on August 31.

On September 4 the *Tarawa* arrived at Mayport, Florida where her air group was released. Seven days later she tied up at Quonset Point, Rhode Island, having logged 71,000 nautical miles.

The *Tarawa* participated in her final major exercise as an attack carrier during November. This operation was termed LANTEX 55.

In January 1955 she entered Boston Naval Yard for conversion to an anti-submarine warfare (ASW) support carrier. She was redesignated CVS-40 during her conversion period. The work was completed in May when she began refresher training near Cuba. The remainder of the year was used to train the crew in ASW tactics. In November the *Tarawa* became flagship of Hunter-Killer Group Four.

"Operation Springboard" began on January 5, 1956, and the *Tarawa* was able to demonstrate her ASW abilities. She established a record by engaging in 694 operational training exercises during the month.

During the summer the *Tarawa* embarked midshipmen from numerous colleges for their annual training cruise, which was completed July 6 when the carrier returned to Quonset Point. After releasing the "middies," she continued operational training off the Atlantic seaboard. Christmas leave was granted to the crew while the carrier was at Boston.

On January 12, 1957, the *Tarawa* began an extensive overhaul at the Boston Navy Yard. She completed her yard period in June and resumed training in the Caribbean with visits to St. Thomas in the Virgin Islands, and Kingston, Jamaica.

Simulated battles with fleet submarines developed the carrier's ASW capabilities and in August she sailed back to home port.

On September 3 the *Tarawa* headed for European waters and participated in the NATO exercises "Strikeback" and "Pipedown." Over 300 warships took part and the operations helped develop the most powerful peacetime fleet in the annals of history.

The carrier returned to Quonset Point in October and learned she had won the coveted Battle Efficiency "E" for the second consecutive year.

On January 6, 1958, the *Tarawa* engaged in "Operation Springboard" after which her crew enjoyed shore leave at the city then known as Ciudad Trujillo and Port of Spain, Trinidad. She returned to home port on February 7 and 2000 Marines came aboard on March 11.

The carrier participated in Operation Lantphiblex off the capes of North Carolina in an effort to further develop the concept of Vertical Envelopment, which was now vital to amphibious warfare.

On May 9 the air group reported aboard at Norfolk and the ship began "Operation Convex," an exercise designed to develop her ASW effectiveness. Just as the operation began, a message was received that Vice President Richard M. Nixon had been threatened by violent rioters in Venezuela. The *Tarawa* immediately embarked a Marine helicopter squadron and sailed to the trouble spot. While en route another message said that Nixon had safely departed the country and the carrier resumed normal duties.

On August 7, the *Tarawa* got underway and later joined other vessels of Task Force 88. Eleven days later she crossed the equator as flagship of the task force.

Tremendous secrecy and excitement was the order of the day as the *Tarawa* stood ready while the *USS Norton Sound AVM-1* began a series of three missile launchings. Later, the carrier played an important role in Project Argus, a scientific feat of incalculable value matched by top secret procedures. Much of the data obtained from the project is still highly classified.

Bow view of *USS Tarawa CVS-40*.

The *Tarawa* arrived at Rio de Janiero on September 15, where the crew enjoyed a five-day rest. Late in September she returned to home port for the remainder of the year. Training operations continued until the annual Christmas leave period began.

Antisubmarine warfare exercises began anew in January 1959 as the carrier cruised between Quonset Point and New York. In April the *Tarawa* began a two-month visit to Norfolk to host the Global Strategy Conference.

During the summer she continued to sharpen her skills by participation in ASW exercises. Scuttlebutt said that she would be decommissioned, but she continued working and training as if to disprove the rumors.

On November 6, 200 high-ranking officers came aboard for a tour during their studies at the National War College. The guests praised the ship and a formal "thank-you" note was sent by the Chief of Naval Operations.

The *Tarawa* put to sea on November 30 for her final operational cruise and assisted in evaluating new ASW equipment. On the morning of December 14 she docked at Quonset Point for the last time. The long feared rumors were now a fact.

Her squadrons were removed on January 15, 1960, and the carrier sailed to the navy yard in Philadelphia. She joined the Atlantic Reserve Fleet and was decommissioned in May 1960.

The *Tarawa* remained in reserve status, but not

commissioned, until May 1, 1961 at which time she was redesignated an Auxiliary Aircraft Transport Carrier—AVT-12.

On June 1, 1967, the *Tarawa* was stricken from the list of Navy ships and was disposed of for scrap.

During 14 years of active naval service the *USS Tarawa AVT-12* received the Navy Occupation Service Medal, the China Service Medal (extended), the Korean Service Medal, the United Nations Service Medal, and the National Defense Service Medal.

MIDWAY CLASS OF 1942

Construction of the *Midway* class was authorized on July 9, 1942. This new class of carrier was to be the largest ever built up to that time, and to distinguish them from smaller carriers of the fleet, they were designated CVB on July 15, 1943.

The first ship of the class *USS Midway CVB-41*, was laid down for construction on October 27, 1943; the second ship of the class, *USS Coral Sea CVB-42* was laid down on December 1, 1943; and a third unnamed ship was laid down as CVB-43. Ten days after the death of President Franklin D. Roosevelt, the name of *CVB-42* was changed to honor the late president and *Coral Sea* was assigned to *CVB-43*. With the completion of the *Coral Sea* on October 1, 1947, the class was complete as follows:

USS *Midway* CVB-41
USS *Franklin D. Roosevelt* CVB-42
USS *Coral Sea* CVB-43

Original statistics at time of commissioning were: Standard displacement, 45,000 tons; full load displacement, 55,000 tons; overall length, 968 feet; beam 113 feet; 136 feet across the flight deck; draft, 32 feet, 9 inches; armament, eighteen 5-inch 54-caliber gun mounts, eighty-four 40mm mounts and eighty-two 20mm antiaircraft mounts. They could carry 137 aircraft, and a complement of 2604 officers and enlisted men. With the addition of the air group, the complement would be increased to 3354.

Built too late for service in the Second World War, the three carriers played a vital part in the develop-ment of jet aircraft aboard carriers in the late forties. In 1947 and 1948, the flight decks of each carrier were strengthened so that they could handle the new jet aircraft. On October 1, 1952, they were reclassified Attack Aircraft Carriers—CVA.

The highly successful modernization programs incorporated in *Essex*-class carriers made it apparent that these improvements would extend to the *Midway* class. The *Franklin D. Roosevelt* entered Puget Sound Naval Shipyard in May of 1954 to be the first of her class to undergo the major conversion, which included an enclosed hurricane bow and an angle (canted) flight deck. She rejoined the fleet on April 6, 1956. The *Midway* entered Puget Sound in September 1955 and her conversion was completed on September 30, 1957. The *Coral Sea* entered the shipyard on April 15, 1957, and work was completed on January 25, 1960. She was the last of the carriers designed during World War II to undergo a major conversion.

The conversions increased the displacement of the carriers. The *Midway* and *Franklin D. Roosevelt* now displace a standard 51,000 tons and full load of 62,000 tons. The *Coral Sea* displaces 52,500 tons standard and 63,400 tons full load. Width across the flight deck is now 147 feet. Regulus guided missiles were added to the FDR. All but ten of the 5-inch, 54-caliber mounts remain, and she can accommodate 50 to 70 aircraft, depending on the size. Her complement exclusive of the air group is 112 officers and 2475 enlisted men.

Aerial view of *USS Midway CVA-41* in turn to port.

40

USS Midway CVA-41 (CVB-41)

The *USS Midway CVB-41* was the forerunner of six battle carriers ordered on July 9, 1942. At the end of World War II, three of the proposed ships were under construction.

The *Midway's* construction began October 27, 1943, at the Newport News Shipbuilding Company in Virginia. Under the sponsorship of Mrs. Bradford W. Ripley, widow of naval aviator Lieutenant Bradford W. Ripley II, the new carrier was launched in the floating drydock in which she had been built on March 20, 1945.

She was commissioned at the Norfolk Navy Yard September 10 and Captain Joseph F. Bolger took command. Also present at this gala ceremony were Assistant Secretary of the Navy Artemus L. Gates, and Lieutenant George Gay—sole survivor of the *USS Hornet's* Torpedo Squadron 8, which struck enemy carriers June 4, 1942 against overwhelming odds.

USS Midway CVB-41, stern under construction.

The *Midway* commemorates the Battle of Midway—one of the most decisive engagements of the Second World War (June 4–6, 1942).

In an attempt to distinguish the *Midway* Class carriers from others, the *Midways* were designated CVB.

Following the usual fitting out procedures at Norfolk, the new carrier began flight operations October 12. An F4U-4 *Corsair* was the first plane to land on her deck eight days later.

The *Midway* began her shakedown cruise off Guantanamo Bay, Cuba, November 7, during which damage control procedures, gunnery, and all of the ship's departments underwent training drills. She returned to Norfolk Navy Yard December 13 for post-shakedown inspection.

Rear Admiral J. H. Cassidy came aboard on February 20, 1946 and the *Midway* became the flagship of Carrier Division One of the Atlantic Fleet. On March 1 she departed Norfolk to participate in "Operation Frostbite," a cold-weather exercise held in the North Atlantic to evaluate certain equipment. The tests were conducted in the 500 miles between Greenland, Labrador, and the Hudson Strait. The results provided invaluable data concerning carrier operations under extreme weather conditions. The frozen carrier returned to Norfolk March 28.

From April 19 to May 27 the *Midway* was actively involved with exercises with the Eighth Fleet near Guantanamo Bay, Culebra Island, and Puerto Rico. She then entered the navy yard at home port for a routine overhaul.

The *Midway* was roaming again on September 2, 1947 with a V-2 rocket on board. This voyage marked the genesis of "Operation Sandy," involving the first shipboard launching of a heavy rocket. Along for this event was Rear Admiral J. J. Balentine and numerous military and scientific observers. While cruising off the Narrows of Bermuda on September 4, the carrier welcomed Admiral W.H.P. Blandy, Commander in Chief, Atlantic Fleet; Dr. F. Hovde, the President of Duke University; and representatives of the Bell and General Electric Research laboratories. Two days later the captured V-2 rocket ignited and roared off the flight deck trailing a long flaming tail. Afterwards, the *Midway* returned to home port, arriving September 9.

On October 29 the carrier departed Norfolk to participate in Atlantic Fleet maneuvers. She began her first Mediterranean cruise and arrived on November 17 at Gibraltar. After visits to Algeria, Malta, Italy, Sicily, and France, she headed for home, and arrived at Norfolk on March 11, 1948.

From January 4, to March 5, 1949, she completed another cruise to the Mediterranean, then resumed carrier qualification training off the Virginia Capes until October 31.

She began another Mediterranean cruise on January 6, 1950, arriving ten days later at Gibraltar for operations with the Sixth Fleet. This was one of her many brief trips, lasting only two months. She sailed back to home port on May 29 and became the flagship of Rear Admiral W. L. Rees, Commander Carrier Division Two. The next eight days were used to evaluate aircraft operations after which she returned to Norfolk and resumed normal training duties off the Virginia Capes.

On July 10 the *Midway* was on her way for more duty with the Sixth Fleet, which included the usual exercises and training schedules. She departed Gibraltar on November 1 and returned to Norfolk nine days later, where, on the 22nd she entered the navy yard. New rapid-fire gun batteries were installed and her flight deck was strengthened to handle the new jets.

Work was completed April 24, 1951, at which time she resumed carrier qualification and gunnery practice off the coast of North Carolina.

On May 22 the *Midway* slipped into position at Guantanamo Bay, Cuba where night carrier qualifications and simulated aerial bombing attacks were conducted. She returned to home port July 10.

Beginning October 22 the *Midway* was busy in a three-week Atlantic Fleet exercise along the eastern seaboard and returned to Norfolk November 15.

The *Midway* began her fifth Mediterranean cruise on January 9, 1952. As flagship of Carrier Division Four, she joined units of the Italian, English, and French Navy for "Operation Grand Slam." On May 5 she sailed back to home port and received a brief overhaul.

During the summer, the *Midway* welcomed Midshipmen from the U.S. Naval Academy and took them on an orientation cruise, which was completed August 1.

On August 26 she was sailing for maneuvers in the North Sea with NATO units. During this activity she visited Scotland on September 10 for two days. The major exercise during this cruise was "Operation Mainbrace," which involved the *USS Wasp CV-18*, *USS Franklin D. Roosevelt CVB-42*, and *USS Wisconsin BB-64*. The exercise was completed on September 24 and the carrier arrived at Cherbourg, France, two days later. The stopover was highlighted by a visit by Cherbourg's mayor on the 29th, after which the carrier began the long voyage home, arriving at Norfolk October 8. While en route she was reclassified CVA—attack aircraft carrier.

On October 24 she entered the navy yard for a brief overhaul and resumed flight operations on November 14.

The *Midway* was sailing for her fifth Mediterranean cruise on December 1 and arrived at the now familiar port at Gibraltar nine days later. As the flagship for Rear Admiral Ingersoll, Commander Carrier Division Four, she participated in "Operation Rendezvous," a NATO exercise. On May 8, 1953, the *Midway* departed Oran, Algeria, for the trip home, arriving at Norfolk eleven days later. On May 29 she received another overhaul, which was completed October 26. Air operations were then conducted near Mayport and Jacksonville, Florida, interspersed with a short cruise to Guantanamo Bay, before she returned to Norfolk on December 19.

On January 4, 1954 the *Midway* again became the flagship of Carrier Division Four, which initiated another cruise to the Mediterranean, where the usual ports of call were made between training exercises. She returned to Norfolk on August 4 and resumed normal duties off the Virginia Capes.

Excitement filled the air on December 27 when the *Midway* departed home port for a cruise around the world. She stopped briefly at Mayport, Florida (December 28–29) then steamed by way of Capetown, South Africa (January 15–17), and Colombo, Ceylon (January 27–29), to join Seventh Fleet units off Formosa on February 6, 1955. She was designated flagship for Rear Admiral R. W. Ruble, who came aboard via a high line from the destroyer *USS Stoddard DD-566* on February 7. The carrier conducted operations with units of Task Force 77 until late June. This included patrols off Formosa with fleet exercises in the South China Sea to the waters off Subic Bay, Okinawa, and the coast of Honshu, Japan.

On June 28 she departed Yokosuka, Japan, for return to the United States, sailing by way of Hawaii. She arrived at Alameda Naval Air Station, California, on July 14. After off-loading aircraft and equipment of Air Group One, she departed July 22 for the Naval Ammunition Depot Bangor, Bremerton, Washington. Then she moved on to Tacoma the 26th and finally moored at Seattle on the 29th. She entered Puget Sound Shipyard on August 8.

The mighty *Midway* was decommissioned May 15, 1955, for a major conversion. For nearly two years the carrier was covered by a swarm of shipyard workers who installed an angle deck, an enclosed hurricane bow, and a streamlined island structure. Included in this massive job were three steam catapults, a newer type of arresting gear, jet blast deflectors, and the largest aviation crane ever installed on any carrier.

On September 30, 1957, she emerged from the yards with 17,000 tons added to her standard displacement.

After the normal sea trials the *Midway* arrived at her new home port at Alameda, California, in mid-December. Five weeks of shakedown training began in January 1958, then on February 27 she landed her first plane since her decommissioning in 1955.

She returned to Puget Sound March 29 for postconversion alterations, which were completed May 19.

On August 16, 1958, she departed for a cruise to the Western Pacific. As flagship for Carrier Division Five she patrolled the region of Formosa for 37 consecutive days. Visits were also made at Hawaii, Okinawa, Japan, Hong Kong, and Subic Bay. On February 24 the *Midway* departed Yokosuka and returned to home port on March 12, 1959.

Her first months at home were spent in drydock for minor repairs followed by four months of routine operations. In August she was off for another Far East cruise. Upon successfully completing an ORI at Pearl

German V2 rocket leaving flight deck and missile in flight
from *USS Midway CVB-41* during Operation Sandy.

Harbor she became a member of the Seventh Fleet on September 14.

During this cruise she steamed over 50,000 miles, logged 16,000 flight hours and 8000 landings—including the 80,000th landing made on her deck when an AD-6 *Skyraider* plopped down.

On March 25, 1960, she returned to Alameda and underwent a five-month yard period at Hunters Point Shipyard in San Francisco.

In August she resumed routine duties off the coast of California, returning to home port in December for holiday leave.

The *Midway* began her third Western Pacific jaunt on February 15, 1961, and cruised the coastline of Vietnam for several weeks. She was prepared for any eventuality during the Laotian crisis, but when the

ceasefire was signed she resumed normal duties near Japan. In September the *Midway* returned to Alameda and spent a month in the shipyard at San Francisco for maintenance.

In January 1962 she made her first visit to San Diego, where pre-deployment operations began. She logged her 100,000th mile of cruising since her 1960 conversion.

The *Midway* departed home port on April 6 for her fourth tour of duty in the Western Pacific with the usual Seventh Fleet exercises and inspections interspersed between ports of call.

On October 20 she returned to San Francisco for five months of overhaul in which she gained a new arresting gear system and lost six of her 11-inch gun mounts.

On June 13, 1963, two test pilots from the Naval Air Test Center, flying an F4A *Phantom* and an F8D *Crusader,* were automatically landed aboard the *Midway,* using the Bell Aerosystem's ANISPN-10 automatic carrier landing system. Thus another "first" was chalked up for the carrier.

November 8 found the *Midway* en route to the Far East where, for six months, she was a unit of the Seventh Fleet and conducted routine exercises and training programs. She returned to Alameda in May 1964, and spent a year of operations with the First Fleet.

While stateside duty took on an atmosphere of tedious training, the situation had altered in the Western Pacific. Communist aggression had erupted in

South Vietnam and the *Midway* prepared for her first combat cruise.

She departed Alameda March 29, 1965, and arrived at Pearl Harbor, where she passed an ORI, thence to the South China Seas where she joined the Seventh Fleet.

On April 16 the *Midway* launched her aircraft for actual combat strikes at the Bai Duc Thon and Xom Ca Trong highway bridges. The next day, her pilots hit other bridges and roads. The air group destroyed the Phoson bridge and Xom Gia highway on April 23.

Two pilots and an air-crewman of Helicopter Combat Support Squadron One aboard the *Midway* received the Distinguished Flying Cross. The U.S. Armed Forces sixth highest award was presented to

Five A4 skyhawk jets circle for landing aboard the attack carrier *USS Midway* after a strike mission over North Vietnam (November 1965).

the three by Rear Admiral Marshall W. White, Commander, Carrier Division Seven. The recipients were Lieutenant Commander Weslie W. Wetzel, Lieutenant (j.g.) Kent M. Vandervelde and Aviation Machinist's Mate First Class Charles V. Bowman.

On November 23 the *Midway* returned to Alameda. During her combat cruise her pilots had destroyed the first MIG interceptors credited to U.S. forces in Southeast Asia.

The *USS Midway* was decommissioned on February 15, 1966, at Hunters Point Naval Shipyard in San Francisco to undergo a $75 million modernization.

After just two weeks short of four years, the *Midway* emerged from the shipyard to become the largest and most modern carrier of her class with operational capabilities equal to those of the newest attack aircraft carriers.

On January 31, 1970, the *Midway* was recommissioned with Captain Eugene J. Carroll, USN, becoming her 24th commanding officer. Eighteen former *Midway* skippers advanced to flag rank. Ten were advanced to Rear Admiral, and one, Rear Admiral Roy M. Isaman, is still on active duty. Eight were advanced to Vice Admiral and two, Vice Admiral Reynold D. Hogle and Vice Admiral Ralph W. Cousins are still on active duty status.

The *Midway*'s most significant improvement is in her ability to launch and recover aircraft approximately one-third heavier than those of her two sister ships. The overall area of the flight deck has been increased from 2.82 to 4.02 acres. The angle deck was lengthened over 25 feet. Three new deck edge elevators were installed and are capable of handling fully loaded aircraft weighing 100,000 pounds.

Compartments below the flight deck have been rearranged and enlarged to accommodate larger and more complex electronics shops. The *Midway*'s combat information center (CIC) and command complex have been updated with the inclusion of the computerized Naval Tactical Data System (NTDS) and the Ships Inertial Navigation System (SINS). These systems enable the carrier to support and operate the newest computer-equipped aircraft. There is a new deck edge bomb elevator and new storage areas for weapons, enabling the most modern weapons to be handled efficiently.

The *Midway*'s modernization was a monumental undertaking, which required extensive structural and technical modifications to the ship. It was the most extensive ship modernization ever undertaken by the Navy, enabling the carrier to be better prepared than ever to add to her outstanding reputation in the Fleet.

The *USS Midway CVA-41* has received the following awards: The Navy Unit Commendation; the Navy Occupation Service Medal; the China Service Medal (Extended); the Armed Forces Expeditionary Medal and the Vietnam Service Medal.

USS Franklin D. Roosevelt CVA-42.

41

USS Franklin D. Roosevelt CVA-42 (CVB-42)

Franklin D. Roosevelt was born on January 30, 1882, at Hyde Park, New York, and it is said that by blood or marriage he was related to eleven former Presidents, including George Washington. He was also the only man to be elected to the Presidency four times.

Mr. Roosevelt's first national service came when Woodrow Wilson appointed him Assistant Secretary of the Navy, where he served from 1913 to 1920. Dur-

ing this time he made highly significant contributions to the Navy's development and its success in World War I.

In July 1920 he was the Democratic Vice Presidential candidate as a running mate of James M. Cox. In 1921 he returned to private life after an attack of poliomyelitis paralyzed him from the waist down. This did not hinder his ambition and after months of struggle he was elected Governor of New York, serving from 1929 to 1933.

In 1932 he defeated Herbert Hoover in a landslide, and became the 32nd President of the United States on March 4, 1933.

The *USS Franklin D. Roosevelt CVB-42* was the first naval vessel to be named in honor of a person. Her keel was laid on December 1, 1943, at the New York Navy Yard. Originally designated *USS Coral Sea*, the name change was effected shortly after President Roosevelt passed away on April 12, 1945, at Warm Springs, Georgia.

Mrs. John H. Towers, wife of the Deputy Commander in Chief, Pacific Fleet, christened the ship on April 29, 1945. Captain Apollo Soucek took command on Navy Day, October 27, when the new carrier was commissioned.

While on her shakedown cruise the *FDR* visited Rio de Janeiro February 1–11, 1946, and represented the United States at the inauguration of the Brazilian President Dutra.

On March 21 she returned to New York for post-shakedown alterations. Upon completion on April 10 the carrier steamed to Norfolk Navy Yard and became the flagship of the Eighth Fleet, commanded by Admiral Marc A. Mitscher. Training operations were then conducted until May 27.

On August 8 the *FDR* deployed for her first Mediterranean cruise, returning to New York October 4 where open house was celebrated on Navy Day 23 days later. A three-month maintenance period followed at Norfolk.

Carrier history was written November 2 when the *FDR* launched a modified U.S. Air Force F-80 *Shoot-*

USS Franklin D. Roosevelt CVA-42.

ing Star. Lieutenant Colonel Marion Carl, USMC, flew the jet once around the ship, then landed. He thus became the first jet pilot to be launched and recovered by an aircraft carrier. Suddenly, all thoughts that carriers were becoming obsolete were discarded and a program was effected to introduce the "jet age" to sea warfare.

On February 3, 1947 the *FDR* went to the Caribbean area for an extended period of Atlantic Fleet maneuvers, during which time another "first" was recorded. On February 11 a helicopter ascended from her deck to transport mail, personnel, and supplies to the submarine *USS Greenfish*. This was the first time a helicopter was operated at sea. On March 18 the carrier entered the naval shipyard at Norfolk for a four-month overhaul.

The *FDR* was off on another Mediterranean voyage on July 14, 1948. A show of strength was demonstrated with allied forces as Navy aircraft assisted in disrupting the "Berlin Blockade."

During the next five years the *FDR* operated from Norfolk and the Mediterranean. Her primary mission was the ever vigilant task of discouraging aggressive tactics of the Soviet Union. While accomplishing this goal she played a large role in the Navy's success in reversing the Communist advance in all countries bordering the seas where she sailed.

Between Mediterranean deployments the *FDR* conducted flight training programs off the Caribbean and the eastern seaboard. On December 3, 1953, she began a major conversion period.

The *FDR* bid farewell to the Norfolk yards on January 7, 1954. She was too large to transit the Panama Canal and was forced to sail around Cape Horn. A short visit was made to San Francisco, then on March 5 she entered Puget Sound Shipyard at Bremerton, Washington.

The big carrier was decommissioned on April 23 to undergo a two-year conversion in which she received a new angle flight deck, an enclosed hurricane bow, three steam catapults, streamlined island structure, and the latest electronics and radar equipment.

She departed the yard with her new look and was recommissioned on April 6, 1956. A short visit was made at San Francisco prior to sailing 'round the Horn to Mayport, Florida, where she arrived on August 8.

The *FDR* trained pilots of Air Group 17 to use the mirror system in carrier landings until October 25, when she departed Florida and arrived at Norfolk two days later.

She was placed on a 72-hour alert when the Suez Crisis erupted and departed on November 7 for the coast of Portugal, where she patrolled the Atlantic seaboard off Europe. The carrier returned to Norfolk December 9 for maintenance.

Mayport, Florida, became her new home port on February 9, 1957. Nine days later she began a series of weather tests in the Gulf of Maine. The effectiveness of catapults, aircraft, and other vital equipment were evaluated in extremely cold weather. Also, this period she launched her first *Regulus* missile. The tests were completed on March 3 and the carrier returned to home port.

Rear Admiral Pirie and his staff came aboard on the 21st and an aerial demonstration was held near Bermuda for President Eisenhower who was aboard the *USS Canberra CAG-2* nearby.

On May 19 the *FDR* sailed back to Norfolk for general repairs, after which she returned to home port, arriving June 8. She resumed fleet training operations with Air Group 17 on June 17.

An unfortunate accident occurred aboard the *FDR* on the morning of June 19 when an explosion in the Number One pump room killed two crewmen and injured 29. Prompt action prevented further damage or injuries and the carrier sailed to Mayport, where the air group was released. She sailed to Norfolk for repairs which were completed on July 27 at which time she was off for another Mediterranean cruise.

Upon arrival at Gibraltar she relieved the *USS Lake Champlain CVS-37* and began training exercises with the Sixth Fleet. She arrived at Cannes, France, in December where the crew celebrated the Christmas holidays.

A4C aboard the *USS Franklin D. Roosevelt* hooked up, ready for launch.

On February 13, 1958, the *FDR* was relieved by the *USS Saratoga CVA-60*. After a fruitless search for a downed Navy plane, the carrier returned to home port on March 5.

The *FDR* departed Mayport April 18 and went to Bayonne. Her upper mast was removed so that she could sail under the Brooklyn and Manhattan Bridges, thence up the river to New York for a four-month overhaul.

August 18–19 she conducted sea trials off the coast of New Jersey and returned to Mayport for normal operations on September 3.

From February 13 to September 1, 1959, the *FDR* accomplished another Mediterranean voyage and participated in the usual Sixth Fleet exercises. Throughout October and November she teamed with other warships in a joint Navy-Air Force weapons system evaluation program.

On January 6, 1960, the *FDR* departed Norfolk with Air Group One aboard for a simulated atomic attack against targets of the eastern United States.

She was off on another Mediterranean cruise 22 days later, where she relieved the *USS Essex CVA-9* on February 12. On March 1 she hosted a visit by the Honorable Simon H. Vissor, the Dutch Minister of Defense.

An unscheduled exercise was conducted April 2 to simulate wartime conditions wherein all planes were armed and launched.

Simulated attacks were also directed against Italian, Greek, and Turkish targets in which the British carrier *HMS Ark Royal* participated.

On July 25, Lieutenant (jg) R. D. Richards landed his A4D *Skyhawk* aboard the *FDR* to log the 95,000th arrested landing.

The *USS Intrepid CVA-11* arrived on August 16 and the *FDR* returned to home port eight days later. On September 17 she reported to the New York Shipyard for an overhaul. She received the Frensel Lens Landing System, which offered numerous advantages over the mirror system then in use. The new system projects a beam of light from an integral stabilized light source and the pilot simply follows the beam to the deck for a landing. Also included during the yard period was an elaborate closed-circuit television system whose identification was known to the crew as WFDR-TV. The station was made possible thanks to the crew's recreation fund.

The *FDR* began another Mediterranean cruise on February 15, 1961, and relieved the *USS Independence CVA-62* on the 23rd at Rota, Spain. A five-day visit to Naples began March 3. Eighteen days later Commander A. R. Hawkins made the 100,000th landing in an A4D *Skyhawk*.

On April 14 a period of antisubmarine warfare exercises began along the coasts of Italy, Greece, and Turkey, where simulated attacks were staged.

The *FDR* received an urgent message on May 20 that an American citizen aboard the civilian liner SS *Atlantic* had suffered an acute stomach disorder. A doctor from the carrier was immediately flown by helicopter to the stricken man. It was decided to return him to the carrier, where the necessary surgery was performed. After two weeks of recovery the patient was transferred to a hospital at Nice, France.

An allied nations NATO team review took place in the Bay of Naples on June 24. Close air support to the task force was provided August 7–14 at southern Sardinia. On the 28th the *FDR* returned to Mayport, Florida.

She was underway on November 19 to join other Second Fleet units in the Caribbean Sea, where a crisis was brewing in the Dominican Republic. During a seven-day show of force off the coast of Santo Domingo, the task force helped to stabilize the conditions.

In February 1962 the *FDR* entered the New York Navy Yard for a two-month overhaul, during which she received a unique closed-circuit TV system used to train pilots during carrier qualifications. The system records the landings on video tape and assists the Landing Signal Officer in directing landing planes.

The *FDR* deployed to the Mediterranean in September. On April 22, 1963, she came home to Mayport

The XFD-1 "Phantom" Navy jet propelled aircraft makes its first take off from the *USS Franklin D. Roosevelt.* This aircraft possesses a top speed of over 500 mph.

The "Phantom" jet is airborne after a run of 360 feet.

and in July went to New York for a five-month overhaul.

Upon completion she was off on another Mediterranean cruise in April 1964 where she engaged in Sixth Fleet exercises along with NATO forces. She returned to Florida on December 22.

During the first half of 1965 the *FDR* operated along the Atlantic seaboard with the Second Fleet. Then, on June 28, she was en route to the Mediterranean again, from which she returned on December 17 in time for the crew to enjoy holiday leave at home.

Strong measures were required to repel Communist aggression in Southeast Asia, particularly North Vietnam's attempted conquest of the free peoples of South Vietnam. To support the U.S. and South Vietnamese efforts, the *FDR* was temporarily assigned to the Seventh Fleet in the Far East.

On June 21, 1966, she departed Mayport and sailed to Rio de Janeiro, then to the Cape of Good Hope, across the Indian Ocean and into the South China Sea, arriving on Yankee Station in the Tonkin Gulf on August 10. That same day she launched attacks against North Vietnamese military targets.

During her tenure in these troubled waters the carrier's air group flew over 7000 missions and destroyed bridges, barges, oil and munitions depots, and railway tracks.

Interspersed with her combat, the *FDR* paid visits to the Philippines, Japan, and Hong Kong. After eight months of combat duty the carrier returned to Mayport, Florida, on February 21, 1967.

At a time when most ships are being considered for retirement, the *FDR* regards herself as entering the prime of life. With periodic modernization she will continue to operate with the biggest and latest carriers in the fleet.

The *Coral Sea* is seen operating off the Atlantic with an F7U-3 "Cutlass" on the port catapult and two XFJ-2 "Furies" on the flight deck for qualifications.

42

USS Coral Sea CVA-43 (CVB-43)

The first *USS Coral Sea CVE-57* was an escort carrier built by the Kaiser Shipbuilding Company of Vancouver, Washington. CVE-57 was originally intended as the *USS Alikula Bay*, but was changed to *Coral Sea* on April 1, 1943, during construction.

The *Coral Sea* was launched May 1, 1943, and commissioned a few months later on August 27. Then, on October 10, 1944, her identity was again revised to *Anzio* and the name *Coral Sea* was assigned to CVB-42, then under construction at the New York Navy Yard.

Upon the death of President Franklin D. Roosevelt on April 12, 1945, CVB-42 was renamed in honor of the late chief executive.

A third unnamed CVB being built since July 10, 1944, at Newport News Shipbuilding and Drydock Company in Virginia, took the name *Coral Sea*. Mrs. Thomas C. Kinkaid, wife of Admiral Kinkaid, who commanded a Cruiser Division in the Battle of the Coral Sea (May 4–8, 1942), christened the new carrier on April 2, 1946.

On October 1, 1947, the *USS Coral Sea CVB 43*

was commissioned with Captain Aaron P. Storrs III, USN, commanding.

The original statistics of the first *Coral Sea* upon commissioning were overall length, 968 feet; extreme breadth, 130 feet; standard displacement, 45,000 tons; draft, 35 feet; speed, 33 knots; accommodations, 379 officers, 3725 enlisted men; armament, eighteen 5-inch 54-calibre mounts and twenty-one 40mm quadruple antiaircraft mounts.

The *Coral Sea* put to sea for trials off the Virginia Capes on December 8, 1947. Her shakedown cruise began January 19, 1948, off the coast of Guantanamo Bay, and the Panama Canal.

A simulated air strike was conducted against the Culegra Island until April 3. The following day the *Coral Sea* returned to Norfolk Navy Yard for post-shakedown alterations.

Midshipmen came aboard June 5. Two days later the *Coral Sea* got underway for Lisbon, Portugal, arriving there 16 days later.

In company with Task Force 84, the carrier slipped through the Straits of Gibraltar and anchored off the French Riviera on June 30, 1948.

After six days, she commenced various training operations. A final midshipmen training period was held near Cuba, then on August 6, 1948, the *Coral Sea* returned to the States. She entered Norfolk Navy Yard on October 7 for an extended overhaul. This work was completed on February 19, 1949, and she left for refresher training off Guantanamo Bay March 18–April 25, 1949.

The *Coral Sea* departed Norfolk on May 3, 1949 and began her first tour of duty with the Sixth Fleet in the Mediterranean eleven days later. During the

A view of the *Coral Sea* CVB-43 December 10, 1947.

cruise she visited the Sicilian ports of Augusta and Palermo, and Naples, Leghorn, and Rapallo on the Italian mainland.

Training exercises were held near Malta; on July 1 the carrier stopped at Cannes, France. July 27–August 1, the crew took a break in their heavy schedule to visit Istanbul, Turkey.

On September 17, the *Coral Sea* bid farewell to Gibraltar and returned to Norfolk on the 25th. The carrier entered the Navy yard for an overhaul until April 6, 1950.

From May 1 to June 18, 1950, the *Coral Sea* conducted a post-yard shakedown off Guantanamo Bay. Vice Admiral Felix B. Stump was copilot of the first North American A-J1, long-range medium bomber to touch down on a carrier flight deck on August 31, 1950. The plane landed aboard the *Coral Sea* with a maximum load to prove that bombers could successfully operate from aircraft carriers.

The *Coral Sea* steamed from Norfolk on September 9, 1950, for another Mediterranean tour. She participated in Sixth Fleet maneuvers near the coast of Sicily and Malta as well as Suda Bay, Crete.

Highlighting the cruise was a visit to Iran and Algeria. On January 22, 1951, the *Coral Sea* was detached from the Sixth Fleet and sailed to Norfolk on February 1.

Less than four weeks later she began a third Mediterranean cruise as flagship of Rear Admiral Daniel V. Gallery, Commander, Carrier Division Six.

The carrier left Norfolk Navy Yard on March 20 and joined the Sixth Fleet again off Gibraltar on April 1.

During this cruise she participated in "Beehive I," the first NATO (North Atlantic Treaty Organization) exercise.

Between training periods, she stopped at Italy, France, Greece, and Turkey. September 22–26 the carrier rested at Lisbon, then returned to Norfolk on October 7, 1951.

From October 10, 1951, to February 12, 1952, the *Coral Sea* underwent a yard overhaul of significance. A special weapons and sonic research team was aboard following the overhaul for tests near the Virginia Capes area.

On March 3, the *Coral Sea* was back at Norfolk to prepare for a fourth cruise to the Mediterranean.

She cleared Norfolk on April 19, and arrived at her destination on the 27th.

After participation in the NATO exercise "Beehive II," she sailed into Split, Yugoslavia, on September 11, 1952. Marshal Josip Broz Tito, president of Yugoslavia, was given a three-hour cruise to observe flight opera-

tions. This was the first time a U.S. aircraft carrier had visited Yugoslavia.

The *Coral Sea* weighed anchor from Split Harbor on September 14, and journeyed to Cannes and Lisbon.

On October 1, 1952, her designation was changed from *CVB-43* to *CVA-43*, then three days later she returned to Norfolk, Virginia. At this time she operated for two months off the Virginia Capes and underwent a short overhaul.

On January 5, 1953, the *Coral Sea* was en route to areas near Mayport and Jacksonville, Florida, for air operations. Rear Admiral C. R. Brown, commander Carrier Division Six, was aboard as she left Mayport on April 26. The carrier arrived at Oran, Algeria, on May 7. On June 24, the *Coral Sea* became one of the first U.S. warships to visit a Spanish port when she sailed into Barcelona. She was active in the NATO Operation "Black Wave" and after a brief stop at Palermo, Sicily, she returned to Norfolk on November 21, 1953.

The *Coral Sea* then entered the naval yards for an extended overhaul, which was completed by March 1954.

Following three months of air operations off Mayport, Florida, and a testing period with members of the Armed Forces Special Weapons Project, the *Coral Sea* became flagship of Rear Admiral E. A. Cruise, Commander, Carrier Division Six, on July 7, 1954, and sailed for Norfolk for air operations near Mayport. She returned to the Mediterranean, arriving off Gibraltar July 27; this marked her sixth Mediterranean cruise. Generalissmo Franco of Spain visited the ship during this time.

The carrier participated in the NATO exercise "Happy Valley," and "Italic Sky II," then returned to the Navy yard at Norfolk December 20, 1954.

The *Coral Sea* operated between Mayport and Norfolk until March 23, 1955, then set a course for her seventh tour with the Sixth Fleet.

The carrier made a port call at and conducted additional NATO exercises off Malta.

On September 29, 1955, she was again docked at Norfolk for overhaul. The yard work was completed February 1, 1956, at which time the mighty ship conducted a refresher training cruise near Guantanamo Bay, Cuba.

The *Coral Sea* sailed from Norfolk on April 9, 1956, assigned to Task Force 24, and took part in exercises off the eastern seaboard of Bermuda. Air operations were launched near Mayport until August 14. Eleven days later the carrier joined the Sixth Fleet at Golfo Di Palmas, Sardinia. During her stay, the *Coral Sea* was active in the NATO exercise, "Whipsaw."

She visited Athens on October 20, where King Paul and Queen Fredericka of Greece came aboard to observe task force and air operations. Ten days later the *Coral Sea* stood ready at Suez, assuring protection of American citizens as well as aiding their evacuation from the dangerous area during the crisis period.

The carrier was back at Norfolk on February 11, 1957. The *Coral Sea* steamed away again on February 26, heading for the West Coast for a major conversion. A stop was made at Santos, Brazil, March 9–13, then she rounded Cape Horn on the 17th.

The crew enjoyed liberty in Talcahuano and Valparaiso, Chile, on March 20th and 25th and liberty calls were made at Balboa, Canal Zone, from March 21 to April 3 and Port Townsend and Tacoma, Washington, April 11–15.

The *Coral Sea* entered Puget Sound Naval Shipyard on April 15 and was decommissioned nine days later.

The massive face-lifting of the *Coral Sea* included a canted deck, enclosed hurricane bow, a streamlined island structure; her displacement was increased to 63,-000 tons. She was the last of the prewar designed carriers to receive the modernization.

On January 26, 1960, the *Coral Sea* was recommissioned and began sea trials off the coast of Washington, then returned to the yards for post shakedown alterations. This was completed on September 19 and she left the yard at San Francisco to begin her initial Far East cruise to relieve the *USS Ticonderoga CVA-14*. The *Coral Sea* became an element of the Seventh Fleet in the tense, troubled Laotian area.

The ever-ready carrier made stops at Iwakuni, Yokosuka, Kobe, and Sasebo, Japan; Buckner Bay, Okinawa; Hong Kong; and Subic Bay, Philippines. She operated near the South China Sea until May 11, 1961, then prepared for the long voyage home. After being relieved by the *USS Bon Homme Richard CVA-31*, the *Coral Sea* sailed from Subic Bay on May 13 and docked at the Naval Air Station, Alameda, California, 14 days later.

On May 30, the *Coral Sea* went through a 40-day overhaul at Hunter's Point Shipyard in San Francisco, after which a month-long midshipman's cruise was held during July, serving 33 NROTC middies from fourteen colleges.

The *Coral Sea* arrived in San Diego on August 18 to participate in the celebration honoring 50 years of naval aviation. More than 26,000 persons toured the ship.

The *Coral Sea* became the first Pacific Fleet carrier to operate with the F4H Phantom II when Lieutenant

A bomb-laden A4C "Skyhawk" is positioned on the catapult for a combat strike over Vietnam.

Commander Patrick L. Working of VF-121 landed in September. Another celebration took place on October 30 when Lieut. Fred M. Backman made the 100,000th arrested landing in an A3D Skyhawk. The ship's bakers prepared a 1058-pound cake for the occasion.

The *Coral Sea* operated off the San Francisco coast for two months in preparation for a second Western Pacific deployment. With Carrier Air Group 15 aboard she departed Alameda on December 15, 1961. A rigorous ORI was observed near Hawaii, then on Christmas Day a luau was held at the Queen's Surf on Wakiki Beach for the 2000 sailors.

On January 8, 1962, the carrier arrived in Subic Bay. Air operations were analyzed by Rear Admiral J. B. Frewen, Royal Navy, seven days later.

Interspersed with operational training, the ship made port calls at Sasebo, Yokosuka, Hong Kong, and Subic Bay.

During April, while engaged in a 16-day at-sea period, the *Coral Sea* travelled 6666 miles, catapulted 1317 aircraft, and landed 1492 (388 at night); CAG-15 flew 5206.6 hours. In addition, 169 propeller aircraft were deck launched. In July the carrier returned to Alameda, California.

While in San Francisco on August 14, Prince Juan Carlos of Spain and Princess Sophia of Greece visited the ship for a close look at an attack carrier.

The *Coral Sea* entered Hunter's Point Shipyard on September 8 for a routine overhaul, which was completed on December 17; then she returned to Alameda four days later to begin the holiday leave period.

On January 3, 1963, she steamed toward San Diego

Flight deck operations are timed almost to the second, so
Coral Sea's flight deck crewmen waste no time in getting
this RF8A Crusader photo reconnaissance plane ready for
an immediate launch. (Photo by LTJG M. J. Perez, USN)

to release crew members for training at fleet schools. Back in San Francisco on February 2, the carrier ran aground. After 8½ hours of struggle by ten tugs the warship was released from her muddy imprisonment.

The *Coral Sea* was again headed for Japan on April 3 to join the Seventh Fleet. After successful completion of the annual ORI at Pearl Harbor, a course was set for Australia on April 19. She crossed the Equator, and the International Date Line six days later, and 3000 sailors became "Golden Shellbacks."

The carrier arrived in Sydney on April 29 and a two-week visit began in honor of the 21st Annual celebration of the Battle of Coral Sea. The Japanese Consul, the Lord Mayor of Sydney, and top ranking Australian armed forces officers paid a visit. Also on hand was a retired Japanese Navy captain who fought opposite the *Coral Sea* commander, Captain Charles E. Roemer, during the actual Battle of Coral Sea.

Usual ports of call were made, followed by a six-week "overseas middie cruise" during July and August. The midshipmen from the U.S. Naval Academy and various colleges came aboard in Yokosuka. The ship departed November 13 for the return voyage home. She slipped under the Golden Gate Bridge on November 25 and tied up at NAS Alameda. This completed eight months of overseas duty and a crowd of 3000 anxious wives, children, and friends of the sailors greeted the ship.

The *Coral Sea* departed Alameda on January 7, 1964, to conduct a ten-day qualification test for new pilots. January also marked the beginning of interrupted stateside duty, which would last a year. The carrier was busy between Alameda and San Diego until June 22, 1964. During this time various training exercises were handled as well as training for midshipmen.

On June 26, the *Coral Sea* entered Puget Sound Shipyard for a brief overhaul, returning to Alameda on July 3. During the four subsequent months the carrier continued her uneventful but vital mission of operational training and air operations along the coasts of Southern and Northern California.

On December 7, 1964, the giant carrier began her fourth Western Pacific cruise. Carrier Air Wing 15 (CAW-15), formerly designated Carrier Air Group 15, was aboard for its fourth cruise with the *Coral Sea*, since the ship's recommissioning in 1960.

A complete ORI was held at Pearl Harbor until January 16, 1965, and the carrier sailed from the yards to join the Seventh Fleet seven days later.

On January 30, 1965, the *Coral Sea* steamed into Subic Bay for a four-hour replenishment.

As Flagship Task Group 77.5—with Rear Admiral Edward C. Outlaw, Commander, Carrier Division One aboard—the *Coral Sea* was ending her operational training and heading for Manila to enjoy a rest, which began February 7.

At 6:12 A.M., the *USS Ranger CVA-61* received orders to assemble all units of the Seventh Fleet. Although no U.S. carrier had launched actual combat strikes since the Gulf of Tonkin incident in August 1964, the crew was tense with anticipation of the impending orders.

The *Coral Sea* was directed to ready her aircraft for possible strike missions. On the evening of February 6 guerrilla attacks were staged against American bases in South Vietnam. Several G.I.'s were killed or wounded.

At 12:40 on February 7, 1965, Task Force 77 received orders to strike North Vietnam; at exactly 3:00 P.M., 20 aircraft from the *Coral Sea* were launched and teamed up with planes from the *Ranger* and *USS Hancock CVA-19* for aerial attacks on the Dong Hoi military barracks, which served as a staging area for Viet Cong infiltrators into South Vietnam. These missions were the initial carrier combat reprisal attacks against North Vietnam and the largest single air combat strikes since the Korean War.

An A4E Skyhawk from the *Coral Sea*'s attack squadron 155 was hit by antiaircraft fire. Lt. Edward A. Dickson, the pilot, was seen ejecting from his stricken craft, but a thorough 48-hour search failed to locate him. Many of the search planes were fired at by Communist shore batteries.

The reprisal attack on Dong Hoi on February 7 was only the first of many such strikes, as future hostile action by North Vietnamese troops harrassed American advisory groups; it was also the first time since her commissioning in 1947 that the *Coral Sea* had launched aircraft in actual combat.

On February 11, 50 *Coral Sea* aircraft armed with conventional ordnance went on a second reprisal mission against the Viet Cong army barracks and staging areas.

Afterwards, three of the carrier's planes failed to return. Lt. Robert Shumaker of VF-154 was captured by the Viet Cong when his F8U Crusader was hit by ground fire. The remaining two pilots were rescued safely.

It was back at Pearl Harbor on January 15 that Captain George L. C. Cassell, USN, had assumed command of the *Coral Sea*. He would command the big carrier during the most crucial days of her 18-year service. During those first 30 days of combat the *Coral Sea* logged 720 hours of continuous operation and

A weary combat pilot returns to the *Coral Sea* at sundown.

steamed over 12,400 miles. Only 32 hours of the 720 was spent in replenishment, and the carrier was able to remain in combat capacity at all times.

The amount of fuel taken aboard was sufficient to allow the carrier to sail from San Francisco, circumnavigate the globe, and return to Norfolk, Virginia. A record-breaking replenishment was made when the *USS Graffias* transferred 252 tons of provisions to the *Coral Sea*.

The *Coral Sea* arrived at Subic Bay on March 6 for a well-deserved rest after logging 2321 arrested gear landings during a 50-day continuous at-sea period.

The sailors had received word five days earlier that for their operations they would be awarded the Armed Forces Expeditionary Medal. On March 15, 1965, the *Coral Sea* departed for her return to the South China Sea.

Rear Admiral Outlaw, Commander Carrier Division One and Commander Task Group 77.5 assumed command of Task Force 77, and on March 19, the *Coral Sea* launched her third strike against military targets in North Vietnam. She was designated to attack supply buildings at Phu Van and Vin Son. This strike was successful, and there was no loss of aircraft.

Dr. Phan Huy Quat, Prime Minister of South Vietnam, came aboard the *Coral Sea* on March 24, 1965. In an address to the crew, Doctor Quat stated: "We in free Vietnam are following with great interest your everyday activities in this part of the world for we know that they are aimed mainly at helping us preserve our independence and territorial integrity in the force of blatant Communist aggression coming from the North. We in free Vietnam are proud to count you among our friends, for friends you are indeed in our hour of greatest need when our very survival as free men is at stake. We are also deeply thankful that you have willingly accepted many sacrifices in serving out here—serving your great country, but also, and more importantly, serving the sacred ideals of liberty and justice."

The *Coral Sea* air group joined planes from the *Hancock* on March 26 to bomb North Vietnamese radar sites at Vinh Son, Cap Mui Ron, Ha Tinh, and Bach Long Island.

One A4D Skyhawk and an F8U Crusader were lost to enemy firepower, but both pilots were rescued.

Four days later, the ship's pilots inflicted heavy damage to a communications station at Bach Long Island. The island, located some 120 miles southeast of Hanoi, was blasted by 60 aircraft, 30 each from the *Hancock* and *Coral Sea*. Over 50 tons of ordnance were dropped and pilots on the mission reported the heaviest ground

fire to date. Three planes were lost.

On March 31, the *Coral Sea* launched 20 attack and 8 support planes on an assault against the radar installations at Cap Mui Ron and Vinh Son. More than 25 tons of bombs fell on each target. The *Coral Sea* was assigned Cap Mui Ron, located 78 miles northwest of the demilitarized zone. Pilots reported heavy damage inflicted and no enemy ground or air resistance was encountered.

A group from the *Coral Sea* and *Hancock* made two separate strikes on a bridge at Dong Phuong Thong on April 3 and dropped 60 tons of ordnance on the structure located 70 miles south of Hanoi. The attacks began at 10 A.M. and 2:30 P.M. The result was one span knocked down and another damaged. During the attacks MIG jets were spotted for the first time by Task Force 77, but no air-to-air combat ensued.

Four days later, Lt. W. M. Roark of VA-153 was shot down on a reconnaissance flight and officially listed as killed in action.

A major strike against the Communists in North Vietnam took place on April 16 when the carriers of Task Force 77 hit the Xom Ca Trang highway bridge 60 miles north of the DMZ. The bridge was knocked out with a Bullpup missile from a *Coral Sea* pilot, and later a second highway bridge was destroyed in the same area.

The *Coral Sea* went to Subic Bay on April 18 for a rest period. Ten days later she was underway for Hong Kong, B.C., arriving April 25. The crew was given five days to view the exotic island and enjoy a few memorable tours.

On May 1, the *Coral Sea* departed Hong Kong to resume air operations off the coast of South Vietnam.

Forty A4 Skyhawks from the *Coral Sea* and *USS Midway CVA-41* were launched May 8 against the Vinh airfield complex in North Vietnam; the airfield was 70 percent destroyed.

The petroleum storage area at Phu Que became a target on May 18. The area, located 125 miles south of Hanoi, was hit by a score of A1 Skyraiders and A4 Skyhawks plus 18 F8U Crusaders.

An air strike composed of more than 50 planes hit the Phuoc Loi Naval Base in North Vietnam on May 20 and heavy damage was inflicted on this base located 165 miles south of Hanoi.

The *Coral Sea* returned to Subic Bay on May 29 for a short visit then sailed to Yokosuka, Japan, arriving on June 5.

While in Yokosuka on June 12, the carrier received the words, "indefinite period of extension in the Far East." For anyone who has ever made a Western Pa-

Loaded with bombs, an A4E "Skyhawk" of Attack Squadron 155 of the *Coral Sea* banks and prepares to make a diving run on a Viet Cong outpost in South Vietnam.

cific cruise on a carrier this was no surprise, because as one sailor expressed it: "It was normal to hear we got extended; no carrier ever returned on the expected date."

The *Coral Sea* departed Yokosuka on June 13. After storing ammunition at Subic Bay, she returned to the South China Sea for air operations with the Seventh Fleet Task Force.

While on a routine reconnaissance mission 40 miles west of Thanh Hoa, North Vietnam, on June 25, Commander Peter Mongilaroi, Commander, Carrier Air Wing 15, was killed in action when his A4C *Skyhawk* was shot down.

The *Coral Sea* observed an upkeep period at Subic Bay July 26–29, then made a second visit to Hong Kong August 4–11.

On August 12, the *Coral Sea* returned to the coast of South Vietnam for continued combat operations.

Lt. (jg) Eward B. Shaw of VA-165 was killed in action when his A1H *Skyraider* was hit by flak after a mission 75 miles north of the DMZ.

The *Coral Sea* sailed again to Subic Bay on September 12, 1965, for a recreation period, at which time 125 students from Columbo University at Olongapo, Zambales, toured the giant warship.

On September 20, the *Coral Sea* departed the Philippine port to resume operations off the Vietnam coast.

Carrier Air Wing 15 set a new record in naval aviation history on October 4, 1965, when Lt. (jg) William J. Kish of VA-155 flew his A4E *Skyhawk* on the carrier's 10,000th combat sortie. No other carrier in the history of the Navy had ever accomplished this amount of combat sorties with one air wing during a single combat cruise.

On October 17, the *Coral Sea* was back at Subic Bay to prepare for her return to the United States. On the next day, the mighty carrier bid farewell to our Filipino friends.

Amidst the water spray from San Francisco fireboats, the *Coral Sea* entered San Francisco Bay on November 1. A 973-foot pennant flew from her mast as the carrier returned from her first war cruise in her 18 years of commissioned service. Twenty days later,

she entered Hunters Point Naval Shipyard for a four-month overhaul.

The *Coral Sea* was released from the yard on March 28 and began an intensive training period prior to a scheduled Western Pacific deployment. The crew's combat readiness was keyed to peak efficiency.

On July 29, 1966, the *Coral Sea* sailed from Alameda on her second Vietnam war cruise. Upon completing a successful ORI at Pearl Harbor, she arrived in Subic Bay via Yokosuka, Japan, on August 20, 1966. For the next 24 hours ammunition, stores, spare parts, and aircraft were loaded in preparation for her assignment in the Yankee Station area.

While en route to the Gulf of Tonkin on August 26, the *Coral Sea* suffered an engineering casualty when a blade from two of her screws was lost. Repairs were

The *USS Mattoponi AO-41* refuels the destroyer *USS Rowan DD-782* and the *Coral Sea* off Yankee Station in the South China Sea.

completed at the Ship Repair Facility in Yokosuka. This task took seven days and on September 8, the *Coral Sea* was en route to the South China Sea.

On September 13, 1966, the *Coral Sea* launched her first combat air strikes of the 1966–67 cruise against Communist military targets on North Vietnam. Emphasis was on communications and supply facilities. During this initial tour of duty on Yankee Station the *Coral Sea* celebrated her 19th birthday.

While in operation on a second duty tour at Yankee Station, the *Coral Sea* received Admiral David L. McDonald, Chief of Naval Operations.

The 161,000th arrested landing was logged on November 16, of which 10,000 had been made since May 1966.

The *Coral Sea* returned to Subic Bay on December 6, where she remained for 12 days, then steamed to Hong Kong for Christmas.

On December 26, she departed that port for return to Yankee Station. The *Coral Sea* continued combat operations into January 1967, then returned to Alameda on February 23, 1967.

The *Coral Sea* was adopted by the City of San Francisco on July 24 in a colorful ceremony in the Rotunda of City Hall. This was the first time a U. S. Navy vessel that did not actually bear the city's name had been extended the hospitality to serve as an official representative of a city.

On July 26, 1967, the *Coral Sea* left Alameda for her third combat tour. With Carrier Air Wing 15 embarked she launched her aircraft in the Gulf of Tonkin against targets in Hanoi and Haiphong. She returned to San Francisco in April 1968. For meritorious service during the period August 13, 1967, to February 19, 1968, the *Coral Sea* and her embarked air wing received the Navy Unit Commendation.

The *Coral Sea*'s fourth combat cruise began on September 7, 1968. The air war had changed considerably since the last cruise. President Johnson had ordered a bombing halt above the 18th parallel so the air group struck transhipment points along highways and ferries. On November 1, 1968, a complete bombing halt was ordered above the 17th parallel. Her last combat mission in the North was to strike the northernmost coastal defense sites on Hon Matt Island. Enemy troop concentrations, storage areas, and supply routes were hit in support of Allied forces in South Vietnam. The *Coral Sea* returned to Alameda, California, on April 18, 1969.

The *USS Coral Sea CVA-43* has received the following awards: The Navy Unit Commendation, the Navy Occupation Service Medal; the National Defense Service Medal; the Armed Forces Expeditionary Medal; the Vietnam Service Medal.

USS *Valley Forge* CV-45.

43

USS Valley Forge LPH-8 (CV-45)

Construction of the *Valley Forge* began on September 7, 1944, at the Philadelphia Naval Shipyard; her name commemorates the winter headquarters of General George Washington during the Revolutionary War.

Mrs. A. A. Vandergrift, wife of the Marine Corps Commandant, christened the carrier November 18, 1945. Captain John W. Harris took command during commissioning ceremonies on November 3, 1946.

On January 24, 1947, the *Valley Forge* departed Norfolk for shakedown operations in the Caribbean. Exhaustive evaluations were made in gunnery, damage control, and engineering departments, while the crew

sharpened their naval seamanship skills. On March 17 the carrier participated in a battle problem, then returned to Norfolk for final post-shakedown alterations, which were completed on July 14.

The *Valley Forge* was then temporarily assigned to the operational development forces for ten days, during which time she embarked Night Composite Squadron Two for experimental tests. Next came a tour with the Pacific Fleet. She transited the Panama Canal on August 5 and sailed into San Diego a short time later.

On October 9 she began the first leg of her first

Western Pacific cruise, arriving at Pearl Harbor to train her air group for two months. Navy Day was celebrated at Hawaii and over 3000 guests toured the ship.

On January 16, 1948, the *Valley Forge* departed the Hawaiian paradise and arrived at Sydney, Australia, 13 days later. Her next stop was Hong Kong on the 18th where the crew enjoyed rest and relaxation. The carrier was assigned to Task Force 38, the first task force to embark on a world cruise since the Great White Fleet was dispatched by Teddy Roosevelt in 1907.

On March 10 the carrier cleared Singapore and was at Ceylon from the 15th to the 17th. The next stop was the Persian Gulf, Ras Tanura, on the 24th. Two days later she and her escorts headed for the Mediter-

ranean. After transiting the Suez Canal (the first carrier to do so) on April 3–4, she arrived at Gibraltar on the 11th. Before returning stateside she paid visits to Portsmouth, England, and Bergen, Norway.

On May 1, 1950 the *Valley Forge* steamed westward from San Diego en route to another peacetime cruise of the Western Pacific. On June 26 she was resting at anchor in Hong Kong harbor; this was the fateful day the Communists invaded the Republic of Korea. The *Valley Forge* was instantly underway for Subic Bay for supplies, thence to the war-torn Korean peninsula.

The initial offensive mission of the Korean conflict was launched from the *Valley Forge* on July 3. These planes provided close air support and bombed North Korean targets. These air strikes continued to November 19 during which time Carrier Air Group 5 flew

Three-Quarters view of the *USS Valley Forge CV-45* with crewmen preparing planes for Korean strike.

5283 combat missions and dropped 1500 tons of ordnance.

On December 1 the carrier returned to home port at San Diego, but due to the increasing war tempo she was off on another patrol two days later. On December 6, with nearly 100 planes of Carrier Air Group 2 aboard, she steamed back to Korea.

On December 22 the carrier joined Task Force 77 for a ten-month cruise. More than 2580 sorties were flown over Seoul, Wonsan, Hungnam, and the Choisan Reservoir.

On March 29, 1951, the *Valley Forge* returned to home port, then underwent an overhaul at the Puget Sound Naval Shipyard.

She became the only carrier to start a third Korean war cruise on December 11. During this tour her air group ran a series of attacks against Communist-operated railroads.

The carrier engaged in "Operation Blueheart" and the air group attacked the Communist capital of Pyongyang.

Ensign John Abbot of the carrier's air group was credited with single-handedly destroying nine locomotives. The destruction of trains was vital in blocking the advance of enemy ground units.

The *Valley Forge* returned to home port on July 3, 1952. Then on January 2, 1953, she launched strikes at enemy targets during her fourth Korean tour. Three months earlier she had been reclassified CVA-45.

Daily air support missions were directed against such familiar battle areas as Finger Ridge and Capital Hill. Main supply arteries were severed along the Korean coast while 3700 tons of bombs rained from *Valley Forge* jets above.

The carrier returned to San Diego on June 25 with the distinct honor of being the only carrier to complete four Korean War cruises. She was awarded the Navy Unit Commendation for exceptionally meritorious service during her operations in Korea from July 3, 1950 to June 5, 1953.

After a brief rest period the *Valley Forge* transited the Panama Canal and reported to the Norfolk Navy Yard for Atlantic Fleet duty.

From August 17 to September 4 she hosted 4000 Midshipmen on a training cruise to Halifax, Nova Scotia. Upon her return she entered Portsmouth Navy Yard for conversion and was redesignated CVS-45 on November 12.

In January 1954 the *Valley Forge* rejoined the Atlantic Fleet and began refresher training near Cuba until July 21, when she deployed for the annual midshipmen cruise.

The carrier sailed to the Mediterranean during September; highlighting this cruise was the NATO ASW exercise "Operation Blackjack." The usual ports of call were visited before she returned to Norfolk on November 11.

On January 3, 1955, the *Valley Forge* began "Operation Springboard" in the Caribbean and the crew was able to enjoy liberty at St. Thomas, Virgin Islands, and Kingston, Jamaica. ASW maneuvers were conducted off the Atlantic seaboard until February 14.

The *Valley Forge* departed Norfolk on September 7 and joined Canadian, British, French, and Portuguese ships in the North Atlantic off the Iberian Peninsula for the NATO ASW exercise, "Operation Springboard." She returned to Norfolk in October.

During the spring of 1956 the carrier conducted ASW operations off the Virginia Capes, and on May 22 participated in "Operation Petticoat." This was a dependents' cruise and the first to be conducted on an ASW carrier in the Atlantic Fleet.

Routine training exercises were held throughout early 1957, and during the summer, West Point Cadets and Annapolis Midshipmen embarked for their annual cruise.

The *Valley Forge* scored another "first" off Guantanamo Bay in October when her landing party was ferried ashore by HR28 Marine helicopters.

During February 1958, she was active in ASW operations off the Atlantic coast. In March, 1392 Marines were embarked to participate in a major amphibious exercise called LANTPHIBEX 1-58.

On April 1 the *Valley Forge* became the flagship of Task Group ALFA, under the command of Rear Admiral John S. Thach.

September 8–October 11 she underwent a yard overhaul at Norfolk, then resumed normal duties on October 19. On November 26 she was back at Norfolk for a four-week maintenance period.

On January 5, 1959 the *Valley Forge* collided with a merchant vessel during very stormy weather conditions. Considerable damage to the carrier's flight deck sent her into the New York Naval Yard, where a section of flight deck from the decommissioned *USS Franklin AVT-8* replaced the damaged portion of the wounded ship.

Anti-submarine warfare training resumed until June 30, when Midshipmen from Annapolis and various civilian colleges came aboard for their two-week cruise.

From October 10 to November 18 the carrier underwent a yard period at the New York Naval Yard, followed by routine ASW operations until December 29.

The *Valley Forge* departed Norfolk on January 21, 1960, to participate in "Operation Skylark" in the Caribbean. A civilian scientist team launched three of the world's largest balloons, which ascended 22 miles and carried nuclear emulsion designed to record primary cosmic rays high above the earth's surface. The scientific phase of this operation was directed by Dr. Marcel Schien of the University of Chicago.

On June 9 a three-month Midshipman cruise began off the Mediterranean and was concluded August 30. During this tour, in July, members of the Central European Nations Treaty Organization (CENTO) came aboard to observe ASW operations.

On December 19, helicopters from the carrier recovered the nose cone of a missile launched from Cape Canaveral. Two days later the tanker SS *Pine Ridge* was breaking up in heavy seas off Cape Hatteras and the *Valley Forge* rushed to the scene and rescued 28 survivors.

The carrier reported to Norfolk on March 6, 1961, for conversion to an amphibious assault ship—LPH (Landing Helicopter Platform). She was officially reclassified LPH-8 on July 1 and departed the shipyard to become part of the newly developed military tactics force of vertical envelopment.

On September 26 she sailed from Norfolk as flagship of the Caribbean Ready Squadron and cruised near the shores of the Dominican Republic October 21–25 and November 18–29. She conducted those operations necessary to prepare for the overthrow of the Trujillo regime.

The *Valley Forge* departed Norfolk on January 6, 1962, and travelled to her new home port at Long Beach, California, arriving on the 23rd. After training for nine weeks off the California coast, she departed on April 16 to join the Seventh Fleet in the Western Pacific. She was designated flagship of Ready Amphibious Task Group 76.5 on May 7.

While operating in the Gulf of Siam ten days later the carrier landed Marines in Thailand, about 400 miles south of Bangkok. These troops were withdrawn in July. The carrier returned to home port in December, and spent the first six weeks of 1963 involved in major amphibious operations. From February 28 to March 12 she participated in "Operation Steel Gate" off Camp Pendleton; April 1–10 it was "Operation Dirt Road" off Hawaii; and June 3–14 it was "Operation Windsock" off Camp Pendleton.

On July 1 she entered the Long Beach Naval Shipyard for a $9 million FRAM II conversion. The acronym means Fleet Rehabilitation and Modernization overhaul. The expensive facelifting was completed on

After part of *Valley Forge LPH-8*; flight deck with Marines during Operation Dirt Road off the coast of Hawaii.

January 27, 1964, and the carrier resumed training out of home port.

On March 20 she deployed for another tour to the Far East. She relieved the *USS Iwo Jima LPH-2* at Buckner Bay, Okinawa, then stopped briefly in Hong Kong. From May 29 to June 7 she was engaged in "Operation LIGTAS," a combined SEATO exercise. On August 5, several North Vietnamese PT-boats attacked the *USS Maddox DD-721* in the Gulf of Tonkin and the *Valley Forge* took station in the South China Sea off the Vietnam coast. Aircraft from the *USS Ticonderoga CVA-14* and *USS Constellation CVA-64* repelled the PT boat attack. After 57 days at sea the *Valley Forge* returned to Subic Bay for maintenance. She was awarded the Armed Forces Expeditionary Medal for her support during the Tonkin Gulf crisis. On November 5 she returned to Long Beach, California.

SILVER LANCE—the largest Navy-Marine Corps operation—was conducted from February 23 to March 12, 1965, and the *Valley Forge* played a major role in the exercise, thereby proving her high state of combat readiness. Following the exercise she sailed to Hawaii.

At Pearl Harbor she received cargo, aircraft, and troops, then proceeded to Yokosuka, Japan, where the planes were off loaded. On April 17 she returned to home port in California.

The Vietnam situation was deteriorating rapidly and on May 24 the *Valley Forge* once again aimed her bow towards the Far East. After a stopover at Okinawa to off load 1700 Marines she headed for home port, arriving July 1.

USS Valley Forge LPH-8.

July 20–22 the carrier participated in Exercise Heliex 66W off Camp Pendleton, California. The purpose of this operation was to provide afloat amphibious training to Marine Corps Reserve Units.

Throughout August the carrier prepared for an extended period of duty in the Western Pacific and on September 1 she departed San Diego and steamed to the troubled waters of the South China Sea. During October and November she underwent an intensive training program including a full scale amphibious landing exercise which was completed on November 4.

The *Valley Forge* departed Subic Bay two days later and joined other Seventh Fleet units near the coast of South Vietnam. She was active in "Operation Blue Marlin," in which she became a standby reserve unit. Throughout December the assault ship embarked Marines who participated in "Operation Dagger Thrust" and "Harvest Moon."

On January 8, 1966, the carrier returned to Subic Bay and then participated in a major amphibious exercise called Hilltop III off Mindoro, Philippines. Afterwards, the *Valley Forge* returned to the coastal waters off Vietnam and began special exercises in "Operation Double Eagle I."

The particular operation was the most elaborate amphibious operation since the Korean conflict. The carrier returned to Subic Bay and was relieved by the *USS Princeton LPH-5*

After a quick jaunt back to Vietnam to deliver supplies, the *Valley Forge* entered the Navy yard at Yokosuka for maintenance and repairs.

She departed Japan on March 26 and sailed to home port at Long Beach, arriving on April 9. In June she resumed amphibious training preparatory to her next Western Pacific cruise.

On August 15, 1966, the *Valley Forge* was flagship

for the largest amphibious exercise held on the West Coast, Exercise Silver Point III. On September 7, the *Valley Forge* left Long Beach for a short cruise to the Western Pacific. After a brief call at Pearl Harbor, she steamed to Okinawa with troops and supplies. She left Okinawa on October 6 and participated in operation Hilltop III off Mindoro. She also took part in rescue operations when two ships collided in Manila Bay on October 25. The *Valley Forge* celebrated her 20th birthday while at sea on November 3, 1966. After a four-day stay at Hong Kong from November 14 to 18, the *Valley Forge* returned to Long Beach on December 1, 1966.

She entered the Long Beach Naval Shipyard on December 18 for a major overhaul, which included the installation of a new flight deck and air conditioning of all major spaces. She left the yard on July 14, 1967, to conduct refresher training under the supervision of the Fleet Training Group out of San Diego. Upon completion of the training exercises, the *Valley Forge* re-entered the Navy Yard at Long Beach for minor repairs.

On November 10, 1967, the *Valley Forge* left Long Beach for another cruise to the Far East. During this cruise, she participated in six operations with units of the Seventh Fleet off Vietnam. They were: Fortress Ridge, Badger Tooth, Badger Catch I, II, III, and Swift Saber. She paid a short visit to Hong Kong, Japan, and the Philippines before returning to Long Beach in February 1968. She set a new record on the cruise of 65 days on the line on Yankee Station.

From March to July 1968 the *Valley Forge* took part in Operations Badger Catch II, III, and Swift Saber. She remained in the Long Beach shipyard in August for upkeep and preparing for her January 1969 deployment to the Western Pacific. Upon her return to Long Beach, the *Valley Forge* resumed ASW operations off the coast of Southern California the remainder of the year. After 23 years of service to her country, the *USS Valley Forge LPH-8* was decommissioned on January 15, 1970, stricken from the list of Navy ships, and disposed of for scrap.

The *Valley Forge LPH-8* received the following awards: The Navy Unit Commendation; the Meritorious Unit Commendation; Navy Occupation Service Medal; China Service Medal; Korean Service Medal with eight battle stars; United Nations Service Medal; National Defense Service Medal; Armed Forces Expeditionary Service Medal; Vietnam Service Medal; and the Republic of Korea Presidential Unit Citation Badge.

The *USS James E. Kyes* DD-787 alongside the *USS Philippine Sea* CV-47 in Korean waters.

44

USS Philippine Sea AVT-11 (CV-47)

The Battle of the Philippine Sea was a violent struggle on June 19–20, 1944, and two months later construction began on the carrier that would commemorate that battle.

The keel of the *USS Philippine Sea CV-47* was laid down on August 19, 1944, at the Bethlehem Steel Company, Quincy, Massachusetts.

Mrs. Albert B. Chandler, wife of the Kentucky Senator, christened the new carrier on September 5, 1945. On May 11, 1946, Captain Delbert S. Cornwell took the helm and the carrier was commissioned.

In June the *Phil Sea* went to Quonset Point, Rhode Island, where Air Group 20 reported aboard, followed by a shakedown cruise near Guantanamo Bay. On November 20, 1946, she returned to the Boston Navy Yard for alterations and to prepare for "Operation High Jump," the Navy's first Antarctic Expedition. Rear Admiral Richard E. Byrd and his staff were embarked on January 2, 1947, and the carrier sailed for Little America.

On January 29 the *Phil Sea* arrived in the Antarctic, where Admiral Byrd and his party were launched from the ship in six R4D planes. The carrier then returned to Quonset Point.

Air Group 9 came aboard in April and began training operations in the Caribbean until July when the carrier sailed into the Brooklyn Navy Yard for an overhaul that was completed in November.

In February 1948 the *Philippine Sea* deployed on her first Mediterranean cruise during which Rear Admiral Ralph Jennings, Commander Carrier Division Four, was aboard with his staff. The carrier operated as a unit of the Sixth Fleet and visited France, Greece, Tunisia, and Sicily before returning to the Boston Navy Yard in June.

Operational Development Force 4 was embarked following the yard overhaul. It was their job to develop a new carrier control approach system. This is a seagoing equivalent to the Ground Control Approach system use at airports. The tests were completed in October and the *Phil Sea* then conducted cold-weather exercises off the Arctic Circle during November and December.

In January 1949 the carrier once again headed for the Mediterranean, where Admiral J. J. Clark, Commander Carrier Division Four, and Air Group 7 were embarked. Operations continued with the Sixth Fleet until May when the carrier returned to Boston for an overhaul.

The last four months of the year were spent in the Caribbean conducting operational development projects with jet aircraft, interspersed with exercises in the North Atlantic with the fleet.

During the first three months of 1950 the *Philippine Sea* handled carrier qualifications off the Atlantic seaboard and the Caribbean. During April and May the carrier hosted the Secretary of the Navy, the Armed Forces Industrial College, the War College, and the Armed Forces Staff College. These various civilian and military guests received a demonstration of the ship's warfare capabilities.

On May 24 the carrier departed Norfolk, and arrived in San Diego via the Panama Canal on June 10. Rear Admiral W. F. Boone, Commander Carrier Division Five, and staff were embarked and Air Group 11 reported aboard on July 3. Two days later the carrier

headed for the Western Pacific via Pearl Harbor to join United Nations Task Force 77. At Hawaii Admiral Boone and his staff left the ship.

The *Philippine Sea* received her first exposure to combat on August 5 as her air group was launched for strikes against railroad and communication centers, in addition to providing air support to Army and Marine ground troops. In November, when the Communists advanced southwards through the middle of the Korean Peninsula, the *Philippine Sea*'s pilots provided air cover during the Marines' withdrawal to Hangnom.

During this cruise the carrier launched as many as 140 daily combat sorties. Thousands of bombs, rockets, and napalm were dropped over strategic enemy targets. Lieutenant Tom Amen of the *Phil Sea*'s air group was the first Navy pilot to down a Russian-built MIG-16.

Rear Admiral E. C. Ewen, Commander Carrier Division One, transferred his flag to the *USS Valley Forge CV-45* on February 25, 1951. One month later the *Philippine Sea* became the flagship of Vice Admiral H. M. Martin, Commander of the mighty Seventh Fleet. Air Group 2 relieved Air Group 11 and the carrier departed Yokosuka to resume operations against the Communists over Formosa.

On June 9 the *Phil Sea* arrived at the San Francisco Naval Shipyard following a record crossing from Yokosuka in 7 days, 13 hours. Next came a three-month overhaul.

On December 31 the *Philippine Sea* sailed from San Francisco to rejoin the United Nations Task Force 77. The most significant operation during this cruise was her participation in strikes against Communist hydroelectric plants at Shiho, Kyson, Fusen, and Kojo. The task force cooperated with Marine Corps and Air Force planes to concentrate on attacks to these targets, which produced 60 percent of the hydroelectric power to Manchuria.

February–July 1952 the *Phil Sea* pilots struck communications, supply, and transportation networks of North Korea. On August 8 the carrier returned to San Diego where on October 1 she was redesignated CVA-47.

On December 15 the *Philippine Sea* deployed on her third Korean war cruise and during the next six months conducted air strikes until July 27, 1953, when the cease fire was signed.

The carrier arrived at Alameda, California, on August 14 and released the air group. Shortly afterwards, she entered the yards at San Francisco for an overhaul.

From January 9 to March 12, 1954, the *Phil Sea* operated off the California coast and was then sched-

USS Philippine Sea with VS-37 flying overhead.

uled for another Western Pacific cruise. She arrived at Manila on April 22 and then cruised the Philippine Seas until June.

The cease fire order of July 21 had terminated the Korean fighting, but Communist planes shot down a Cathay-Pacific Airways passenger plane near Hainan Island off the China coast. The carrier rushed to rescue survivors. Five days later two F4Us and 11 ADs from the *Phil Sea* were attacked by a pair of Chinese fighter planes. The American pilots were under strict orders to engage in combat only if attacked so the AD pilots returned the fire and destroyed the two aggressors.

The carrier received a short yard period in Yokosuka, then in November she returned to San Diego.

In April 1955, Air Group 2 came aboard and the carrier deployed on her fifth Western Pacific cruise, arriving at Yokosuka on May 2, where she began operations

with the Seventh Fleet. Joint exercises were held with the Chinese Nationalist Forces off Formosa. On November 11 the *Phil Sea* departed Yokosuka and returned to San Diego 12 days later.

While en route to home port on November 15 she received word of her reclassification to CVS-47. She went to the yards for installation of ASW equipment and on January 1, 1956, began antisubmarine warfare maneuvers off the coast of California.

For the next three years the *Philippine Sea* was active with the Second Fleet in San Diego and the Seventh Fleet in the Far East. In December 1958 she was decommissioned in the San Diego Group of the Pacific Reserve Fleet. On May 15, 1959, she was redesignated AVT-11—Auxiliary Aircraft Transport. On December 1, 1969, the *Philippine Sea* was stricken from the list of Navy ships and disposed of for scrap.

Aerial of *USS Philippine Sea CVA-47* at sea off North Korea.

The *USS Philippine Sea AVT-11* has received the Navy Unit Commendation; China Service Medal (extended); Korean Service Medal; United Nations Service Medal; National Defense Service Medal; and the Republic of Korea Presidential Unit Citation Badge.

SAIPAN CLASS OF 1943

Construction of two new light carriers, the *USS Saipan CVL-48* and *USS Wright CVL-49*, was authorized on September 18, 1943. The design of the two ships was similar to the *Independence*-class light carriers but major differences put them into a class of their own.

The hull below the main deck was designed like the hulls of the *Baltimore*-class heavy cruisers. The major difference between the *Saipan* class and *Independence* class light carriers is that the Saipan class ships were designed, laid down, and built as light carriers, whereas the *Independence*-class carriers were originally laid down as light cruisers and reordered to be completed as aircraft carriers.

The *Saipan* was commissioned on July 14, 1946, and the *Wright* on February 9, 1947. When commissioned the carriers displaced 14,500 tons standard and 19,600 tons full load. Overall length, 684½ feet; beam 77 feet; draft, 28 feet; width, 109 feet; armament, two 40mm quadruple mounts and nine 40mm twin mounts; aircraft, 50; complement, 234 officers and 1487 enlisted men.

Built too late to see service in the Second World War, both ships operated as training carriers and saw service in the Korean waters following the cease fire. The *Wright* was decommissioned on March 15, 1956 and placed in the Bremerton Group of the Pacific Reserve Fleet. She remained in the mothball fleet until March 15, 1962, on which date she entered drydock in the Puget Sound Naval Shipyard to undergo conversion to a command ship. She was redesignated CC-2 on September 1, 1962 and recommissioned *USS Wright CC-2* on May 11, 1963.

The *Saipan* was decommissioned on October 3, 1957, and placed in the Bayonne, New Jersey, Group of the Atlantic Reserve Fleet. A contract was granted to the Alabama Dry Dock and Shipbuilding Company of Mobile, Alabama, on February 13, 1963 to convert the *Saipan* into a command ship. The *Saipan* entered the shipyard on March 30, 1963 and was redesignated CC-3 on January 1, 1964. While under conversion to a command ship, the *Saipan* was redesignated a Major Communications Relay Ship AGMR-2 on September 1, 1964. Her name was changed to *Arlington* on April 8, 1965, and she was commissioned *USS Arlington AGMR-2* on August 27, 1965.

While in Reserve, the *Saipan* and *Wright* were reclassified AVT-6 and AVT-7, respectively, but neither of the two ships saw service in the capacity of Auxiliary Aircraft Carriers.

Both ships still have the original statistics except they no longer carry aircraft and the complement is 746 men plus 1000 for the staff of command or communications personnel.

Aerial of *USS Saipan CVL-48* entering New York Harbor (April 1948).

45

USS Arlington AGMR-2 (CVL-48)

The *USS Arlington AGMR-2*, presently a major communications ship, was originally commissioned and served for 12 years as an aircraft carrier bearing the name *USS Saipan CVL-48*.

Her keel was laid in New Jersey at the New York Shipbuilding Company and on July 8, 1945, Mrs. John W. McCormack, wife of the Congressman from Massachusetts and then Majority Leader of the House of Representatives (Mr. McCormack later served as Speaker of the House) christened the new light carrier.

Captain John G. Crommelin took command on July 14, 1946, and the *USS Saipan CVL-48* was commissioned into the U.S. Navy at Philadelphia.

The *Saipan* was the prototype of a new type of aircraft carrier and her name commemorates the Battle for Saipan, fought in the Marianas from June 15 to

July 9, 1944. Her hull design is that of a modified *Baltimore*-class heavy cruiser.

As a light carrier the *Saipan* stretched out 684 feet with an extreme width at the flight deck of 115 feet. She displaced 14,500 tons with a draft of 28 feet and could maintain 30 knots. The carrier carried 234 officers and 1487 enlisted men. The main armament battery was never installed but she did have five 40mm quadruple antiaircraft mounts and ten twin 40mm mounts. She could serve 50 airplanes effectively.

On August 17, 1946, the *Saipan* was underway from Philadelphia to begin her first series of air operations. Her Air Officer, Commander Harden, was the first to land aboard the new carrier when he flew an F4U *Corsair* to the ship on August 18. The carrier arrived at Pensacola, Florida, 13 days later, and spent eight months training student aviators.

Naval aviation cadets on board the *USS Saipan CVL-48;*
flight deck officer gives the signal to a cadet as he prepares
to take off in an SNJ.

By April 4, 1947, the carrier had logged more than 12,000 arrested landings. She returned to Norfolk on May 5, then steamed to Philadelphia for a yard overhaul that was completed October 23.

She sailed back to Pensacola and resumed air training until December 17. Four days later she returned to Norfolk and joined the Operational Development Force to assist in the development of jet operational techniques.

The *Saipan* took a break in this schedule on February 7, 1948, and went to La Guaira, Venezuela. Aboard at the time was Mr. MacLeish, the U.S. Minister and special representative of President Harry S Truman, and would attend the Presidential Inaugural cere-

monies at Caracas on February 15. The carrier then returned briefly to Norfolk on the 24th.

On April 18 the *Saipan* arrived at New York and relieved the *USS Mindoro CVE-120* as flagship of Carrier Division Seventeen. The next day she headed for Quonset Point, arriving May 3 and embarked Fighter Squadron 17A. That afternoon she launched FH-1 jets and thereby introduced the first complete squadron of jet fighters into regular fleet operations from an aircraft carrier. Five days later she went back to Norfolk and the Commander of Carrier Division Seventeen transferred his flag back to the *Mindoro*.

A cursory Operational Development cruise was made off the New England coast. From June 30 to

November 1 the carrier was at Norfolk for an over-haul.

On January 27, 1949 the *Saipan* began training operations off Guantanamo Bay and returned to Norfolk March 10.

On May 10 the carrier began a training cruise to Canada with Naval Reservists aboard. She arrived six days later at Quebec and hosted 1500 Canadians, who toured the ship on the 17th. One of the visitors was U.S. Ambassador Steinhardt, and Brigadier General Jean Allard, HMRCA. The carrier returned to Norfolk on May 28, and continued operations off the Virginia Capes, interspersed with brief cruises to Pensacola and Cuba.

On March 6, 1951, the *Saipan* was designated flagship of Carrier Division 14 and deployed for a tour of duty with the Sixth Fleet in the Mediterranean. Ports of call included Gibraltar, Italy, Algiers, and Sicily. On June 8 she returned to Norfolk and later resumed training operations off the Florida coast.

The *Saipan* departed Norfolk on January 21, 1952, for operations near Greenland. In February she participated in convoy exercises near Trinidad. From June 3 to August 4 she hosted a Midshipman cruise to Torquay, England; Dublin, Ireland, and Guantanamo

Bay. Upon her return to Norfolk she underwent an overhaul from August 26 to December 11. Training operations resumed off Guantanamo Bay until June 8, 1953, when the *Saipan* joined the *USS Missouri BB-63* for a Midshipman training cruise. Ports of call were made at Santos, Brazil, the Panama Canal, and Cuba. On August 4 the carrier returned to Norfolk and prepared for a world cruise.

The *Saipan* departed Norfolk on September 28, transited the Panama Canal and arrived at Yokosuka, Japan, via San Diego and Hawaii on November 30. She tied up at Inchon, Korea, on February 21, 1954, where she received the 8th Army's Chief of Staff, Brigadier General T. L. Sherburne.

The *Saipan* supported Marine Division assault landing exercises off Iwo Jima before returning to Yokosuka on March 27. She was at sea again on April 13 and arrived at Tourane Bay, French Indo-China, five days later. She then visited Manila, Japan, Singapore, Columbo, and Aden. After transiting the Panama Canal she went to Naples, Ville Franche, Barcelona, and Lisbon. On July 9, she headed for the States, arriving at Mayport, Florida on July 24.

On October 13 the *Saipan* rushed to the scene of Hurricane Hazel, which had all but destroyed Haiti.

USS Saipan underway at sea.

USS Arlington AGMR-2.

For seven days the carrier launched mercy flights, providing food, medicine, and doctors to the unfortunate victims. The government there voted the *Saipan* a member of the Order of Merit of the Republic of Haiti on October 22, before the carrier returned to Norfolk.

From November 1, 1954, to March 14, 1955, the *Saipan* received an overhaul, then began refresher training near Guantanamo Bay. She arrived at Pensacola on June 6 for duty as a training carrier with the Naval Air Training Command.

Another mercy mission began on September 30 when the *Saipan* rushed to British Honduras—the victim of Hurricane Janet. En route to the disaster area she was ordered to divert her course towards Mexico and assist the citizens of Tampico and Vera Cruz, where damage was more severe than at Honduras. Upon arrival, the *Saipan* launched aircraft for eight days, delivering a million pounds of food and medicine and 81 medical teams. Over 3000 individual helicopter flights were conducted, which rescued 6171 persons. The *Saipan* was presented a scroll of Honor and Merit for her humanitarian efforts from the Mexican Red Cross.

On October 12 the carrier resumed her training duties at Pensacola and continued until April 1, 1957.

Tragedy struck on February 5, 1957, when Captain William R. Kane, the *Saipan's* commanding officer, was killed during a crash landing attempt at Kaysville, Georgia. He was succeeded by Captain Geoffrey P. Norman.

The *Saipan* departed the Pensacola Naval Training Base on April 1, 1957, after serving there for ten years and eight months. She entered the Bayonne Annex of the New York Shipyard four days later to begin overhaul prior to deactivation. On October 30 she was officially placed in reserve and stripped of her commission.

On May 15, 1959 the *Saipan* was reclassified AVT-6 —Auxiliary Aircraft Transport. She remained in the Reserve Fleet until March 30, 1963, when she was moved to the Alabama Drydock and Shipbuilding Company for conversion to a Command Ship with a new designation, CC-3. While the conversion process was taking place she was again reclassified to AGMR-2, which made her a major communications ship on September 1, 1964. At the final stage of the overhaul the ship received a new name on April 8, 1965. She was now the *USS Arlington AGMR-2.*

On August 12, 1966 the *Arlington* departed Mobile, Alabama, and entered the yards at Portsmouth, Virginia. Fifteen days later she was recommissioned with Captain Charles A. Darrah in command.

From September to December the *Arlington* remained at the Norfolk Navy Yard for alterations. Her dimensions were now altered from her days as a carrier.

The *Arlington* has an overall length of 684 feet. Her width (antenna deck) is 115 feet and beam (main deck) is 77 feet 5 inches. She displaces 14,500 tons with a draft of 28 feet and a speed of 33 knots. Her propulsion comes from steam turbines providing 120,000 total shaft horsepower with four screws. The crew comprises 47 officers and 948 enlisted men.

The mission of the *Arlington* is to serve as an Operational Communications Relay Ship. She provides the Fleet with modern, reliable, rapid, and secure communications, and is capable of operating for long periods of time at sea. She can augment existing shore-based communications services or substitute for services that become incapacitated. Equipped with a special antenna system she can act as an extension of vital fleet communications in areas where shore facilities do not exist.

In early January 1967, the *Arlington* departed Norfolk Navy Yard to begin training operations near Guantanamo Bay.

She operated with the Second Fleet for the next three years as a major communications replay ship, then she steamed for San Diego, where on January 14, 1970, she was decommissioned and placed in the San Diego Reserve Group of the Pacific Reserve fleet.

As the *USS Saipan CVL-48* the *Arlington* has received the Korean Service Medal, United Nations Service Medal, and the National Defense Service Medal.

USS Wright CVL-49.

46

USS Wright CC-2 (CVL-49)

The current *USS Wright AGMR-3* is the second U.S. Navy vessel named to honor the Wright Brothers.

The first *USS Wright AZ-1* was commissioned on December 16, 1920. Named for Wilbur Wright (1867–1912), the ship served as tender and flagship of Air Squadrons, Scouting Force, U.S. Atlantic Fleet and flagship for the Commander of that unit. On December 1, 1925, she was redesignated AV-1 (heavier than air

tender) and participated in the salvage operations of the *USS S-4* on March 17, 1927.

Captain Ernst J. King (later Fleet Admiral and the Navy's first CNO) was the ship's skipper at that time. In addition to Captain King, the list of commanding officers of the *Wright* is a Naval Who's Who: Commander Lamar R. Leahy (May 5, 1923–May 8, 1925); Captain Ernest D. McWhorter (June 1, 1928–June 8,

1929); Commander Aubrey W. Fitch (May 24–July 7; 1930); Lieutenant Commander DeWitt C. Ramsey (June 21–29, 1932); and Commander Marc A. Mitscher (May 29, 1937–Nov. 5, 1938).

All of these officers would later attain the rank of Admiral and lead the Navy through formidable struggles to victory in the Pacific during World War II.

The *Wright* saw action in that war, and on February 1, 1945, she was renamed *San Clemente AG-79* so that the name of *Wright* could be assigned to a new light aircraft carrier, *CVL-49*, then under construction. On August 19, 1948 the *San Clemente* was sold for scrap.

The keel of *CVL-49* was laid down on August 22, 1944. Mrs. Harold S. Miller, niece of the Wright brothers, christened the new carrier on September 1, 1945.

This ship would honor both Wilbur and Orville for their aviation accomplishments. On September 9, 1947, the *USS Wright CVL-49* was commissioned under the command of Captain Frank T. Ward.

The *Wright's* overall length was 684 feet with an extreme width at the flight deck of 115 feet. She displaced 14,500 tons with a draft of 28 feet and her speed was 33 knots. The carrier provides spaces for 234 officers and 1553 enlisted men. Armament consisted of a secondary battery of two 40mm quadruple mounts and nine 40mm twin mounts. No main battery was ever installed.

On March 18, 1947, the *Wright* departed Philadelphia and arrived for duty with the Naval Air Training Command, Pensacola, Florida, on March 31. Air defense drills, gunnery practice, and carrier qualifications for new pilots was the order of the day.

Throughout the summer the carrier embarked a total of 1081 Naval Reservists during three separate training cruises, each lasting two weeks. A Midshipmen cruise was made in September, and on October 15 she hosted 62 Army officers for a demonstration of naval flight operations.

On October 24, the *Wright* returned to the Philadelphia Navy Yard for post-shakedown alterations, which were completed November 17. She returned to Pensacola on December 23 and resumed training duties. Following one year in this role she steamed to Norfolk on January 26, 1949, for a four-month overhaul. In May, a brief refresher cruise was made to Cuba, and by August 1 she was again at Norfolk.

Two weeks of antisubmarine warfare training was held at Narragansett Bay, after which air operations began out of Quonset Point, Norfolk, Key West, and Pensacola. The *Wright* continued this duty until January 7, 1951, at which time she was relieved by the

USS Cabot CVL-28 at Pensacola. The *Wright* had qualified 2794 pilots for carrier operations, during which time she logged 20, 825 landings.

The *Wright* began her first Mediterranean cruise on January 10 and joined the Sixth Fleet at Gibraltar eleven days later. During this tour she was active in fleet training exercises and visited Algeria, Sicily, Crete, Lebanon, and France. On March 19, the *Wright* departed Golfe Juan and returned to Newport, Rhode Island, 12 days later. An extended yard overhaul began at Norfolk followed by a refresher cruise off Guantanamo Bay, Cuba.

From February 25 to March 21, 1952, the carrier participated in a convoy exercise beginning at Newport and continuing to Trinidad and the Panama Canal Zone.

June 9–27 the *Wright* was flagship of Carrier Division 14 and joined Hunter-Killer Task Group 8.4 for ASW operations off the Atlantic coast. On August 26 she rendezvoused with the Second Task Fleet for combined defense exercises with NATO forces.

The *Wright* returned to Quonset Point on July 1 and hosted several Naval Reserve units during ASW tactics. She continued this task until August 26, when she teamed with the Second Task Fleet commanded by Vice Admiral Felix B. Stump, en route to northern Europe. Four days later, she was temporarily detached from the task force and sailed to Port Lyautey, French Morocco, arriving September 4. Her mission was to shuttle equipment and personnel of Squadron VMF (N) 114 to that port. Upon completion she rejoined the task force on September 6 and sailed into the Firth of

USS Wright CC-2 (ex-CVL-49).

Clyde, Scotland, four days later. The *Wright* joined a combined defense exercise with two British destroyers in NATO's "Operation Mainbrace." Also participating were the British aircraft carriers *HMS Illustrious R-87* and *HMS Eagle R-05*. The group arrived at Rotterdam, Holland, on September 25. Four days later the *Wright* departed and sailed to Newport, arriving October 9.

From October 1952 to February 1954 the carrier held carrier qualifications off the Virginia Capes. On February 21 she arrived off Golfe Juan, France, for a month of training with the Sixth Fleet, returning to Norfolk in April. Carrier qualifications continued from May through July in the Gulf of Mexico and Mayport, Florida. On July 31 she entered the Philadelphia Navy Yard for a four-month overhaul.

On January 4, 1954 the *Wright* began refresher training off Guantanamo Bay until February 10. After 6½ years of Atlantic duty she departed Norfolk on April 5 to join the Pacific Fleet. She transited the Panama Canal and arrived at Yokosuka, Japan, on May 28 via San Diego and Hawaii.

Training operations were continuously held with the Seventh Fleet during this cruise and a short rest was taken at Hong Kong September 24–30. The *Wright* departed Yokosuka on October 15 and arrived at San Diego 14 days later. She then went to Long Beach for an overhaul, which was completed February 23, 1955.

As a member of Carrier Division 17, the *Wright* took part in air operations out of San Diego until May, then joined the *USS Mount McKinley AGC-27* as flagship of Task Group 7.3 to conduct the atomic test "Operation Wigwam" in the Pacific. On May 20 she returned to San Diego. She sailed to Mare Island Naval Shipyard on July 14 to undergo deactivation procedures. Then she went to the yards at Puget Sound on October 17 for the final phase of her decommissioning. The *Wright* was zipped up in mothballs on March 15, 1956, and berthed with the Bremerton group of the Pacific Reserve Fleet. On May 15, 1959, she was reclassified AVT-7—Auxiliary Aircraft Transport.

The *Wright* was moved on March 15, 1962, from her snug berth and underwent a major conversion as a command vessel. It took one year to complete the $16 million job. On September 1 she was reclassified CC-2.

On May 11, 1963, the *Wright* was recommissioned with Captain John L. Arrington at the helm. Rear Admiral Allan L. Reed, Assistant Chief of Naval Operations, called the *Wright* "the most capable command ship the world has ever known."

The carrier took a one-day jaunt for sea trials on May 28. Additional tests were held on June 12. On July 6 she was underway to conduct electronic tests. From that day to July 16 a test was run for cinching a calibration buoy in the Strait of Juan de Fuca between Vancouver, British Columbia, and Port Angeles, Washington. She returned to Puget Sound on the 19th.

On July 31 the *Wright* went to sea with the Pacific Fleet Inspection and Survey Board, which would evaluate preliminary acceptance trials. She returned to the yards on August 1. From August 30 to September 2 she paid a visit to Seattle, where the ship hosted an open house. On September 6 she was back at North Island Naval Air Station in San Diego.

For the next three weeks she underwent an extensive training schedule with members of the Pacific Fleet. On September 27 she headed for Puget Sound, arriving three days later.

On November 20, 1963 the *Wright* tied up alongside Bangor Pier at the Naval Ammunition Depot Bangor, Bremerton, Washington, to take on munitions. The Naval Ammunition Depot Bangor is located 13 miles north and west of Bremerton and the Puget Sound Naval Shipyard on the east side of Hood Canal. The ammunition depot has been engaged in ordnance operations on the Kitsap peninsula since 1908. Its mission is the receipt, storage and issue of ammunition to the fleet and other armed forces. The Depot is considered one of the Navy's principal outloading points because of unexcelled deep-water berthing facilities and isolated location.

Any ship that is to enter the Puget Sound Naval Shipyard at Bremerton for a yard overhaul stops at the Depot to offload ammunition. Upon completion of the yard period, the ship returns to Bangor and takes on ammunition prior to returning to the fleet.

It usually takes three days to offload ammunition from an aircraft carrier. Those who have spent those three days at Bangor have found the climate to be mild and damp, with rainfall quite heavy sometimes six or seven months of the year. But the lush green of the countryside and the bright colors of the maple and dogwood trees in autumn make a colorful and beautiful contrast to the various shades of the green conifers.

After munitions were loaded aboard, the *Wright* made a brief stop in Seattle, and was then underway on November 26 for Balboa, Canal Zone. While en route she received a distress call from the Israeli merchantship *SS Velos*, which requested medical aid. After changing course, the *Wright* intercepted the *Velos* later that afternoon and the ship's medical officer was flown aboard to treat a seaman.

On December 7 the *Wright* anchored at Panama Bay where later in the day she transited the Panama Canal and docked at Cristobal, where the crew enjoyed liberty. Two days later the *Wright* was officially transferred to the operational command of the Atlantic Fleet. A three-day visit was made to the Virgin Islands before she headed for Norfolk, arriving on the 15th.

Routine operations was held off the Atlantic coast until February 26, 1964, when she entered the yards at Norfolk. A four-month overhaul followed, which was completed in June.

Throughout the summer and into November she visited Annapolis, New York, and Boston, then headed back to Norfolk on December 21 for the holidays.

On January 5, 1965, the *Wright* conducted normal operations off the Virginia Capes. During the next month she cruised that area with periodic stops at Hampton Roads. On February 27 she again docked at the Norfolk Navy Yard and remained until August. She received a new communications system, which was tested through October and November. She returned to Norfolk on November 24.

The new SVLF communications system underwent another evaluation during January 1966, then on February 14 she sailed into Port Everglades, Florida, for a three-day visit. A local hospital was in need of blood and the crew donated 40 pints to the blood bank. The *Wright* returned to Norfolk on February 17.

From April 27 to May 25 she underwent a restricted availability test at Norfolk and received major alterations. Following the yard work she began testing her newly received TROPO antenna.

As a command ship the *Wright* serves as a mobile command post for top echelon commands for area or world-wide military operations. Facilities are provided for instant world-wide communications and rapid automatic exchange, processing, storage, and display of vital command data. On the after end of her flight deck are facilities for three helicopters.

The *USS Wright* as *CVL-49* received the Navy Occupation Service Medal; Korean Service Medal; United Nations Service Medal; and the National Defense Service Medal.

The keel of the USS *United States* CVA-58 was laid down for construction at the Newport News Shipbuilding and Dry Dock Company on April 14, 1949. She was to have a standard displacement of 65,000 tons; an overall length of 1090 feet; a flight deck length of 190 feet, capable of increase to 236 feet by means of retractable extensions. Speed was to be in excess of 33 knots and her expected cost was $189 million. On April 23, 1949, 19 days after the keel laying, construction of the *United States* was halted.

Fifteen months after cancellation of the *United States*, construction of a new class of carriers was authorized with the names *Forrestal* and *Saratoga* assigned to the first two hulls to be constructed.

The first carrier to be designed and built after the Second World War was ordered on July 12, 1951. She was named to honor the late Secretary of Defense James Forrestal. Original design included an axial flight deck and a small island structure that could be lowered during flight operations. By the time the *Forrestal's* keel was laid on July 14, 1952, new improved designs were developed, changing the carrier's earlier appearance. With the success of the experimental angle deck on the *Antietam,* an improved canted deck was included in the new design of the *Forrestal.* The island structure was also redesigned as a fixed structure. Four deck edge elevators and three

separate launching areas were included.

As compared with the *Midway*-class carriers in size, the *Forrestal* class is approximately 80 feet longer. Elevators are much larger and catapults and arresting gears are much more powerful. With the commissioning of the USS *Independence* CVA-62 on April 3, 1959, the *Forrestal* class was completed with four carriers:

USS *Forrestal* CVA-59   USS *Ranger* CVA-61
USS *Saratoga* CVA-60   USS *Independence* CVA-62

The cost for each ship was *Forrestal*, $218 million; *Saratoga*, $182 million; *Ranger*, $189,311,000; the *Independence*, $200 million.

The four carriers have a standard displacement of 60,000 tons and a full load displacement of 76,000 tons. Overall lengths are as follows: *Forrestal*, 1039 feet; *Saratoga*, 1046 feet; *Ranger* and *Independence* 1047 feet. They have a draft of 37 feet; beam 129½ feet; width across the flight deck, 252 feet. The armament consists of four 5-inch 54-calibre dual-purpose mounts. Depending on size, between 60 and 90 aircraft can be accommodated. Complement is 119 officers and 2540 enlisted men. The complement in wartime can be raised to 428 officers and 4155 enlisted men.

The *Forrestal* has entered her 14th year in commission and has undergone some modifications as have the other three carriers in the class. The forward 5 inch 54 calibre gun sponsons were removed from all four ships.

USS Forrestal CVA-59 ready to launch an F8H while on operations in the Caribbean Sea.

47

USS Forrestal CVA-59

James Vincent Forrestal was born on February 15, 1892, in Beacon, New York. He attended Dartmouth and Princeton before enlisting in the Navy in May 1917, and served in the U.S. and overseas until his discharge as a lieutenant in July two years later.

James Forrestal went to work in banking in New York City until June 1940, when he entered government service as an administrative assistant to President Roosevelt.

In August he became Under Secretary of the Navy and in May 1944 he was appointed the Secretary of the Navy. Forrestal was acclaimed for his brilliant work in building the world's largest Navy. In September 1947 he became the first Secretary of Defense,[1] a position he held until his resignation in March 1949.

1. The Department of Defense was created September 18, 1947. The Departments of the Army, Navy, and Air Force were thus combined into a single executive department.

Launching of the *USS Forrestal CVA-59* at Newport News,
Virginia. Mrs. James Forrestal, sponsor, christening ship.

The first of a new class of aircraft carriers was authorized for construction on July 12, 1951 and would honor the Secretary. The new carrier would incorporate techniques developed subsequent to World War II and was built from the keel up with an angle flight deck and an enclosed hurricane bow.

The keel was laid on June 14, 1952, at the Newport News Shipbuilding Company in Virginia. On December 11, 1954, Mrs. James V. Forrestal, christened the first postwar aircraft carrier, and on October 1, 1955, she was commissioned with Captain Roy L. Johnson commanding.

On January 3, 1956, Commander R. L. Werner made the first landing aboard the new carrier in his JF-3 *Fury* jet. Commander Werner was the C.O. of the carrier's first embarked air group.

A ten-week shakedown cruise began off Guantanamo Bay on January 24, 1956, and was completed on March 28. Following a final inspection by the Commander, Naval Air Force, Atlantic Fleet, she returned to the yards on May 4 where her original propeller shafts were replaced to improve performance.

From June to November the *Forrestal* qualified pilots for carrier operations. When the Egyptian crisis flared early in November, the carrier bolstered the deployed forces of the Atlantic Fleet. She returned to Norfolk in time to enjoy the Christmas holidays.

On January 23, 1957, the *Forrestal* departed Mayport, Florida, and began her first cruise to the Mediterranean. Assigned to the Sixth Fleet, she participated in underway demonstration cruises witnessed by numerous military observers from various nations. Stopovers were made at ten ports where curious spectators got a great view of the U.S. Navy's newest aircraft carrier. On July 22 the *Forrestal* returned to the States and entered the Portsmouth Navy Yard for maintenance.

Next came a month of training exercises off the North Carolina coast in August. Also, preparations were made for her September–October NATO exercise called "Strikeback." A brief rest came following these operations in the North Sea and the carrier visited Southhampton, England.

Over 65,000 Englishmen lined the dock when the carrier departed. The remainder of the year was spent in maneuvers off the Virginia Capes.

Early in 1958 the *Forrestal* was at the Norfolk Navy Yard, followed by operational training off the coasts of North Carolina, Georgia, and Florida.

On September 2 she departed Norfolk and sailed into Augusta Bay, Sicily, on the 16th to relieve the *USS Saratoga CVA-60*. While in Naples Harbor in October the *Forrestal* made naval history by repairing a major failure in her Number One catapult. This was the first time such an extensive repair effort had been accomplished away from a naval yard, and was handled through the combined efforts of the ship's crew and civilian technicians from the States.

While anchored at Barcelona, Spain, on December 2, Rear Admiral Roy L. Johnson relieved Rear Admiral Charles P. Griffin as Commander, Carrier Division Four. Johnson was no stranger to the carrier, as he had served as her first skipper in 1955.

In February 1959 there was a breakdown in the Number Two catapult, which resulted in another work period at Naples. When completed, the carrier participated in "Exercise Big Deal."

In March the *USS Franklin D. Roosevelt CVA-42* sailed into Pollensa Bay, Mallorca, to relieve the *Forrestal*. On March 12 the carrier returned to Norfolk and received her first inspection by the Bureau of Inspection and Survey.

On April 1, the *Forrestal* entered the yards at Norfolk for her first regular overhaul. While there, on May 9, Captain Samuel K. Brown, Jr., became the new commanding officer.

Following the yard work the carrier logged six weeks of refresher training off Guantanamo Bay, after which she resumed her normal pilot qualification duties. A weapons evaluation exercise was held in November followed by a one-day dependents' cruise before the holiday leave periods were granted.

On January 28, 1960, the *Forrestal* departed Norfolk for her third Mediterranean voyage, arriving at Cannes,

France, on February 14. She relieved the *USS Saratoga* on that date and on April 28 Captain R. E. Riera relieved Captain Brown.

The carrier visited seven countries and ten ports, and received her Battle Efficiency "E" before returning to Norfolk on August 3.

She moved to Hampton Roads on September 9, prior to entering the drydock at Norfolk. On October 30 she went to sea again with Secretary of the Navy John B. Connally aboard. The following day she was back at Norfolk to receive eight additional guests who observed flight operations. The Christmas holidays were spent at Norfolk where the crew received liberty.

In January 1961, the *Forrestal* sailed again and relieved the *Saratoga* on February 14 at Pollensa Bay. This was her fifth Mediterranean cruise and the crew was elated to learn that the Battle Efficiency "E" had been won for the second consecutive time. The carrier also captured Departmental "E's" in Gunnery, Operations, Engineering, and Air Operation. The Communications department was awarded its Green "C" award.

On March 21, Archbishop Makarios, President of Cyprus, came aboard at Limassol, as a guest of Vice Admiral George W. Anderson, Jr., Commander, Sixth Fleet, and Rear Admiral F. Massey, Commander Carrier Division Four.

On June 16, Captain Donald M. White became the new commanding officer at Palermo, Sicily, in a change of command ceremony witnessed by Undersecretary of the Navy Paul B. Fay.

On August 9, Secretary of the Navy John B. Connally again visited the ship and addressed the crew over the carrier's closed-circuit TV system.

Carrier Air Group 8 set a record 26,000 total flying hours during this cruise. Upon return to the States in September the carrier received an extensive overhaul a Portsmouth. Her arresting gear system was modified and the forward gun mounts were removed. She received an engine test facility, which was installed on the fantail.

On January 13, 1962, she departed the yards for a refresher cruise at Guantanamo Bay and for the next six weeks she tested all her shipboard equipment during underway exercises. While on a three-month Caribbean cruise she visited Haiti and participated in Project Mercury, in which John Glenn became the first American to orbit the earth.

In April Vice President Lyndon B. Johnson visited the *Forrestal* and reviewed a demonstration of the Navy's strategic mission on the high seas. A week later she joined the Second Fleet Atlantic exercise, Operation Lantphibex 1–62, and afterwards made a brief stop at Trinidad's Port of Spain.

On August 3 the *Forrestal* departed Norfolk and joined other carriers in the Mediterranean for "Operation Riptide III," which demonstrated the Navy's ability to interchange with NATO forces. Aircraft from France, the United Kingdom, and Portugal were used as the weapons teams and pilots worked as one unit. Upon conclusion of the exercise the *Forrestal* remained in the area for seven months.

While at Cannes, the carrier treated 300 children to a two day gala party.

Following various exercises with the Sixth Fleet the carrier then steamed to home port, arriving at Norfolk on March 2, 1963. She had travelled 48,000 nautical miles while her air group had logged 23,000 flight hours during 10,300 missions.

The carrier underwent a short maintenance period, then on May 4, Captain D. H. Guinn took over as the new C.O. One week later the *Forrestal* maneuvered up the narrow southern branch of the Elizabeth River and into a Norfolk drydock. She remained until June while minor repairs were made.

Throughout the summer the *Forrestal* operated from home port while qualifying pilots and providing additional training for her own air group. On September 9 she teamed with units of Task Force 23 and went to Boston for the annual convention of the East Coast Navy League. She was the largest ship that ever tied up at Boston. She returned to home port on September 19.

November found the *Forrestal* cruising the Eastern Seaboard with other units of the Second Fleet, before returning to homeport for holiday leaves.

On July 10, 1964, the carrier departed Norfolk and relieved the *USS Enterprise CVA (N)-65* at Pollensa Bay, Mallorca. She resumed normal duties with the Sixth Fleet and visited familiar ports. In March 1965, the *USS Shangri-La CVA-38* relieved the *Forrestal*, which returned to home port 12 days later to conclude seven months of overseas duty.

Stateside duties once again consisted of qualifying pilots for carrier operations.

Miss America of 1965, Vonda Kay Van Dyke of Phoenix, visited the *Forrestal* on May 11 at the Portsmouth Naval Shipyard. On August 14 a dependents' cruise was taken and ten days later the big ship was at sea heading for another Mediterranean voyage, with her first port of call at Naples.

While riding anchor at Genoa the *Forrestal* celebrated her tenth birthday on October 1. Throughout November and December she participated in various NATO exercises.

On January 15, 1966, the *Forrestal's* helicopter squadron (HG-2) rescued four U.S. Air Force officers from their wrecked plane atop Mount Helmos in Greece. On the 24th the carrier departed Taranto, Italy, with other ships of Task Group 60.2. General quarters was sounded on February 2 in a series of drill competitions. She returned to Naples three days later, and during a stop at Rome some of the crew attended an audience given by Pope Paul VI. Neighboring Pompeii, the Isle of Capri, and Mount Vesuvius also attracted the ship's company. On March 30 the *Forrestal* arrived at a designated position to await her relief carrier, *USS Saratoga*. Upon its arrival the *Forrestal* began briefing the *Saratoga's* officers and crew on recent operations, weapons air operations, engineering, and administration aspects of the Mediterranean deployments. Then the *Forrestal* transited the Gibraltar Strait on March 31 and headed homeward.

The Pier 12 area was inundated with cheering, eager friends and relatives as the giant carrier tied up on April 7. In nearby Portsmouth a $50 million overhaul was scheduled. Ammunition was removed April 11–14, then she steamed up the Elizabeth River and into the yards on April 15. By July 10, a third of the work had been accomplished and the carrier moved out of drydock.

The highly sophisticated Naval Tactical Data System (NTDS) arrived August 1, and upon its installation the carrier became the most modern ship afloat. With the NTDS she can launch and recover aircraft electronically and is also able to locate, identify, and track planes in her vicinity. Most valuable, however, is its ability to guide the *Forrestal's* planes to enemy planes more effectively than conventional radar systems.

The *Forrestal* celebrated her birthday in the shipyard with a cake measuring 11 feet in length and weighing over 4000 pounds. It was shaped like the carrier and devoured by the crew. On that occasion, Michael V. Forrestal, son of the late Secretary, addressed the crew.

On December 10–11 a simulated "cruise" was made at dockside preliminary to the actual drills to be used in future deployment.

On January 7, 1967, the *Forrestal* prepared for sea trials. Two days later she steamed to the Virginia Capes for five days of post-trial repairs, returning to the yards on the 14th.

It was 10:51 Saturday morning, July 29, 1967. The *Forrestal* was preparing for her second launch of the day off the coast of North Vietnam. During the preceding four days over 150 missions had been completed by Carrier Air Wing 17 against enemy targets. Aircrewmen were hustling about the deck to prepare planes for the launch. It would never come.

Suddenly smoke was seen on the aft section of the flight deck. At 11.01 a tremendous explosion rocked the 80,000-ton carrier. Twelve *Skyhawks,* seven *Phantoms* and two *Vigilantes* were in the disaster area and were fueled, armed, and manned with their engines whining. For some mysterious reason an A4 *Skyhawk* fuel tank was punctured and the stream of escaping fuel was instantly set ablaze. The entire aft portion of the carrier was engulfed in flames within seconds.

Lieutenant Commander Robert Browning was one of the pilots ready for launch. He was sitting in his plane when suddenly he heard a "whoosh," and saw an explosion in front of him. Two A4s instantly became balls of flame. A bomb dropped from one and rolled to a stop only six feet from the burning JP-5 jet fuel.

Browning leaped from his plane, ducked under the tails of two *Skyhawks* and ran up the flight deck towards the island. He was twice knocked down by explosions before he reached it.

In the immediate area were the destroyers *USS Rupertus DD-851* and *USS George K. MacKenzie DD-836,* which acted as plane guards. Also nearby were the *USS Oriskany CVA-34* and *USS Bon Homme Richard CVA-31.*

As the fuel-fed fires licked at the planes, attempts were made to extinguish the inferno. A chief petty officer, armed only with a small fire extinguisher, ran towards the bomb that had fallen from the *Skyhawk.* The chief and several members of a firefighting team nearby were killed when the bomb exploded. Shrapnel from the bomb was scattered 400 feet.

Lieutenant Commander Browning said he watched a dozen men run into the fire before the bomb went off.

Another explosion jarred the ship, giving the feeling that the whole stern had left the vessel. Rafts, fuel tanks, drop tanks, and debris of every description littered the water below. A helicopter from the *Oriskany* arrived to rescue crewmen, who had jumped, fallen or were knocked off the carrier.

Continuous explosions aboard the vessel rocked the helicopter and Lieutenant David Clements, the pilot, described the aft end of the carrier as "a mass of twisted steel with holes in the flight deck, a vacant space where there had been many aircraft, and a towering column of black smoke and flames."

At 11:47 A.M. the flight deck conflagration was under control. It was finally extinguished at 12:15 A.M. Fires continued on the 01 and 02 levels and in hangar bay three. This hangar bay fire was fed by clothing, bed-

ding, and other flammables, and the smoke and flames hampered a search for shipmates trapped in compartments.

Ensign Robert Schmidt, a 24-year-old engineering officer, said, "My work really wasn't the exciting kind of thing; just keeping the fire from spreading into any other areas. My people were doing all kinds of dirty work, moving into areas where the water was so hot it was almost boiling. OBA (oxygen breathing apparatus) windows started fogging up and the people could hardly see anything. Yet these kids went into the deeper areas of the ship endangering their own lives. . . ."

At 1:48 P.M. fires in the 01, 02 and 03 levels were still burning, but all the ship's machinery and steering gear were operational.

The after radio compartment was evacuated at 2:12 P.M. because of dense smoke and water. Fires at the 01 level were put out at that time.

The *Forrestal* set course for a rendezvous with the hospital ship *USS Repose* at 2:47. The Commander of Task Force 77 directed the carrier to proceed to Subic Bay after meeting the *Repose.*

By 8:30 P.M. the fires were still burning but were now under control. The flames in the 02 and 03 levels were still too hot for people to enter and holes were cut into the flight deck for access to compartments below.

Ensign Schmidt and his damage control party continued their efforts and stormed into the burning compartments. "I asked for volunteers," stated Schmidt, "and immediately had two or three men follow me back into the guts of the fire. Several times people would come up to me and ask, 'What can I do?' 'How can I help?' At first, I couldn't find work for all the people who wanted to help. I can't have enough praise for the sailors I supervised. They fought the fires and did all the dirty jobs. These kids worked all night, 24–28 hours, containing the fire. I have nothing but praise for the American sailor."

A chief petty officer in the hangar deck asked for five volunteers as he ran with water-soaked clothes from the fire area. Thirty men volunteered and rolled 250-pound bombs to the edge of the deck and pushed them over. Lieutenant Otis Knight, who only weighed 130 pounds, carried a 250-pound bomb to the edge and released it. His shipmates are certain that he could never repeat that feat.

At 8:33 fires in the 02 level were finally under control and by 8:54 medical evacuation to the *USS Repose AH-16* was in progress. On July 30 at 12:20 P.M. all the fires were extinguished.

The tragedy slowly permeated the minds of the

Crewmen fight the raging fires aboard the *Forrestal* on
July 29, 1967, after an initial freak blast triggered the
explosion of fully armed and fueled aircraft being prepared
for a launch against North Vietnam.

Holes in the *Forrestal*'s flight deck attest to the tremendous
force of the explosions of July 29, 1967.

This A-4C "Skyhawk" was one of many aircraft destroyed
by the fires and explosions of July 29, 1967.

Heroic firemen play a hose on the raging fires, intent on saving their ship, knowing well the dangers they encounter.

crewmen aboard the blackened carrier. They were tired, but could not sleep and roamed aimlessly about the vessel, lending a hand where needed. Volunteers were still requested and men who were completely fatigued raced through the passageways to assist working parties.

Four gaping holes marred the flight deck, 26 aircraft were destroyed or jettisoned, and 31 others were damaged. The most shocking statistic was that 132 crewmen were dead, 62 injured, and two missing.

As the crippled carrier steamed slowly toward Subic Bay, a memorial service was held in Hangar Bay One. Following the benediction by Chaplains Geoffrey Gaugham and David Cooper, 13 Marines fired three volleys from their rifles. Upon the ship's arrival at Subic Bay, weary crewmen contemplated the events of the horror-filled day.

Surviving pilots, who had been awaiting launch in their planes, recalled efforts to escape the conflagration. Lieutenant (jg) Don Dameworth of VA-106 managed to jump to safety on the port catwalk, which resulted only in a twisted knee.

Lieutenant (jg) David Dollarhide of VA-46 broke his hip when he leaped from his Skyhawk. J. M. Payne, a 19-year-old airman of VF-11 picked up Dollarhide and hauled him midway to the island where both men fell. AT3 Deloren Massey then rushed out and aided both men to the sick bay.

Lieutenant Commander John McCain of VA-46 was hit by flying shrapnel as he jumped from his plane and hurried across the deck.

Lieutenant Commander Fred White of the same squadron managed to crawl from his plane, and as others rushed to aid him the first bomb explosions were heard. Lieutenant Commander Herb Hope of CVW-17, flying VA-46, escaped from his plane and made it to the net.

AE3 Bruce Mulligan, a 22-year-old VA-106 crewman, was all the way aft when he heard the explosions. He pivoted, saw a fireball coming at him and hit the deck. He was able to crawl forward when suddenly hit by shrapnel. Undaunted by his injuries, he helped a friend to sick bay, then returned to the flight deck. "Back aft of the island," he said, "we started throwing missiles and rockets over the side. After that was done I looked around for some of my buddies and I could only find one. So we decided to help them fight the fire and got the fire hoses aft. My buddy and I stayed aft for I don't know how long. We got separated and some officer said later to leave.

"I went back to the island and got my hands taken care of and stayed there. I was kind of groggy. I found another of my buddies and we went back aft again to help with the fire. By this time they were working on the holes in the flight deck.

"Once again, one of our officers in the squadron found me and took me down to the forecastle to rest. I stayed there for about ten minutes, then went back aft again. I stayed back there until I just passed out and my buddy dragged me out of there."

Thomas Lawler escaped from his shop on the 03 level when the first explosion occurred and said the overhead "began to glow like it was on fire." For hours afterwards he we busy disarming aircraft in the hangar bays. "I don't believe," he says, "that we were in any very great danger in hangar bay three. The only thing that worried me slightly at all was on the first trip in the hangar bay, when you could see practically nothing at all. We kept hearing a gushing, a loud gurgling sound and we couldn't quite determine what that was, and the unknown always worries me a little. . . ."

Shipfitter Chief Daniel N. Ringer, said, "I figured we could fight [the flight deck fire] from down below. Right then we didn't know it was as bad as it was.

First, we cooled down the hangar bay doors. We couldn't get them open and had to go through the side. Around 1800, Ensign Schmidt said they were having trouble on the flight deck and asked if I'd go up and see if I could help them out. I tried to get in one way but couldn't do it. We put saltwater on the bulkhead and it turned to steam, and we couldn't go any farther. I received permission from DC (damage control) Central to cut holes in the flight deck with a torch. I don't know exactly how many we cut, ten or twelve. We finally cooled the bulkheads down enough so we could get at them from the sides. The men just started going in. That's what you're taught at boot camp. Get the fire out."

Seaman Milton Parker, age 21, stated, "When the fire started I was on the 09 level just watching flight operations. I looked at the fantail and saw a drop tank fall off one of the A4s and all of a sudden there was fire everywhere. I headed towards my GQ station on the second deck aft, but couldn't get there because the after portion of the ship was secured. So I manned the hoses on the flight deck from about ten minutes after 11 until 2200 [10:00 P.M.] when I got relieved. The next morning I reported back down to the hangar bay to see if I could help back in Bay Three. I started fighting fires back there and tried to get back into some of the compartments to try and get some of the guys out of there. All our training worked. When the fire started, they called out just the most experienced men. I am a nozzle man so I went in and started hosing down some of the holes in the flight deck. It was very hot. I lost both soles off my shoes when I stepped in some melted metal. I put on some flight deck shoes and went back in."

Lieutenant (jg) Robert Cates, an explosive ordnance officer, recalled, "When I saw the fire start, I ran back to the island to start breaking out fire hoses. We didn't realize then that there was any ordnance involved.

"About the time we got to the island structure, the first bomb went off. I knew what it was right away. I'd heard them go off before. So I asked for, and received, permission to jettison all the bombs on the bomb farm.

"Mr. Smith and Wilson jettisoned the para-flare lockers on the catwalk on the starboard side. I went under an A5 and started to pull missiles on elevator Number Three. They were about ten feet from a burning A5. There was so much debris we couldn't pull them out.

"So I went out on the flight deck and started helping move the planes. We moved an A3 up forward and got a couple of helos out of the way and I was able to

get at the missiles. We started pulling the missile parts off the elevator and took them forward to some other people who jettisoned them.

"About that time I noticed there was a 500-pound bomb and a 750-pound bomb in the middle of the flight deck. They had been on fire. They hadn't detonated or anything . . . they were just sitting there smoking. So I went up and defused them and had them jettisoned.

"About this time, Black, my other man, came up to the flight deck so we started picking up everything we could find that had explosives and threw them over the side. We continued our way aft, taking what ordnance we found off aircraft and threw it over the side.

"We found a hole that had been blown down to the 03 level where a 500-pound bomb was still live and had a fuse in it. Black volunteered to go down and defuse it. We lowered him on a rope and he unscrewed the fuse and pulled it out. We had to leave the bomb there because there was too much fire in the compartment. That 500-pound bomb worried me. I decided that the best thing we could do was pull it out of the compartment. Black tied a rope around a tractor and I put the other end around my waist and tied it around the bomb . . . and we managed to get it over the side.

"Black had a lot of guts when he went down into that hole to defuse the bomb. And I remember seeing Chief Farrier, the crash crew chief, running past me with a CO2 bottle in his hand. He tried to put the fire out on the aircraft . . . he was killed instantly."

D. Harvey, chief radarman of the OI Division, said, "No order needed to be given twice . . . few orders were needed. To move a hose, one only had to grab hold and start pulling. Yellow shirts, red shirts, sailors in dungarees, pilots in flight gear—any one not otherwise occupied—would grab on and move where they were told to. These men seldom knew the man next to them and had never trained together at anything like this, yet there was no confusion. They saw what was needed and did it.

"Men of all ranks and rates exercised initiative and courage in doing their jobs. Seamen and commanders both directed hoses into smoke-filled holes, aware all the time that more bombs were down there and could explode anytime.

"Frequently, a crew would turn their hoses on a group working next to them to cool them off and keep their shoes from burning. Many, when relieved at one hose, would simply take up station on another. Most of the men on the *Forrestal's* flight deck have not yet voted."

Lieutenant (jg) Frank Guinan, sat on the deck next

A view of the port stern corner of the flight deck starting from about frame 240 of the *Forrestal* while in Subic Bay, Philippines on August 1, 1967.

A personal message from Lyndon B. Johnson was sent after the tragedy to the skipper of the *Forrestal*, Captain Beling. The message stated: "I want you and the men of your command to know that the thoughts of the American people are with you at this tragic time. We all feel a great sense of personal loss. The devotion to duty and courage of your men have not gone unnoticed. The sacrifices they have made shall not be in vain."

Captain Beling also commended the crew: "I am most proud of the way the crew reacted. The thing that is foremost in my mind is the concrete demonstration that I have seen of the worth of American youth. I saw many examples of heroism. I saw and subsequently heard of not one example of cowardice."

Fifty-seven hours after the fire began, the first phase of the repair effort began. Planners and estimators from the States met the carrier when she limped into Subic Bay. No time was wasted in evaluating the damage and the time required to put the ship in condition for the trip to Norfolk.

The Naval Repair Facility at Subic Bay put every available worker to the task and an 8-day deadline was set and met with time to spare.

When the *Forrestal* departed, her flight deck had been patched sufficiently to enable her to launch and recover aircraft if necessary. The third and most important phase of the repair work began at Norfolk when the ship's 115-ton Number Four elevator was removed and placed on the blocks. Larger sections of the maimed flight deck were also removed.

More than 600 men worked during three shifts, six days a week, to get the carrier into some image of her former self.

to his room. He was too tired to get up and go inside. "It seems unreal," said he, and added, "nobody had better say to me that American youth is lazy. I saw men working today who were not only injured, but thoroughly exhausted and had to be carried away."

USS Saratoga CVA-60.

48

USS Saratoga CVA-60

On December 16, 1952, the keel of the *USS Saratoga CVA-60* was laid at the New York Naval Shipyard in Brooklyn. The carrier was launched on October 8, 1955, under the sponsorship of Mrs. Charles S. Thomas, wife of the Secretary of the Navy.

Captain Robert J. Stroh took command and the *Saratoga* was commissioned on April 14, 1956. Among the guests at this ceremony was Moses Arnold, CWO (Retired), who had served on the previous *USS Saratoga CV-3.*

As sea trials began, the new carrier shuttled between the yards and ocean, conducting evaluations in engineering, flight operations, steering, and gunnery. On August 18 the *Saratoga* began shakedown operations near Guantanamo Bay. Final sea trials were conducted December 3–5 while members of the Board of Inspection and Survey put the ship through final acceptance maneuvers.

The *Saratoga* was sent to the New York Shipyard on December 19 for post-shakedown alterations.

In April 1957, the carrier steamed to her new home port at Mayport, Florida. On June 6, President Dwight D. Eisenhower and members of his cabinet came aboard to observe flight operations.

A history-making flight was made by two F8U *Crusader* jets when they were launched from the *USS Bon Homme Richard CVA-31* off the San Diego coast, and touched down on the *Saratoga* in the Atlantic—a distance of 2530 miles. This was the highlight of the Presidential visit, and the 3 hour 20 minute flight was the first Pacific to Atlantic, carrier to carrier, non-stop flight ever accomplished.

President Eisenhower commented: "The *Saratoga* looks good. We know, just as you do, that she is good. Good sailing and to all of you, good luck on the important task you are performing in defense of our country."

On September 3, the *Saratoga* departed home port and headed for a European cruise, during which she participated in the NATO exercise, "Strikeback." More than 150 warships of every type and many aircraft took an active role in this operation, which demonstrated the overall combat readiness of the forces embarked for the Allied Command Nations. They included the United States, Canada, Netherlands, Norway, and the United Kingdom. The *Saratoga* returned to home port on October 22.

On February 1, 1958, the carrier sailed to the Mediterranean, where she joined the mighty Sixth Fleet. When Jordan threatened the rebel forces in Lebanon, the Fleet stood ready for any consequence. More than 10,000 flights were launched from the *Saratoga* and other carriers operating in the troubled waters.

Highlighting this cruise was a visit by the Royal Hellenic Majesties, King Paul and Queen Fredericka of Greece. The royal couple and guests observed the carrier's air power on June 16.

The *Saratoga* returned to Mayport, Florida on October 1, then steamed to Norfolk for a routine overhaul. Afterwards, she resumed training operations in the Caribbean Sea.

Another Mediterranean cruise began August 15, 1959. During "Operation Monsoon," the *Saratoga*'s aircraft provided President Eisenhower with protective cover while he reviewed the Sixth Fleet.

Christmas and New Years were celebrated in

USS Saratoga CVA-60.

Cannes, France, after which the carrier was back at sea for a NATO exercise called "Big Deal II." She returned to home port in Florida on February 26, 1960.

Another overhaul was conducted followed by flight operations near Mayport until August 22. The carrier then departed for another Mediterranean cruise, where she participated in a simulated nuclear attack with the British carriers *HMS Ark Royal* and *HMS Hermes.*

On January 23, 1961, a fire broke out in the Number Two main machinery room, presumably engendered by a ruptured fuel line. Damage control parties acted quickly and had the flames smothered in 120 minutes. The tragedy left its calling card, however, for seven men were killed. The *Saratoga* returned to home port on February 25, then headed to Norfolk for repairs.

At midnight, May 24, disaster again plagued the *Saratoga* when the West German ore ship *Bernd Leonhardt* collided with the carrier 35 miles off the North Carolina coast. No serious damage was sustained, however, and the two vessels limped back to the yards for repairs.

"Narrow Gauge" experiments were conducted during June and tested a novel flight deck lighting system. Five light bars were installed on either side of the carrier's centerline and spaced along the landing area at 40-foot intervals. Flood lights were placed every 50 feet along both sides of the deck and under the overhang of the deck to illuminate the hull surface of the water during the landing tests.

On November 28 the *Saratoga* was once again headed for a tour with the Sixth Fleet and many crewmembers visited Rome, Paris, Munich, Madrid, and the French and Spanish Alps. Normal NATO exercises were conducted throughout the cruise and on May 11, 1962, the carrier returned to home port.

She arrived at Norfolk on June 30 to begin a five-month overhaul. Her arresting gear system was modernized to handle heavier aircraft, while the crew's berthing and recreation facilities were improved. A Pilot Landing Aid Television (PLAT) system was installed to assist pilots in carrier operations. The *Saratoga* returned to Mayport late in November.

Orders sent the carrier to patrol Guantanamo Bay, Cuba throughout December, subsequent to the Cuban crisis. She returned to home port shortly before the Holiday Season to celebrate her first Christmas at home in three years.

On March 29, 1963, the *Saratoga* began her fifth Mediterranean cruise, during which she received Fleet Excellence Awards in communications and operations. The crew visited France, Spain, and Turkey, and on October 25, 1964, the carrier sailed back to home port

To keep a tradition alive, the *Saratoga* has a black stripe painted down her funnel as did the old *Sara Maru.*

for a full year of stateside duty. She received new electronic equipment in November, which enabled her to receive direct photographic transmissions from the TIROS weather satellite. The equipment underwent a year of testing and the second weather satellite, NIMBUS, then became operational.

In January 1964 the *Saratoga* began three weeks of operations in the Caribbean. An epoch-making "first" was set in February when the new A6A *Intruder* squadron VA-75 was embarked for carrier qualifications.

In March the carrier spent three days at West Palm Beach, Florida, and was the first major Navy ship to visit that area in recent years. More than 20,000 visitors viewed the *Saratoga* in May during Armed Forces Day and the carrier's marching unit joined the traditional Fifth Avenue parade.

Following a short term of carrier qualifications in June the *Saratoga* went to Norfolk for a routine overhaul, which included installation of the second Integrated Operational Intelligence System (IOIS). This was developed to meet the requirements for speed, flexibility, accuracy, and rapid recovery of stored intelligence data. The complete system is comprised of the RA-5C Reconnaissance Attack Weapons System and an Integrated Operational Intelligence System, which is designed to provide a tactical commander with a complete background of information on a target area. The IOIS is also capable of gathering reconnaissance data day or night in all types of weather.

In mid-September the newly equipped carrier began sea trials. A one-day visit to Mayport was made before she returned to the yards for completion of repairs to engineering spaces.

A sixth deployment to the Mediterranean began on November 28, during which time she participated in NATO exercises with the French, Spanish, and Royal Dutch Navy.

While at various major European ports the carrier welcomed civilian visitors. On July 12, 1965, she returned to home port and resumed normal operations.

On September 2 she entered the Jacksonville Naval Shipyard for maintenance followed by a two-week shakedown cruise off the Florida coast. She returned to Mayport early in December.

During January and February 1966 the *Saratoga* was involved in normal operations. On March 11 she steamed to Roosevelt Roads, Puerto Rico, for an Operational Readiness Inspection (ORI). On March 30 she departed for Pollensa Bay, Mallorca, to relieve the *USS Forrestal CVA-59*. The *Saratoga's* Mediterranean voyage was keyed to high training and visits were made to Malta, Istanbul, Naples, and Greece. She arrived at Barcelona on September 24, remaining there until October 3. After a brief pause at Mallorca she was relieved by the *USS Shangri-La CVA-38* on October 15 and returned to home port where she arrived eleven days later.

The *Saratoga* received an overhaul, which was completed on March 28, 1967. She departed Mayport for six weeks of refresher training near Guantanamo Bay as flagship of Carrier Division Six.

On May 6 she set a precedent by launching three experimental aircraft: an XC-14A transport; a CH-54 *Chinook* helicopter; and an OV-10A *Bronco* counterinsurgency attack plane.

The next day the *Saratoga* arrived at Pollensa Bay,

The Navy's latest A7A Corsair II is launched from the *Saratoga* May 5, 1969, while operating off the Atlantic seaboard. F-4 Phantoms await their turn.

Mallorca, and relieved the *USS Shangri-La*. As Arab-Israeli tensions became strained and the Near East seemed destined for war, the carrier steamed into the Eastern Mediterranean south of Crete and stood by for possible assistance. Fighting erupted along Israel's borders on June 5 and the *Saratoga* remained on station until the conclusion of the Six-Day War.

For the next three months the *Saratoga* conducted flight operations. During one of the scheduled exercises she teamed with units of the Spanish Air Force for day and night operations.

After being relieved by the *Shangri-La,* the *Saratoga* headed for the States. While en route she encountered one of the most violent storms ever recorded in the North Atlantic. She arrived at Mayport on December 6 and remained in port during the holidays.

On January 8, 1968, the *Saratoga* entered the Philadelphia Navy Yard for her first major overhaul since commissioning. Installed was the latest electronics and communications equipment. The job required ten months of work at a cost of $40 million. She departed the yards on January 31, 1969, and spent a few days testing the new systems at sea before returning to home port on February 17.

At the end of the month the *Saratoga* began eight weeks of refresher training near Guantanamo Bay. On April 12 she hosted 34 dignitaries representing 14 NATO countries. Also aboard were the Under Secretary of the Navy, John W. Warner, and the Chief of Naval Operations, Admiral Thomas H. Moorer. All witnessed a surface and air power demonstration in honor of the 20th Anniversary of NATO. Afterwards, the carrier returned to Mayport for three weeks of maintenance.

On May 14 she was off again and hosted President Richard M. Nixon on Armed Forces Day. The President's helicopter landed aboard the carrier at 1:00 P.M. on May 17, the second time in the carrier's thirteen year history that a President of the United States had been piped aboard.

She returned to Mayport on May 29 and began training for her next Mediterranean tour, for which she got underway during July 1969.

The *USS Saratoga CVA-60* maintains the proud tradition of her gallant forerunner, which wrote history in the Pacific during World War II. Prior to that conflict the former *Saratoga CV-3* had a wide black stripe down the center of her stack which distinguished her from her sister, the *USS Lexington CV-2*.

The present *Saratoga* carries a black stripe down her island structure.

For her participation in the Cuba crisis, the *Saratoga* was awarded the Armed Forces Expeditionary Medal.

USS Ranger CVA-61.

49

USS Ranger CVA-61

The keel of the *USS Ranger CVA-61* was laid on August 2, 1954 at the Newport News Shipbuilding Company. She is the eighth Naval vessel to carry the name, which honors the first carrier designed and built from the keel up as an aircraft carrier—the *USS Ranger CV-4*.

The new ship was launched September 29, 1956, under the sponsorship of Mrs. Arthur W. Radford, wife of the Admiral who was then serving as the Chairman of the Joint Chiefs of Staff.

On August 10, 1957, the *Ranger* was commissioned at Norfolk under the command of Captain Charles T. Booth II.

The *Ranger* has an overall length of 1046 feet; extreme beam 236 feet; extreme width at the flight deck 249 feet 6 inches. She displaces 53,300 tons and her draft is 37 feet. She carries 466 officers and 3360 enlisted men at a speed of 34 knots.

On October 3, 1957, the *Ranger* joined the Atlantic Fleet and departed the next day for Guantanamo Bay for shakedown operations. With Attack Squadron 85 aboard, the ship's first air operation came October 14 when Captain Booth made the first landing in a TF-1. Commander M. P. Deputy, leader of VF-12, touched down in an A4D *Skyhawk* on October 25 to make the first jet landing.

The *Ranger* was engaged in extensive exercises and air operations along the eastern seaboard and the Caribbean until June 20, 1958. On that day she went to sea with 200 Naval Reserve Officer Candidates for a two-month training cruise. This tour took the carrier around Cape Horn. She arrived at her new home port at Alameda, California on August 20.

The rest of the year was spent conducting carrier qualifications for Air Group 14. On January 3, 1959, she departed home port and sailed to Okinawa via Hawaii where she became the flagship of Rear Admiral H. H. Caldwell, Commander Carrier Division Two. As a unit of the Seventh Fleet the *Ranger* conducted air operations with Naval units of the Southeast Treaty Organization out of Subic Bay, Philippines.

President Garcia of the Philippines and SEATO military officers came aboard on May 2 for a one-day cruise. This was followed by a special weapons warfare exercise and patrol along the southern seaboard of Japan.

At Yokosuka on June 19, members of the Japanese Imperial Family—Princess Chi Chi bu and Prince and Princess Takamatsu—boarded the *Ranger*, along with Japanese Government officials, to observe air demonstrations with the USS *Shangri-La CVA-38*.

When the crisis between Nationalist China and Communist China reached a boiling point on July 5, the *Ranger* stood ready for any eventuality and patrolled the east coast of Taiwan. The situation abated four days later and the carrier resumed normal fleet operations before returning to Alameda on July 27.

The *Ranger* was active off the California coast during the next six months. Day and night training brought the ship's crew and air group to a high state of battle efficiency. Air Group 9 underwent intensive training and qualified new pilots for carrier duty.

On February 6, 1960, during a Far East tour, the pilots logged 17,000 hours in the air while the *Ranger* steamed as a member of the Seventh Fleet.

The crew participated in the "People to People" program and donated five tons of clothing plus several thousand dollars to charitable and social agencies in the Far East. On August 30 the *Ranger* returned to home port. Following a maintenance period and routine training off the western seaboard, she made another cruise to the western Pacific from August 11, 1961, to March 8, 1962.

On November 9 the *Ranger* departed Alameda for brief operations in the Hawaiian area, then headed for Okinawa where she engaged in simulated warfare. During this exercise her striking group was opposed by shore-based aircraft and submarines. Additional maneuvers were conducted with the carrier USS *Kitty Hawk CVA-63* and the British carrier HMS *Hermes* near the Philippines. While at Hong Kong the *Ranger* was the stage for a full-scale production of the Gilbert and Sullivan musical comedy, *HMS Pinafore*, which was presented by a Chinese college theatre group.

On May 1, 1963, the *Ranger* steamed into the South China Sea to support contingent operations in Laos. As the tension eased she resumed normal duties. A one-day cruise was held for 150 members of the Japanese-American Society, which is dedicated to increasing knowledge and cultural exchanges between the two nations.

The carrier departed Yokosuka on June 3 for the United States. Later that afternoon she was shadowed by Soviet *Badger* jet bombers. They were intercepted by the *Ranger's* fighters at a distance of 100 miles from the ship. The *Ranger* arrived at Alameda on June 14.

The carrier entered the San Francisco Naval Yard on August 7 for an extensive overhaul. The job was completed on February 10, 1964, and she left the yards with a larger flight deck to handle newer jets. Also installed was a Nose Wheel Catapult system.

A refresher training cruise began March 25, which took the carrier to Hawaii on June 19. She returned to home port on July 10.

On August 5 she departed for the western Pacific. Tension in the South China Sea reached a climax at the time of the *Ranger's* departure from California. The USS *Maddox DD-731* had been assaulted by North Vietnamese PT Boats on August 2. After a second unprovoked attack two nights later, aircraft from the USS *Ticonderoga CVA-14* arrived on the scene. Thus, a new and critical phase of Seventh Fleet operations began. On August 5, the USS *Constellation CVA-64* and USS *Ticonderoga* made retaliatory strikes on the PT boat bases. This was the result of a direct order from President Lyndon Johnson.

An eight-hour layover was made at Pearl Harbor before the *Ranger* journeyed to Subic Bay, then on to Yokosuka where she became the flagship of Rear Admiral Miller, Commander of Task Force 77 on October 17.

During the next few months she cruised the troubled waters of the South China Sea; she spent one continu-

USS *Ranger* CVA-61 passing beneath the Golden Gate Bridge while entering the San Francisco harbor (October 1958).

ous period of 65 days "on the line" striking selected military targets in North Vietnam.

General William Westmoreland came aboard on March 9, 1965, to confer with Admiral Miller. The conference was followed by air strikes on enemy targets until April 13. The *Ranger* would have continued to send out sorties, but a fuel line ruptured in one of her machinery spaces, necessitating a return to Subic Bay, where she arrived two days later.

On April 20 she departed homeward bound and reached home port on May 6.

In the air war against North Vietnam, Carrier Air Group 9 was very active. Pilots from VA-93 and VA-94 flew their A4C *Skyhawks* into the hostile regions as VA-95 handled the bombing runs. F4B *Phantoms* from

VF-92 and VF-96 provided air cover during these missions while airborne support came from VAH-2, VAW-11 and VFP-63. Photographic coverage of the missions was the responsibility of VFP-63, which flew RF8A *Crusaders* and RVAH-5 *Vigilantes*.

During her tour of duty 151 underway replenishments at sea provided the carrier with 21 million gallons of fuel and 2600 tons of food supplies.

The *Ranger* was a guest of the San Francisco Naval Shipyard from May 13 to September 30, 1965, followed by refresher training.

On December 10 she left home port for her sixth Western Pacific cruise and her second tour of duty off the Vietnam coast. Strikes were launched on January 15, 1966, but the most important sortie came on June

USS Ranger—One of the Ranger's catapult crews hooks an F4 Phantom to one of the ship's four catapults prior to a strike into Vietnam. The Ranger was operating in the South China Sea at the time. The Phantom belongs to VF-143 whose home base is Miramar, California.

29 when the Ranger planned and executed the first attacks against the Haiphong fuel storage facilities. Air Wing 14 handled the mission during a precisely controlled effort and achieved success without any damage to their planes.

Other significant targets were the Phu Lang military area—a two square mile region where 40 percent of the oil and ordnance storage facilities were destroyed. Repeated strikes were launched against the Than Hoa, Quang Soui, and Nghia Dong military complexes. The Ranger spent 218 days with the Seventh Fleet; 179 of these days were spent at sea, with 136 days in combined combat operations. Only two ports were visited and comprised 26 days at Yokosuka, Japan and 23 days at Subic Bay. On August 25, after logging 99,000 nautical miles, the Ranger returned to Alameda. She remained there until September 28 when she departed for Puget Sound, arriving two days later.

The Ranger received an extensive overhaul, which was completed on May 30, 1967; she then resumed normal training duties out of her home port of San Diego. This training period continued for five months and sharpened the skills of all concerned.

Attack Carrier Air Wing Two embarked on September 15, bringing their new A7A Corsair II jet planes and UH-2C Seasprite turboprop rescue helicopters. Following a refresher training period for the new air wing, the Ranger proceeded to engage in a major fleet exercise called "Moon Festival." The operation began October 9 and was completed eight days later.

On November 4, 1967, the Ranger departed home port and steamed to Japan, arriving at Yokosuka on the 21st. Three days later she relieved the USS Constellation and began duty with the Seventh Fleet. She sailed to the Philippines to pick up the Commander of Carrier Division Three on November 30 and left Subic Bay on December 1 for combat operations in the Tonkin Gulf.

The Ranger arrived on station December 3 and went to work sending air strikes against North Vietnamese targets. In the succeeding five months the Ranger pilots of Air Wing 2 hit ferries, bridges, airfields, and numerous military targets. A welcome break came on April 8 when the carrier visited Yokosuka, but within three days she was back on Yankee Station.

Rear Admiral John P. Weinel, Commander Carrier Division Three, embarked on the Ranger, stated that the Ranger's Carrier Air Wing Two was "The most sophisticated air wing ever to deploy aboard a carrier." The all-jet air wing included Attack Squadron 147, flying the Navy's newest light-attack bomber, the A7A Corsair II, on its maiden combat mission. Air strikes over North Vietnam were unexpectedly interrupted when the Ranger was called in to the Sea of Japan following the North Korean seizure of the intelligence ship USS Pueblo AGER-2. For 30 days the Ranger operated with other ships off the Korean coast, then she returned to the Gulf of Tonkin to resume combat operations against North Vietnam. The Ranger returned to Alameda, California, on May 25, 1968.

Five days after returning home, the Ranger steamed for Puget Sound Naval Shipyard, Bremerton, Washington, for a two-month overhaul. Upon her return to Alameda in August, the Ranger began training operations in preparation for her fourth combat cruise.

The Ranger left Alameda on October 26, 1968, for a return to Vietnam. Because of the November 1, 1968 bombing halt, the carrier's air wing concentrated their efforts in air support to the Allied ground forces in South Vietnam.

Just 11 days before the Ranger was scheduled to return home, a North Korean MIG fighter jet shot down a U.S. Navy EC-121 intelligence-gathering aircraft, killing all 31 crew members aboard. The Ranger was ordered to leave the Gulf of Tonkin and steam to the Korean waters. As part of Task Force 71, the Seventh Fleet's northern striking force, the Ranger operated in both the Sea of Japan and the Yellow Sea. Following a short visit to Subic Bay, for off loading of

An A1 (Skyraider) approaches the *USS Ranger CVA-61* for an arrested landing.

excess ordnance and on loading supplies, the *Ranger* returned to Alameda, California on May 17, 1969.

A two-month overhaul in the Hunters Point Naval Shipyard in San Francisco followed the carrier's return home. In August the *Ranger* commenced training and pilot qualifications off the coast of Northern California. She left Alameda in October 1969 for a seven-month deployment to the Western Pacific to support the combat operations against North Vietnam in the Gulf of Tonkin.

The *USS Ranger CVA-61* has received the following awards: The Navy Unit Commendation; the Meritorious Unit Commendation; the National Defense Service Medal; the Armed Forces Expeditionary Medal; and the Vietnam Service Medal.

USS Independence CVA-62.

50

USS Independence CVA-62

On July 1, 1955, the keel of the *USS Independence CVA-62* was laid at the New York Shipyard in Brooklyn. Mrs. Thomas S. Gates, wife of the Secretary of the Navy, christened the carrier and she was launched on June 6, 1958.

Principal speaker during commissioning ceremonies on July 10, 1959, was Admiral Arleigh A. Burke, Chief of Naval Operations. Captain R. Y. McElroy, Jr., USN, became the new carrier's first skipper.

The *Independence*, named to commemorate her predecessor, the former light carrier *USS Indepen-*dence CVL-22, began shakedown operations in the Caribbean Sea area during March. All phases of shipboard trials were conducted, including gunnery practice, damage control, and engineering exercises.

After post-shakedown alterations, the *Independence* was loaded with ammunition and aviation fuel, then sailed from Norfolk Navy Yard on November 30, 1959, bound for a new home port at Mayport, Florida.

Until March 4, 1960, she operated between Mayport and Norfolk, assigned to carrier qualifications duties for training new pilots.

A change of command for Commander Carrier Division Two took place aboard the carrier on March 4 when Rear Admiral Ray C. Needham relieved Rear Admiral William A. Sutherland Jr. During the months that followed, the *Independence* operated near the Virginia Capes area.

On June 9, midshipmen from the U.S. Naval Academy came aboard for a six-week summer cruise. The carrier returned to the yards at Norfolk in mid June 1960.

The *Independence* began her first Mediterranean cruise on August 4, 1960, as a member of the Sixth Fleet. She participated in the NATO exercises "Ship-Ring," "Flash-Back," "Set-Back," and "Dead-Beat." Visits were made at Rota and Barcelona, Spain; Athens, Greece; Cannes, France; and Naples, and Palermo, Italy. During this cruise, the *Independence* was active in the people-to-people program, in which 1397 orphans were hosted and 166 flag rank officers and general visitors came aboard. The total guest list numbered 17,500.

The carrier was back at Norfolk on March 3, 1961, after logging 37,092 nautical miles.

Following additional carrier qualification training for pilots near Mayport, Fla., the carrier returned to the Norfolk Navy Yard to play host to the Azalea Queen of 1961, Miss Lynda Bird Johnson, daughter of the then Vice President of the U.S. Two hundred and fifty people came aboard to celebrate the occasion.

Back in the Caribbean area, the *Independence* kept close contact with the American citizens in Cuba and the Guantanamo Naval Base. The modern attack carrier was considered a main defense in deterring aggression.

The *Independence* entered the Norfolk Navy Yard for a six-month availability and upkeep. Shortly afterwards, NROTC and Naval Academy personnel came aboard and the "Big I" began a training cruise for both enlisted men and officers.

On July 4, 1961, the sleek carrier was host to thousands of civilians at the New York Navy Yard. She sailed two days later to begin Second Fleet maneuvers.

More than a thousand wives and children were aboard on July 17 for a Dependents' Cruise. They received a first-hand view of shipboard operations and the vital mission that their husbands were fulfilling in the defense of their country.

On August 4, the *Independence* deployed on her second tour of duty in the Mediterranean. The usual ports were visited and USO shows were held on the ship during the cruise. Over 13,000 visitors toured the carrier during open-house periods. The carrier partici-

pated in the NATO exercises "Checkmate I" and "Checkmate II" and on December 19 she returned to her berth at Norfolk.

By January 14, 1962, the *Independence* was conducting carrier qualifications again and the new F4H Phantom II was hoisted aboard for the first at-sea flights of the jet.

Another Dependents' Cruise was held off the Virginia Capes on March 24, 1962. Many sailors were rotated to other duties and new men took their places on board. When a ship in the Navy conducts a cruise for the wives, children, or girlfriends of the crew, there is always something new to see and learn.

The *Independence* departed Norfolk in April 1962 on her third Mediterranean cruise, reaching Gibraltar in May. She relieved the USS *Saratoga* CVA-60 on May 15.

General David M. Shoup, Commandant of the United States Marine Corps, visited the *Independence* to familiarize himself with the shipboard life of the Marines. Marines compose a small but vital function in the successful and safe operation of a ship like the "Big I." As the watchdogs of the Navy, the Leathernecks maintain a close and alert eye on the Special Weapons Sections of many warships.

On July 5, the *Independence* was host to Princess Grace and Prince Rainier of Monaco. The Royal Family plus officers and men of the carrier were entertained by the National Orchestra Opera of Monte Carlo.

The major exercise under the NATO program in late July 1962 was "Operation Full Swing." On August 19 the word that the entire crew had been anxiously waiting to hear was received—the USS *Forrestal* CVA-59 had arrived to relieve the "Big I." This meant a return to the United States. The *Independence* nudged up along Pier 12 at Norfolk on August 30, 1962.

In October, the "Big I" participated in amphibious operations off Vieques, near Puerto Rico. When President John F. Kennedy announced the blockade of Cuba, the *Independence* stood ready in the event of a serious outbreak of aggression. She was again at Norfolk on November 20 after 43 days of continuous sailing and 20 days of consecutive air operations.

In December 1962, the carrier entered the Norfolk Navy Yard for her first major overhaul since commissioning. During this period, Miss Jacquelyn Jeanne Mayer, Miss American 1963, visited the ship. Repairs were completed in May and the *Independence* began a six-week refresher training cruise in the Caribbean.

The "Big I" deployed on her fourth Mediterranean cruise on August 6, 1963, and the usual NATO exercises were conducted. An eight-day visit to Beirut, Lebanon began on September 30.

The *Independence* was at sea when the news was received that the President of the United States, John F. Kennedy, had been assassinated. The carrier anchored in Golfo di Palmas, Sardinia on November 23 for a fleet conference. Homage was then paid by the ship's crew on the flight deck.

On December 11, the *Independence* was at Livorno, Italy, where many of the ship's crew visited Pisa and Florence. In March 1964, the "Big I" returned to Norfolk. While operating off the Virginia Capes in May, several SA3H helicopters were embarked to test their ability as Antisubmarine craft for use aboard attack aircraft carriers.

On July 1, the carrier arrived in New York to hold open-house for thousands of people visiting the Worlds Fair.

The *Independence* arrived at Mayport, Florida, on August 22, 1964. A month later she steamed to the North Atlantic to participate in the NATO exercise Teamwork. Afterwards, she headed for Gibraltar on October 4 to relieve the *USS Franklin D. Roosevelt CVA-42* for a four-week period of duty in the Mediterranean.

On November 5, the "Big I" arrived at Norfolk and underwent a two-month restricted availability. On February 10, she departed Norfolk to join Task Force 77 in the South China Sea. This was her first deployment to the Western Pacific and she was the first Atlantic Fleet carrier to see action in the Vietnam conflict. For 40 days, the *Independence* operated off Yan-

The USS Independence enroute to New York City on June 3, 1964, for a visit to the New York Worlds Fair.

An E1B (Willy Fudd) lands on the *Independence* following a mission in the Gulf of Tonkin off the coast of Vietnam.

kee Station, launching aircraft against enemy positions in North Vietnam. Brief calls were made at Singapore, the Philippines, and Hong Kong.

The *Independence* operated with the *USS Coral Sea CVA-43, USS Oriskany CVA-34, USS Midway CVA-41*, and the *USS Bon Homme Richard CVA-31*, conducting daily strikes against military targets both north and south of the 17th parallel. The "Big I's" Attack Squadron 72 was credited with destroying the first operational Surface-to-Air Missile (SAM) site in North Vietnam on October 17, 1965.

During this Vietnam cruise, the *Independence* received ammunition, fuel, and food during underway replenishments while flight operations continued. Credit for this vital force goes to the Service Force Pacific Fleet, which plays a highly important but often unsung part in replenishing various ships operating throughout the Pacific.

Many dignitaries visited the "Big I" while operating with Task Force 77, including Secretary of Defense Robert S. McNamara, Chief of Naval Operations Admiral David L. McDonald, General William Westmoreland, Commander of the U.S. Forces in Vietnam, and Premier of the Republic of Vietnam, Lt. Gen. Nguyen Cao Ky.

On December 13, 1965, the *Independence* returned to her home port in Norfolk, after steaming more than 68,000 miles.

In February 1966, she entered the Norfolk Navy Shipyard to undergo repairs and overhaul.

Early in April, the carrier resumed training opera-

tions in the Caribbean. Nearly 3000 dependents embarked for a family cruise on May 10. Later that month, aviation history was made aboard the *Independence* when the first VTOL (Vertical Takeoff and Landing) jet aircraft took off from the attack carrier. The tri-service experimental aircraft, called the "Kestrel," was developed jointly by the United States, the United Kingdom, and the Federal Republic of Germany.

On June 13, 1966, the *Independence* departed Norfolk for her fifth Mediterranean deployment. She relieved the *USS America CVA-66* on July 1 in Pollensa Bay, Mallorca, Spain, and became the flagship of Task Force 60 of the Sixth Fleet.

The *Independence* returned to Norfolk on February 1, 1967. She entered the Portsmouth Naval Shipyard in March to undergo an extensive and extended overhaul.

The overhaul took nine months during which time the carrier's hull and machinery were completely refurbished, including the armament and ordance systems. A new computer provided for an automatic accounting of all supply material. The *Independence* also received the new Navy Tactical Data System, which provided the commanding officer with fast, accurate, comprehensive information on which to base tactical decisions.

Sea trials and refresher training began on November 7 off the Virginia Capes and continued throughout the remainder of the year.

The carrier departed Norfolk on January 8, 1968, for Guantanamo Bay to conduct training exercises in the Caribbean. Additional operations were held off the Florida coast and the North Carolina Capes.

F4B Phantom II number "205" of VF-84 is launched from the *USS Independence* on a strike over Vietnam (July 1965).

She returned to Norfolk on March 16, 1968, to prepare for Sixth-fleet duty in the Mediterranean. On April 26, 1968, she headed for Pollensa Bay, Majorca, in the Balearic Islands, where she arrived May 9.

The "Big I's" crew have a nickname for their ship, "The latest of the Greatest," and she has lived up to this reputation daily as a major unit of the Atlantic Fleet.

The *USS Independence CVA-62* has received the following awards: The Navy Unit Commendation (Vietnam); National Defense Service Medal; Navy Expeditionary Medal; Armed Forces Expeditionary Medal; Vietnam Service Medal with one star.

Construction of the *USS Kitty Hawk CVA-63* was authorized in 1956. Although her design was that of the *Forrestal* class, major improvements separated the ship into a class of her own. She was commissioned on April 29, 1961. With the completion of the *USS John F. Kennedy CVA-67*, the class was complete as follows:

USS Kitty Hawk CVA-63
USS Constellation CVA-64
USS America CVA-66
USS John F. Kennedy CVA-67

The ships differ in appearance from the *Forrestal* class in that the island structures are smaller and are set further aft. Construction of the *Constellation* was delayed when a fire damaged her in December 1960. The completion of the *John F. Kennedy* was delayed because of a discussion over whether to make the carrier conventional or nuclear. The *Kitty Hawk's* estimated cost was $217,963,000.

The displacements of the four carriers are *Kitty Hawk* and *Constellation*, 60,000 tons standard and 75,200 tons full load; *America*, 60,300 tons standard and 78,250 full load; *Kennedy*, 61,000 tons standard and 83,000 full load. Overall length: *Kitty Hawk*, 1062 feet; *Constellation*, 1072 feet; *America* and *Kennedy*, 1047 feet. Beam is 130 feet; width across the flight deck, 252 feet (260 feet across the flight deck of the *Constellation*). The carriers can accommodate 70 to 90 aircraft depending on size. Missiles: two twin terrier surface to air launchers in *Kitty Hawk, Constellation,* and *America;* 2 twin Tartar surface to air launchers in the *Kennedy*. Complement, 120 officers and 2600 enlisted men. With airwing embarked, complement is between 4800 to 5000 men. Speed: in excess of 35 knots.

USS Kitty Hawk CVA-63.

51

USS Kitty Hawk CVA-63

On December 17, 1903, just outside Kitty Hawk, North Carolina, Orville and Wilbur Wright completed the first successful flight in history in which a machine carrying a man raised itself into the air by its own power. This initial heavier-than-air flight marked the birth of aviation.

Four additional flights were accomplished that eventful day. The first only lasted twelve seconds and the strange craft flew a distance of 120 feet at an altitude of two feet!

The first Navy vessel to be named in honor of the historic site where the ingenious Wright brothers took to the air was the *USS Kitty Hawk AVP-1*. She was constructed in 1932 and served in a civilian status until June 25, 1941, when the Navy acquired her for the purpose of transporting aircraft, equipment, and ammunition to various Pacific bases.

The keel of the present day *USS Kitty Hawk CVA-63* was laid on December 27, 1956 in the docks of the New York Shipbuilding Corporation, Camden, New Jersey.

Mrs. Neil H. McElroy, wife of the former Secretary of Defense, christened the ship on May 21, 1960.

Capt. William F. Bringle assumed command on April 29, 1961, and the *Kitty Hawk* was commissioned at the Philadelphia Naval Shipyard.

The *Kitty Hawk* has a full load displacement of 80,000 tons and is 1047 feet, 6 inches long with an extreme beam of 252 feet. Her speed is in excess of 30 knots. The flight deck covers an area of 176,234 square feet. No wood was used in building the hull or the flight deck planking. The carrier can accommodate 4000 crew members.

The *Kitty Hawk* was originally designed as a *Forrestal*-class carrier but eventually evolved into a class of her own. The major difference which separates her from the Forrestal class is the installation of four Terrier guided missile batteries on the *Kitty Hawk's* after section. The missiles are surface-to-air (SAM) and are dispatched from dual aim launchers. Another difference is that the *Kitty Hawk* has a smaller island structure, which is located further aft of the flight deck.

On July 15, 1961, the *Kitty Hawk* left Philadelphia for her first taste of sea duty. Commander Thomas, flying a "TF" Trader, made the first takeoff on July 17, 1961; later the same day, he also completed the first landing.

On July 22, the *USS Robert K. Huntington DD-781* came alongside the *Kitty Hawk* and the new carrier began her first at-sea fueling operations. The *Kitty Hawk* returned to Norfolk Navy Shipyard on July 24, 1961.

The *Kitty Hawk* left Norfolk on August 11, bound for her new assignment with the Pacific Fleet. As she passed the North Carolina town she was named after, four A4D aircraft from the ship's air group flew in a salute over the Wright Brothers' Memorial.

During the cruise around South America, the *Kitty Hawk* made quite a few friends while distributing food and medical supplies to the needy persons of Brazil. While in Trinidad on September 18, 1961, Rear Admiral Reed, Commander, South Atlantic Forces, visited the ship.

On September 27, the carrier arrived in Rio de Janeiro, Brazil, where more than 25,000 persons toured the ship. As she pulled away from the harbor, over 1,500,000 people lined Copacabana and Leblon Beaches to wave farewell. This was on October 1, 1961.

The *Kitty Hawk* rounded Cape Horn seven days later and pulled in to Valparaiso, Chile, on October 13. While in port, the crew rebuilt a school house. Visitors were taken aboard to view air operations off the coast of Chile.

When the carrier was at Peru on October 20, the

President of Peru and the Governor of Callaces visited the ship for two days. The final South American port the ship visited was Lima, Peru, where bullfights were held in honor of the carrier.

The *Kitty Hawk* arrived in San Diego on November 1, 1961, and more than 20,000 people looked the carrier over.

In December, the *Kitty Hawk* entered the San Francisco Naval Shipyard to undergo a six-month post-shakedown overhaul. She left the yards on May 5, 1962, and began a two-week sea trial period before returning to San Diego. The carrier conducted a three-week cruise to Hawaii, then during July and August she operated off the coast of Southern California.

On September 13, 1962, the carrier deployed on her first Western Pacific cruise and duty with the Seventh Fleet. A Commander-in-Chief Pacific Weapons Demonstration was staged for representatives of all the free nations of Asia.

During the cruise, the *Kittl Hawk* visited Sascho, Iwakuni, Beppu, Kobe, and Yokosuka, Japan; Manila and Subic Bay, Philippines; and Hong Kong.

In December, Bob Hope and his USO show entertained the crew and another dignitary, Cardinal Spellman, paid the ship a visit.

Several Russian aircraft made over-flights to observe the ship.

On April 2, 1963, the *Kitty Hawk* returned to her home port of San Diego, pulling alongside Quay Wall at the North Island Naval Air Station.

On June 6, 1963, the *Kitty Hawk* became a "Floating White House," when President John F. Kennedy came on board to observe the First Fleet Weapons Demonstration. From the flight deck, the President viewed 18 ships plus countless aircraft during the maneuvers. Included in the Presidential party were Secretary of the Navy Fred Korth and Under Secretary of the Navy Paul B. Fay. The President spent the night aboard ship.

On October 17, the *Kitty Hawk* deployed on her second cruise to the Far East. During the cruise, she participated in two large scale amphibious operations; "Big Dipper" and "Back Pack." The purpose was to provide air support for assault ground forces. Included with the U.S. ships were forces from Nationalist China. The operations also showed the way in which American and Allied forces can cooperate.

The *Kitty Hawk* established quite a few records during the cruise. An All-Navy transfer record for at-sea loading of attack cargo stores of 75.5 tons per hour was set with the *USS Castor AKS-1*. In late March, the 15,000th arrested gear landing was logged. On April 3,

1964, the carrier was awarded the Battle Efficiency "E" Excellency awards. Other awards were presented to the Air and Communications departments.

On July 20, the *Kitty Hawk* returned to San Diego and her home port of North Island. From the mainmast flew a 1069-foot homeward-bound pennant. Naval regulations permits a vessel to fly such a pennant upon returning to the States after serving nine or more months deployment. It is believed to be the second largest homeward bound pennant ever flown. The *USS Essex CVS-9* (then CV-9) had flown a 1538-foot pennant upon returning from Japan at the close of World War II. A directive, not in effect at that time, now requires that the size of a homeward-bound pennant be no longer than the length of the ship.

On August 15, 1965, the *Kitty Hawk* arrived at the Puget Sound Naval Shipyard, Bremerton, Washington, to undergo a $14 million eight-month overhaul. The day following her arrival, she was host to more than 27,000 people during an Open House.

During her overhaul period, the *Kitty Hawk* was fitted out with an Integrated Operational Intelligence Center (IOIC), an Automatic Landing System, a new Airborne System Support Center (ASSC), and a Naval Tactical Data System (NTDS). Of all the new equipment installed, the NTDS is the most modern and sophisticated. It is a data-processing and communications system that evaluates enemy threats and recommends counter-moves to shipboard commanders in millionths of a second. The multi-unit computer system enables ships to exchange information at extremely high speeds.

NTDS was designed to meet the demands of modern warfare, in which aircraft and missiles may approach a task force at speeds of thousands of miles an hour. It anticipates simultaneous attacks on fleet units from several quarters at several altitudes, in numbers that would saturate the plots with grease pencil transparencies now in use in Combat Information Centers. The system works at fantastic speeds. Uncorrelated information coming from a variety of sources goes into data-processing equipment located on board ship. At this point, such functions as detection, location, tracking speed, identity and size of friendly and enemy contacts are worked out in transistorized computers that form the "brain" of the system. The "answers" are displayed automatically on scopes installed in the Combat Information Center (CIC) where command and operating personnel monitor the tactical situation and issue the required commands. The display of such information makes it readily possible for key personnel to understand quickly the immediate situation, thus permitting a concentration of judgment for effective weapon assignment to threats against the ship. More than this, computer installations within the task force, interconnected by means of radio equipment using advanced communications technique, will exchange tactical information at high speeds. As a result, the task force commander, as well as individual unit commanders, are provided with a complete overall tactical picture of the task force situation in addition to the picture for local information sources. The system is capable of incorporating all anti-war weapons now in use or under development by the Navy.

On March 3, 1965, the *Kitty Hawk* began a five-day sea trial period off the Strait of Juan De Fuca. All systems checked out and the carrier returned to the yards on March 8. As the yard period came to a close, the Bremerton Community Symphony Orchestra came aboard and performed a full-scale concert for the ship's crew as a farewell gesture.

The *Kitty Hawk* steamed out of the Puget Sound Shipyard on April 28 and returned to her home port at North Island, San Diego, California.

On June 3, the *Kitty Hawk* and her crew took part in the production of a Walt Disney movie, *Lt. Robin Crusoe, USN*. Several crewmembers had parts in the film, and after its completion it was premiered on the *Kitty Hawk's* hangar deck. This was the first time a full-length feature film was ever premiered on a U.S. Navy ship of the line.

The *Kitty Hawk* deployed on her third Western Pa-

The *USS Kitty Hawk* arriving at Yokosuka, Japan, on October 10, 1962, on her first tour of duty with the Seventh Fleet in the Western Pacific.

cific cruise on Oct. 19, 1965. By this time, the situation in Vietnam required the increased involvement of U.S. forces. The Pearl Harbor Evaluation Team that had inspected the carrier's Operational Readiness Inspection had given the *Kitty Hawk* an 87 percent excellence score. On November 23, the *Kitty Hawk* became flagship of the Commander, Attack Carrier Striking Force, U.S. Seventh Fleet. Rear Admiral James R. Reedy broke his flag out while the carrier was in Subic Bay. Provisions were loaded aboard and the *Kitty Hawk* prepared for duty off the coast of Vietnam.

While operating in the South China Sea on December 6, 1965, a fire erupted in the number three main machinery room. Two men were killed and 29 injured in the smoke-filled blaze. At the time the fire started, the ship was conducting air operations over Vietnam. Flight operations were not interrupted and damage was minor, due to the efficiency of the fire fighting teams.

While the carrier was operating off the Vietnam coast on December 17, a USO show, which included Miss Martha Raye, arrived on board to entertain the crew, who would not be home this Christmas.

The *Kitty Hawk*'s Vietnam service during the 1965–1966 Western Pacific cruise was highly impressive. During the period November 1965 to May 1966, Carrier Air Wing Eleven (CAW-11) dropped a total of 10,731 tons of explosives on designated enemy targets. This is the most tonnage dropped on enemy areas by any one carrier in the history of naval aviation. Men of the *Kitty Hawk*'s air group were awarded 861 Air Medals, 19 Navy Commendation Medals, five Distinguished Flying Crosses, two Purple Hearts and one Silver Star.

Rear Admiral James R. Reedy, Commander of the Seventh Fleet's Carrier Strike Force, presented the awards during an unforgettable flight deck ceremony.

On April 19, 1966, Lieutenant Commander Raymond C. Vehorn and Lieutenant (jg) John H. Hurlburt made the 50,000th arrested gear landing aboard the *Kitty Hawk*. On May 21, the ship celebrated her fifth birthday in Subic Bay. Open House was held for the people of Subic Bay and town officials of Olongapo Zambales.

The ammunition ship, *USS Pyro AE-24* and the *Kitty Hawk* shattered all fleet records on May 11, when ordnance was transferred at the rate of 238 tons per hour during an underway replenishment in the Gulf of Tonkin. The previous record-holder was the *USS Oriskany CVA-34*.

On June 13, 1966, the *Kitty Hawk* returned to San Diego, California. More than a thousand people stood on the Quay Wall pier to greet the carrier. Many of those waiting were anxious friends and family of the crew.

For her Vietnam service, the *Kitty Hawk* was awarded the Navy Unit Commendation and the Vietnam Service Medals.

Upon her return from the Western Pacific, the *Kitty Hawk* began air operations and training off the coast of Southern California in preparation for her next Far Eastern cruise.

The *Kitty Hawk* received an extensive modification of complex equipment, then conducted operations near the coast of Southern California until November 5, 1966. On that day she left San Diego for the Western Pacific.

A brief stopover was made at Hawaii, then the carrier headed for Yokosuka, Japan, arriving on November 19. At Japan, Rear Admiral David C. Richardson, Commander, Attack Carrier Striking Force, Seventh Fleet, came aboard with his staff.

After a replenishment stop at Subic Bay, the carrier returned to Yankee Station for air strikes over North Vietnam on December 5.

Major transshipment points and storage facilities were hit. No target was overlooked in an effort to prevent the flow of manpower and supplies from North Vietnam to the Communist guerrilla forces in the south.

On January 2, 1967, the carrier's crew enjoyed a short rest period at Subic Bay; they were back on station on the 18th.

Heavy multi-carrier attacks on Dong Phong Thuong rendered the entire area useless to the enemy. A trio of bridges at Ninh Binh felt the effect of bombs and rockets released by Carrier Air Wing 11.

North Vietnam was struck again on February 14, after which the carrier returned to Subic Bay.

A week-long visit to Hong Kong enlivened the spirits of the crew, then on March 3, the carrier was again positioned at Yankee Station.

Attacks were directed at Hon Gai and Bac Giang, where numerous bridges were damaged or destroyed. A series of strikes on a major iron and steel complex at Thai Nguyen began on March 11. The Haiphong powerplant was the victim on the 20th and Kep airfield and surrounding supply depots were hit for three consecutive weeks.

On the *Kitty Hawk*'s final mission during this cruise, her planes hit the Army supply depot at Van Dien and the powerplant at Bac Giang. The *USS Constellation CVA-64*, sister ship of the *Kitty Hawk*, arrived at Subic Bay on May 24 and took over. The *Kitty*

An F4B Phantom II clears the *Kitty Hawk*'s flight deck on a combat strike over Vietnam. Two Phantom jets stand ready for launch as an RA5C Vigilante is prepared for a catapult launch.

Hawk then returned to Yokosuka, Japan for a ten-day visit.

A minor collision with the oiler *USS Platte AO-24*, occurred on June 16 during refueling operations in the mid-Pacific. Only slight damage was done and the carrier continued to her home port at North Island, San Diego, arriving June 20. Next she went to the Long Beach Shipyard for overhaul and repairs.

During this period the *Kitty Hawk*'s engineering plant was completely refurbished and the most modern electronics equipment was installed.

Following refresher training and air operations near San Diego, the *Kitty Hawk* departed on November 17, 1967, to begin her fifth Western Pacific cruise. She arrived at Pearl Harbor on the 23rd, and, following readiness instructions, steamed to Yokosuka on November 30.

On December 23, the "Hawk's" Air Wing Eleven commenced combat strikes. Her stay on the line was 61 days and this is believed to be a record for on-station operations at Yankee Station off Vietnam. The air wing struck major enemy targets, including the Kien An airfield, a communications center, and the Long Vi thermal power plant. On March 31, 1968, bombing was restricted to areas south of the 20th parallel. The *Kitty Hawk*'s aircraft swept into North Vietnam's "Panhandle" region destroying two enemy surface-to-air (SAM) missile sites, a radar intercept site, and a camouflaged MIG-17 on the ground. Numerous cargo barges carrying supplies south were also destroyed.

In June 1968, the *Kitty Hawk* returned to San Diego after seven months in Southeast Asia. She underwent a two-month restricted yard availability in San Diego for repairs, then began training operations off the coast of California with units of the First Fleet in September of 1968.

The *Kitty Hawk* left San Diego on December 26, 1968 to begin her fourth Vietnam cruise and her sixth cruise to the Western Pacific. On January 5, while in Pearl Harbor, the *Kitty Hawk* and her embarked Air Wing Eleven received the Presidential Unit Citation for the 1967–1968 cruise. The citation, signed by President Lyndon B. Johnson, is the highest award a unit can receive and the *Kitty Hawk* is the first ship to be so awarded for Vietnam service.

The *USS Kitty Hawk CVA-63* has received the following awards: The Presidential Unit Citation; the Navy Unit Commendation (Vietnam); the National Defense Service Medal; the Armed Forces Expeditionary Medal; and the Vietnam Service Medal with four stars.

USS Constellation CVA-64 departs Pearl Harbor for second West Pacific Cruise. Starboard beam view (May 1964).

52

USS Constellation CVA-64

On September 14, 1957, construction began on the *USS Constellation CVA-64* at the New York Naval Shipyard, Brooklyn, N. Y.

Mrs. Christian A. Herter, wife of the then-Secretary of State, christened the new carrier on October 8, 1960. Capt. Thomas J. Walker took command on Navy Day, October 27, 1961, and the *Connie* was commissioned.

The present *Constellation* is named in honor of the U.S. Frigate of the same name, which was the first U.S. Navy ship. The frigate was named after a national symbol of importance—the circle of stars in the original American flag. The Continental Congress in 1777 stated "that the flag of the United States be thirteen stripes, alternate, red and white; that the Union be thirteen stars, white in a blue field, representing a new constellation."

From the day Captain Walker took command until January 25, 1962, the *Connie* operated from the New York Naval Shipyard. Builder's trials were conducted November 4–6, 1961, and Preliminary Acceptance trials from November 27 to December 2. Final Acceptance trials were held January 16–18, 1962.

On January 25, the *Constellation* departed New York for the Norfolk Navy Yard, arriving six days later. While en route, she test fired her Terrier booster vehicles to determine blast effects on the ship's structure and launching systems. At Norfolk, the carrier underwent a degaussing and deperming operations.

An interruption in shakedown operations came when the *Connie* was designated as recovery ship for Project Mercury. Extensive astronaut and capsule recovery practice was conducted, but foul weather postponed the project and the carrier resumed shakedown exercises.

On February 1, 1962, during Project Mercury, the first arrested landing was logged on the *Connie*. The A4D was flown by Commander George C. Watkins of Air Group Thirteen.

The *Constellation* arrived at Guantanamo Bay on March 14 and began flight operations. While at Roosevelt Roads, Puerto Rico, at 2:49 P.M., March 11, the carrier fired a Terrier missile to intercept a drone target. The launch and intercept were successful and this event marked the first time a Terrier had been launched from an aircraft carrier to intercept a target moving at supersonic speed. Another missile shot was conducted on April 17–18 and further flight operations training continued until May 3.

The *Connie* sailed from Cuba on May 4 and arrived at the New York Naval Shipyard on the 16th for final post-shakedown alterations.

Tension filled the air and spirits were high as word was received that the *Connie* would soon embark on a 15,000 mile cruise, taking her to a new home port at San Diego via Cape Horn.

On July 12, 1962, the carrier bid farewell to Norfolk and began the initial leg of her South American cruise. The *Connie's* first port of call was Trinidad. She crossed the equator on August 4, arriving in Rio de Janeiro, Brazil five days later.

Carrier Air Group Five demonstrated a jet fly-by over Copacabana Beach, which was witnessed by an estimated 500,000 Brazilians.

The *Constellation* rounded Cape Horn on August 19, and paid a short visit at Valparaiso, Chile, before steaming to the Panama Canal Zone on September 3, 1962. The *Connie* became the first large U.S. Navy vessel in ten years to hold open-house, and during the three-day lay-over more than 50,000 visitors came aboard. The new carrier sailed again on September 6 and made another stop four days later at Acapulco, Mexico.

On September 17, the *Constellation* arrived at her new home port of San Diego, and pulled alongside Quay Wall at North Island Naval Station.

Air Group Fourteen came aboard on November 19, and on the same day the first change of command was observed when Captain Walker was relieved by Capt.

Stanley W. Vejtasa. Two days later the *Connie* sailed for a three-week mid-Pacific cruise to Hawaii, where she underwent a vigorous flight operations and strike capabilities period. During January 1963, she took part in a Weapons Training Exercise and Nuclear Strike Training Exercise.

On February 23, the *Constellation* began her first Western Pacific cruise. After passing an Operational Readiness Inspection at Pearl Harbor, she steamed for Subic Bay, and joined the U.S. Seventh Fleet.

On March 23, the *Connie* arrived at Subic Bay and Rear Admiral Ralph H. Shifley, Commander, Carrier Division, Seventh Fleet, came aboard with his staff. While operating in the South China Sea on April 5, Admiral Shifley was relieved by Rear Admiral Thomas W. South. Five days later, the carrier arrived in Hong Kong for a three-day rest and relaxation period for the crewmen.

Throughout the Western Pacific cruise, the *Connie's* overseas homeport was Yokosuka. On April 20, while in port, the Commander of Carrier Division Five and his staff were received with Rear Admiral L. J. Kirn in command.

The carrier's next stop was the large industrial port of Kobe, Japan, where hundreds of visitors came aboard to see the modern aircraft carrier.

On June 3, the *Constellation* arrived at Iwakuni, Japan, and another "first" was entered in the log as a wedding took place. An officer and his fiancee were the first to be married on the carrier in ceremonies that took place on the forecastle.

From June 26 to July 3, the carrier was at Sasebo, Japan, and on July 11 she arrived at Buckner Bay, Okinawa.

While operating near Taiwan on July 25, 1963, President and Madame Chiang Kai Shek of the Republic of China came aboard for a one-day visit. The carrier returned to Yokosuka on August 24 to prepare for her trip to the United States.

The *Constellation* sailed into San Diego, California, on September 10, 1963. Captain Vejtasa was relieved by Capt. Frederic A. Bardshar on November 9.

Carrier Division Group Nine was commissioned on board on January 15, 1964, with Rear Admiral S. Guest in command. Flight operations and carrier qualifications were conducted throughout January and February. On March 2, the *Connie* began a three-week training cruise to Hawaii, then returned to San Diego on the 24th.

Nearly 3000 crewmen and their families heard the world-famous evangelist Billy Graham deliver the Sunday morning sermon on May 3 aboard the *Constella-*

USS Constellation CVA-64.

tion. Two days later, the carrier sailed for her second tour of duty in the Far East.

Following the normal Operational Readiness Inspection at Pearl Harbor, the *Connie* arrived in the South China Sea on June 6, 1964. A seven-day rest period began on July 27 when the ship dropped anchor in Hong Kong Harbor.

While at sea on August 4, the *Connie* launched strikes against patrol boats attacking an American destroyer in the Gulf of Tonkin and also assisted the *USS Ticonderoga CVA-14* in these strikes. The unprovoked attack by North Vietnamese P.T. Boats on two American warships occurred in international waters.

Additional air strikes were launched on August 5, against patrol boat bases in Communist North Viet-

nam. The *Connie* spent the majority of this cruise operating off the coast of South Vietnam.

On November 27, 1964, Capt. George H. Mahler III relieved Captain Bardshar as commanding officer. On the same day, crewmen of the carrier were awarded the Armed Forces Expeditionary Medal and those who had been a part of the Gulf of Tonkin operations were presented the Navy Unit Commendation which read:

"For exceptionally meritorious service in support of operations in the Gulf of Tonkin during the period August 2–5, 1964. By participating in immediate, determined and successful air strike counter attack operations against the North Vietnamese torpedo boats and supporting facilities Task Group 77.6 demonstrated the firm intent of the United States to maintain freedom of the seas and to take all necessary measures in defense of peace in Southeast Asia. The outstanding professional and technical competence and effective teamwork displayed by all members of Task Group 77.6 in carrying out this action were in keeping with the highest traditions of the United States Naval Service.

"All personnel attached to and serving Task Group 77.6 during the above period, including Commander, Carrier Division Nine; Commander, Destroyer Squadron 19, and members of staffs, air groups, and squadrons and detachments actually present and participating in the above action, are hereby authorized to wear the Navy Unit Commendation Ribbon. (Signed) *Paul H. Nitze*, Secretary of the Navy."

On January 20, 1965, the *Constellation* departed Yokosuka and returned to her home port in San Diego on February 1.

A month of upkeep began, and on March 22 the carrier was underway for the Puget Sound Naval Shipyard in Bremerton, Washington, where she would undergo an eight-month overhaul.

After unloading ammunition at Bangor, Wash., the *Connie* sailed into Puget Sound on March 31 and entered drydock #6 on May 14.

The massive overhaul that followed cost $19 million. The *Connie* was fitted out with an Automatic Landing System, an Inertial Navigation System, an Integrated Operational Intelligence System, and a Naval Tactical Data System.

Upon completion of yard work, the updated carrier returned to the Naval Ammunition Depot Bangor, Bremerton, Wash., to load explosives. Three days later, she went to San Diego for refresher training.

Capt. William D. Houser assumed command of the *Constellation* on January 29, 1966. Three months of operational training took place near the Southern California coast until May 12, when the carrier sailed for her third Western Pacific cruise.

From May 17 to 22 the *Connie* conducted her ORI at Pearl Harbor. She departed Hawaii on May 23 and arrived at Yokosuka, Japan, on June 1.

The *Constellation* became the flagship of Task Force 77, and on June 7 she sailed from Yokosuka to take her position in the Yankee station off the coast of South Vietnam.

On October 19, 1966, jets from the *Constellation* took advantage of a break in monsoon rains over North Vietnam and destroyed or damaged at least 14 barges and tugboats near Haiphong.

While on the line on "Yankee Station" from June 15th to November 9th, 1966, the carrier's air wing sank 22 North Vietnamese PT boats and damaged 13 others, destroyed 75 bridges, demolished 272 supply vehicles and damaged 337 others, and destroyed 304 barges and damaged 513 others to help stem the flow of military supplies between Communist North Vietnam and the Viet Cong and North Vienamese units in South Vietnam.

Daily air strikes were launched against heavily defended North Vietnamese transportation and supply dumps. From the *Constellation's* flight deck flew the aircraft that struck the Do Son, Dong Nham, and Haiphong petroleum storage areas, the Vong Bi thermal power plant, and the Ninh Binh and Thanh Hoa transhipment and storage areas.

The *Connie* left Yokosuka on November 9 arriving in San Diego on December 3, 1966. The anxious crew members hastily left the ship to meet friends and relatives after a tedious seven-month deployment.

The *Connie* and her Air Wing received their second Navy Unit Commendation for Vietnam service, which read in part: ". . . for outstanding professionalism, initiative and unstinting devotion to duty . . . in carrying out numerous major strikes on significant military objectives in North Vietnam and inflicted extensive damage on these important and strategic targets during their May–November 1966 deployment."

A yard overhaul was completed and the carrier operated off the California coast. She departed San Diego in April 1967, and returned to Yankee Station on May 18.

The carrier's A6A Intruders blasted Kim Nac bridge at Dai Thuy; petroleum storage areas at Haiphong were also struck, as well as the Cat Bi airfield and Thi Long railroad bridge.

On June 2, 1967, the Do Va freight transshipment port received heavy damage. On June 20, aircraft from the *Connie* and *Enterprise* hit a railroad yard and bridge near Haiphong plus a SAM site. Into July the *Connie* did her share in the Vietnam campaign. The Vinh power plant was severely damaged on July 25 after the target was first raked by eight-inch guns on the *USS St. Paul CA-73.*

On August 7 pilots from the *Connie* hit military barracks outside Haiphong plus ammunition dumps and a motor pool. As Communist MIG-21 jets rose to intercept the *Connie's* pilots, two were downed by air-to-air missiles from an F4C Phantom II. Two days of strikes ten miles south of the Red Chinese border on August 13–14 destroyed the Loc Binh highway bridge and a railroad bypass bridge at Lang Son. The latter was under construction by the North Vietnamese to link their main rail supply line into Red China.

The outstanding efforts of Carrier Air Wing 14 did

An F8U landing on canted deck during flight operations.
USS Constellation CVA-64.

not go unrewarded. They successfully slowed the movement of the enemy war supplies and reinforcements into South Vietnam. On October 9 they broke through an intensive flak barrage and smashed military barracks. Van Dien vehicle depot south of Hanoi was left in flames on October 26. Two days later a three-pronged strike blasted a freight transshipment point at Chi Lai, a barge repair yard at Kien An, and the Cat Bi airfield.

On October 30, Kien An field and strategic fuel storage areas at Haiphong received another destructive

visit from the *Connie's* flyers. The flight leader of this strike commented: "Three large fireballs erupted, one through the other. It looked like the Great Pumpkin had arrived."

On November 7, 1967, the Haiphong area was smashed again. The nearby Ninh Ngoai boat works was damaged and a 30-car train was wrecked. The *Connie's* last major strike took place on the 8th when the Dong Lo transshipment point near Hanoi was hit, resulting in the destruction of many buildings.

Following a short stop at Subic Bay and Yokosuka, the big carrier steamed for home, arriving in San Diego on December 4, 1967.

The *USS Constellation CVA-64* received her third Navy Unit Commendation for her services from May 18 to November 26, 1967.

While conducting training exercises off California on February 17, 1968, the *Connie* was visited by President Johnson. The President attended religious services the next morning and was briefed by the carrier's senior officers. Later, President Johnson spoke to the crew saying: "Three times this ship has stood on Yankee Station. I am proud to say to your Captain, to all the officers and men of the *Constellation,* well done."

The *USS Constellation CVA-64* has received the Navy Unit Commendation (Vietnam); the Meritorious Unit Commendation; National Defense Service Medal; Naval Expeditionary Medal; Armed Forces Expeditionary Medal; and the Vietnam Service Medal with three stars.

NUCLEAR POWER: THE ENTERPRISE

USS Enterprise CVAN-65 (May 1964).

53

USS Enterprise CVA (N)-65

On December 2, 1942, a team of eminent scientists, under the direction of Enrico Fermi, ushered in the atomic age when they produced the first sustained chain reaction.

As many had feared, the terrific force of this energy was destined for release in the form of a lethal weapon —the A-Bomb.

At the end of World War II it was necessary to develop other, more powerful, bombs. But at the same time, this newly discovered power could also be channeled into more protective and humane uses.

And so it was that a precedent was established when the eighth ship to bear the name *Enterprise* was authorized for construction. The *USS Enterprise CVA*

(N)-65 was built at the Newport News Shipbuilding Company; her keel was laid on February 4, 1958, and she slid down the ways on September 24, 1960, to become the first aircraft carrier to be powered by nuclear energy.

Mrs. William B. Franke, wife of the Secretary of the Navy, christened this mighty addition to the Fleet.

On October 29, 1961 the *Enterprise* began six days of builder's and pre-acceptance sea trials; this was also the first time that both evaluations had been combined into one test period. The new carrier transcended the expectations of everyone and her trial speed was over 40 miles per hour.

"I think we've hit the jackpot!" exclaimed Admiral

George W. Anderson, Jr., Chief of Naval Operations.

The *Enterprise* was officially commissioned on November 25, 1961. John B. Connally, Jr., Secretary of the Navy, remarked that she was as worthy as her forerunner (*USS Enterprise CV-6*) of World War II fame and said, "she will reign a long, long time as Queen of the Seas."

Captain Vincent Paul de Poix became her first commanding officer.

The overall length of the *Enterprise* measures 1101 feet with a beam of 133 feet. Her extreme width at the flight deck is 252 feet. She has a full load displacement of 86,000 tons with a draft of 35 feet. Her crew comprises 400 officers and 4200 enlisted men. The distance from her keel to the mast top equals that of a 25-story building and the ship is powered by eight nuclear reactors which require refueling only once every three years. She can handle 100 aircraft, launching them at a rate of four per minute from four catapults.

On January 12, 1962, she went to sea for duty with the Fleet. Five days later, Commander George C. Talley, Jr., leader of Air Group One, made the first landing flying an F8U *Crusader* jet.

Upon completion of carrier qualification exercises she became a unit of the Project Mercury Recovery Force off Bermuda. This second effort to launch a man into space was postponed and she returned to Norfolk.

The *Enterprise* departed home port on February 5 and sailed to Guantanamo Bay, Cuba, via Mayport, Florida, where she received Heavy Attack Squadron 7. Another group, Fighter Squadron 102, was already aboard.

On February 15, Lieutenant John Brockner of that squadron made the carrier's 1000th landing.

Shakedown operations were completed on April 5 and the "Big E" returned to homeport three days later. On April 14, President John F. Kennedy came aboard to watch a demonstration of the Second Fleet's capabilities. Also aboard for this event were numerous foreign diplomats and U.S. Congressmen.

On June 25 the *Enterprise* officially became a member of the Second Fleet. With Carrier Air Group Six embarked, she held training exercises in the western Atlantic, which ended on July 4 when she sailed into Boston. Open house was held and 12,000 Bostonians came aboard. The carrier departed the next day to participate in her first full-scale exercise as a unit of Task Force 24.

During the operation she launched long-range aircraft "strikes" at land targets and was active in anti-air warfare before returning to Norfolk on July 12.

On August 3 she sailed again and arrived in the Mediterranean ready for duty with the Sixth Fleet. She took part in an exercise called "Riptide III," which included aircraft and ships from France, the United Kingdom, the U.S., and Portugal. On August 16 she provided close air support to amphibious troops landing at Sardinia, then made her first foreign port of call at Cannes, France.

During September the *Enterprise* participated in a NATO exercise in the Aegean Sea along with 24 ships of the Sixth Fleet plus units of the United Kingdom, Greece, and Turkey. The objective was to simulate attacking and defending an amphibious force as it inched towards its target area. *Enterprise* pilots were able to develop their skills in both conventional and nuclear warfare tactics. After concluding this cruise the "Big E" reported to the Second Fleet on October 2, and returned to Norfolk nine days later.

On October 12 she became the flagship of Rear Admiral J. T. Hayward, Commander Carrier Division Two. Meanwhile, the Cuban crisis was precipitated by the arrival of Soviet missiles to that island. Within a week the "Big E" took up a position near Cuba.

President Kennedy announced the quarantine of Cuba on October 22. This blockade remained in effect until November 21, when Russia withdrew the offensive weapons under the eyes of the U.S. Navy task force. The *Enterprise* returned to home port on December 7 and conducted carrier suitability trials for the new A6A and E2A aircraft.

On February 6, 1963, the carrier was underway again. The next day she was joined by the *USS Bainbridge DLG (N)-251*, a nuclear-powered frigate. The "Big E" relieved the *USS Forrestal CVA-59* on February 16 at Pollensa Bay. After training exercises in the Mediterranean she went to Cannes on February 25 and remained until March 4.

On March 11 she arrived at Athens and was visited by King Paul I and Queen Fredericka of Greece. Then the "Big E" joined in combined air defense exercises at Palmero, Sicily.

While at Cannes on July 20 Captain Frederick H. Michaelis relieved Captain de Poix and two days later a visit was made by Under Secretary of the Navy, Paul B. Fay, Jr.

During this period the *Enterprise* participated in a four-day exercise called "Poopdeck II," which was followed by an air support strike for amphibious landing exercises off Southern Sardinia.

On August 24 the crew of the "Big E" watched the arrival of the *USS Independence CVA-62*, which would relieve them. The *Enterprise* returned to home port on

USS Enterprise CVAN-65.

September 4. Four days later the crew learned that they had been awarded the Battle Efficiency "E" and the Air Department had garnered their "E" for battle readiness.

The *Enterprise* departed Norfolk on February 6, 1964, and relieved the *USS Independence* on the 22nd at Golfo de Palma. On the evening of February 25 she made a high-speed run to meet the Finnish Ship *SS Verna Paulin*. A helicopter transported the carrier's medical officer to the merchant vessel to render aid to a seaman injured in a fall.

The carrier joined Amphibious Task Force 61 March 11–14 for a combined ASW and air defense exercise off Turkey and Italy. The "Big E" was off Cyprus March 14–21, during a time of political unrest on the island. After a while the carrier resumed normal duties.

On May 13 the *Enterprise* rendezvoused with the *USS Bainbridge* and *USS Long Beach* to form the first nuclear-powered task force. At that time the "Big E" and the *Long Beach* were the only two ships in the Atlantic Fleet with the Navy Tactical Data System (NTDS). They conducted the initial tests and evaluations of this system and followed that with an ASW exercise, "Fairgame II," held off France and Corsica. On July 24 the *USS Forrestal* relieved the "Big E" at Pollensa Bay.

The *Enterprise, Long Beach,* and *Bainbridge* were designated Task Force One on July 31 and steamed by Gibraltar to begin a 30,565-mile journey around the world. To demonstrate the advantages of nuclear-powered surface vessels, the task force performed the entire 65-day globe-circling voyage without receiving any fuel, food, or other provisions while en route. This same fleet could not be accomplished by a task force of conventionally powered ships.

This epoch-making cruise was titled "Operation Sea Orbit." The ships welcomed visits on August 3–5 from dignitaries representing Senegal, Sierra Leone, and

Liberia while cruising south along the African coast. Then the "Big E" crossed the equator, and in true Naval tradition, 4300 "Pollywogs" were initiated into the status of "Shellbacks." On the last day of August the carrieer was west of Australia, where a beach flyover was made over Perth and Fremantle.

On September 4 the "Big E" stopped at Sydney for a three-day stopover and was visited by the Prime Minister of Australia, Sir Robert Menzies. The carrier transited the South Pacific to Cape Horn September 9–17 and crossed the International Date Line on the 10th. An air power demonstration was conducted for dignitaries from Buenos Aires, Argentina and Montevideo, Uruguay on September 21. The carrier steamed north through the Caribbean on the following day on her last leg of the cruise.

On October 2 Air Wing Six was launched and on the following day the carrier arrived at Norfolk while thousands cheered from the dock.

During her eight-month cruise she had steamed 74,-943 miles. Navy Secretary Paul Nitze came aboard and addressed the crew.

The trio of ships that made up the nuclear powered task force sailed 5155 miles in 8 days, 9 hours, and 52 minutes, at an average speed of 25 knots. They had established a new speed record during the voyage and the *Enterprise* crew learned that they had once again earned the Battle Efficiency "E" for the year, as well as the Battle "E" for her air weapons, engineering, and reactor departments.

These awards were presented by Vice Admiral Ramsey on October 9. After a one-day dependents' cruise, the carrier went into drydock at Newport News for her first overhaul. While there she received the Integrated Operational Intelligence System (IOIS). Also installed was a Satellite Navigation System developed by Johns Hopkins University. Other modifications included a remodeling of all aviation electronics shops. The old port missile sponson was converted into a 280-man compartment. All four of her drive shafts were removed and two were replaced.

On February 17, 1965, the *Enterprise* left the drydock and got underway for sea trials on June 22 to conduct carrier qualifications off the Virginia Capes.

The carrier sailed to Guantanamo Bay on July 16 to prepare for an Operational Readiness Inspection (ORI). The next day, Captain Michaelis was relieved by Captain James L. Holoway. The "Big E" returned to home port after the training period and ORI.

The *Enterprise* departed on October 9 and sailed to the South China Sea for participation in the Vietnam turmoil.

She rounded the Cape of Good Hope and entered the Indian Ocean on October 14. She arrived at Leyte on November 27.

On December 2 the "Big E" prepared for air strikes against the Viet Cong. Rear Admiral Henry L. Miller, Commander Carrier Division Three, aboard the *Enterprise,* sent the following message to the Secretary of the Navy: "I have the distinct honor and pleasure to announce to you that the first nuclear-powered task force group in your Pacific Fleet and the United States Navy engaged the enemy in South Vietnam." The "Big E," with all-jet Air Wing 11, struck hard against the Viet Cong installations in the Third and Fourth Corps areas.

Commander O. E. Krueger, leader of VA-94, became the first pilot of Air Wing Nine to enter combat when he led a strike with A4s against Viet Cong strongholds near Bien Hoa. On December 2 the pilots attacked enemy positions along the entire 450-mile length of South Vietnam. During this time they dropped 167 tons of bombs and rockets. They struck again the next day and set a new record of strikes launched in a single day.

On December 14, then-United States Ambassador Henry Cabot Lodge escorted then-South Vietnamese Premier Nguyen Ky (currently the country's Vice President) and his staff aboard the *Enterprise.* Two days later, air strikes were sent against roads, bridges, and supply centers to interdict the flow of enemy arms and ammunition. For the first time in aerial warfare, the emplacements had to be struck before the targets could be hit, for they were heavily defended by complex antiaircraft systems.

On December 22 the *Enterprise* pilots, along with those of the *USS Kitty Hawk CVA-63* and *USS Ticonderoga CVA-14,* attacked the Yong Bi power plant, which produced two-thirds of all the electrical power for Hanoi and the sea port at Haiphong. The raid was a complete success and on Christmas Day a truce was made to invite the North Vietnamese government to open peace negotiations.

The *Enterprise* and *Bainbridge* received world-wide attention as the largest and most powerful warships of the fleet. The presence of the "Big E" at Yankee and Dixie stations and the Tonkin Gulf was felt by all. Their speed, detection systems, and operational capabilities proved to exceed original estimates during their first week on the line.

The first big strike of the New Year came on January 8, 1966. A total of 116 sorties against Viet Cong targets in all four corps areas in South Vietnam were launched from the "Big E," *Ticonderoga* and *Hancock.* Operations continued until the 15th when the *Enterprise* went for a short rest to Subic Bay. She was back on Dixie Station on February 4 to strike enemy strongholds.

She shifted to Yankee Station seven days later and sent strikes against VC supply depots in the North.

On February 20 strikes were launched against the Bai Thuong barracks near Thanh Hoa and a storage area near Vinh. Three days later pilots from the "Big E" and the *Kitty Hawk* struck enemy troop concentrations and supply areas south of the DMZ. That same day the *Enterprise* departed Yankee Station for a ten-day rest at Subic Bay. While there, on March 6, Astronaut Walter Schirra and his wife visited the carrier. A visit was also made by Philippine President Ferdinand E. Marcos five days later.

The "Big E" departed March 13 for joint exercises with units of the Chinese Nationalists of Taiwan. Generalissimo Chaing Kai Shek came aboard for a brief visit before the carrier went back to Yankee Station on March 16.

The monsoon season was at its peak, bringing low foggy ceilings and thunderstorms, but the air group was able to fly through the heavy AA fire and bad weather to hit their assigned targets. A typical escape was that of Lieutenant Greenwood of VF-92. Captain Holloway described this incident saying, "Lieutenant Greenwood was making a high-speed, low-altitude attack on a bridge in North Vietnam when his jet was hit by enemy antiaircraft fire and burst into flames. Realizing that his aircraft was flyable, but mortally damaged, he climbed through the overcast and turned eastward to the Gulf of Tonkin. His intention was to remain with the plane as long as possible in an effort to get well out over the Gulf, to bail out. The low cloud cover prevented him from seeing whether he was over land or water. When he could no longer control his burning aircraft, Lieutenant Greenwood ejected and, after descending through the low clouds, found himself entering the water just a few hundred yards off the hostile shoreland. He could see armed men putting to sea in powered junks and sampans heading for his position.

"As soon as Greenwood's plane had been hit, the rescue forces had been alerted and were now converging on the location of the downed pilot. It was late in the day, and in the gloom of the low overcast, Lieutenant Greenwood's position in the water was difficult to pinpoint. One rescue plane had him in sight, but was damaged and driven off by the heavy fire from shore and from the boats closing in on the downed pilot. As Greenwood lighted his last flare, a helicopter spotted him and approached for pickup.

The nearest enemy boat was only 150 yards away and firing on Greenwood and the helicopter. With the waist gunner using his 50 caliber machine gun and the pilot firing his tommy gun, the helicopter held off the armed sampan long enough to hoist Greenwood to safety."

For almost a week, beginning April 22, the nuclear carrier's air wing struck enemy supply centers at Vinh. The carrier then retired from the line and headed for Subic Bay when a message was received to assist a downed aircraft between Hong Kong and the Liuchow Peninsula. Afterwards, the carrier sailed into Subic Bay for a six-day rest.

The *Enterprise* shifted operations to Dixie Station on April 28 and struck the enemy at the Mekong Delta. On May 31 she was again at Yankee Station and conducted a major strike against a military supply complex at Nam Dinh, only 30 miles from Hanoi. After six successive missions, massive wreckage was all that remained.

On June 5 the "Big E" was ready to come home. Since December 2, 1965, she had launched 13,020 combat sorties and delivered 8000 tons of ordance on selected targets. On June 10 she departed Subic Bay for the States.

One of the biggest welcome-home celebrations took place on June 21 as the *Enterprise* slipped under the Golden Gate Bridge. Whistles chirped as fire boats shot geysers into the air and a flotilla of small craft escorted her up the bay. The "Big E" docked at Alameda Naval Air Station, where family and friends roared with happiness. The Mayors of San Francisco, Oakland, and Alameda proclaimed an *Enterprise* Day.

On June 30 the carrier entered the San Francisco Naval Shipyard for maintenance. Her catapults were completely overhauled and several compartments were updated to handle the new E2A *Hawkeye* and A6A *Intruder* aircraft that would be used on future cruises.

Following a refresher training period off the coast of Southern California, the *Enterprise* departed Alameda on November 19. After an ORI off Hawaii she arrived at Subic Bay on December 8 and then proceeded to Yankee Station, arriving nine days later.

Air strikes were launched on December 27 against enemy infiltration routes north of the DMZ. Railroads were hit at Vinh Pho Can and storage areas at Ninh Binh and Van Coi received heavy damage.

Throughout January 1967 the carrier's air wing conducted armed coastal reconnaissance and destroyed enemy waterborne supply boats and coastal highway bridges.

Aircraft from the *Ticonderoga* teamed with the *En-*

terprise's pilots February 4–5 to hit the Thanh Hoa trans-shipment complex and it was learned later that major reconstruction would be required before it could again function properly.

The Grumman A6A *Intruder* are extremely efficient in bad weather. Guided to their targets by computerized systems, the *Intruder* crews actually preferred night flights and rainy days for their missions.

An eight-day ceasefire for the Vietnamese Tet holiday began February 8, which gave the enemy AA gunners time to reinforce their positions. During the night of February 24, several *Intruder* jets flew into the heart of an intense AA and surface to air missiles to complete a successful attack on thermal power plants at Bac Giang and Hon Gai. These targets were vital to North Vietnamese defense capabilities and the impact rendered from the attacks signaled a new phase in the air war. The Ha Ton Naval Supply complex was struck fifteen days later.

For many months, the RVAH-7 pilots flew unarmed photo missions in the wake of the carrier's attacking planes and necessarily faced the same enemy fire as their armed companions. On June 6, about 35 miles southwest of Hanoi, the photo teams took some excellent pictures, which revealed several heavily camouflaged SAM missiles on trailers. The next day a strike force was launched to destroy the missiles, and after the strike there remained only smoking rubble.

The Hon Gia railyard and supply depot was hit June 12–13. The "Big E" departed the line on June 20 and arrived three days later at Subic Bay. She departed June 26 for the States, arriving at Alameda on July 6.

Captain Kent L. Lee relieved Captain Holloway on July 11 and the carrier began an overhaul at San Francisco. Upon completion she conducted air operations and refresher training off the California coast until December.

On January 3, 1968, the *Enterprise* departed Alameda and following an ORI at Hawaii she steamed to Sasebo, Japan. She was the first nuclear-powered surface vessel to visit that part of the world, and when she arrived on January 19—in company with the nuclear guided missile frigate USS *Truxtun DLG(N)-35*—she was met with demonstrations by left-wing extremist groups.

On January 23, 1968 the "Big E" departed Sasebo and that afternoon received word that the USS *Pueblo AGER-2* had been seized by North Koreans off Wonsan. The carrier quickly headed north in response to orders and her air group was prepared to assist in any way necessary. Following a period of watchful waiting in the Sea of Japan, the carrier sailed southwards.

Air strikes were launched on February 21 when the *Enterprise* arrived at Yankee Station. Three days later strikes were sent at the port facility on Hanoi's Red River. The war was carried deeper into North Vietnam's panhandle on the 26th when planes struck a highway bridge near Dong Hoi.

On March 2 a thermal power plant northeast of Haiphong was blasted. Beginning March 9, three days of strikes smashed the Ninh Giang cargo transshipment and storage area near Haiphong. Kien, an airfield near that city, was the target on the 15th and the field was cratered by numerous bombs.

After a brief rest at Subic Bay the "Big E" returned to Yankee Station on March 26 and blasted the Vinh airfield and Cam Pha transformer station. The next day damage was inflicted to oil storage tanks in the same area.

With the advent of President Johnson's bombing limitations in April, Air Wing Nine concentrated interdiction strikes near Vinh and the border area along the DMZ. On May 20, the "Big E" retired from the line and after a brief stop at Subic Bay, anchored in Hong Kong Harbor to give her crew a week of rest and relaxation. Interdiction strikes were then resumed until June 26, on which day, the carrier steamed for home, arriving at Alameda on the 18th of July 1968.

Nine days after her return home, the *Enterprise* steamed for the Puget Sound Naval Shipyard, Bremerton, Washington, for a minor overhaul. She left Bremerton on September 28 and conducted underway training from October 9 to November 21.

On January 9, 1969, the *Enterprise* left Alameda to begin her fourth deployment to the Western Pacific. While conducting Operation Readiness Inspection (ORI) off Hawaii on January 14, the carrier suffered an unfortunate accident in which explosions and fires took the lives of 28 crewmen, 15 aircraft and extensive damage to the flight deck. The yard workers at Pearl Harbor joined forces with the ship's crew and the carrier was repaired in half of the original estimated time. After five days of sea trials off Hawaii, the *Enterprise* set course for Subic Bay, arriving on March 27. She reached the Gulf of Tonkin on March 31 and immediately began launching her aircraft against the enemy in South Vietnam.

The "Big E" steamed into the Sea of Japan on April 16 when the North Koreans shot down a Navy EC-121 reconnaissance aircraft. She arrived off the coast of Korea on April 20 and joined three other carriers as flagship of the newly reinstated Task Force 71. By late April, three of the carriers had left, but the *Enterprise*

AIH(AD-6) aircraft of VA-65, commanded by CDR. H. W. Swinburn, at the ready with 12 250-pound and one 500-pound MCBR bomb. Flight deck of *USS Enterprise CVAN-65* at sea.

remained, conducting special flight operations. After 47 days at sea, the carrier was relieved by the *USS Kitty Hawk CVA-63*, and returned to Subic Bay for a five-day rest period. She left Subic Bay on May 21 and proceeded to the Republic of Singapore for a five-day visit to the city-state on the Malayan Peninsula.

The *Enterprise* returned to Yankee Station on May 31 and remained on the line up to June 15 then after two days at Subic Bay, returned to Alameda on July 2, 1969. The "Big E" left Alameda on July 14 to undergo an extended yard period at Norfolk, Virginia. Over 2800 men of the carrier became "Shellbacks" when the carrier rounded Cape Horn. A short visit was paid to Rio de Janeiro, Brazil, during the voyage to Norfolk. The yard period will last for one year and the ship will have her nuclear cores replaced. The present cores lasted four years, the new ones to be installed will power the *Enterprise* for over 10 years.

The *USS Enterprise CVA(N)-65* has received the Navy Unit Commendation; National Defense Service Medal; Navy Expeditionary Medal; Armed Forces Expeditionary Medal; Vietnam Service Medal with four bronze stars; and the Vietnamese Campaign Service Medal.

KITTY HAWK CLASS: HULL NUMBERS 66, 67

Starboard bow aerial view of the *USS America CVA-66* underway off the U.S. Naval Base, Guantanamo Bay, Cuba, during her shakedown training course (June 1965).

54

USS America CVA-66

The *USS America CVA-66* is one of the Navy's newest carriers. She was contracted for by the Newport News Shipbuilding Company of Virginia on November 25, 1960, and her keel was laid January 9, 1961.

Mrs. David L. McDonald, wife of the Chief of Naval Operations, christened the new ship on February 1, 1964. As Mrs. McDonald smashed the traditional champagne bottle across the bow, the Naval Air Force Atlantic Fleet Band played "Anchors Aweigh" and thousands of spectators cheered the eventful occasion.

The name *America* was the personal choice of the late President John F. Kennedy. When he assigned it to CVA-66 it marked the first time a ship so named was designed and built specifically for the U.S. Navy. Over 37 months prior to her launching, the *America* had begun to take a definite form. Rivet guns joined bending steel and welders to produce an eerie sound of breathing while pumping life into the hull.

Four giant deck elevators, each weighing 150 tons, were installed. A plane can be moved from the hangar deck to the flight deck in only 45 seconds. In the space of one minute, a plane can be loaded, moved up to the flight deck, unloaded and the giant elevator returned to the hangar deck.

The *America's* 300-ton island structure was erected on the center of the flight deck. A 24-inch margin was deleted from the base of the structure and rewelded when the island was permanently positioned.

Moving the island housing was equivalent to moving a five-story building along a 102-foot sliding way. The 52-foot-tall island was placed upon a greased wooden sliding and a crawler crane pulled the load along the deck. The 102-foot journey took 23 minutes.

Subsequent to the gala launching, the *America* was moved to a fitting-out pier where a year was used to put on the finishing touches.

She successfully completed the builders' trials on November 20, 1964. At 9:00 A.M., December 1, she slipped away from her berth and got underway for preliminary acceptance tests. During the builders' evaluations November 18–20, Captain Lawrence Heyworth, Jr., the prospective commanding officer, was aboard and voiced his approval of the carrier's performance.

The *America* is conventionally powered and carried a price tag of $156 million. She is a modified *Forrestal*-class vessel, but numerous improvements and inherent operational abilities put her in a class of her own. The two major differences between her and the *Forrestal* class are elevator configurations and a modernized island structure.

The *America* has a standard displacement of 64,000 tons and displaces 77,600 tons fully loaded. Her length stretches out 1047½ feet with a width at flight deck of 252 feet. Her flight deck covers 4.5 acres. She has two massive anchors, each weighing 30 tons; each link of her anchor chain weighs 391 pounds.

She houses two twin terrier missile launches, and her aircraft are launched from a quartet of C-13 steam catapults. Four geared turbines are rotated by eight Foster Wheeler Boilers that supply the power to turn four huge propellers, each standing 21 feet high.

Her crew consists of 470 officers and 4434 enlisted men plus a contingent of 61 U.S. Marines.

Attempting to compare the giant size of the *America* is easy. For instance, if the Eiffel Tower was laid on her flight deck, the Paris landmark would overhang a mere five feet. The carrier is twice the length of the Washington Monument and the gigantic Empire State Building is only 202½ feet taller than the length of the *USS America*.

Electronic systems of a highly sophisticated nature maintain the carrier's operational efficiency. The combined output of all electronic equipment aboard the ship is equal to 200 powerful radio stations operating

Starboard beam aerial view of the *USS America* CVA-66 operating off the capes of Virginia (April 1965).

simultaneously. Her potential generating power will satisfy the needs of a city with over one million inhabitants. The *America* has 24,350 lighting fixtures and 1400 telephones.

On January 23, 1965, the *USS America* was placed into commission at Norfolk with Captain Lawrence Heyworth, Jr., taking command. She departed March 16 for a six-week training schedule off the Virginia Capes. During this period on April 5, Commander Kenneth B. Austin, the *America's* executive officer, made the first landing in an A4 *Skyhawk.*

Air Wing Six reported aboard on May 1 and the carrier headed for the Caribbean for two months of ORI training and received an excellent rating, the highest mark ever won by a combat ship during the past three years.

On July 1 the *America* returned to Norfolk for post-shakedown alterations. Fourteen days later she was designated flagship of Carrier Division Two and participated in Second Fleet operations until August 21. She went through another ORI during October off Guantanamo Bay, Cuba, and again won an excellent rating. The proud carrier returned to home port on October 27.

Normal flight operations were conducted off the Virginia Capes throughout November, then on the 30th the *America* departed Norfolk and arrived at Pollensa Bay on December 9. She steamed into the Mediterranean Sea the following day and spent the next seven months as an integral member of the Sixth Fleet. Various training exercises were conducted, inter-

An E-1B "Tracer" air early warning aircraft being towed from the elevator onto the hangar deck of the *America*, March 31, 1965.

spersed with gala port calls. On July 1, 1966, the carrier headed for home, and arrived nine days later at Norfolk.

From July 15 to August 28 she was at the yards for an overhaul, which was completed on September 20. She resumed normal duties near Guantanamo Bay.

During November and December the *America* participated in a major Second Fleet exercise called "Operation Lantiflex 66." Afterwards she went back to Norfolk.

On January 10, 1967, the carrier departed home port and sailed to the Mediterranean, where she operated in the Ionian Sea. Word was received that she had been awarded the coveted Battle Efficiency "E" for 1966.

Tension was building between Israel and Arab forces and Egypt had placed troops in the Gaza Strip and demanded the withdrawal of U.N. Peace Keeping forces. The Israeli forces beefed up their troops and both forces were then on constant alert. The United Arab Republic closed the Gulf of Aqaba to Israeli ships.

The *America's* anxious crew watched the latest developments on the carrier's closed circuit WMAR-TV. On the morning of June 2, 1967 a Soviet destroyer armed with surface-to-air missiles continuously zigzagged through the carrier's formation.

Vice Admiral William I. Martin, Commander of the mighty Sixth Fleet, sent a message to the intruder stating that its behavior had disrupted the carrier's operations and was hampering its freedom of movement on the high seas. The destroyer then departed the area but was shortly replaced by another Soviet destroyer, which remained for the next few days.

News of war between the Arabs and Israelis reached the *America* on the morning of June 5 as the carrier was receiving fuel from the *USS Truckee AO-147.* By evening, general quarters had been sounded and an advanced state of readiness was established.

While sailing 15 miles north of the Sinai Peninsula in International Waters, the technical research ship *USS Liberty AGTR-5* was accidentally attacked by Israeli torpedo boats and jet fighters. The attack came at 2:00 P.M. on June 8. The *America* received a message from the stricken *Liberty* but was unable to learn the identification of the attackers.

The *America's* flight deck erupted into a bustle of activity as F4B *Phantoms* were launched to ward off further attacks on the *Liberty.*

A message from Tel Aviv was received and it was learned of the tragic error of the attack. The carrier recalled her planes.

An A-4E from Naval Air Test Center, Patuxent River, Maryland, landing aboard the *USS America* for carrier suitability trials.

Even though the assault upon the *Liberty* was unintentional, 34 American sailors had been killed and 75 seriously wounded.

At 6:00 A.M. the destroyers *USS Davis DD-937* and *USS Massey DD-778* rendezvoused with the *Liberty* to assist in helping the wounded. Participating were two corpsmen from the *America.*

By 10:30 a pair of *America* helicopters arrived and began transporting the more seriously wounded men to the carrier. One hour later the *America* pulled up alongside the *Liberty,* 350 miles south of Souda Bay, Crete, where 50 wounded sailors were taken aboard.

Fighting between the Israelis and Arabs continued. As the Israeli forces edged closer to victory, the Arabs accused the Sixth Fleet of providing air cover

for Israeli ground troops. This charge was absolutely false, but was nevertheless reported by the newsmen in the area.

Memorial services for the men of the *Liberty* were conducted on June 10, but the *America* remained on station several more days before resuming routine flight operations. The *America* steamed through the Strait of Gibraltar on September 12 and returned to Norfolk on the 20th after eight months in the Mediterranean. She immediately entered the Norfolk Navy Shipyard for overhaul until January 6, 1968, then spent the next few months training with the Second Fleet.

On April 10, 1968, the *America* left Norfolk for her first Western Pacific deployment. After a brief visit

View of the *USS America CVA-66* underway in Hampton, Virginia.

to Rio de Janeiro, she continued her voyage through the South Atlantic and the Indian Ocean to the South China Sea, arriving at Subic Bay, Philippine Islands on May 21. The *America* launched her embarked Carrier Air Wing Six over North Vietnam to interdict water and highway supply traffic up to May 31, 1968. She spent four months on Yankee Station in the Gulf of Tonkin. Her off the line ports of call between combat operations were, Hong Kong, the Philippines, and Yokosuka, Japan. Her final period on Yankee Station was from September 28 to October 30. After a four-day stay in Subic Bay, the *America* began her long trip home on November 3, 1968.

Ports of call on her return to the U.S. included Sydney, Wellington (New Zealand), and Rio de Janeiro. The *America* returned to Norfolk on December 16, 1968. On January 8, 1969, she left Norfolk for ten days of carrier qualifications for new pilots off the coast of Jacksonville, Florida. On January 23, 1969, the *America* celebrated her fourth birthday. She entered the Norfolk Naval Shipyard, Portsmouth, Virginia, the following day for an extensive overhaul.

The *John F. Kennedy* shortly after being launched on May 27, 1967 at the Newport News Shipbuilding and Dry Dock Company, Newport News, Virginia.

55

USS John F. Kennedy CVA-67

The U.S. Navy's newest aircraft carrier carries the name of the 35th President of the United States. Ironically, while Kennedy, a strong advocate of sea power, was the chief executive, funds were allocated in 1963 for construction of a new attack aircraft carrier to be designated CVA-67, but no name had been chosen.

On June 6, 1963, President Kennedy stood on the flight deck of the *USS Kitty Hawk CVA-63* and addressed the officers and crew, recalling the 1962 Cuban quarantine. "Events of October 1962," he said, "indicated as they had all through history, that control of the sea means security. Control of the seas can mean

Miss Caroline Kennedy, daughter of the late President, christens the *USS John F. Kennedy CVA-67*, named in honor of her father. Looking on are her mother, Mrs. John F. Kennedy, and her brother John. May 27, 1967.

peace. The United States must control the seas if it's to protect your security and those countries which stretch thousands of miles away that look upon you on the ship and the sister ships of the United States Navy."

John Fitzgerald Kennedy was born May 29, 1917 at Brookline, Massachusetts. He was commissioned an Ensign in the U.S. Naval Reserve in 1942. While commanding torpedo patrol boat PT-109 on August 1, 1942, his craft was rammed by a Japanese destroyer. Despite injuries to himself, he swam for hours while holding a shipmate, and finally reached shore. After nine days of struggle in enemy-held territory, Kennedy

lead his crew to safety. For "outstanding courage, endurance and leadership which contributed to the saving of several lives," John F. Kennedy was awarded the Navy and Marine Corps Medal. On October 10, 1942, he was promoted to Lieutenant (j.g.), then to full Lieutenant on October 1, 1943.

After the war Kennedy returned to his prewar job as a correspondent for the *Chicago Herald American* and the International News Service.

Elected to Congress in 1946, he represented the 11th Congressional District of Massachusetts until elected to the Senate seven years later.

John F. Kennedy was elected President of the

An F-4 "Phantom II" is readied for launch from the *John F. Kennedy* on October 22, 1968.

United States on November 8, 1960, but would not serve his full term in office. Tragedy struck on November 23, 1963, while he rode in a motorcade greeting the citizens of Dallas. An assassin's bullets reached out and found the President and the country's leader was pronounced dead at Parkland Hospital a short time later. His body was laid to rest at Arlington National Cemetery on November 25, 1963.

It was appropriate that President Lyndon Johnson designated CVA-67 as the *John F. Kennedy* in respect for the late President.

The keel was laid on October 22, 1964, at the Newport News Shipbuilding Company and she was launched on May 27, 1967, after being christened by Miss Caroline Kennedy, daughter of the late President. Mrs. John F. Kennedy served as Matron of honor as 32,000 people witnessed the epochal event.

On September 7, 1968, the *USS John F. Kennedy CVA-67* was officially placed in commission and Cap-

tain Earl P. Yates became the new carrier's skipper.

The carrier had completed two brief sea trials prior to her commissioning, and on August 30, 2447 enlisted men boarded her and became the "plank owners."

The overall length of the *Kennedy* is 1051 feet with a standard displacement of 80,000 tons, and a speed in excess of 30 knots. Her width measures 252 feet and her massive flight deck contains 4.56 acres. She accommodates 411 officers and 4174 enlisted men, and can carry more than 85 aircraft, which are launched from four catapults.

On October 21, 1968, the *Kennedy* went to sea for the first time as a commissioned ship. She held training and shakedown operations off the coast of Virginia.

Commander H. L. Marr, commander of Carrier Air Wing One, was the first to take off and land aboard the ship in an A4C *Skyhawk* on October 22, 1968.

The *Kennedy* was refueled on the same day by the *USS Waccamaw AO-109.* Another precedent for the carrier was established the following day when she refueled the destroyer *USS Fox DD-779.*

On November 2 a six-week training cruise began off Guantanamo Bay, Cuba and ports of call included Montego Bay, Jamaica.

During January and February 1969 the *Kennedy* prepared for her first Mediterranean cruise. As flagship of Carrier Division Two, and with Carrier Air Wing One aboard, the *Kennedy* departed for that destination on March 3, 1969.

If someone in a foreign port asked a sailor of the new carrier his sense of values in today's troubled times, he may quote his ship's namesake, John F. Kennedy, who once said ". . . Any man who may be asked in this century what he did to make his life worth while, I think I can respond with a good deal of pride and satisfaction: I served in the United States Navy."

NUCLEAR POWER: THE NIMITZ CLASS

56

USS Chester W. Nimitz CVA (N)-68

Chester W. Nimitz was born on February 24, 1885, in Fredericksburgh, Texas. Ironically his original ambition was to attend West Point, but a dearth of vacancies in his county and a competitive examination for Annapolis made him decide to try the Naval Academy. He was graduated in 1905, third in his class. His first assignment was with the China Station and his first command was the gunboat *USS Panay*, predecessor to the *USS Panay PR-5*, which was sunk December 12, 1937, nearly precipitating hostilities. He was 27 years old when commander of the Atlantic Submarine Flotilla in 1912–13. In August of 1926, Nimitz established the first Naval Reserve Officers Training Corps (NROTC) at the University of California.

Ten days after the attack on Pearl Harbor, President Franklin D. Roosevelt appointed Admiral Nimitz as Commander in Chief of the Pacific Fleet. Master strategist that he was Nimitz took a broken fleet and molded it into the strongest armada ever to be assembled in time of war. His calculating common sense and reasoned good opinion of his fellow men were exploited to the full in getting them to do their work for him.

Nimitz was promoted to Fleet Admiral on December 15, 1944. His area of command during the Second World War covered 65 million square miles, bounded on the North by Alaska and in the East by North America. Nimitz will be remembered for his brilliant strategy in directing the Pacific war to full victory, but history will perhaps recall his best at one of the proudest moments of his career—signing the Japanese Surrender Articles on the USS Missouri BB-63 in Tokyo Bay September 2, 1945, as the United States Representative. After the war, Nimitz was appointed Chief of Naval Operations on November 26, 1945. After serving in this capacity for two years he retired to his home in Berkeley, California. Fleet Admiral Nimitz died on February 20, 1966.

On March 31, 1967, a little over a year after Admiral Nimitz's passing, congress authorized the construction of the USS Chester W. Nimitz CVA(N)-68. She would be the first of three new nuclear carriers to form the Nimitz Class of 1967.

As of this writing, a second Nimitz class carrier to undergo construction in 1970 will be named in honor of the late President Dwight D. Eisenhower.

The Nimitz was laid down for construction on June 22, 1968, at the Newport News Shipbuilding and Dry Dock Company of Newport News, Virginia. Present at the keel laying were: his widow; a son, Rear Ad-miral Chester W. Nimitz, Jr. (Ret); and three daughters, Miss Ann Nimitz, Sister M. Aquinas, and Mrs. James Lay, wife of Captain (Ret) Lay.

The keel laying of the Nimitz took place 26 years after the Battle of Midway, a significant turning point in the Second World War and a highlight in the distinguished career of Admiral Nimitz. The three aircraft carriers that played a decisive role in the Battle of Midway—the USS Enterprise CV-6, USS Hornet CV-8 and the USS Yorktown CV-5—were built some 400 yards south of shipway 11 where the Nimitz is being built.

The Nimitz-class aircraft carriers will displace 95,100 tons full load; overall length, 1092 feet; beam, 134 feet; they will be able to carry in excess of 90 aircraft depending on the size at a speed of 30 knots. They will have an armament of three Basic Defence Missile Systems (BPDMS) launchers with Sparrow III missiles. They will be powered by two pressurized water-cooled nuclear reactors, whereas the Enterprise is powered by four nuclear reactors. Estimated cost of the Nimitz is set at $544 million. The nuclear reactors of the Nimitz class will enable the ships to steam for 13 years and some one million miles before "refueling." (That is, when the reactors' cores have to be replaced with new ones.)

PART II
The Fledglings

When the Langley *began carrier operations in early 1922, existing aircraft were used, for no carrier aircraft had been designed at that time. Many types of aircraft operated on the* Langley *during the period 1922–1927. In the Early Planes section (pp. 411–415) eight of these aircraft are identified. All were biplanes and were designed as "convertibles"—that is, designed with wheels or floats. By 1927, when the* Lexington *and* Saratoga *joined the fleet, the transition period was just about over and aircraft designed for carrier suitability appeared.*

The "Fledgling" aircraft are broken down into classes such as Fighter Aircraft, Scout Dive Bombers, Torpedo Bombers, Attack Aircraft, ASW Early Warning Aircraft, and Observation and Scout Aircraft. Only carrier aircraft procured in sufficient number to equip at least one squadron are included. In several aircraft, types designed later were also used on aircraft carriers and designations of the later models that operated on carriers appear in the Notes below the photograph of the original aircraft.

1

Early Planes

Designation: DH-4B
Type: Observation
Manufacturer: Dayton-Wright
Engine: Liberty
Horse Power:
Top Speed: 122 mph
Length: 30' 2"

Span: 42' 6"
Gross Weight: 4214 lbs.
First Order: 1918
First Delivery: May 24, 1918
Last Delivery:
Number Procured: 332
First Delivery to
Operating Unit: July 14, 1918, Miami

Notes: DH-4B-One DH-4B was converted to DH-4B by the Naval Aircraft Factory prior to acceptance.

Designation: VE-7SF
Type: Fighter-Trainer
Manufacturer: Lewis & Vought, NAF
Engine: Hispano
Horse Power: 180
Top Speed: 115 mph
Length: 24' 5"

Span: 34' 1"
Gross Weight: 2100 lbs.
First Order: 1920
First Delivery: May 27, 1920
Last Delivery: Jan.–March 1924
Number Procured: 29
First Delivery to
Operating Unit: July 26, 1920.
Mitchell Field, Garden City

Notes: Originally procured as a trainer, some were converted to fighters.

Designation: DT-2
Type: Torpedo Bomber
Manufacturer: Naval Air Factory
Engine: Liberty
Horse Power: 450
Top Speed: 105 mph
Length: 37' 8"

Span: 50'
Gross Weight: 7217 lbs.
First Order: 1921
First Delivery: May 12, 1922
Last Delivery: 1924
Number Procured: 67
First Delivery to
Operating Unit: Dec. 12, 1922 VT-2

Designation: VE-9H
Type: Observation-Trainer
Manufacturer: Chance-Vought
Engine: Wright E-3
Horse Power: 180
Top Speed: 118 mph
Length: 24' 6"

Span: 34' 1"
Gross Weight: 2175 lbs.
First Order: 1922
First Delivery: June 24, 1922
Last Delivery: July 10, 1923
Number Procured: 21
First Delivery to
Operating Unit: June 24, 1922
USS Nevada BB-36

Notes: VE-9's were originally procured as trainers. Some of these aircraft were converted to fighters.

Designation: CS-1
Type: Torpedo Bomber
Manufacturer: Curtiss-Martin
Engine: Wright
Horse Power: 525
Top Speed: 102 mph
Length: 38' 5"

Span: 52' 3"
Gross Weight: 7934 lbs.
First Order: 1922
First Delivery: Unknown
Last Delivery: Jan. 9, 1926
Number Procured: 83
First Delivery to
Operating Unit: Dec. 20, 1923 VS-3

Designation: FB-1
Type: Fighter
Manufacturer: Boeing
Engine: Curtiss D-12
Horse Power: 400
Top Speed: 167 mph
Length: 23' 6"

Span: 32'
Gross Weight: 2949 lbs.
First Order: 1923
First Delivery: Dec. 1, 1925
Last Delivery: Jan. 21, 1927
Number Procured: 43
First Delivery to
Operating Unit: Dec. 25, 1922 VF-2

Designation: UO-1
Type: Observation
Manufacturer: Chance-Vought
Engine: U-8-D
Horse Power: 250
Top Speed: 109 mph
Length: 29' 3"

Span: 34' 1"
Gross Weight: 2608 lbs.
First Order: 1922
First Delivery: July–Oct. 1922
Last Delivery: April–June 1927
Number Procured: 163
First Delivery to
Operating Unit: June 14, 1924.
USS Tennessee BB-43

Notes: UO-1 UO-5 and FU-1

In Flight: Jan. 22, 1924
Designation: TS-1
Type: Fighter
Manufacturer: Curtiss, NAF
Engine: Lawrance J-1
Horse Power: 200
Top Speed: 116 mph
Length: 24' 10"

Span: 25'
Gross Weight: 2089 lbs.
First Order: 1921
First Delivery: May 9, 1922
Last Delivery: Oct. 8, 1923
Number Procured: 43
First Delivery to
Operating Unit: Dec. 9, 1922
USS Langley CV-1

2

Fighter Aircraft

Designation: FB-5
Type: Fighter
Manufacturer: Boeing
Engine: Packard 2A-1500
Horse Power: 525
Top Speed: 169 mph
Length: 23' 2"

Span: 32'
Gross Weight: 3196 lbs.
First Order: 1925
First Delivery: Dec. 1, 1925
Last Delivery: Dec. 1, 1927
Number Procured: 43
First Delivery to
Operating Unit: Dec. 25, 1925 VF-2

Designation: F6C-3 Hawk
Type: Fighter
Manufacturer: Curtiss
Engine: Curtiss D-12
Horse Power: 400
Top Speed: 154 mph
Length: 22' 7"

Span: 31' 6"
Gross Weight: 2963 lbs.
First Order: 1925
First Delivery: Aug. 7, 1925
Last Delivery: June 10, 1927
Number Procured: 75
First Delivery to
Operating Unit: Sept. 30, 1925 VF-2

Notes: F6C-4

Designation: FU-1
Type: Fighter
Manufacturer: Chance-Vought
Engine: Wright R-790
Horse Power: 220 mph

Top Speed: 125 mph
Length: 24' 4"
Span: 34' 4"

Designation: F2B-1
Type: Fighter
Manufacturer: Boeing
Engine: Pratt & Whitney R-1340
Horse Power: 410
Top Speed: 158 mph
Length: 22' 11"
Span: 30' 1"

Gross Weight: 2814 lbs.
First Order: 1926
First Delivery: Dec. 5, 1926
Last Delivery: Feb. 24, 1928
Number Procured: 33
First Delivery to
Operating Unit: Dec. 2, 1927 VF-1B

Designation: F3B-1
Type: Fighter
Manufacturer: Boeing
Engine: Pratt & Whitney R-1340-B
Horse Power: 450
Top Speed: 155 mph
Length: 24' 10"
Span: 33'
Gross Weight: 2884 lbs.

First Order: 1927
First Delivery: March 7, 1927
Last Delivery: Jan. 17, 1929
Number Procured: 74
First Delivery to
Operating Unit: Oct. 17, 1927 VF-1B
Notes: F3B-1 taking off from *Saratoga* CV-3
on February 7, 1929

Designation: F7C-1 Seahawk
Type: Fighter
Manufacturer: Curtiss
Engine: Pratt & Whitney R-1340B
Horse Power: 450
Top Speed: 153 mph
Length: 22' 2"
Span: 32' 8"

Gross Weight: 2962 lbs.
First Order: 1927
First Delivery: August 28, 1927
Last Delivery: Jan. 3, 1929
Number Procured: 18
First Delivery to
Operating Unit: Dec. 28, 1928 VF-5M

Designation: F4B-1
Type: Fighter
Manufacturer: Boeing
Engine: Pratt & Whitney R-1340-C
Horse Power: 450
Top Speed: 166 mph
Length: 20' 7"
Span: 30'

Gross Weight: 2718 lbs.
First Order: 1928
First Delivery: May 8, 1929
Last Delivery: Jan. 28, 1933
Number Procured: 188
First Delivery to
Operating Unit: VB-1B Aug. 8, 1929
Notes: F4B-2, 3, & 4

Designation: F4B-4
Type: Fighter
Manufacturer: Boeing
Engine: Pratt & Whitney R-1340-D
Horse Power: 500

Top Speed: 184 mph
Length: 20' 4"
Span: 30'
Gross Weight: 3107 lbs.

Designation: F8C-4 Helldiver
Type: Fighter
Manufacturer: Curtiss
Engine: Pratt & Whitney R-1340-C
Horse Power: 450
Top Speed: 137 mph
Length: 25' 11"
Span: 32'

Gross Weight: 3783 lbs.
First Order: 1927
First Delivery: Jan. 2, 1928
Last Delivery: Nov. 1931
Number Procured: 151
First Delivery to
Operating Unit: Jan. 21, 1928 VO-7M

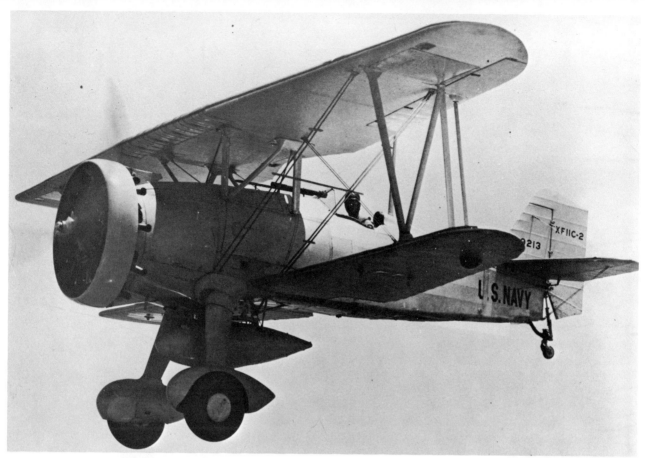

Designation: XF11C-2 Hawk
Type: Fighter
Manufacturer: Curtiss
Engine: Wright SR-1820-F
Horse Power: 600
Top Speed: 192 mph
Length: 22' 7"
Span: 31' 6"

Gross Weight: 4078 lbs.
First Order: 1932
First Delivery: April 16, 1932
Last Delivery: Nov. 12, 1934
Number Procured: 57
First Delivery to
Operating Unit: April 28, 1933 VF-1B

Designation: FF-1
Type: Fighter
Manufacturer: Grumman
Engine: Wright SR-1820-F
Horse Power: 600
Top Speed: 208 mph
Length: 25'
Span: 34' 6"

Gross Weight: 4470 lbs.
First Order: 1931
First Delivery: Dec. 30, 1931
Last Delivery: Nov. 1, 1933
Number Procured: 28
First Delivery to
Operating Unit: June 21, 1933 VF-5B

Designation: BF2C-1
Type: Fighter
Manufacturer: Curtiss
Engine: Wright R-1820-04
Horse Power: 700

Top Speed: 225 mph
Length: 23'
Span: 31' 6"
Gross Weight: 4555 lbs.
Notes: Formerly F11C

Designation: F2F-1
Type: Fighter
Manufacturer: Grumman
Engine: Pratt & Whitney R-1535-72
Horse Power: 650
Top Speed: 231 mph
Length: 21' 2"
Span: 28' 6"

Gross Weight: 3789 lbs.
First Order: 1932
First Delivery: Oct. 10, 1933
Last Delivery: August 2, 1935
Number Procured: 56
First Delivery to
Operating Unit: Feb. 19, 1935 VF-2B

Designation: F3F-1
Type: Fighter
Manufacturer: Grumman
Engine: PWA R-1535-84
Horse Power: 650
Top Speed: 226 mph
Length: 23' 5"
Span: 32'
Gross Weight: 4108 lbs.

First Order: 1934
First Delivery: March 22, 1935
Last Delivery: May 10, 1939
Number Procured: 164
First Delivery to
Operating Unit: April 3, 1936 VF-4
Notes: F3F2 and 3
Landing on *USS Ranger CV-4*

Designation: F3F-3
Type: Fighter
Manufacturer: Grumman
Engine: PWA R-1820-22
Horse Power: 850

Top Speed: 239 mph
Length: 23' 2"
Span: 32'
Gross Weight: 4535 lbs.

Designation: F2A Buffalo
Type: Fighter
Manufacturer: Brewster
Engine: PWA R-1820-40
Horse Power: 1000
Top Speed: 284 mph
Length: 26' 4''
Span: 35'

Gross Weight: 6321 lbs.
First Order: 1936
First Delivery: Dec. 1937
Last Delivery: April 1942
Number Procured: 503
First Delivery to
Operating Unit: Dec. 8, 1939 VF-3
Notes: F2A1, 2 & 3

Designation: F2A-1 Buffalo
Type: Fighter
Manufacturer: Brewster
Engine: PWA R-1820-22
Horse Power: 850

Top Speed: 271 mph
Length: 26'
Span: 35'
Gross Weight: 5043 lbs.

Designation: F4F-3 Wildcat
Type: Fighter
Manufacturer: Grumman
Engine: R-1830-76
Horse Power: 1100
Top Speed: 298 mph
Length: 29' 11"
Span: 38'

Gross Weight: 6206 lbs.
First Order: 1936
First Delivery: Nov. 1937
Last Delivery: May 1945
Number Procured: 7905
First Delivery to
Operating Unit: Dec. 4, 1941 VF-41
Notes: F4F 4 and 7

Designation: FM-1 Wildcat
Type: Fighter
Manufacturer: Eastern Aircraft
Engine: R-1830-86
Horse Power: 1100

Top Speed: 275 mph
Length: 28' 9"
Span: 38'
Gross Weight: 7406 lbs.
Notes: FM2

Designation: F6F-3 Hellcat
Type: Fighter
Manufacturer: Grumman
Engine: Pratt & Whitney R-2800-10W
Horse Power: 2000
Top Speed: 324 mph
Length: 33' 7"
Span: 42' 10"

Gross Weight: 11,381 lbs.
First Order: 1941
First Delivery: June 26, 1942
Last Delivery: November 1945
Number Procured: 12,275
First Delivery to
Operating Unit: Jan. 16, 1943 VF-9
Notes: F6F5

Designation: F4U-1 Corsair
Type: Fighter
Manufacturer: Chance-Vought
Engine: R-2800-8
Horse Power: 2000
Top Speed: 341 mph
Length: 33' 5"
Span: 41'
Gross Weight: 11,117 lbs.

First Order: 1938
First Delivery: May 29, 1940
Last Delivery: January 1953
Number Procured: 12,620
First Delivery to
Operating Unit: Oct. 3, 1942 VF-12
Notes: First combat on Feb. 13, 1943 VMF-124 at Bougainville. F4U-4, F4U-5

Designation: F3A-1 Corsair
Notes: Brewster version of the F4U

Designation: FG-1D Corsair
Type: Fighter
Notes: Goodyear version of the F4U

Designation: FR-1 Fireball
Type: Fighter
Manufacturer: Ryan Aero
Engine: WAC R-1820-72W GE-I-16 jet
Horse Power: 1300
Top Speed: 1300, 1610
Length: 32' 4"
Span: 40'

Gross Weight: 9958 lbs.
First Order: 1943
First Delivery: June 25, 1944
Last Delivery: November 1945
Number Procured: 69
First Delivery to
Operating Unit: March 1945 VF-66 Pacific

Designation: FH-1
Type: Fighter
Manufacturer: McDonnell
Engine: 2 Westinghouse 19xB-2-B
Thrust: 1600 lbs. each
Top Speed: 479 plus
Length: 38' 10"
Span: 40' 9"
Gross Weight: 9820 lbs.

First Order: 1943
First Delivery: Jan. 26, 1945
Last Delivery: May 1948
Number Procured: 61
First Delivery to
Operating Unit: July 23, 1945 VF-17A
Atlantic
Notes: Formerly FD-1

Designation: FJ-1 Fury (straight wing)
Type: Fighter
Manufacturer: North American
Engine General Electric J47-GE-2
Thrust: 4000 lbs.
Top Speed: 960 mph (plus)
Length: 37' 6"
Span: 37' 1"
Gross Weight: 18,000 lbs.
First Order: 1945
First Delivery: Sept. 11, 1946
Last Delivery: April 1948
Number Procured: 33
First Delivery to
Operating Unit: Nov. 18, 1947 VF-5A Pacific

Designation: F2H-1 Banshee
Type: Fighter
Manufacturer: McDonnell
Engine: 2 Westinghouse J-34-WE-22
Top Speed: 600 mph
Length: 40' 2"
Span: 41' 7"
Gross Weight: 14,000 lbs.
First Order: 1945
First Delivery: Jan. 11, 1947
Last Delivery: Aug. 1953
Number Procured: 894
First Delivery to
Operating Unit: Mar. 1949 VF-171 Atlantic
Notes: F2H2

Designation: F9F-2 Panther Straight Wing
Type: Fighter
Manufacturer: Grumman
Engine: Pratt & Whitney J42-P-6
Top Speed: 625 miles p h plus
Length: 40'
Span: 38'
Gross Weight: 15,750 lbs.

First Order: 1946
First Delivery: Nov. 24, 1947
Last Delivery: Dec. 12, 1952
Number Procured: 1388
First Delivery to
Operating Unti: May 8, 1949 VF-51 Pacific
Notes: F9F-3

Designation: QF-9G Cougar
Type: Fighter
Manufacturer: Grumman
Engine: Pratt & Whitney J48-P-8
Top Speed: 690 plus
Length: 40' 6"
Span: 34' 6"
Gross Weight: 20,000 lbs.

First Order: 1951
First Delivery: Sept. 20, 1951
Last Delivery: Dec. 1959
Number Procured: 1985
First Delivery to
Operating Unit: Nov. 1952 VF-32 Atlantic
Notes: Formerly F9F-6. Swept wing version
of the Panther.

Designation: F7U-3 Cutlass
Type: Fighter
Manufacturer: Chance-Vought
Engine: 2 Westinghouse J46-WE-8
Top Speed: 650 plus
Length: 44' 3½"
Span: 39' 8½"
Gross Weight: 18,210 lbs.
First Order: 1946

First Delivery: Sept. 27, 1948
Last Delivery: Dec. 1955
Number Procured: 305
First Delivery to
Operating Unit: Dec. 54 VF-81 & VF-83 Atlantic and VF-122 and VF124 Pacific
Notes: In Jan. 1952 F7U-1 was assigned to Advanced Training Command at NAS Corpus Christi.

Designations: F6A Skyray
Type: Fighter
Manufacturer: Douglas
Engine: Pratt & Whitney J-57-P8
Thrust: 9700 lbs.
Top Speed: Mach 0.95
Length: 45' 5"
Span: 33' 6"

Gross Weight: 21,000 lbs.
First Order: 1948
First Delivery: Jan. 25, 1951
Last Delivery: December 1958
Number Procured:
First Delivery to
Operating Unit: April 16, 1956 VC-3 Pacific
Notes: Formerly F4D-1

Designation: F8U-1 Crusader
Type: Fighter
Manufacturer: Chance-Vought
Engine: Pratt & Whitney J57-P-4A Turbojet
Thrust: 16,200 lbs.
Top Speed: Mach 2 1,000 plus mph
Length: 54' 3"
Span: 35' 8"

Gross Weight: 27,500 lbs.
First Order: 1953
First XFF Delivery: December 28, 1956
Number Procured: 318 F8U-1; built
Notes: W. Paul Thayer
Ling-Tempco Vought Inc.
P. O. Box 5907
Dallas, Texas 75222

Designation: F4B Phantom II
Type: Fighter
Manufacturer: McDonnell
Engine: Two General Electric J79-GE-8
Thrust: 16,500 lbs. each
Top Speed: Mach 2.6

Lenght: 58' 3"
Span: 38' 5"
Gross Weight: 46,000 lbs.
First Order: 1954
First Delivery: May 27, 1958
Notes: Formerly F4H-1

Designation: F3F Demon
Type: Fighter
Manufacturer: McDonnell
Engine: Allison J71-A-2
Length: 58' 11"
Span: 35' 4"

Gross Weight: 33,000 lbs.
Notes: Formerly F3H
McDonnell Douglas
Box 516
St. Louis, Missouri 63166

3

Scout Dive Bombers

Designation: BM-1
Type: Scout Dive Bomber
Manufacturer: Martin, NAF
Engine: Pratt & Whitney SF-1690-C
Horse Power: 600
Top Speed: 143 mph
Length: 28' 6"
Span: 41'
Gross Weight: 6143 lbs.

First Order: 1928
First Delivery: June 6, 1929
Last Delivery: Jan. 1933
Number Procured: 35
First Delivery to
Operating Unit: July 1, 1932, USS Lexington CV-2
Notes: BM2

Designation: SF-1
Type: Scout Dive Bomber
Manufacturer: Grumman
Engine: Wright R-1820-84
Horse Power: 700
Top Speed: 207 mph
Length: 24' 4"
Span: 34' 6"
Gross Weight: 5074 lbs.

First Order: 1931
First Delivery: Aug. 19, 1932
Last Delivery: Dec. 12, 1934
Number Procured: 35
First Delivery to
Operating Unit: Mar. 30, 1934 VF-2B
12, 1935
Notes: SF-1 landing on *Lexington* CV-2 April
12, 1935

Designation: BG-1
Type: Scout Dive Bomber
Manufacturer: Great Lakes
Engine: Pratt & Whitney R-1690-44
Horse Power: 600
Top Speed: 186 mph
Length: 28' 4"
Span: 36'

Gross Weight: 6221 lbs.
First Order: 1932
First Delivery: June 1933
Last Delivery: November 1935
Number Procured: 61
First Delivery to
Operating Unit: Oct. 24, 1934 VB-3B

Designation: SBU-1
Type: Scout Dive Bomber
Manufacturer: Chance-Vought
Engine: Pratt & Whitney R-1535-80
Horse Power: 700
Top Speed: 200 mph
Length: 27' 10"
Span: 33' 3"

Gross Weight: 5520 lbs.
First Order: 1932
First Delivery: June 22, 1933
Last Delivery: Aug 1937
Number Procured: 126
First Delivery to
Operating Unit: Nov 20, 1935 VS-3B

Designation: SBC-3
Type: Scout Dive Bomber
Manufacturer: Curtiss
Engine: PWA R-1535-94
Horse Power: 750
Top Speed: 212 mph
Length: 27' 5"
Span: 34'

Gross Weight: 4456
First Order: 1932
First Delivery: June 14, 1934
Last Delivery: April 1941
Number Procured: 258
First Delivery to
Operating Unit: July 17, 1937 VS-5
Notes: SBC-4

Designation: SB2U-1 Vindicator
Type: Scout Dive Bomber
Manufacturer: Chance-Vought
Engine: PWA R-1535-96
Horse Power: 750
Top Speed: 242 mph
Length: 34'
Span: 42'

Gross Weight: 6777 lbs.
First Order: 1934
First Delivery: Jan. 4, 1936
Last Delivery: July 1941
Number Procured: 170
First Delivery to
Operating Unit: Dec. 30, 1937 VB-3
Notes: SB2U-2; 3

Designation: SB2U-3 Vindicator
Type: Scout Dive Bomber
Manufacturer: Chance-Vought
Engine: PWA 1535-2
Horse Power: 750

Top Speed: 182 mph
Length: 34'
Span: 42'
Gross Weight: 7932 lbs.

Designation: BT-1 (SBD)
Type: Scout Dive Bomber
Engine: PWA R-1535-94
Horse Power: 750

Top Speed: 215 mph
Length: 31' 8"
Span: 41' 6"
Gross Weight: 6978 lbs.

Designation: SBN-1
Type: Scout Dive Bomber
Manufacturer: Brewster
Engine: PNA R-1820-38
Horse Power: 850
Top Speed: 237 mph
Length: 27' 10"
Span: 39'

Gross Weight: 6238 lbs.
First Order: 1934
First Delivery: May 21, 1938
Last Delivery: Mar 23, 1942
Number Procured: 31
First Delivery to
Operating Unit: May 31, 1938 VB-3

Designation: SBD-1 Dauntless
Type: Scout Dive Bomber
Manufacturer: Douglas
Engine: PWA R-1820-32
Horse Power: 450
Top Speed: 234 mph
Length: 31' 9"
Span: 39'

Gross Weight: 7698
First Order: 1934
First Delivery: Aug. 19, 1935
Last Delivery: Aug. 1944
Number Procured: 5356
First Delivery to
Operating Unit: April 11, 1938 VB-5
Notes: SBD-1, 2, 3, 4, 5 and 6

Designation: SBD-5 Dauntless
Type: Scout Dive Bomber
Manufacturer: Northrop Douglas
Engine: WAC R-1820-60
Horse Power: 1200

Top Speed: 223 mph
Length: 33'
Span: 41' 7"
Gross Weight: 10,080

Designation: SBD-6 Dauntless
Type: Scout Dive Bomber
Manufacturer: Northrop, Douglas
Engine: WAC R-1820-66
Horse Power: 1350

Top Speed: 244 mph
Length: 33'
Span: 41' 7"
Gross Weight: 10,773

Designation: SB2C-1 Helldiver
Type: Scout Dive Bomber
Manufacturer: Curtiss
Engine: WAC R-2600-8
Horse Power: 1500
Top Speed: 278 mph
Length: 36' 4"
Span: 49' 9"
Gross Weight: 13,140 lbs.

First Order: 1939
First Delivery: Dec 18, 1940
Last Delivery: Oct 1945
Number Procured: 6649
First Delivery to
Operating Unit: Dec. 15, 1942 VS-9
Notes: First combat with VB-17 in attack on
Rabaul on November 11, 1943
SB2C-2, 3, 4, 5

Designation: SB2C-5 Helldiver
Type: Scout Dive Bomber
Manufacturer: Curtiss
Engine: WAC R-2600—20
Horse Power: 1900

Top Speed: 267 mph
Length: 36' 8''
Span: 49' 9''
Gross Weight: 14,415 lbs.

Designation: SB2A-2 Buccaneer
Type: Scout Dive Bomber
Manufacturer: Brewster
Engine: WAC R-2600-8
Horse Power: 1700
Top Speed: 259 mph
Length 39' 2''
Span: 47'

Gross Weight: 13,068 lbs.
First Order: 1939
First Delivery: June 17, 1941
Last Delivery: February 1944
Number Procured: 771
First Delivery to
Operating Unit: Unknown
Notes: SB2A-3

Designation: SBF-1 Helldiver
Notes: SBF 1, 3-4
Fairchild of Canada version of the SB2C
Same Specifications

Designation: SBW-1 Helldiver
Notes: SBW-1, 3, 4, & 5
Canadian Car and Foundry version of the SB2C
Same Specifications

Designation: BTD-1 Destroyer
Type: Scout Dive Bomber
Manufacturer: Douglas
Engine: Wright R-3350-14
Horse Power: 2250
Top Speed: 319 mph
Length: 38' 7''
Span: 45'

Gross Weight: 18,140 lbs.
First Order: 1941
First Delivery: April 8, 1943
Last Delivery: October 1945
Number Procured: 30
First Delivery to
Operating Unit: Unknown

4

Torpedo Bombers

Designation: T3M-1
Type: Torpedo Bomber
Manufacturer: Martin
Engine: Wright T-3B
Horse Power: 575
Top Speed: 109 mph
Length: 41' 9"
Span: 52' 4"
Gross Weight: 8994 lbs.

First Order: 1925
First Delivery: July 27, 1926
Last Delivery: 1927
Number Procured: 124
First Delivery to
Operating Unit: Sep 7, 1926 VT-1
Notes: T3M-1 taking off from *Lexington* CV-2
April 6, 1928
T3M-2

Designation: T4M-1
Type: Torpedo Bomber
Manufacturer: Martin/Great Lakes
Engine: Pratt & Whitney R-1690
Horse Power: 525
Top Speed: 116 mph
Length: 35' 8"
Span: 53'
Gross Weight: 6599 lbs.

First Order: 1927
First Delivery: May 20, 1927
Last Delivery: Dec 29, 1931
Number Procured: 153
First Delivery to
Operating Unit: Aug 8, 1928 VT-2B
Notes: T4M-1 taking off from *Saratoga* CV-3
on Jan 6, 1932

Designation: TG-2
Type: Torpedo Bomber
Manufacturer: Great Lakes
Engine: Pratt & Whitney R-1690
Horse Power: 525
Top Speed: 116 mph
Length: 34' 11"

Span: 53'
Gross Weight: 7852 lbs.
Notes: (T4M TE-1
TG-2 built by Great Lakes on subcontract
from Detroit Aircraft Co.
TG-2 taking off from *Saratoga* CV-3 on December 1, 1932

Designation: TBD-1 Devastator
Type: Torpedo Bomber
Manufacturer: Douglas
Engine: PWA R-1830-64
Horse Power: 850
Top Speed: 192 mph
Length: 35'
Span: 50'

Gross Weight: 9251 lbs.
First Order: 1934
First Delivery: April 15, 1935
Last Delivery: Nov. 1939
Number Procured: 130
First Delivery to
Operating Unit: Oct. 5, 1937 VT-3

Designation: TBF-1 Avenger
Type: Torpedo Bomber
Manufacturer: Grumman
Engine: R-2600-8
Horse Power: 1500
Top Speed: 254 mph
Length: 41'
Span: 54' 2"
Gross Weight: 13,813 lbs.

First Order: 1940
First Delivery: Aug. 1, 1941
Last Delivery: Sept. 1945
Number Procured: 9836
First Delivery to
Operating Unit: March 25, 1942 VT-8
Notes: TBF first saw action on June 4, 1942,
during the Battle of Midway by shore based
unit of VT-8

Designation: TBM-1C
Notes: Same specifications as TBF-1
TBM3

Designation: TBY-2 Seawolf
Type: Torpedo Bomber
Manufacturer: Chance-Vought
Engine: Pratt & Whitney R-2800-22
Horse Power: 2100
Top Speed: 292 mph
Length: 39′ 2″

Span: 56′ 11″
Gross Weight: 17,491 lbs.
First Order: 1940
First Delivery: Dec. 22, 1941
Last Delivery: Sept. 1945
Number Procured: 181

5

Attack Aircraft

Designation: AD-4 Skyraider
Type: Attack
Manufacturer: Douglas
Engine: Wright R-3350-26W
Horse Power: 2700
Top Speed: 365 mph
Length: 38' 2"
Span: 50'

Gross Weight: 14,716 lbs.
First Order: 1944
First Delivery: Mar. 18, 1945
Last Delivery: March 1947
Number Procured: 3160
First Delivery to
Operating Unit: Dec. 6 1946 VA-19A Pacific
Notes: AD 1, 2, 3, 4

Designation: A-1G Skyraider
Type: Attack
Manufacturer: Douglas
Engine: Wright R-3350-26WA
Top Speed: 365 mph

Length: 38' 10½"
Span: 50'
Gross Weight: 10,500 lbs.
Notes: Formerly A4D-5N Night Attack

Designation: AM-1 Mauler
Type: Attack
Manufacturer: Martin
Engine: Pratt & Whitney R-4360-4W
Horse Power: 3000
Top Speed: 316 mph
Length: 41' 3"
Span: 50' 1"

Gross Weight: 20,166 lbs.
First Order: 1944
First Delivery: Aug. 26, 1944
Last Delivery: October 1949
Number Procured: 152
First Delivery to
Operating Unit: March 1, 1948 VA-17A
Atlantic

Designation: Guardian AF2-S
Type: Attack
Manufacturer: Grumman
Engine: Pratt & Whitney R-2800-48
Horse Power: 2300
Top Speed: 280 mph
Length: 43' 2''
Span: 60'

Gross Weight: 17,327 lbs.
First Order: 1945
First Delivery: Dec. 19, 1946
Last Delivery: March 1953
Number Procured: 389
First Delivery to
Operating Unit: Oct. 18, 1950 VS-25 Pacific

Designation: AJ-1 Savage
Type: Attack
Manufacturer: North American
Engine: Two Pratt & Whitney R-2800-44W
One J-33-A10
Horse Power: 2300/4600 Thrust
Top Speed: 392 mph
Length: 63' 5''
Span: 71' 5''

Gross Weight: 35,742 lbs.
First Order: 1946
First Delivery: July 3, 1948
Last Delivery: June 1954
Number Procured: 143
First Delivery to
Operating Unit: Sept. 13, 1949 VC-5 Pacific
Notes: AJ-2

Designation: A3D Skywarrior
Type: Attack Bomber
Manufacturer: Douglas
Engine: Two Pratt & Whitney J-57-P-10
Thrust: 11,000 lbs. each
Top Hpeed: 630 mph
Length: 73' 6"
Span: 72' 6"

Gross Weight: 38,000 lbs.
First Order: 1949
First Delivery: Oct. 22, 1952
First Delivery to
Operating Unit: March 31, 1956 VAH-1 Atlantic
Notes: Formerly A3D-2

Designation: A4 Skyhawk
Type: Attack
Manufacturer: Douglas
Engine: Wright J65-W-4
Thrust: 7800 lbs.
Top Speed: 664 mph
Length: 39'

Span: 27' 6"
First Order: June 22, 1954
First Delivery to
Operating Unit: Pac. and Atl. fleets 1956
Notes: Formerly A4D-1

Designation: EF-10B Skynight
Type: Fighter
Manufacturer: Douglas
Engine: 2 Westinghouse J46
Length: 50'
Span: 45'
First Order: 1946

First Delivery: Mar. 23, 1948
Last Delivery: Oct. 1953
Number Procured: 268
First Delivery to
Operating Unit: Feb. 1951 VC-3 Pacific
Notes: Formerly F3D-2

Designation: A5A Vigilante
Type: Attack
Manufacturer: North American
Engine: Two General Electric J-79-GE-8
Thrust: 10,900 lbs. each
Top Speed: Mach 2.1
Length: 75' 10"
Span: 53'

Gross Weight: 60,000 lbs.
First Order: Aug. 31, 1958
Number Procured: 55
First Delivery to
Operating Unit: June 16, 1961 NAS Sanford, Florida
Notes: Formerly A3J-1. A5A's being converted to RA-5C configuration.

Designation: A6A Intruder
Type: Attack
Manufacturer: Grumman
Engine: Two Pratt & Whitney J-52-P-8A
Thrust: 9300 lbs. each
Top Speed: Mach 0.95
Length: 54' 7"
Span: 53'

Gross Weight: 25,684 lbs.
First Order: 1959
First Delivery: April 19, 1960
First Delivery to
Operating Unit: Feb. 1, 1963 VA-42 NAS Oceana
Notes: Formerly A2F-1.

Designation: A7A Corsair II
Type: Attack
Manufacturer: Ling-Temco Vought
Engine: Pratt & Whitney TF30-P-6
Thrust: 11,350 lbs.
Length: 46' 1½"
Span: 38' 9"

Gross Weight: 14,857 lbs.
First Order: 1964
First Delivery: Sept. 27, 1965
First Delivery to
Operating Unit: Sept. 13, 1966. US Naval Air Training Command, Patuxent River, Maryland

Designation: RA-5C Vigilante
Type: Carrier Base Attack Dual Reconnaissance
Manufacturer: North American
Engine: Two General Electric J-79-GE-8
Thrust: 10,900 lbs. each
Top Speed: Mach 2.1
Length: 75' 10"

Span: 53'
Gross Weight: 80,000 lbs.
First Order: June 30, 1962
First Delivery to
Operating Unit: VAH-3 NAS Sanford, Florida.
January 1964
Notes: Formerly A3J-C. Dual reconnaissance version of the A5A

6

ASW Early Warning Aircraft

Designation: S2D Tracker
Type: ASW Search and Attack
Manufacturer: Grumman
Engine: Two Wright R-1820-82-WA
Horse Power: 1525
Top Speed: 265 mph
Length: 43' 6"

Span: 72' 7"
Gross Weight: 18,315 lbs.
First Order: 1958
First Delivery: May 20, 1959
Number Procured: 215
Notes: Formerly S2F-3

Designation: S2E Tracker
Type: ASW Search and Attack
Manufacturer: Grumman
Engine: Two Wright R-1820-82-WA
Horse Power: 1525
Top Speed: 265 mph
Length: 43' 6"

Span: 72' 7"
Gross Weight: 18,315 lbs.
First Delivery to
Operating Unit: Oct. 1962 VS-41
Notes: Formerly S2F-3S. Similar to the S2D but much more advanced ASW equipment.

Designation: C-1A Trader
Type: General Utility Transport-Trainer
Manufacturer: Grumman
Engine: Two Wright R-1820-82-WA
Horse Power: 1525
Top Speed: 265 mph

Length: 43' 6"
Span: 72' 7"
Gross Weight: 18,315 lbs.
Notes: Formerly TF-1. A general utility-trainer version of the S2B Tracker.

Designation: E1B Tracer
Type: Airborne early warning and fighter direction
Manufacturer: Grumman
Engine: Two Wright R-1820-82-WA
Horse Power: 1525
Top Speed: 265 mph

Length: 43' 6"
Span: 72' 7"
Gross Weight: 18,315 lbs.
Notes. Formerly WF-2. A modification of the TF Trader for early warning and fighter duties direction. Has a complete new tail assembly with twin fin and rudders.

Designation: E2A Hawkeye
Type: Airborne Early Warning Aircraft
Manufacturer: Grumman
Engine: Two Allison T56-A8/8A turbojet
Top Speed: 297 mph
Length: 56' 4"

Span: 80' 7"
Gross Weight: 36,063 lbs.
First Order: Jan. 19, 1964
First Delivery to
Operating Unit: VAW-11 San Diego NAS
Notes: Formerly W2F-1.

7

Observation and Scout Craft

Designation: UO-5
Type: Observation
Manufacturer: Chance-Vought
Engine: Wright R-790
Horse Power: 220

Top Speed: 122 mph
Length: 24′ 4″
Span: 34′ 4″
Gross Weight: 2506 lbs.

Designation: OC-2 Falcon
Type: Observation Scout
Manufacturer: Curtiss
Engine: Pratt & Whitney R-1340
Horse Power: 410
Top Speed: 138 mph
Length: 28'
Span: 38'

Gross Weight: 4020 lbs.
First Order: 1927
First Delivery: Jan. 2, 1928
Last Delivery: Nov. 1931
Number Procured: 151
First Delivery to
Operating Unit: Jan. 21, 1928 VO-7M

Designation: O2U-1
Type: Observation
Manufacturer: Chance-Vought
Engine: Pratt & Whitney R-1340
Horse Power. 410
Top Speed: 150 mph
Length: 24' 7"
Span: 34' 6"

Gross Weight: 3389 lbs.
First Order: 1926
First Delivery: Nov. 18, 1926
Last Delivery: Feb. 25, 1930
Number Procured: 291
First Delivery to
Operating Unit: Nov. 18, 1927 VO-7M
Notes: O2U-1, 2, 3, 4.

Designation: O2U-4
Type: Observation
Manufacturer: Chance-Vought
Engine: Pratt & Whitney R1340C
Horse Power: 450

Top Speed: 138 mph
Lenght: 25' 1"
Span: 36'
Gross Weight: 3997 lbs.

Designation: O3U-1
Type: Observation-Scout
Manufacturer: Chance-Vought
Engine: Pratt & Whitney R-1340-C
Horse Power: 450
Top Speed: 144 mph
Length: 26' 1"
Span: 36'
Gross Weight: 3999 lbs.

First Order: Jan. 18, 1930
First Delivery: June 1930
Last Delivery: July 1935
Number Procured: 329
First Delivery to
Operating Unit: July 31, 1930 USS Nevada
BB-36
Notes: O3U-3 and 6

Designation: SU-1
Type: Scout
Manufacturer: Chance-Vought
Engine: Pratt & Whitney R-1690-C
Horse Power: 600
Top Speed: 170 mph

Length: 26' 3"
Span: 36'
Gross Weight: 4502 lbs.
Notes: SU-1, 2, 3 and 4
Formerly O3U-2

Designation: SU-4
Type: Scout
Manufacturer: Chance-Vought
Engine: Pratt & Whitney R-1690-42
Horse Power: 600

Top Speed: 168 mph
Length: 27' 11"
Span: 35'
Gross Weight: 4765 lbs.

PART III

Medals and Commendations

1

Presidential Unit Citation: Alphabetical Listing

The following is a complete alphabetical listing of Navy and Marine Corps squadrons awarded the Presidential Unit Citation while embarked in aircraft carriers during the Second World War. Only one squadron, Torpedo Squadron Eight, was actually cited in the award by name; all other squadrons were cited under the name of the carriers in which they were embarked.

Air Groups

Air Group 1: See USS *Yorktown CV-10*
Air Group 2: See USS *Hornet CV-12*
Air Group 3: See USS *Yorktown CV-10*
Air Group 4: See USS *Bunker Hill CV-17* and
    USS *Essex CV-9*
Air Group 5: See USS *Yorktown CV-10*
Air Group 8: See USS *Bunker Hill CV-17*
Air Group 9: See USS *Essex CV-9* and
    USS *Lexington CV-16*
Air Group 9 (2): See USS *Yorktown CV-10*
Air Group 11: See USS *Hornet CV-12*
Air Group 15: See USS *Essex CV-9*
Air Group 16: See USS *Lexington CV-16*
Air Group 17: See USS *Bunker Hill CV-17*
Air Group 17 (2) See USS *Hornet CV-12*
Air Group 19: See USS *Lexington CV-16*
Air Group 20: See USS *Lexington CV-16*
Air Group 21: See USS *Belleau Wood CVL-24*
Air Group 24: See USS *Belleau Wood CVL-24*
Air Group 29: See USS *Cabot CVL-28*
Air Group 30: See USS *Belleau Wood CVL-24*
Air Group 31: See USS *Cabot CVL-28*
Air Group 31 (2): See USS *Belleau Wood CVL-24*
Air Group 45: See USS *San Jacinto CVL-30*
Air Group 49: See USS *San Jacinto CVL-30*

Air Group 51: See USS *San Jacinto CVL-30*
Air Group 83: See USS *Essex CV-9*
Air Group 84: See USS *Bunker Hill CV-17*
Air Group 88: See USS *Yorktown CV-10*
Air Group 94: See USS *Lexington CV-16*

Bombing Fighter Squadrons

Bombing Fighter Squadron 3: See USS *Yorktown CV-10*
Bombing Fighter Squadron 9: See USS *Lexington CV-16* and USS *Yorktown CV-10*
Bombing Fighter Squadron 17: See USS *Hornet CV-12*
Bombing Fighter Squadron 88: See USS *Yorktown CV-10*
Bombing Fighter Squadron 94: See USS *Lexington CV-16*

Bombing Squadrons

Bombing Squadron 1: See USS *Yorktown CV-10*
Bombing Squadron 2: See USS *Hornet CV-12*
Bombing Squadron 3: See USS *Yorktown CV-10*
Bombing Squadron 4: See USS *Bunker Hill CV-17* and USS *Essex CV-9*
Bombing Squadron 5: See USS *Yorktown CV-10*
Bombing Squadron 8: See USS *Bunker Hill CV-17*
Bombing Squadron 9: See USS *Essex CV-9*, USS *Lexington CV-16*, and USS *Yorktown CV-10*
Bombing Squadron 11: See USS *Hornet CV-12*
Bombing Squadron 15: See USS *Essex CV-9*
Bombing Squadron 16: See USS *Lexington CV-16*
Bombing Squadron 17: See USS *Bunker Hill CV-17* and USS *Hornet CV-12*

Bombing Squadron 19: See *USS Lexington CV-16*
Bombing Squadron 20: See *USS Lexington CV-16*
Bombing Squadron 83: See *USS Essex CV-9*
Bombing Squadron 84: See *USS Bunker Hill CV-17*
Bombing Squadron 88: See *USS Yorktown CV-10*
Bombing Squadron 94: See *USS Lexington CV-16*

Composite Squadron

Composite Squadron 24: See *USS Belleau Wood CVL-24*

Fighter Squadrons

Fighter Squadron 1: See *USS Yorktown CV-10*
Fighter Squadron 2: See *USS Hornet CV-12*
Fighter Squadron 3: See *USS Yorktown CV-10*
Fighter Squadron 4: See *USS Bunker Hill CV-17* and *USS Essex CV-9*
Fighter Squadron 5: See *USS Yorktown CV-10*
Fighter Squadron 6: See *USS Belleau Wood CVL-24*
Fighter Squadron 8: See *USS Bunker Hill CV-17*
Fighter Squadron 9: See *USS Essex CV-9, USS Lexington CV-16* and *USS Yorktown CV-10*
Fighter Squadron 11: See *USS Hornet CV-12*
Fighter Squadron 15: See *USS Essex CV-9*
Fighter Squadron 16: See *USS Lexington CV-16*
Fighter Squadron 17: See *USS Hornet CV-12*
Fighter Squadron 18: See *USS Bunker Hill CV-17*
Fighter Squadron 19: See *USS Lexington CV-16*
Fighter Squadron 20: See *USS Lexington CV-16*
Fighter Squadron 21: See *USS Belleau Wood CVL-24*
Fighter Squadron 24: See *USS Belleau Wood CVL-24*
Fighter Squadron 29: See *USS Cabot CVL-28*
Fighter Squadron 30: See *USS Belleau Wood CVL-24*
Fighter Squadron 31: See *USS Cabot CVL-28* and *USS Belleau Wood CVL-24*
Fighter Squadron 45: See *USS San Jacinto CVL-30*
Fighter Squadron 49: See *USS San Jacinto CVL-30*
Fighter Squadron 51: See *USS San Jacinto CVL-30*
Fighter Squadron 83: See *USS Essex CV-9*
Fighter Squadron 84: See *USS Bunker Hill CV-17*
Fighter Squadron 88: See *USS Yorktown CV-10*
Fighter Squadron 94: See *USS Lexington CV-16*

Marine Fighter Squadrons

Marine Fighter Squadron 124: See *USS Essex CV-9*
Marine Fighter Squadron 213: See *USS Essex CV-9*
Marine Fighter Squadron 221: See *USS Bunker Hill CV-17*
Marine Fighter Squadron 451: See *USS Bunker Hill CV-17*

Night Fighter Squadrons

Night Fighter Squadron 76: See *USS Bunker Hill CV-17, USS Hornet CV-12,* and *USS Lexington CV-16*
Night Fighter Squadron 77: See *USS Essex CV-9,* and *USS Yorktown CV-10*

Torpedo Squadrons

Torpedo Squadron 1: See *USS Yorktown CV-10*
Torpedo Squadron 2: See *USS Hornet CV-12*
Torpedo Squadron 3: See *USS Yorktown CV-10*
Torpedo Squadron 4: See *USS Belleau Wood CVL-24,* and *USS Bunker Hill CV-17* and *USS Essex CV-9*
Torpedo Squadron 5: See *USS Yorktown CV-10*
Torpedo Squadron Eight: 4 June 1942—Air Battle of Midway
Torpedo Squadron 8: See *USS Bunker Hill CV-17*
Torpedo Squadron 9: See *USS Essex CV-9, USS Lexington CV-16,* and *USS Yorktown CV-10*
Torpedo Squadron 11: See *USS Hornet CV-12*
Torpedo Squadron 15: See *USS Essex CV-9*
Torpedo Squadron 16: See *USS Lexington CV-16*
Torpedo Squadron 17: See *USS Bunker Hill CV-17* and *USS Hornet CV-12*
Torpedo Squadron 19: See *USS Lexington CV-16*
Torpedo Squadron 20: See *USS Lexington CV-16*
Torpedo Squadron 21: See *USS Belleau Wood CVL-24*
Torpedo Squadron 24: See *USS Belleau Wood CVL-24*
Torpedo Squadron 29: See *USS Cabot CVL-28*
Torpedo Squadron 30: See *USS Belleau Wood CVL-24*
Torpedo Squadron 31: See *USS Belleau Wood CVL-24* and *USS Cabot CVL-28*
Torpedo Squadron 45: See *USS San Jacinto CVL-30*
Torpedo Squadron 49: See *USS San Jacinto CVL-30*
Torpedo Squadron 51: See *USS San Jacinto CVL-30*
Torpedo Squadron 83: See *USS Essex CV-9*
Torpedo Squadron 84: See *USS Bunker Hill CV-17*
Torpedo Squadron 88: See *USS Yorktown CV-10*
Torpedo Squadron 94: See *USS Lexington CV-16*

2

Navy Unit Commendation: Alphabetical Listing

The following is a complete alphabetical listing of Naval air units and squadrons awarded the Navy Unit Commendation while embarked in aircraft carriers. For eligibility dates, see the carriers listed as cited the Navy Unit Commendation.

Air Groups

Air Group 6: See *USS Enterprise CV-6*
Air Group 7: See *USS Hancock CV-19*
Air Group 10: See *USS Enterprise CV-6*
Air Group 14: See *USS Wasp CV-18*
Air Group 20: See *USS Enterprise CV-6*
Air Group 22: See *USS Cowpens CVL-25*
Air Group 23: See *USS Langley CVL-27*
Air Group 25: See *USS Cowpens CVL-25*
Air Group 32: See *USS Langley CVL-27*
Air Group 44: See *USS Langley CVL-27*
Air Group 46: See *USS Cowpens CVL-25*
Air Group 50: See *USS Cowpens CVL-25*
Air Group 80: See *USS Hancock CV-19*
Air Group 81: See *USS Wasp CV-18*
Air Group 86: See *USS Wasp CV-18*
Air Group 90: See *USS Enterprise CV-6*

Air Task Groups

Air Task Group 1: See *USS Valley Forge CVA-45*

Airborne Early Warning Wings

Airborne Early Warning Wing 11 Detachment B See *USS Ticonderoga CVA-14*
Airborne Early Warning Wing 11 Detachment F See *USS Constellation CVA-64*

Attack Carrier Air Wings

Attack Carrier Air Wing 2: See *USS Midway CVA-41*
Attack Carrier Air Wing 7: See *USS Independence CVA-62*
Attack Carrier Air Wing 16: See *USS Oriskany CVA-34*

Attack Squadrons

Attack Squadron 52: See *USS Ticonderoga CVA-14*
Attack Squadron 55: See *USS Ticonderoga CVA-14*
Attack Squadron 56: See *USS Ticonderoga CVA-14*
Attack Squadron 144: See *USS Constellation CVA-64*
Attack Squadron 145: See *USS Constellation CVA-64*
Attack Squadron 146: See *USS Constellation CVA-64*

Bombing Squadrons

Bombing Squadron 6: See *USS Enterprise CV-6* and *USS Hancock CV-19*
Bombing Squadron 7: See *USS Hancock CV-19*
Bombing Squadron 10: See *USS Enterprise CV-6*
Bombing Squadron 14: See *USS Wasp CV-18*
Bombing Squadron 20: See *USS Enterprise CV-6*
Bombing Squadron 80: See *USS Hancock CV-19*
Bombing Squadron 81: See *USS Wasp CV-18*
Bombing Squadron 86: See *USS Wasp CV-18*

Bombing Fighter Squadrons

Bombing Fighter Squadron 6: See *USS Hancock CV-19*
Bombing Fighter Squadron 86: See *USS Wasp CV-18*

Torpedo Squadron 20: See *USS Enterprise CV-6*
Torpedo Squadron 22: See *USS Cowpens CVL-25*
Torpedo Squadron 23: See *USS Langley CVL-27*
Torpedo Squadron 25: See *USS Cowpens CVL-25*
Torpedo Squadron 32: See *USS Langley CVL-27*
Torpedo Squadron 44: See *USS Langley CVL-27*
Torpedo Squadron 46: See *USS Cowpens CVL-25*
Torpedo Squadron 50: See *USS Cowpens CVL-25*

Torpedo Squadron 80: See *USS Hancock CV-19*
Torpedo Squadron 81: See *USS Wasp CV-18*
Torpedo Squadron 86: See *USS Wasp CV-18*

Jtf Nucleus Staff

Jtf-122 Nucleus Staff: See *USS Boxer LPH-4*

3

Presidential Unit Citation: By Carrier

USS Enterprise CV-6

7 December 1941–15 November 1942:
Gilbert and Marshall Islands Raid, Wake Island Raid, Marcus Island Raid, Battle of Midway, Occupation of Guadalcanal, Battle of Stewart Islands, Battle of Santa Cruz Islands, Battle of Solomon Islands.

USS Essex CV-9

Air Group Nine (VF-9, VB-9 and VT-9)
  31 August 1943: Marcus.
  5–6 October 1954: Wake.
  11 November–5 December 1943: Gilberts, Rabaul.
  29 January–23 February 1944: Marshalls, Truk, Marianas.
Air Group Fifteen (VF-15, VB-15, VT-15 and Part of VFN-77)
  19–23 May 1944: Wake, Marcus.
  11 June–8 August 1944: Marianas, Bonins.
  6 September–14 November 1944: Philippines, Palau, Ryukyus, Formosa, and Luzon.
Air Group Four (VF-4, VB-4, and VT-4)
  14–16 Oecember 1944: Luzon.
Air Group Four (VF-4, VT-4, VMF-124 and VMF-213)
  3–22 January 1945: Philippines, Formosa, China Sea, Ryukyus.
  16 February–1 March 1945: Japan, Bonins.
Air Group Eighty-Three (VF-83, VB-83, and VT-83)
  18 March–24 May 1945: Ryukyus, Japan.
  10 July–15 August 1945: Japan.

USS Yorktown CV-10

31 August 1943–15 August 1945
Air Group Five (VF-5, VB-5, and VT-5)

31 August 1943: Marcus.
5–6 October 1943: Wake.
10 November–5 December 1943: Gilberts.
29 January–23 February 1944: Marshalls, Truk, Marianas.
29 March–30 April 1944: Palau, Hollandia, Truk.
Air Group One (VF-1, VB-1, VT-1, and Part of VFN-77)
  11 June–28 July 1944: Marianas, Bonins, Yap.
Air Group Three (VF-3, VB-3, and VT-3)
  11–19 November 1944: Luzon.
  14–16 December 1944: Luzon.
  3–22 January 1945: Philippines, Formosa, China Sea, Ryukyus.
Air Group Three (VF-3, VBF-3, and VT-3)
  16–25 February 1945: Japan, Bonins.
Air Group Nine (VF-9, VBF-9, VB-9, and VT-9)
  18 March–9 June 1945: Ryukyus, Japan.
Air Group Eighty-Eight (VF-88, VBF-88, VB-88, and VT-88)
  10 July–15 August 1945: Japan.

USS Hornet CV-12

Air Group Two (VF-2, VB-2, VT-2, and Part of VFN-76)
  29 March–1 May 1944: Palau, Hollandia, Truk.
  11 June–5 August 1944: Marianas, Bonins, Yap.
  6–24 September 1944: Philippines, Palau.
Air Group Eleven (VF-11, VB-11, and VT-11)
  10 October–22 November 1944: Ryukyus, Formosa, Philippines, Luzon.
  14–16 December 1944: Luzon.
  3–22 January 1945: Philippines, Formosa, China Sea, Ryukyus.
Air Group Seventeen (VF-17, VBF-17, VB-17, and VT-17)

16 February–10 July 1945: Japan, Bonins, Ryukyus.

USS Lexington CV-16

18 September 1943–15 August 1945
Air Group Nine (VF-9, VBF-9, VB-9, and VT-9)
  16 February–1 March 1945: Japan, Bonins, Ryukyus.
Air Group Sixteen (VF-16, VB-16, and VT-16)
  18 September 1943: Tarawa.
  5–6 October 1943: Wake.
  19 November–5 December 1943: Gilberts.
Air Group Sixteen (VF-16, VB-16, VT-16, and Part of VFN-76)
  18 March–30 April 1944: Palau, Hollandia, Truk.
  11 June–5 July 1944: Marianas.
Air Group Nineteen (VF-19, VB-19, VT-19, and Part of VFN-76)
  18 July–5 August 1944: Marianas, Palau, Bonins.
  6 September–6 November 1944: Philippines, Palau, Yap, Ryukyus, Formosa, Luzon.
Air Group Twenty (VF-20, VB-20, and VT-20)
  14–16 December 1944: Luzon.
  3–22 January 1945: Philippines, Formosa, China Sea, Ryukyus.
Air Group Ninety-Four (VF-94, VBF-94, VB-94, and VT-94)
  20 June 1945: Wake.
  10 July–15 August 1945: Japan.

USS Bunker Hill CV-17

11 November 1943–11 May 1945: In the South, Central, Southwest and Western Pacific.
Air Group Seventeen (VF-17, VB-17, VT-17, and Part of VFN-76)
  11 November 1943–23 February 1944: Rabaul, Gilberts, Nauru, Kavieng, Marshalls, Truk, Marianas.
Air Group Eight (VF-8, VB-8, VT-8, and Part of VFN-76)
  29 March–30 April 1944: Palau, Hollandia, Truk.
  11 June–5 August 1944: Marianas, Bonins, Palau.
  6 September–21 October 1944: Philippines, Palau, Yap, Ryukyus, Formosa.
Air Group Four (VF-4, VB-4, and VT-4)
  11–25 November 1944: Luzon.
Air Group Eighty-Four (VF-84, VB-84, VT-84, VMF-221, and VMF-451)
  16 February–11 May 1945: Japan, Bonins, Ryukyus.

USS Belleau Wood CVL-24

18 September 1943–15 August 1945
Air Group Twenty-Four (VF-24, VC-24, and Part of VF-6)

18 September 1943: Tarawa.
5–6 October 1943: Wake.
19 November–5 December 1943: Gilberts.
Air Group Twenty-Four (VF-24 and VT-24)
  29 January–23 February 1944: Marshalls, Truk, Marianas.
  29 March–1 May 1944: Palau, Hollandia, Truk.
  11–24 June 1944: Marianas.
Air Group Twenty-One (VF-21 and VT-21)
  8–18 September 1944: Palau, Philippines.
  10–25 October 1944: Ryukyus, Formosa, Philippines.
Air Group Thirty (VF-30 and VT-30)
  16 February–10 June 1945: Japan, Bonins, Ryukyus.
Air Group Thirty-One (2) (VF-31 and VT-31)
  10 July–15 August 1945: Japan.

USS Cabot CVL-28

29 January 1944–8 April 1945
Air Group Thirty-One (VF-31 and VT-31)
  29 January–16 February 1944: Marshalls, Truk.
  29 March–30 April 1944: Palau, Hollandia, Truk.
  11 June–5 August 1944: Marianas, Bonins, Yap.
  6–24 September 1944: Philippines, Palau, Yap.
Air Group Twenty-Nine (VF-29 and VT-29)
  10 October–25 November 1944: Ryukyus, Formosa, Philippines, Luzon.
  14–16 December 1944: Luzon.
  3–22 January 1945: Philippines, Formosa, China Sea, Ryukyus.
  16–25 February 1945: Japan, Bonins.
  18 March–8 April 1945. Ryukyus, Japan.

USS San Jacinto CVL-30

19 May 1944–15 August 1945
Air Group Forty-Five (VF-45, and VT-45)
  14–16 December 1944: Luzon.
  3–22 January 1945: Philippines, Formosa, China Sea, Ryukyus.
  16 February–27 April 1945: Japan, Ryukyus, Bonins.
Air Group Forty-Nine (VF-49, and VT-49)
  12 May–10 June 1945: Ryukyus, Japan.
  10 July–15 August 1945: Japan.
Air Group Fifty-One (VF-51, and VT-51)
  19–23 May 1944: Wake and Marcus.
  11 June–5 August 1944: Marianas, Bonins, Palau, Yap.
  31 August–18 September 1944: Bonins, Palau, Yap.
  10 October–22 November 1944: Ryukyus, Formosa, Luzon, Philippines.

USS Kitty Hawk CVA-63

23 December 1967–1 June 1968
Attack Carrier Air Wing Eleven CVW-11 (VA-75, VA-112, VA-114, VF-114, VF-213, HATRON 4 Detachment 63, Reconnaissance Attack Squadron 11, Carrier Early Warning Squadron 114, Helicopter Combat Support Squadron 1 Detachment 63

4

Navy Unit Commendation: By Carrier

USS Enterprise CV-6

Air Group Six (VF-6, VB-6, VT-6)
19 November–5 December 1943: Gilberts.
Air Group Ten (VF-10, VB-10, VT-10)
29 January–20 February 1944: Marshalls and Truk.
Air Group Ten (VF-10, VB-10, VT-10 and Part of VFN-10)
20 March–30 April 1944: Palau, Hollandia, Truk.
11 June–5 July 1944: Marianas.
Air Group Twenty (VF-20, VB-20, VT-20 and Part of VFN-78)
31 August–18 September 1944: Bonins, Palau, Yap.
Air Group Twenty (VF-20, VB-20, VT-20)
10 October–22 November 1944: Philippines, Ryukyus, Formosa, Luzon.
Air Group Ninety (VFN-90, VTN-90*)
6–22 January 1945: Philippines, Formosa, China Sea, Ryukyus.
16 February–19 March 1945: Japan, Bonins, Ryukyus.
7–13 April 1945: Ryukyus.
7–14 May 1945: Ryukyus.

USS Essex CVA-9

21 August 1951–5 March 1952: Korea
CVG-5.
21 August 1951–5 March 1952.

USS Ticonderoga CVA-14

Task Group 77.5:
2–5 August 1964: Gulf of Tonkin.
CAW-5 (VA-51, VA-52, VA-53, VA-55, VA-56, VAH-4 Det B, VAP-61 Det, VAW-11 Det. B, VFP-63 Det B, and HU-1 Det B.)

USS Wasp CV-18

Air Group Fourteen (VF-14, VB-14, VT-14 and Part of VFN-77)
19–23 May 1944: Wake, Marcus.
11 June–27 July 1944: Marianas, Bonins, Palau.
6 September–6 November 1944: Philippines, Palau, Yap, Ryukyus, Formosa, Luzon.
Air Group Eighty-One (VF-81, VB-81, VT-81)
Luzon: 14–19 November 1944
14–16 December 1944
Air Group Ninety-One (VF-81, VT-81)
3–22 January 1945: Philippines, Formosa, China Sea, Ryukyus.
Air Group Eighty-One (VF-81, VT-81, VMF-216, VMF-217)
16 February–1 March 1945: Japan, Bonins, Ryukyus.
Air Group Eighty-Six (VF-86, VBF-86, VB-86, VT-86)
Japan: 18–21 March 1945
18 July–15 August 1945

USS Hancock CV-19

Air Group Seven (VF-7, VB-7, VT-7)
10 October–25 November 1944: Ryukyus, Formosa, Philippines, Luzon.
14–16 December 1944: Luzon.
3–22 January 1945: Philippines, Formosa, China Sea, Ryukyus.
Air Group Eighty (VF-80, VB-80, VT-80)
16 February–1 March 1945: Japan, Bonins, Ryukyus.
Air Group Six (VF-6, VBF-6, VB-6, VT-6)
18 March–6 April 1945: Ryukyus, Japan.
20 June 1945: Wake.
10 July–15 August 1945: Japan.

USS Boxer LPH-4

Nucleus JTF-122 Staff embarked:
  26–30 April 1965: Dominican Republic Crisis

USS Cowpens CVL-25

Air Group Twenty-Five (VF-25, VC-25 and Part of
    VF-6)
  5–6 October 1943: Wake.
  19 November–5 December 1943: Gilberts.
Air Group Twenty-Five (VF-25, VT-25)
  29 January–23 February 1944: Marshalls.
  29 March–1 May 1944: Palau, Hollandia, Truk.
  11 January–1 July 1944: Marianas, Bonin.
Air Group Twenty-Two (VF-22, VT-22)
  6 September–19 November 1944: Philippines, Palau,
    Yap, Ryukyus, Formosa, Luzon.
  14–16 December 1944: Luzon.
  3–22 January 1945. Philippines, Formosa, China Sea,
    Ryukyus.
Air Group Forty-Six (VF-46, VT-46)
  16 February–1 March 1945: Bonins, Japan, Ryukyus.
Air Group Fifty (VF-50, VT-50)
  20 June 1945: Wake.
  10 July–15 August 1945: Japan.

USS Langley CVL-27

Air Group Thirty-Two (VF-32, VT-32)
  29 January–23 February 1944: Marshalls.
  29 March–30 April 1944: Palau, Hollandia, Truk.
  11 June–8 August 1944: Marianas, Bonins.
  6–24 September 1944: Philippines, Palau, Yap.
Air Group Forty-Four (VF-44, VT-44)
  10 October–25 November 1944: Ryukyus, Formosa,
    Philippines, Luzon.
  14–16 December 1944: Luzon.
  3–22 January 1945: Philippines, Formosa, China Sea,
    Ryukyus.
Air Group Twenty-Three (VF-23, VT-23)
  16–25 February 1945: Japan, Bonins.
  18 March–11 May 1945: Japan, Ryukyus.

USS Bon Homme Richard CVA-31

Korea: 22 June–18 December 1952
CVG-7:
22 June–18 December 1952.

USS Leyte CVA-32

Korea: 9 October 1950–19 January 1951
CVG-3:
9 October 1950–19 January 1951.

USS Oriskany CVA-34

10 May–6 December 1965: Southeast Asia.
CVW-16:
10 May–6 December 1965.

USS Princeton CVA-37

Korea: 5 December 1950–10 August 1951
        15 April–18 October 1952
        13 March–15 May 1953
        11 June–27 July 1953
CVG-19: 5 December 1950–10 August 1951
        15 April–18 October 1952
CVG-15: 13 March–15 May 1953
        11 June–27 July 1953

USS Coral Sea CVA-43

Southeast Asia: 7 February–18 October 1965.
CVW-15:
7 February–18 October 1965: Southeast Asia.

USS Midway CVA-41

Southeast Asia: 16 April–4 November 1965.
CVW-2:
16 April–4 November 1965.

USS Valley Forge CVA-45

Korea: 3 July–18 November 1950
       11 December 1951–11 June 1952
       1 January–5 June 1953
CVG-5:
3 July–18 November 1950
1 January–5 June 1953
Air Task Group One:
11 December 1951–11 June 1952

USS Philippine Sea CVA-47

Korea: 4 August 1950–31 May 1951

31 January–27 July 1953
CVG-11:
4 August 1950–31 May 1951
CVG-2:
31 March–31 May 1951
CVG-9:
31 January–27 July 1953

USS Ranger CVA-61

Southeast Asia: 10 January–6 August 1966.
CVW-14:
10 January–6 August 1966.

USS Independence CVA-62

Southeast Asia: 5 June–21 November 1965.

CVW-7:
5 June–21 November 1965.

USS Kitty Hawk CVA-63

Southeast Asia: 26 November 1965–14 May 1966.
CVW-11:
26 November 1965–14 May 1966.

USS Constellation CVA-64

Task Group 77.6:
  2–5 August 1964: Gulf of Tonkin
  CAW-14 (VA-144, VA-145, VA-146, VAH-10, VAP-
    61, VAW-11 Det F, VF-142, VF-143, VFP-63
    Det F, HU-1 Det F)

5

Meritorious Unit Commendation

USS Intrepid CVS-11

6 July 1968–16 January 1969

USS Hornet CVS-12

24 October 1968–2 May 1969

USS Hancock CVA-19

20 January–14 July 1967

USS Kearsarge CVS-33

11 July–11 December 1966
12 October–28 May 1968

USS Princeton LPH-5

23 March–2 August 1966
6 March–27 May 1968

USS Valley Forge LPH-8

30 August 1965–9 April 1966
7 September–1 December 1966

USS Ranger CVA-61

3 December 1967–9 May 1969

USS Constellation CVA-64

14 June 1968–23 January 1969

6

Mexican Service Medal

USS Jupiter AC-3*

Vera Cruz: 27 April–9 July 1914
         6 April 1916
      12–23 April 1916

* USS *Jupiter AC-3* was converted to the *USS Langley CV-1* in 1921–1922.

7

World War I Victory Medal

USS Jupiter AC-3

The *USS Jupiter AC-3* served as a transport during the First World War during the period 23 May–26 June 1917. Later, in 1921–1922, the *USS Jupiter* was converted into the U.S. Navy's first aircraft carrier and renamed *USS Langley CV-1*.

8

American Defense Service Medal

USS *Langley AC-3*

USS *Lexington CV-2*

USS *Saratoga CV-3*

USS *Ranger CV-4*

USS *Yorktown CV-5*

USS *Enterprise CV-6*

USS *Wasp CV-7*

USS *Hornet CV-8*

The *Ranger, Yorktown,* and *Wasp* were awarded the American Defense Service Medal with Bronze "A" for actual or potential belligerent contact with the Nazi Forces in the Atlantic during the periods indicated:

USS Ranger CV-4

USS Ranger and embarked Air Group (VF-42, VS-41 and VS-42) for service during the period 24–September–20 October 1941.

USS Yorktown CV-5

USS Yorktown and embarked Air Group (VB-5, VS-21, and VT-5) during the periods indicated: 21 September–11 October 1941; 31 October–4 November 1941.

USS Wasp CV-7

USS Wasp and embarked Air Group for service during the periods indicated: 1–9 August 1941; 23 September–17 October 1941

9

American Area Campaign Service Medal

USS *Langley AV-3*
USS *Lexington CV-2*
USS *Saratoga CV-3*
USS *Ranger CV-4*
USS *Yorktown CV-5*
USS *Enterprise CV-6*
USS *Wasp CV-7*
USS *Hornet CV-8*
USS *Essex CV-9*
USS *Yorktown CV-10*
USS *Intrepid CV-11*
USS *Hornet CV-12*
USS *Franklin CV-13*
USS *Ticonderoga CV-14*
USS *Randolph CV-15*
USS *Lexington CV-16*

USS *Bunker Hill CV-17*
USS *Wasp CV-18*
USS *Hancock CV-19*
USS *Bennington CV-20*
USS *Independence CVL-22*
USS *Princeton CVL-23*
USS *Belleau Wood CVL-24*
USS *Cowpens CVL-25*
USS *Monterey CVL-26*
USS *Langley CVL-27*
USS *Cabot CVL-28*
USS *Bataan CVL-29*
USS *San Jacinto CVL-30*
USS *Bon Homme Richard CV-31*
USS *Shangri La CV-38*

10

Asiatic-Pacific Area Campaign Service Medal

USS Lexington CV-2

Pacific Raids 1942:
  Air action off Bougainville, 20 February 1942
  Salamaua–Lae Raid, 10 March 1942
Battle of Coral Sea 4–8 May 1942

USS Saratoga CV-3

Guadalcanal–Tulagi Landings, 7–9 August 1942
Capture and defense of Guadalcanal, 10 August–
  1 September 1942
Eastern Solomons Operation, 23–25 August 1942
Treasury–Bougainville Operation:
  Buka–Bonis Strike, 1–2 November 1943
  Rabaul Strike, 11 November 1943
Gilbert Islands Operation 18–30 November 1943
Marshall Islands Operation:
  Occupation of Kwajalein and Majuro Atoll,
  29 January–8 February 1944
  Occupation of Eniwetok Atoll, 17 February–2 March
  1944
Asiatic-Pacific Raids 1944:
  Sabang Raid, 19 April 1944
  Soerabaja Raid, 17 May 1944
Iwo Jima Operation:
  Assault and occupation of Iwo Jima, 15–21 February
  1945
  5th Fleet Raids against Honshu and the Nansei
  15–16 February 1945, 25 February 1945–1 March
  1945

USS Yorktown CV-5

Pacific Raids 1942:
  Marshall–Gilbert Raids, 1 February 1942

Salamaua–Lae Raid, 10 March 1942
Battle of Coral Sea 4–8 May 1942
Battle of Midway 3–6 June 1942

USS Enterprise CV-6

Pearl Harbor–Midway, 7 December 1941 (Only planes
  which operated over Pearl Harbor)
Submarine Assessment–Hawaiian Area: 10 December
  1941
Pacific Raids 1942:
  Marshall–Gilbert Raids, 1 February 1942
  Wake Island Raid, 24 February 1942
  Marcus Island Raid, 4 March 1942
Battle of Midway, 3–6 June 1942
Guadalcanal–Tulagi Landings (Including first salvo),
  7–9 August 1942
Capture and defense of Guadalcanal, 10–25 August
  1942
Eastern Solomons (Stewart Island), 23–25 August 1942
Santa Cruz Operation, 26 October 1942
Guadalcanal (Third Salvo), 12–15 November 1942
Rennel Island, 29–30 January 1943
Gilbert Islands Operation, 19 November–4 December
  1943
Marshall Islands Operation:
  Occupation of Kwajalein and Majuro Atolls, 29
  January–8 February 1944
  Attack on Jaluit Atoll, 20 February 1944
Asiatic–Pacific Raids 1944:
  Truk Attack, 16–17 February 1944
  Palau, Yap, Ulithi, Woleai, Raid, 30 March–1 April
  1944
  Truk, Satawan, Ponape Raid, 29 April–1 May 1944
Hollandia Operation (Aitape–Humboldt Bay–Tanah-
  merah Bay) 21–24 April 1944

Marianas Operation:
Capture and occupation of Saipan, 11–14 June 1944
Battle of the Philippine Sea, 19–20 June 1944
Western Caroline Operation:
Raids on Volcano–Bonin Islands and Yap Islands,
31 August–8 September 1944
Capture and Occupation of Southern Palau Islands,
6 September–24 October 1944
Assaults on the Philippine Islands,
9–24 September 1944
Leyte Operation:
3rd Fleet Supporting Operations Okinawa Attacks,
10 October 1944
Northern Luzon and Formosa Attacks,
11–14 October 1944
Luzon Attacks,
15 October 1944
17–19 October 1944
13–14 November 1944
19 November 1944
Luzon Operation:
Formosa Attacks,
3–4 January 1945
9 January 1945
15 January 1945
Luzon Attacks, 6–7 January 1945
China Coast Attacks,
12 January 1945
16 January 1945
Iwo Jima Operation:
5th Fleet Raids Against Honshu and the Nansei
Shoto,
15–16 February 1945
25 February 1945
1 March 1945
Assault and Occupation of Iwo Jima,
23 February–12 March 1945
Okinawa Gunto Operation:
5th and 3rd Fleet Raids in Support of Okinawa
Gunto Operation, 17 March–15 May 1945

USS Wasp CV-7

Guadalcanal–Tulagi Landings, 7–9 August 1942
Capture and Defense of Guadalcanal,
10 August–15 September 1942

USS Hornet CV-8

Battle of Midway, 3–6 June 1952
Buin-Faisi-Tonolai Raid, 5 October 1942
Capture and Defense of Guadacanal, 16 October 1942
Santa Cruz Operation, 26 October 1942

USS Essex CV-9

Pacific Raids 1943:
Marcus Island Raid, 31 August 1943
Wake Island Raid, 5–6 October 1943
Treasury–Bougainville Operation:
Rabaul Strike, 11 November 1943
Gilbert Islands Operation:
19 November–4 December 1943
Marshall Islands Operation:
29 January 1944–8 February 1944
Asiatic–Pacific Raids 1944:
Truk Attack, 16–17 February 1944
Marianas Attack, 21–22 February 1944
Marianas Operation:
Capture and Occupation of Saipan,
11–24 June 1944
First Bonins Raid, 15–16 June 1944
Battle of the Philippine Sea, 19–20 June 1944
Capture and Occupation of Guam,
12 July–15 August 1944
Tinian Capture and Occupation,
20 July–10 August 1944
Western Caroline Islands Operation:
Capture and Occupation of Southern Palau Islands,
6 September–14 October 1944
Assaults on the Philippine Islands,
9–24 September 1944
Leyte Operation:
3rd Fleet Supporting Operations Okinawa Attack,
10 October 1944
Battle of Surigao Strait, 24–26 October 1944
Northern Luzon and Formosa Attacks,
11–14 October 1944
Luzon Attacks,
15 October 1944
17–19 October 1944
5–6 November 1944
19–25 November 1944
14–16 December 1944
Visayas Attacks, 21 October 1944
Luzon Operation:
Formosa Attacks,
3–4 January 1945
9 January 1945
15 January 1945
21 January 1945
Luzon Attacks, 6–7 January 1945
China Coast Attacks,
12 January 1945
16 January 1945
Nansei Shoto Attacks, 22 January 1945
Iwo Jima Operation:

Assault and Occupation of Iwo Jima,
  15 February–4 March 1945
5th Fleet Raids against Honshu and the Nansei
Shoto,
  15–16 February 1945
  25 February 1945
  1 March 1945
Okinawa Gunto Operation:
  5th and 3rd Fleet Raids in Support of Okinawa
  Gunto Operation, 17 March–30 May 1945
Third Fleet Operations against Japan,
  10 July–15 August 1945

USS Yorktown CV-10

Pacific Raids 1943:
  Marcus Island Raid, 31 August 1943
  Wake Island Raid, 5–6 October 1943
Gilbert Islands Operation,
  19 November–4 December 1943
Marshall Islands Operation:
  Occupation of Kwajalein and Majuro Atolls,
  29 January–8 February 1944
Asiatic–Pacific Raids 1944:
  Truk Attack, 16–17 February 1944
  Marianas Attack, 21–22 February 1944
  Palau, Yap, Ulithi Woleai Raids,
  30 March–1 April 1944
Hollandia Operation (Aitape–Humboldt Bay–Tanah-
  merah Bay), 21–24 April 1944
Marianas Operation:
  Capture and Occupation of Saipan, 11–24 June 1944
  First Bonins Raid, 15–16 June 1944
  Battle of the Philippine Sea, 19–20 June 1944
  Second Bonins Raid, 24 June 1944
  Third Bonins Raid, 3–4 July 1944
  Capture and Occupation of Guam,
  12 July–15 August 1945
  Palau, Yap, Ulithi Raid, 25–27 July 1944
Leyte Operation:
  Luzon Attacks,
    13–14 November 1944
    19–22 November 1944
Luzon Operation:
  Luzon Attacks, 6–7 January 1945
  Formosa Attacks,
    3–4 January 1945
    9 January 1945
    15 January 1945
    21 January 1945
  China Coast Attacks,
    12 January 1945
    16 January 1945

Nansei Shoto Attack, 22 January 1945
Iwo Jima Operation:
  Assault and Occupation of Iwo Jima,
  15 February–1 March 1945
5th Fleet Raids against Honshu and the Nansei
Shoto,
  15–16 February 1945
  25 February 1945
  1 March 1945
Okinawa Gunto Operation:
  5th and 3rd Fleet Raids in Support of Okinawa
  Gunto Operation, 17 March–11 June 1945
Third Fleet Operation against Japan,
  10 July–15 August 1945

USS Intrepid CV-11

Marshall Islands Operation:
  Occupation of Kwajalein and Majuro Atolls,
  29 January–8 February 1944
Asiatic–Pacific Raids 1944:
  Truk Attack, 16–17 February 1944
Western Caroline Islands Operation:
  Capture and Occupation of Southern Palau Islands,
  6 September–14 October 1944
  Assaults on the Philippine Islands,
  9–24 September 1944
Leyte Operation:
  3rd Fleet Supporting Operations Okinawa Attack,
  10 October 1944
  Northern Luzon and Formosa Attacks,
  13–14 October 1944
  Battle of Surigao Strait, 24–26 October 1944
  Luzon Attacks,
    15 October 1944
    17–19 October 1944
    5–6 November 1944
    19–25 November 1944
  Visayas Attack, 21 October 1944
Okinawa Gunto Operation:
  5th and 3rd Fleet Raids in Support of Okinawa
  Gunto Operation, 17 March–16 April 1945

USS Hornet CV-12

Asiatic–Pacific Raids 1944:
  Palau, Yap, Ulithi, Woleai Raids,
  30 March–1 April 1944
  Truk, Satawan, Ponape Raid, 29 April–1 May 1944
Hollandia Operation (Aitape–Humboldt Bay–Tanah-
  merah Bay), 21–24 April 1944
Marianas Operation:
  Capture and Occupation of Saipan, 11–24 June 1944
  First Bonins Raid, 15–16 June 1944

Battle of the Philippine Sea, 19–20 June 1944
Second Bonins Raid, 24 June 1944
Third Bonins Raid, 3–4 July 1944
Capture and Occupation of Guam,
    12 July–15 August 1944
Fourth Bonins Raid, 4–5 August 1944
Western Caroline Islands Operation:
  Capture and Occupation of Southern Palau Islands,
    6 September–4 October 1944
  Assaults on the Philippine Islands,
    9–24 September 1944
Western New Guinea Operation:
  Morotai Landings, 15 September 1944
Leyte Operation:
  3rd Fleet Supporting Operations Okinawa Attack,
    10 October 1944·
  Battle of Surigao Strait, 24–26 October 1944
  Luzon Attacks,
    15 October 1944
    17–19 October 1944
    5–6 November 1944
    13–14 November 1944
    19 November 1944
Luzon Operation:
  Luzon Attacks, 6–7 January 1945
  Formosa Attacks,
    3–4 January 1945
    9 January 1945
    15 January 1945
    21 January 1945
  China Coast Attacks,
    12 January 1945
    16 January 1945
  Nansei Shoto Attack, 22 January 1945
Iwo Jima Operation:
  Assault and Occupation of Iwo Jima,
    15 February–4 March 1945
  5th Fleet Raids against Honshu and the Nansei Shoto,
    25 February 1945
    1 March 1945
Okinawa Gunto Operation:
  5th and 3rd Fleet Raids in Support of Okinawa
  Gunto Operation, 17 March–11 June 1945

USS Franklin CV-13

Marianas Operation:
  Third Bonins Raid, 3–4 July 1944
  Capture and Occupation of Guam,
    12 July–15 August 1944

Palau, Yap, Ulithi Raid, 25–27 July 1944
Fourth Bonins Raid, 4–5 August 1944
Western Caroline Islands Operation:
  Raids on Volcano, Bonin Islands and Yap Islands,
    31 August–8 September 1944
  Capture and Occupation of Southern Palau Islands,
    6 September–14 October 1944
  Assaults on the Philippine Islands,
    9–24 September 1944
Leyte Operation:
  3rd Fleet Supporting Operations Okinawa Attack,
    10 October 1944
  Northern Luzon and Formosa Attacks,
    11–14 October 1944
  Luzon Attacks,
    15 October 1944
    17–19 October 1944
  Battle of Surigao Strait, 24–26 October 1944
Okinawa Gunto Operation:
  5th and 3rd Fleet Raids in Support of Okinawa
  Gunto Operation, 17 March–11 May 1945

USS Ticonderoga CV-14

Western Caroline Islands Operation:
  Capture and Occupation of Southern Palau Islands,
    6 September–14 October 1944
  Assaults on the Philippine Islands,
    9–24 September 1944
Leyte Operation:
  Luzon Attacks,
    5–6 November 1944
    13–14 November 1944
    19–25 November 1944
    14–16 December 1944
Luzon Operation:
  Luzon Attacks, 6–7 January 1945
  Formosa Attacks,
    3–4 January 1945
    9 January 1945
    15 January 1945
    21 January 1945
  China Coast Attacks,
    12 January 1945
    16 January 1945
Okinawa Gunto Operation:
  5th and 3rd Fleet Raids in Support Okinawa Gunto
  Operations, 24 May–11 June 1945
Third Fleet Operations against Japan,
    21 July–15 August 1945

USS Randolph CV-15

Iwo Jima Operation:
  5th Fleet Raids against Honshu and the Nansei Shoto,
    25 February 1945–1 March 1945
  Assault and Occupation of Iwo Jima, 15 February–
    1 March 1945
Okinawa Gunto Operation:
  5th and 3rd Fleet Raids in Support of Okinawa
  Gunto Operation, 8 April–29 May 1945
Third Fleet Operations against Japan,
    10 July–15 August 1945

USS Lexington CV-16

Pacific Raids 1943:
  Tarawa Island Raid, 18 September 1943
  Wake Island Raid, 5–6 November 1943
Gilbert Islands Operation:
  19 November–4 December 1943
Marshall Islands Operation:
  Mille Atoll, 18 March 1944
Asiatic-Pacific Raids 1944:
  Palau, Yap, Ulithi, Woleai Raid,
    30 March–1 April 1944
  Truk, Satawan, Ponape Raid, 29 April–1 May 1944
Hollandia Operation (Aitape-Humboldt Bay-Tanah-
    merah Bay), 21–24 April 1944
Marianas Operation:
  Capture and Occupation of Saipan, 11–24 June 1944
  Battle of the Philippine Sea, 19–20 June 1944
  Capture and Occupation of Guam,
    12 July 1944–15 August 1944
  Palau, Yap, Ulithi Raid, 25–27 July 1944
  Fourth Bonins Raid, 4–5 August 1944
Western Caroline Islands Operation:
  Capture and Occupation of Southern Palau Islands,
    6 September–14 October 1944
  Assault on the Philippine Islands,
    9–24 September 1944
Leyte Operation:
  3rd Fleet Supporting Operations Okinawa Attack,
    10 October 1944
  Northern Luzon and Formosa Attacks,
    11–14 October 1944
  Visayas Attacks, 21 October 1944
  Battle of Surigao Strait, 24–26 October 1944
  Luzon Attacks,
    15 October 1944
    17–19 October 1944
    5–6 November 1944

19–25 November 1944
Luzon Operation:
  Luzon Attacks, 6–7 January 1945
  Formosa Attacks,
    3–4 January 1945
    9 January 1945
    15 January 1945
    21 January 1945
  China Coast Attacks,
    12 January 1945
    16 January 1945
  Nansei Shoto Attack, 22 January 1945
Iwo Jima Operation:
  5th Fleet Raids against Honshu and the Nansei Shoto,
    15–16 February 1945
    25 February 1945
    1 March 1945
  Assault and Occupation of Iwo Jima,
    15 February–4 March 1945
Third Fleet Operations against Japan,
    10 July–15 August 1945

USS Bunker Hill CV-17

Treasury-Bougainville Operation:
  Rabaul Strike, 11 November 1943
Gilbert Islands Operation: 19 November–8 December
    1943
Bismarck-Archipelago Operation:
  Kavieng Strikes,
    25 December 1943
    1 January 1944
    4 January 1944
Marshall Islands Operation:
  Occupation of Kwajalein and Majuro Atolls,
    29 January–8 February 1945
Asiatic-Pacific Raids 1944:
  Truk Attack, 16–17 February 1944
  Marianas Attack, 21–22 February 1944
  Palau, Yap, Ulithi, Woleai Raid,
    30 March–1 April 1944
  Truk, Satawan, Ponape Raid, 29 April–1 May 1944
Hollandia Operation (Aitape-Humboldt Bay-Tanah-
    merah Bay), 21–24 April 1944
Marianas Operation:
  Capture and Occupation of Saipan, 11–24 June 1944
  Battle of the Philippine Sea, 19–20 June 1944
  Capture and Occupation of Guam,
    12 July–15 August 1944
  Palau, Yap, Ulithi Raid, 25–27 July 1944
Western Caroline Islands Operation:

Capture and Occupation of Southern Palau Islands,
    6 September–14 October 1944
Assaults on the Philippine Islands,
    9–24 September 1944
Leyte Operation:
    3rd Fleet Supporting Operations Okinawa Attacks,
    10 October 1944
Northern Luzon and Formosa Attacks,
    13–14 October 1944
Luzon Attacks,
    15 October 1944
    17–19 October 1944
    13–14 November 1944
    14–16 December 1944
Iwo Jima Operation:
    5th Fleet Raids against Honshu and the Nansei
    Shoto,
        16 February 1945
        25 February 1945
        1 March 1945
    Assault and Occupation of Iwo Jima,
        15 February–4 March 1945
Okinawa Gunto Operation:
    5th and 3rd Fleet Raids in Support of Okinawa
    Gunto Operation, 17 March–28 May 1945

USS Wasp CV-18

Western New Guinea Operation:
    Morotai Landings, 14 September 1944
Marianas Operation:
    Capture and Occupation of Saipan, 7–24 June 1944
    First Bonins Raid, 15–16 June 1944
    Battle of the Philippine Sea, 19–20 June 1944
    Capture and Occupation of Guam,
        12 July–9 August 1944
    Palau, Yap, Ulithi Raid, 25–27 July 1944
Western Caroline Islands Operation:
    Capture and Occupation of Southern Palau Islands,
        6 September–14 October 1944
    Assault on the Philippine Islands,
        9–24 September 1944
Leyte Operation:
    3rd Fleet Supporting Operation Okinawa Attack,
        10 October 1944
    Battle of Surigao Strait, 24–26 October 1944
    Northern Luzon and Formosa Attacks,
        11–14 October 1944
    Luzon Attacks,
        15 October 1944
        17–19 October 1944
        5–6 November 1944

13–14 November 1944
19–22 November 1944
14–16 December 1944
Luzon Operation:
    Luzon Attacks, 6–7 January 1945
    Formosa Attacks,
        3–4 January 1945
        9 January 1945
        15 January 1945
        21 January 1945
    China Coast Attacks,
        12 January 1945
        16 January 1945
    Nansei Shoto Attack, 22 January 1945
Iwo Jima Operation:
    Assault and Occupation of Iwo Jima,
        15 February–4 March 1945
    5th Fleet Raids against Honshu and the Nansei
    Shoto,
        15–16 February 1945
        25 February 1945
        1 March 1945
Okinawa Gunto Operation:
    5th and 3rd Fleet Raids in Support of Okinawa
    Gunto Operation, 17–22 May 1945
Third Fleet Operations against Japan, 26 July–15
    August 1945

USS Hancock CV-19

Leyte Operation:
    3rd Fleet Supporting Operation Okinawa Attack,
        10 October 1944
    Northern Luzon and Formosa Attacks,
        11–14 October 1944
    Luzon Attacks,
        18–19 October 1944
        19–25 November 1944
        14–16 December 1944
    Visayas Attacks, 20–21 October 1944
    Battle of Samar, 25–26 October 1944
Luzon Operation:
    Luzon Attacks, 6–7 January 1945
    Formosa Attacks,
        3–4 January 1945
        9 January 1945
        15 January 1945
        21 January 1945
    China Coast Attacks,
        12 January 1945
        16 January 1945
    Nansei Shoto Attack, 22 January 1945

Iwo Jima Operation:
Assault and Occupation of Iwo Jima,
15 February–4 March 1945
5th Fleet Raids against Honshu and the Nansei Shoto,
15–16 February 1945
25 February 1945
1 March 1945
Third Fleet Operations against Japan,
10 July–15 August 1945

USS Bennington CV-20

Iwo Jima Operation:
Assault and Occupation of Iwo Jima,
15 February–4 March 1945
5th Fleet Raids agains Honshu and the Nansei Shoto,
15–16 February 1945
25 February 1945
1 March 1945
Okinawa Gunto Operation:
5th and 3rd Fleet Raids in Support of Okinawa Gunto Operation, 17 March–11 June 1945
Third Fleet Operations against Japan,
10 July–15 August 1945

USS Independence CVL-22

Pacific Raids 1943:
Marcus Island Raid, 31 August 1943
Wake Island Raid, 5–6 October 1943
Treasury-Bougainville Operation:
Rabaul Strike, 11 November 1943
Gilbert Islands Operation: 19–20 November 1943
Western Carolina Islands Operation:
Capture and Occupation of Southern Palau Islands,
6 September–14 October 1943
Leyte Operation:
3rd Fleet Supporting Operations Okinawa Attack,
10 October 1944
Northern Luzon and Formosa Attacks,
13–14 October 1944
Visayas Attacks, 21 October 1944
Luzon Attacks,
15 October 1944
17–19 October 1944
5–6 November 1944
19–25 November 1944
14–16 December 1944
Battle of Surigao Strait, 24–26 October 1944
Luzon Operation:

Formosa Attacks,
3–4 January 1945
9 January 1945
15 January 1945
21 January 1945
China Coast Attacks,
12 January 1945
16 January 1945
Nansei Shoto Attack, 22 January 1945
Okinawa Gunto Operation:
5th and 3rd Fleet Raids in Support of Okinawa Gunto Operation, 17 March–11 June 1945
Third Fleet Operations against Japan,
10 July–15 August 1945

USS Princeton CVL-23

Pacific Raids 1943:
Tarawa Island Raid, 18 September 1943
Treasury-Bougainville Operation:
Buka-Bonis Strike, 1–2 November 1943
Rabaul Strike, 5 November 1943
Rabaul Strike, 11 November 1943
Gilbert Islands Operation: 10–20 November 1943
Marshall Islands Operation:
Occupation of Kwajalein and Majuro Atolls,
29 January–8 February 1944
Occupation of Eniwetok Atoll,
17 February–2 March 1944
Asiatic-Pacific Raids 1944:
Palau, Yap, Ulithi, Woleai, Raid,
30 March–1 April 1944
Truk, Satawan, Ponape Raid, 29 April–1 May 1944
Hollandia Operation (Aitape-Humboldt Bay- Tanah-merah Bay), 21–24 April 1944
Marianas Operation:
Capture and Occupation of Saipan, 11–24 June 1944
Battle of the Philippine Sea, 19–20 June 1944
Capture and Occupation of Guam,
12 July–15 August 1944
Western Caroline Islands Operation:
Capture and Occupation of Southern Palau Islands,
6 September–14 October 1944
Assaults on the Philippine Islands,
9–24 September 1944
Leyte Operation.
3rd Fleet Supporting Operations Okinawa Attack,
10 October 1944
Northern Luzon and Formosa Attacks,
11–14 October 1944
Luzon Attacks,
15 October 1944

17–19 October 1944
Visayas Attacks, 21 October 1944
Battle of Surigao Strait, 24 October 1944

USS Belleau Wood CVL-24

Pacific Raids 1943:
    Tarawa Island Raid, 18 September 1943
    Wake Island Raid, 5–6 October 1943
    Gilbert Islands Operation:
        19 November–4 December 1944
Marshall Islands Operation:
    Occupation of Kwajalein and Majuro Atolls
        29 January–8 February 1944
Asiatic-Pacific Raids 1944:
    Truk Attack, 16–17 February 1944
    Marianas Attack, 21–22 February 1944
    Truk, Satawan, Ponape Raid, 29 April–1 May 1944
Hollandia Operation (Aitape-Humboldt Bay-Tanah-
    merah Bay): 21–24 April 1944
Marianas Operation:
    Capture and Occupation of Saipan, 11–24 June 1944
    First Bonins Raid, 15–16 June 1944
    Battle of the Philippine Sea, 19–20 June 1944
    Second Bonins Raid, 24 June 1944
    Capture and Occupation of Guam,
        12 July–15 August 1944
Western Caroline Islands Operation:
    Capture and Occupation of Southern Palau Islands,
        6 September–14 October 1944
    Assaults on the Philippine Islands,
        9–24 September 1944
Western New Guinea Operations:
    Morotai Landings, 15 September 1944
Leyte Operations:
    3rd Fleet Supporting Operations Okinawa Attack,
        10 October 1944
    Northern Luzon and Formosa Attacks,
        11–14 October 1944
    Luzon Attacks,
        15 October 1944
        17–19 October 1944
    Battle of Surigao Strait, 24–26 October 1944
Iwo Jima Operation:
    5th Fleet Raids against Honshu and the Nansei
Shoto,
        15–16 February 1945
        25 February 1945
        1 March 1945
    Assault and Occupation of Iwo Jima,
        15 February–4 March 1945
Third Fleet Operations against Japan,
    10 July–15 August 1945

USS Cowpens CVL-25

Pacific Raids 1943:
    Wake Island Raid, 5–6 October 1943
Gilbert Islands Operation:
    19 November–4 December 1944
Marshall Islands Operation:
    Occupation of Kwajalein and Majuro Atolls,
        31 January–3 February 1945
Asiatic-Pacific Raids 1944:
    Truk Attack, 16–17 February 1944
    Marianas Attacks, 21–22 February 1944
    Palau, Yap, Ulithi, Woleai Raid,
        30 March–1 April 1944
Western New Guinea Operation:
    Morotai Landings, 15 September 1944
Marianas Operation:
    Capture and Occupation of Saipan, 11–24 June 1944
    First Bonins Raid, 15–16 June 1944
    Battle of the Philippine Sea, 19–20 June 1944
Western Caroline Islands Operation:
    Capture and Occupation of Southern Palau Islands,
        6 September–14 October 1944
    Assaults on the Philippine Islands,
        9–24 September 1944
Leyte Operation:
    3rd Fleet Supporting Operations Okinawa Attack,
        10 October 1944
    Northern Luzon and Formosa Attacks,
        11–14 October 1944
    Luzon Attacks,
        15 October 1944
        17–19 October 1944
        5–6 November 1944
        13–14 November 1944
        19–25 November 1944
        14–16 December 1944
Luzon Operation:
    Luzon Attacks, 6–7 January 1945
    Formosa Attacks,
        3–4 January 1945
        9 January 1945
        15 January 1945
        21 January 1945
    China Coast Attacks,
        12 January 1945
        16 January 1945
    Nansei Shoto Attack, 22 January 1945
Iwo Jima Operations:
    5th Fleet Raids against Honshu and the Nansei
Shoto,
        15–16 February 1945
        25 February 1945

1 March 1945
Assault and Occupation of Iwo Jima,
   15 February–4 March 1945
Third Fleet Operations against Japan,
   10 July–15 August 1945

USS Monterey CVL-26

Gilbert Islands Operation:
   19 November–8 December 1943
Bismarck–Archipelago Operation:
   Kavieng Strike,
      25 December 1943
      1 January 1944
Asiatic–Pacific Raids 1944:
   Truk Attack, 16–17 February 1944
   Marianas Attack, 21–22 February 1944
   Palau, Yap, Woleai, Ulithi Raid,
      30 March–1 April 1944
   Truk, Satawan, Ponape Raid, 29 April–1 May 1944
Marshall Islands Operation:
   Occupation of Kwajalein and Majuro Atolls,
      29 January–8 February 1944
Hollandia Operation (Aitape–Humboldt Bay–Tanah-
   merah Bay), 21–24 April 1944
Marianas Operation:
   Capture and Occupation of Saipan, 11–24 June 1944
   Battle of the Philippine Sea, 19–20 June 1944
   Third Bonins Raid, 3–4 July 1944
Western New Guinea Operation:
   Morotai Landings, 15 September 1944
Western Caroline Islands Operation:
   Capture and Occupation of Southern Palau Islands,
      6 September–14 October 1944
   Assaults on the Philippine Islands,
      9–24 September 1944
Leyte Operation:
   Third Fleet Supporting Operations Okinawa Attack,
      10 October 1944
   Northern Luzon and Formosa Attacks,
      11–14 October 1944
   Luzon Attacks,
      15 October 1944
      17–19 October 1944
      24–26 October 1944
      13–17 November 1944
      19 November 1944
      14–16 December 1944
Okinawa Gunto Operation:
   5th and 3rd Fleet Raids in Support of Okinawa
   Gunto Operation, 9–30 May 1945
Third Fleet Operations against Japan:
   10 July–15 August 1945

USS Langley CVL-27

Marshall Islands Operation:
   Occupation of Kwajalein and Majuro Atolls,
      29 January–8 February 1944
   Occupation of Eniwetok Atoll,
      17 February–2 March 1944
Hollandia Operation (Aitape–Humboldt Bay–Tanah-
   merah Bay), 21–24 April 1944
Asiatic–Pacific Raids 1944:
   Palau, Yap, Ulithi, Woleai Raid,
      30 March–1 April 1944
   Truk, Satawan, Ponape Raid, 29 April–1 May 1944
Marianas Operation:
   Capture and Occupation of Saipan, 11–24 June 1944
   First Bonins Raid, 15–16 June 1944
   Battle of the Philippine Sea, 19–20 June 1944
   Capture and Occupation of Guam,
      12 July–15 August 1945
Western Carolines Islands Operation:
   Capture and Occupation of Southern Palau Islands,
      6 September–14 October 1944
   Assaults on the Philippine Islands,
      9–24 September 1944
Leyte Operation:
   3rd Fleet Supporting Operations Okinawa Attack,
      10 October 1944
   Northern Luzon and Formosa Attacks,
      11–14 October 1944
   Luzon Attacks,
      15 October 1944
      17–19 October 1944
      5–6 November 1944
      13–14 November 1944
      19–25 November 1944
      14–15 December 1944
   Visayas Attacks, 21 October 1944
   Battle of Surigao Strait, 24–26 October 1944
Luzon Operation:
   Formosa Attacks,
      3–4 January 1945
      9 January 1945
      15 January 1945
      21 January 1945
   Luzon Attacks, 6–7 January 1945
   China Coast Attacks,
      12 January 1945
      16 January 1945
   Nansei Shoto Attack, 22 January 1945
Iwo Jima Operation:
   Assault and Occupation of Iwo Jima
      15 February–1 March 1945
   5th Fleet Raids against Honshu and the Nansei

Shoto,
    15–16 February 1945
    25 February 1945
    1 March 1945
Okinawa Gunto Operation:
5th and 3rd Fleet Raids in Support of Okinawa
Gunto Operation, 17 March–24 May 1945

USS Cabot CVL-28

Marshall Islands Operation:
    Occupation of Kwajalein and Majuro Atolls,
        29 January–8 February 1944
Asiatic–Pacific Raids 1944:
    Truk Attack, 16–17 February 1944
    Palau, Yap, Ulithi, Woleai Raid,
        30 March–1 April 1944
    Truk, Satawan, Ponape Raid, 29 April–1 May 1944
Hollandia Operation (Aitape–Humboldt Bay–Tanah-
    merah Bay), 21–24 April 1944
Marianas Operation:
    Battle of the Philippine Sea, 19–20 June 1944
    Third Bonins Raid, 3–4 July 1945
    Capture and Occupation of Saipan, 11–24 July 1944
    Capture and Occupation of Guam,
        12 July–15 August 1944
    Palau, Yap, Ulithi Raid, 25–27 July 1944
    Fourth Bonins Raid, 4–5 August 1944
Western Caroline Islands Operation:
    Capture and Occupation of Southern Palau Islands,
        6 September–14 October 1944
    Assaults on the Philippine Islands,
        9–24 September 1944
Leyte Operation:
    3rd Fleet Supporting Operations Okinawa Attack,
        10 October 1944
    Northern Luzon and Formosa Attacks,
        13–14 October 1944
    Luzon Attacks,
        15 October 1944
        5–6 November 1944
        19–25 November 1944
    Visayas Attack, 21 October 1944
    Battle of Surigao Strait, 24–26 October 1944
Luzon Operation:
    Formosa Attacks,
        3–4 January 1945
        9 January 1945
        15 January 1945
        21 January 1945
    Luzon Attacks, 6–7 January 1945
    China Coast Attacks,

    12 January 1945
    16 January 1945
Nansei Shoto Attacks, 22 January 1945
Iwo Jima Operation:
    5th Fleet Raids against the Nansei Shoto and
    Honshu,
        15–20 February 1945
        25 February 1945
        1 March 1945
    Assault and Occupation of Iwo Jima,
        15 February–1 March 1945
Okinawa Gunto Operation:
    5th and 3rd Fleet Raids in Support of Okinawa
    Gunto Operation, 17 March–9 April 1945

USS Bataan CVL-29

Hollandia Operation (Aitape–Humboldt Bay–Tanah-
    merah Bay): 21–24 April 1944
Asiatic–Pacific Raids 1944:
    Truk, Satawan, Ponape Raid, 29 April–1 May 1944
Marianas Operation:
    Capture and Occupation of Saipan, 11–24 June 1944
    First Bonins Raid, 15–16 June 1944
    Battle of the Philippine Sea, 19–20 June 1944
    Second Bonins Raid, 24 June 1944
Okinawa Gunto Operation:
    5th and 3rd Fleet Raids in Support of Okinawa
    Gunto Operation, 17 March–30 May 1945
Third Fleet Operations against Japan,
    10 July–15 August 1945

USS San Jacinto CVL-30

Marianas Operation:
    Capture and Occupation of Saipan, 11–24 June 1944
    Battle of the Philippine Sea, 19–20 June 1944
    Capture and Occupation of Guam,
        12 July–15 August 1944
    Palau, Yap, Ulithi, Raids, 25–27 July 1944
    Fourth Bonins Raid, 4–5 August 1944
Western Caroline Islands Operation:
    Raids on Volcano–Bonin Islands and Yap Islands,
        31 August–8 September 1944
    Capture and Occupation of Southern Palau Islands,
        6 September–14 October 1944
    Assaults on the Philippine Islands,
        9–24 September 1944
Leyte Operation:
    3rd Fleet Supporting Operations Okinawa Attack,
        10 October 1944
    Northern Luzon and Formosa Attacks,

11–14 October 1944
Luzon Attacks,
   15 October 1944
   17–19 October 1944
   13–14 November 1944
   19 November 1944
   14–16 December 1944
Battle of Surigao Strait, 24–26 October 1944
Luzon Operation:
  Formosa Attacks,
   3–4 January 1945
   9 January 1945
   15 January 1945
   21 January 1945
  Luzon Attacks, 6–7 January 1945
  China Coast Attacks,
   12 January 1945
   16 January 1945

Iwo Jima Operation:
  Assault and Occupation of Iwo Jima,
   15 February–4 March 1945
  5th Fleet Raids against Honshu and the Nansei Shoto,
   25 February 1945
   1 March 1945
Okinawa Gunto Operation:
  5th and 3rd Fleet Raids in Support of Okinawa Gunto Operation, 17 March–11 June 1945
Third Fleet Operations against Japan,
   10 July–15 August 1945

USS Bon Homme Richard CV-31

Third Fleet Operations against Japan,
   10 July–15 August 1945

European-African-Middle Eastern Area Campaign Service Medal

USS Ranger CV-4

USS Wasp CV-7

North African Operation:
  Algeria–Morocco Landings, 8–11 November 1942
Escort, anti-submarine, armed guard and
special operations:
  Norway Raid, 2–6 October 1943

Reinforcement of Malta:
  3–16 May 1942
  14–21 April 1942

12

World War II Victory Medal

USS Saratoga CV-3
USS Ranger CV-4
USS Enterprise CV-6
USS Essex CV-9
USS Yorktown CV-10
USS Intrepid CV-11
USS Hornet CV-12
USS Franklin CV-13
USS Ticonderoga CV-14
USS Randolph CV-15
USS Lexington CV-16
USS Bunker Hill CV-17
USS Wasp CV-18

USS Hancock CV-19
USS Bennington CV-20
USS Independence CVL-22
USS Belleau Wood CVL-24
USS Cowpens CVL-25
USS Monterey CVL-26
USS Langley CVL-27
USS Cabot CVL-28
USS Bataan CVL-29
USS San Jacinto CVL-30
USS Bon Homme Richard CV-31
USS Shangri La CV-38

13

Navy Occupation Service Medal

USS Essex CV-9

2–3 September 1945 "A"

USS Yorktown CV-10

2 September–9 October 1945 "A"

USS Intrepid CV-11, CVA-11

25 October–3 December 1945 "E"
8 June–31 July 1955 "E"
1 August–25 October 1955 "E"

USS Hornet CVA-12

20 May–1 June 1954 "E"

USS Ticonderoga CV-14

2–20 September 1945 "A"
28 December 1945–7 January 1946 "A"

USS Randolph CV-15, CVA-15

2–15 September 1945 "A"
2 November–13 December 1954 "E"
13 February–26 July 1954 "E"
10 December 1954–10 June 1955 "E"

USS Lexington CV-16

2–22 September 1945 "A"
10 October–3 December 1945 "A"

USS Wasp CV-18, CVA-18

26–27 November 1945 "E"
2 June–6 September 1952 "E"
4–26 October 1953 "E"

USS Hancock CV-19

2 September–9 October 1945 "A"

USS Bennington CV-20, CVA-20

12–21 October 1945 "A"
2–22 September 1945 "E"
6 October 1953–16 February 1954 "A"

USS Independence CVL-22

2–23 September 1945 "A"
7–9 October 1945 "A"
1–4 December 1945 "A"

USS Belleau Wood CVL-24

2–20 September 1945 "A"
11–20 October 1945 "A"

USS Cowpens CVL-25

2 September–7 October 1945 "A"
4–14 January 1945 "A"

USS Monterey CVL-26

2–11 November 1945 "A"

USS Cabot CVL-28

2 September–15 October 1945 "A"
21 January–17 March 1945 "E"

USS Bataan CVL-29

2–15 September 1945 "A"

USS San Jacinto CVL-30

2–3 September 1945 "A"

USS Boxer CV-21, CVA-21

29 September–4 October 1945 "A"
8 December 1945–3 January 1946 "A"
9–10 May 1946 "A"
29 January–5 February 1950 "A"
1–8 April 1950 "A"

USS Bon Homme Richard CV-31

2–27 September 1945 "A"
7–9 October 1945 "A"

USS Leyte CV-32, CVA-32

7 April–6 June 1947 "E"
7 August–13 November 1947 "E"
16 September 1949–17 January 1950 "E"
13 May–15 August 1950 "E"
22 September–10 December 1951 "E"
5 September 1952–26 January 1953 "E"

USS Kearsarge CV-33

8 June–24 September 1948 "E"

USS Oriskany CV-34

27 May–26 September 1951 "E"

USS Antietam CV-36, CVA-36, CVS-36

8 December 1945–3 January 1946 "A"
1 July–17 October 1953 "E"
19 January–1 March 1955 "E"

USS Princeton CV-37

27 September–11 October 1946 "A"

20–25 November 1948 "A"

USS Shangri-La CV-38

2 September–19 October 1945 "A"

USS Lake Champlain CVA-39

16–18 November 1953 "E"
8 October 1954–7 April 1955 "E"
19 September–25 October 1955 "E"

USS Tarawa CV-40, CVA-40

27 September–12 October 1946 "A"
4–8 January 1947 "A"
7 December 1951–2 June 1952 "E"
20 January–26 June 1953 "E"
26 November 1953–14 January 1954 "E"

USS Midway CVB-41, CVA-41

13 November 1947–4 March 1948 "A"
11 January–22 February 1949 "E"
16 January–15 May 1950 "E"
20 July–1 November 1950 "E"
21 January–27 April 1952 "E"
10 December 1952–8 May 1953 "E"
14 January 1954–26 July 1954 "E"

USS Franklin D. Roosevelt CVB-42, CVA-42

12 August–30 September 1946 "E"
23 September 1948–15 January 1949 "E"
21 January–8 May 1951 "E"
22 September 1951–26 January 1952 "E"
2 October–11 December 1952 "E"
21 June–26 November 1953 "E"

USS Coral Sea CVB-43, CVA-43

12 May–19 September 1949 "E"
22 September 1950–23 January 1951 "E"
30 March–24 September 1951 "E"
27 April–4 October 1952 "E"
7 May–14 October 1953 "E"
24 July–11 December 1954 "E"
5 April–31 July 1955 "E"
1 August–21 September 1955 "E"

USS Valley Forge CV-45   USS Philippine Sea CV-47

14 October–1 November 1945 "A"   27 February–19 June 1948 "E"
                                            11 January–15 May 1949 "E"

14

China Service Medal (Extended)

USS Essex CV-9, CVA-9

19–24 July 1952
24 January–13 February 1955

USS Yorktown CVA-10

5–21 September 1954
7–9 November 1954
24 January–13 February 1955

USS Intrepid CV-11

2–9 October 1945

USS Hornet CVA-12

21–30 July 1954
5–21 September 1954
7–9 November 1954

USS Wasp CVA-18

9–10 January 1954
18–19 January 1954
25 March–5 April 1954
26 January–13 February 1955

USS Hancock CVA-19

Only to personnel who actually participated in operational flights over Chinese Waters, including the Taiwan and Formosa Straits.
25–27 September 1955
8–10 November 1955
19–21 January 1956
1 February 1956

USS Bennington CVA-20

Only those who actually participated in operational flights over Chinese Waters, including the Taiwan and Formosa Straits and/or engaged in training flights with the Armed Forces of NGRC.
16–20 January 1956
14–18 March 1956

USS Boxer CV-21

7 October–6 November 1945
23 November–6 December 1945
1–6 May 1946
12 May–4 June 1946
11–16 February 1950

USS Kearsarge CV-33, CVA-33

30 October 1952
24 January–13 February 1953
1 February 1956
4–5 April 1956

USS Oriskany CV-34

30 October 1952

USS Antietam CV-36

8 September–15 October 1946
1 May–4 June 1946
14 August–9 September 1947

USS Princeton CV-37, CVA-37

15–30 October 1946

29 October–16 November 1948
3–14 February 1955

USS Shangri-La CVA-38

Awarded to only those who actually participated in operational flights over Chinese Waters, including the Taiwan and Formosa Straits and/or engaged in training flights with Armed Forces of NGRC.
14–15 March 1956

USS Tarawa CV-40, CVA-40

14–30 October 1946
29 October–14 December 1948
29 May–2 June 1954

USS Midway CVA-41

6–13 February 1955

USS Valley Forge CV-45

11 February–17 March 1948
19–24 June 1950

USS Philippine Sea CV-47, CVA-47

11–13 April 1951
19–24 July 1952
19 August 1954

15

Antarctica Service Medal

USS Philippine Sea CVA-47

Operation Highjump—24 January–3 February 1947

16

Korean Service Medal

USS Essex CVA-9

Dates of the *Essex* in Korean Waters:
  15 August–11 March 1952
  26 July 1952–26 January 1953
  1 January–14 February 1954
  26 April–9 March 1954
  26–28 June 1954
Korean Conflict Engagements:
  United Nations Summer–Fall Offensive:
  22 August–19 September 1951
  3 October 1951
  14–21 November 1951
  Second Korean Winter:
  22 November–12 December 1951
  28 December 1951–1 February 1952
  20 February–5 March 1952
  Third Korean Winter:
  8 December 1952–10 January 1953

USS Yorktown CVA-10

Dates of the *Yorktown* in Korean Waters:
  14 November 1953–17 February 1954

USS Wasp CVA-18

Dates of the *Wasp* in Korean Waters:
  10 November 1953–7 January 1954
  20 January–11 February 1954
  12–21 April 1954

USS Boxer CVA-21

Dates of the *Boxer* in Korean Waters:

14 September–26 October 1950
26 March–9 April 1951
16 April–8 October 1951
10 March–9 September 1952
30 April–9 August 1953
22 August–11 November 1953
3–18 June 1954
24–27 July 1954
Korean Conflict Engagements:
  North Korean Aggression:
  18 September–26 October 1950
  Inchon Landing:
  13–17 September 1950
  First United Nations Counter Offensive:
  26 March–9 April 1951
  Communist China Spring Offensive:
  2 March–7 June 1951
  17 June–8 July 1951
  United Nations Summer–Fall Offensive:
  9–18 July 1951
  28 July–22 August 1951
  4 September–3 October 1951
  Second Korean Winter:
  31 March–30 April 1952
  Korean Defense Summer–Fall 1952:
  14–26 May 1952
  11 June–6 July 1952
  4–8 August 1952
  25 August–4 September 1952
  Korea Summer–Fall 1953:
  12 May–19 July 1953
  4–27 July 1953

USS Leyte CVA-32

Dates of the *Leyte* in Korean Waters:

3 October–26 January 1951
Korean Conflict Engagements:
North Korean Aggression:
9–29 October 1950
Communist China Aggression:
6 November–25 December 1950
8–19 January 1951

USS Kearsarge CVA-33

Dates of the *Kearsarge* in Korean Waters:
8 September–29 October 1952
31 October 1952–5 January 1953
19 January–28 February 1953
2 August–15 September 1953
28 September–15 November 1953
30 November 1953–2 January 1954
Korean Conflict Engagements:
Korean Defense Summer–Fall 1952:
18 September–18 October 1952
31 October–30 November 1952
Third Korean Winter:
1–4 December 1952
18 December 1952–1 January 1953
19 January–22 February 1953

USS Oriskany CVA-34

Dates of the *Oriskany* in Korean Waters:
17–28 October 1952
31 October 1952–29 March 1953
11 April–2 May 1953
15 October 1953–15 March 1954
25 March–6 April 1954
Korean Conflict Engagements:
Korean Defense Summer–Fall 1952:
31 October–19 November 1952
Third Korean Winter:
4–24 December 1952
10 January–11 February 1953
4–29 March 1953
11–25 April 1953

USS Antietam CVA-36

Dates of the *Antietam* in Korean Waters:
4 October–16 April 1952
Korean Conflict Engagements:
United Nations Summer–Fall Offensive:
15 October–14 November 1951
Second Korean Winter:
28 November–28 December 1951

18 January–6 February 1952
20 February–19 March 1952

USS Princeton CVA-37

Dates of the *Princeton* in Korean Waters:
1 December 1950–16 August 1951
14 April–20 October 1952
27 February–16 May 1953
31 May–7 September 1953
Korean Conflict Engagements:
Communist China Aggression:
5 December 1950–24 January 1951
First United Nations Counter Offensive:
25 January–4 April 1951
18–21 April 1951
Korean Conflict Engagements:
Communist China Spring Offensive:
22 April–19 May 1951
2 June–1 July 1951
United Nations Summer–Fall Offensive:
14 July–10 August 1951
Second Korean Winter:
30 April 1952
Korean Defense Summer–Fall 1952:
1–13 May 1952
4–26 June 1952
6 July–3 August 1952
4–16 October 1952
Third Korean Winter:
13–31 March 1953
Korea Summer–Fall 1953:
1–15 May 1953
18 June–27 July 1953

USS Lake Champlain CVA-39

Dates of the *Lake Champlain* in Korean Waters:
9 June–27 July 1953
10–17 October 1953
Korean Conflict Engagement:
Korea Summer–Fall 1953:
13–27 June 1953
13–27 July 1953

USS Tarawa CVA-40

Dates of the *Tarawa* in Korean Waters:
15 February–15 March 1954
26 March–15 April 1954

USS Valley Forge CVA-45

Dates of the *Valley Forge* in Korean Waters:
    27 June–23 November 1950
    16 December 1950–30 March 1951
    4 December 1951–20 June 1952
    22 December 1952–16 March 1953
    28 March–10 June 1953
Korean Conflict Engagements:
  North Korean Aggression:
    2 July–12 September 1950
  Communist China Aggression:
    3–19 November 1950
    22 December 1950–24 January 1951
  Inchon Landing:
    13–17 September 1950
  First United Nations Counter Offensive:
    25 January–26 March 1951
  Second Korean Winter:
    9 December 1951–17 January 1952
    1–20 February 1952
    5 March–2 April 1952
    16–30 April 1952
  Korean Defense Summer–Fall 1952:
    1–14 May 1952
    26 March–11 June 1952
  Third Korean Winter:
    2–22 January 1953
    29 March–11 April 1953
  Korea Summer–Fall 1953:
    1–14 May 1953
    27 May–6 June 1953

USS Philippine Sea CVA-47

Dates of the *Philippine Sea* in Korean Waters:
    1 August–8 April 1950
    15 August–2 June 1951
    20 January–12 July 1952
    25 January–31 July 1953
    12–18 April 1954
    2–16 July 1954
Korean Conflict Engagements:
  North Korean Aggression:
    4 August–12 September 1950
    9–23 October 1950
  Communist China Aggression:
    16 November 1950–24 January 1951
  Inchon Landing:
    13–17 September 1950
  First United Nations Counter Offensive:

    25 January–13 March 1951
    3–21 April 1951
  Communist China Spring Offensive:
    22 April–3 May 1951
    17–30 May 1951
  Second Korean Winter:
    30 January–20 February 1952
    19 March–16 April 1952
  Korean Defense Summer–Fall 1952
    14 May–4 June 1952
    23 June–6 July 1952
  Third Korean Winter:
    31 January–4 March 1953
    20 March–17 April 1953
  Korean Summer–Fall 1953:
    15–27 March 1953
    4 June–4 July 1953
    17–27 July 1953

USS Bon Homme Richard CVA-31

Dates of the *Bon Homme Richard* in Korean Waters:
    28 May–6 December 1951
    18 June–24 December 1952
Korean Conflict Engagements:
  Communist China Spring Offensive:
    28 March–17 June 1951
    1–8 July 1951
  United Nations Summer-Fall Offensive:
    9–28 July 1951
    10 August–5 September 1951
    19 September–18 October 1951
    31 October–27 November 1951
  Second Korean Winter:
    28–29 November 1951
  Korean Defense Summer-Fall 1952:
    23–26 June 1952
    3 July–4 August 1952
    9–18 August 1952
    4–18 September 1952
    12 October–5 November 1952
    24–29 November 1952
  Third Korean Winter:
    1–17 December 1952

USS Bataan CVL-29

Dates of the *Bataan* in Korean Waters:
    28 November 1950–13 June 1951
    11 February–11 August 1951
    15 November 1952–10 May 1953
    14–18 August 1953

Korean Conflict Engagements:
  Communist China Aggression:
    16 December 1950–24 January 1951
  First United Nations Counter Offensive:
    25 January–22 March 1951
    31 March–6 April 1951
    9–15 April 1951
    19–21 April 1951
  Communist China Spring Offensive:
    22–26 April 1951
    1–10 May 1951
    19 May–3 June 1951
  Second Korean Winter:
    30 April 1952
  Korean Defense Summer-Fall 1952:
    1–10 May 1952
    7–15 June 1952
    26 June–3 July 1952
    13–22 July 1952
    1–2 August 1952

  Third Korean Winter:
    16 March 1953
    26 March–4 April 1953
    11–20 April 1953
    27–30 April 1953
  Korea Summer-Fall 1953:
    1–6 May 1953

USS Saipan CVL-48

Dates of the *Saipan* in Korean Waters:
  30–November 1953–10 February 1954
  20 February–15 March 1954
  27 March–13 April 1954
  25 April–25 May 1954

USS Wright CVL-49

Dates of the *Wright* in Korean Waters:
  28 May–27 July 1954

17

United Nations Service Medal

USS *Essex CVA-9*
USS *Yorktown CVA-10*
USS *Wasp CVA-18*
USS *Boxer CVA-21*
USS *Bataan CVL-29*
USS *Bon Homme Richard CVA-31*
USS *Leyte CVS-32*
USS *Kearsarge CVA-33*
USS *Oriskany CVA-34*

USS *Antietam CVS-36*
USS *Princeton CVA-37*
USS *Lake Champlain CVA-39*
USS *Tarawa CVA-40*
USS *Valley Forge CVA-45*
USS *Philippine Sea CVA-47*
USS *Saipan CVL-48*
USS *Wright CVL-49*

18

Navy Expeditionary Medal

USS Essex CVS-9

Cuba:

    13–26 April 1961
    21–23 October 1962

USS Randolph CVS-15

Cuba:

    20 April–11 May 1961
    15–31 May 1961
    9–15 June 1961

USS Boxer LPH-4

Cuba:

    24 July–3 August 1961
    21 March–6 April 1961
    16–27 April 1962
    30 April–3 May 1962

    28–30 June 1962
    25–27 July 1962

USS Shangri-La CVA-38

Cuba:

    3–11 June 1961
    14–18 June 1961

USS Independence CVA-62

Cuba:

    19–29 April 1961
    18–23 October 1962

USS Enterprise CVA(N)-65

Cuba:

    19–23 October 1962

19

Armed Forces Expeditionary Medal

USS Essex CVS-9

Lebanon:
    16 July–1 August 1958
    11–20 August 1958
Taiwan:
    16–27 September 1958
Cuba:
    24 October–15 November 1962

USS Yorktown CVS-10

Vietnam:
    8–26 February 1965
    20 March–28 April 1965
Korea:
    23 January–22 March 1968

USS Hornet CVS-12

Quemoy and Matsu Islands:
    14–15 July 1959
    24–25 July 1959
    21–23 October 1962
    15–16 November 1962
Korea:
    19–27 April 1969

USS Ticonderoga CVA-14

Taiwan:
    12–15 November 1958
    20–22 November 1958
    5–8 December 1958
    29 December 1958–1 January 1959

Laos:
    26–30 September 1961
Quemoy and Matsu Islands:
    10–14 October 1961
Vietnam:
    27 September–1 October 1961
    16–17 October 1961
    23 April–1 May 1963
    2–5 August 1964
    11 August–22 September 1964
    7–29 October 1964
    2–6 November 1964
    21–28 November 1964
Korea:
    23 January–22 March 1968
    20–27 April 1969

USS Randolph CVS-15

Cuba:
    24 October–7 November 1962
    23–30 November 1962

USS Lexington CVS-16

Taiwan:
    15–17 August 1958
    27 August–16 September 1958
    26 September–15 October 1958
    10–15 November 1958
    27–28 November 1958
Quemoy and Matsu Islands:
    28 June–2 July 1959
    11–16 July 1959
    17–19 October 1959

20–21 December 1961
Vietnam:
    15–23 December 1960
    1–8 January 1961
    28 February–6 March 1962

USS Wasp CVS-18

Lebanon:
    16 July–11 August 1958
    21–31 August 1958
    16–17 September 1958
Cuba:
    2–19 November 1962

USS Hancock CVA-19

Taiwan:
    23 August–9 September 1958
Quemoy and Matsu Islands:
    14–17 September 1959
Vietnam:
    10–14 March 1962
    16–20 May 1962
    28 August–6 September 1963
    3–10 November 1963
    7 December 1964–4 May 1965

USS Bennington CVS-20

Taiwan:
    12 October–2 November 1958
    24 November–3 December 1958
Vietnam:
    16–19 December 1960
    21–22 December 1960
    3–7 January 1961
    14–18 May 1962
    17–26 May 1965

USS Boxer LPH-4

Cuba:
    24 October–6 December 1962
Dominican Republic:
    28 April–1 June 1965

USS Bon Homme Richard CVA-31

Vietnam:
    22–27 March 1961
    5–13 March 1964

12–14 May 1964
5–10 June 1964
13–17 June 1964
24–27 September 1964
31 August–6 November 1964
14–21 November 1964
23 November 1964
27 November 1964
29–30 November 1964
1–4 December 1964
7 December 1964
9–16 December 1964
26 May–3 July 1965

USS Kearsarge CVS-33

Vietnam:
    11 August–24 September 1964
Korea:
    23 January–22 March 1968

USS Oriskany CVA-34

Quemoy and Matsu Islands:
    30 September–2 October 1959
    9–12 October 1960
Vietnam:
    6–12 September 1963
    4–9 November 1963
    7 May–2 June 1965
    10 June–3 July 1965

USS Princeton LPH-5

Taiwan:
    27 August–16 September 1958
    14–22 October 1958
Vietnam:
    25–26 January 1962
    14–17 April 1962
    13–17 April 1963
    24 April–3 May 1963
    28 August–12 September 1963
    27 October–9 November 1964
    16 November–10 December 1964
    26 December 1964–31 January 1965
    9–28 February 1965
    9 March 1965
    16–23 April 1965
    2–13 May 1965

USS Shangri-La CVA-38

Taiwan:
  30 August–1 September 1958
  3–27 September 1958
  15–16 October 1958
  21–29 October 1958
  7–9 August 1959

USS Lake Champlain CVS-39

Cuba:
  18 November–5 December 1962

USS Midway CVA-41

Taiwan:
  6–10 September 1958
  12–29 September 1959
  12–30 October 1958
  11–15 November 1958
  30 November–12 December 1958
Vietnam:
  24–25 March 1961
  28 March–7 April 1961
  8 April–11 May 1965
  19 May–28 June 1965

USS Franklin D. Roosevelt CVA-42

Vietnam:

USS Coral Sea CVA-43

Vietnam:
  29 April–9 May 1961
  12–19 January 1962
  24–27 January 1962
  2 February–4 March 1965
  16 March–16 April 1965
  2–27 May 1965
  23 June–3 July 1965
Korea:
  23 January–22 March 1968

USS Valley Forge LPH-8

Vietnam:
  14–21 May 1962

  30 June–4 July 1962
  16–17 June 1964
  5 August–28 September 1964
  7–14 October 1964

USS Saratoga CVA-60

Cuba:
  3–20 December 1962

USS Ranger CVA-61

Quemoy and Matsu Islands: 24–25 June 1960
Vietnam:
  1–4 May 1963
  19–20 September 1964
  1–9 October 1964
  28 November–30 December 1964
  17 January–17 March 1965
  4–13 April 1965
Korea:
  23 January–22 March 1968
  20–22 March 1969
  20–27 April 1969

USS Independence CVA-62

Cuba: 24 October–20 November 1962
Vietnam: 29 June–3 July 1965

USS Kitty Hawk CVA-63

Quemoy and Matsu Islands: 15–16 November 1962
Vietnam: 20 May–10 June 1964

USS Constellation CVA-64

Vietnam:
  6 June–13 July 1964
  4 August–21 September 1964
  29 October–23 November 1964

USS Enterprise CVA(N)-65

Cuba: 24 October–3 December 1962
Korea:
  23 January–22 March 1968
  20 April–11 May 1969

20

Vietnam Service Medal

USS Yorktown CVS-10

26 February–25 March 1966
14–27 April 1966
31 May 1966
3–4, 11–12 June 1966
25 June–3 July 1966

USS Intrepid CVS-11

14 May–15 June 1966
8 June–

USS Ticonderoga CVA-14

4 November–2 December 1965
22 December 1965–14 January 1966
22 January–16 February 1966
6–31 March 1966
10–21 April 1966

USS Hancock CVA-19

17 December 1965–

USS Bennington CVS-20

29 July–17 August 1965
27 August–10 September 1965

USS Boxer LPH-4

9–17 September 1965
20–23 May 1966

USS Bon Homme Richard CVA-31

18 July–13 August 1965
10 September–1 October 1965
8–29 October 1965
13 November–17 December 1965

USS Oriskany CVA-34

4–20 July 1965
9 August–12 September 1965
30 September–19 October 1965
29 October–27 November 1965

USS Princeton LPH-5

1–9 September 1965
23 March–8 April 1966
21 April–8 May 1966

USS Midway CVA-41

22 July–26 August 1965
11 September–9 October 1965
18 October–5 November 1965

USS Franklin D. Roosevelt CVA-42

USS Coral Sea CVA-43

4–24 July 1965
11 August–11 September 1965
21 September–15 October 1965

USS Valley Forge LPH-8

6–7 October 1965
7–18 November 1965
25 November–25 December 1965
6, 26–31 January 1966
1–28 February 1966
1, 8 March 1966

USS Ranger CVA-61

15–31 January 1966
1–12, 23–28 February 1966
1–22 March 1966
12–30 April 1966
1–9, 30–31 May 1966
1 June 1966–

USS Independence CVA-62

4 July–10 August 1965
26 August–23 September 1965

14 October–12 November 1965

USS Kitty Hawk CVA-63

25 November–23 December 1965
15 January–4 February 1966
18 February–15 March 1966
1–29 April 1966
8–23 May 1966

USS Constellation CVA-64

14 June–13 July 1966

USS Enterprise CVA(N)-65

2 December 1965–14 January 1966
4–23 February 1966
16 March–12 April 1966
22 April–14 May 1966
23 May–6 June 1966

21

Philippine Liberation Campaign Ribbon

USS *Enterprise* CV-6—1 Star
USS *Essex* CV-9—1 Star
USS *Yorktown* CV-10—1 Star
USS *Intrepid* CV-11
USS *Hornet* CV-12—1 Star
USS *Franklin* CV-13
USS *Ticonderoga* CV-14—1 Star
USS *Lexington* CV-16—2 Stars
USS *Bunker Hill* CV-17
USS *Wasp* CV-18—2 Stars

USS *Hancock* CV-19
USS *Independence* CVL-22—2 Stars
USS *Princeton* CVL-23
USS *Belleau Wood* CVL-24—
USS *Cowpens* CVL-25—2 Stars
USS *Monterey* CVL-26
USS *Langley* CVL-27—2 Stars
USS *Cabot* CVL-28—2 Stars
USS *San Jacinto* CVL-30—2 Stars

Republic of the Philippines Presidential Unit Citation Badge

USS *Enterprise* CV-6
USS *Essex* CV-9
USS *Yorktown* CV-10
USS *Intrepid* CV-11
USS *Hornet* CV-12
USS *Franklin* CV-13
USS *Ticonderoga* CV-14
USS *Randolph* CV-15
USS *Lexington* CV-16
USS *Bunker Hill* CV-17

USS *Wasp* CV-18
USS *Hancock* CV-19
USS *Independence* CVL-22
USS *Princeton* CVL-23
USS *Belleau Wood* CVL-24
USS *Cowpens* CVL-25
USS *Monterey* CVL-26
USS *Langley* CVL-27
USS *Cabot* CVL-28
USS *San Jacinto* CVL-30

23

Republic of Korea Presidential Unit Citation Badge

USS Essex CVA-9

15 August 1951–11 March 1952
8 July 1952–26 January 1953

USS Bataan CVL-29

28 November 1950–12 June 1951
11 February 1952–11 August 1952
15 February 1953–10 May 1953

USS Boxer CVA-21

15 September 1950–26 October 1950
26 March 1951–8 October 1951
10 March 1952–9 September 1952
30 April 1953–27 July 1953

USS Bon Homme Richard CVA-31

15 May 1951–6 December 1951
18 June 1952–24 December 1952

USS Leyte CVS-32

5 October 1950–19 January 1951

USS Kearsarge CVA-33

8 September 1952–28 February 1953

USS Oriskany CVA-34

17 October 1952–30 April 1953

USS Antietam CVS-36

4 October 1951–27 July 1953

USS Princeton SVA-37
1 December 1950–16 August 1951
14 April 1952–21 October 1952
27 February 1953–27 July 1953

USS Lake Champlain CVA-39

9 June 1953–27 July 1953

USS Valley Forge CVA-45
1 December 1950–16 August 1951
14 April 1952–21 August 1952
27 February 1953–27 July 1953

USS Philippine Sea CVA-47

1 August 1950–31 May 1951
20 January 1952–12 July 1952
25 January 1953–27 July 1953

24

Republic of Vietnam Presidential Unit Citation

USS *Yorktown CVS-10*
USS *Intrepid CVS-11*
USS *Ticonderoga CVA-14*
USS *Hancock CVA-19*
USS *Bennington CVS-20*
USS *Boxer LPH-4*
USS *Bon Homme Richard CVA-31*
USS *Oriskany CVA-34*
USS *Princeton LPH-5*

USS *Midway CVA-41*
USS *Franklin D. Roosevelt CVA-42*
USS *Coral Sea CVA-43*
USS *Valley Forge LPH-8*
USS *Ranger CVA-61*
USS *Independence CVA-62*
USS *Kitty Hawk CVA-63*
USS *Constellation CVA-64*
USS *Enterprise CVA(N)-65*

PART IV
Appendices

1

A Brief History of the United States Fleets

At the time of the commissioning of the Navy's first aircraft carrier (the *USS Langley CV-1*) in 1922, the United States Navy was formed into two fleets: The U.S. Fleet and the Asiatic Fleet. By 1931 the Navy had 15 battleships, 3 aircraft carriers, 18 cruisers, 78 destroyers, 55 submarines and 115 lesser combatant and non-combatant ships. They were unequally divided between the two fleets.

The U.S. Fleet comprised the Battle Force and the Scouting Force. The Battle Force included the latest battleships, aircraft carriers, a cruiser division and a few destroyer divisions, and was based in the Pacific. The Scouting Force, based in the Atlantic and the Caribbean, operated with the remaining cruisers and destroyers plus a Training Squadron consisting of older battleships. The submarines and Base Force (also called the train, which were the auxiliaries that supplied the fleet—such as tenders and tug boats) were divided between the Pacific Battle Force and Atlantic Scouting Force.

The Asiatic Fleet was much smaller and consisted of the South China Patrol based at Chefoo, and the Yangtze River Gunboat Flotilla based at Shanghai. Nineteen destroyers formed the South China Patrol, and the Navy's gunboats, twelve subchasers and several auxiliaries formed the Yangtze River Gunboat Flotilla.

In January of 1941, the Atlantic Squadron was formed, consisting of four battleships, four cruisers, one carrier and a destroyer squadron. From November 1, 1940, to February 1, 1941, the Atlantic Squadron was called the Patrol Force, United States Fleet. On February 1, 1941, the Patrol Force, United States Fleet was renamed the Atlantic Fleet and the U.S. Fleet was renamed the Pacific Fleet.

Units of the Atlantic and Pacific Fleets were divided into smaller "Forces" and operated in designated areas. The predominant part of the old U.S. Fleet had operated in the Pacific for nearly ten years. On March 1, 1941, a shift was made, and three battleships, four light cruisers and one carrier were transferred from the Pacific Fleet to the Atlantic Fleet, mainly because of the U-Boat menace in the Atlantic.

On February 19, 1943, Admiral Ernest J. King issued a directive stating that the U.S. Fleet would be composed of numbered fleets, effective March 15, 1943. On that day, the South Pacific Force, Pacific Fleet was renamed the Third Fleet; the South Atlantic Force, Atlantic Fleet was renamed the Fourth Fleet; the Central Force, Pacific Fleet was renamed the Fifth Fleet; the Naval Forces Southwest Pacific became the Seventh Fleet and the Eighth Fleet came from the Northwest Africa Force.

While the First, Second and Sixth Fleets established by the directive issued by Admiral King, came from no previously established "Force" as the above numbered fleets, their predecessors were the task forces which fought the Japanese and German submarine menace in the early months of the Second World War. The Task Forces numbered 10 to 19 in late 1942 and in early 1943 were usually associated with escort convoys from the Pacific coast to North, Central and South Pacific ports. In similar fashion, the Task Forces numbered 20 to 29 either escorted inshore and transoceanic convoys in the Atlantic Theater or were part of the commands roving the seas in search of U-Boats.

The Ninth Fleet included a miscellany of commands and so it continued to be during its short existence. The Ninth Fleet could have been nicknamed the "paper fleet" because it served administrative purposes for the most part.

On May 20, 1943, the Tenth Fleet was established to

become the Navy's Antisubmarine Warfare command. During its early months, the Tenth Fleet operated under a shroud of mystery for the most part. It was a fleet without ships in that it had recourse to every vessel of the U.S. Navy with the power to commandeer whatever forces when and where needed for ASW operations. All ASW units and groups were shifted to the Tenth Fleet. Most of the credit for winning the Battle of the Atlantic—destroying the U-Boats—can be credited to the Tenth Fleet. On June 15, 1945, the Tenth Fleet was dissolved.

On January 1, 1947, the operating forces of the Navy were reorganized, incident to the processes of streamlining the Navy, reducing command overhead and simplifying the fleet organization in the light of war experience. All numbered fleets were abolished except for one task fleet in each ocean, the First Task Fleet in the Pacific and the Second Task Fleet in the Atlantic.

The Sixth Task Fleet was reestablished on June 1, 1948, to succeed Commander Naval Forces, Mediterranean. The Seventh Task Fleet was reestablished on August 1, 1949, as a successor to Commander Naval Forces, Western Pacific. Later, the four fleets were directed to drop the word "Task" from their titles.

Today, the First Fleet operates from the West Coast to Hawaii. Units of the First Fleet train for rotation duty with the Seventh Fleet which operates in the Western Pacific from Hawaii north to the Arctic and south to the Antarctic. The Second Fleet operates off the Western Atlantic and trains for rotation duty with the Sixth Fleet which operates in the underside of Europe with Headquarters at Villafranche.

2

Deployment of the United States Fleets

Basic Organization of the United States Fleets
Effective March 15th 1943[1]

Fleet Number	Authority	Task Force No.s	Assignment or use
FIRST FLEET	CINCPAC	TF's 10–19	Pacific Fleet major surface combatant task forces.
SECOND FLEET	CINCLANT	TF's 20–29	Atlantic Fleet under Commander in Chief Atlantic.
THIRD FLEET	CINCPAC	TF's 30–39	Pacific Fleet assigned to Commander South Pacific.
FOURTH FLEET	CINCLANT	TF's 40–49	Atlantic Fleet assigned to Commander South Atlantic.
FIFTH FLEET	CINCPAC	TF's 50–59	Pacific Fleet major amphibious, escort and service task forces Hawaiian Sea Frontier; Hawaiian Dept.; and Air Pacific.
SIXTH FLEET	CINCLANT	TF's 60–69	Atlantic Fleet for Central and North Atlantic task forces.
SEVENTH FLEET	COMINCH	TF's 70–79	Assigned to Commander Southwest Pacific.
EIGHTH FLEET	COMINCH	TF's 80–89	Assigned to Commander Naval Forces North African Waters.
NINTH FLEET	COMINCH	TF's 90–99	Used for US Naval Forces in Europe; Southeast Pacific Force; Naval Transportation Service.
U.S. FLEET	COMINCH	TF's 00–09	Used for task forces directly under COMINCH or under the Commanders of the Sea Frontiers.

1. All but the First and Second Fleets were abolished January 1, 1947. The Sixth Fleet was reestablished June 1, 1948 and the Seventh Fleet was reestablished August 1, 1949.

3

An Attack Carrier's Deployment

Facts of Interest of an Attack Carrier's Deployment to the Western Pacific: The below example is the West-Pac cruise of the *USS Ticonderoga CVS-14,* her last cruise as a CVA, February 1, to September 18, 1969.

Navigation

97	Days on station in waters off Vietnam
181	Days at sea
48	Days in port
73,846	Navigation miles steamed

Engineering

78,015	Engine miles steamed
19,554,569	Gallons of fresh water expended
15,251,341	Gallons of fresh water made
16,016,719	Gallons of feed water made
31,268,060	Total gallons of water made

Deck

11,845,000	Gallons of jet fuel taken aboard
240,000	Gallons of aviation gas taken aboard
52	Fueling operations at sea
117	Underway replenishments
1.3	Average hours alongside support ships daily

Flight Operations

11,000	Arrested landings

Supply

$7,000,000	Cash disbursed
$833,255	Ship's store sales
2,061,720	Meals served
161,000	Loaves of bread baked
49,650	Pounds of coffee consumed
860,000	Pounds of meat consumed
138,000	Dozen eggs consumed
1,102,600	Cold drinks sold
900,000	Pounds of laundry washed

Weapons

206	Tons per average underway replenishment
198.8	Tons per hour average underway replenishment
8,375	Tons ordnance handled

Medical

15,751	Outpatients
15,196	Prescriptions
9,792	Immunizations
2,883	X-rays
726	Eye examinations (including prescriptions)
9,088	Laboratory procedures
529	Surgical procedures
684	Glasses ordered

Dental

8,046	Patient sittings
7,482	Permanent restorations
157	Prosthetic appliances
1,069	Surgical procedures
1,188	Fluoride treatments
29,329	Total procedures

Aircraft Intermediate Maintenance

18,314	Total items processed
111	Total operating days
165	Total items per operating day

Photo Laboratory

133,000	Feet of film processed
15,566	Prints made for intelligence purposes

Communications

150,000	Messages handled
200	Messages of birth to new fathers

Post Office

$1,320,139.66	Total amount of money orders sold
285,486	Total pounds of mail handled

Chaplin's Office

450	Number of religious services
22,295	Total attendance at religious services
140	Sunday school classes or discussion groups conducted
17,623	Attendance at Sunday services
290	Weekly religious services conducted
4,750	Attendance at weekly religious services
73	Helicopter transfers of chaplains (Holy Helo)

4

Numerical List of Aircraft Carriers

Aircraft carriers in numerical order with the original hull number and classification in the far left column.

CV-1 LANGLEY (ex JUPITER)
Built at Mare Island Navy Yard,
Vallejo, California
Keel Laid: October 18, 1911
Launched: October 24, 1912
Commissioned: April 7, 1913 USS *Jupiter AC-3*
Conversion to CV authorized July 11, 1919
Commissioned USS *Langley CV-1* March 20, 1922
Commander K. Whiting (Acting)
Captain S. H. R. Doyle, Commanding July 16, 1922
Sunk by Japanese February 27, 1942 south of Java.

CV-2 LEXINGTON (ex CC-1)
Built at Fore River Shipbuilding Co., Quincy, Massachusetts.
Keel Laid: August 8, 1921
Launched: October 3, 1925
Conversion to CV authorized July 1, 1922
Commissioned: December 14, 1927
Captain A. W. Marshall, Commanding
Sunk by American destroyers after the battle of the Coral Sea May 8, 1942.

CV-3 SARATOGA (ex CC-3)
Built at New York Shipbuilding Corporation, Camden, New Jersey
Keel Laid: September 25, 1920
Launched: April 7, 1925
Conversion to CV authorized: July 1, 1922
Commissioned: November 16, 1927
Captain H. E. Yarnell, Commanding
Sunk by initial blast at the A-Bomb test in the Bikini Lagoon July 25, 1946

CV-4 RANGER
Built at Newport News Shipbuilding and Dry Dock Company, Newport News, Virginia
Keel Laid: September 26, 1931
Launched: February 25, 1933
Commissioned: July 4, 1934
Captain A. L. Bristol, Commanding
Decommissioned: October 18, 1946,
Atlantic Reserve Fleet
Stricken from list of Navy ships and sold for scrap January 28, 1947

CV-5 YORKTOWN
Built at Newport News Shipbuilding and Dry Dock Company, Newport News, Virginia
Keel Laid: May 21, 1934
Launched: April 4, 1936
Commissioned: September 30, 1937
Captain E. D. McWhorter, Commanding
Sunk by American destroyers following the Battle of Midway June 7, 1942

CV-6 ENTERPRISE
Built at Newport News Shipbuilding and Dry Dock Company, Newport News, Virginia
Keel Laid: July 16, 1934
Launched: October 3, 1936
Commissioned: May 12, 1938
Captain N. H. White, Jr., Commanding
Decommissioned: February 17, 1947,
Atlantic Reserve Fleet
Reclassified CVA October 1, 1952
Reclassified CVS July 1953
Stricken from list of Navy ships and sold for scrap July 1, 1958

CV-7 WASP
Built at Bethlehem Shipbuilding Corporation,

Quincy, Massachusetts
Keel Laid: April 1, 1936
Launched: April 4, 1939
Commissioned: April 25, 1940
Captain J. W. Reeves, Jr., Commanding
Sunk by American destroyers following the Battle of Santa Cruz September 15, 1942.

CV-8 HORNET
Built by Newport News Shipbuilding and Dry Dock Company, Newport News, Virginia
Keel Laid: September 25, 1939
Launched: December 14, 1940
Commissioned: October 20, 1941
Captain M. A. Mitscher, Commanding
Sunk by American destroyers and Japanese Navy off Guadalcanal October 24, 1942.

CV-9 ESSEX
Built at Newport News Shipbuilding and Dry Dock Company, Newport News, Virginia
Keel Laid: April 28, 1941
Launched: July 31, 1942
Commissioned: December 31, 1942
Captain D. B. Duncan, Commanding
Decommissioned: January 9, 1947,
Pacific Reserve Fleet
Recommissioned: September 15, 1951
Reclassified CVA: October 1, 1952
Reclassified CVS: March 8, 1960
Decommissioned: December 31, 1969
Inactive—Pacific Reserve Fleet

CV-10 YORKTOWN (ex BON HOMME RICHARD)
Built at Newport News Shipbuilding and Dry Dock Company, Newport News, Virginia
Keel Laid: December 1, 1941
Launched: January 21, 1943
Commissioned: April 15, 1943
Captain J. J. Clark, Commanding
Decommissioned: January 9, 1947,
Pacific Reserve Fleet
Reclassified CVA: October 1, 1952
Recommissioned: December 15, 1952
Reclassified CVS: September 1, 1957
Decommissioned: July 1970
Inactive—Atlantic Reserve Fleet

CV-11 INTREPID
Built at Newport News Shipbuilding and Dry Dock Company, Newport News, Virginia
Keel Laid: December 1, 1941
Launched: April 26, 1943
Commissioned: August 16, 1943
Captain T. L. Sprague, Commanding
Decommissioned: March 22, 1947,

Pacific Reserve Fleet
Reclassified CVA: October 1, 1952
Recommissioned: October 15, 1954
Reclassified CVS: March 31, 1962
Active—Atlantic Fleet

CV-12 HORNET (ex KEARSARGE)
Built at Newport News Shipbuilding and Dry Dock Company, Newport News, Virginia
Keel Laid: August 3, 1942
Launched: August 30, 1943
Commissioned: November 29, 1943
Captain M. R. Browning, Commanding
Decommissioned: January 15, 1947,
Pacific Reserve Fleet
Recommissioned: September 11, 1952
Reclassified CVA: October 1, 1952
Reclassified CVS: July 27, 1958
Decommissioned: July 1970
Inactive—Pacific Reserve Fleet

CV-13 FRANKLIN
Built at Newport News Shipbuilding and Dry Dock Company, Newport News, Virginia
Keel Laid: December 7, 1942
Launched: October 14, 1943
Commissioned: January 31, 1944
Captain J. N. Shoemaker, Commanding
Decommissioned: February 17, 1947,
Atlantic Reserve Fleet
Reclassified CVA: October 1, 1952
Reclassified CVS: July 1953
Reclassified AVT-8: May 15, 1959
Stricken from list of Navy ships and sold for scrap October 1, 1964

CV-14 TICONDEROGA (ex HANCOCK)
Built at Newport News Shipbuilding and Dry Dock Company, Newport News, Virginia
Keel Laid: February 1, 1943
Launched: February 7, 1944
Commissioned: May 8, 1944
Captain D. Kiefer, Commanding
Decommissioned: January 9, 1947,
Pacific Reserve Fleet
Reclassified CVA: October 1, 1952
Recommissioned: September 11, 1954
Reclassified CVS: October 1, 1969
Active—Pacific Fleet

CV-15 RANDOLPH
Built at Newport News Shipbuilding and Dry Dock Company, Newport News, Virginia
Keel Laid: May 10, 1943
Launched: June 29, 1944
Commissioned: October 9, 1944

Captain F. L. Baker, Commanding
Decommissioned: June 1947,
Atlantic Reserve Fleet
Reclassified CVA: October 1, 1952
Recommissioned: July 1, 1953
Reclassified CVS: March 31, 1959
Decommissioned: February 13, 1969
Inactive—Atlantic Reserve Fleet

CV-16 LEXINGTON (ex CABOT)
Built at Bethlehem Steel Company,
Quincy, Massachusetts
Keel Laid: September 15, 1941
Launched: September 26, 1942
Commissioned: February 17, 1943
Captain F. B. Stump, Commanding
Decommissioned: April 23, 1947,
Pacific Reserve Fleet.
Reclassified CVA: October 1, 1952
Recommissioned: August 15, 1955
Reclassified CVS: October 1, 1962
Reclassified CVT: July 1, 1969
Active—Navy training carrier Pensacola, Florida

CV-17 BUNKER HILL
Built at Bethlehem Steel Company,
Quincy, Massachusetts
Keel Laid: September 15, 1941
Launched: December 7, 1942
Commissioned: May 25, 1943
Captain J. J. Ballentine, Commanding
Decommissioned: January 1947,
Pacific Reserve Fleet
Reclassified CVA: October 1, 1952
Reclassified CVS: July 1953
Reclassified AVT-9: May 15, 1959
Stricken from list of Navy ships November 1, 1966.
Berthed at North Island—test ship for the Naval
Electronics Laboratory, San Diego, California.

CV-18 WASP (ex ORISKANY)
Built at Bethlehem Steel Company,
Quincy, Massachusetts
Keel Laid: March 18, 1942
Launched: August 17, 1943
Commissioned: November 24, 1943
Captain C. A. F. Sprague, Commanding
Decommissioned: February 17, 1947,
Atlantic Reserve Fleet
Recommissioned: September 10, 1951
Reclassified CVA: October 1, 1952
Reclassified CVS: November 1, 1956
Active—Atlantic Fleet

CV-19 HANCOCK (ex TICONDEROGA)
Built at Bethlehem Steel Company,

Quincy, Massachusetts
Keel Laid: January 26, 1943
Launched: August 17, 1943
Commissioned: April 15, 1944
Captain F. C. Dickey, Commanding
Decommissioned: May 9, 1947,
Pacific Reserve Fleet
Reclassified CVA: October 1, 1952
Recommissioned: February 15, 1954
Decommissioned: April 16, 1956 for
Major Conversion.
Recommissioned: November 15, 1956
Active—Pacific Fleet

CV-20 BENNINGTON
Built at Newport News Shipbuilding and Dry
Dock Company, Newport News, Virginia
Keel Laid: December 15, 1942
Launched: February 26, 1944
Commissioned: August 6, 1944
Captain J. B. Sykes, Commanding
Decommissioned: November 8, 1946,
Atlantic Reserve Fleet
Reclassified CVA: October 1, 1952
Recommissioned: November 13, 1952
Reclassified CVS: June 30, 1959
Decommissioned: January 15, 1970
Inactive—Pacific Reserve Fleet

CV-21 BOXER
Built at Newport News Shipbuilding and
Dry Dock Company, Newport News, Virginia
Keel Laid: September 13, 1943
Launched: December 14, 1944
Commissioned: April 16, 1945
Captain D. F. Smith, Commanding
Reclassified CVA: October 1, 1952
Reclassified CVS: November 15, 1955
Reclassified LPH-4: January 30, 1959
Decommissioned December 1, 1969 and stricken
from the list of Navy ships and sold for scrap.

CV-22 INDEPENDENCE (ex AMSTERDAM CL-59)
Built at New York Shipbuilding Corporation,
Camden, New Jersey
Keel Laid: May 1, 1941
Launched: August 22, 1942
Reclassified CV: January 10, 1942
Commissioned: January 1, 1943
Reclassified CVL: July 15, 1943
Captain G. R. Fairlamb, Jr., Commanding
Decommissioned: August 28, 1946, Kwajalein
Sunk by U. S. Navy in tests of new aerial and
undersea weapons off coast of California
January 29, 1951

524

CV-23 PRINCETON (ex TALLAHASSEE CL-61)
Built at New York Shipbuilding Corporation,
Camden, New Jersey
Keel Laid: June 2, 1941
Reclassified CV: February 16, 1942
Launched: October 18, 1942
Commissioned: February 25, 1943
Reclassified CVL: July 15, 1943
Captain G. R. Henderson, Commanding
*Sunk by American ships during Battle of Leyte
Gulf, October 24, 1944.*

CV-24 BELLEAU WOOD (ex NEW HAVEN CL-76)
Built at New York Shipbuilding Corporation,
Camden, New Jersey
Keel Laid: August 11, 1941
Reclassified CV: February 16, 1942
Launched: December 6, 1942
Commissioned: March 31, 1943
Reclassified CVL- July 15, 1943
Captain A. M. Pride, Commanding
Decommissioned: January 23, 1947,
Pacific Reserve Fleet
Loaned to Spain Sept. 1953 to Sept. 1960
*Stricken from list of Navy ships and sold for scrap
September 1960.*

CV-25 COWPENS (ex HUNTINGTON CL-77)
Built at New York Shipbuilding Corporation,
Camden, New Jersey
Keel Laid: December 17, 1941
Reclassified CV: March 27, 1942
Commissioned: May 28, 1943
Captain R. P. McConnell, Commanding
Reclassified CVL: July 17, 1943
Decommissioned: February 11, 1947,
Atlantic Reserve Fleet
Reclassified AVT-1: May 15, 1959
*Stricken from list of Navy ships and sold for scrap
November 1, 1959.*

CV-26 MONTEREY (ex DAYTON CL-78)
Built at New York Shipbuilding Corporation,
Camden, New Jersey
Keel Laid: December 29, 1941
Reclassified CV: March 27, 1942
Launched: February 28, 1943
Commissioned: June 17, 1943
Captain L. T. Hundt, Commanding
Reclassified CVL: July 15, 1943
Decommissioned: February 11, 1947,
Atlantic Reserve Fleet
Recommissioned: September 15, 1950
Decommissioned: January 5, 1956,
Atlantic Reserve Fleet

Reclassified AVT-2: May 15, 1959
Inactive—Atlantic Reserve Fleet

CVL-27 LANGLEY (ex FARGO CL-85 ex CROWN POINT)
Built at New York Shipbuilding Corporation,
Camden, New Jersey
Keel Laid: April 11, 1942
Reclassified CV: March 27, 1943
Launched: May 22, 1943
Reclassified CVL: July 15, 1943
Commissioned: August 31, 1943
Captain W. M. Dillon, Commanding
Renamed *LaFayette* and loaned to France January 1951 to March 1963.
*Stricken from the list of Navy ships and sold for
scrap May 1963.*

CVL-28 CABOT (ex WILMINGTON CL-79)
Built at New York Shipbuilding Corporation,
Camden, New Jersey
Keel Laid: March 13, 1942
Reclassified CV: June 2, 1942
Launched: April 4, 1943
Reclassified: CVL: July 15, 1943
Commissioned: July 24, 1943
Captain M. F. Schoeffel, Commanding
Decommissioned February 11, 1947,
Atlantic Reserve Fleet
Recommissioned: October 27, 1948
Decommissioned: January 21, 1955,
Atlantic Reserve Fleet
Reclassified AVT-3: May 15, 1959
Inactive—Atlantic Reserve Fleet

CVL-29 BATAAN (ex BUFFALO CL-99)
Built at New York Shipbuilding Corporation,
Camden, New Jersey
Keel Laid: August 31, 1942
Reclassified CV: June 2, 1942
Reclassified CVL: July 15, 1943
Launched: August 1, 1943
Commissioned: November 17, 1943
Captain V. H. Schaeffer, Commanding
Decommissioned: May 11, 1947,
Atlantic Reserve Fleet
Recommissioned: May 13, 1950
Decommissioned: 1954, Pacific Reserve Fleet
Reclassified AVT-4: May 15, 1959
*Stricken from list of Navy ships and sold for scrap
September 1, 1959.*

CVL-30 SAN JACINTO (ex NEWARK CL-100
        ex REPRISAL)
Built at New York Shipbuilding Corporation,
Camden, New Jersey
Keel Laid: October 26, 1942

Reclassified CV: June 2, 1942
Reclassified CVL: July 15, 1943
Launched: September 26, 1943
Commissioned: December 15, 1943
Captain H. M. Martin, Commanding
Decommissioned: January 1947,
Pacific Reserve Fleet
Reclassified AVT-5: May 15, 1959
Inactive—Pacific Reserve Fleet

CV-31   BON HOMME RICHARD
Built at New York Navy Yard, New York, N. Y.
Keel Laid: February 1, 1943
Launched: April 29, 1944
Commissioned: November 26, 1944
Captain A. O. Rule, Commanding
Decommissioned: January 9, 1947,
Pacific Reserve Fleet
Recommissioned: January 15, 1951
Reclassified CVA: October 1, 1952
Decommissioned: May 15, 1953 for
Major Conversion.
Recommissioned: September 6, 1955
Active—Pacific Fleet

CV-32   LEYTE (ex CROWN POINT)
Built at Newport News Shipbuilding and Dry
Dock Company, Newport News, Virginia.
Keel Laid: February 21, 1944
Launched: August 23, 1945
Commissioned: April 11, 1946
Captain H. F. MacComsey, Commanding
Reclassified CVA: October 1, 1952
Reclassified CVS: July 1953
Decommissioned and reclassified
AVT-10: May 15, 1959
Inactive—Atlantic Reserve Fleet

CV-33   KEARSARGE
Built at New York Navy Yard, New York, N. Y.
Keel Laid: March 1, 1944
Launched: May 5, 1945
Commissioned: March 2, 1946
Captain F. J. McKenna, Commanding
Decommissioned: June 16, 1950,
Pacific Reserve Fleet
Recommissioned: February 15, 1952
Reclassified CVA: October 1, 1952
Reclassified CVS: October 1, 1958
Decommissioned: February 13, 1970
Inactive—Pacific Reserve Fleet

CV-34   ORISKANY
Built at New York Navy Yard, New York, N. Y.
Keel Laid: May 1, 1944
Launched: October 13, 1945

Commissioned: September 25, 1950
Captain P. H. Lyons, Commanding
Reclassified CVA: October 1, 1952
Active—Pacific Fleet

CV-35   REPRISAL
Built at New York Navy Yard, New York, N. Y.
Keel Laid: July 1, 1944
Construction cancelled August 12, 1945.

CV-36   ANTIETAM
Built at Philadelphia Navy Yard, Philadelphia,
Pennsylvania
Keel Laid: March 15, 1943
Launched: August 20, 1944
Commissioned: January 28, 1945
Captain J. R. Tague, Commanding
Decommissioned: June 21, 1949,
Pacific Reserve Fleet
Recommissioned: January 17, 1951
Reclassified CVA: October 1, 1952
Reclassified CVS: July 1953
Decommissioned: May 8, 1963
Inactive—Atlantic Reserve Fleet

CV-37   PRINCETON
Built at Philadelphia Navy Yard, Philadelphia,
Pennsylvania
Keel Laid: September 14, 1943
Launched: July 8, 1945
Commissioned: November 18, 1945
Captain J. M. Hoskins, Commanding
Decommissioned: June 21, 1949,
Pacific Reserve Fleet
Recommissioned: August 28, 1950
Reclassified CVA: October 1, 1952
Reclassified CVS: November 12, 1953
Reclassified LPH-5: March 2, 1959
*Decommissioned, stricken from list of Navy ships
and sold for scrap January 30, 1970*

CV-38   SHANGRI-LA
Built at Norfolk Navy Yard, Portsmouth,
Virginia
Keel Laid: January 15, 1943
Launched: February 24, 1944
Commissioned: September 15, 1944
Captain J. D. Barner, Commanding
Decommissioned: November 7, 1947,
Pacific Reserve Fleet
Recommissioned: May 10, 1951
Decommissioned: September 1952 for
Major Conversion
Reclassified CVA: October 1, 1952
Recommissioned: January 10, 1955
Reclassified CVS: July 1, 1969

Active—Atlantic Fleet

CV-39 LAKE CHAMPLAIN
Built at Norfolk Navy Yard, Portsmouth,
Virginia
Keel Laid: March 15, 1943
Launched: November 2, 1944
Commissioned: June 3, 1945
Captain L. C. Ramsey, Commanding
Decommissioned: March 1946,
Atlantic Reserve Fleet
Recommissioned: September 19, 1952
Reclassified CVA: October 1, 1952
Reclassified CVS: August 1, 1957
Decommissioned: May 2, 1966,
Atlantic Reserve Fleet
Stricken from list of Navy ships and sold for scrap
December 1, 1969

CV-40 TARAWA
Built at Norfolk Navy Yard, Portsmouth,
Virginia
Keel Laid: March 1, 1944
Launched: May 12, 1945
Commissioned: December 8, 1945
Captain A. I. Malstrom, Commanding
Decommissioned: June 30, 1949,
Atlantic Reserve Fleet
Recommissioned: February 3, 1951
Reclassified CVA: October 1, 1952
Reclassified CVS: January 10, 1955
Decommissioned and reclassified AVT-12:
May 1, 1960, Atlantic Reserve Fleet
Stricken from the list of Navy ships and sold for
scrap June 1, 1967.

CV-41 MIDWAY
Built at Newport News Shipbuilding and
Dry Dock Company, Newport News, Virginia
Keel Laid: October 27, 1943
Launched: March 20, 1945
Reclassified CVB: July 15, 1943
Commissioned: September 10, 1945
Captain J. F. Bolger, Commanding
Reclassified CVA: October 1, 1952
Decommissioned: May 1955
Recommissioned: September 10, 1957
Decommissioned: February 14, 1966
for Major Modernization.
Recommissioned: January 31, 1970
Active—Pacific Fleet

CV-42 FRANKLIN D. ROOSEVELT (EX CORAL SEA)
Built at New York Navy Yard, New York, N. Y.
Keel Laid: December 1, 1943
Reclassified CVB: July 15, 1943

Commissioned: October 27, 1945
Captain A. Soucek, Commanding
Reclassified CVA: October 1, 1952
Decommissioned: April 23, 1954
for Major Conversion
Recommissioned: April 6, 1956
Active—Atlantic Fleet

CV-43 CORAL SEA
Built at Newport News Shipbuilding and
Dry Dock Company, Newport News, Virginia
Reclassified CVB: July 15, 1943
Keel Laid: July 10, 1944
Launched: April 2, 1946
Commissioned: October 1, 1947
Captain A. P. Storrs III, Commanding
Reclassified CVA: October 1, 1952
Decommissioned: April 24, 1957 for
Major Conversion.
Recommissioned: September 26, 1960
Active—Pacific Fleet

CVB-44 Construction cancelled January 11, 1943

CV-45 VALLEY FORGE
Built at Philadelphia Navy Yard, Philadelphia,
Pennsylvania
Keel Laid: September 7, 1944
Launched: November 18, 1945
Commissioned: November 3, 1946
Captain J. W. Harris, Commanding
Reclassified CVA: October 1, 1952
Reclassified CVS: November 12, 1953
Reclassified LPH-8: July 1, 1961
Decommissioned, stricken from the list of Navy
ships and sold for scrap January 15, 1970.

CV-46 IWO JIMA
Built at Philadelphia Navy Yard, Philadelphia,
Pennsylvania
Keel Laid: January 29, 1945
Construction cancelled August 12, 1945

CV-47 PHILIPPINE SEA (EX WRIGHT)
Built at Bethlehem Steel Company,
Quincy, Massachusetts
Keel Laid: August 19, 1944
Launched: September 5, 1945
Commissioned: May 11, 1946
Captain D. S. Cornwell, Commanding
Reclassified CVA: October 1, 1952
Reclassified CVS: November 5, 1955
Decommissioned: December 1958,
Pacific Reserve Fleet
Stricken from list of Navy ships and sold for scrap
December 1, 1969.

CVL-48 SAIPAN

Built New York Shipbuilding Corporation,
Camden, New Jersey
Keel Laid: July 10, 1944
Launched: July 8, 1945
Commissioned: July 14, 1946
Captain J. G. Crommelin, Commanding
Decommissioned: October 30, 1957,
Pacific Reserve Fleet
Reclassified AVT-6: May 15, 1959
Reclassified CC-3: January 1, 1964
Reclassified AGMR-2: September 1964
Renamed *Arlington*: April 8, 1965
Recommissioned: August 27, 1966
Decommissioned: January 14, 1970
Inactive—Pacific Reserve Fleet

CVL-49 WRIGHT
Built at New York Shipbuilding Corporation,
Camden, New Jersey
Keel Laid: August 21, 1944
Launched: September 1, 1945
Commissioned: February 9, 1947
Captain F. T. Ward, Commanding
Decommissioned: March 15, 1956,
Pacific Reserve Fleet
Reclassified AVT-7: May 15, 1959
Reclassified CC-2: September 1, 1962
Recommissioned: May 11, 1953
Active—Atlantic Fleet

CV-50-55 Construction cancelled March 27, 1945

CVB-56-57 Construction cancelled March 28, 1945

CV-58 UNITED STATES
Construction cancelled April 23, 1949

CVA-59 FORRESTAL
Built at Newport News Shipbuilding and
Dry Dock Company, Newport News, Virginia
Keel Laid: July 14, 1952
Launched: December 11, 1954
Commissioned: October 1, 1955
Captain R. L. Johnson, Commanding

CVA-60 SARATOGA
Built at New York Navy Yard, New York, N. Y.
Keel Laid: December 16, 1952
Launched: October 8, 1955
Commissioned: April 14, 1956
Captain R. J. Stroh, Commanding
Active—Atlantic Fleet

CVA-61 RANGER
Built at Newport News Shipbuilding and
Dry Dock Company, Newport News, Virginia
Keel Laid: August 2, 1954
Launched: September 29, 1956
Commissioned: August 10, 1957

Captain C. T. Booth II, Commanding
Active—Pacific Fleet

CVA-62 INDEPENDENCE
Built at New York Navy Yard, New York, N. Y.
Keel Laid: July 1, 1955
Launched: July 10, 1958
Commissioned: January 10, 1959
Captain R. Y. McElroy, Jr., Commanding
Active—Pacific Fleet

CVA-63 KITTY HAWK
Built at New York Shipbuilding Corporation,
Camden, New Jersey
Keel Laid: December 27, 1956
Launched: May 21, 1960
Commissioned: April 29, 1961
Captain W. F. Bringle, Commanding
Active—Pacific Fleet

CVA-64 CONSTELLATION
Built at New York Naval Shipyard,
Brooklyn, New York
Keel Laid: September 14, 1957
Launched: October 8, 1960
Commissioned: October 27, 1961
Captain T. J. Walker, Commanding
Active—Pacific Fleet

CVA(N)-65 ENTERPRISE
Built at Newport News Shipbuilding and
Dry Dock Company, Newport News, Virginia
Keel Laid: February 2, 1958
Launched: September 24, 1960
Commissioned: November 25, 1961
Captain V. P. de Poix, Commanding
Active—Pacific Fleet

CVA-66 AMERICA
Built at Newport News Shipbuilding and
Dry Dock Company, Newport News, Virginia
Keel Laid: January 9, 1961
Launched: February 1, 1964
Commissioned: January 23, 1965
Captain L. Heyworth Jr., Commanding
Active—Atlantic Fleet

CVA-67 JOHN F. KENNEDY
Built at Newport News Shipbuilding and
Dry Dock Company, Newport News, Virginia
Keel Laid: October 22, 1964
Launched: May 27, 1967
Commissioned: September 7, 1968
Captain E. P. Yates, Commanding
Active—Atlantic Fleet

CVA(N)-68 CHESTER W. NIMITZ
Newport News Shipbuilding and Dry Dock
Company of Newport News, Virginia

Keel Laid: June 22, 1968
Under construction
CVA(N)-69 DWIGHT D. EISENHOWER
    To be built by the Newport News Shipbuilding

and Dry Dock Company, Newport News, Virginia
CVA(N)-70 Un-named, to be built by Newport News Shipbuilding and Dry Dock Company, Newport News, Virginia

Index to Campaigns and Battle Engagements